AMERICAN
WAR LIBRARY

★ The American Revolution ★

WEAPONS
OF WAR

AMERICAN
WAR LIBRARY

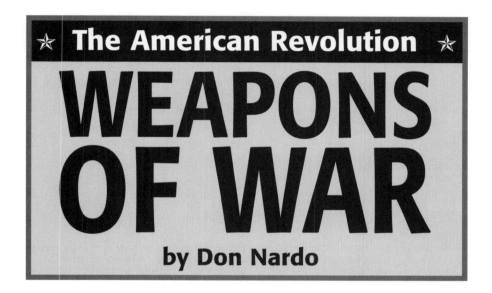

★ The American Revolution ★

# WEAPONS OF WAR

by Don Nardo

LUCENT
BOOKS®

THOMSON
★
GALE

San Diego • Detroit • New York • San Francisco • Cleveland • New Haven, Conn. • Waterville, Maine • London • Munich

THOMSON

————— ✦ —————™

GALE

On cover: "Engagement Between the *Bouhomme Richard* and
the *Sevapis* of Flamborough Head," by Richard Willis 1779.

© 2003 by Lucent Books. Lucent Books is an imprint of The Gale Group, Inc.,
a division of Thomson Learning, Inc.

Lucent Books® and Thomson Learning™ are trademarks used herein under license.

*For more information, contact*
Lucent Books
27500 Drake Rd.
Farmington Hills, MI 48331-3535
Or you can visit our Internet site at http://www.gale.com

**LIBRARY OF CONGRESS CATALOGING-IN-PUBLICATION DATA**

Nardo, Don, 1947-
    Weapons of war / by Don Nardo.
       p. cm. — (American war library. American Revolution series)
Includes bibliographical references and index.
    ISBN 1-59018-226-X (alk. paper)
    1. United States. Continental Army—History—Juvenile literature. 2. Great Britain.
Army—History—Revolution, 1775-1783—Juvenile literature. 3. United States. Continental
Army—Weapons systems—History—Juvenile literature. 4. Great Britain. Army—Weapons
systems—History—18th century—Juvenile literature. 5. United States. Continental
Army—Drill and tactics—History—Juvenile literature. 6. Great Britain. Army—Drill and
tactics—History—18th century—Juvenile literature. 7. United States—History—Revolu-
tion, 1775-1783—Manpower—Juvenile literature. 8. United States—History—Revolution,
1775-1783—Equipment and supplies—Juvenile literature. 9. Military weapons—United
States—History—18th century—Juvenile literature. 10. Military weapons—Great Britain—
History—18th century—Juvenile literature. I. Title. II. Series.
    E259 .N36 2003
    973.3—dc21
                                       2002007293

# ⋆ Contents ⋆

Foreword . . . . . . . . . . . . . . . . . . . . . . . . . . . . . . . . 7

Introduction: The Deciding Factors in the
 American Victory 9

Chapter 1: Muskets and Other Firearms . . . . . . . . . . . . . 16

Chapter 2: Bayonets and Other Bladed Weapons . . . . . . 32

Chapter 3: Formal and Informal Battle Tactics . . . . . . . . 47

Chapter 4: British and American Artillery . . . . . . . . . . . . 63

Chapter 5: Ships and Naval Warfare . . . . . . . . . . . . . . . . 79

Chapter 6: Spies and Military Intelligence . . . . . . . . . . . . 93

Notes . . . . . . . . . . . . . . . . . . . . . . . . . . . . . . . . . . . 109

Glossary . . . . . . . . . . . . . . . . . . . . . . . . . . . . . . . . . 113

For Further Reading . . . . . . . . . . . . . . . . . . . . . . . . . 115

Major Works Consulted . . . . . . . . . . . . . . . . . . . . . . . 116

Additional Works Consulted . . . . . . . . . . . . . . . . . . . . 119

Index . . . . . . . . . . . . . . . . . . . . . . . . . . . . . . . . . . . 121

Picture Credits . . . . . . . . . . . . . . . . . . . . . . . . . . . . . 127

About the Author . . . . . . . . . . . . . . . . . . . . . . . . . . . 128

# A Nation Forged by War

The United States, like many nations, was forged and defined by war. Despite Benjamin Franklin's opinion that "There never was a good war or a bad peace," the United States owes its very existence to the War of Independence, one to which Franklin wholeheartedly subscribed. The country forged by war in 1776 was tempered and made stronger by the Civil War in the 1860s.

The Texas Revolution, the Mexican-American War, and the Spanish-American War expanded the country's borders and gave it overseas possessions. These wars made the United States a world power, but this status came with a price, as the nation became a key but reluctant player in both World War I and World War II.

Each successive war further defined the country's role on the world stage. Following World War II, U.S. foreign policy redefined itself to focus on the role of defender, not only of the freedom of its own citizens, but also of the freedom of people everywhere. During the cold war that followed World War II until the collapse of the Soviet Union, defending the world meant fighting communism. This goal, manifested in the Korean and Vietnam conflicts, proved elusive, and soured the American public on its achievability. As the United States emerged as the world's sole superpower, American foreign policy has been guided less by national interest and more on protecting international human rights. But as involvement in Somalia and Kosovo proves, this goal has been equally elusive.

As a result, the country's view of itself changed. Bolstered by victories in World Wars I and II, Americans first relished the role of protector. But, as war followed war in a seemingly endless procession, Americans began to doubt their leaders, their motives, and themselves. The Vietnam War especially caused people to question the validity of sending its young people to die in places where they were not particularly wanted and for people who did not seem especially grateful.

While the most obvious changes brought about by America's wars have been geopolitical in nature, many other aspects of society have been touched. War often does not bring about change directly, but acts instead like the catalyst in a chemical reaction, accelerating changes already in progress.

Some of these changes have been societal. The role of women in the United States had been slowly changing, but World War II put thousands into the workforce and into uniform. They might have gone back to being housewives after the war, but equality, once experienced, would not be forgotten.

Likewise, wars have accelerated technological change. The necessity for faster airplanes and a more destructive bomb led to the development of jet planes and nuclear energy. Artificial fibers developed for parachutes in the 1940s were used in the clothing of the 1950s.

Lucent Books' American War Library covers key wars in the development of the nation. Each war is covered in several volumes, to allow for more detail and context, and to provide volumes on often neglected subjects, such as the kamikazes of World War II, or weapons used in the Civil War. As with all Lucent Books, notes, annotated bibliographies, and appendixes such as glossaries give students a launching point for further research. In addition, sidebars and archival photographs enhance the text. Together, each volume in the American War Library will aid students in understanding how America's wars have shaped and changed its politics, economics, and society.

# The Deciding Factors in the American Victory

**V**ictory in the age-old enterprise of warfare usually depends on a complex combination of factors. These often include the quality and destructive potential of the weapons of one or both sides, the quantities of these weapons, and the numbers of troops involved and the degree of their training. The size of the territory that troops must defend or occupy (large territories being more difficult either to defend or conquer and hold) is another factor. Others include: the strategies and battlefield tactics employed by the war leaders; the distribution and availability of sufficient horses, ships, troop transports, food, boots, ammunition, and other supplies; the quality of the military intelligence (information gathered by spies) of both sides; the unity and solidarity, or lack thereof, of the attackers or defenders; and the fighting spirit displayed by the attackers or the defenders or both.

All these factors came into play during the American Revolution, the war by which

Britain's North American colonies gained their independence. And it is striking that in most aspects of warfare, the British started out with the upper hand. The military and material disadvantages and difficulties the Americans faced at the outset of the fighting were daunting. Also, the enemy they faced was the most powerful empire on earth. It is not surprising, therefore, that a majority of people on both sides viewed the chances of the rebellion succeeding as slim at best. Still, the patriots possessed a few advantages of their own, which made victory possible in the end. These advantages were, on the whole, less obvious and less tangible from a military standpoint than those of the British; and that may explain why so many people expected Britain to win the conflict.

## Weapons, Troops, and Training

In considering the military advantages and disadvantages of both sides, one finds that the kinds of weapons and battle tactics employed were not a major factor in the outcome. In general, both the British and Americans employed the same weapons. These included muskets, rifles, swords, bayonets, cannons, and warships. Moreover, both sides used these weapons in more or less the same ways.

One American disadvantage at the beginning of the war had less to do with the types of weapons used and more with their quantities. The patriots started out with fewer muskets and far fewer cannons than the British. The Americans also began with no standing, uniformly trained and disciplined army to match that of Britain. They had thousands of militiamen scattered across the former colonies; but these were part-time soldiers with little or no formal training. According to military historian Ian V. Hogg, "The two things needed by an armed force to convert it from a rabble to a viable combat unit are training and discipline; and until these two were acquired, most of the hurriedly-raised American forces were of negligible worth." [1] In addition, the patriots had almost no navy, a severe disadvantage considering that Britain had the largest, finest navy in the world.

The Americans tried to address these problems. Congress called for the manufacture of large numbers of standardized

*American militiamen skirmish with British regulars in Lexington's town square in April 1775.*

muskets. And it raised a standing army of regular soldiers. At first they lacked proper training, but the commander in chief, George Washington, rapidly remedied this situation, and by 1778 the American army had achieved more or less parity with the British forces in training and discipline. Still, the number of American troops remained small. By 1781, Britain's forces in North America totaled almost forty-nine thousand, including more than thirty-nine thousand infantry (foot soldiers); while American forces were often as low as five thousand men. Furthermore, the Americans failed to create an effective navy. In 1776 Congress ordered the construction of thirteen warships, but nearly all of these had been destroyed or captured by 1781.

## Patriots vs. Loyalists

Another serious American disadvantage during the war, one often underestimated today, was a lack of solidarity. Simply put, not all the local inhabitants were patriots. Despite a number of British abuses of the colonies in recent years, some Americans could not imagine no longer being British and did not want to split with the mother country. Because they were still loyal to Britain, they became known as loyalists. (The British called them Tories.) Their numbers were larger than most people today realize. Of about two million five hundred thousand people living in the new nation in 1776, leading patriot John Adams estimated that about a third, or nearly eight hundred fifty thousand, were loyal to the

king. (Another third, he said, were patriots like himself. The rest did not care who governed them.)

The existence of such large numbers of loyalists in the country made fighting a war against Britain extremely difficult. First, the loyalists lived everywhere—in all the cities and throughout the countryside. Considering the patriots to be traitors to the British crown, many loyalists spied on their neighbors and reported what they saw and heard to the British. Moreover, almost fifty thousand loyalists fought on the British side against the patriots. Therefore, the American Revolution was not only a war for independence but also a true civil war in which neighbor fought neighbor. And as noted historians Henry S. Commager and Richard B. Morris point out, many patriots felt threatened enough to resort to harsh measures against loyalists.

The very strength of loyalism in America condemned it to persecution. Had the loyalists been few in number, weak and disorganized, the patriots might have ignored them, or have contented themselves with making sure that they could do no harm. But they were numerous and powerful, strong enough at times to take the offensive against the patriots and endanger the success of the Revolution. It was not, therefore, surprising that even before Independence the Patriots moved to frustrate, intimidate, punish and, if possible, wipe out loyalism. . . . The treatment of the loyalists was harsh,

*A group of patriots force a loyalist out of town, a scene often repeated across the colonies.*

but harshness has almost always characterized the treatment of those who were on the wrong, or losing, side of a revolution. From the point of view of the patriots, the loyalists were traitors and therefore worse than open enemies. Nor can the judicious historian deny that the patriots had considerable justification for their attitude and their actions. Loyalists were numerous enough to be dangerous; they did in fact give aid to the enemy; many were spies and informers, many more sold food supplies to the British; thousands fought in the British ranks. [2]

Considering these disadvantages, as well as others, it is no wonder that many Americans, not to mention most British, felt that America had almost no chance of winning the war. A respected New York man, Charles Inglis, summed up this view in a popular pamphlet in 1776, warning: "Devastation and ruin must mark the progress of this war. Our seacoasts and ports will be ruined, and our ships taken. Torrents of blood will be spilled and thousands [of people] reduced to beggars." [3]

## America's Superior Size and Spirit

The fact that such prophets of doom turned out to be wrong can be attributed to a mixture of American strengths and

British weaknesses. First, the former colonists inhabited a huge country; even though it was confined mainly to a strip of land sandwiched between the Atlantic Ocean and the Appalachian Mountains, it was several times larger than Britain. And America's potential natural resources—such as farmland, timber, minerals, and metals—were staggering. More important, the country was so large that the British could not hope to control it completely without a gigantic army of occupation; and maintaining such large forces across the expanse of an ocean was beyond the abilities of any nation at the time.

Indeed, even the smaller army Britain managed to send to North America was beset by problems in organization and logistics (maintenance and distribution of supplies and troops). And these problems seriously impaired Britain's war effort. "Almost everything the British soldier ate, wore, rode, or fired had to be transported from Britain by ship," Ian Hogg writes, "since there was insufficient material in the colonies." In addition, Britain's

administrative machine was split between . . . [numerous] semi-autonomous agencies . . . all of whom had some vital function which they jealously guarded, and all of whom, to a greater or lesser degree, overlapped the functions and responsibilities of some other agency. All this ensured a fine climate for rivalry. . . . [The system] proved totally unable to adapt to the needs of the fighting troops, which, in consequence, never managed to produce the results demanded of them. [4]

## Another Potent Weapon—Propaganda

In addition to guns, swords, cannons, warships, and spies, both the British and Americans employed no less potent a weapon—propaganda. An excellent example occurred in the hours and days following the war's opening battles, fought at Lexington and Concord on April 19, 1775, as pointed out by noted historians Henry Commager and Richard Morris (in their book *Spirit of 'Seventy-Six*):

> Lexington and Concord was what the patriots had been waiting for. The British had taken the offensive; the British had fired the first shot. Not only this, but the British had been guilty of atrocities to boot—arson and pillage and rapine and murder. All this the Americans alleged, and doubtless believed [although none of it was true]. We think of propaganda as a modern development, but there is very little that [we] could teach the patriots of 1775 about propaganda. The Massachusetts Committee of Safety hurried its version over to England, and broadcast it throughout the colonies. Never before had news traveled so fast. Israel Bissel, a regular postrider, was off on the morning of the nineteenth with the stirring tale; that noon . . . he reached Worcester, and his horse fell dead. The next day he was in New London. Then on to New Haven, and by the twenty-third he reached New York. . . . Other couriers sped the news to New Hampshire [and other colonies]. . . . Everywhere the news of Lexington and Concord strengthened the hands and fired the hearts of the patriots.

Finally, the British soldiers who went, many of them reluctantly, to put down the rebellion were unable to match the spirit of the American troops, who felt they were fighting for their homes and freedom. And significantly, a fair number of British military officers were aware of this important American advantage. As early as April 1775, a British captain wrote to his father overseas, saying that the rebels, though "the most absolute cowards on the face of the earth," were nonetheless "worked up to such a degree of enthusiasm and madness that they are easily persuaded the Lord is to assist them in whatever they undertake, and that they must be invincible."[5] British general Thomas Gage agreed, telling Britain's secretary of war:

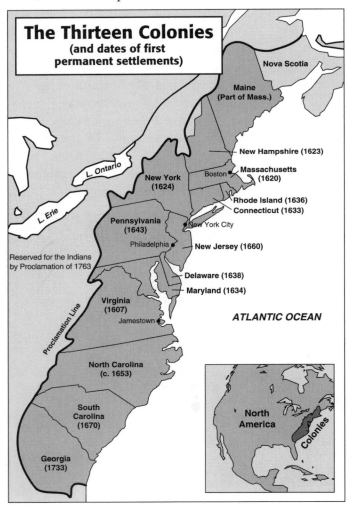

**The Thirteen Colonies**
**(and dates of first permanent settlements)**

Nova Scotia

Maine (Part of Mass.)

L. Ontario

New Hampshire (1623)

New York (1624)

Boston

Massachusetts (1620)

L. Erie

Rhode Island (1636)
Connecticut (1633)

Pennsylvania (1643)

New York City

Philadelphia

New Jersey (1660)

Reserved for the Indians by Proclamation of 1763

Delaware (1638)

Maryland (1634)

Virginia (1607)

Proclamation Line

Jamestown

ATLANTIC OCEAN

North Carolina (c. 1653)

South Carolina (1670)

North America

Colonies

Georgia (1733)

These people show a spirit and conduct against us they never showed against the French [in the recently fought French and Indian War], and everybody has judged of them from their former appearance and behavior [i.e., underestimated them] . . . which has led many into great mistakes. They are now spirited up by a rage and enthusiasm as great as ever people were possessed of, and you must proceed in earnest [i.e., send a lot more troops and supplies] or give the business up . . . Your Lordship would be astonished to see the tract of country they have entrenched and fortified.[6]

At least Gage believed the British might win the war if enough men, weapons, and supplies were brought to bear. By contrast, another British leader,

*Colonists demonstrate their spirit with a cheer after setting fire to a British merchant ship.*

Sergeant Adair, saw the ultimate futility of the British war effort, telling Parliament: "It is my opinion that we cannot conquer America; I have not a doubt that we cannot acquire or maintain a beneficial sovereignty over her by violence and force."[7] As it turned out, Adair was right. No matter what weapons and tactics were used, or how many loyalists the patriots had to contend with, or how superior the British navy was, the size and spirit of the country created in July 1776 ultimately proved to be the deciding factors in the American victory.

# Chapter 1

# Muskets and Other Firearms

The principal firearms used by both sides in the American Revolution were the musket (or firelock), rifle, and pistol. Numerous versions and styles of each existed, some independently crafted, others mass produced. These weapons could be deadly. Yet armies rarely relied on them alone, since they were slow loading and, with the exception of rifles in the hands of expert marksmen, not very accurate. So soldiers used them in combination with various bladed weapons and artillery (cannons and other big guns).

## From Matchlock to Flintlock

Of the main firearms, the musket was by far the most common, being one of the two main weapons wielded by foot soldiers. (The other was the bayonet.) As imperfect as they were, the muskets available by the opening of the Revolution were the end result of about four centuries of technical evolution. The first version appeared in Europe in the mid- to late 1300s. It was so long and heavy that it had to be supported by a pole or wooden framework and usually required two men to operate. Smaller versions that could be carried and fired by a single infantry soldier were in use in the 1400s, but they were inaccurate and took so long to load that a soldier was rarely able to fire more than ten or twelve shots per hour.

The most significant early innovation in musket technology was the matchlock mechanism, introduced in the mid- to late 1400s. Earlier muskets had been ignited by a piece of smoldering rope, the "match," which the gunmen blew on and touched to a hole in the barrel, igniting the gunpowder inside. In the matchlock, by contrast, a metal lever bolted to the top of the barrel held the smoldering match in place. When the gunner pulled the trigger, a spring snapped the lever back so that the match touched and ignited a small amount of powder in a tiny pan. The flash then penetrated a hole in the barrel igniting the powder inside and firing the gun.

Various improvements were made in the matchlock over the years, but the next major technical innovation in musketry did not occur until the mid- to late 1600s. This was the flintlock. It ignited the powder in its pan with sparks from a piece of flint hitting against steel, which increased both the relia-

---

*A fifthteenth-century soldier fires a primitive musket with a smoldering "match" attached.*

bility and loading speed of the weapon. Military historian Archer Jones explains:

The flint, held by the spring-loaded hammer, struck a blow against a plate attached to the cover of the pan, opening the pan as it simultaneously caused sparks which ignited the powder and fired the musket. The mechanism proved much more reliable than the matchlock, initially firing two-thirds of the time as against the matchlock's 50 percent rate. Subsequent improvements enabled the musket to fire 85 percent of the time. The flintlock greatly increased the rate of fire, a process speeded up by the use of an oblong paper cartridge that contained the ball and the proper amount of powder. With the old matchlock, a musketeer first filled his pan from a powderhorn; opened a small wooden cartridge and emptied its powder into the cloth from his hat; took his ramrod [a wooden or metal stick] and rammed the cloth and ball down upon it, and fastened it to the lock, ready to fire at last. With a flintlock the musketeer bit off the end of the cartridge with his teeth, retaining the ball in his mouth; used some powder from the cartridge to fill the pan and poured the remainder down the barrel, following it with the ball from his mouth and the paper of the cartridge; he then used his ramrod to drive the paper and ball down on the powder, and he was ready to fire. Instead of one round a minute, the soldier with a flintlock with paper cartridge could fire two or three or even more rounds in a minute.[8]

The simpler loading process of the flintlock also altered the composition of infantry formations. Before, two musketeers required at least a yard between them to load properly. By contrast, the easier-loading flintlock required as little as twenty-two inches between men, so that a general could double the number of soldiers in each rank (line)

on the battlefield. In turn, this increased the firepower of each rank. Still another improvement in the flintlock was the use of stronger metal alloys for the barrel. This allowed for larger, more powerful powder charges, which increased the velocity of a one-ounce musket ball to about one thousand feet per second, making it more lethal than slower-moving balls.

## Muskets of the Revolution

Flintlock muskets began to be manufactured in quantity in the 1690s, and the British and French standardized their own military ver-

*A modern reenactor loads an authentic Long Land Service Musket, or "Brown Bess."*

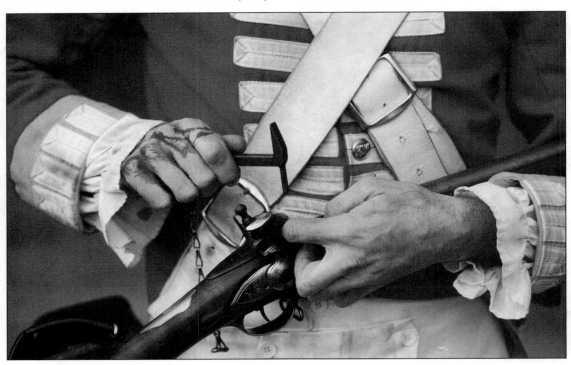

sions in the early 1700s. In the years that followed, the standard British military firearm was the Long Land Service Musket, more commonly known as the "Brown Bess." It weighed about eleven pounds and its barrel was forty-six inches long. The weapon fired a ball weighing a little over an ounce to an effective range of about two hundred yards. In the mid-1760s, the Short Land Service Musket, also referred to as the Brown Bess, appeared, with a barrel thirty-nine to forty inches in length. Better-balanced than the Long Land version, the Short Land musket at first supplemented and over time slowly replaced the Long Land. Therefore, British soldiers were armed with both versions during the Revolution.

The Brown Bess and the slightly lighter (at just under ten pounds) standard French service musket were also commonly used by Americans in the mid-1700s. Somewhat less common in America was a Prussian (German) musket with a forty-three-inch barrel and a Dutch musket. Much more prevalent, however, were nonstandardized muskets made in limited numbers in small American and European workshops. These weapons came in a wide variety of lengths, weights, styles, bores, and calibers. (The bore is the inside of the barrel and the caliber is the specific width of the bore.) This bewildering diversity of muskets presented no difficulty in peacetime. As Ian Hogg points out:

It mattered little to a New England farmer if his musket happened to have a bore of .63 [inch] or .72, or some other odd caliber, governed entirely by the boring bit that happened to be handy when the gunsmith made the weapon. The farmer made his own bullets in a mold provided by the same gunsmith, and his expenditure [use] of ammunition was negligible compared to his ability to mold more during his non-hunting periods. [9]

Thus, when American militiamen left their farms and businesses to fight, they carried muskets of varying designs and effectiveness. This situation was adequate for a few impromptu battles, but not for fighting a prolonged war that required arming large numbers of disciplined soldiers with weapons of standard reliability and effectiveness. To this end, in July 1775 the infant U.S. Congress called for the manufacture of standardized muskets to be overseen by the various Committees of Safety, groups set up in the colonies to implement defensive measures. The resolution stated:

It [is] recommended to the Colonies that they set and keep their gunsmiths at work to manufacture good firelocks with bayonets. Each firelock [is] to be made with a good bridle lock, of $\frac{3}{4}$ inch bore and of good substance to the breech. The barrel [is] to be 3 feet 8 inches in length, the bayonet to be 18 inches in the blade, with a steel ramrod . . . the price to be fixed by the Assembly or Convention [i.e.,

Congress] or Committee of Safety of each Colony.[10]

*A colonist fires his musket in this reenactment. Such weapons frequently misfired.*

At first, the American service musket was similar to the British Brown Bess, with a barrel length of forty-four inches (half way between the Long Land and Short Land versions). But in time the Committees of Safety adopted a musket closer in design to the lighter French version.

## Musket Drills and Commands

Supplying the soldiers of one's army with muskets was one thing, and making sure that the weapons were used proficiently and effectively was another. Firing a flintlock required a series of precise steps executed in a specific order; if the gunman made a mistake in any single step, the weapon failed to fire. And too many misfires on the battlefield could spell defeat for an army. Consequently, the British rigorously drilled their musketeers in the actions of carrying, shouldering, loading, aiming, firing, and reloading their weapons. During training, and often on the battlefield, too, a junior officer in charge of an infantry unit issued a verbal command for each action. This excerpt from an official British war manual, *Exercise of the Firelock*, illustrates the extraordinary degree of complexity and precision involved in each action:

Upon the command "Prime and Load," make a quarter face [turn] to the right . . . at the same time bringing down the firelock to the priming position, with the left hand at the well, the side-brass touching the right hip, the thumb of the right hand placed in front of the hammer with the fingers clenched, the firelock nearly horizontal. Open the pan. . . . Upon the command "Handle Cartridge," 1st, draw the cartridge from the pouch. 2nd, bring it to the mouth, holding [it] between the forefinger and thumb, and bite off the top of the cartridge. On the command "Prime," 1st, shake out some powder into the pan and place the three last fingers on the hammer. 2nd, shut the pan. . . . 3rd, seize the small [part] of the butt with the above three fingers. Upon the command "About," turn the piece nimbly round to the loading position, meeting the muzzle [front] with the heel of the hand, the butt within two inches of the ground, and the flat of it against the left ankle. 2nd, place the butt on the ground without noise, raise the elbow square with the shoulder, shake the powder into the barrel [of the musket], putting in after it the paper and ball. 3rd, drop the right elbow close to the body and seize the head of the ramrod. . . . Upon the command "Draw Ramrods," 1st, force the ramrod half [way] out and seize it back-handed exactly in the middle. . . . 2nd, draw it entirely out . . . [and] turning it at the same time to the front, put it one inch into the barrel. Upon the command "Ram Down Cartridge," 1st, push the ramrod down till the second finger touches the muzzle. Second, press the ramrod lightly towards you and slip the two fingers and thumb to the point, then grasp [it] as before. 3rd, push the cartridge well down to the bottom. 4th, strike it two very quick strokes with the ramrod. [11]

This and similar manuals go on in the same manner, providing exact instructions for each command. The chain of steps involved may seem overly complicated to the modern observer who is accustomed to the more simple operation of modern guns. However, through repeated drills and practice, eighteenth-century British soldiers became adept at performing these steps almost as second nature.

At first, most of the musketeers of the American regular army lacked this kind of precise instruction and the formal drilling that accompanied it. And this deficiency contributed to several defeats the patriots suffered in the early stages of the war. In 1778, however, General Washington assigned an experienced Prussian soldier, named Baron Frederick von Steuben, the task of instituting systematic musket training and drills. Von Steuben trained the Americans in European, or "Continental," methods and tactics and subsequently issued a manual that remained standard in the United States Army well into the nineteenth century. This excerpt covers the actions of cocking, aiming, and firing a flintlock musket:

[To cock the firelock] turn the barrel opposite to your face, and place your thumb upon the cock, raising the elbow square at this motion. Cock the firelock by drawing down your elbow, immediately placing your thumb upon the breech-pin, and the fingers under the guard. [To aim the firelock] step back about six inches with the right foot, bringing the left toe to the front; at the same time drop the muzzle and bring up the butt-end of the firelock against your right shoulder; place the left hand forward on the swell of the stock, and the forefinger of the right hand before the trigger, sinking the muzzle a little below level, and with the right eye looking along the barrel. [To fire the firelock] pull the trigger briskly, and immediately after bringing up the right foot, come to the priming position, placing the heels even, with the right toe pointing to the right, the lock opposite the right breast, the muzzle directly to the front and as high as the hat, the left hand just forward of the feather-spring, holding the piece firm and steady; and at the same time seize the cock with the forefinger and thumb of the right hand, the back of the hand turned up.[12]

## Early Rifles: Advantages and Disadvantages

Although the musket could be effective when operated correctly and fired in large numbers simultaneously, it possessed a serious drawback stemming from the nature of

*Baron von Steuben shows a group of American soldiers how to load and fire their muskets.*

## Ranks of Muskets Alternating Fire

This excerpt from Baron von Steuben's Revolutionary War manual, used by American troops in the war, is titled "Position of Each Rank in the Firings." It instructs musket-bearing soldiers in the proper coordination of two or more ranks of men alternating their fire so as to maximize the destructive effect on the enemy.

Front Rank! Make Ready! One motion.

Spring the firelock briskly to a recover, as soon as the left hand seizes the firelock above the lock, the right elbow is to be nimbly raised a little, placing the thumb of that hand upon the cock, the fingers open by the plate of the lock, and as quickly as possible cock the piece, by dropping the elbow, and forcing down the cock with the thumb, immediately seizing the firelock with the right hand, close under the lock; the piece to be held in this manner perpendicular, opposite the left side of the face, the body kept straight, and as full to the front as possible, and the head held up, looking well to the right.

Take Aim! Fire!

As before explained.

Rear Rank! Make Ready! One motion.

Recover and cock as before directed, at the same time stepping about six inches to the right, so as to place yourself opposite the interval of the front rank.

Take Aim! Fire!

As before explained.

its bore. The inside walls of the barrel were smooth, hence the common term "smoothbore musket." For various technical reasons, the ball was smaller than the bore; for example, the Long Land Service Musket had a caliber of .753 inch, but the ball it fired was .70 inch across. The space between the edge of the ball and inside of the barrel, in this case .053 inch, was called windage. The problem was that the windage allowed the ball to meander from side to side as it moved down the barrel so that it exited the gun slightly off center, contributing to its inaccuracy.

In contrast, another firearm used in the Revolution—the rifle—largely eliminated this drawback. The term rifle is derived from the weapon's "rifling," or set of spiral grooves etched into the inside walls of the barrel. When the weapon fired, the ball spun through the grooves and exited the gun spinning; at the same time, the ball made a tight fit in the bore, almost eliminating the windage. The result was a much more accurate shot. Another advantage of the rifle, Hogg explains, was its

greater range and velocity, due again to the tight fit of the ball. The musket ball's windage allowed a proportion of the propelling gas to rush past and be wasted in muzzle blast, whereas the rifle ball, firmly lodged in the rifling, sealed all the gas behind it and extracted every available scrap of performance from the powder. [13]

It is unknown when the concept of rifling a gun was first introduced. Early specimens

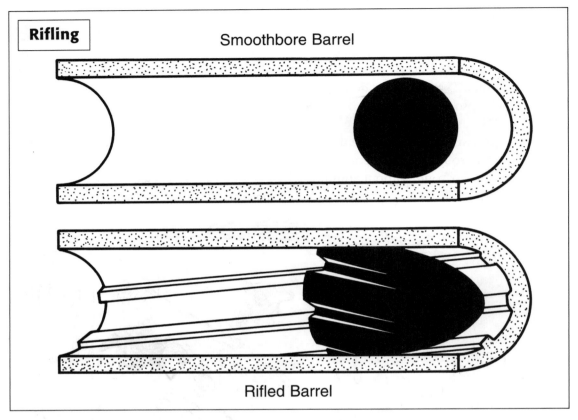

**Rifling**

Smoothbore Barrel

Rifled Barrel

dating from the 1540s have survived. However, the manufacturing technique required special tools and much skill, so the rifle was not widely adopted until the 1600s, and even then remained mainly a hunter's weapon. The rifle reached the American colonies in the early 1700s when German and Swiss gunsmiths emigrated across the Atlantic and set up shop. At first they were large weapons with calibers ranging from .5 to .7 inches; but over time American frontiersmen demanded lighter guns with smaller bores, so a more distinctly American version with a bore of .45 inch became

common. Because most of the gunsmiths who made this version lived in Pennsylvania's Lancaster County, it became known as the Pennsylvania Rifle. (The romantic but less accurate term "Kentucky Rifle," which is better known today, was not applied to the weapon until the early nineteenth century.)

The main reason that the rifle remained only a supplement to the less accurate musket in the American Revolution was that the rifle took much longer to load. The rifleman first had to force the ball into the rifling near the muzzle, often with a mallet, and then use his ramrod to push it farther down into the barrel. Most riflemen could get off only one shot per minute, or two at best. That was enough time for an enemy soldier to close in and bayonet the rifleman before he was finished reloading; so the rifle was impractical in large battles. In fact, American general Anthony Wayne wrote to a colleague that he "would almost as soon face an enemy with a good musket and bayonet without ammunition," than with a rifle.[14]

## Sharpshooting Riflemen

Nevertheless, riflemen were highly effective as long-range sharpshooters who could pick off individual enemy soldiers, especially officers. In a battle fought at Bemis Heights, New York, in September 1777, a famous squad of riflemen under Daniel Morgan successfully killed several English officers at long

*An American gunsmith and his assistants manufacture muskets and rifles one at a time.*

range. After the battle, the defeated British commander, General John Burgoyne, recalled:

> The enemy had with their army great numbers of marksmen, armed with rifle-barrel pieces [i.e., rifles]. These, during the engagement, hovered upon the flanks [sides] in small detachments, and were very expert in securing themselves and in shifting their ground. In this action, many placed themselves in high trees in the rear of their own line, and there was seldom a minute's interval of smoke in any part of our line without officers being taken [picked] off by single shots. [15]

Another British officer, George Hanger, whom the Americans took prisoner about a month later at Saratoga, New York, had a chance to meet some of these notorious sharpshooters. "I have many times asked the American backwoodsmen what was the most their best marksmen could do," he later wrote.

> They have constantly told me that an expert rifleman, provided he can draw good and true sight . . . can hit the head of a man at 200 yards. I am certain that, provided an American rifleman was to get a perfect aim at 300 yards at me standing still, he most undoubtedly would hit me, unless it was a very windy day. [16]

## An Incredible Shot

A British officer, George Hanger, who was captured by the Americans at Saratoga and survived the war, later penned this compelling eyewitness account (from his book written for sportsmen) describing the amazing skill of an American rifleman:

Colonel Tarleton, and myself, were standing a few yards out of a wood, observing the situation of a part of the enemy which we intended to attack. . . . It was absolutely a plain field between us and mill; not so much as a single bush on it. Our orderly-bugler stood behind us about three yards. . . . A[n American] rifleman passed over the mill-dam, evidently observing two officers, and laid himself down on his belly; for in such positions, they always lie, to take a good shot at a long distance. He took a deliberate and cool shot at my friend, at me, and at the bugle-horn man. Now observe how well this fellow shot. It was in the month of August, and not a breath of wind was stirring. Colonel Tarleton's horse and mine, I am certain, were not anything like two feet apart. . . . A rifle-ball passed between him and me; looking directly to the mill I . . . observed the flash of the powder. I directly said to my friend, "I think we had better move." . . . The words were hardly out of my mouth when the bugle-horn man behind me . . . jumped off his horse and said, "Sir, my horse is shot." The horse staggered, fell down, and died. . . . Now speaking of this rifleman's shooting, nothing could be better. . . . I have passed several times over this ground and ever observed it with the greatest attention; and I can positively assert that the distance he fired from at us was full 400 yards!

*From his hiding place in a tree, an American sharpshooter kills two British soldiers.*

It was Hanger's good fortune never to be hit by an American rifleman. The fate of one British officer who *was* so hit turned out to be one of the great ironies of the war. Long a gun enthusiast as well as a soldier, Scotsman Patrick Ferguson invented his own version of the rifle, which modern experts believe was the most effective firearm made in the eighteenth century.

Reportedly, it could fire four to six shots per minute, making it faster, as well as more accurate, than any musket. In April 1776, Ferguson demonstrated his rifle to his superiors, who were impressed enough to have him make one hundred more. To test the new weapon, in September 1777 Ferguson led a unit of a hundred British riflemen into battle at Brandywine Creek, in Pennsylvania. Unfortunately, he was seriously wounded before his men could prove themselves and the British unwisely disbanded the unit. If they had instead replaced all their muskets with Ferguson rifles, they might have won the war.[17]

As for Ferguson, he recovered and fought the Americans again, in October 1780, at Kings Mountain, near the border of North and South Carolina. The great rifleman was done in by swarms of his American counterparts. One of them, James Collins, later recalled:

> On examining [Ferguson's body] . . . it appeared that almost fifty rifles must have been leveled at him at the same time. Seven rifle balls had passed through his body, both his arms were broken, and his hat and clothing were literally shot to pieces.[18]

Sharpshooting riflemen like those who slew Ferguson did not always kill their opponents, however. Indeed, they were skilled enough to be highly selective and aim to wound when they felt the occasion warranted it. In January 1778, for example, Pennsylvania frontiersman John McCasland, an expert marksman, wounded and captured a Hessian (German) mercenary soldier to prevent him from looting. "On one occasion," MacCasland later wrote when applying for a military pension,

sixteen of us were ranging about hunting Hessians, and we suspected Hessians to be at a large and handsome mansion house in Bucks County, Pennsylvania, about sixteen miles from Philadelphia. We approached near the house and discovered a large Hessian standing in the yard with his gun, as a sentinel we supposed, and by a unanimous vote of the company present it was agreed on that Major McCorman or myself, who were good marksmen, should shoot him. . . . We cast lots, and it fell to my lot to shoot the Hessian. I did not like to shoot a man down in cold blood. The company present knew I was a good marksman, and I concluded to break his thigh. I shot with a rifle and aimed at his hip. He had a large iron tobacco box in his breeches pocket, and I hit the box, the ball glanced, and it entered his thigh and scaled the bone of the thigh on the outside. He fell and then rose. We scaled the yard fence and surrounded the house. They [the Hessian and his companions] saw their situation and were evidently disposed to surrender. They could not speak English, and we could not understand their language. . . . They were twelve in number. We took them prisoners and carried them to Valley Forge and delivered them up to General Washington.[19]

## Flintlock Pistols

Paralleling the development and use of flintlock muskets and rifles was that of flintlock pistols. To load and fire such a pistol required the same precise and laborious series of steps involved in using other flintlock weapons. And similarly, rifled pistols were more accurate than smoothbore versions. Although most were muzzle loaded, some had barrels that unscrewed, allowing them to be breech loaded (that is, from the back), which eliminated the need for a ramrod. Being smaller, the typical pistol naturally lacked the firepower of a musket or rifle; to compensate somewhat, some gunsmiths made versions with double barrels.

In peacetime, most pistols manufactured before the mid-nineteenth century were used for individual self-defense, protecting one's home, or dueling. In wartime, most infantrymen did not carry pistols, partly because it was too difficult for a soldier to carry and use both pistols and muskets, and also because belt holsters had not

*The spring-loaded hammer and plate are clearly visible on this surviving flintlock pistol.*

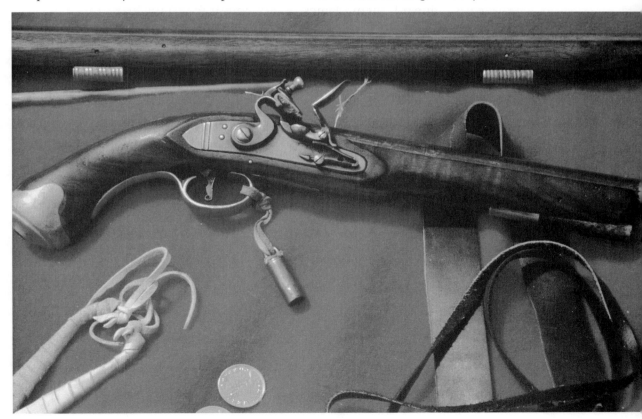

yet been invented. The weapon was limited mainly to officers, who customarily did not carry muskets or rifles; sailors, who used pistols in the hand-to-hand combat that occurred when they boarded enemy ships; and cavalrymen, who found a pistol easier to wield than a musket or rifle while charging on horseback. Unlike the officer or sailor, the cavalryman had to worry about the weapon's discharge frightening his horse. A 1778 military manual, *The Discipline of the Light Horse,* gave this advice about acclimating a horse to the sound and smell of its rider's pistol:

> To [get your] horse [used] to [the discharge of] firearms, first put a pistol . . . in . . . with his feed, [get him used] to the sound of the lock and pan [i.e., cocking the weapon]; after which, when you are upon him, show it [the pistol] to him, presenting it forwards, sometimes on one side, sometimes on the other; when he is reconciled to that, proceed to flash in the pan [ignite the powder]; after which, put a small charge into the piece, and so continue augmenting it [increasing the size of the charge] by degrees. . . . If he seems uneasy, walk him forwards a few steps slowly, and then stop, [move him] back, and caress him.[20]

In the opening years of the war, American cavalrymen and sailors used mainly British-made pistols, which at the time were the most common version in the former colonies. As time went on, however, pistols were imported from numerous foreign countries. The most popular were Dutch versions, which featured calibers ranging

## Craftsmanship of Pistols

In this excerpt from *Weapons of the American Revolution and Accouterments,* military historian Warren Moore tells about the diverse craftsmen involved in the manufacture of the British and American pistols used in the war.

The tradesmen involved in the fabrication of pistols consisted of a barrelforger, locksmith, wood stocker or carver, engraver, and metalsmith. Almost all English pistols had the maker's name engraved or stamped across the lockplate, and sometimes on the barrel also. Some of the later firms made the entire gun in their shops, employing workers from all of the trades mentioned above. Others were simply assemblers of parts which were made to their specifications by the respective specialists, the finished product being assembled by workers in their shops. Gunsmiths engaged in making military arms for the British government followed strict specifications, and supplied either the finished weapon, or else batches of finished parts which were later assembled. . . . Of course, there were a number of American-made pistols used in the Revolution. . . . The stocks of these were usually made of native woods such as maple or cherry. . . . For the most part they incorporated a British- or European-made lock. . . . In contrast to the handsome appearance and expert workmanship of English pistols, most of the American pistols were extremely plain.

from .65 to .69 inches, barrels eleven to fifteen inches long, and a weight of just over three pounds; and French versions, which came in a wide variety of designs and sizes. The most common pistol used by Americans in the later years of the war was a French version with a caliber of .65 inch, a nine-inch barrel, and a weight of roughly two and a half pounds.

Thus, the pistols of the American Revolution were a mix of weapons that were made in many countries. It was not until 1799, well after the end of the war, that the U.S. government instituted a standardized army pistol. Manufactured by Simeon North of Connecticut, it closely followed the design of a 1777 French version.

# Chapter 2

# Bayonets and Other Bladed Weapons

**B**laded, or edged, weapons are generally defined as those featuring an exposed, sharpened metal surface suitable for slicing, hacking, or stabbing an enemy. The principal bladed weapons of the American Revolution included the bayonet, the sword and dagger, the halberd (or poleax), the spear (or pike, or spontoon), and the hatchet (a one-handed ax, also called a tomahawk). It is important to emphasize that at the time of the Revolution firearms had not yet replaced bladed weapons in battle—an evolutionary process that began in late medieval times and was not completed until the twentieth century. In fact, bladed weapons were just as prominent in, and crucial to, combat as firearms in the American Revolution.

## Evolution of the Bayonet

The importance of bladed weapons in the American war for independence is most clearly exemplified by the bayonet. Although muskets and rifles played major roles in battle in this period, the bayonet, more than any other weapon, determined the winners of most of the infantry engagements of the eighteenth century. The most characteristic feature of the large battles of the American Revolution was long lines of soldiers facing off with bayonets attached to their muskets. After discharging their muskets one or more times, the troops charged the enemy, attempting to stab them with their bayonets. And it was not uncommon for one side to fall back and retreat before this dreaded bladed onslaught.

A brief summary of the evolution of the bayonet reveals why it was used this way, as well as why it was so widely effective and feared. In effect, it was a later substitute for the pike, a long spear used by infantry in ancient and medieval times. In the 1300s and 1400s, a few armies, most notably that of the Swiss, developed large infantry formations of soldiers bearing outstretched pikes. Armed soldiers creating a forest of bristling spearpoints proved to be a formidable defensive barrier on the battlefield; and it was extremely lethal when it marched forward on the offensive. Later, in the 1500s and 1600s, generals combined units of musketeers with their pikemen. The musketeers, whose guns were still very slow loading and therefore vulnerable to enemy infantry and especially cavalry, stood inside a protective barrier of pikes. The pikemen kept the enemy at bay while the gunmen reloaded.

With the appearance of faster loading, more reliable flintlock muskets in the 1600s, guns became much more effective on the battlefield. But they were still not reliable or lethal enough to stop a large cavalry charge by themselves. Rows of pikes

were still needed for that. A few military innovators recognized that the best solution was somehow to combine both weapons into one. And the result was the introduction of the bayonet, a bladed weapon that simulated the end of a pike and could also be mounted on a musket.

The exact origins of the bayonet are unclear. But the first version used in warfare, called a plug bayonet, was apparently made in France in the mid-1600s. It was essentially a long dagger with a tapering handle; the term "plug" referred to the fact that the soldier

*An American bayonet charge devastates the British at Cowpens in January 1781.*

stuffed the handle into the muzzle of his musket, plugging it. In this way, he converted his gun into a pikelike weapon. This allowed a general to convert his pikemen into musketeers, thereby increasing the firepower of his army while maintaining a way to stop cavalry charges; namely, when enemy cavalry threatened, the gunmen fired off a round and then quickly inserted their bayonets, creating a wall of steel to fend off the horsemen.

It soon became clear, however, that plug bayonets had a serious disadvantage. After they had been inserted, the muskets could not be fired. So the troops could alternate either as gunmen or as quasi-pikemen, but they could not be both at the same time. What was needed was a bayonet that could be permanently attached to a musket while leaving the barrel free for firing. And that need was fulfilled when the socket bayonet appeared, again in France, in the late 1600s. According to noted military historian George C. Neumann, it

> employed a metal sleeve that slipped over the muzzle of the gun. A narrow neck branching out from the sleeve's upper end supported the blade. Since the blade was now offset from the bore and parallel to the barrel, the musket could be loaded and fired while the bayonet remained in place. Versions of the new socket design were widely adopted by both the English and French armies just after 1700—although the "plug" continued in use for at least another decade. [21]

## American Adoption of Bayonets

The bayonet caught on quickly in Europe and became one of the two principal infantry weapons (the other being the musket itself) used there in the early 1700s. However, bayonets did not achieve the same popularity in Britain's American colonies during the same period. This was probably because most of the fighting the colonists had engaged in over the years had consisted of informal skirmishes against Indians, in which bayonets were of little or no use.

The Americans had their first major exposure to bayonets in the French and Indian War, fought in North America between 1754 and 1763. But most of the fighting was between trained British and French troops and few colonists gained any real experience with the weapon. For these reasons, at the outset of their war for independence the Americans lacked both appreciation for, and skill with, what was at the time the most reliable weapon in the British arsenal.

This shortcoming was not lost on American war planners. In 1775, Congress recommended that each state see that its militia had supplies of bayonets. The regular army commanded by George Washington needed bayonets even more, since these troops would bear the brunt of the fighting with the highly trained British regulars. There was a rush, therefore, to find and/or produce as many bayonets as possible. Some of those used by American soldiers in the war were captured from British troops or arsenals;

others were purchased from the French, Germans, and other Europeans; and still others were manufactured in American forges and workshops. At first, the American-made versions were patterned after British models; but as time went on, they increasingly resembled French bayonets.

While the Americans accumulated bayonets and began training with them, they learned firsthand how devastating these weapons could be, not only on the open battlefield but also in surprise attacks. The so-called Paoli Massacre was a prime example. In mid-September 1777, George Washington tried to maneuver his army to attack the British near Philadelphia. In the meantime, he sent General Anthony Wayne with a small force to attack the enemy from the rear. Unfortunately, local loyalists discovered Wayne's camp at Paoli, and alerted the British. Just after midnight on September 21, British redcoats bristling with bayonets fell on the camp. The unprepared American soldiers suffered heavy casualties, as reported a few days later by an American major, Samuel Hay:

[It was] a scene of butchery. All was confusion. . . . I need not go on to give

*This reenactor, authentically dressed as an American private, wields a socket bayonet.*

the particulars, but the enemy rushed on with fixed bayonets and made the use of them they intended. So you may figure to yourself what followed. The party lost 300 privates in [those] killed,

## Bayonets Take Stony Point

On July 15, 1779, 1,350 American troops commanded by General Anthony Wayne captured the fort at Stony Point, on the west side of the Hudson River in New York, using only bayonets. British losses totaled 63 killed, 70 or more wounded, and 543 captured. According to another American officer, Nathaniel Greene (as quoted in Henry Johnston's *The Storming of Stony Point*):

> The attack was made about midnight and conducted with great spirit and enterprise, the troops marching up in the face of an exceeding heavy fire with cannon and musketry, without discharging a gun. This is thought to be the perfection of discipline and will forever immortalize Gen. Wayne, as it would do honor to the first general in Europe. . . . The darkness of the night favored the attack and made our loss much less than might have been expected. The whole business was done with fixed bayonets. Our loss in killed and wounded amounted to ninety men, including officers—eight only of which were killed. . . . The enemy made little resistance after our people [armed with their bayonets] got into the works; their cry was, "Mercy, mercy, dear, dear Americans!"

wounded, and missing, besides commissioned and non-commissioned officers. . . . The 22nd, I went to the ground to see the wounded. The scene was shocking—the poor men groaning under their wounds, which were all by stabs of bayonets and cuts of . . . swords. Col. Grier was wounded in the side by a bayonet, superficially slanting to the breast bone. Captain Wilson's stabbed in the side. . . . Andrew Irvine was run through the fleshy part of the thigh with a bayonet.[22]

### The Sword

Next to the bayonet, the most important bladed weapon used in the American Revolution was the sword. Until the advent of widespread use of the bayonet in the early 1700s, the sword was a standard tool of warfare in Europe, the Near East, and elsewhere for at least five thousand years. Most often it was used as a backup weapon to supplement the spear, bow and arrow, lance, pike, or some other primary weapon. Moreover, off the battlefield the sword had considerable social and family value, especially in late medieval and early modern Europe. "To the civilian," Neumann explains,

> it represented his social standing in a highly stratified [class-conscious] society; to the officer it indicated his status and rank—as well as a means of defending his honor in the duel. . . . Family swords also represented strong emotional ties, as many of them are found listed for chosen heirs in 18th century wills.[23]

By the beginning of the American war for independence, however, many, if not most, British and other European infantrymen no longer carried swords into battle. This was because their bayonets performed roughly the same cutting and stabbing functions. There were some exceptions, including grenadiers (elite infantry units), drummers and fifers, and officers. But by the end of the war, all of these had largely stopped carrying swords except for certain officers. In contrast, American infantry were somewhat slower to abandon swords. In the opening year of the war, Congress called for soldiers to carry swords and hatchets in addition to bayonets. Although many ordinary foot soldiers gradually stopped wearing swords during the conflict, American officers were actually required to carry them throughout the war.

The situation was different outside the infantry. For the cavalry soldier of this period

*An American officer uses his sword to try to fend off a bayonet attack.*

the saber, a formidable slashing sword, was the primary offensive weapon; it was seen as more reliable and lethal than the horseman's other main weapon, the pistol. The superiority of the saber was ably summarized by Epaphras Hoyt, a noted Massachusetts cavalry captain, in his *Treatise on the Military Art:*

> It is generally agreed by experienced officers, that firearms are seldom of any great utility to cavalry in an engagement, while they are drawn up in regiments, squadrons, or other considerable bodies. Indeed, there is little hope for success from any who begin their attack with the fire of carbines [rifles] or pistols; numerous examples could be cited from military history to show their ineffi-

ciency. It is by the right use of the sword that they [cavalrymen] are to expect victory. This is indisputably the most formidable and useful weapon of cavalry. Nothing decides an engagement sooner than charging briskly with this weapon in hand. By this mode of attack, a body of cavalry will generally rout one that receives it with pistols ready to fire.[24]

Hundreds of different styles and sizes of cavalry swords (as well as other kinds of swords) existed. But the most popular type used by American horse soldiers in the Revolution was a light saber with a curved blade. The blade varied in length from thirty-two and one-half to thirty-six and one-half inches and was attached to the pommel (knob on the saddle's front) by a

## Major Sword Types

The swords used in the American Revolution by American, British, French, German, and other fighters fell into seven general categories:

The first—hangers—included swords with short blades (averaging about twenty-five inches), having one or two sharpened edges; they were originally used by ordinary infantry soldiers, but by the time of the Revolution they had become mainly officers' weapons. The second type, hunting swords, were designed for nonmilitary tasks, but were sometimes worn by both land and naval officers off the battlefield as symbols of their rank. Short sabers, having blades averaging twenty-eight to thirty-two inches in length, were single-edged weapons used mostly by infantry officers in combat. The

fourth type, the small sword, was a weapon with a thin, straight blade designed for thrusting; it was worn mainly by well-to-do gentlemen off the battlefield, especially in America, and required a great deal of skill and training to use properly. The basket-hilted sword, of Scottish origin, was most often a large broadsword, a weapon with a long, straight, double-edged blade, used by both foot soldiers and horsemen. The sixth category consisted of cavalry swords; the two main types were long sabers with single-edged blades designed for slashing, and double-edged broadswords. Finally, the naval cutlass, used mainly by sailors, was like a saber, only shorter and with a wider hand guard on the hilt.

*This American cavalry officer brandishes a saber, a formidable slashing weapon.*

small metal nut. The saber wielded by Epaphras Hoyt himself, which is preserved in Memorial Hall in Deerfield, Massachusetts, is of this type.

Sailors also used swords. The naval version of the weapon came to be called a cutlass in the second half of the eighteenth century. The blade of a cutlass, generally a bit shorter than that of a cavalry saber, was straight or slightly curved and had a cutting edge on one side only. The hilt had an unusually wide guard to protect the hand in the close-in fighting common in naval boarding tactics. The average seaman carried his cutlass naked (without a sheath) by thrusting it through his belt.

Most of the time soldiers and sailors drew their swords only during battle. However, occasionally these weapons were used to kill unarmed civilians or prisoners in cold blood. Today many Americans are surprised to learn that such atrocities were perpetrated by both sides during the American Revolution. In this excerpt from his gripping narrative of the battle of Haw River in February 1781, in which American troops defeated a force of loyalists (Tories), American fighter Moses Hall describes such nefarious use of swords:

The evening after our battle with the Tories, we having a considerable number of prisoners, I recollect a scene which made a lasting impression upon my mind. I was invited by some of my comrades to go and see some of the prisoners. We went to where six were standing together. Some discussion taking place, I heard some of our men cry out, "Remember Buford" [a reference to an earlier massacre carried out by the Tories],

## The English Bayonet

In this excerpt from his informative book, *Swords and Blades of the American Revolution,* military historian George C. Neumann describes the standard English bayonet, which emerged about 1720 and remained more or less unchanged until the early nineteenth century.

Its total length was just over 21 inches. The 4-inch long socket had an outside diameter of slightly more than one inch, and a rear reinforcing ring. Its blade approximated 17 inches from the tip to the base guard and was triangular in cross section (i.e., for stabbing instead of cutting), with a flat top surface. . . . Across the blade's end (where it joined the neck) was a raised triangular base guard. Standard Brown Bess muskets of the 18th century had a top rectangular bayonet stud. The bayonet socket included a three-step slot through which the stud slid.

and the prisoners were immediately hewed to pieces with broadswords. At first I bore the scene without any emotion, but upon a moment's reflection, I felt such horror as I never did before nor have since, and, returning to my quarters and throwing myself upon my blanket, I contemplated the cruelties of war until overcome and unmanned by a distressing gloom from which I was not relieved until commencing our march next morning.[25]

### Knives, Daggers, and Hatchets

The use of bladed weapons smaller than swords was widespread in the American Revolution. Most American men carried knives of one type or another both on and off the battlefield. Perhaps most common was the belt knife, with a single-edged blade designed mainly for cutting; it was most often used as a tool—for skinning game, chopping food, whittling, and so forth—but it could also be used as a weapon to stab or scalp someone. A person carried a belt knife either in a leather sheath that attached to the belt or naked in the belt.

Daggers were slightly bigger knives designed specifically for fighting. Such a weapon usually had a symmetrical tapering blade, averaging six to ten inches in length, with two sharp edges, so that it could be used both to slash and stab. Many American soldiers, especially frontiersmen and militiamen, carried daggers; and some of them preferred to use them instead of bayonets in hand-to-hand combat. Some British fighters also carried daggers. Most notable was the dirk, of Scottish origin, with a thin, single-edged blade measuring twelve to seventeen inches long.

The hatchet, or small one-handed ax, was a common tool and weapon in colonial America. The terms hatchet, half-ax, belt-ax, and tomahawk (from an Indian word) were used more or less interchangeably in the colonies in the eighteenth century. Both settlers and soldiers used hatchets for clearing brush and cutting down small trees. And the hatchet's value as a personal weapon became clear early on. Metal hatchets were particularly valuable to white Europeans in the prosperous trade with American Indians, since they were superior to traditional stone tomahawks and therefore much in demand among Native Americans. One white trader, Sir William Johnson, estimated that he sold about ten thousand hatchets to Indians in the year 1765 alone.

During the American Revolution, a majority of American fighters carried hatchets. Many in the militia and regular infantry had them, and they were standard backup weapons for riflemen. Some British infantrymen also carried the belt-ax as a backup. Because of the secondary role it played, few descriptions of the hatchet's use in battle have survived, but the following exception vividly shows how lethal it—as well as the knife—could be in a fight. In the summer of 1778, an American, David Welch, who was serving in Vermont, took part in a fight to the death with one of

*Hatchets and knives play key roles in this battle between colonists and Indians.*

Britain's Native American allies. Happening on two American Indians beside a campfire in the woods, Welch crept up on them. "I drew my gun," he later wrote,

> and whilst lying thus flat on the ground, I took deliberate aim at one of the Indians and shot him dead. The other Indian instantly sprung upon his feet, seizing his gun, and started to run. Without reflecting upon the consequence, I immediately ran after him, having my gun unloaded. The Indian made but a few leaps after I started before he turned and fired upon me, but his fire missed . . . by several feet. He then dropped his gun and came at me with his tomahawk. I encountered him with my empty gun. The first blow which he aimed with his tomahawk I warded off with my gun, and in doing it I was so fortunate as to hook the deadly weapon from him. It fell upon the ground rather behind me. I was then encouraged and sprung to get the tomahawk, in which effort I succeeded. Whilst I was yet bent in picking up the tomahawk, the Indian, who had drawn his knife, gave me a cut, giving me a deep but short wound upon my right leg a little above my knee. He then aimed a second stroke at me with the same weapon. This blow I warded off with my left hand, in doing which I received a wound between the thumb and forefinger. About the same instant, with the tomahawk I hit him a blow on the head which brought him to the ground, and with another blow after he had fallen I made sure he was beyond doing me any further harm. [26]

## The Survival of Pole Arms

Another class of bladed weapons used in the American Revolution, collectively called pole arms, included the halberd and various types of spears (including the pike and spontoon). The halberd, or poleax, was a long spear with an axlike blade mounted near the end. It was common on battlefields in late medieval times across most of Europe and its metal blades came in a bewildering variety of decorative shapes. An infantryman could use the spearpoint of his halberd to jab at and penetrate an enemy's armor, or he could swing the weapon with two hands like a giant ax. Not surprisingly, one well-placed stroke of this weapon could bring down a horse and its rider.

By the mid- to late 1600s, with the development of massed units of musketeers, followed by the emergence of the bayonet, the halberd became more or less obsolete as a weapon. However, history has shown that traditional military weapons tend to die very slowly. Soldiers in Europe and America retained the halberd for another century or so, mainly as a symbol of rank. Usually, a sergeant carried it, although soldiers and officials of other ranks did so, too, on ceremonial occasions. The fact that many halberds of the American Revolution had finely sharpened blades indicates that they were still used in battle, though probably only rarely.

As for pikes, the very long versions wielded by the Swiss in late medieval times

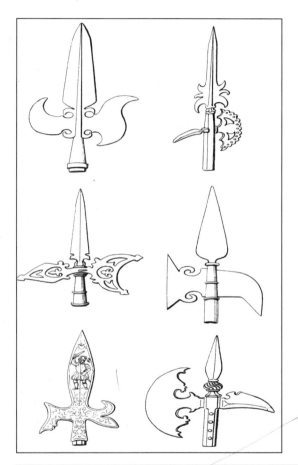

were replaced by the line of musket–bayonet men that emerged in the late 1600s and early 1700s. However, a shorter pike, or big spear—the spontoon (or espontoon)—survived as a standard tool of warfare in Europe and America. Mostly it was an infantry officer's weapon. British and American officers did not ordinarily carry muskets or rifles on the battlefield. The rationale was that the complicated actions of loading and firing would divert their attention too much from observing the battle and giving orders. So officers carried spontoons, which became their symbol. George Washington later explained why he felt the spear was essential for an American officer:

> As the proper arming of officers would add considerable strength to the Army, and the officers themselves derive great confidence from being armed in the time of action, the General orders everyone of them to provide himself with a half pike or spear as soon as possible—firearms, when made use of, withdrawing their attention too much

*Drawings of eighteenth-century halberds illustrate the wide variety of blade styles.*

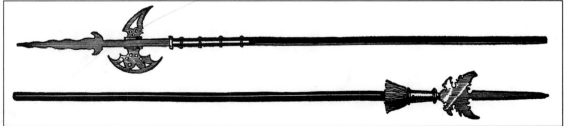

from their men, and to be without either, has a very awkward and unofficer-like appearance.[27]

Still, Washington, like some other American leaders, including Anthony Wayne, was not content to relegate spears solely to officers and advocated their use by some ordinary infantry soldiers as well. Those troops with bayonets obviously did not need to carry spears. However, Washington worried about the safety and effectiveness of his units of riflemen, since rifles had no bayonets. He reasoned that the spear would make a good auxiliary weapon for riflemen to help protect them against cavalry charges; so in early June 1777 he wrote to Daniel Morgan, leader of the famous Morgan's Riflemen, telling him: "I have sent for spears, which I expect shortly to receive and deliver [to] you, as a defense against horse[men]; till you are furnished with these, take care not to be caught in such [a] situation as to give them any advantage over you."[28] The spears arrived a week later, but Washington was not totally satisfied with them. He had ideas for improvements, as he indicated in a letter to the American committee in charge of procuring weapons:

> The spears have come to hand, and are very handy and will be useful to the Rifle Men. But they would be more conveniently carried, if they had a sling fixed to them; they should also have a spike in the butt end to fix them in the ground and they would then serve as a rest for the rifle. The iron plates which fix the spear head to the shaft should be at least eighteen

## The Resurrection of Battle Pikes?

Pikes were used by some American soldiers during the Revolution. This was because the Continental Congress and some of the individual colonial governments were convinced they were not outmoded, as the British and French believed. Pennsylvania and Maryland ordered them by the thousands; and the Pennsylvania leaders issued the following recommendation (quoted in Harold Peterson's *Arms and Armor in the Colonial Period*) for their use by infantry.

It has been regretted by some great soldiers . . . that the use of pikes was ever laid aside, and many experienced officers of the present time agree . . . that it would be very advantageous in our modern wars to resume that weapon, its length reaching beyond the bayonet, and the compound force of the files [of soldiers carrying pikes] . . . rendering a charge made with them insupportable by any battalion armed only in the common manner. At this time, therefore . . . the use of pikes in one or two rear ranks is recommend[ed]. . . . Every [metal]smith can make these, and therefore the country may soon be supplied with many of them. . . . When an army is to encamp, they may . . . be used as tent poles, and save the trouble of carrying them. The Committee of Safety will supply examples to those battalions who are disposed to use them.

inches long to prevent the shaft from being cut through with the stroke of a horseman's sword. Those only, intended for the Rifle Men, should be fixed with slings and spikes in the end; those for the Light Horse[men] need neither. There will be 500 [spears] wanted for the Rifle Men as quick as possible.[29]

The committee forwarded Washington's letter to Benjamin Fowler, the man in charge of manufacturing the weapons. He made a drawing that incorporated the commander in chief's suggestions and indicated that he would quickly get to work implementing them; further, he would have the batch of five hundred spears intended for Morgan's riflemen ready as soon as possible. Regrettably, no evidence survives to confirm that Morgan and his men actually used these spears in the battle of Saratoga, which took place a few months later.

However, there is no question that some American fighters used such spears in com-

*Rifleman Daniel Morgan may have issued spears to some of his men.*

bat situations in the war. They played an especially prominent role in numerous naval engagements, where spears were used liberally to supplement firearms and cutlasses.

*Spear-like poles add a layer to the American defenses erected at Saratoga.*

According to an account in a Pennsylvania newspaper, in a naval skirmish that took place in May 1776, "great execution was done by the spears. One man, with that weapon, is positive of having killed nine of the enemy."[30] In these ways, swords, axes, and spears, among the oldest weapons known to humanity, played their part in the emergence of what eventually became the strongest, most advanced nation of the modern era.

# Chapter 3

# Formal and Informal Battle Tactics

The tactics employed by the British and American soldiers who fought in the American Revolution have long been a subject of interest and discussion among scholars and students alike. Numerous books and articles are published each year describing various battles of the war. And a number of reenactment groups gather annually to restage some of the more pivotal battles with authentic replicas of the costumes and weapons of that era.

One common popular myth these works and groups dispel is that the Revolution was mainly a clash of old-fashioned, formal European tactics and unorthodox, informal American guerrilla tactics. In this scenario, the Americans usually fought individually or in small groups and hid behind rocks and trees. From these hiding places, they sniped at the British troops, who invariably marched along in the open in rigid formation, as gullible as sitting ducks.

The reality was almost always quite different. In the vast majority of engagements, the opposing armies faced each other in the open in the traditional European manner. American soldiers did employ guerilla-type tactics at times, including sniping, ambushes, and raids on houses and villages. These were most often carried out by members of the militia, ordinary citizens who fought on a temporary basis and then returned to their homes and farms. But more commonly, groups of militia supplemented the ranks of the regular, standing American army. The American regulars trained in and used the standard infantry and cavalry tactics of the era—although both the Americans and British employed cavalry sparingly in the war, partly because of the general ruggedness of the terrain. So American troops, including militiamen, used formal battle tactics more often than informal ones.

## A Countryside in Arms

Still, the role played by groups of militia when they operated on their own and employed more informal guerilla tactics was crucial to the American war effort. This mode of fighting was largely a new phenomenon in modern warfare, one for which the British were unprepared. As historian Jeremy Black explains, it reflected the unique situation of the rebellious colonies.

The American war was the first example of a transoceanic conflict fought between a European colonial power and subjects of European descent, and the first example of a major revolutionary war, a struggle for independence in which the notion of the citizenry under arms played a crucial role. The creation of the new state was accompanied by the creation of a new type of army; both reflected a more dynamic and egalitarian [equal] society than that of Europe.[31]

Most often, American militia groups acting on their own used what is best described as harassment and containment tactics. On the one hand, they patrolled the countryside, guarding farms, villages, and supply depots from British foragers (supply gatherers). This severely restricted the ability of the British to live off the land and forced them to import more food from across the ocean, a more difficult and expensive proposition.

Militiamen (and sometimes regular soldiers) also harried, threatened, and/or restrained local loyalists, keeping them from supplying or otherwise helping the British. At times, particularly in the Carolinas in the last two years of the war, such antiloyalist tactics could be brutal and cruel, though the patriots maintained they were necessary. James Collins, an American soldier who took part in several raids against loyalists, later recalled:

## The Influence of Military Manuals

A large portion of the military tactics used by the British in the eighteenth century were originally codified in official regulations issued in 1728. These had been heavily influenced by military manuals, especially *A Treatise on Military Discipline* by Humphrey Bland. First published in 1727, Bland's work was reprinted several times before the outbreak of the American Revolution. In this excerpt, he tells how to divide a battalion into smaller units called platoons:

The Major is to order the Men to fix their Bayonets, it being the custom to perform the Firings with the Bayonets fix'd on the Muzzle; which, however, may be omitted in common Exercise, if the Commanding Officer thinks proper; but never on Service. When the Bayonets are fixed, the Battalion is to be divided into Platoons; the Number of which must depend upon the strength of the Battalion, and the particular Firings you intend to perform. Neither is a Platoon composed of any fixed number of Files but may be more or less, according as the Battalion will allow of it; However a Platoon is seldom composed of less than 10 Files, which are 30 Men, or more than 16 Files, which are 48 Men; because a Platoon composed of less than 10 Files would not be Weight enough to do any considerable Execution; and those above 16 Files would be too great a Body of Men for an Officer to manage upon Service.

*British foragers raid an American home during the intense fighting in the Carolinas.*

We would meet at a time and place appointed, probably at a church, schoolhouse, or some vacant building, generally in the afternoon, lay off our circuit and divide into two or more companies and set off after dark. Wherever we found any Tories, we would surround the house. One party would force the doors and enter, sword in hand, extinguish all the lights if there were any, and suffer no lights to be made, when we would commence hacking the man or men that were found in the house, threatening them with instant death, and occasionally making a furious stroke as if to dispatch them at once, but taking care to strike the wall or some object that was in the way, they generally being found crouched up in some corner, or about the beds. Another party would mount the roof of the house and commence pulling it down. Thus, the dwelling

*American soldiers and loyalists skirmish. Both patriots and loyalists resorted to brutal tactics.*

house, smoke houses and kitchen, if any, were dismantled and torn down. . . . The poor fellows, perhaps expecting instant death, would beg hard for life, and make any promise on condition of being spared, while their wives or friends would join in their entreaties. . . . There were none of the poor fellows much hurt, only they were hacked about their heads and arms enough to bleed freely.[32]

Not only did the militia harass many loyalists, nullifying their effect on the war effort, they also contained the British army largely in the coastal sections of the country. Practically every time British troops marched inland from the sea, hundreds and sometimes thousands of militiamen and other locals rose up to fight them. Disconcerted, the British typically halted their inland advance.

The main reason this tactic worked so well against the British was that having to face a whole countryside of angry, armed people was completely new to them. Back in Europe, an army on the march could expect to move safely through the country-side until it met up with enemy troops and engaged in a pitched battle. The frightened local townspeople and peasants almost always hid or ran away. Seeing the American countryside in arms made the British nervous, even fearful, so that for most of the war they avoided venturing too far inland, preferring to stay near the coast. There, the closeness of their ships and supply lines made them feel safer.

These fears were not without foundation. On occasion the efforts of local militiamen and other patriots helped to bring about a major British defeat and ended an important strategic campaign. A clear example occurred in 1777. Britain's General John Burgoyne led an army southward from Canada by way of Lake Champlain (on the border between New York and Vermont). His goal was to invade and conquer northern New York and the New England states. But Burgoyne soon encountered the awesome power of a countryside in arms. Seemingly out of nowhere, groups of local patriots harassed and attacked his supply trains. Large groups of militiamen also continually reinforced the ranks of American regulars, who otherwise would have been outnumbered and unable to stop the British advance. "Wherever the King's forces point," Burgoyne complained to another British leader,

> militia, to the number of three or four thousand, assemble in twenty-four hours. They bring with them their sub-sistence [food and other supplies], etc., and, the alarm over, they return to their farms. The Hampshire Grants [what is now Vermont] in particular, a country unpeopled and almost unknown in the last war [the French and Indian conflict], now abounds in the most active and most rebellious race of the continent, and hangs like a gathering storm upon my left. In all parts [of the countryside] the [rebels'] industry and management in driving cattle and removing corn [to keep these supplies out of British hands] are indefatigable [untiring] and certain. . . . Mr. [General Horatio] Gates [the American commander opposing Burgoyne] is now strongly posted . . . with an army superior to mine . . . [with] as many militia as he pleases.[33]

Burgoyne's assessment that he was in dire trouble was correct. He lost so many men—through death, wounding, or desertion—that he finally could not go on; and on October 17, 1777, he had no choice but to surrender to Gates.

## Cowardly or Practical Tactics?

In most of the battles of Burgoyne's upstate New York campaign, American militiamen fought alongside Gates's regulars. But isolated British units sometimes found themselves ambushed or sniped at by rebel militiamen acting on their own, especially in wooded areas. When that happened at various times and places in the war, the

British were quick to label their opponents cowards who would not come out and "fight like men." Complained one British soldier in 1775: "They are a cowardly set that will not fight but when fenced by trees, houses or trenches."[34]

In that same year another British soldier recorded such guerilla tactics in more detail. Following the fight at Concord Bridge, on April 19, 1775—the second armed clash of the war after the skirmish on Lexington green earlier that same day—American militiamen relentlessly harassed the British during the latter's march back to Boston. "We set out upon our return," recalled one of the British regulars, John Barker.

Before the whole [British unit] had quitted the town we were fired on from houses and behind trees, and before we had gone one-half mile we were fired on from all sides, but mostly from the rear, where people had hid themselves in houses till we had passed and then fired. The country was an amaz-

*Britain's General John Burgoyne surrenders to American commander Horatio Gates.*

## Militia Against Regulars

The skirmish in Lexington on April 19, 1775, constituting the first battle of the American Revolution, was an example of untrained militiamen facing a line of highly trained British regulars. The outbreak of violence was due partly to the way each side viewed the other. The patriots saw the British redcoats as bullies and intruders; the British felt they were dealing with dangerous rebel troublemakers. The following excerpt is from an eyewitness account by Reverend Jonas Clark (from Charles Hudson's *History of the Town of Lexington*):

> When within about a quarter of a mile of the meeting-house [where the American militia had assembled], they [the British] halted and the command was given to prime and load; which being done, they marched on till they came up to the east end of said meeting-house, in sight of our militia . . . who were about 12 or 13 rods [200 feet] distant. . . . Upon this, our men dispersed—but many of them not so speedily as they might have done, not having the most distant idea of such brutal barbarity and more than savage cruelty from the troops of a British king, as they immediately

> experienced! For, no sooner did they come in sight of our company, but one of them, supposed to be an officer of rank, was heard to say to the troops. "Damn them!/ We will have them!" Upon which the troops . . . rushed furiously towards our men. About the same time, three [British] officers . . . advanced on horseback to the front of the body, and coming within 5 or 6 rods [about 90 feet] of the militia, one of them cried out, "Ye villains, ye Rebels, disperse!"—or words to this effect. . . . The second of these officers, about this time, fired a pistol towards the militia as they were dispersing. The foremost, who was within a few yards of our men, brandishing his sword and then pointing towards them, with a loud voice said to the troops, "Fire! By God, fire!"—which was instantly followed by a discharge of arms from the said troops, succeeded by a very heavy and close fire upon our party. . . . Eight were left dead upon the ground! Ten were wounded. The rest of the company, through divine goodness, were (to a miracle) preserved unhurt in this murderous action!

ing[ly] strong one, full of hills, woods, stone walls, etc., which the rebels did not fail to take advantage of, for they were so concealed there was hardly any seeing them. In this way we marched between nine and ten miles, their numbers increasing from all parts, while our's was reducing by deaths, wounds and fatigue, and we were totally surrounded with such an incessant fire as it's possible to conceive; our ammunition was likewise near expended.[35]

While these tactics seemed cowardly to the British regulars, to local militiamen, who lacked the high degree of organization and training of the British troops, they seemed the safer and more practical approach. This was particularly true of riflemen. These marksmen with their slow-loading guns were most effective when they fired from behind some kind of cover. At the battle of Long Island on August 27, 1776, a British captain, William Congreve, witnessed such tactics and later wrote:

*American troops take advantage of natural cover in the battle of Kings Mountain.*

I found the enemy numerous and supported by the 6-pounders [cannon]. However, by plying them smartly with grapeshot their guns were soon drawn off, but the riflemen being covered by trees and large stones had very much the advantage of us, who were upon the open ground . . . [and had] not the [British] light infantry . . . come up [to help us] in time I believe we should all have been cut off. [36]

Similar informal tactics that took advantage of natural obstacles were employed by the American riflemen who defeated the British at Kings Mountain in October 1780. A sixteen-year-old rifleman, Thomas Young, later recalled:

The orders were at the firing of the first gun, for every man to raise a whoop, rush forward, and fight his way [up the hill] as best he could. When our division came up to the northern base of the mountain, Colonel Roebuck drew us a little to the left and commenced the attack. I well remember how I behaved. Ben Hollingworth and myself took right up the side of the mountain, and fought from tree to tree, our way to the summit. I recollect I stood behind one tree and fired until the bark was nearly all knocked off, and my eyes pretty well filled with it.[37]

## The Long Red Line

Such tactics were the exception rather than the rule during the war. For the most part, the opposing armies met in the open and employed formal lines of musket–bayonet men, the infantry formation that dominated European warfare by the early 1700s. This type of fighting came to be called linear warfare (since the term linear refers to the use of lines). By the time of the American Revolution, linear tactics had become an established ritual of war. Honorable generals and officers were expected to follow standard rules, which were set down in minute detail in numerous military manuals and handbooks of the period. Indeed, the desire to uphold such honor was a major factor in the decision of the American commander in chief, George Washington, to employ linear tactics against the British. (Conversely, this explains why many British officers thought the more informal tactics of the American militia were cowardly.)

In the early 1700s, it was customary for an army's infantrymen to form a line five ranks deep on the battlefield. But by the outset of the Revolution, the British had reduced the depth of their standard line to three or four ranks; and the Americans typically used only two ranks. Field artillery (cannons on movable carriages) were usually interspersed at intervals among the infantry. Cavalry units, their men armed with sabers and pistols, placed themselves behind or on the flanks (sides) of the infantry. "The basic objective," George Neumann explains,

was to pierce the opponent's ranks and disrupt the formation by frontal assault, or, better yet, to maneuver into a position of hitting on the flank to "roll up" his battle line. Such formalized procedure in an age of aristocratic chivalry led to "posts of honor," which were jealously sought by senior brigades and regiments. These included the two flank positions in line of battle, the advance during the attack, and at the rear when retreating. . . . The battle usually opened with artillery fire. Then one side would begin a steady disciplined advance with fixed bayonets, halt about 50 to 100 yards from their opponent and deliver one or a series of volleys—to which the others would reply. But since the inaccurate smoothbore musket was still more a defensive than an offensive weapon, the climax came when one side charged with the bayonet, backed when possible by sword-swinging cavalry. Despite advances in firearms, the classic 18th century battle was still decided by the clash of edged weapons at close quarters.[38]

The "long red line" of British musket–bayonet men in their red coats became a familiar sight to American fighters. British linear formations seemed especially formidable to the rebels in the first two years of the war, when most American troops still lacked proper training in formal tactics. At times, the oncoming British appeared relentless and unstoppable, since no matter how many times they were repulsed, their ranks would reform and renew the assault. This was the case in the famous battle of Bunker Hill (actually fought on Breed's Hill) in Boston on June 17, 1775. The Americans, who had fortified the hilltop, watched grimly as the rows of redcoats marched toward them, keeping step to the beat of drummers. According to the account of an American defender named Peter Thacher:

> Having sent out large flank guards in order to surround [the American position], they [the British] began a very slow march towards our lines. . . . The provincials [Americans] in the redoubt [fortified area on the hilltop] and the lines reserved their fire till the enemy had come within about ten or twelve yards and then discharged [their muskets] at once upon them. The fire threw their body into very great confusion, and all of them after having kept a fire for some time retreated in very great disorder down to the point where they landed, and some of them even got into their boats. At this time their officers were observed by spectators on the opposite shore to come down and then to use the most passionate gestures, and even to push forward the men with their swords. At length, by their exertions, the troops were again rallied and marched up to the entrenchments. The Americans reserved their fire and a second time put the regulars to flight, who once more retreated . . . to the boats. The same or greater exertions were now again observed to be made by their officers, and having formed once more they . . . determined now, it appeared, to make a decisive effort. . . . The ammunition of the provincials was expended, [and] the enemy advanced on three sides . . . at once. . . . Can it be wondered at, then, that the word was given [for the Americans] to retreat? . . . With very great signs of exultation [triumph] the British troops . . . took possession of the hill. [39]

Untrained American troops fared even worse against British bayonet charges. At Camden, in South Carolina, on August 16, 1780, the American militiamen who were supporting the regular army under Horatio Gates fled the field in disarray before the onrushing British bayonets. Garret Watts, one of those who ran, remembered that

> I was among the nearest to the enemy; that a man named John Summers was my file leader; that we had orders to wait for the word to commence firing;

that the militia were in front and in feeble condition at that time. They were fatigued. . . . They had been fed a short time previously on molasses entirely. I can state on oath that I believe my gun was the first gun fired, notwithstanding the orders, for we were close to the enemy, who appeared to maneuver [with their bayonets] in contempt of us, and I fired without thinking except that I might prevent the man opposite from killing me. The discharge and loud roar soon became general from one end of the line to the other. Amongst other things, I confess I was amongst the first that fled. The cause of that I cannot tell, except that everyone I saw was about to do the same. It was instantaneous. There was no effort to rally, no encouragement to fight. Officers and men joined in the flight. [40]

*American forces put attacking lines of British redcoats to flight at Bunker Hill.*

*Horatio Gates, pictured on his horse, fled the field at Camden in August 1780.*

Indeed, Gates himself fled with the militia and did not stop until he had covered sixty miles; needless to say, this display of bad judgment ended his military career.

## American Mastery of Tactics

Fortunately, the American rout at Camden turned out to be the exception rather than the rule. It was largely attributable to the militia's lack of training and group discipline; while by contrast, the American regulars at Camden stood their ground and maintained good order, though they were soundly defeated in the end. In fact, once the American regulars began training and drilling in linear tactics they were usually able to stand up to their British counterparts. At the battle of Long Island, fought on August 27, 1776, the Americans surprised the British by forming classic linear battle lines, as recalled by an unknown American participant in the fray:

The enemy then advanced to us, when Lord Stirling, who commanded, immediately drew up in a line and offered them battle in the true English taste. The British then advanced within about 300 yards of us and began a very heavy fire from their cannon and mortars, for both the balls and shells flew very fast, now and then taking off a head. Our men stood it amazingly well, not even one showed a disposition to shrink. Our orders were not to fire till the enemy came within 50 yards of us; but when they perceived we stood their fire so coolly and resolutely, they declined coming any nearer, though treble [three times] our number. [41]

Despite their impressive battle line and raw courage, the Americans eventually had to retreat from Long Island, which they did in well-ordered fashion. Yet their mastery of linear tactics, which had allowed them to face the legendary British lines without flinching, had foreshadowed American victories to come. Perhaps none was more decisive and inspiring than that at Cowpens, in the Carolinas, on January 17, 1781. The sides were evenly matched and the battlefield open, flat, and unobstructed; military experts then and now agree that the American win was due almost entirely to a superior display of tactics and discipline, qualities

that before this had usually been associated with the British army.

The British commander, cavalry leader Colonel Banastre Tarleton (who was notorious for his brutal terror raids on civilians), had a force of some one thousand one hundred British regulars and Tories. He arranged his battle line in the standard manner, with his infantry in the middle and cavalry units (in this case consisting of about fifty men each) on the flanks. In contrast, his opponent, the famous rifleman Daniel Morgan, had about one thousand men, including a mix of militia, regulars, and a few horsemen. Morgan organized his

## Variations in British Tactics

In the early 1770s, Major General William Howe introduced some variations in discipline and tactics into standard British practices, feeling that these would help British troops better adapt to fighting in North America. He trained his men to march and fight in two ranks, as well as the usual three or four, and to march into battle in open order (with at least an arm's length between individual soldiers). One of Howe's subordinates described the new rules this way (as quoted in Stuart Reid's *British Redcoat*):

It is the Major General's wish, that the troops under his command may practice forming from two to three and four deep; and that they should be accustomed to charge in all those orders. In the latter orders, of the three and four deep, the files will, in course, be closer, so as to render a charge of the greatest force. The Major General also recommends to regiments the practice of dividing the battalions, by wings or otherwise, so that one line may support the other when an at-

tack is supposed; and, when a retreat is supposed, that the first line may retreat through the intervals of the second, the second doubling up its divisions for the purpose, and forming again in order to check the enemy who may be supposed to have pressed the first line. The Major General would approve also of one division of a battalion attacking in the common open order of two deep, to be supported by the other compact division as a second line, in a charging order of three or four deep. The gaining the flanks also of a supposed enemy, by the quick movements of a division in common open order, while the compact division advances to a charge; and such other evolutions, as may lead the regiments to a custom of depending on and mutually supporting each other; so that should one part be pressed or broken, it may be accustomed to form again without confusion, under the protection of a second line, or any regular formed division.

own troops into three lines. In the front he placed his militia; behind them were his regulars, commanded by Colonel John E. Howard; and in the rear were the cavalry, led by Colonel William Washington.

Seeing that Morgan had put his militia up front, the overconfident Tarleton was certain that the British would win the day. A hearty bayonet charge, he reasoned, would send the Americans packing, as had occurred at Camden. However, Morgan had wisely anticipated this possibility. He had told his militiamen, many of whom were crack shots, to fire two volleys at the oncoming British and then swiftly move to the rear of the American army. The British would then have to contend with the better-trained and battle-hardened American regulars and horsemen. "Hold your fire till they're a hundred paces away," Morgan ordered his militiamen.

Give 'em two shots! Just two shots! Don't fire over their heads. Get the epaulettes [shoulder decorations worn by officers] and the sergeants. Hit their middles. Then you can move off to the left. . . .

*Pictured are American militiamen on their way to fight Tarleton at Cowpens.*

Move off and get around behind the hill. . . . Two shots right in the gizzard. Hit 'em in the head if it's easier! Same as shooting turkeys![42]

When the British front line came within a hundred yards of the American front line, Morgan's plan went into effect. The militiamen fired their two volleys, killing and wounding many in the front British rank, then quickly moved toward the rear. At the same time, men from Tarleton's second rank filled the gaps in his front rank, which then marched forward at the American regulars. But to the surprise of the British, Morgan's troops suddenly pulled back, as if retreating. Sensing victory, the British regulars charged forward wildly, their ranks losing much of their order in the process. This was Morgan's and Howard's golden opportunity. They ordered their men to halt, turn, and fire on the onrushing enemy at nearly point-blank range. After this devastating barrage, the American regulars immediately launched into a spirited bayonet charge that shattered the British lines. At the same time, Morgan's militiamen, now fully rested, stepped forward in orderly fashion from their rear position and fired at will into the crumbling British ranks. Desperate, Tarleton tried to use his small cavalry force to attack the American flanks, but Colonel Washington's own horsemen charged forward and routed them. In the words of one American soldier:

In a few moments Colonel Washington's cavalry was among them like a

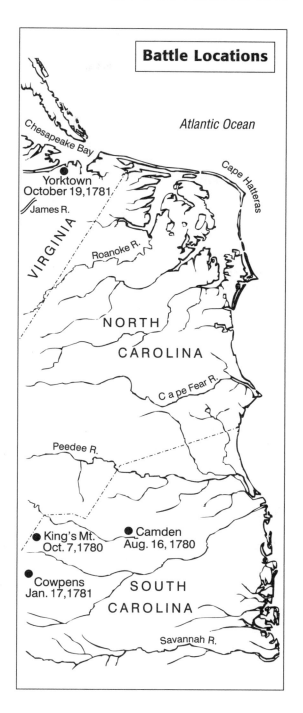

**Battle Locations**

Atlantic Ocean

Chesapeake Bay

Cape Hatteras

Yorktown
October 19, 1781

James R.

VIRGINIA

Roanoke R.

NORTH

CAROLINA

Cape Fear R.

Peedee R.

● King's Mt.
Oct. 7, 1780

● Camden
Aug. 16, 1780

● Cowpens
Jan. 17, 1781

SOUTH

CAROLINA

Savannah R.

whirlwind, and the poor fellows began to keel from their horses without being able to remount. The shock was so sudden and violent they could not stand it, and immediately betook themselves to flight. There was no time to rally, and they appeared to be as hard to stop as a drove of wild . . . steers going to a Pennsylvania market. [43]

The results of the battle were stunning. Of Tarleton's force of eleven hundred men, a hundred had been killed, two hundred wounded, and more than six hundred captured. By contrast, American casualties were a mere twelve killed and sixty wounded. Tarleton was one of the few British who managed to escape (after engaging in a brief saber fight with Colonel Washington). In Tarleton's mind, his overwhelming defeat was merely a fluke; in the end, he and his countrymen would surely bring the rebels to their knees. But he was dead wrong. In only a few short years the Americans had managed to master the tactics that had helped to make the British army hugely effective and widely feared. The tide of war had turned in the patriots' favor and now nothing on earth could stop it.

# Chapter 4

# British and American Artillery

**B**oth sides in the American Revolution employed the same kinds of cannons, more formally known as artillery or ordnance. There were three major classes of ordnance, as well as numerous sizes in each class, and one class or size was often better suited than others to a specific military situation or goal. For example, some artillery, generally referred to as field pieces, worked best on the open battlefield. Others were more effective for destroying walls and buildings during sieges. And still others, called naval ordnance, were designed for or adapted to the peculiar needs of warships.

Despite these differences in application, all types of artillery in use in the eighteenth century had certain basic traits and features in common. First, they were cast from either iron or bronze. Second, they were smoothbore and muzzle-loading, like a musket. Third, also like muskets and other hand-held guns, artillery worked with gunpowder, a premeasured amount of which was loaded from a paper or cloth container called a cartridge.

All types of ordnance fired metal projectiles, which were usually round. The single, solid, nonexplosive variety was informally called a cannonball, but in military terms it was referred to as shot. A cluster of small iron balls that scattered after firing was called grape

*Various types of British and American ordnance fired iron cannonballs like these.*

shot, while a hollow ball filled with gunpowder designed to detonate on impact was called a shell. Other things that all types of ordnance had in common: the gunner fired his cannon by inserting a lighted match into a vent in the rear and the firing of the weapon produced a strong recoil that made it jump backwards, so that it had to be repositioned before firing again.

## The Three Classes of Ordnance

These, then, were the realities that artillery gunners had to deal with when using any weapon in the three general classes of ordnance. The first class was called simply the artillery gun. It had a long barrel in relation to its caliber, was used for firing at targets within plain sight (as on the battlefield), and its trajectory—the path taken by its projectile—was flat, or not too high. The gunner aimed the weapon by sighting along two notches, one located near the muzzle, the

other near the back. If he wanted less elevation (to make the cannon shoot lower, with a flatter trajectory), he shoved one or more quoins (wooden wedges) under the back of the barrel, which lowered the angle of the muzzle. (A few of the guns used in the Revolution were equipped with a screw mechanism that eliminated the need for quoins.)

The main reason that artillery guns had more or less flat trajectories was the way they sat in their carriages. A typical artillery gun carriage of the day consisted of an axle with two wheels attached to the ends. Resting on the middle of the axle were one or two pieces of timber, the backs of which were attached to a team of horses for transport or rested on the ground when the weapon was in use. The gun itself was fastened to the tops of the timbers. So when the timbers holding the gun touched the ground in the back, the weapon could not be angled upward any higher.

## Molly and the Cannonball

One of the most interesting footnotes to the use of artillery in the American Revolution occurred at the battle of Monmouth, in New Jersey, in June 1778. Molly Pitcher, a camp follower who supplied the American troops with water, bravely took over her husband's job as artillery gunner when he was wounded and then herself had a narrow brush with death. This eyewitness account is attributed to American soldier Joseph P. Martin in his memoir of the war.

One little incident happened during the heat of the cannonade, which I was eyewitness to, and which I think would be unpardonable not to mention. A woman whose husband belonged

to the Artillery [company], and who was then attached to a piece [i.e., operated a cannon] in the engagement, attended with her husband at the piece the whole time. While in the act of reaching for a cartridge and having one of her feet as far before the other as she could step, a cannon shot from the enemy passed directly between her legs without doing any other damage than carrying away all the lower part of her petticoat. Looking at it with apparent unconcern, she observed that it was lucky it did not pass a little higher, for in that case it might have carried away something else, and [she] continued her occupation.

*An artillery piece rests on the historic site of the battle of Saratoga.*

The second major class of ordnance, the howitzer, was capable of firing at a higher angle than a gun. This was partly because the howitzer had a larger caliber and shorter barrel, which made it easier to maneuver on a carriage. The weapon had a bigger caliber and shorter barrel because it was designed to fire shells. Being hollow, a shell was more fragile than solid shot, so the charge that propelled the shell had to be smaller, to keep it from rupturing the shell's casing. The smaller the explosion, the shorter the barrel-length needed to ac-commodate it. Thus, the barrel of an average howitzer was five to seven times its caliber, compared with fifteen to twenty-five times for a gun. Howitzers were the cannons of choice for firing over obstacles like trees, houses, and low hills to reach a target.

The third class of artillery was the mortar, which also fired a powder-filled shell rather than solid shot. A mortar was a short,

*American cannons at Valley Forge, where Washington's army spent the winter of 1777–1778.*

stumpy cannon that fired at high angles, allowing its shells to pass over the high walls of forts and fortified towns and drop downward on the desired target. Most mortar barrels were only one to three calibers long; so if a mortar's caliber was ten inches, its barrel was somewhere between ten and thirty inches long. This made the mortar by far the shortest of all cannons.

Unlike the situation with guns and howitzers, the size of the powder charges mortar gunners used varied considerably, depending on the range desired. As Ian Hogg explains:

The whole concept of range determination changed when mortars were used. Instead of having a fixed charge and varying the elevation of the piece to pitch the projectile to the desired range, the mortar used a fixed elevation—45 degrees—and varied the charge in order to altar the range.[44]

Because the mortar's angle of elevation was fixed, it was mounted on a simple, stationary holder. Essentially it was a large block of wood with a curved recess carved in the top to accommodate the back end of the cannon. The whole assembly, weighing anywhere from about five hundred to eight thousand five hundred pounds, depending on the weapon's size, could be lifted onto a wagon or boat for transport. Another consequence of the mortar's fixed elevation was the manner in which the gunner aimed it. "Sighting was done," Hogg continues,

by scribing or painting a line down the top surface of the mortar barrel to coincide with axis of the bore; this was aligned with the target by the gunner standing behind and holding a plumb-line in his hand. He sighted so that he

saw the target on the far side of the plumb-line and had the axis line of the mortar barrel also in alignment with his plumb-line. This showed that the mortar was pointing at the target and, more important, that it was truly upright and not canted over to one side or another. [45]

## Mobility of Artillery

Although guns, howitzers, and mortars could be highly effective if aimed well and/or fired at the proper angle, they shared one major problem: Namely, most were extremely heavy and therefore difficult

*An old engraving shows a mortar mounted in a simple, stationary holder.*

to transport overland. It must be remembered that few roads existed in the American colonies, and most were unpaved. Dirt roads and fields were often uneven, with holes and gullies, and when it rained they turned to mud. As a result, the artillery carriages, dragged by horses, moved very slowly across the countryside, sometimes so slowly they could not keep up with the infantry. This meant the foot soldiers had either to slow down to keep pace with their ordnance or move ahead of it and wait for it to catch up. Both options prolonged a campaign and frustrated the participants.

The problem of artillery's lack of mobility was addressed in contemporary military manuals dealing with ordnance. Perhaps the most famous and influential example was *A Treatise on Artillery,* first published in 1757 by John Muller, an artillery master who had been born in Germany and emigrated to England in his youth. Muller realized that most cannons were too heavy for the major-

ity of existing roads and that the great number of horses involved further complicated matters. In his manual he warned his readers:

All the carriages made use of in the artillery have shafts; and to prevent the great length of those that require a great number of horses, the rule is to draw [the artillery] by pairs [of horses standing] abreast, which is an absurdity nowhere else to be met with; for when the road is frequented by carriages drawn by two horses abreast there is always a ridge in the middle, which the shaft horse, endeavoring to avoid, treads on one side, whereby the wheels catch against the ruts, and stop the carriage; and when the fore [front] horses bring them back, he treads on the other side, where the same happens again; so that the shaft horse, instead of being useful any other ways than to support the shafts, becomes a hindrance to the rest.[46]

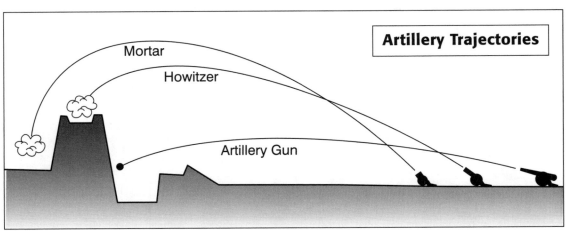

*This drawing illustrates the lack of speed and mobility of a typical artillery train.*

Moreover, it was not only the cannons themselves that slowed an army down. The carriages bearing the weapons made up only part of a long artillery train that also included dozens or even hundreds of wagons carrying shot, shells, gunpowder, tools, spare parts, and various other ordnance supplies. Military historian H.C.B. Rogers describes some of the typical vehicles that made up such a train:

A tumbril was a two-wheel cart to carry pioneers' and miners' tools. A powder cart also had two wheels, and contained shot lockers and space for four barrels of powder. An ammunition wagon was considerably larger, with four wheels. . . . The block carriage consisted of two long beams lengthwise on four wheels and was used to carry guns which were too heavy to be moved on their own carriages. A sling wagon was a four-wheel vehicle, with rack and handle mounted in the center, for moving mortars and heavy guns over short distances from

*Henry Knox's men drag fifty cannons from Fort Ticonderoga to Boston.*

one position to another. The forge cart originally had two wheels, but it was so difficult to keep it steady that they were replaced by four. It was equipped with bellows, tool space, iron plate for the fireplace, wooden trough for water, an iron plate for cinders, and another iron plate to stop the flame from setting fire to the cart. There was also a gin, a sort of portable crane for lifting ordnance on and off their carriages or mortar beds.[47]

## Creation of American Artillery Units

However daunting a problem, the difficulty of moving an artillery train through the countryside was the least of the worries facing American gunners at the outset of the Revolution. Much more pressing was the lack of good ordnance. Moreover, there was no formal artillery corps or organization in the colonies, a shortcoming that did not bode well for the American war effort.

Fortunately, a small number of patriots had knowledge of artillery, and one of them, Henry Knox, of Boston, caught George Washington's attention. After the battle of Bunker Hill, in which Knox took part, Washington asked him to create an American artillery force. Almost immediately, Knox showed that he was the right person for the job. He managed to transport fifty cannons captured from the British at Fort Ticonderoga, in upstate New York, to Boston, where they were eventually instrumental in driving the British out of the city.

Knox then turned his attention to organizing the widely scattered colonial artillery men and collecting enough ordnance for them to use. In mid-1776, Knox created four artillery regiments. Each regiment eventually consisted of ten companies, the size of a company depending on the number and caliber of the ordnance it possessed. A typical artillery company had between six and ten artillery guns or howitzers. To find these weapons, at first Knox had to resort to the proverbial beg, borrow, and steal method. His men scoured the colonies collecting whatever they could find and whenever possible confiscated British cannons.

Knox fully realized that these makeshift methods would not do in the long run, and he pressed for American forges to manufacture their own cannons. One forge in Pennsylvania produced about sixty artillery pieces in 1776. However, Knox also recognized that cannon-making facilities in different areas would turn out ordnance of widely varying sizes and calibers, making it more difficult for him to standardize American artillery. So he established a central cannon factory in Springfield, Massachusetts, where the dimensions and calibers of ordnance were tightly supervised.

Knox's artillery units soon became the most effective branch of the infant American military establishment. This was partly due to efficient organization and just plain hard work. But innovation was also a key factor. The Americans tried to increase the mobility of the ordnance used to support infantry on the battlefield by making smaller, lighter, more portable cannons. Known as Galloper Guns, some of these cannons could be pulled by a single horse. (However, some of the weapon's mobility was offset because its ammunition had to be carried in wagons, which were as slow as ever.)

Although resourceful, another innovation of American artillery men proved less useful in the long run. This was the "floating battery," a flat-bottomed barge that carried cannons to strategic positions in rivers. Hogg provides the following description of the first such battery, built on the Charles River near Boston, and explains why the idea never quite caught on:

A 12- or 18-pounder . . . was fitted at bow and stern, firing through embrasures [openings] which could be closed by wooden doors. A three-pounder was mounted at each side of the stern, and four ½-pounder swivel guns were mounted on top of the superstructure. Musketry ports were cut in the sides, while propulsion was by a bank of oars on each side. These two craft were used to bombard British positions in Boston in September and October 1775, but their effect was negligible. With the British abandonment of Boston in the following year the floating batteries became redundant and were dismantled.

*Henry Knox, who established an American cannon-making plant in Springfield, Massachusetts.*

Similar batteries were also built in Pennsylvania and used in various actions along the line of the Delaware River, but the practice was never widespread, since the peculiar conditions suited to the use of floating batteries occurred but rarely.[48]

## Artillery Tactics

Even with innovations such as Galloper Guns and floating batteries, the use of artillery on the battlefield in the war was usually not decisive. In general, military commanders employed guns and howitzers in two ways. First, these weapons protected an army's deployment onto the battlefield. In other words, a general needed to move his infantry and cavalry units into the desired positions without risking harassment or sudden attack by the enemy; and a screen of artillery field pieces provided cover for troop movements. Artillery pieces also took part in actual combat, most often by firing on enemy formations, softening them for the attack of infantry and cavalry.

The key to the effectiveness of such tactics was, of course, the mobility of the artillery involved. Here, the gunners of the American Revolution sometimes attempted to implement the tactical advances recently introduced by Prussian leader Frederick the Great in Europe's Seven Years' War (1756–1763). In fact, the American development of Galloper Guns was directly inspired by Frederick's innovations, summarized by military historian Albert Manucy:

To keep pace with cavalry movements, he [Frederick] developed a horse artillery that moved rapidly along with the cavalry. His field artillery had only light guns and howitzers. With these improvements he could establish small batteries at important points in the battle line, open the fight, and protect the deployment of his columns with light guns. What was equally significant, he could change the position of his batteries according to the course of the action. Frederick sent his 3- and 6-pounders ahead of the infantry. Gunners dismounted 500 paces from the enemy and advanced on foot, pushing their guns ahead of them, firing incessantly and using grape shot during the latter part of their advance. Up to closest range they went, until the infantry caught up, passed through the artillery line, and stormed the enemy position. Remember that battle was pretty formal, with musketeers standing or kneeling in ranks, often in full view of the enemy![49]

In such combat situations, field gunners sometimes fired randomly into the enemy ranks, hoping to wreak whatever

*Prussia's Frederick the Great, who developed a light, mobile artillery force.*

havoc they could. But the better generals and artillery commanders tried to concentrate their fire on points of weakness in the enemy lines. They were influenced by a noted French artillery expert, the Chevalier du Teil, who had written: "It is necessary to multiply the artillery on the points of attack which ought to decide the victory." To secure "decisive results," he said, "it is necessary to assemble the greatest number of troops, and a great quantity of artillery, on the points where one wishes to force the enemy." Further, to make sure these are the weak points, one should distract the enemy by implementing "false attacks" at other points in his line.[50]

## Effects of Field Artillery

When applied properly, attacks by field pieces could be effective not only because of the physical damage they did but also because they frightened, confused, and demoralized the enemy. A Prussian soldier who encountered Austrian artillery in a battle fought prior to the outbreak of the American Revolution left behind this riveting testimony:

A storm of shot and howitzer shells passed clear over our heads, but more than enough fell in the ranks to smash a large number of our men. . . . I glanced aside just once and I saw an NCO [noncommissioned officer] torn apart by a shell nearly. The sight was frightful enough to take away my curiosity. . . . [Then we advanced] through long corn, which reached as far as our necks, and as we came nearer we were greeted with a hail of canister [shells] that stretched whole clumps of our troops on the ground. We still had our muskets on our shoulders and I could hear how the canister balls clattered against our bayonets.[51]

Field artillery was also sometimes effective in less formal skirmishes involving fewer troops and having no overall battle plan. Joseph P. Martin, an American soldier who took part in the chaotic fighting on Long Island in 1776, left behind this account of dueling artillery pieces in such a skirmish:

We overtook a small party of the artillery, here dragging a heavy twelve-pounder upon a field carriage, sinking half way to the naves [wheel hubs] in the sandy soil. They plead[ed] hard for some of us to assist them to get in their piece [i.e., move it closer to the action]; our officers, however, paid no attention to their entreaties, but pressed forward towards a creek, where a large party of Americans and British were engaged. By the time we arrived, the enemy had driven our men into the creek, or rather mill-pond (the tide being up), where such as could swim got across; those that could not swim, and could not procure anything to buoy them up, sunk. The British, having several field pieces stationed by a brick house, were pouring the canister [shells] and grape [shot] upon the Americans like a shower of hail. They would doubtless have done them much more damage than they did but for the twelve-pounder mentioned above; the men, having gotten it within sufficient distance to reach them, and opening a fire upon them, soon obliged them to shift their quarters.[52]

## The Artillery Barrage at Yorktown

Perhaps the most devastating use of artillery consisted of barrages of besieged forts and towns by mortars, sometimes supplemented by howitzers. The American offensive on Yorktown, facing Chesapeake Bay in southern Virginia, an action which brought about the British surrender and ended the war, was the most memorable example. By March 1781 the Americans had won a succession of victories in the Carolinas. This forced the leading British

general, Charles Cornwallis, to move his forces to Virginia; and in April he established new headquarters at Yorktown. Soon, a large allied force of American and French troops commanded by General Washington converged on Yorktown. Cornwallis now found himself trapped between the American and French troops on his land side and a fleet of French ships, armed with cannons, anchored in the bay.

It was at this point that the American and French artillery came to the fore. On

## British Artillery Guns

This chart, based on information compiled by scholar Ian Hogg (in his *Armies of the American Revolution*), lists the various iron artillery guns used by the British in the era of the American war for independence:

| Name | Caliber inches | Length feet | inches | Weight pounds | Range yards |
|---|---|---|---|---|---|
| 3-pounder | 2.90 | 4 | 6 | 725 | 1,400 |
| 6-pounder | 3.67 | 6 | 0 | 1,650 | 1,500 |
| 6-pounder | 3.67 | 8 | 0 | 2,200 | 1,500 |
| 9-pounder | 4.20 | 7 | 0 | 2,300 | 1,800 |
| 9-pounder | 4.20 | 7 | 6 | 2,425 | 1,800 |
| 12-pounder | 4.62 | 7 | 6 | 2,925 | 1,800 |
| 12-pounder | 4.62 | 8 | 6 | 3,125 | 1,800 |
| 12-pounder | 4.62 | 9 | 0 | 3,200 | 1,800 |
| 12-pounder | 4.62 | 9 | 6 | 3,400 | 1,800 |
| 18-pounder | 5.29 | 9 | 0 | 4,000 | 2,300 |
| 18-pounder | 5.29 | 9 | 6 | 4,200 | 2,300 |
| 24-pounder | 5.82 | 9 | 0 | 4,750 | 2,400 |
| 24-pounder | 5.82 | 9 | 6 | 4,900 | 2,400 |
| 24-pounder | 5.82 | 10 | 0 | 5,200 | 2,400 |
| 32-pounder | 6.41 | 9 | 6 | 5,500 | 2,900 |
| 32-pounder | 6.41 | 10 | 0 | 5,800 | 2,900 |
| 42-pounder | 6.95 | 9 | 6 | 6500 | 3,100 |
| 42-pounder | 6.95 | 10 | 0 | 6,700 | 3,100 |

September 28, 1781, allied cannons opened fire on Yorktown from both sides. On the land side, the artillery were at first placed at a distance of a thousand yards, but as the days passed and the enemy's defenses weakened, the Americans moved their cannons closer. By October 10, the barrage was more intense than ever. Cornwallis was so worried about being hit by the shot and shells that he moved into a makeshift bunker dug beneath the garden of the house he had been using. Yet the British gunners in the town must be credited for firing back, even though their shells did little damage. American surgeon, James Thacher, later recalled:

> From the tenth to the fifteenth, a tremendous and incessant firing from the Amer-

*American cannons blast away at British positions in Yorktown in September 1781.*

## Washington Cheats Death

During the furious, weeks-long American and French artillery barrage of the British at Yorktown, in September to October 1781, American soldier John Suddarth witnessed a remarkable act of courage by Commander-in-Chief George Washington (quoted in John Dann's *The Revolution Remembered*).

> During the progress of these works [i.e., the siege of Yorktown], [I] witnessed a deed of personal daring and coolness in General Washington which he never saw equaled. During a tremendous cannonade from the British in order to demolish our breastworks [mounds of earth piled up around the town], a few days prior to the surrender, General Washington visited that part of our fortifications behind which [I] was posted and, whilst here, discovered that the enemy were de-stroying their property and drowning their horses, etc. Not, however, entirely assured of what they were doing, he took his [spy]glass and mounted the highest, most prominent, and most exposed point of our fortifications, and there stood exposed to the enemy's fire, where shot seemed flying almost as thick as hail and were instantly demolishing portions of the embankment around him for ten or fifteen minutes, until he had completely satisfied himself of the purposes of the enemy. During this time his aides, etc., were remonstrating [arguing] with him with all their earnestness against this exposure of his person and once or twice drew him down. He severely reprimanded them and resumed his position. When satisfied, he dispatched a flag to the enemy, and they desisted from their purpose.

ican and French batteries is kept up, and the enemy return the fire, but with little effect. A red-hot shell from the French battery set fire to the *Charon*, a British 44-gun ship, and two or three smaller vessels at anchor in the river, which were consumed in the night. From the banks of the river, I had a fine view of this splendid conflagration. The ships were enwrapped in a torrent of fire, which spread with vivid brightness among the combustible rigging, and running with amazing rapidity to the tops of the several masts, while all around was thunder and lightning from our numerous cannon and mortars, and in the darkness of the night, presented one of the most sublime and magnificent spectacles which can be imagined. Some of our shells, overreaching the town, are seen to fall into the river, and bursting, throw up columns of water like shooting of the monsters of the deep.[53]

The modest British defensive efforts eventually proved fruitless since the American and French artillery continued to pound the town with increasing fury. A German officer serving under Cornwallis later described the devastating barrage of October 17:

At daybreak the enemy bombardment resumed, more terribly strong than ever before. They fired from all positions without letup. Our command, which was in the Hornwork, could hardly tolerate the enemy bombs, howitzer, and cannonballs any longer. There was nothing to be seen but bombs and cannonballs raining down on our entire line. [54]

This virtual rain of death convinced Cornwallis that his position was hopeless and two days later he surrendered his entire army to General Washington. After this major defeat, which was brought about almost entirely by artillery fire, the British no longer had the stomach to go on. The Americans had won their freedom from Britain.

# Chapter 5

# Ships and Naval Warfare

**N**oted scholar of American history Henry S. Commager once called the story of naval warfare in the American Revolution "a nautical version of David and Goliath."[55] This is a fitting description considering that throughout the conflict Britain enjoyed complete military superiority on the seas. In 1775, when fighting broke out in Lexington and Concord, the British Royal Navy possessed 131 warships carrying between 60 and 100 guns (naval cannons), 98 more with from 20 to 56 guns, and 41 smaller fighting vessels, for a total of 270 warships. By war's end, the fleet boasted 478 ships, 174 of which carried 60 to 100 guns and 198 of which had 20 to 56 guns. In addition, Britain's fleet of cargo vessels was more than seven thousand strong throughout the war.

Not all of these ships were in North American waters, of course, as the Royal Navy also guarded England and patrolled the world's seas. Yet British war leaders could count on a veritable never-ending stream of replacements when they lost either warships or cargo vessels. The warships they committed to the fight against the American rebels usually dominated the colonies' coasts. These vessels often blockaded American

*Typical of British naval firepower was this array of cannons on the warship* Victory.

79

ports, keeping supplies and other overseas aid from reaching the Americans. They could also ferry British troops quickly from one place to another, landing them at strategic locations and keeping them well supplied.

In contrast, the Americans began the war with almost no navy to speak of. They had no large warships equipped with long rows of cannons and were able at first to assemble only a few dozen small schooners (sailboats) and cargo ships, either state- or privately owned. Although Congress quickly instituted the Continental navy, which implemented a crash program for building warships, these vessels were far fewer in number and carried considerably less ordnance than their British counterparts. Only four carried forty or more guns and most had fewer than twenty-eight guns. Moreover, even this inadequate showing pushed American war planners to their limit. "Individual ships of small size might be built and equipped," naval historian Jack Coggins points out,

but the construction of a large fleet of ships capable of lying in the line of battle, with their attendant frigates [warships with twenty to forty-four guns] and smaller craft, was entirely beyond any but a first-class power. For the revolted colonies, torn with war and internal dissentions and jealousies and all but penniless, to attempt such a thing was out of the question. Nor, if by some miracle the ships themselves could be constructed, were there gun foundries capable of arming them.[56]

Making matters worse, far fewer American than British military officers had combat experience. "The raw material was there," Coggins continues, however,

while of the [American] captains and mates many were men of great experience and skill, it should be noted that although there were many colonials capable of commanding a merchant vessel, few had actually been in combat. Naval command calls for other qualities besides seamanship. Few merchant captains, used to independent command, could adapt to naval discipline, while none knew anything of tactics. As it was also unfortunately true that many of those appointed to command owed their preferment to political "pull" and favoritism, the Continental navy was, with a few brilliant exceptions, poorly officered. Had the commanders been of the same caliber as the ships, the naval record would have been brighter.[57]

Considering the American navy's deficiencies of ships, guns, and experienced officers, it is not surprising that by the time its ally, the French fleet, began to make a difference in North America (in 1781), almost all of the larger American warships had been sunk or captured. Still, the American captains and sailors had fought with amazing daring and acquitted themselves surprisingly well. In their short tenure in the war they had attacked British communications and overseas commerce, raided the coasts of the

*Land-based American cannons fire on British ships, which ruled the waves.*

British Isles and various British colonies, hindered enemy troop movements, (thereby saving several American states from being overrun), and sunk or captured some two hundred British ships, mostly cargo vessels. In addition, American privateers (armed private ships) sank or captured another six hundred enemy merchant ships.

## Birth of the U.S. Navy

From a modern vantage, the construction of a navy by the American rebels seems a natural and inevitable step in their bold attempt to break away from Britain and establish

## Proper Record-Keeping Aboard Ship

These sections of the *Rules for the Regulation of the Navy of the United Colonies of North-America,* composed in 1775 by the Naval Committee, deal with the obligation of the captain and other authorities to keep accurate personnel records and make sure that the property of crewmen killed in action went to their next of kin.

The Captain shall before he sails make return to and leave with the Congress, or such person or persons as the Congress appoint for that purpose, a complete list of all his officers and men, with the time and terms of their entering; and during his cruise, shall keep a true account of the desertion or death of any of them, and of the entering of others; and after his cruise, and before any of them are paid off, he shall make return of a complete list of the same, including those who shall remain onboard his ship. . . . Any officer, seaman or others entitled to wages or prize-money, may have the same paid to his assignee, provided the assignment be attested by the Captain or commander, the master or purser of the ship, or a chief magistrate of some county or corporation. . . . The Captain or purser shall secure the clothes, bedding and other things of such persons as shall die or be killed, to be delivered to their executors or administrators. All the papers, charter parties, bills of lading, passports and other writings whatever, found on board any ship or ships which shall be taken [captured] shall be carefully preserved, and the originals sent to the court of justice for maritime affairs, appointed, or to be appointed by Congress for judging concerning such prize or prizes.

their own nation. History had shown them, after all, that ships could be among the most potent weapons in warfare. Yet the truth is that the infant American fleet was almost stillborn in its docks. At first, many of the founding fathers were convinced that building a navy was a waste of time and money, since any attempt to oppose the mighty Royal Navy would surely be suicidal. Finally, in late August 1775, one colonial assembly—that of Rhode Island—had the gumption to make a formal proposal to Congress that warships be built. "This assembly is persuaded," the resolution stated,

that the building and equipping [of] an American fleet as soon as possible would greatly and essentially [help to preserve] the lives, liberty, and property of the good people of these colonies; and therefore instruct their delegates to use their whole influence, at the ensuing [meeting of] Congress, for building, at Continental expense, a fleet of sufficient force for the protection of these colonies.[58]

On October 5, Congress agreed to appoint a committee of three—John Adams, John Langdon, and Silas Deane—to consider naval preparedness. Adams later remembered:

The opposition was very loud and vehement. Some of my colleagues appeared greatly alarmed by [the idea of sending warships against the British]. . . . It was [like] an infant taking a mad bull by the horns; and what was more profound and remote, it was said it would ruin the character and corrupt the morals of our seamen. [59]

Despite these objections, the committee plowed forward. On October 30, Congress added four more members to the group, at which time it became officially known as the Naval Committee. Adams and the others worked fast. And on December 11, 1775, they recommended to Congress that the patriots build thirteen warships—five with thirty-two guns, five with twenty-eight guns, and three with twenty-four guns—all to be ready for action in 1776.

In the meantime, however, there was a more immediate need for ships to intercept British supplies bound for Boston and other American cities. Luckily, George Washington had already foreseen this necessity. Between early September and late November of 1775, he had acquired seven small merchant vessels and outfitted them with whatever ordnance he could find. (This army-controlled squadron was one of three small ones that supplemented the main ocean-going fleet; the other two patrolled Lake Champlain, in upstate New York, and the Mississippi River, respectively.)

## High Standards of Discipline

The first ship in Washington's fleet was the *Hannah,* a schooner outfitted with four small cannons. Its captain, Nicholas Broughton, received the following instructions:

You, being appointed a Captain in the Army of the United Colonies of North America, are hereby directed to take the command of a detachment of said Army and proceed on board the schooner *Hannah,* at Beverly, lately fitted out and equipped with arms, ammunition and provisions, at the Continental expense. You are to proceed, as commander of said schooner, immediately on a cruise against such vessels as may be found on the high seas

*John Adams, who served on the Naval Committee, as he appeared in old age.*

or elsewhere, bound inwards and outwards, to or from Boston . . . and to take and seize all [British] vessels laden with soldiers, arms, ammunition or provisions . . . or which you shall have good reason to suspect are in such service.[60]

These may seem like rather tall orders for a ship so small and lacking in ordnance. Yet they reflect both how seriously patriot leaders like Washington and Adams took the British threat and the degree of professionalism they wanted to instill in the emerging American naval forces. In spite of their obvious material shortcomings, Broughton and other American ship captains were expected to follow high standards and impose and maintain efficient organization and strict discipline aboard their vessels. To ensure this, on November 28, 1775, the Naval Committee issued an official set of naval rules and regulations. The document begins:

The Commanders of all ships and vessels belonging to the Thirteen United Colonies are strictly required to show in themselves a good example of honor and virtue to their officers and men, and to be very vigilant in inspecting the behavior of all such as are under them, and to discountenance and suppress all dissolute, immoral and disorderly practices; and also, such as are contrary to the rules of discipline and obedience, and to correct those who are guilty of the same according to the usage of the sea.[61]

Some of these "rules of discipline and obedience" were spelled out by the Naval Committee this way:

If any shall be heard to swear, curse or blaspheme the name of God, the Captain is strictly enjoined to punish them for every offence, by causing them to wear a wooden collar or some other shameful badge of distinction, for so long a time as he shall judge proper. If he [the offender] be a commissioned officer he shall forfeit one shilling for each offence, and a warrant or inferior officer, six-pence. He who is guilty of drunkenness (if a seaman) shall be put in irons until he is sober, but if an officer, he shall forfeit two days pay. No Commander shall inflict any punishment upon a seaman beyond twelve lashes upon his bare back with a cat of nine-tails [a kind of whip]; if the fault shall deserve a greater punishment, he is to apply to the Commander in Chief of the navy in order to the trying of him by a court martial, and in the meantime he may put him under confinement. . . . Any officer, seaman or marine, who shall begin to excite, cause, or join in any mutiny or sedition in the ship to which he belongs on any pretence whatsoever, shall suffer death or such other punishment as a court-martial shall direct. None shall presume to quarrel with, or strike his superior officer, on pain of such punishment as a court-martial shall order to be inflicted. . . . All murder shall be punished with death. All robbery and theft shall be punished at the discretion of a court-martial. [62]

## American Naval Ordnance

Of course, professionalism and discipline alone were not enough to challenge a fighting force as strong as the British navy. More than anything else, American ships needed effective ordnance. But at the outset of the war the rebels had few large cannons in their possession, and Washington needed most of these for his land army. To equip his small fleet of schooners, Washington managed to borrow or capture a few small artillery pieces. But outfitting the new frigates Congress had ordered for main fleet was far more problematic. Colonial foundries were simply not up to the task of producing big, standardized, reliable naval ordnance in large quantities. To make up for this shortfall, the rebels captured whatever British cannons they could and bought more from France (although many of the French guns turned out to be outdated and sometimes unreliable). Meanwhile, Benedict Arnold, who had charge of the small Lake Champlain fleet, armed several of his vessels with artillery pieces captured from the British at Fort Ticonderoga.

*Benedict Arnold, who commanded the small American fleet on lake Champlain.*

*These drawings show typical naval ordnance of the late eighteenth century.*

Even when American ships managed to find enough cannons, there was no guarantee they would be effective in battle. Seamen trained in firing them were in short supply in the colonies. Also, such guns were cumbersome and difficult to aim, especially from the rolling deck of a ship. Sights were either nonexistent or inefficient; the large amount of windage in the barrels of naval ordnance practically ensured that the paths of the cannonballs would be off-target; and in the time lag between the order to "Fire!" and the actual explosion of the charge, both the attacking ship and its opponent moved in unpredictable ways, further hindering accuracy. Because of these factors, the warships of the day were equipped with as many big guns as possible; the hope was that a massive artillery barrage would do enough damage to the enemy to make up for the lack of accuracy of individual cannons.

In addition to problems relating to accuracy, naval gunners faced considerable difficulties simply in firing their weapons. The typical loading and firing sequence included many steps, all of which were important; if any one of them was accomplished improperly, the gun might misfire, injuring the gunners, or not fire at all. According to Jack Coggins:

On being called to quarters (action stations) by beat of drum or bugle call, the gun crew first cast off the lashings with which the guns were always securely fastened to the ship's side when not in use. (A gun which broke loose from its fastenings in a rough sea was a terrible menace and might, by crashing through the side, actually endanger the ship.) The gun was run in and the tampion, or wooden plug used to keep out spray and moisture, was taken out of the muzzle. A cartridge—a cylindrical bag of powder, often made of flannel—was brought up to the gun from the magazine below decks by a young "powder monkey," whose duty it was to keep one or more guns supplied. The cartridge was rammed all the way down the bore, and a ball was taken from the shot racks which lined the bulwarks and hatchways and rammed down on the charge. . . . A lighted slow match, made of cotton wick soaked in lye, or some other substance, was twisted about a forked stick some three feet long (the linstock). . . . When the gun captain thought his piece was well and truly laid on the target he sidestepped smartly to avoid the backward rush of the cannon in recoil and ordered the glowing end of the match brought down on the vent. There was a poof of flame and smoke from the vent, followed almost instantaneously by the flash and roar of the gun, which ran back until checked by the breeching [a heavy rope that secured the gun to the ship's side]. Before reloading, any sparks or smoldering pieces of cartridge were extinguished by swabbing out the bore with a wet sponge, usually made of sheepskin fixed to the end of a wooden staff. [63]

## Boldness in Place of Firepower

Though British gunners faced these same problems, British ships had far more naval ordnance and larger numbers of trained seamen than American ships did. But while the rebels were clearly outgunned, they did not shy away from adopting bold strategies and tactics. And sometimes their sheer audacity paid off. The first American naval mission of the war—that of Captain Broughton and his *Hannah*—is an example. The little warship left port on September 5, 1775, and on its second day out spotted a large British merchantship, the *Unity*, bound for Boston and heavily loaded with lumber and other valuable supplies. Broughton later reported how he accomplished the first American capture of an enemy ship in the war:

> Next morning, I saw a ship under my lee quarter; I perceived her to be a large ship. I tacked and stood back for the land; soon after I put about and stood towards her again and found her a ship of no force [i.e., equipped with few or no cannons]. I came up with her, hailed, and asked where she came from; was answered, from Piscataqua, and bound to

## U.S. Warships of the American Revolution Carrying Twenty-Four or More Cannons

| Name of Ship | Number of Cannons | Source | Fate |
|---|---|---|---|
| Alfred | 24 | Bought | Captured |
| Raleigh | 32 | Built | Captured |
| Hancock | 32 | Built | Captured |
| Warren | 32 | Built | Destroyed |
| Washington | 32 | Built | Destroyed |
| Randolph | 32 | Built | Destroyed |
| Providence | 28 | Built | Captured |
| Trumbull | 28 | Built | Captured |
| Congress | 28 | Built | Destroyed |
| Virginia | 28 | Built | Captured |
| Effingham | 28 | Built | Destroyed |
| Boston | 24 | Built | Captured |
| Montgomery | 24 | Built | Destroyed |
| Delaware | 24 | Built | Captured |
| Indien | 40 | Built | Sold |
| Deane | 32 | Built | Name changed to *Hague;* retired in 1783 |
| Queen of France | 28 | Bought | Destroyed |
| Alliance | 32 | Built | Sold |
| Confederacy | 32 | Built | Captured |
| Bonhomme Richard | 42 | Bought | Destroyed |
| Pallas | 32 | Borrowed | Returned after war |
| Serapis | 44 | Captured | Sold |
| America | 74 | Built | Given to France in 1786 |
| Bourbon | 36 | Built | Sold |

Boston. I told him he must bear away and go into Cape Ann [north of Boston]; but being very loath [i.e., because he was reluctant], I told him if he did not I should fire on her. On that she bore away and I have brought her safe into Cape Ann Harbor.[64]

Other small craft in Washington's squadron, along with some state- and privately owned craft, scored similar successes in the months that followed. Not only did they capture dozens of enemy merchant ships, on occasion their prizes had British troops aboard.

### A Spirit of Enterprise

Even more daring were the strategies adopted for some of the larger American warships after they were completed in 1776. Patriot leader Robert Morris urged John

Paul Jones, one of the more experienced captains in the American fleet, to attack the British in the West Indies and Florida in an effort to draw British warships away from American cities. "Destroying their settlements," Morris wrote,

> spreading alarms, showing and keeping up a spirit of enterprise that will oblige them to defend their extensive possessions at all points, is of infinitely more consequence to the United States of America than all the plunder that can be taken. If they divide their force, we shall have elbow room and, that gained, we shall turn about and play our parts to the best advantage, which we cannot do now, being constantly cramped in one part [of the country] or another. It has long been clear to me that our infant fleet cannot protect our own coasts; and the only effectual relief it can afford us is to attack the enemy's defenseless places and thereby oblige them to station more of their ships in their own countries, or to keep them employed in following ours, and either way, we are relieved so far as they do it. [65]

Jones obtained positive results with this strategy and then went a step further by carrying the naval war to the enemy's very shores. He executed a series of daring raids on English and Irish coasts beginning in April 1778 and captured a small British warship, the *Drake*, in the process. The following year, he captured seventeen enemy

merchant vessels off the British coast and then took on the British warship *Serapis*, outfitted with forty-four guns. In a furious battle, Jones's smaller ship, the *Bonhomme Richard*, exchanged fire with the enemy at point-blank range. Then, when the captain of the *Serapis* called for the Americans to surrender, Jones delivered his now famous reply: "I have not yet begun to fight!" [66] The battle continued and two hours later it was the *Serapis* that surrendered to Jones.

*John Paul Jones leads the crew of the* Bonhomme Richard *to victory in 1779.*

# The First American Submarine

In 1775, David Bushnell, a Connecticut farm boy with remarkable mechanical skills, invented a primitive submarine, which he named the *American Turtle.* Between 1776 and 1778, he tested the vehicle in New York and Philadelphia waters but was unable to achieve any measurable success, mainly because it was too difficult to operate. This contemporary document (quoted in volume 2 of Commager and Morris's *Spirit of 'Seventy-Six*) provides a thumbnail sketch of a weapon far ahead of its time.

Bushnell's machine was composed of several pieces of large oak timber, scooped out and fitted together, and its shape . . . [like] that of a round clam. It was bound around thoroughly with iron bands, the seams were corked, and the whole was smeared over with tar, so as to prevent the possibility of the admission of water to the inside. It was of capacity to contain one engineer, who might stand or sit, and enjoy sufficient elbow room for its proper management. The top or head was made of a metallic composition, exactly suited to its body, so as to be watertight; this opened upon hinges, and formed the entrance to the machine. Six small pieces of thick glass were inserted in this head for the admission of light. In a clear day and clear sea water . . . he could see to read at the depth of three fathoms. To keep it upright and properly balanced, seven hundred pounds of lead were fastened to its bottom, two hundred pounds of which were so contrived as to be discharged at any moment, to increase the buoyancy of the machine. But to enable the navigator when under water to rise or sink at pleasure, there were two forcing pumps, by which water could be pressed out at the bottom; and also a spring, by applying the foot to which a passage was formed for the admission of water. . . . The navigator steered by rudder, the tiller of which passed through the back of the machine at a water joint, and in one side was fixed a small pocket compass. . . . In the night when no light entered through the head, this compass . . . was all that served to guide the helmsman in his course.

---

*Early schematic drawings of David Bushnell's submarine, the* American Turtle.

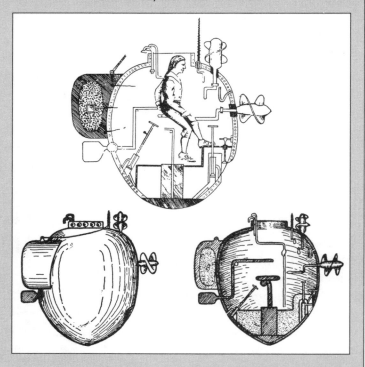

*Crewman from the sunken American warship* Philadelphia *scramble ashore during the battle of Lake Champlain.*

Meanwhile, no less bold was the American confrontation with the British on Lake Champlain. In October 1776, at Valcour Bay, Benedict Arnold's small naval squadron engaged a superior enemy force in hopes of delaying a British invasion of New York and New England from the north. As Arnold himself described the David-and-Goliath-like encounter:

Yesterday morning at eight o'clock, the enemy's fleet, consisting of [two ships] mounting sixteen guns . . . one schooner of fourteen guns, two of twelve, two sloops, a bomb-ketch, and a large vessel . . . carrying one twelve or eighteen-pounder in their bows, appeared off Cumberland Head. We im-

mediately prepared to receive them. . . . At eleven o'clock they ran under the lee of Valcour and began the attack. The schooner, by some bad management, fell to leeward and was first attacked; one of her masts was wounded, and her rigging shot away. The captain thought prudent to run her [aground] on the point of Valcour, where all the men were saved. They boarded her, and at night set fire to her. At half-past twelve the engagement became general and very warm [intense]. Some of the enemy's ships . . . beat and rowed up within musket-shot of us. They continued a very hot fire with round and grape shot until five o'clock, when they thought proper to retire to about six or seven hundred yards distance, and continued the fire until dark. The [American vessels] *Congress* and *Washington* have suffered greatly; the latter lost her first lieutenant killed, captain and master wounded. The *New York* lost all her officers, except her captain. The *Philadelphia* was hulled [poked with holes] in so many places that she [sank] in about one hour after the engagement was over. The whole [number of Americans] killed and wounded amounts to about sixty.[67]

Though the Americans were swept from the lake and lost the battle, the time it had taken the British to amass their lake fleet and square off with Arnold forced them to put off, and eventually to cancel, their invasion. In the words of noted nineteenth-century naval historian Alfred T. Mahan, "Never had any force, big or small, lived to better purpose, or died more gloriously. . . . [Later crucial American victories were] due to the invaluable year of delay secured to them by their little navy on Lake Champlian."[68] Indeed, a fitting epitaph for the entire American naval effort in the war would be: It showed uncommon boldness and courage in the face of vastly superior enemy numbers and weaponry, and in so doing secured a heroic niche in history.

# Chapter 6

# Spies and Military Intelligence

oday the work of intelligence organizations like the U.S. Central Intelligence Agency (CIA), which collects military and political information through the use of spies and other means, is taken for granted. Many people are surprised, though, to learn that such organizations have operated for centuries. In fact, secret intelligence gathering and other spy activities were among the most potent weapons used by both sides, but especially by the patriots, in the American Revolution.

Only a few months after the opening battles of the conflict, at Lexington and Concord, members of the Continental Congress recognized the need for collecting intelligence about the enemy; and on November 29, 1775, they formed the Committee of Secret Correspondence. Its members included some of the major American founding fathers: Pennsylvania's Benjamin Franklin, Virginia's Benjamin Harrison, and New York's Robert Livingston. Two years later, Congress changed the committee's name to the Com-

mittee of Foreign Affairs, though its secret activities remained the same. These activities included sending secret agents behind enemy lines and also abroad to collect intelligence; analyzing that information and making estimates of enemy troop strengths; conducting covert (undercover) operations, including sabotage; spreading misinformation to deceive the enemy; creating and breaking codes designed to hide secret information; intercepting and opening private mail; and funding privateers (armed, privately owned ships) to capture or destroy enemy ammunition and supplies.

Besides the committee that authorized these activities, Congress appointed another committee in June 1776 to decide what to do about British agents caught spying on Americans. Its members included John Adams, Thomas Jefferson, and Robert Livingston, among others. At the time, no law existed to handle cases of civilian espionage (spying); and American military leaders felt that the existing punishments for military spying were not severe enough. In August, the committee made its recommendations to Congress, which immediately enacted the first U.S. espionage act. It read:

> Resolved, that all persons not members of, nor owing allegiance to, any of the United States of America, as described in a resolution to the Congress of the 29th of June last, who shall be found lurking as spies in or about the fortification or encampments of the armies of the United States, or of any of them, shall suffer death, according to the law and usage of nations, by sentence of a court martial, or such other punishment as such court martial may direct. [69]

As time went on, some patriot leaders expressed the view that the act needed to include Americans who turned traitor and spied on their countrymen. So on February 27, 1778, Congress expanded the law to include any "inhabitants of these states" whose intelligence activities gave aid to the enemy. [70]

The passage of the espionage law pleased the commander in chief of the American army—George Washington. More than any other figure of the period, he dominated American intelligence efforts, often recruiting spies and dispatching them on their missions himself. Many personal experiences taught him that good intelligence work was vital to the war effort. One of the more disturbing incidents occurred in Sep-

tember 1777 when the Americans suffered a defeat at Brandywine, in Pennsylvania. In a letter to the president of the Congress, Washington wrote:

> Sir: I am sorry to inform you, that in this day's engagement, we have been obliged to leave the enemy masters of the field. Unfortunately the intelligence received of the enemy's advancing up the Brandywine, and crossing at a ford about six miles above us, was uncertain and contradictory, notwithstanding all my pains to get the best. This prevented my making a disposition, adequate to the force with which the enemy attacked us on the right; in consequence of which the troops first engaged, were obliged to retire before they could be reinforced. [71]

It is ironic that less than two months before this disaster, in a letter to one of his officers, Washington had made the seminal and now famous statement that would set the tone for the future of American intelligence activities:

> The necessity of procuring good intelligence is apparent & need not be further urged. All that remains for me to add is that you keep the whole matter as secret as possible. For upon secrecy, success depends in most enterprises of the kind, and for want of it, they are generally defeated, however well planned & promising a favorable issue. [72]

## Foreign Agents

One way that Washington, as well as the members of the Committee of Secret Correspondence, attempted to ensure better intelligence collection was to recruit skilled, methodical, and cautious agents. Some of these agents spied in the colonies, while others did so abroad, including in England.

The first agent the committee enlisted for foreign work was Arthur Lee, a doctor from Stratford, Connecticut. Franklin and his colleagues sent Lee to England in December 1775, telling him: "It is considered of utmost

*A messenger informs General Washington of the American defeat at Brandywine.*

consequence to the cause of liberty that the Committee be kept informed of developments in Europe."[73] The committee also hired W.F. Dumas, a Swiss journalist working in the Netherlands. Dumas used secret letter drops (depositing letters in prearranged spots) to report back to the committee, as well as to exchange information with Lee in London.

Another important American foreign agent in the war's early years was Silas Deane. A former delegate to the Continental Congress, Deane went to France disguised as a Bermudian merchant. There, he worked with French merchants to find and recruit French privateers to help disrupt British supply lines. Deane also worked secretly with Lee, and eventually with Franklin himself (when Franklin was appointed a commis-

sioner to France in 1776), to win the French over to the American cause, an effort that eventually succeeded.

In addition, Deane looked to recruit people for sabotage operations against targets in England. The only known mission that succeeded involved a young American house painter, James Aitken, who met with Deane in Paris late in 1776. Deane helped the other man obtain a phony passport and the two men planned an operation in which Aitken, using fire bombs he had designed, would destroy British shipyards in England. An official CIA report summarized the results of Aitken's mission:

> In late November 1776, Aitken landed at Dover [on England's southern coast], and on December 7 he ignited a fire at

## The Necessity of Good Intelligence

This letter (quoted in volume 8 of *The Writings of George Washington*) written by George Washington on July 26, 1777 to a subordinate, Colonel Elias Dayton, ends with Washington's now famous and often quoted declaration of the importance of military intelligence.

> The reason of my being thus particular in describing Lord Stirling's route, is, because I wish you to take every possible pains in your power, by sending trusty persons to Staten Island in whom you can confide, to obtain intelligence of the enemy's situation & numbers—what kind of troops they are, and what guards they have—their strength & where posted. . . . You will also make some enquiry how many boats are & may be certainly [used] to transport the troops, in case

the enterprise [should] appear advisable. You will, after having assured yourself upon these matters, send a good & faithful officer to meet Lord Stirling with a distinct and accurate account of every thing—as well respecting the numbers & strength of the enemy—their situation etc.—as about the boats, that he may have a general view of the whole, and possessing all the circumstances, may know how to regulate his conduct in the affair. The necessity of procuring good intelligence is apparent & need not be further urged. All that remains for me to add is, that you keep the whole matter as secret as possible. For upon secrecy, success depends in most enterprises of the kind, and for want of it, they are generally defeated, however well planned & promising a favorable issue.

the Portsmouth dockyard that burned from late in the afternoon until the following morning, destroying twenty tons of hemp, ten one-hundred-fathom cables, and six tons of ship cordage. After failing to penetrate the security at Plymouth, Aitken proceeded to Bristol, where he destroyed two warehouses and several houses. On January 16, 1777, the British cabinet met in emergency session and urged immediate measures to locate the mysterious "John the Painter." . . . Guards were augmented at all military facilities and arsenals, and a reward was posted. By January 20 the cabinet, again in extraordinary session, discussed suspending *habeas corpus* and placing the country under martial law. Five days later the reward was increased to one thousand pounds and newspapers reported panic throughout England.[74]

## Domestic Spying

Meanwhile, spies recruited by either the committee or General Washington and his officers infiltrated British-held territories in the American colonies. Some disguised themselves as seemingly innocent or harm-

*Arthur Lee, an American doctor and spy, collected intelligence in Europe.*

less individuals; once behind enemy lines, they gathered information by snooping around sensitive areas and/or talking to unsuspecting British soldiers or local loyalists.

Like Silas Deane, Robert Townsend also pretended to be a merchant. Townsend's cover name, known only to a handful of Americans, including his boss Washington, was "Culper, Junior." At a New York coffeehouse frequented by British officers, Townsend often overheard their conversations and duly

## The Congressional Oath of Secrecy

American leaders early on recognized that it was important to ensure that no intelligence was leaked by any of their number who might be privy to secret information. To guard against this possibility, on November 9, 1775, the Continental Congress adopted an oath of secrecy (quoted in the CIA's *Intelligence in the War of Independence*) that reads as follows:

Resolved, that every member of this Congress considers himself under the ties of virtue, honor and love of his country, not to divulge, directly or indirectly, any matter or thing agitated or debated in Congress, before the same shaft have been determined, without the leave of the Congress; nor any matter or thing determined in Congress, which a majority of the Congress shall order to be kept secret; and that if any member shall violate this agreement, he shall be expelled from this Congress, and deemed an enemy to the liberties of America, and liable to be treated as such, and that every member signify his consent to this agreement by signing the same.

passed on valuable tidbits of information to another spy, Samuel Woodhull, whose cover name was "Culper, Senior." Woodhull's job was to get the intelligence to General Washington's staff. Scholar John Bakeless, an expert on espionage in the war, outlines the usual careful, roundabout, and effective method employed by the so-called Culper spy ring:

If Woodhull happened to visit New York when intelligence was ready, Townsend gave it to him orally, to be written down later. . . . Otherwise Townsend turned his reports over to a currier, usually Austin Roe, who made the fifty-mile ride to [the Long Island town where Woodhull lived]. . . . As a precaution, the currier did not visit Woodhull's house, but left the messages in a box, buried in an open field. In due course, Lieutenant Caleb Brewster, a veteran of the whaling trade, crossed Long Island Sound [in a boat] . . . received the reports from Woodhull, and returned to Connecticut, where

[American cavalrymen delivered] them to Washington's headquarters.[75]

Among the other American intelligence agents who successfully used disguises and stealth to accomplish their missions was John Honeyman. Sometimes he pretended to be a butcher; other times he posed as a loyalist or an American traitor. He not only collected much valuable information about British military activities in New Jersey but also took part in a crucial deception operation. In December 1776, following Washington's instructions, Honeyman pretended to be an American being hunted for treason. He fell in with the British and Hessians in the Trenton area, who believed him when he claimed that Washington's troops were in no shape to fight. This ruse was a major factor in the American victory at Trenton following Washington's surprise crossing of the Delaware River on December 26.

Another successful American agent,

Nancy Morgan Hart, was one of several women who spied for the patriots. She took advantage of her unusual physical attributes—being tall, muscular, and cross-eyed—by assuming the identity of a mentally ill homeless man. Managing to penetrate the British lines in Augusta, Georgia, she gained valuable information about the enemy defenses there. Hart was a tough customer, even by male standards. When some loyalists found out she was a spy and attacked her home, she captured them all, turned them in to the patriots, and witnessed their execution.

## Risk of Capture and Death

The missions described above were all successful. But several others ended in failure, and the risk of an agent being caught and/or killed was ever present. Indeed, the British were as skilled in ferreting out spies in their midst as the Americans were, so espionage was always a dangerous game. One American agent, John L. Mersereau, son of one of Washington's officers, had a series of hair-raising escapes, including one that took place on Staten Island in 1778. "[I] sometimes carried

*Formidable American spy Nancy Morgan Hart captures loyalists entering her home.*

intelligence to the Jersey shore in person," Mersereau later recalled.

At one time, learning that my father was at Elizabethtown and having important intelligence to communicate and further instructions to receive, I repaired in the night an old skiff which lay among the grass on a part of the island not then guarded by the British and passed over and had an interview with my father. But when my business was concluded it was too late to return that night, and I remained on the Jersey side the next day, concealed in a barn. During my absence, the British had noticed the absence of the old skiff and placed a sentry near the place where I had embarked and expected to land on my return. I landed there without knowing the place was guarded. The sentry hailed, and I fled on my hands and feet to a ditch, along which I could run without being much exposed to his fire. He fired his musket just as I got into the ditch, and his ball struck a post just over my head. I then jumped out of the ditch and ran directly to my lodgings. The sentinel, with others, pursued me and reached the outer door just as I entered my room. Had they persevered, I must have been discovered and taken. It happened, however, that a British "Major Tenpenny" (so-called) quartered at the same house and, being drunk at the time, countermanded further search, swearing "there were no rebels in the house where he lodged," or words to that effect. [76]

Mersereau was lucky to escape in one piece. However, others were not as fortunate, among them James Aitken, the American saboteur who had successfully burned docks and warehouses in southern England. Constantly on the run from British authorities, Aitken was eventually apprehended with some of his bomb-making materials still on his person. He refused to admit that he was behind the sabotage, but the British soon managed to find his forged passport and other damning evidence. And on March 10, 1777, they hanged him at Portsmouth dockyard, scene of his first "crime."

Undoubtedly the most famous case of an American spy's capture and execution was that of Nathan Hale. A captain in the Connecticut militia, in 1776 Hale responded to General Washington's request for a volunteer to gather information in British-held New York. Unfortunately, as spies go Hale was a rank amateur, having no training or experience, no undercover contacts in New York, and no way to communicate with his American superiors. As later remembered by his close friend Stephen Hempstead, Hale was captured and hanged before he made it back with the intelligence he had collected:

Captain Hale had changed his uniform for a plain suit of citizens' brown clothes, with a round broad-brimmed hat; assum-

*Washington gives Nathan Hale instructions before sending him on his fateful mission.*

ing the character of a Dutch schoolmaster, leaving all his other clothes, commission, public and private papers with me, and also his silver shoe buckles, saying they would not comport with his character of schoolmaster, and retaining nothing but his college diploma, as an introduction to his assumed calling. Thus equipped, we parted for the last time in life. He went on his mission . . . [saying that] he expected to return . . . if he succeeded in his object [mission]. The British army had, in the meantime, got possession of New York, whither he also passed, and [he] had nearly executed his mission, and was passing through the British picket guard between the lines of the two armies, within a mile and a half of his own quarters,

*The British hang would-be American spy Nathan Hale on September 26, 1776.*

when he was stopped at a tavern at a place called the "Cedars." Here there was no suspicion of his character being other than he pretended, until most unfortunately he was met in the crowd by . . . [his] own relation [Samuel Hale of Portsmouth, New Hampshire] (but a Tory and a renegade). . . . He recognized him and most inhumanely and infamously betrayed him, divulging his true character, situation in the army, etc. . . . Then without any formality or trial or delay, they hung him instantaneously, and sent a [message] over to our army, stating that "they had caught such a man within their lines this morning, and hung him as a spy."[77]

Ironically, Hale was the least successful of all the American spies in the war, yet he became the most celebrated of their number, mainly because of the defiant last words attributed to him. According to Captain William Hull of Connecticut, who witnessed the execution on September 26, 1776:

> My station was near the fatal spot, and I requested the Provost Marshal to permit the prisoner to sit [with me] while he was making the necessary preparations. Captain Hale entered. He was calm, and bore himself with gentle dig-

nity. . . . He asked for writing materials, which I furnished him. He wrote two letters, one to his mother and one to a brother officer. He was shortly after summoned to the gallows. [Only] a few persons were around him, yet his characteristic dying words were remembered. He said, "I only regret that I have but one life to lose for my country."[78]

## The Exploits of Double Agents

General Washington had realized the risks of sending an amateur like Nathan Hale to gather intelligence but evidently thought the chances of success outweighed those risks. By contrast, Washington would never have allowed someone so inexperienced to get in-

volved in the most dangerous spy game of all—counterintelligence. This is the domain of the double agent, someone who pretends to spy for one side but is really spying for the other. To be successful, a double agent must be able to fool many people while secretly transmitting information for extended periods. It is work that requires exceptional skill and attention to detail.

Perhaps the most successful American double agent of the American Revolution was Enoch Crosby, a veteran soldier in Washington's army. In August 1776, Crosby managed to gain the confidence of a New York loyalist who believed he shared his views. This allowed Crosby to infiltrate a secret loyalist military company aiding the British against the Americans. He reported

## Ballad of a Spy Hero

After Nathan Hale's death, he became a martyr to the American cause and inspired much adulation, including the popular ballad excerpted here (quoted in volume 1 of Commager and Morris's *Spirit of 'Seventy-Six*):

> He warily trod on the dry rustling leaves, As he passed through the wood; as he passed through the wood; And silently gained his rude launch on the shore, As she played with the flood; as she played with the flood. . . .
>
> The guards of the camp, on that dark, dreary night, Had a murderous will; had a murderous will. They took him and bore him afar from the shore, To a hut on the hill; to a hut on the hill.
>
> No mother was there, nor a friend who could cheer, In that little stone cell; in that

> little stone cell. But he trusted in love, from his father above. In his heart, all was well; in his heart, all was well. . . .
>
> They took him and bound him and bore him away, Down the hill's grassy side; down the hill's grassy side. 'Twas there the base hirelings, in royal array, His cause did deride; his cause did deride.
>
> Five minutes were given, short moments, no more, For him to repent; for him to repent; He prayed for his mother, he asked not another. To Heaven he went; to Heaven he went.
>
> The faith of a martyr, the tragedy showed, As he trod the last stage; as he trod the last stage. And Britons will shudder at gallant Hale's blood, As his words do presage; as his words do presage.

the whereabouts of the group's next meeting to the patriots, who captured the loyalists, including Crosby (to maintain his cover). He then "escaped" and returned to his loyalist "friends" and soon afterward joined another loyalist military unit. Thanks to Crosby, this group met the same fate as the first one. The daring double agent repeated the same kind of operation at least four times before the loyalists began to grow suspicious of him. (Crosby's exploits became the model for James Fenimore Cooper's 1821 book, *The Spy,* the first novel about espionage written in English.)

Another successful American double agent, Captain David Gray, pretended to be a deserter, and to make his cover look as authentic as possible General Washington actually put him on the American deserters' list. A British intelligence officer, Colonel Beverly Robinson, believed Gray's story and enlisted him as his own spy-courier. Thereafter, when told to deliver secret messages to other British agents, Gray first made sure his American superiors had read them, then passed them along to the British spies as ordered. For more than two years Gray successfully penetrated the highest levels of the British secret service in North America. Eventually, General Washington recalled him and, to restore his reputation among his countrymen, struck his name from the deserters' list.

Still another accomplished American double agent, Dr. Edward Bancroft, of Massachusetts, began his career in espionage after making the acquaintance of Benjamin Franklin, whose secret committee was always on the lookout for fresh spy talent. According to Henry Commager and Richard Morris:

When Franklin went to France, Bancroft arranged to act as his spy; later he made the same arrangements with Silas Deane, to whom he had been commended by the Committee of Secret Correspondence and with whom he became on terms of intimacy. Meantime Bancroft had been appointed agent for the British government—at the handsome salary of £1,000 per year—and a most successful agent he was. Just to add to his interests—and rewards—he speculated heavily [made numerous bets] on [the outcomes brought about by] the secret information which he obtained through espionage. To top it, Bancroft had himself appointed secretary of the American Peace Commission which negotiated the final settlement with England![79]

Counterintelligence worked both ways, of course. And General Washington was duly concerned about British spies who might have infiltrated American circles or American traitors working undercover for the British. In a note written on March 24, 1776, he told aides:

There is one evil I dread, and that is, their spies. I could wish, therefore, the most attentive watch be kept. . . . I wish a dozen or more of honest, sensible and

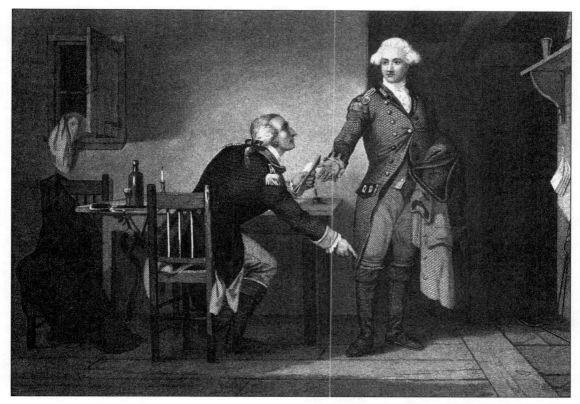

*Benedict Arnold urges his accomplice, Major John Andre, to conceal documents in his boot.*

diligent men, were employed . . . in order to question, cross-question etc., all such persons as are unknown, and cannot give an account of themselves in a straight and satisfactory line. . . . I think it a matter of importance to prevent them from obtaining intelligence of our situation.[80]

Washington's worries about British spies and American traitors were validated with a vengeance when one of the most accomplished American generals, Benedict Arnold, began working with the British in 1780. Arnold was bitter over what he

deemed unfair treatment by his superiors; he was also deeply in debt and needed money. So he began hatching secret plans with the British to betray West Point, a post he commanded. Luckily for the Americans, the plot was revealed when Major John Andre, a British agent who transmitted Arnold's messages, was caught in the act. His cover blown, Arnold fled to the enemy's ranks, where he became a British general. This left Andre to face the consequences of spying and getting caught. American intelligence

*Major John Andre suffers death by hanging after being caught spying.*

question, unwilling to give him a true answer. When I could no longer evade this importunity, I said to him that I had a much loved classmate in Yale College by the name of Nathan Hale, who entered the army with me in the year 1776. After the British troops had entered New York, General Washington wanted information respecting the strength, position & probable movements of the enemy. Captain Hale tendered his services, went into New York, and was taken just as he was passing the outposts of the enemy. Said I, with emphasis, "Do you remember the sequel to this story?" "Yes," said Andre. "He was hanged as a spy, but you surely do not consider his case and mine alike." I replied, "Precisely similar will be your fate." He endeavored to answer my remarks, but it was manifest he was more troubled than I had ever seen him before.[81]

As Tallmadge had predicted, on October 2, 1780, Andre met the same fate as Nathan Hale—death by hanging.

## Secret Writing Methods

If Arnold's message had been somehow unreadable or undecipherable, West Point may have fallen and Major Andre may not have been hanged. The reality was that many other secret messages passed during the war *were* rendered unreadable by various methods. For example, American spy Silas Deane used an invisible ink made from cobalt chloride, glycerin, and water. Even

expert Benjamin Tallmadge later recalled escorting Andre to his trial:

> As we progressed on our way to Tappan [New York] . . . Major Andre was very inquisitive to know my opinion as to the result of his capture. In other words, he wished me to give my opinion as to the light in which he would be viewed by General Washington, and a military tribunal. . . . I endeavored to evade this

more effective was the so-called sympathetic stain, invented by James Jay, a doctor and brother of the famous patriot John Jay. The stain consisted of one chemical for writing a message, which quickly became undetectable to the eye, and another chemical that when applied to the paper revealed the message. General Washington promoted use of the stain, saying that it would render a spy's "communications less exposed to detection, but relieve the fears of such persons as may be entrusted in its conveyance."[82]

Eventually, the British captured some papers revealing that the Americans in the New York area were using sympathetic stain. Realizing that some other way to hide information from the enemy had to be found, Benjamin Tallmadge, who often oversaw the members of the Culper spy ring, devised an effective numerical substitution code. According to the CIA's report:

Tallmadge took several hundred words from a dictionary and several dozen names of people or places and assigned each a number from 1 to 763. For example, 38 meant attack, 192 stood for fort, George Washington was identified as 711, and New York was replaced by 727. An American agent posing as a deliveryman transmitted the messages to other members of the ring. One of them, Anna Strong, signaled

## William Johnson's Successful Deception

One of the most effective deception operations of the war was conducted by American agent William Johnson, who convinced the British that General Washington planned to attack them in New York. This kept them from committing troops to his real objective, Yorktown. According to a later recollection by Johnson (as quoted in John Dann's *The Revolution Remembered*):

The next evening we received a letter from General Washington directing us to go to New York immediately and circulate as well as we could the information that he intended to attack New York, Staten Island, and Paulus Hook. In company with a young man hired for the purpose, [I] proceeded that night to Bergen Point, where Colonel Ward's regiment . . . [was] garrisoned. [I] called upon the colonel and communicated to him the intended attack of General Washington. The colonel, upon this . . . conveyed [me] in his barge to a British galley which was lying in the kills [creeks] opposite Colonel Ward's garrison. [I] communicated the same information to the officer commanding the galley, who immediately conveyed [me] in his barge to New York and introduced [me] to General Birch, who was in command of the British troops there. [I] informed the general that a friend of their cause had sent him from Morristown to let them know of General Washington's intended attack. He thanked [me] for the information and said [I] ought to be well rewarded for it. [I] then went to Mr. Savage and from thence to the mayor's to get a permit and returned home. The British troops did not leave New York as was contemplated, and General Washington, instead of making those attacks, immediately proceeded to the South, where the surrender of the British army ended the Revolutionary struggle.

the messages' location with a code involving laundry hung out to dry. A black petticoat indicated that a message was ready to be picked up, and the number of handkerchiefs identified the cove on Long Island Sound where the agents would meet.[83]

The use of this and other numerical substitution codes was so successful that by the end of the war, several prominent patriots, including John Jay, Robert Livingston, and John Adams, were using them.

Methods of secret writing, as well as other espionage practices developed during the American Revolution, helped the patriots to win the war. They also laid the foundation of the U.S. intelligence community, which has played a crucial role in nearly every war the country has fought since that time.

# ☆ Notes ☆

## Introduction: The Deciding Factors in the American Victory

1. Ian V. Hogg, *Armies of the American Revolution*. Englewood Cliffs, NJ: Prentice-Hall, 1975, p. 24.
2. Henry S. Commager and Richard B. Morris, eds., *The Spirit of 'Seventy-Six: The Story of the American Revolution as Told by Participants,* vol. 1. New York: Bobbs-Merrill, 1958, p. 333.
3. Quoted in William Dudley, ed., *The American Revolution: Opposing Viewpoints.* San Diego, CA: Greenhaven Press, 1992, pp. 154–155.
4. Hogg, *Armies of the American Revolution,* p. 16.
5. G.D. Scull, ed., *Memoir and Letters of Captain W. Glanville Evelyn, of the Fourth Regiment from North America, 1774–1776.* Oxford: James Parker, 1879, pp. 53–55.
6. Clarence E. Carter, ed., *The Correspondence of General Thomas Gage,* vol. 2. New Haven: Yale University Press, 1931–1932, pp. 686–687.
7. Quoted in Commager and Morris, *Spirit of 'Seventy-Six,* vol. 1, p. 264.

## Chapter 1: Muskets and Other Firearms

8. Archer Jones, *The Art of War in the Western World.* New York: Oxford University Press, 1987, pp. 269–270.
9. Hogg, *Armies of the American Revolution,* p. 64.
10. Quoted in Harold L. Peterson, *Arms and Armor in Colonial America.* Mineola, NY: Dover, 2000, p. 183.
11. Quoted in Hogg, *Armies of the American Revolution,* pp. 45–46.
12. Baron Frederick von Steuben, *Baron von Steuben's Revolutionary War Drill Manual.* Mineola, NY: Dover, 1985, pp. 99–100.
13. Hogg, *Armies of the American Revolution,* p. 66.
14. Quoted in Samuel E. Morison, *The Oxford History of the American People.* New York: Oxford University Press, 1965, p. 232.
15. Quoted in Jeremy Black, *Warfare in the Eighteenth Century.* London: Cassell, 1999, p. 118.
16. George Hanger, *Colonel George Hanger to All Sportsmen.* London: Stockdale, 1814, pp. 207–210.
17. The fate of all but one of these prototypes of Ferguson's remarkable rifle is unknown. The single surviving weapon, found years later in a New England attic, now rests in the museum at Morristown National Historic Park, in New Jersey.
18. Quoted in Hugh F. Rankin, ed., *The American Revolution.* New York: Putnam, 1964, p. 263.

19. Quoted in John C. Dann, ed., *The Revolution Remembered: Eyewitness Accounts of the War for Independence.* Chicago: University of Chicago Press, 1980, p. 156.

20. Quoted in Warren Moore, *Weapons of the American Revolution and Accoutrements.* New York: Promontory Press, 1967, p. 10.

## Chapter 2: Bayonets and Other Bladed Weapons

21. George C. Neumann, *Swords and Blades of the American Revolution.* Harrisburg, PA: Stackpole Books, 1973, pp. 22–23.

22. Quoted in Commager and Morris, *Spirit of 'Seventy-Six,* vol. 1, pp. 622–623.

23. Neumann, *Swords and Blades,* p. 51.

24. Epaphras Hoyt, *Treatise on the Military Art.* Brattleborough, VT: Smead, 1798, p. 101.

25. Quoted in Dann, *The Revolution Remembered,* p. 202.

26. Quoted in Dann, *The Revolution Remembered,* p. 275.

27. Quoted in John C. Fitzpatrick, ed., *The Writings of George Washington,* vol. 10. Washington, DC: U.S. Government Printing House, 1933–1944, p. 190.

28. Quoted in Fitzpatrick, *Writings of George Washington,* vol. 8, p. 236.

29. Quoted in Fitzpatrick, *Writings of George Washington,* vol. 8, p. 272.

30. Quoted in Peterson, *Arms and Armor in Colonial America,* p. 294.

## Chapter 3: Formal and Informal Battle Tactics

31. Black, *Warfare in the Eighteenth Century,* p. 112.

32. James Collins, *Autobiography of a Revolutionary Soldier,* ed. John M. Roberts. Clinton, LA: Feliciana Democrat, 1859, p. 24.

33. Quoted in Commager and Morris, *Spirit of 'Seventy-Six,* vol. 1, pp. 577–578.

34. Quoted in Black, *Warfare in the Eighteenth Century,* p. 114.

35. Quoted in Rankin, *American Revolution,* pp. 29–30.

36. Quoted in Black, *Warfare in the Eighteenth Century,* p. 118.

37. Quoted in Rankin, *American Revolution,* p. 261.

38. Neumann, *Swords and Blades,* pp. 18–19.

39. Quoted in Commager and Morris, *Spirit of 'Seventy-Six,* vol. 1, pp. 127–128.

40. Quoted in Dann, *The Revolution Remembered,* pp. 194–195.

41. Quoted in Henry Onderdonk, *Revolutionary Incidents of Suffolk and King's Counties: With an Account of the Battle of Long Island and the British Prisons and Prison-Ships at New York.* New York: Leavitt, 1849, pp. 147–148.

42. Quoted in Kenneth Roberts, *The Battle of Cowpens: The Story of 900 Men Who Shook an Empire.* Garden City, NY: Doubleday, 1958, p. 87.

43. Collins, *Autobiography,* pp. 264–265.

## Chapter 4: British and American Artillery

44. Hogg, *Armies of the American Revolution,* p. 131.

45. Hogg, *Armies of the American Revolution,* p. 132.

46. John Muller, *A Treatise on Artillery.* Originally published 1756. Reprint: Ottawa, CN: Museum Restoration Service, 1965, p. 58.

47. H.C.B. Rogers, *A History of Artillery.* Secaucus, NJ: Citadel Press, 1975, pp. 71–72.

48. Hogg, *Armies of the Revolution,* p. 137.

49. Albert Manucy, *Artillery Through the Ages: A Short Illustrated History of Cannon, Emphasizing Types Used in America.* Washington, DC: U.S. Government Printing Office, 1949, p. 11.

50. Quoted in Robert S. Quimby, *The Background of Napoleonic Warfare: The Theory of Military Tactics in Eighteenth-Century France.* New York: AMS Press, 1968, p. 296.

51. Quoted in Jones, *Art of War,* pp. 298–299.

52. Joseph P. Martin, *Private Yankee Doodle: Being a Narrative of Some of the Adventures, Dangers, and Sufferings of a Revolutionary Soldier.* Originally published in 1830. Reprint: ed. George E. Scheer. Boston: Little, Brown, 1962, p. 21.

53. James Thacher, *A Military Journal During the American Revolutionary War, from 1775–1783, Describing Interesting Events and Transactions of this Period.* Boston: Cottons and Barnard, 1827, pp. 283–284.

54. Quoted in Black, *Warfare in the Eighteenth Century,* p. 124.

## Chapter 5: Ships and Naval Warfare

55. Commager and Morris, *Spirit of 'Seventy-Six,* vol. 2, p. 912.

56. Jack Coggins, *Ships and Seamen of the American Revolution.* Harrisburg, PA: Stackpole Books, 1969, p. 21.

57. Coggins, *Ships and Seamen,* p. 21.

58. *Rhode Island Records, 1772–1777,* vol. 7. State archives, Providence, RI, p. 369.

59. Quoted in Charles F. Adams, ed., *The Works of John Adams, Second President of the United States: With a Life of the Author, Notes and Illustrations,* vol. 3. Boston: Little, Brown, 1850–1856, p. 8.

60. Quoted in Gardner W. Allen, *A Naval History of the American Revolution,* vol. 1. Gansevoort, NY: Corner House, 1970, p. 60.

61. *Rules for the Regulation of the Navy of the United Colonies of North-America.* Originally published in 1775. Reprint: Washington, DC: Naval Historical Foundation, 1944, p. 3.

62. *Rules,* pp. 4–5.

63. Coggins, *Ships and Seamen,* pp. 149–150.

64. Quoted in Allen, *Naval History,* vol. 1, pp. 60–61.

65. Quoted in Commager and Morris, *Spirit of 'Seventy-Six,* vol. 2, pp. 919–920.

66. Quoted in Commager and Morris, *Spirit of 'Seventy-Six,* vol. 2, p. 948.

67. Quoted in Commager and Morris, *Spirit of 'Seventy-Six,* vol. 1, p. 222.

68. Quoted in Commager and Morris, *Spirit of 'Seventy-Six,* vol. 1, p. 220.

## Chapter 6: Spies and Military Intelligence

69. Quoted in Central Intelligence Agency, *Intelligence in the War of Independence.* Washington, DC: Central Intelligence Agency, n.d.g, p. 3.
70. Quoted in CIA, *Intelligence,* p. 4.
71. Quoted in Fitzpatrick, *Writings of George Washington,* vol. 9, p. 207.
72. Quoted in Fitzpatrick, *Writings of George Washington,* vol. 8, p. 85.
73. Quoted in CIA, *Intelligence,* p. 7.
74. CIA, *Intelligence,* p. 9.
75. John Bakeless, *Turncoats, Traitors, and Heroes: Espionage in the American Revo-lution.* Philadelphia: Lippincott, 1953, p. 228.
76. Quoted in Dann, *The Revolution Remembered,* pp. 349–350.
77. Quoted in Onderdonk, *Revolutionary Incidents,* pp. 48–50.
78. Quoted in Maria Hull Campbell, *Revolutionary Services and Civil Life of General William Hull; Prepared from His Manuscripts.* New York: Appleton, 1848, p. 38.
79. Commager and Morris, *Spirit of 'Seventy-Six,* vol. 2, p. 743.
80. Quoted in CIA, *Intelligence,* pp. 10–11.
81. Quoted in Rankin, *American Revolution,* pp. 208–209.
82. Quoted in CIA, *Intelligence,* p. 15.
83. CIA, *Intelligence,* p. 16.

# ⭐ Glossary ⭐

**artillery:** Cannons; or ordnance.

**bore:** The inside of a gun's barrel.

**breech:** The back end of a gun's barrel.

**caliber:** The specific width of a gun's bore.

**covert:** Undercover.

**cutlass:** A single-edged sword, somewhat shorter than a saber, that became a standard sailor's weapon by the second half of the eighteenth century.

**dirk:** A dagger of Scottish origin having a thin, single-edged blade.

**espionage:** Spying or intelligence work.

**flank:** The side or wing of a military formation. To "outflank" the enemy is to move one's own troops around his flanks, exposing them to attack from side and rear as well as front.

**flintlock:** A mechanism for firing a gun in which a piece of flint strikes a piece of steel, producing a spark that ignites the gunpowder.

**frigate:** A sailed-driven warship equipped with between twenty and forty-four cannons.

**grape shot:** A mass of small iron balls fired by a cannon.

**grenadier:** Originally an infantry soldier who threw grenades at the enemy; but by the time of the American Revolution an elite infantry soldier who used more conventional weapons.

**gun:** In terms of artillery, a cannon with a long barrel that fired shot in low trajectories, best suited for use on an open battlefield where targets were in plain sight.

**halberd:** A long spear with an axlike blade attached at or near the front end.

**howitzer:** A cannon with a barrel length falling between those of artillery guns and mortars; a howitzer could fire somewhat higher than an artillery gun.

**intelligence:** In military terms, information accumulated about one's enemy by spying or other means.

**linear tactics:** The European or Continental tactical system in which opposing lines of soldiers, usually equipped with muskets and bayonets, marched toward each other in the open.

**matchlock:** A mechanism for firing a gun in which pulling the trigger brings a lighted match into contact with a small pan of gunpowder, which flashes and ignites the gunpowder inside the barrel.

**mortar:** A cannon with a wide, short barrel designed for firing shells in a high trajectory, usually over fortress or city walls.

**musket (or firelock):** An early gun with a smooth bore that fired by means of either a matchlock or flintlock mechanism.

**muzzle:** The front end of a gun's barrel.

**ordnance:** Artillery; or cannons.

**pike:** A very long spear.

**plug bayonet:** An early kind of bayonet that was inserted into the barrel of a musket, plugging it and rendering it incapable of firing.

**pole arm:** Any of a class of weapons featuring a blade attacked to a pole, including spears, pikes, halberds, and spontoons.

**quoins:** Wooden wedges placed under one end of a cannon to raise its elevation.

**ramrod:** A stick used by early gunmen to push the powder and ball down into the gun barrel.

**rifle:** A gun with a rifled bore, that is, a barrel that has a set of spiral grooves etched on its inside.

**saber:** A slashing sword used mainly by cavalrymen.

**schooner:** A large sailboat.

**shell:** A metal container filled with gunpowder fired from a cannon.

**shot:** Solid balls fired from cannons, or lead balls or pellets fired from muskets or rifles.

**smoothbore:** A firearm, such as the musket, having a barrel with a smooth inside surface.

**socket bayonet:** A type of bayonet that attached to the outside of the barrel of a gun so that the weapon could be fired without removing the bayonet.

**spontoon:** A long spear or short pike, often having a fancily shaped blade.

**squadron:** A group of ships, usually part of a larger fleet.

**tampion:** A wooden plug stuffed into the barrel of a naval cannon when not in use, to keep out moisture.

**windage:** In firearms, the space between the edge of the ball (or bullet) and the inside of the barrel.

# ☆ For Further Reading ☆

Isaac Asimov, *The Birth of the United States, 1763–1816*. Boston: Houghton Mifflin, 1974. One of the most prolific and gifted American popular writers here delivers a highly informative survey of the main events and characters of the American Revolution and early decades of the United States.

Bruce Bliven, Jr., *The American Revolution*. New York: Random House, 1986. A commendable synopsis of the U.S. war of independence, aimed at junior-high-school readers.

Deborah Kent, *Lexington and Concord*. Danbury, CT: Children's Press, 1997. Aimed at young readers, this is an excellent overview of the opening battles of the American Revolution.

Don Nardo, *Opposing Viewpoints Digests: The American Revolution*. San Diego: Greenhaven Press, 1998. A collection of extensively documented essays containing a wide range of opinions and debates about the conflict between Britain and its American colonies.

Diane Smolinski, *Land Battles of the Revolutionary War*. Crystal Lake, IL: Heinemann Library, 2001. A fine overview of the major land battles fought in the war, including Trenton, Cowpens, and Yorktown.

———, *Revolutionary War Soldiers*. Crystal Lake, IL: Heinemann Library, 2001. Another excellent book about the Revolutionary War by Smolinski, this one covers the enlistment, weapons, uniforms, training, and duties of the soldiers who fought in the war.

Gail B. Stewart, *The Revolutionary War*. San Diego: Lucent Books, 1991. One of the best current writers for young adults does a fine job chronicling the main events of the war between Britain and its American colonies.

Linda R. Wade, *Early Battles of the American Revolution*. Edina, MN: Abdo, 2001. An effective synopsis of the initial engagements fought in the American war of independence.

Brian Williams, *George Washington*. New York: Marshall Cavendish, 1988. The events leading to the founding of the United States and beyond are traced in this general biography of the Revolutionary War general and first U.S. president. Reading level is junior high school.

Marco Zlatich, *General Washington's Army, Vol. 1: 1775–1778*. Oxford: Osprey, 1994.

———, *General Washington's Army, Vol. 2: 1779–1783*. Oxford: Osprey, 1995. Two handsomely illustrated books showing full-color reconstructions of the uniforms and weapons used by the American soldiers during the revolution. Highly recommended.

# ✯ Major Works Consulted ✯

## Modern Sources

Gardner W. Allen, *A Naval History of the American Revolution.* 2 vols. Gansevoort, NY: Corner House, 1970. A large, detailed study of the naval engagements of the war.

John Bakeless, *Turncoats, Traitors, and Heroes: Espionage in the American Revolution.* Philadelphia: Lippincott, 1953. One of the two classic modern studies of espionage during the war for independence (the other being Carl van Doren's book; see below), this is an information-packed, absorbing read.

Jeremy Black, *Warfare in the Eighteenth Century.* London: Cassell, 1999. A handy general overview of the weapons, tactics, and military advancements of the century in which the American Revolution took place.

Charles K. Bolton, *The Private Soldier Under Washington.* Gansevoort, NY: Corner House, 1997. Perhaps the best general study of the average American soldier in the war for independence, including information about recruitment, camps, weapons, training, and more.

Jack Coggins, *Ships and Seamen of the American Revolution.* Harrisburg, PA: Stackpole Books, 1969. An excellent synopsis of the warships and sailors that fought in the war, including data on shipbuilding, weapons, experiments with submarines, and descriptions of major battles.

Edward Countryman, *The American Revolution.* New York: Hill and Wang, 1985. Arguably the most authoritative single-volume general history of the American war for independence, this is a large, richly documented, and engrossing study. Highly recommended.

Robert A. Gross, *The Minutemen and Their World.* New York: Hill and Wang, 1976. A well-written, well-documented summary of the men who fought in the colonial—and later state—militia during the American Revolution.

Ian V. Hogg, *Armies of the American Revolution.* Englewood Cliffs, NJ: Prentice-Hall, 1975. This excellent overview of the military aspects of the war contains numerous color illustrations.

Archer Jones, *The Art of War in the Western World.* New York: Oxford University Press, 1987. An excellent academic, though nonscholarly treatment of the history of Western warfare by a respected military historian. Jones devotes a long, well-organized chapter to the infantry tactics of the eighteenth century, which characterized much of the fighting in the American Revolution.

Robin May, *The British Army in North America, 1775–1783*. Oxford: Osprey, 1997. A fine, beautifully illustrated overview of British troops during the American Revolution, focusing mainly on their units and uniforms, but also including information on recruitment and pay.

Warren Moore, *Weapons of the American Revolution and Accoutrements*. New York: Promontory Press, 1967. One of the better general synopses of the hand-held weapons of the war and the accessories carried by their users.

George C. Neumann, *Swords and Blades of the American Revolution*. Harrisburg, PA: Stackpole Books, 1973. A very clearly written and informational study of the bayonets, swords, daggers, axes, halberds, and spears used in the conflict. Highly recommended.

Carl van Doren, *Secret History of the American Revolution*. Clifton, NJ: Augustus M. Kelley, 1973. A fulsome telling of the spies, traitors, and other individuals who gathered intelligence for both sides in the war.

W.J. Wood, *Battles of the Revolutionary War, 1775–1781*. New York: Da Capo Press, 1995. This is one of the better general overviews of the major battles fought in the conflict.

## Primary Sources

The following volumes (or sets of volumes) are invaluable mines of primary source materials, some of them personal memoirs or military manuals, others official town records, and still others compilations containing dozens or hundreds of complete or partial letters, pamphlets, newspaper articles, journals, and so on, from the years of the American Revolution.

Charles F. Adams, ed., *The Works of John Adams, Second President of the United States: With a Life of the Author, Notes and Illustrations*. 10 vols. Boston: Little, Brown, 1850–1856.

Humphrey Bland, *A Treatise on Military Discipline*. New York: Hugh Gaine, 1759.

Maria Hull Campbell, *Revolutionary Services and Civil Life of General William Hull; Prepared from His Manuscripts*. New York: Appleton, 1848.

Clarence E. Carter, ed., *The Correspondence of General Thomas Gage*. 2 vols. New Haven: Yale University Press, 1931–1932.

Central Intelligence Agency, *Intelligence in the War of Independence*. Washington, DC: Central Intelligence Agency, n.d.g. Contains numerous quotations from contemporary letters and other documents, many of them secret at the time.

James Collins, *Autobiography of a Revolutionary Soldier*. Ed. John M. Roberts. Clinton, LA: Feliciana Democrat, 1859.

Henry S. Commager and Richard B. Morris, eds., *The Spirit of 'Seventy-Six: The Story of the American Revolution as Told by Participants*. 2 vols. New York: Bobbs-Merrill, 1958.

John C. Dann, ed., *The Revolution Remembered: Eyewitness Accounts of the War for*

*Independence.* Chicago: University of Chicago Press, 1980.

William Dudley, ed., *The American Revolution: Opposing Viewpoints.* San Diego, CA. Greenhaven Press, 1992.

John C. Fitzpatrick, ed., *The Writings of George Washington.* 39 vols. Washington, DC: U.S. Government Printing House, 1933–1944.

George Hanger, *Colonel George Hanger to All Sportsmen.* London: Stockdale, 1814.

Epaphras Hoyt, *Treatise on the Military Art.* Brattleborough, VT: Smead, 1798.

Charles Hudson, *History of the Town of Lexington, Middlesex County, Massachusetts, from Its First Settlement to 1868.* Boston: Houghton Mifflin, 1913.

Henry P. Johnston, *The Storming of Stony Point on the Hudson, Midnight, July 15, 1779: Its Importance in the Light of Unpublished Documents.* New York: White, 1900.

Joseph P. Martin, *Private Yankee Doodle: Being a Narrative of Some of the Adventures, Dangers, and Sufferings of a Revolutionary Soldier.* Originally published in 1830. Reprint: Ed. George E. Scheer. Boston: Little, Brown, 1962.

Samuel E. Morison, ed., *Sources and Documents Illustrating the American Revolution, 1764–1788, and the Formation of the Federal Constitution.* Oxford: Clarendon Press, 1953.

Richard B. Morris, ed., *The American Revolution, 1763–1783: A Bicentennial Collec-* *tion.* Columbia: University of South Carolina Press, 1970.

John Muller, *A Treatise on Artillery.* Originally published 1756. Reprint: Ottawa, CN: Museum Restoration Service, 1965.

Henry Onderdonk, *Revolutionary Incidents of Suffolk and King's Counties: With an Account of the Battle of Long Island and the British Prisons and Prison-Ships at New York.* New York: Leavitt and Company, 1849.

Howard H. Peckham, ed., *Sources of American Independence.* 2 vols. Chicago: University of Chicago Press, 1978.

Hugh F. Rankin, ed., *The American Revolution.* New York: Putnam, 1964.

*Rhode Island Records, 1772–1777.* State archives, Providence, RI.

*Rules for the Regulation of the Navy of the United Colonies of North-America.* Originally published in 1775. Reprint: Washington, DC: Naval Historical Foundation, 1944.

G.D. Scull, ed., *Memoir and Letters of Captain W. Glanville Evelyn, of the Fourth Regiment from North America, 1774–1776.* Oxford: James Parker, 1879.

Baron Frederick von Steuben, *Baron von Steuben's Revolutionary War Drill Manual.* Mineola, NY: Dover, 1985.

James Thacher, *A Military Journal During the American Revolutionary War, from 1775–1783, Describing Interesting Events and Transactions of This Period.* Boston: Cottons and Barnard, 1827.

# ★ Additional Works Consulted ★

David F. Butler, *United States Firearms: The First Century, 1776–1875*. New York: Winchester Press, 1971.

Martha Byrd, *Saratoga: Turning Point of the American Revolution*. Philadelphia: Auerbach, 1973.

Philip Davidson, *Propaganda and the American Revolution, 1763–1783*. New York: W.W. Norton, 1973.

Thomas Flexner, *George Washington*. Boston: Little, Brown, 1968.

Albert N. Hardin, Jr., *The American Bayonet, 1776–1964*. Philadelphia: Riling and Lentz, 1964.

B.P. Hughes, *British Smooth Bore Artillery: The Muzzle-Loading Artillery of the 18th and 19th Centuries*. Harrisburg, PA: Stackpole, 1969.

Pauline Maier, *From Resistance to Revolution*. New York: Knopf, 1972.

Albert Manucy, *Artillery Through the Ages: A Short Illustrated History of Cannon, Emphasizing Types Used in America*. Washington, DC: U.S. Government Printing Office, 1949.

Samuel E. Morison, *The Oxford History of the American People*. New York: Oxford University Press, 1965.

Harold L. Peterson, *Arms and Armor in Colonial America*. Mineola, NY: Dover, 2000.

———, *The Treasury of the Gun*. New York: Golden Press, 1962.

Robert S. Quimby, *The Background of Napoleonic Warfare: The Theory of Military Tactics in Eighteenth-Century France*. New York: AMS Press, 1968.

Stuart Reid, *British Redcoat, 1740–1793*. Oxford: Osprey, 1996.

Kenneth Roberts, *The Battle of Cowpens: The Story of 900 Men Who Shook an Empire*. Garden City, NY: Doubleday, 1958.

H.C.B. Rogers, *A History of Artillery*. Secaucus, NJ: Citadel Press, 1975.

———, *The Mounted Troops of the British Army*. London: Seeley, 1959.

———, *Weapons of the British Soldier*. London: Seeley, 1960

John Shy, *Toward Lexington: The Role of the British Army in the Coming of the American Revolution*. Princeton: Princeton University Press, 1965.

———, *A People Numerous and Armed: Reflections on the Military Struggle for American*

*Independence.* New York: Oxford University Press, 1976.

Robert W. Tucker and David, C. Hendrickson, *The Fall of the First British Empire.* Baltimore: Johns Hopkins University Press, 1982.

Irwin Unger, *These United States: The Questions of Our Past, Volume I.* Boston: Little, Brown, 1978.

Howard Zinn, *A People's History of the United States.* New York: HarperCollins, 1980.

Adams, John
  appointed to
    Congressional
    Committee on civilian
    espionage, 93
  appointed to Naval
    Committee, 82–83
  on numbers of loyalists
    and patriots in colonies,
    11
  use of numeric codes by,
    108
Adair, Sergeant, 15
Aitken, James "John the
  Painter"
  capture and death of, 100
  sabotage operations by,
    96–97
America
  artillery units created in,
    70–72
  map of thirteen colonies
    of, 14
  natural resources and, 13
  size of, as factor in war,
    12–13
  use of bayonets in, 34–36
American Indians, 41
American Peace
  Commission, 104
American Revolutionary
  War
  as a civil war, 11
  first battle of, 53
  first transoceanic conflict, 48

foundation for U.S.
  intelligence community
  laid during, 108
Americans
  advantages possessed by, 9
  disadvantages of, 10
  fear of British using linear
    tactics, 56
  guerrilla battle tactics used
    by, 47
  increase mobility of
    ordnance by, 71
  lack of good ordnance
    and, 70–71
  lack of solidarity and, 11
  lack of training as
    musketeers, 21
  mastery of formal battle
    tactics, 58–62
  parity of troops with
    British achieved by, 11
  rifle made by, 24
  spirit of, 14
  victory in Carolinas by, 75
  victory at Cowpens and, 59
American Turtle
  (submarine), 90
Andre, Major, 106
Armies of the American
  Revolution (Hogg), 75
Arms and Armor in the Colonial
  Period (Peterson), 44
Arnold, Benedict, 85
  betrayal of America by,
    105–106

naval battle at Valcour Bay
  and, 91
artillery
  artillery gun, 64
  central cannon factory for,
    71
  effects of, 74
  "floating battery," 71–72
  howitzer, 65
  mobility of, 67–69
  mortar, 65–67
  problems of accuracy of
    naval, 86–87
  support train of, 69–70
  tactics for, 72–74
  three major types of, 63
  trajectories of, 68
  at Yorktown, 75–78
Augusta, Georgia, 99

Bakeless, John
  on Culper spy ring, 98
Bancroft, Edward, 104
Barker, John
  account of American
    guerrilla tactics, 52–54
Battle of Bunker Hill, 71
  British battle tactics at, 56
Battle of Haw River, 39
Battle of Lake Champlain,
  91
Battle of Long Island, 53
  American use of
    traditional battle tactics
    at, 58

artillery at, 74
Battle of Monmouth, 64
bayonet, 43
  effect on tactics by, 32
  pike, 32–33
  plug type, 33–34
  socket type, 34
Bemis Heights, New York, 25
Bergen Point, 107
Black, Jeremy
  on uniqueness of the Revolution, 48
Bland, Humphrey
  on military manuals, 48
*Bonhomme Richard* (ship), 89
Boston, Massachusetts, 52, 56, 70, 71
Brandywine Creek, Pennsylvania, 28
  lack of military intelligence at, 94
Breed's Hill, 56
Brewster, Caleb, 98
Bristol, England, 97
British
  defeat at Lake Champlain, 51
  feelings of, assured success by, 12
  lack of preparation for guerrilla tactics, 58
  loyalists and, 11–12
  major defeat of, by American militia, 51
  pistols of, 30
  superiority of, 9
*British Redcoat* (Reid), 59
Broughton, Nicholas, 87
  instructions to, 83–84
Bucks County, Pennsylvania, 28
Bunker Hill, 57

Burgoyne, John
  on sharpshooters, 26
  surrender of, 51, 52
Bushnell, David, 90

Camden, South Carolina, 56
  American regulars at, 58
Cape Ann, 88
cavalry
  saber and, 38
  use in battle, 47
Central Intelligence Agency (CIA), 93
  report on Tallmadge's numeric code, 107–108
Charles River, 71
*Charon* (gunship), 77
Chesapeake Bay (Virginia), 75
Clark, Reverend Jonas
  on Battle of Lexington Green, 53
Coggins, Jack
  on difficulties of building the Continental navy, 80
  on loading and firing of naval artillery, 86
Collins, James
  on militia tactics against loyalists, 48–50
  report of Ferguson's death, 28
Commager, Henry S.
  ballad about Nathan Hale, 103
  on Bancroft as double agent, 104
  on history of American Revolutionary naval warfare, 79
  on persecution of loyalists, 11–12
  on use of propaganda, 13

Committee of Foreign Affairs, 93–94
Committee of Safety, 44
  standardization of muskets by, 19–20
Committee of Secret Correspondence, 93, 104
  recruitment of skilled agents by, 95–97
Concord, Massachusetts, 13
  guerrilla tactics used at, 52–54
*Congress* (ship), 92
Congreve, William
  on riflemen at Long Island, 53–54
Connecticut, 31, 98, 100
Continental Congress
  use of pikes and, 44
  establishment of intelligence agency by, 93
  oath of secrecy taken by, 98
  spy from, 96
Continental navy
  birth of, 81–83
  boldness of, 87–88, 91–92
  early in the war, 10
  first submarine, 90
  lack of trained artillerymen, 86
  ordnance of, 85–87
  swords of, 39
  use of spears in, 45–46
  warships of, 88
Cooper, James Fenimore, 104
Cornwallis, Charles
  movement of troops to Virginia by, 75
Cowpens, 59
  description of battle at, 60–62

Crosby, Enoch, 103–104
Cumberland Head, 91

Dann, John
on courage of Washington
at Yorktown, 77
on William Johnson's
deception, 107
Dayton, Elias, 96
Deane, Silas
appointment to Navy
Committee, 82
sabotage operations by,
96–97
as spy contact, 104
use of invisible ink by, 106
Deerfield, Massachusetts,
39
Delaware River, 72, 98
Discipline of the Light Horse,
The (military manual)
on acclimating a horse to
the pistol, 30
Dover, England, 96
Drake (warship), 89
Dumas, W.F., 96
Dutch
musket, 19
pistols of, 30–31

Elizabethtown, 100
Exercise of the Firelock (war
manual), 20–21

Ferguson, Patrick, 27–28
flintlock pistols
American standardization
of, 31
use of, 29–30
Fort Ticonderoga, 70, 71,
85
Fowler, Benjamin, 45
Franklin, Benjamin, 93, 104

Frederick the Great
(Prussian leader), 72
French, 96
bayonets purchased from,
35
pistols, 31
plug bayonet and, 33–34
service musket of, 19
socket bayonet and, 34
French and Indian War, 34,
51

Gage, Thomas
on patriots' spirit, 14–15
Galloper Guns, 72
Gates, Horatio
Burgoyne surrenders to,
52
career ending mistake of,
56–58
Germans, 24
bayonets purchased from,
35
Gray, David, 104
Great Britain
bureaucracy and, 15
superiority on the seas, 79
surrender after Yorktown
by, 75, 107
Green, Nathaniel
on bayonet attack on
Stony Point, 36

Hale, Nathan, 100–103, 106
Hale, Samuel, 102
Hall, Moses
use of sword in battle,
39–40
Hampshire Grants, 51
Hanger, George
on accuracy of rifle
sharpshooters, 26
Hannah (schooner), 83, 87

Harrison, Benjamin, 93
Hart, Nancy Morgan, 99
hatchet
as backup weapon,
41–42
names for, 40–41
Hay, Samuel
on butchery at Paoli by
bayonets, 35–36
Hempstead, Stephen
on Nathan Hale's mission,
100–101
Hessians, 98
History of the Town of
Lexington (Hudson), 53
Hogg, Ivan V.
chart of artillery used by
British, 75
on lack of standardization
of muskets, 19
on needs of American
armed forces, 10–11
on range of mortar, 66
on sighting of mortar, 67
Hollingworth, Ben, 55
Honeyman, John, 98
Hook, Paulus, 107
Howard, John E., 60
Howe, William, 59
Hoyt, Epaphras
on use of the saber by
cavalry, 38
Hudson, Charles
on Battle of Lexington
Green, 53
Hudson River, 36
Hull, William
on execution of Nathan
Hale, 102–103

Inglis, Charles
on British attitude of
military superiority, 12

*Intelligence in the War of Independence* (Central Intelligence Agency), 98
Irvine, Andrew, 36

Jay, John, 107, 108
Jay, James
  sympathetic stain invented by, 107
Jefferson, Thomas, 93
Johnson, Sir William
  on Native American use of tomahawk, 51
  successful deception by, 107
Johnston, Henry
  on bayonets at Stony Point, 36
Jones, Archer
  on workings of flintlock, 17–18
Jones, John Paul
  raids on English and Irish coasts, 89
  results of raids on Indies and Florida, 89

Kings Mountain
  death of Ferguson at, 28
  use of riflemen at, 54–55
knives and daggers, 40
Knox, Henry, 70–72
  creating of artillery regiments by, 71

Lake Champlain, 51, 92
  fleet at, 85
  naval confrontation at, 91
  naval patrols of, 83
Lancaster County, Pennsylvania, 24
Langdon, John, 82
Lee, Arthur, 95–96

Lexington, 13, 52
  first battle of Revolution at, 53
  picture of skirmish in, 10
Livingston, Robert, 93, 108
Long Island Sound, 98

Mahan, Alfred T.
  on naval battle at Valcour, 92
Manucy, Albert
  on Frederick The Great's innovations, 72–73
Martin, Joseph P.
  account of Molly Pitcher, 64
  on use of artillery in skirmish, 74
Maryland, 44
Massachusetts Committee of Safety, 13
McCasland, John, 28
McCorman, Major, 28
Memorial Hall, 39
Mersereau, John L., 99–100
military intelligence, 9
  counterintelligence, 103–106
  Culper spy ring, 97–98
  dangers of, 99
  domestic spying, 87–99
  encrypted messages and, 106–108
  first novel about, 104
  foreign agents and, 95–97
  punishment for civilian spies, 93–94
militia
  containment of British army by, 50–51
  guerrilla tactics used by, 47–48
  at Lexington, 53, 55

persecution of loyalists by, 48–50
Mississippi River, 83
Moore, Warren
  on craftsmanship of pistols, 30
Morgan, Daniel, 44, 59
  on use of rifles in defeat of Burgoyne, 16, 26
Morgan's Riflemen, 44
Morris, Richard B.
  on appointment of Bancroft as double agent, 104
  ballad about Nathan Hale, 103
  order to attack West Indies and Florida, 89
  on persecution of loyalists, 11
  on use of propaganda, 13
Morris, Robert, 88–89
Muller, John
  on difficulty of transporting artillery, 68
muskets, 43
  American standard version, 20
  combined with bayonet, 33–34
  drawback of design of, 22–23
  drills for, 20–22
  flintlock and, 17–18
  history of, 16
  lack of standardization of, 19
  Long Land Service Musket, 19
  matchlock mechanism and, 16–17
  Short Land Service Musket "Brown Bess," 19

Naval Committee, 83
  issue of naval rules by,
    84–85
Neumann, George C.
  on the English bayonet, 40
  objectives of linear tactics,
    55
  on sword as symbol of
    social standing, 36
  on use of socket bayonet, 34
New England, 51
New Jersey, 64, 98
New York, 51, 71, 98
*New York* (ship), 92
North, Simeon, 31

Paoli Massacre, 35
Pennsylvania, 44, 72
Peterson, Harold
  on use of pikes in the
    Revolution, 44
Philadelphia, Pennsylvania,
  28, 35
*Philadelphia* (ship), 91–92
Piscataqua, New
  Hampshire, 87
Pitcher, Molly, 64
pole arms
  halberd, 32, 42–43
  pikes, 43–44
  use of, by navy, 46
  use of spear by riflemen,
    44
Portsmouth, England, 97
Portsmouth, New
  Hampshire, 102
Prussia, 19

Reid, Stuart
  on variations in British
    tactics, 59
*Revolution Remembered, The*
  (Dann), 77, 107

Rhode Island, 82
rifle
  advantages of, 23–24
  disadvantages of, 24–25
  effectiveness of, 53
  Pennsylvania "Kentucky"
    Rifle, 24
  sharpshooters, snipers
    and, 25–28
Robinson, Beverly, 104
Roe, Austin, 98
Roebuck, Colonel, 54
Rogers, H.C.B.
  description of vehicles in
    artillery train, 69–70
Royal Navy (British)
  size of, 79
  use in the Revolution, 79–80
*Rules for the Regulation of the
  Navy of the United Colonies
  of North America* (Naval
  Committee), 82

Saratoga, 26, 46, 65
*Serapis* (warship), 89
Seven Years' War, 72
Scotland, 40
South Carolina
  battle locations in, 61
*Spirit of 'Seventy-six*
  (Commager and Morris,
  Richard), 13, 103
Springfield, Massachusetts,
  71
*Spy, The* (Cooper), 104
Staten Island, New York, 99,
  107
Stirling, Lord, 58
Stony Point, New York, 36
*Storming of Stony Point, The*
  (Johnston), 36
Strong, Anna, 107–108
Suddarth, John

on courage of Washington
    at Yorktown, 77
Summers, John, 56
Swiss, 24
  infantry formation of,
    32–33
  pikes and, 43
sword, 32
  cutlass, 39
  light saber, 38–41
  major types of, 38
  social value of, 36
  troops use of, 37
*Swords and Blades of the
  American Revolution*
  (Neumann), 40

tactics, 9
  effect of flintlock on, 18
  myths about American
    Revolutionary, 47
  traditional, 55–62
  variations of British, 59
Tallmadge, Benjamin, 106
  numerical encryption
    devised by, 107–108
Tarleton, Banastre, 59
Tarleton, Colonel, 26
Teil, Chevalier du
  on use of artillery, 73
Tenpenny, Major, 100
Thacher, James
  on artillery use at
    Yorktown, 76–77
Thacher, Peter
  on British battle tactics at
    Bunker Hill, 56
Townsend, Robert "Culper
  Junior," 97
*Treatise on Artillery, A*
  (Muller), 68
*Treatise on Military Discipline,
  A* (Bland), 48

*Treatise on the Military Art* (Hoyt), 38
Trenton, New Jersey, 98

*Unity* (merchant ship), 87
U.S. Congress
  establishment of Naval Committee by, 82
  standardization of muskets by, 19
U.S. espionage act, 94

Valcour Bay, 91
Valley Forge, 28, 66
Vermont, 41
von Steuben, Baron Frederick, 21–23

Ward, Colonel, 107
Washington, George, 100
  acquisition of merchant ships by, 83
  appointment of Knox by, 71
  commissioning of bayonets by, 34–35

espionage and, 104–107
forces at Yorktown, 75
on importance of spear, 43–44
on necessity of good military intelligence, 94
Paoli Massacre and, 35
remedy for lack of musket training, 21
spear for riflemen, 44–45
training of troops and, 11
use of linear tactics, 55
at Valley Forge, 28, 66
Washington, William, 60–63
*Washington* (ship), 92
Watts, Garret
  on battle at Camden, 56–58
Wayne, Anthony, 35
  capture of, 36
  on disadvantages of the rifle, 25
  use of spear by infantry, 44
weapons
  bladed, 32–46
  as factor in warfare, 9
  firearms, 16–31

military intelligence, 93–108
propaganda as, 13
types used in the Revolution, 10
unity as, 14
*Weapons of the American Revolution and Accoutrements* (Moore), 30
Welch, David
  description of fight with tomahawk, 41–42
West Point, 106
women, 64
  as spies, 99
Woodhull, Samuel "Culper Senior," 98
*Writings of George Washington, The* (George Washington), 96

Yale College, 106
Yorktown, 107
  artillery at, 75–78
Young, Thomas
  as rifleman at Kings Mountain, 54

# ★ Picture Credits ★

Cover photo: © Bridgeman Art Library

Joe Bernier, 24

© Bridgeman Art Library, 7

Dover Publishers, Inc., 32, 33, 37, 41, 43(both), 63(top), 67, 69, 75, 76, 81, 86, 90, 102

Hulton/Archive by Getty Images, 85, 91

Alan Iglesias, 61, 68

Chris Jouan, 14

Library of Congress, 16, 17, 22, 47, 50, 52, 54, 57, 60, 70, 72, 79 (top), 83, 88, 89, 105, 106

© Bob Krist/CORBIS, 35

© Kelly-Mooney Photography/CORBIS, 20

© David Muench/CORBIS, 46, 65

North Wind Pictures, 9, 12, 15, 25, 27, 29, 45, 49, 58, 63 (bottom), 66, 73, 93, 95, 97, 99, 101

© Paul A. Souders/CORBIS, 18

© Ted Spiegel/CORBIS, 39

Stock Montage, 10

© Adam Woolfitt/CORBIS, 79 (bottom)

## ★ About the Author ★

Historian and award-winning author Don Nardo has written many books for young adults about American history and government, including *The Declaration of Independence, The Mexican-American War, The Bill of Rights,* and biographies of Thomas Jefferson, Andrew Johnson, and Franklin D. Roosevelt. Mr. Nardo lives with his wife, Christine, in Massachusetts.

# Understanding
## Data Communications
## and Networks

# THE PWS SERIES IN COMPUTER SCIENCE

ABERNETHY AND ALLEN, *Experiments in Computing: Laboratories for Introductory Computer Science in Think Pascal*

ABERNETHY AND ALLEN, *Experiments in Computing: Laboratories for Introductory Computer Science in Turbo Pascal*

ABERNETHY AND ALLEN, *Exploring the Science of Computing*

AGELOFF AND MOJENA, *Essentials of Structured BASIC*

BAILEY AND LUNDGAARD, *Program Design with Pseudocode, Third Edition*

BELCHER, *The COBOL Handbook*

BENT AND SETHARES, *BASIC: An Introduction to Computer Programming, Fourth Edition*

BENT AND SETHARES, *BASIC: An Introduction to Computer Programming with Apple, Third Edition*

BENT AND SETHARES, *Microsoft BASIC: Programming the IBM PC, Third Edition*

BENT AND SETHARES, *QBASIC*

BENT AND SETHARES, *QuickBASIC: An Introduction to Computer Science Programming with the IBM PC*

BORSE, *FORTRAN 77 and Numerical Methods for Engineers, Second Edition*

CLEMENTS, *68000 Family Assembly Language*

CLEMENTS, *Principles of Computer Hardware, Second Edition*

COBURN, *Visual BASIC Made Easy*

COSNARD AND TRYSTRAM, *Parallel Algorithms and Architecture*

DECKER AND HIRSHFIELD, *Pascal's Triangle: Reading, Writing, and Reasoning About Programs*

DECKER AND HIRSHFIELD, *The Analytical Engine: An Introduction to Computer Science Using HyperCard 2.1, Second Edition*

DECKER AND HIRSHFIELD, *The Analytical Engine: An Introduction to Computer Science Using ToolBook*

DECKER AND HIRSHFIELD, *The Object Concept*

DERSHEM AND JIPPING, *Programming Languages: Structures and Models, Second Edition*

DROZDEK AND SIMON, *Data Structures in C*

EGGEN AND EGGEN, *An Introduction to Computer Science Using C*

FIREBAUGH AND MICHIE, *Artificial Intelligence: A Knowledge-Based Approach, Second Edition*

FLYNN AND McHOES, *Understanding Operating Systems*

GIARRATANO AND RILEY, *Expert Systems: Principles and Programming, Second Edition*

HENNEFELD, *Using Microsoft and IBM BASIC: An Introduction to Computer Programming*

HENNEFELD, *Using Turbo Pascal 6.0–7.0, Third Edition*

HOLOIEN AND BEHFOROOZ, *FORTRAN 77 for Engineers and Scientists, Second Edition*

HOUSE, *Beginning with C*

JAMISON, RUSSELL, AND SNOVER, *Laboratories for a Second Course in Computer Science: ANSI Pascal*

JAMISON, RUSSELL, AND SNOVER, *Laboratories for a Second Course in Computer Science: Turbo Pascal*

LOUDEN, *Programming Languages: Principles and Practice*

MARTINS, *Introduction to Computer Science Using Pascal*

MEARS, *BASIC Programming with the IBM PC, Second Edition*

MOJENA, *Turbo Pascal*

MOJENA AND AGELOFF, *FORTRAN 77*

PAYNE, *Advanced Structured BASIC: File Processing with the IBM PC*

PAYNE, *Structured BASIC for the IBM PC with Business Applications*

PAYNE, *Structured Programming with QuickBASIC*

POLLACK, *Effective Programming in Turbo Pascal*

POPKIN, *Comprehensive Structured COBOL, Fourth Edition*

RILEY, *Advanced Programming and Data Structures Using Pascal*

RILEY, *Using MODULA-2*

RILEY, *Using Pascal: An Introduction to Computer Science I*

ROB, *Big Blue BASIC: Programming the IBM PC and Compatibles, Second Edition*

ROJIANI, *Programming In BASIC for Engineers*

ROOD, *Logic and Structured Design for Computer Programmers, Second Edition*

RUNNION, *Structured Programming in Assembly Language for the IBM PC and PS/2, Second Edition*

SHAY, *Understanding Data Communications and Networks*

SMITH, *Design and Analysis of Algorithms*

STUBBS AND WEBRE, *Data Structures with Abstract Data Types and Ada*

STUBBS AND WEBRE, *Data Structures with Abstract Data Types and Pascal, Second Edition*

SUHY, *CICS using COBOL: A Structured Approach*

WANG, *An Introduction to ANSI C on UNIX*

WANG, *An Introduction to Berkeley UNIX*

WANG, *C++ with Object-Oriented Programming*

WEINMAN, *FORTRAN for Scientists and Engineers*

WEINMAN, *VAX FORTRAN, Second Edition*

WHALE, *Data Structures and Abstraction Using C*

ZIRKEL AND BERLINGER, *Understanding FORTRAN 77 & 90*

# UNDERSTANDING DATA COMMUNICATIONS AND NETWORKS

**William A. Shay**

University of Wisconsin—Green Bay

**PWS Publishing Company**

I (T) P    An International Thomson Publishing Company

Boston • Albany • Bonn • Cincinnati • Detroit • London • Madrid • Melbourne • Mexico City
New York • Paris • San Francisco • Singapore • Tokyo • Toronto • Washington

PWS PUBLISHING COMPANY
20 Park Plaza, Boston, Massachusetts 02116-4324

I $\left(T\right)$ P$^{\text{TM}}$  International Thomson Publishing
The trademark ITP is used under license.

*For more information, contact*:

**PWS Publishing Co.**
**20 Park Plaza**
**Boston, MA 02116**

Thomas Nelson Australia
102 Dodds Street
South Melbourne, 3205
Victoria, Australia

International Thomson Publishing Japan
Hirakawacho Kyowa Building, 31
2-2-1 Hirakawacho
Chiyoda-ku, Tokyo 102
Japan

Nelson Canada
1120 Birchmount Road
Scarborough, Ontario
Canada M1K 5G4

International Thomson Editores
Campos Eliseos 385, Piso 7
Col. Polanco
11560 Mexico D.F., Mexico

International Thomson Publishing GmbH
Königswinterer Strasse 418
53227 Bonn, Germany

International Thomson Publishing Europe
Berkshire House I68-I73
High Holborn
London WC1V 7AA
England

International Thomson Publishing Asia
221 Henderson Road
#05-10 Henderson Building
Singapore 0315

**Library of Congress Cataloging-in-Publication Data**

Shay, William A.
    Understanding data communications and networks / William A. Shay.
        p. cm.
    Includes bibliographical references and index.
    ISBN 0-534-20244-6
    1. Data transmission systems.    2. Computer networks.    I. Title.
TK5105.S49   1994
004.6—dc20

94-31432
CIP

This book is printed on recycled, acid-free paper.

*Sponsoring Editor:* Michael J. Sugarman
*Developmental Editor:* Mary Thomas
*Production Editor:* Abigail M. Heim
*Marketing Manager:* Nathan Wilbur
*Manufacturing Coordinator:* Lisa Flanagan
*Editorial Assistant:* Benjamin Steinberg

*Interior Designer:* Abigail M. Heim
*Interior Illustrator:* Pure Imaging
*Cover Designer:* Marshall Henrichs
*Typesetter:* Pure Imaging
*Cover Printer:* New England Book Components
*Text Printer and Binder:* Quebecor Printing/Martinsburg

Printed and bound in the United States of America
94  95  96  97  98  99—10  9  8  7  6  5  4  3  2  1

**TO DANIEL AND TIMOTHY**

# Contents

**CHAPTER 1** **Introduction to Communications, Standards, and Protocols**     **1**

**1.1** **WHY STUDY COMMUNICATIONS?**     **1**

A Brief History   1   •   Applications   3   •   Issues   6

**1.2** **COMPUTER NETWORKS**     **7**

Common Bus Topology   9   •   Star Topology   10   •   Ring Topology   10   •   Fully Connected Topology   12   •   Combined Topologies   13

**1.3** **STANDARDS AND STANDARDS ORGANIZATIONS**     **14**

The Need for Standards   14   •   Agencies   15

**1.4** **OPEN SYSTEMS AND THE OSI MODEL**     **17**

Overview of the Model   20   •   Physical Layer   23   •   Data Link Layer   27   •   Network Layer   30   •   Transport Layer   31   •   Session Layer   37   •   Presentation Layer   42   •   Application Layer   44   •   Summary   46

**1.5** **THE FUTURE OF DATA COMMUNICATIONS**     **47**

**REVIEW QUESTIONS   51   •   EXERCISES   52   •   REFERENCES   54**

**CHAPTER 2** **Transmission Fundamentals**     **55**

**2.1** **COMMUNICATIONS MEDIA**     **56**

Conductive Metal   58   •   Optical Fiber   60   •   Wireless Communications   65   •   Summary   76

**2.2   Communication Services and Devices        76**

Telephone System   76

**2.3   Codes        86**

ASCII Code   87  •  EBCDIC Code   92  •  Baudot, Morse, and BCD Codes   92

**2.4   Analog and Digital Signals        96**

Digital Encoding Schemes   96  •  Analog Signals   99  •  Data Rate   105

**2.5   Modulation and Demodulation        109**

Digital-to-Analog Conversion   111  •  Analog-to-Digital Conversion   116

**2.6   Modems and Modem Standards        119**

Signal Constellation   120  •  Intelligent (Hayes Compatible) Modems   124

**2.7   Summary        126**

**Review Questions   128  •  Exercises   130  •  References   133**


**Chapter 3   Data Communication                                   135**

**3.1   Transmission Modes        136**

Serial and Parallel Transmission   136  •  Asynchronous and Synchronous Transmission   137  •  Simplex, Half-Duplex, and Full-Duplex Communications   140

**3.2   Interface Standards        141**

RS-232 Interface   142  •  RS-232 Subsets   145  •  Null Modems   146  •  RS-449 Interface   147  •  X.21 Interface   149

**3.3   Multiplexing        151**

Frequency Division Multiplexing (FDM)   153  •  Time Division Multiplexing   155  •  Statistical Multiplexers   157  •  T-1 Carrier   159

**3.4   Contention Protocols        162**

Aloha Protocols   163  •  Carrier Sense Multiple Access (CSMA)   167  •  Collision Detection   170  •  Token Passing   173

**3.5   Data Compression        178**

Huffman Code   180  •  Run Length Encoding   183  •  Relative Encoding   185  •  Lempel-Ziv Encoding   185  •  Summary of Compression Techniques   187

**3.6   Summary        188**

**Review Questions   189  •  Exercises   191  •  References   194**

**CHAPTER 4**    **Data Security and Integrity**                        **195**

4.1    **INTRODUCTION**        **195**

4.2    **PARITY CHECKING**        **196**
Parity Checking Analysis   197   •   Double-Bit Error Detection   198   •
Burst Error Detection   198

4.3    **CYCLIC REDUNDANCY CHECKS**        **200**
Polynomial Division   201   •   How CRC Works   202   •   Analysis of
CRC   204   •   CRC Implementation Using Circular Shifts   208

4.4    **HAMMING CODES**        **210**
Single-Bit Error Correction   210   •   Multiple-Bit Error
Correction   212   •   Comparison of Error Detection and Error
Correction   214

4.5    **ENCRYPTION AND DECRYPTION**        **214**
Caesar Cipher   215   •   Poly-alphabetic Cipher   217   •
Transposition Cipher   220   •   Bit-Level Ciphering   221   •
Data Encryption Standard   222   •   Key Distribution and
Protection   226

4.6    **PUBLIC KEY ENCRYPTION**        **228**
RSA Algorithm   229   •   Digital Signatures   231   •   Summary
of Encryption Methods   233

4.7    **VIRUSES, WORMS, AND HACKING**        **234**
Infecting Files   235   •   Memory Resident Viruses   237   •   Virus
Sources   237   •   Internet Worm   238   •   Computer Hackers   240

4.8    **SUMMARY**        **241**

       **REVIEW QUESTIONS   243   •   EXERCISES   245   •   REFERENCES   247**

**CHAPTER 5**    **Protocol Concepts**                        **249**

5.1    **INTRODUCTION**        **249**

5.2    **BASIC FLOW CONTROL**        **250**
Signaling   250   •   Frame-Oriented Control   253   •   Protocol
Efficiency   257

5.3    **SLIDING WINDOW PROTOCOLS**        **260**
Frame Format   262   •   Go-back-n Protocol   263   •   Selective
Repeat Protocol   270   •   Sliding Window Protocol Efficiency   278   •
Summary of Protocols   281

**5.4  PROTOCOL CORRECTNESS      281**
Finite State Machines   282   •   Petri Nets   288

**5.5  DATA LINK CONTROL PROTOCOLS      292**
High-Level Data Link Control (HDLC)   293   •   Binary Synchronous
Communications (BSC) Protocol   301   •   Summary: Data Link
Protocols   306

**5.6  CASE STUDY: KERMIT      306**

**5.7  SUMMARY      313**

REVIEW QUESTIONS   314   •   EXERCISES   316   •   REFERENCES   320


**CHAPTER 6   Local Area Networking                              321**

**6.1  NETWORK TOPOLOGIES      321**

**6.2  ETHERNET: IEEE STANDARD 802.3      324**
Relation to OSI   325   •   Ethernet Components   325   •   Cable
Specifications   328   •   Frame Format   330   •   Efficiency   331

**6.3  TOKEN RING: IEEE STANDARD 802.5      335**
Token and Frame Formats   337   •   Reserving and Claiming
Tokens   339   •   Ring Maintenance   344   •   Fiber Distributed Data
Interface (FDDI)   347   •   Slotted Rings   351   •   Efficiency   351

**6.4  TOKEN BUS: IEEE STANDARD 802.4      352**
Token Bus Operations   354   •   Prioritizing Frames   359

**6.5  INTERCONNECTING LANs      362**
Layer 1 Connections   364   •   Layer 2 Connections   365   •
Bridging Different Types of LANs   366   •   Bridge Routing   368   •
Summary   381

**6.6  CASE STUDY: NOVELL NETWARE      381**
NetWare Configuration   382   •   Running Novell NetWare   383   •
Security and Integrity   385   •   Selected Novell Commands   388   •
Login Scripts   389   •   NetWare 4.0   391

**6.7  SUMMARY      392**

REVIEW QUESTIONS   394   •   EXERCISES   396   •   REFERENCES   399

**CHAPTER 7** Wide Area Networks **401**

**7.1** **INTRODUCTION** **401**

**7.2** **NETWORK ROUTING** **404**
Routing Tables 405 • Types of Routing 406 • Dijkstra's
Algorithm 409 • Bellman-Ford Algorithms 412 • Hierarchical
Routing 417 • Routing Information Protocol (RIP) 421 • Summary
of Routing Techniques 422 • Congestion and Deadlock 422

**7.3** **PUBLIC DATA NETWORKS: THE X SERIES PROTOCOLS** **427**
Packet Switched Network Modes 427 • X.25 Public Data Network
Interface Standard 431 • Triple X Standard for Non-X.25 Devices 436

**7.4** **INTERNET PROTOCOL** **440**
Overview of TCP/IP 440 • DoD Internet Protocol 441 • Internet
Control Message Protocol 450 • ISO Internet Protocol 451

**7.5** **TRANSPORT PROTOCOLS** **452**
DoD Transmission Control Protocol 454 • User Datagram
Protocol 464 • OSI Transport Protocols 464

**7.6** **WIDE AREA NETWORKS IN OPERATION** **466**

**7.7** **SUMMARY** **474**

**REVIEW QUESTIONS** **476** • **EXERCISES** **478** • **REFERENCES** **480**

**CHAPTER 8** Additional Network Protocols **482**

**8.1** **TCP APPLICATIONS** **482**
Client-Server Model 482 • Virtual Terminal 485 •
TELNET 486 • File Transfers 490 • SNMP—Simple Network
Management Protocol 500

**8.2** **ELECTRONIC MAIL: X.400 AND X.500 STANDARDS** **503**
X.400 Mail Standards 505 • X.500 Directory Service 512 •
Summary 516

**8.3** **INTEGRATED SERVICES DIGITAL NETWORK (ISDN)** **517**
ISDN Services 518 • ISDN Architecture 520 • Protocols 521 •
Broadband ISDN (BISDN) 530 • Summary 531

8.4   **Systems Network Architecture (SNA)          532**

Lower Layers   533   •   Path Control   533   •   Transmission
Control   541   •   Data Flow Control   544   •   Higher Layers   546

**Review Questions   548   •   Exercises   550   •   References   551**


**Glossary          554**

**Acronyms          584**


**Index          587**

# PREFACE

## Purpose

*Understanding Data Communications and Networks* is designed for junior level students in a computer science program who have a minimum of two semesters of programming (through data structures) and a knowledge of precalculus or discrete mathematics. It covers all the standard topics found in a typical introductory course in data communications and computer networks, such as transmission media, analog and digital signals, data transmissions, multiplexing, network topologies, data security, Ethernets, token rings, and wide area network protocols. This book is designed to help the reader understand:

- the differences, advantages, and disadvantages of different transmission media;
- analog and digital signals, modulation and demodulation techniques, and how modems work;
- the need for error detection and correction, the mechanisms used, and their advantages and disadvantages;
- standards such as RS232, RS449, HDLC, SDLC, DES, X.25, OSI, SNA, IEEE 802.3, IEEE 802.4, IEEE 802.5, and TCP/IP, standards organizations, and why standards are needed;
- local area networks and contention strategies for shared transmission media;
- packet-switched networks and routing strategies;
- the effect of noise on efficient and effective communication, and error detection and correction techniques used to deal with it;
- the need for flow control and various ways of enforcing it;
- how networks may be connected and ways to devise routing strategies to allow a dynamic and flexible design;
- worms and viruses and how they can affect a system;

- the need for security, and various encryption techniques; and
- data compression techniques.

While it would certainly be difficult to cover all these subjects in a one-semester course, the range allows instructors flexibility in choosing the topics best suited for their students.

An *Instructor's Solutions Manual*, with answers to review questions and exercises, is available from the publisher.

## Organization and Outline

This text offers a mix of theory, which provides a foundation for further study, and application, which brings students closer to the realities of communication systems and networks. In fact, several chapters end with a case study devoted to a specific application. All students should benefit from the applications, and the more theoretical material will challenge the more ambitious students.

Each chapter serves as a base on which to build the next. For example, when studying multiplexing, contention, or compression, students should have an understanding of how signals propagate through different media. When studying local area networks, they should understand problems of contention on multiple-access lines, noisy channels, and flow control. When studying wide area network protocols, they should understand local area network protocols and why these are not suitable to larger networks. Essentially, the text uses a bottom-up approach.

**Chapter 1** provides an introduction to the field, touching on current issues and applications in the field of communications and networks. It describes the needs for standards and lists relevant standards organizations, then defines a model that many believe will be the foundation of future communications systems, the Open System Interconnect.

**Chapters 2 and 3** deal mainly with kinds of transmission media, signal types, and data transmission, including modulation techniques and modems, interface standards, multiplexing, contention, and data compression interface. **Chapter 4** covers the security and integrity of transmitted data. Together these chapters form the "data communications" part of the text.

**Chapter 5** begins the "computer networks" part by discussing protocols that regulate the flow of information among stations. It also presents some of the standard protocols used in local area networks. **Chapter 6** covers local area networks (LANs), discussing the standards that define Ethernets and token ring and token bus networks. It then addresses the issues of connecting multiple LANs and the problems of ensuring that information gets to its intended destination, and closes with a discussion of Novell NetWare, one of the most popular LAN managers.

**Chapter 7** covers wide area networks (WANs) and the need for protocols different from LAN protocols. It outlines different ways of routing information within a network and gives significant attention to three common protocols, X.25 packet switched networks, the Internet protocol (IP), and the transmission control protocol (TCP). Chapter 7 finishes with a brief description of many wide-area networks currently in use. Finally, **Chapter 8** covers applications and additional protocols such as the TCP/IP applications, X.400 email standards, ISDN (a worldwide digital network standard), and IBM's System Network Architecture (SNA).

The exercises at the end of each chapter are divided into two groups. The first group, **Review Questions**, contains questions for which answers can be obtained directly from the corresponding chapter. This encourages the reader to go back through the text and pick out what the author or instructor believes is important. I believe this method to be better pedagogically than simply listing important topics at the end, which encourages students to read textbooks as they would a novel—linearly. Learning complex material, however, often requires reading, rereading, and going back through the text to sort out and understand different concepts.

But "factual" questions are not enough. The second group, **Exercises**, contains questions that challenge readers to apply what they have learned and to compare, make logical deductions, and consider alternatives.

## Acknowledgments

An undertaking such as writing a text is rarely, if ever, an individual effort. Many people have contributed and have given me valuable ideas, information, and/or support during this project. I especially would like to recognize the following people:

To the reviewers of this text,

| | |
|---|---|
| Abdullah Abonamah<br>*University of Akron* | James E. Holden<br>*Clarion University* |
| George W. Ball<br>*Alfred University* | Judith Molka<br>*University of Pittsburgh* |
| Mehran Basiratmand<br>*Florida International University* | Dan O'Connell<br>*Fredonia College—SUNY* |
| Ron Bates<br>*DeAnza College* | Jon L. Spear |
| Bruce Derr<br>*Syracuse University* | Janet M. Urlaub<br>*Sinclair Community College* |
| Mohammad El-Soussi<br>*Santa Barbara City College* | David Whitney<br>*San Francisco State University* |

I took all of your comments and suggestions seriously, and incorporated many into the final manuscript.

My thanks also to:

David Kieper, Computing and Information Technology, University of Wisconsin—Green Bay, who answered a lot of my questions, often acted as a sounding board, and helped me phrase some complex descriptions in (I hope) understandable ways; and

Lance Leventhal, who helped get me started on this book and provided some early feedback.

Michael Sugarman, computer science editor at PWS: Your efforts certainly contributed to keeping the writing/reviewing process on schedule. Your professionalism is greatly appreciated.

All the other people at PWS, including Abby Heim, Ken Morton, Mary Thomas, Ben Steinberg, Lisa Flanagan, Nathan Wilbur, and Liz Clayton: Your contributions and efforts helped make a manuscript into a book.

My family, Judy, Danny, and Timmy: You sacrificed a lot while I spent many late and weekend hours in my home office getting the manuscript ready. I appreciate the words of encouragement (and all the little hugs from Timmy who didn't quite understand why I locked myself in my office), which certainly helped me through this arduous process.

Members of the CMP 465 class of the 1994 spring semester at Alfred University, where this book was class-tested in manuscript form: Thank you for your thoughtful comments and suggestions.

Finally, to those who will eventually read this text, I would very much appreciate your opinion. Please feel free to send any comments to William Shay, Department of Information and Computing Science, University of Wisconsin—Green Bay, Green Bay WI 54311-7001, or via email at shayw@uwgb.edu.

*William A. Shay*

# Understanding Data Communications and Networks

# CHAPTER 1

## INTRODUCTION TO COMMUNICATIONS, STANDARDS, AND PROTOCOLS

*Different words mean the same thing. Same words mean different things. It is not the exact definition but how the concept works*—Ken Sherman, *Data Communications*

## 1.1   Why Study Communications?

Why should we study communications? The many reasons range from "It is an interesting field" to "I have to know how to connect my PC to the company's network." But one of the most compelling reasons is that communication technology has invaded virtually every aspect of daily life, from professional and educational uses to purely recreational ones. It has become so pervasive that we either take it for granted or are simply not aware of its applications.

### A BRIEF HISTORY

The field of communications is certainly not new: People have been communicating since early humans grunted and scratched pictures on cave walls. For thousands of years people communicated using little more than words, parchments, stone tablets, and smoke signals. The primary forms of sending information were based on the auditory and visual senses. You either heard someone speaking or saw the letters and symbols that defined a message.

Communications changed drastically in 1837, when Samuel Morse invented the telegraph. This invention made it possible to send information using electrical impulses over a copper wire. Messages were sent by translating each character into a sequence of long or short electrical impulses (or the less technical terms of dots and dashes) and transmitting them. This association of characters with electrical impulses was called the Morse code. The ability to send information with no obvious verbal or visual medium began a sequence of events that forever changed the way people communicate.

In 1876 Alexander Graham Bell took the telegraph one step further. Rather than converting a message into a sequence of dots and dashes, he showed that a voice could be converted directly to electrical energy and transmitted over a wire using continuously varying voltages. At the wire's other end the electrical signals were converted back to sound. The result was that a person's voice could be transmitted electronically between two points as long as a physical connection existed between them. To most people whose lives were based only on what they could see and hear, this invention was absolutely incredible and seemed magical.

The earliest telephones required a different pair of wires for each phone to which you wished to connect. In order to place a call a person had to first connect the telephone to the correct wires and then hope the person on the other end was there listening. There were no bells or signaling devices to interrupt dinner. That changed with the invention of the switchboard (Figure 1.1), a switching device that connected lines between two telephones. Callers simply picked up the phone and recited the number of the person they wished to call. Telephones had not yet evolved to the point where people had to perform manual activities such as dialing numbers or pushing buttons. Establishing connections was voice activated. That is, an operator heard the number and then used a switchboard to connect one person's phone lines with another person's lines.

During the next 70 years the telephone system grew to the point where the telephone is a common device in a home. Most of us do not even think about how the telephone system works. We know we can dial a number and be connected to just about anywhere in the world.

FIGURE 1.1    **Early Switchboards**

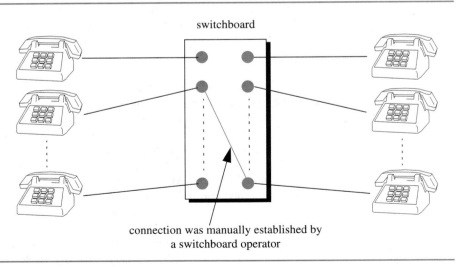

switchboard

connection was manually established by
a switchboard operator

Another event important to communications occurred in 1945 with the invention of the first electronic computer, the **ENIAC (Electronic Numerical Integrator and Calculator)**. Designed for computing ballistics tables for World War II, it was the first device that could actually process information electronically. Although the ENIAC played no direct role in data or computer communications, it did show that calculations and decision making could be done electronically, an important ability in today's communication systems.

The relation between computers and communications began to emerge after the invention of the transistor in 1947 allowed smaller and cheaper computers to be built. The new generation of computers that emerged during the 1960s made new applications such as processing and routing telephone calls economically feasible. In addition, more businesses were buying computers and developing applications, and the need to transfer information between them began to grow.

The first communication system between computers was simple but reliable, and it is still used today. Basically, it involved writing information from one computer onto a magnetic tape, throwing the tape into the back of the car, then transporting the tape to another computer. Once there, the other computer could read the information on the tape. This was a very reliable form of communication, assuming the person driving the car didn't get into an accident or leave the windows open while driving through a car wash.

Another milestone in electronic communications occurred shortly after the invention of the integrated circuit and the personal computer (PC). The ability to have computing power on a desk generated an entirely new way of storing and retrieving information. The 1980s saw the infusion of millions of PCs into virtually every business, company, school, and organization and into many homes as well. The fact that so many people now had computers generated the need to make information even more easily accessible. Today, computers and communications have progressed to the point where most businesses or schools can no longer function without them. Our almost total dependence on them demands that we understand them and their abilities and limitations.

### APPLICATIONS

Transferring data between computers is just one area of communications. For example, most people are aware that a television uses an antenna or cable to bring signals into a home. But that is the last step in a worldwide communication system that began in 1962 with **Telstar**, a communication satellite designed to transfer telephone and television signals between the United States and Europe. Telstar showed that transmitting information between continents was both technologically and economically feasible.

Many communication satellites transmit television signals today. Figure 1.2 shows a common system. A transmitter in one part of the world sends a signal to an orbiting satellite, which relays the signal to receivers in other parts. Signals from the receiver are sent to broadcast towers and are transmitted locally using an **FCC (Federal Communications Commission)** approved frequency. An antenna receives the signals and relays them to the television set in your home.

Television antennas are not the only way to receive signals. Many homes subscribe to a cable television service that brings signals into the home using a coaxial cable. In addition, many people purchase their own receiving dishes and receive satellite signals directly.

Other communications applications are **local area networks (LANs)** and **wide area networks (WANs)**, systems that allow multiple computers to communicate over short (LAN) or long (WAN) distances. Once connected, users can send data files, login to remote computers, or send mail (**email** or **electronic mail**). With email, a person can send personal or business messages from one computer to another. The email system stores messages on a computer disk where someone else can read them.

The phenomenal growth of email, which sends and receives messages electronically, has caused some people to predict it will eventually replace postal service. This is not likely to happen in the foreseeable future, but email is used extensively by many professionals.

With email, it is possible to send a message to remote locations from the privacy of your own home; Figure 1.3 shows how. A person with a PC and modem at home can access his or her company's computer. This computer is connected to a local area network that allows a message to be sent to any person connected to it. The local area network also connects to a wide area network that allows a message to be sent across the country or to other countries. Local area networks at the other

FIGURE 1.2    **Television Reception**

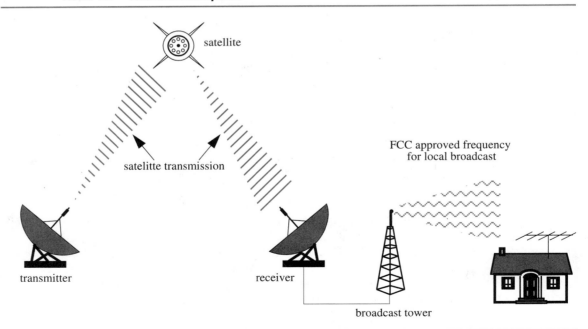

FIGURE 1.3    **Electronic Mail Connections**

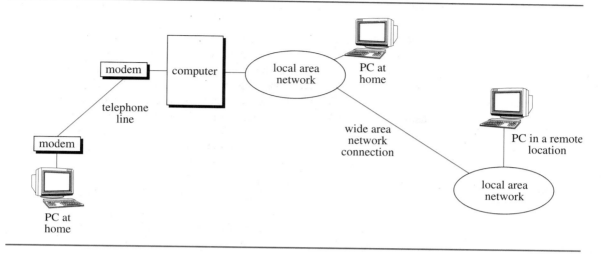

end can route a transmitted message to any connected PC. An individual on that end with a PC and modem can receive the message at home.

The following additional applications are described only briefly here. References 1, 2, 3, and 4 provide more detailed, but not too technical, descriptions of them. We will discuss some of these topics more fully in later chapters.

- **Facsimile machines (fax).** A fax machine creates an electronic equivalent of an image on a sheet of paper and it then sends the image over telephone lines. A fax machine at the other end re-creates the original paper's image. The fax is widely used to send letters, charts, and diagrams in minutes.

- **Voice and video communications**. LANs, used to connect PCs and other devices, transfer data primarily. Communication systems can also transmit voice and video images. Many companies often manage their own telephone systems or **private branch exchanges (PBX)** (discussed further in Section 2.1). Video communications can be used to play a tape or receive a video transmission from outside and relay the signals throughout a company or organization. Video communication has special needs because it typically requires the sending of 30 images per second, and each image requires a large amount of information to maintain crisp pictures with true color.

- **Teleconferencing**. Many people are no doubt painfully aware of the number of business meetings or conferences that occur each day. One of the most difficult aspects of planning such meetings is making sure everyone who needs to be present can attend. When the necessary people are in different parts of the country, they must make arrangements to travel to the meeting site. Teleconferencing involves setting up video cameras and televisions at different locations so that people at each location can see and hear each other. In effect, they "attend" meetings or conferences without leaving their individual locations. Figures and charts needed for presentations also can be broadcast for all to see.

- **Cellular telephones.** The telephone is certainly the most extensive communication system. Until the 1960s, however, the two communicating sites had to be connected physically. At that time, the telephone system started to use satellite and microwave towers to send signals. Still, for a while those making and receiving the calls had to use a telephone that was connected physically to a local office. That changed with the invention of the cellular telephone, a device that connects to the telephone system using radio waves. It allows people to make telephone calls from their cars, the office picnic, or the ballpark—any place with sending and receiving towers nearby. Section 2.1 discusses cellular telephones further.

- **Information services.** Those with a PC and modem can subscribe to many different information services. **Bulletin boards** (data banks) allow the free exchange of some software, files, or other information. Other services allow users to get stock quotations and make transactions electronically or to examine airline schedules and make reservations. Other services archive much of the information that travels a wide area network such as the Internet. They also allow a user to login and search for information using key words or topics. The service can then provide information detailing the location of documents dealing with the indicated topic.

## ISSUES

These new technological developments have created many issues of concern. For example, we have used the word *connect* and its various forms many times in the previous discussion. But how do we connect? What do we use to make a connection? Do we use wire, cable, or optical fiber? Can we connect without them? Chapter 2 discusses many options.

Communication technology is like traffic planning in a large city. Roads allow you to get where you want to go, but they must be able to handle large amounts of traffic, especially in a large city. Designers must strike a balance between flow and cost. A ten-lane highway circling the city will provide better traffic flow than a six-lane highway, but are more lanes worth the extra cost? The answer probably is yes in the largest cities but no in the smaller ones. Communication systems are similar. They must allow a certain amount of information to be transmitted, but just how much depends on the applications. The amount of information we need to send will affect how devices are connected. Chapters 3 and 6 discuss different ways to connect devices.

Once we decide how to connect we must establish some rules for communication. City streets are of little use without traffic signals or laws to control traffic. The same is true for communications systems. Whether the primary medium is a cable or through the air, we need to know that many sources will want to send information. We need some rules to prevent messages from colliding or to specify what to do when they do collide. Chapters 3, 5, and 6 discuss ways to provide orderly communications.

Ease of use is another concern. Most people will not use a technology if it is difficult to use. For example, most people who purchased VCRs never learned to program them, at least until "VCR plus" was available. For a communication system or network to be viable, the information must be readily accessible. But how accessible do we want it? Should anyone be able to look at it? If it's an on-line library catalog, yes. If it's financial information for your retirement or investment account, no.

Communications systems must be secure. We must realize that the easy exchange of information invites unauthorized and illegal use of it. How can we make information accessible to those who need it yet prevent anyone else from seeing it? This is especially tough when the unauthorized people have many resources and make concerted efforts to break security measures. As the sensitivity of the information increases, security measures become more sophisticated. No system, however, is perfectly safe. Consequently, laws that provide for severe penalties were passed to help deter such activities. Chapter 4 deals with security.

Even if we deal with all of the issues and manage to connect computers to provide the most efficient, cost effective, secure, and easy transfer of information, one problem remains: Many computers are incompatible. In some cases transferring information from one computer to another is like moving a transmission from one car to another. If both cars are Ford Escorts you can do it, but if one is an Escort and the other is a Grand Prix you will have some problems.

One heavily researched area today is the development of **open systems**. If fully implemented, an open system would allow any two computers to exchange information as long as they are connected. Given the diversity among computer systems, this is a very ambitious goal. Section 1.4 describes open systems and a popular open-system model.

Finally, we return to the question: Why study data communications? Simply, it's a field that is experiencing and will experience tremendous growth. There is a desperate need for people who understand it and can help shape its future.

## 1.2    Computer Networks

During the 1950s, most computers were similar in one respect. They had a main memory, a CPU, and peripherals (Figure 1.4). The memory and CPU were central to the system. Since then a new generation of computing has emerged in which computation and data storage need not be centralized. A user may retrieve a program from one place, run it on any of a variety of processors, and send the result to a third location.

A system connecting different devices such as PCs, printers, and disk drives is a **network**. Typically, each device in a network serves a specific purpose for one or more individuals. For example, a PC may sit on your desk providing access to information or software you need. A PC may also be devoted to managing a disk drive containing shared files. We call it a **file server**. Often a network covers a

FIGURE 1.4     **Communicating Devices in a Computer System**

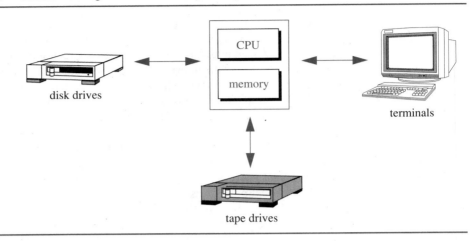

small geographic area and connects devices in a single building or group of build-ings. Such a network is a **local area network (LAN)**. A network that covers a larger area such as a municipality, state, country, or the world is called a **wide area network (WAN)**.

To illustrate a network's use, suppose a small business has connected several devices as shown in Figure 1.5. A company executive is planning a presentation to the board of directors that includes an analysis of last month's sales. The data resides in a file server, the statistical software to analyze sales runs on a PC, and a program forecasting future sales runs only on the mainframe. The executive can transfer the sales figures from the file server to a PC (Step 1 in Figure 1.5). She can then run the statistical software, send the results to the mainframe, and run the forecasting soft-ware (Step 2). When the results are generated, she can transfer them back to the PC (Step 3), where she can format the data for presentation. Finally, she can print her charts on a laser printer (Step 4).

The arrangement in Figure 1.5 is a simple scheme that works for one person. Most networks, however, involve many people using many PCs, each of which can access any of many printers or servers. With all of these people accessing informa-tion, their requests inevitably will conflict. Consequently, the devices must be con-nected in a way that permits an orderly transfer of information for all concerned. A good analogy is a street layout in a large city. With only one person driving it mat-ters little where the streets are, which ones are one-way, where the traffic signals are, or how they are synchronized. But with thousands of cars on the streets during the morning rush hour, a bad layout will create congestion that causes major delays. The same is true of computer networks. They must be connected in a way that allows data to travel among many users with little or no delay. We call the connection strategy the **network topology**. The best topology depends on the types of devices and user needs. What works well for one group may perform dismally for another.

FIGURE 1.5    **Variety of Connected Computing Devices**

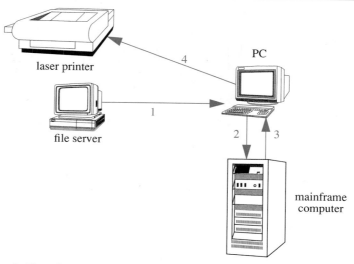

Step 1:  Transfer data from file server to PC  and run statistical software.
Step 2:  Transfer results from Step 1 to mainframe and run forecasting program.
Step 3:  Transfer results from Step 2 back to PC for printer formatting.
Step 4:  Send results to laser printer.

## COMMON BUS TOPOLOGY

Figure 1.6 shows a **common bus topology** (or simply **bus topology**) connecting devices such as workstations, mainframes, and file servers. They communicate
through a single bus (one or more parallel lines). A common approach gives each
device an interface that listens to the bus and examines its data traffic. If an interface
determines that data is destined for the device it serves, it reads the data from the bus
and transfers it to the device. Similarly, if a device wants to transmit data, the interface circuits sense when the bus is empty and then transmit data. This is not unlike
waiting on a freeway entrance ramp during rush hour. You sense an opening and either quickly dart to it or "muscle" your way through, depending on whether you're
driving a subcompact or a large truck.

Sometimes, two devices try to transmit simultaneously. Each one detects an
absence of traffic and begins transmitting before becoming aware of the other
device's transmission. The result is a collision of signals. As the devices transmit
they continue to listen to the bus and detect the noise resulting from the collision.
When a device detects a collision it stops transmitting, waits a random period of
time, and tries again. This process, called **carrier sense, multiple access with collision detection (CSMA/CD)** is discussed along with other ways to access common
media in Sections 3.4 and 6.2.

FIGURE 1.6    **Common Bus Topology**

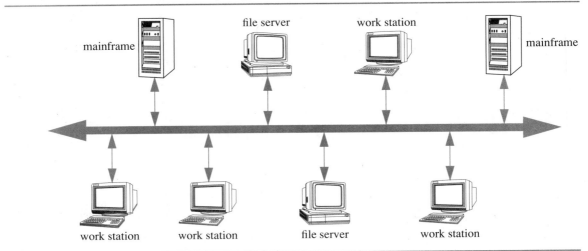

One popular common bus network is the **Ethernet**. Its common bus typically is the **Ethernet cable**, which consists of copper, optical fiber, or combinations of both (although recent developments allow connections using microwave and infrared technology). Its design allows terminals, PCs, disk storage systems, and office machines to communicate. A major advantage of the Ethernet is the ability to add new devices to the network easily.

## STAR TOPOLOGY

Another common connecting arrangement is the **star topology** (Figure 1.7). It uses a central computer that communicates with other devices in the network. Control is centralized; if a device wants to communicate, it does so only through the central computer. The computer, in turn, routes the data to its destination. Centralization provides a focal point for responsibility, an advantage of the star topology. The bus topology, however, has some advantages over a star topology. The lack of central control makes adding new devices easy since no device must be aware of others. In addition, the failure or removal of a device in a bus network does not cause the network to fail. In the star topology, the failure of the central computer brings down the entire network.

Star topologies often involve a single mainframe computer that services many terminals and secondary storage devices. With appropriate terminal emulation software, PCs can communicate with it. Data transfers between terminals or between terminals and storage devices occur only through the main computer.

## RING TOPOLOGY

In a **ring topology** (Figure 1.8), devices are connected circularly. Each one can communicate directly with either or both of its neighbors but nobody else. If it wants to

FIGURE 1.7     **Star Topology**

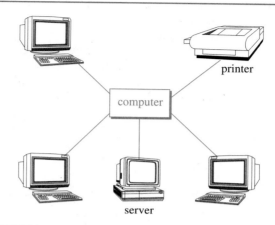

communicate with a device farther away, it sends a message that passes through each device in between.

A ring network may be either **unidirectional** or **bidirectional**. Unidirectional means that all transmissions travel in the same direction. Thus, each device can communicate with only one neighbor. Bidirectional means that data transmissions travel in either direction, and a device can communicate with both neighbors.

Ring topologies such as IBM's **token ring network** often connect PCs in a single office or department. Applications from one PC thus can access data stored on

FIGURE 1.8     **Ring Topology**

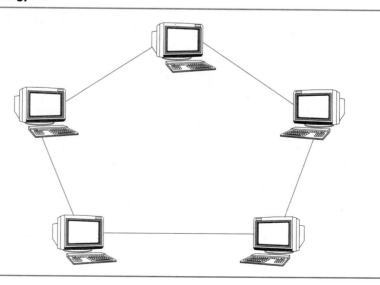

others without requiring a mainframe to coordinate communications. Instead, communications are coordinated by passing a token (predefined sequence of bits) among all the stations in the ring. A station can send something only when it receives the token.

A disadvantage of the ring topology is that when one station sends to another, all stations in between are involved. More time is spent relaying messages meant for others than in, for example, a bus topology. Moreover, the failure of one station causes a break in the ring which affects communications among all the stations. Ways to deal with such problems and other aspects of token rings are discussed further in Sections 3.4 and 6.3.

## FULLY CONNECTED TOPOLOGY

The **fully connected topology** (Figure 1.9) has a direct connection between every pair of devices in the network. This is an extreme design. Communication becomes very simple as there is no competition for common lines. If two devices want to communicate, they do so directly without involving other devices. The cost of direct connections between every pair of devices is high, however. Furthermore, many connections may be vastly underutilized. If two devices rarely communicate, the physical connection between them is seldom used. In such cases, a more economical approach is for the two to communicate indirectly, eliminating the underused line.

FIGURE 1.9    **Fully Connected Topology**

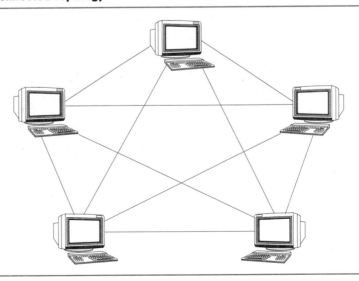

FIGURE 1.10    **Combined Topology**

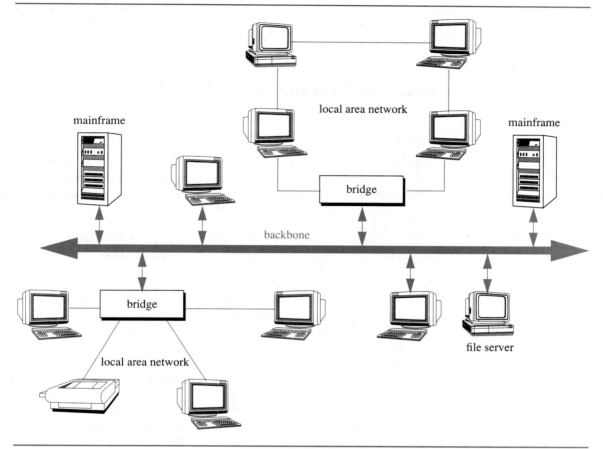

## COMBINED TOPOLOGIES

Many computer networks use combinations of the various topologies. Figure 1.10 shows a possible combination. It has a common bus, sometimes called the **backbone**, which allows users to access mainframes and high-volume or frequently accessed storage. Groups of users such as research scientists, accountants, or sales personnel, however, may have specialized needs and use a LAN most of the time. Periodically, they may want to access high-volume storage or the computing power of a mainframe, but the requirements are not frequent enough to justify connecting each PC to the backbone.

A compromise design identifies several LANs connecting PCs and other devices in a ring, star, or bus topology. Devices within a LAN communicate according to the rules defined by its topology. If a PC must communicate with a device in another LAN, it can do so using a **bridge** that connects the two LANs. As we will see in Chapter 6, different LANs use different rules to communicate, and the bridge is needed to convert between them.

## 1.3    Standards and Standards Organizations

### THE NEED FOR STANDARDS

You might think that the primary problem in establishing communications between two computers is simply making sure that the data bits get from one computer to the other. However, since computers are often very different from one another, the transfer process is actually much more complex, like moving an automobile transmission from a Cadillac to a Toyota. All automobiles are based on the same principles, but different models have unique features appealing to a different style and market, and the same is true of computers. Companies design and manufacture computers in different styles and for different applications. Most follow the same general principles, but specifics reflect the thinking and philosophy of many people. Computers have different architectures, understand different languages, store data in different formats, and communicate at different rates. Consequently, there is much incompatibility, and communication is difficult.

This raises a basic question: How can computers communicate at all? They communicate the same way trade representatives from different countries do. Each person speaks a different language, so they need translators. Furthermore, they need to observe a **protocol** that defines the rules and the manner in which they begin and proceed with discussions. If all involved do not agree to a protocol, the discussions become chaotic. An orderly discussion occurs only if the participants follow the rules. Similarly, if computers are to communicate, they need protocols to determine which one "speaks" and translators to account for different languages. The next step is to define the protocols. Here lies another problem: Protocols are great, but if the principal parties involved follow different protocols, they might as well follow none. If the necessary people could agree on a common protocol, it could become a standard protocol and everyone could use it. Unfortunately, this is a lot like getting everyone to agree on a computer architecture, which we know didn't happen. Getting a diverse group of people to agree on anything is difficult. Different groups have different goals and ideas about which protocol best meets those goals. Consequently, many different standards have evolved and been used over the years.

There are two types of standards. **Defacto standards** are those that exist by virtue of their widespread use. That is, they have become so common that vendors know that producing products consistent with them will have a large market. Many IBM products have become defacto standards. The second type of standard is one that is formally recognized and adopted by an agency that has achieved national or worldwide recognition. Those who wish to see their work become a standard write a proposal and submit it to an agency for consideration. Typically, if the proposal has merit and widespread acceptance, the agency will make suggestions and send it back to its originators for modifications. After several rounds of suggestions and modifications the proposal will be adopted or refused. If approved, the standard gives vendors a model on which to produce new products.

## AGENCIES

The use of agencies certainly puts some order in the rapidly expanding field of communications. Hundreds of standards are approved for different aspects of communications, however, making incompatibility among different types of devices an ongoing problem. For example, many PC users purchase a modem (a device allowing a computer to send and receive signals over a telephone line) to connect to a company or university computer. If the wrong modem is used, however, communication will not happen. More than a dozen standards describe different ways to send and receive signals over the telephone, and if the two modems use different standards there will be no connection. Chapter 2 discusses this problem fully.

The following agencies are important to the field of computer networks and data communications:

- **American National Standards Institute (ANSI)**. ANSI is a private, nongovernmental agency whose members are manufacturers, users, and other interested companies. It has nearly 1000 members and is itself a member of the International Standards Organization, or ISO (described in this list). ANSI standards are common in many fields. In Chapter 6 we discuss the fiber distributed data interface (FDDI), a standard for local area networks using optical fiber. Another standard (discussed in Chapter 2) is the American Standard Code for Information Interchange (ASCII), used by many computers for storing information.

- **Comité Consultatif Internationale de Télégraphique et Téléphonique (CCITT)**. The English equivalent is the International Consultative Committee for Telephony and Telegraphy. The committee is an agency of the International Telecommunications Union division, a United Nations agency. Its members include various scientific and industrial organizations, telecommunication agencies, telephone authorities, and the ISO. CCITT has produced numerous standards dealing with network and telephone communications. Two well-known sets of standards are the V series and X series. The V series deals with telephone communications. Chapter 2 discusses some V standards that describe how a modem generates and interprets analog telephone signals. The X series deals with network interfaces and public networks. Examples include the X.25 standard for interfacing to a packet switched network (discussed in Chapter 7) and the X.400 standard for electronic mail systems (discussed in Chapter 8). There are many other X and V standards; Reference 5 provides an extensive list.

- **Electronic Industries Association (EIA)**. The members of EIA include electronics firms and manufacturers of telecommunications equipment. It is also a member of ANSI. The EIA's primary activities deal with electrical connections and the physical transfer of data between devices. The most well known standard is the RS-232 (also called EIA 232) standard, which most PCs use for communicating with other devices such as modems or printers. The EIA 232 standard is discussed in Chapter 3.

- **Institute of Electrical and Electronic Engineers (IEEE).** The IEEE is the largest professional organization in the world and consists of computing and engineering professionals. It publishes many different journals, runs conferences, and has a group that develops standards. Perhaps its best known work in the communications field is its project 802 LAN standards. Discussed in Chapter 6, the 802 standards define the communication protocols for bus and ring networks.

- **International Standards Organization (ISO).** The ISO is a worldwide organization consisting of standards bodies from many countries such as ANSI from the United States. One of ISO's most significant activities is its work on open systems, which define the protocols that would allow any two computers to communicate independent of their architecture. One well-known model is the **open systems interconnect (OSI)** a seven-layer organization of protocols. Many believe that OSI will be the model used for all future communications. Many of its lower layers already have been implemented and are in widespread use. The higher layers are in various stages of development. We will discuss the OSI model in the next section.

- **National Institute of Standards and Technology (NIST).** Formerly the **National Bureau of Standards** (**NBS**), the NIST is an agency of the United States Department of Commerce. It issues standards the federal government uses for equipment purchases. It also develops standards for many physical quantities such as time, length, temperature, radioactivity, and radio frequencies. One important standard with security applications is the **data encryption standard (DES)** a method of encrypting or changing information into a form that cannot be understood. The DES standard has been manufactured in chips used in communications devices. The standard, discussed in Chapter 4, is complex as well as controversial (some believe the National Security Agency purposely weakened it in order to prevent encryption techniques that it could not solve).

- **International Business Machines (IBM).** Although not a standards agency, IBM should be listed because so much of its work has become de facto standards. Notable examples include its systems network architecture (SNA) and the Extended Binary Coded Decimal Interchange Code (EBCDIC). SNA is a protocol model designed to allow IBM computers and equipment to communicate. We will discuss it in Chapter 8, but in many ways it is similar to the OSI model. The EBCDIC code (discussed in Chapter 2) is an alternative to ASCII for storing data and is commonly used on IBM mainframes (although its PCs commonly use the ASCII code).

These agencies are by no means the only standards bodies, but they are the ones most pertinent to data communication and networks. Reference 6 contains a much larger list of standards bodies.

## 1.4    Open Systems and the OSI Model

We have stated that protocols allow otherwise incompatible systems to communicate. Given two specific systems, the definition of a protocol is fairly straightforward. The problem becomes bigger and more difficult as the number of different types of systems increases. A set of protocols that would allow any two different systems to communicate regardless of their underlying architecture is called an **open system**. The ISO has addressed the problem of allowing many devices to communicate and has developed its **open systems interconnect (OSI)** model. If fully developed, it would allow any two computers to communicate as long as they are connected.

The OSI model is a seven-layer model (Figure 1.11). Each layer performs specific functions and communicates with the layers directly above and below it. Higher layers deal more with user services, applications, and activities, and the lower layers deal more with the actual transmission of information.

FIGURE 1.11    **OSI's ISO Layered Protocol Model**

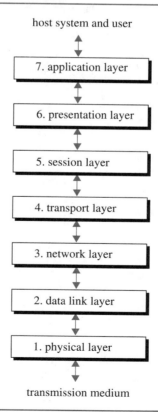

The purpose of layering the protocol is to separate specific functions and to make their implementation transparent to other components. This layering allows independent design and testing of each component. For example, the data link layer and physical layer perform separate functions. The physical layer performs a service to the data link layer. Furthermore, the data link layer does not care how the service is performed but just that it is done. This way, if changes occur in how the physical layer is implemented, the data link layer (and all higher layers) is unaffected. This approach applies to any two consecutive layers and is the same as that behind the modular programming (or top-down design) style that you learned in your first programming class.

Compare the process to a meeting among several heads of state. Each leader needs to make his or her thoughts known, but the ideas often must be recast in appropriate diplomatic language to avoid offending someone. Furthermore, if they all speak a different language, one language must be chosen as the primary form of communication. Figure 1.12 illustrates a possible three-layer protocol involving a crisis that two of the leaders are trying to resolve. One leader adamantly states that

FIGURE 1.12     **Communication Protocol Between Two Heads of State**

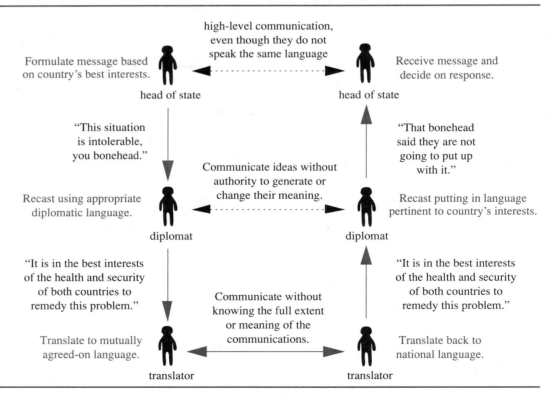

FIGURE 1.13  **Communication Using the OSI Seven-Layer Protocol**

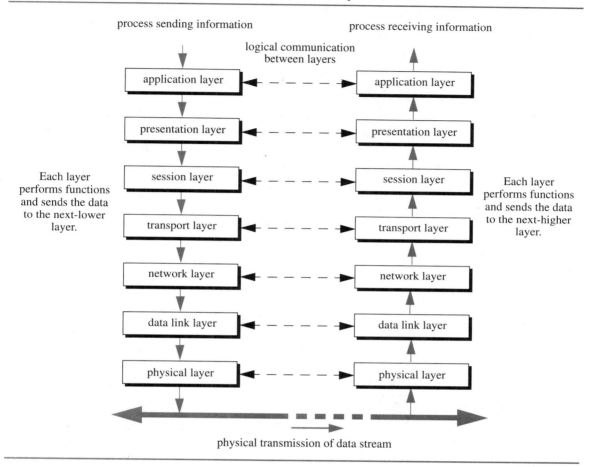

**process sending information**                    **process receiving information**

logical communication
between layers

Each layer
performs functions
and sends the data
to the next-lower
layer.

| application layer | ← – – – → | application layer |
| presentation layer | ← – – – → | presentation layer |
| session layer | ← – – – → | session layer |
| transport layer | ← – – – → | transport layer |
| network layer | ← – – – → | network layer |
| data link layer | ← – – – → | data link layer |
| physical layer | ← – – – → | physical layer |

Each layer
performs functions
and sends the data
to the next-higher
layer.

physical transmission of data stream

he is not going to tolerate the situation. The diplomat recasts the message into a less-threatening tenor and a translator translates the message to the chosen language. On the other side, another translator translates back to a specific language. The diplomat receives the message and tells the head of state what it really means.

In a sense, the two leaders are communicating directly, even though the message actually passes through other individuals. The OSI model works similarly. The lowest level, the physical layer, deals with actual data transmission. The highest level deals with the computer system connected to the network. Each layer in between corresponds to a different level of abstraction in data communications and defines certain functions and protocols.

Two otherwise incompatible sites, each running the OSI model, can communicate with each other (Figure 1.13). Logically, each layer communicates directly with its counterpart at the other site. Physically, each layer communicates with the layers immediately above and below it. When a process wants to send information, it starts by handing it over to the application layer. That layer performs its functions and sends the data to the presentation layer. It, in turn, performs its functions and gives the data to the session layer. This process continues until the physical layer receives the data and actually transmits it.

On the receiving end, the process works in reverse. The physical layer receives the bit stream and gives it to the data link layer. The data link layer performs certain functions and sends the data to the network layer. This process continues until the application eventually receives the information and gives it to the receiving process. The two processes appear to communicate directly, with each layer appearing to communicate directly with its counterpart at another network node. In reality, all data is broken into a bit stream and transmitted between physical layers.

This process is a bit like sending a letter, where you communicate with the letter's recipient by addressing the envelope and dropping it in a mailbox. As far as you are concerned, the activity is then complete: The communication is independent of how the letter is eventually routed or whether it goes by truck, plane, train, boat, or carrier pigeon. You know the letter will arrive and you can simply wait for a response.

## OVERVIEW OF THE MODEL

The highest layer, the **application layer**, works directly with the user or application programs. Note that it is not the same as an application program. The application layer provides user services such as electronic mail, file transfers, remote job entry, and resource allocation. For example, the application layer on one end should appear to send a file directly to the application layer on the other end independent of the underlying network or computer architectures.

The application layer also defines the protocols that allow access to a full screen text editor from different types of terminals. The reason is that different types of terminals use different control sequences for cursor control. For example, just moving the cursor may involve arrow keys or special key combinations. Ideally, we would like to make such differences transparent to the user.

The **presentation layer** is responsible for presenting data in a format its user can understand. For example, suppose two different computers use different numeric and character formats. The presentation layer translates data from one representation to another and insulates the user from such differences. In effect, the presentation layer determines the difference between data and information. After all, networks exist so users can exchange information, not raw bit streams. Users do not want to be concerned with different formats; they would prefer to concentrate on the informational content and what it means to them.

The presentation layer also can provide security measures. It may encrypt data before handing it to the lower layers for transfer. The presentation layer at the other end would decrypt the data after receiving it. The user need never know the data was altered. This is especially important in wide-area networks (ones that span large geographic distances) where unauthorized access is a serious problem.

The **session layer** allows applications on two different computers to establish a session or logical connection. For example, a user may logon to a remote system and may communicate by alternately sending and receiving messages. The session layer helps coordinate the process by informing each end when it can send or must listen. This is a form of synchronization.

The session layer also handles error recovery. For example, suppose a user is sending the contents of a large file over a network that suddenly fails. When it is operational again, must the user start retransmitting from the beginning of the file? The answer is no, because the session layer lets the user insert checkpoints in a long stream. If a network crashes, only the data transmitted since the last checkpoint is lost.

The session layer also brackets operations that must appear to the user as a single transaction. A common example is the deletion of a record from a database. Although the user sees the deletion as a single operation, it actually may involve several. The record must be found and subsequently deleted by altering pointers and addresses and perhaps entries in an index or hash table. If a user is accessing a database through a network, the session layer makes sure that all low-level operations are received before the deletion actually begins. If the database operations were applied one at a time as they were received, a network failure could compromise the database's integrity by changing some pointers but not others (you may recall your introductory data structures class, where incorrect programs did not change all of your pointers) or by deleting a record but not a reference to it.

The fourth layer is the **transport layer**. It is the lowest layer that deals primarily with end-to-end communications (the lower layers dealing with the network itself). The transport layer may determine which network to use for communication. A computer may be connected to several that may differ in speed, cost, and type of communication, the choice often depending on many factors. For example, does the information consist of a long continuous stream of data? Or does it consist of many intermittent transfers? The telephone network is appropriate for long, continuous data transfers. Once a connection has been established, it is maintained until the transfer is complete.

Another approach divides the data into small packets (subsets of the data) and transfers them intermittently. In such cases, a constant connection between two points is unnecessary. Instead, each packet may be transmitted independently through the network. Consequently, when the packets arrive at the other end they must be reassembled before their contents are passed to the layer above. One problem is that if the packets follow different routes there is no guarantee that they will arrive in the order in which they were sent (just as there is no guarantee that a letter mailed on Monday will arrive before one mailed on Tuesday) or that they will all arrive. Not only must the receiver determine the correct order of incoming packets, it also must verify it got them all.

The **network layer** deals with routing strategies. For example, in a bidirectional ring network, there are two paths between any two points. A more complex topology may have many routes from which to choose. Which ones are fastest, cheapest, or safest? Which ones are open or uncongested? Should an entire message follow the same route, or should parts of it be transferred independently?

The network layer controls the **communications subnet**, the collection of transmission media and switching elements required for routing and data transmission. The network layer is the highest layer in the subnet. This layer may also contain accounting software for customer billing. Remember, networks exist to allow users to communicate. As with most services, someone must pay. The fee depends on the amount of data transmitted and possibly the time of day. The network layer can maintain such information and handle billing.

The **data link layer** supervises the flow of information between adjacent network nodes. It uses error detection or correction techniques to ensure that a transmission contains no errors. If the data link detects an error, it can either request a new transmission or, depending on the implementation, correct the error. It also controls how much information is sent at a time: Too much and the network becomes congested; too little and the sending and receiving ends experience excessive waits.

The data link layer also recognizes a format. Data is often transmitted in **frames**, which consist of a group of bytes organized according to a specified format. The data link layer marks the beginning and end of each outgoing frame with unique bit patterns and recognizes these patterns to define an incoming frame. It then sends error-free frames to the previous layer, the network layer.

Finally, the **physical layer** transmits data bits over a network. It is concerned with the physical or electrical aspects of data communications. For example, is the medium copper cable, optical fiber, or satellite communications? How can data be transferred physically from point A to point B? The physical layer transmits data bits received from the data link layer in streams without regard to their meaning or format. Similarly, it receives bits without analyzing them and gives them to the data link layer.

In summary, the lowest three layers deal primarily with the details of network communications. Together, they provide a service to the upper layers. The upper layers deal with end-to-end communications. They define the communication protocols between two users, but are not concerned with the low-level details of data transmission. Some network implementations may not use all seven layers or may combine some of the functions from different layers. Try to remember that OSI is a model (albeit an important one), and not all network protocols adhere to it exactly. Table 1.1 contains a summary of the functions we have discussed so far.

TABLE 1.1    **Summary of OSI Layers**

| LAYER | FUNCTIONS |
|---|---|
| 7. Application | Provides electronic mail, file transfers, and other user services. |
| 6. Presentation | Translates data formats, encrypts and decrypts data. |
| 5. Session | Synchronizes communicating users, recovers from errors, and brackets operations. |
| 4. Transport | Determines network, may assemble and reassemble packets. |
| 3. Network | Determines routes, manages billing information. |
| 2. Data link | Detects or corrects errors, defines frames. |
| 1. Physical | Transmits physical data. |

### PHYSICAL LAYER

The physical layer has two primary aspects: transmission media and connection strategies. The transmission media define how signals are sent. Typical options are twisted wire pairs, coaxial cable, optical fiber, satellites, microwave towers, and radio waves. Each option has different electrical or electromagnetic properties that make it suitable for different situations. A full description of transmission media requires discussions of analog and digital transmissions, bandwidth, signal-to-noise ratios, broadband, baseband, voice grade transmissions, and even Fourier analysis. They warrant their own chapter and are covered in Chapter 2.

The physical layer also covers the connection strategy. We know that two computers must be connected in order to communicate. How they are connected is a design issue. For example, consider the network in Figure 1.14. The **connection strategy** of the physical layer answers the question: "If node A wants to communicate with node F, how do we connect them?" Care must be taken to distinguish this problem from determining the route, or network path. If the lines represent physical connections, there are four routes along which data may travel from node *A* to node *F*. (Can you list them?) The network layer will determine which one is best, but the physical layer determines how the two end-points are actually connected via the chosen route.

There are three connection strategies: circuit switching, message switching, and packet switching. In **circuit switching**, once a connection is made between two nodes, it is maintained until one of them terminates it. In other words, the connection is dedicated to the communication between the two parties. Circuit switching used to be common in the telephone system (Figure 1.15) and is still present in some old telephone switches.

How does it work? A person at node *A* wants to talk to someone at node *F*. The person at *A* requests a connection to *F*. In a telephone network, dialing a number

FIGURE 1.14    **Sample Computer Network**

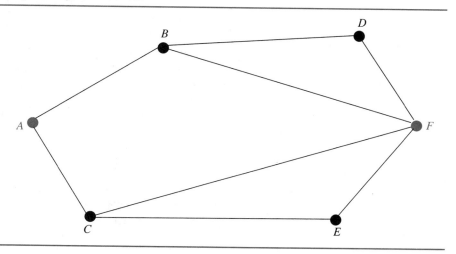

FIGURE 1.15    **Dedicated Circuit Connecting A and F**

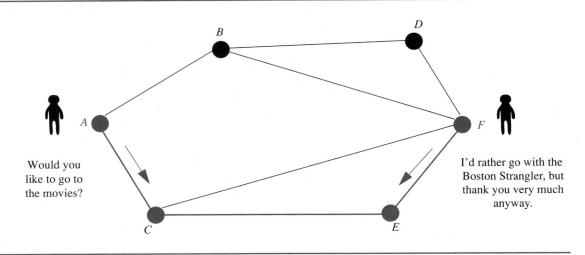

makes the connection. In a computer network, the user enters appropriate commands to connect to a specified location. Either way, logic at node *A* must determine the next node in a route that leads to *F*. This process involves factors such as the cost of the connection and the availability of different paths. For example, a telephone call from San Francisco to Los Angeles is not normally routed through Miami. However, if the lines between the two cities are congested, the connection may be indirect; for example, through Sacramento.

In Figure 1.15, node *A* has determined that *C* is a better choice than *B* in the route from *A* to *F*. Thus, node *A* connects to node *C*. Node *C*, in turn, proceeds similarly. It might choose node *F*, or it might decide to go through node *E*. Again, cost and existing connections affect the choice. In this case, node *C* connects to node *E*. Finally, *E* connects to *F*. The connection is made, and node *F* may be willing to accept it. In the telephone system, you accept a connection by picking up the receiver and saying "hello." In a computer network, appropriate commands are used to "accept" connections. If node *F* does not respond (e.g., busy signal or no answer), node *A* terminates the request.

If node *F* accepts the connection, information may be exchanged. The person at node *A* asks, "Do you want to go the movies?" The person at node *F* responds by saying, "I'd really love to go with you, but my canary just died and I'm in mourning. Ask me some other time when I'm out of town."

Circuit switching requires that the route be determined and the connection made before any information is transmitted. Also, the network maintains the connection until a node terminates it. This type of connection is most useful when the communications between the two nodes is continuous; that is, when node *A* "says" something and node *F* "hears" almost immediately, with virtually no transmission delay. This is not always the best way to communicate, however. First of all, if node *A* calls node *F*, *F* must answer. Otherwise, *A* cannot send any information. Second, suppose nodes *A* and *F* exchange information infrequently. (Did you ever experience long periods of silence during a telephone conversation?) In that case, the connection is underused.

**Message switching** is an alternative to circuit switching. A network uses message switching to establish a route when a message (a unit of information) is sent. For example, suppose node *A* sends the message "Will you go to the movies with me?" to node *F*. Node *A* attaches the location or address of *F* to the message and looks for the first node in the route. As Figure 1.16, shows, node *A* chooses node *C*. As before, the choice depends on cost and the availability of connections. Node *A* sends the message (along with the address of *F*) to *C*. The message is stored there temporarily, while logic looks for another node. It sends the message to node *E*, where it is again stored temporarily. Finally, logic at *E* locates node *F* and sends the message to its final destination.

How are message switching and circuit switching different?

- In message switching, the message is stored temporarily at each node. In circuit switching, the node simply acts as a switching device to route the data. For example, your telephone conversations are not stored at intermediate locations (unless someone is listening and recording your conversation!). The transmission delays resulting from message switching make this connection strategy unsuitable for telephone networks. Delays in voice transmission would make conversations very difficult.

FIGURE 1.16     **Message-Switched Network**

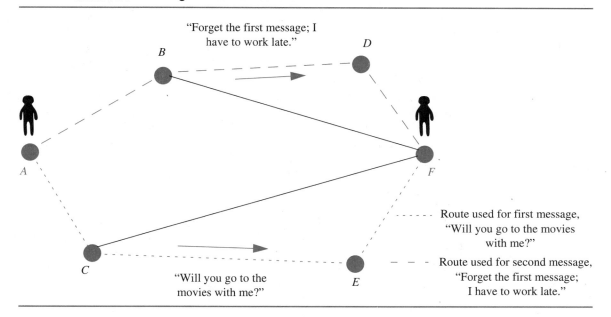

"Forget the first message; I have to work late."

B

D

A

F

C

"Will you go to the movies with me?"

E

- - - - - Route used for first message, "Will you go to the movies with me?"

— — — Route used for second message, "Forget the first message; I have to work late."

- In circuit switching, a single route is dedicated to the exchange of all messages between two routes. In message switching, different messages may travel over different routes. Suppose node *A* wanted to send a second message, "Forget the first message; I have to work late," to node *F*. Since routing is often time dependent, *A* might choose *B* for the first node in the route. The message then goes to nodes *D* and *F*. Different messages thus can share common connections over time, providing a higher utilization.

- Circuit switching requires that both parties be ready when data is sent. Message switching does not. The message may be sent and stored for later retrieval.

The third connection strategy, **packet switching**, minimizes the effects of problems caused by long messages on message switched networks. Long messages may exceed the buffering capacity at a node, or connections between adjacent nodes may be tied up for long periods. A failure in a connection may mean the loss of the entire message. Networks that use this approach are called packet switched networks.

Suppose a user at node *A* wants to send a message to node *F*. If the message is long, it is divided into fixed-size units called packets. Their size is design dependent. Each packet contains its destination address and is routed there by network protocols. When the packets all arrive, they are reassembled. Like message switching, a connection between the two end-points is not maintained. The fixed size of the packets facilitates the necessary buffering at intermediate network nodes.

The two common routing methods in packet switched networks are the **datagram** and the **virtual circuit** . In the **datagram** approach, each packet is transmitted independently. That is, network protocols route each one as though it were a separate message. This allows routing strategies to consider changing conditions within the network. Congestion on certain routes may cause rerouting. (Chapter 7 discusses routing strategies in more detail.)

In the **virtual circuit** approach, network protocols establish a route (virtual circuit) before sending any packets. The delivery of the packets using the same route ensures that the packets arrive in order and without error. The process is similar to circuit switching, with one important difference: The route is not dedicated. That is, different virtual circuits may share a common network connection. Logic at each node must store received packets and schedule them for transmission.

Datagrams have a disadvantage when the message consists of many packets because independent routing represents a lot of overhead. In such cases, a virtual circuit may be more efficient. Another disadvantage of datagrams is that packets may not arrive in the order in which they were sent. Consider the network shown in Figure 1.17. Suppose the user at node *A* wants to send a message consisting of three packets to node *F*. Logic at node *A* decides to route packets $P_1$ and $P_2$ to node *C*. However, as it examines possible routes for $P_3$, it determines that the route through *C* has become congested. Therefore, it sends $P_3$ to node *B*. Packets $P_1$ and $P_2$ then travel to nodes *E* and *F* while packet $P_3$ goes directly from *B* to *F*. Depending on network traffic, *F* could receive the packets in the order $P_1$, $P_3$, $P_2$ and must reassemble them in the correct order.

**FIGURE 1.17    Packet Switched Network**

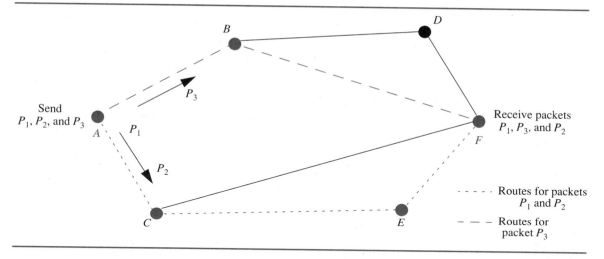

On the other hand, the sensitivity to changing conditions may be an advantage. Routing $P_3$ differently made the packets arrive out of order, but $P_3$ may have arrived much sooner than it would have otherwise. In networks with a lot of traffic, a good route may turn bad quickly if every node begins to send over it—just as a major expressway from the suburbs to the center of a large city is a good route at 5:00 A.M. but very congested at 7:00 A.M.

We will discuss routing strategies and protocols for packet switched network more fully in Chapter 7. For now, Table 1.2 provides a comparison among the three connection strategies we have presented.

## DATA LINK LAYER

While the physical layer sends and receives data, the **data link layer** sits above it and makes sure that it works correctly. For example, what happens if two nodes simultaneously try to transmit data along the same line (**contention**)? How does a node know the data it has received is correct (error detection/correction)? Could electrical interference such as that caused by an electrical storm or voltage fluctuations have changed some bits? If the interference changed a packet's destination, how does a node know it did not receive something it should have?

**Contention** occurs when two or more nodes want to transmit over the same medium at the same time. There are several ways to handle it. Some bus networks use a method called **collision detection**. Collision detection does not prevent multiple nodes from transmitting simultaneously over a common bus. Rather, it is a response to simultaneous transmissions, or **collisions**. Typically, if a device sends something that collides with another transmission, sensing circuits detect the collision, and the device tries to send again later.

TABLE 1.2     **Comparison of Connection Strategies**

| STRATEGY | ADVANTAGES | DISADVANTAGES |
| --- | --- | --- |
| Circuit switching | Speed. It is appropriate when transmission delays are unacceptable. | Since network connections are dedicated, all other routes must avoid them. Both users must be present during communications, such as during a telephone conversation. |
| Message switching | Routes are not dedicated and may be reused immediately after the transmission of a message. The recipient need not accept the message immediately. | Messages generally take longer to reach their destination. Problems also can occur with long messages, as they must be buffered at intermediate nodes. The end of a message travels a route chosen earlier based on conditions that may no longer be true. |
| Packet switching | If congestion develops, the datagram approach to packet switching may choose alternate routes for parts of the message. Thus, network routes are utilized better. | More overhead since each packet is routed separately. Routing decisions must be made for each packet. Packets may arrive out of order in the datagram approach. |

Sometimes a device tries to avoid collisions by listening to the bus activity. If the bus is busy, the device does not transmit. If the circuits detect no activity on the bus, the device goes ahead and transmits. If two devices both sense no activity on the bus and transmit simultaneously, a collision occurs. We call this method of resolving contention **carrier sense multiple access with collision detection (CSMA/CD)**. In effect, it reduces the number of collisions but does not eliminate them. Section 3.4 discusses this approach in detail, and Section 6.2 discusses it as it relates to the ethernet LAN standard.

**Token passing** is another contention scheme that prevents collisions. Here, a unique bit stream, called a **token**, circulates among all network nodes. If a node wants to transmit, it must wait until it receives the token and must append the token to the end of the message. It also changes token control bits to indicate that the token is in use. The message is sent to its destination, and the receiving node now has the token. Depending on the protocol, that station may seize the token and send a message if it has one, or it may send the token to the next node.

Ring networks often use token passing, as shown in Figure 1.18. The token circulates clockwise around the ring. Node *E* currently has the token; therefore, only it can send a message. Because the token is unique, collisions cannot occur. Drawbacks do exist, however: A token may get lost or duplicated or may be hogged by a node. Chapter 6 discusses ways to deal with such events.

Token passing is not limited to rings. It can be used with any network topology by numbering the nodes and circulating the token among them in numerical order. Device numbering is easiest to do in ring or linear networks, however. Section 3.4 discusses token passing and some of its variations, and Sections 6.3 and 6.4 discuss it as it relates to the token ring and token bus LAN standards.

The physical layer sends bit streams across the network. But how does the receiver know whether it has received the correct data? Bad connections, faulty lines, or electrical interference all can affect transmissions. The data link layer executes **error detection/correction** algorithms. With error detection the receiving data link layer determines whether an error has occurred and, if so, typically requests that the information be retransmitted. With error correction the data link layer has the ability to set the damaged bits to their correct value.

Perhaps the simplest detection method uses a **parity bit**, an extra bit attached to each sequence of data bits, or **frame**. For example, an **even parity** makes the total number of 1 bits (including itself) even. That is, if the frame has an odd number of 1 bits, the parity bit is 1. If it has an even number, the parity bit is 0. (There is an analogous definition for **odd parity**.) Consider the frames in Figure 1.19. The first frame has four 1 bits. Therefore, its even parity bit is 0. The second frame has five 1 bits, so its even parity bit is 1. The parity bit is transmitted with the frame and the receiver checks the parity. If it finds an odd number of 1 bits, an error has occurred.

The problem with parity bits is that errors can go undetected. For example, if two bits change during transmission, the number of 1 bits remains even. Thus, parity

FIGURE 1.18    **Token Ring Network**

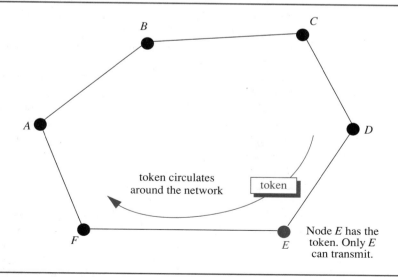

token circulates
around the network

token

Node *E* has the
token. Only *E*
can transmit.

FIGURE 1.19     **Parity Bits**

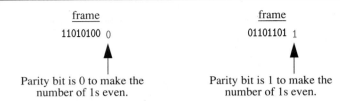

bits can detect single but not double errors. There are other more sophisticated techniques that deal with multiple bit errors. Sections 4.2–4.4 discuss several of them in greater detail.

### NETWORK LAYER

The **network layer** provides the transport layer with the ability to establish end-to-end communications. This ability allows the transport layer to do its tasks without worrying about the details of sending information back and forth between the two stations. It is a lot like making a telephone call without worrying about the details of telephone switching equipment. This process, which often requires communication across multiple intermediate nodes, can be quite difficult. There are several common protocols, but they are too complex to discuss here, and we delay them to later chapters. For example, Section 7.3 discusses packet switched networks and the X.25 protocol, and Section 7.4 discusses the Internet protocol.

The network layer contains algorithms designed to find the best route between two points. We mentioned route determination when we described switching techniques. We indicated that route determination considers factors such as connection costs and availability of lines as it tries to find the quickest and cheapest route to a particular node. For example, Figure 1.20 shows a network containing several routes from $A$ to $F$. Each line connecting two nodes represents the cost, indicated by the numbers on the lines. Going from $A$ to $F$ through $B$ and $D$ results in a total cost of 16. Going through $B$ and $E$ instead results in a cost of only 12. In general, the network layer determines which route is best. There are many different ways to approach routing. Section 7.2 discusses several of them, and Section 6.5 discusses routing as it applies to LAN interconnections. References 7 and 8 also discuss many approaches.

Successful routing is often more difficult than it seems at first. Courses in discrete mathematics and data structures typically cover algorithms designed to find the best or cheapest routes through a graph. They make assumptions that are often not true in real networks, however. They assume that a graph's nodes and the costs of edges connecting them do not change. In dynamic environments both assumptions are often false. New stations and nodes can enter the network regularly and affect both existing routes and their costs. Algorithms must be robust enough to respond to changing conditions.

Even when they do respond, other problems occur. A good route may attract a lot of traffic and overload the computers on it. The resulting congestion often results in

FIGURE 1.20    **Route Costs**

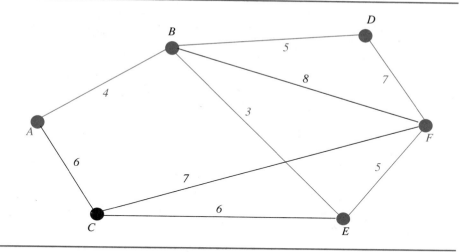

some of the traffic being eliminated. This seems severe, but when a network node has too much information to handle it often has little choice. In this case, the network layer protocol must be able to inform the sender when part of a message is lost.

Other problems can occur when information traveling one route is detoured because changing conditions generated a new best route. The information then may travel that route, only to be detoured again. In an extreme case, information can be detoured continually, causing an endless flow of information throughout the network to bounce from node to node. It is the electronic equivalent of a panhandler looking for a place to call home.

### TRANSPORT LAYER

The **transport layer** represents a transitional layer. The three layers below transport deal primarily with network communications (Figure 1.21). Each node between a sending and a receiving node executes its protocols to ensure the information is being transmitted correctly and efficiently. The transport layer and the three layers above it provide user services. They execute primarily at the sending and receiving nodes to ensure information arrives at the destination and to acknowledge its arrival to the sending node.

One of the transport layer's functions is to provide a reliable and efficient network connection. It allows the three layers above it to perform their tasks independent of a specific network architecture. At the same time, it relies on the lower three layers to control actual network operations. It makes sure information gets from the source to the eventual destination. The major responsibility of this layer is to provide the session layer with a network connection, or **transport connection**. Most important, the transport layer provides reliable and efficient communications. In practice, networks are often unreliable; that is, there is no guarantee that the connections will not fail. What

FIGURE 1.21    End-To-End Connection with Intermediate Nodes

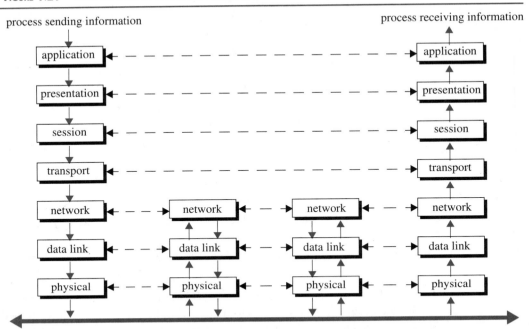

happens if a data packet is lost? What if a packet is significantly delayed? How do these problems affect users? The transport layer insulates the session layer from many details of the network. We discuss the specifics of a common transport protocol, TCP (transmission control protocol), in Chapter 7.

Transport functions include multiplexing, buffering, and connnection management. The transport layer can establish multiple connections (**multiplexing**) to the network. Data is divided and parts of it are sent to separate network nodes, a process called **downward multiplexing** (Figure 1.22). Why transport data this way? Suppose someone wants to transfer a large file. Network connections limit the amount of data that can be sent through a single node. The transport layer, however, can establish connections to multiple nodes and thus increase the overall transmission rate.

In **upward multiplexing** (Figure 1.23), several transport users share a single node. This method applies when a user wants a constant connection to the network, but cannot afford it. The sharing may cause a delay, but it has little effect if network accesses are infrequent.

The transport layer also handles **buffering** at network nodes. An interesting aspect here is that buffering may occur at either the destination or the source node. When a sending transport layer receives data from the session layer for transmission, it divides it into units called **transport protocol data units** (**TPDUs**). The transport protocol sends them to the receiving transport layer (via the lower layers), where they eventually are routed to the receiving session layer.

FIGURE 1.22    **Downward Multiplexing**

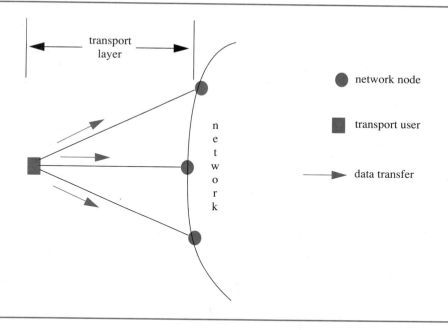

FIGURE 1.23    **Upward Multiplexing**

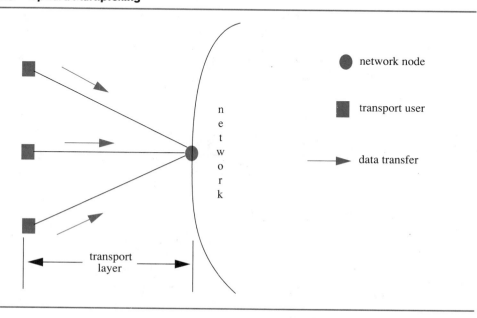

A transport protocol typically requires the acknowledgment of each received TPDU. This is especially useful in packet switching networks where packets may be delayed or even lost due to a network failure. Suppose transport user *A* wants to send several TPDUs to user *B*. In some cases, the TPDUs are buffered at the source and queued for transmission by the lower layers. The transport layer waits for an acknowledgment for each TPDU, but does not remove them from the buffer. If the protocol requires an acknowledgment for each TPDU, the sending transport layer waits for it. If it does not occur within a period of time, the sender retransmits the TPDU which is possible only if it is still in the buffer.

When a receiving transport layer receives a TPDU, it holds the TPDU until the session layer is ready for it. Keep in mind, there is no guarantee the session layer will accept it immediately. If the receiver knows the sender is buffering all TPDUs, it may elect to use a single buffer to save space. The disadvantage of this choice is that the receiver may have no room for subsequent TPDUs until the one being held is delivered to the session layer. In this case the receiver ignores the TPDU, and refuses to acknowledge their reception. The sender receives no acknowledgment and eventually retransmits the TPDUs.

If the network is reliable (that is, errors are few), the TPDUs may instead be buffered at the destination. If the sender knows the receiver is buffering the data, the sender need not do so. It reasons that there is little need to hold on to something once it is sent. After all, the chances of it arriving quickly and safely are high. It's a bit like not keeping a copy of every letter you mail because you are afraid the post office will lose it and you will have to remail it.

**Connection management** is the protocol by which the transport layer establishes and releases connections between two nodes. At first glance, making and releasing connections may seem easy, but it is deceptively tricky. For example, suppose the transport layer is trying to establish a connection between users *A* and *B*. You might think the connection is as simple as (1) user *A* requesting a connection to user *B* and (2) user *B* indicating readiness for a connection, after which (3) a connection occurs. (Figure 1.24). This is a **two-way handshake protocol** for establishing a connection. The problem is that it does not always work because of potential delays in either *A*'s request or *B*'s response.

**FIGURE 1.24    Two-Way Handshake Protocol to Establish a Connection**

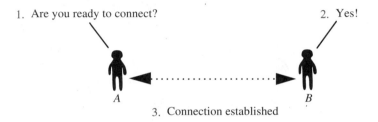

1. Are you ready to connect?          2. Yes!

*A*                                    *B*

3. Connection established

FIGURE 1.25    **Failure of a Two-Way Handshake Protocol**

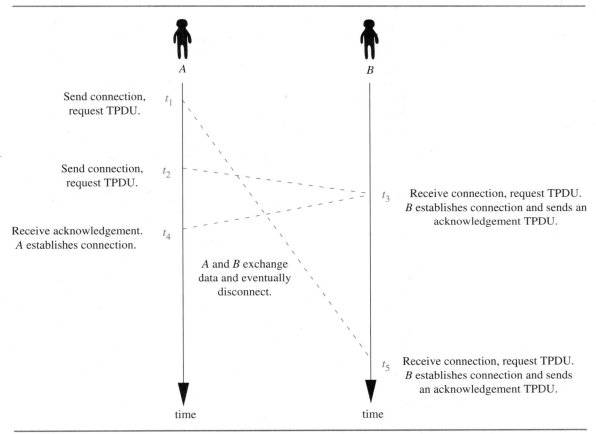

For example, consider the timing shown in Figure 1.25. Note that requests and acknowledgments are made by transmitting special TPDUs. At time $t_1$, user $A$ requests a connection. However, for some reason, perhaps due to network congestion or a problem at an intermediate site, the request is delayed. User $A$, thinking the message is lost, makes another connection request at time $t_2$. User $B$ receives the second request at time $t_3$ and promptly acknowledges it. User $A$ receives the acknowledgment at time $t_4$, and the connection is made. No problem so far.

Users $A$ and $B$ do whatever they are supposed to do and eventually disconnect. However, the first connection request is still floating around somewhere. Suppose it finally arrives at user $B$ at time $t_5$. User $B$ thinks it is another request and acknowledges it. As far as $B$ is concerned there is another connection, but this time it is unintentional. Worse yet, consider what could happen if user $A$ sent a data TPDU during the first connection that was seriously delayed. Not receiving an acknowledgment, user $A$ would have retransmitted it. But the first request is still somewhere in the network. What happens if $B$ finally gets it after time $t_5$? User $B$ thinks it is another TPDU and responds to it. How serious is this problem? Imagine if the connections were private ones to Swiss banks, and the data packets requested deposits of $5 million. Bank officials will not be happy paying interest on a bogus $5-million deposit.

The problem may be solved in two ways. The first is to send a sequence number with every TPDU. It may be based on a counter or clock that increases each time. The second is to use a **three-way handshake protocol**, designed by Tomlinson (Reference 9). It works like this:

- User $A$ transmits a TPDU requesting a connection. Its sequence number is $x$.
- User $B$ transmits a TPDU acknowledging both the request and sequence number. Its sequence number is $y$.
- User $A$ acknowledges the acknowledgment by including sequence numbers $x$ and $y$ in its first data TPDU.

Let's see how this works in a case similar to that of Figure 1.25. Figure 1.26 shows the details. At time $t_1$, user $A$ sends TPDU $x$ requesting a connection. However, as before, the TPDU is delayed. User $A$, receiving no acknowledgment, sends another TPDU at time $t_2$. This is TPDU $y$. User B receives TPDU $y$ at time $t_3$. It acknowledges by sending TPDU $z$, which contains sequence number $y$. User $A$ receives TPDU $z$ at time $t_4$. It acknowledges sequence numbers $y$ and $z$ by including them in its first data TPDU. Everything works so far.

Suppose, as before, users $A$ and $B$ disconnect, and TPDU $x$ arrives at user $B$ at time $t_5$. User $B$ thinks it is another request and acknowledges it by sending TPDU $w$ which contains sequence number $x$. When user $A$ receives this TPDU, it realizes something is wrong because it has not requested a connection. Even if it had requested a second connection, the acknowledged sequence number would not match the one used with the connection request. Either way, $A$ does not acknowledge. Meanwhile, user $B$ is waiting for the acknowledgment. Suppose $B$ subsequently receives a delayed data TPDU from a previous connection. The TPDU will not contain the sequence number $w$ that $B$ sent previously. Consequently, $B$ ignores it and no connection is made.

Terminating connections also can be a problem because of delayed or lost TPDUs. Basically, both parties must agree to disconnect before doing so. A similar three-way handshake protocol is used. In theory, it works as follows:

- User $A$ requests a disconnect.
- User $B$ acknowledges the request.
- User $A$ acknowledges the acknowledgment and disconnects.
- When user $B$ receives the acknowledgment, it disconnects.

As before, problems can occur if a request or acknowledgment is lost. In part, this is handled by having $A$ and $B$ set timers. If either $A$'s request or $B$'s acknowledgment is lost, $A$ will retransmit the request after the timer expires. If $A$'s acknowledg-

FIGURE 1.26    **Three-Way Handshake Protocol**

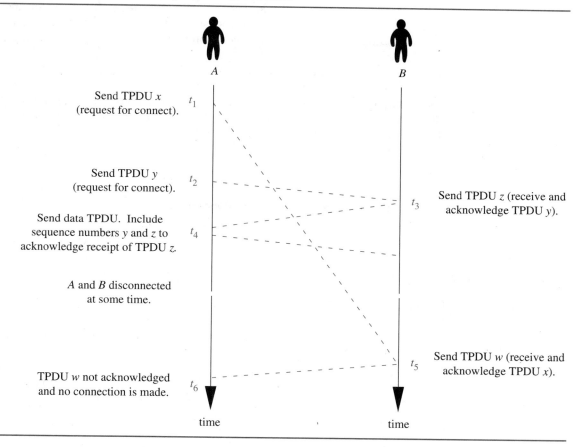

Send TPDU $x$ (request for connect). $t_1$

Send TPDU $y$ (request for connect). $t_2$

$t_3$ Send TPDU $z$ (receive and acknowledge TPDU $y$).

Send data TPDU. Include sequence numbers $y$ and $z$ to acknowledge receipt of TPDU $z$. $t_4$

$A$ and $B$ disconnected at some time.

$t_5$ Send TPDU $w$ (receive and acknowledge TPDU $x$).

TPDU $w$ not acknowledged and no connection is made. $t_6$

time                          time

ment is lost, $B$ will disconnect when its timer expires. We will discuss a specific transport protocol (transmission control protocol, or TCP) in Chapter 7. Reference 7 and 10 give much more attention to transport protocols.

## SESSION LAYER

The next three layers deal primarily with user services and functions. (The previous four layers focused on communications.) The session layer contains the protocols necessary to establish and maintain a connection, or session, between two end-users. The difference between the transport and session layers is often unclear at first. The transport layer provides the session layer with a connection between two nodes, and we just stated that the session provides a connection between users. What is the difference? Figure 1.27 shows an analogy that should help clear up any confusion.

In the figure an executive is asking her secretary to call a customer. The executive is analogous to the session layer and the secretary to the transport layer. Thus, the request in (a) is similar to requesting a session. The executive requests the connection but does not get involved with technical details such as looking up the phone number or dialing it. In (b), the secretary makes the call and thus initiates procedures to establish the transport connection. The process of dialing and initiating the connection is independent of the way the telephone company's switching circuits actually route the call. But again, transport layers don't care about such details. When the call is completed in (c) the transport connection is made. However, the session is not established until the executive finally gets on the phone in (d).

FIGURE 1.27     **Requesting and Establishing a Session Connection**

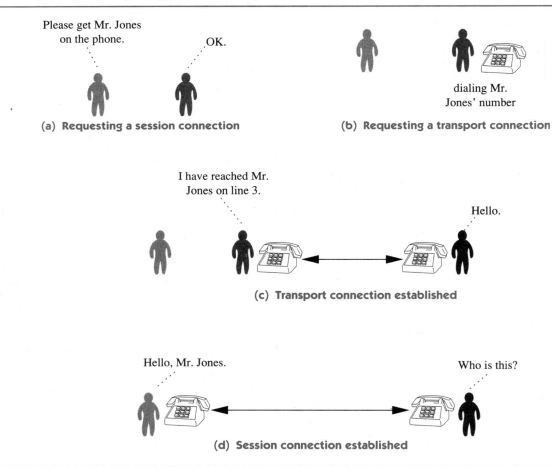

FIGURE 1.28    **Multiple Sessions Using One Transport Connection**

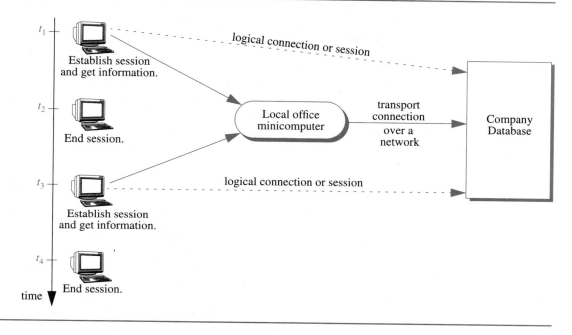

Figure 1.28 shows another example related to computer communications. A large company with offices all over the world has all its essential data and software on a mainframe computer at a central location. Each office (airline reservation systems, major brokerage companies, banks, and so on) has its own front-end processor that communicates with the company's mainframe over a network. Through the processor, regional office employees frequently access the mainframe for short periods. These are the sessions that the session layer provides. Because of the frequent access, the transport layer maintains a single transport connection between the minicomputer and mainframe. Each session uses the same transport connection, a system that is more efficient than negotiating a new connection every time a user wants to access the mainframe.

Don't interpret Figure 1.28 as a form of multiplexing. A transport connection services only one session at a time. A second session can use the transport connection only when the first session is finished.

If the transport connection is disrupted due to a network failure, the session layer can request another transport connection without disrupting the session. This is analogous to the executive in Figure 1.27 being disconnected from her client and then waiting on the telephone while the secretary calls a second time.

Three operations promote orderly communications and allow the session layer to define logical units of information: dialog management, synchronization points, and activities.

**Dialog management:** Most communications are **full duplex**; that is, data transmissions can go in two directions at the same time. In **half-duplex** communications, data can go in either direction, but transmissions must alternate. This is the common personal communication protocol: You normally take turns talking (unless the conversation is between two politicians, neither of whom ever bothers to listen).

If desired, the session layer can manage half-duplex communications. Through the exchange of a data token, it will coordinate conversations (or data exchanges) so that only one user can send at a time. Only the user with the token can send data. When the session layer establishes a session, one user initially gets the token. He or she is the sender, and the other is the receiver. As long as the sender has the token, he or she can send data. If the receiver wants to transmit data, he or she can request the token. The sender decides when to give it up. On acquiring the token, the receiver becomes the sender.

**Synchronization points:** In many cases, a session allows a user to transmit large amounts of data. Some questions you might ask are: What happens if an error occurs after much of the data has been transmitted? Is everything lost? Must I start over from the beginning? The lower layers handle some of the problems of lost packets, but received packets still must percolate up through the OSI layers. What happens if an error occurs there? For example, a file might be transmitted successfully and then lost due to a disk error when the receiving user is writing it. This error has nothing to do with network communication per se, and the lower layers cannot deal with it.

The session layer user can prevent large losses by defining synchronization points within the data stream. They divide the data into distinct **dialog units**. More important, they also define recovery points in case an error occurs. There are two types of synchronization points: **major** and **minor**. Figure 1.29 shows major synchronization points that define separate dialog units.

At each major synchronization point, the receiving session layer must acknowledge that the dialog unit has been received successfully by the intended user. This

**FIGURE 1.29**    **Major Synchronization Points Defining Dialog Units**

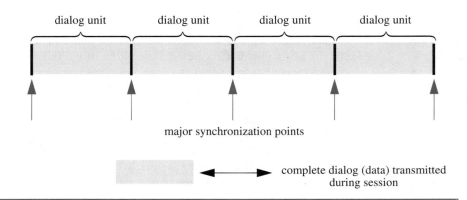

**FIGURE 1.30    Minor Synchronization Points Within a Dialog Unit**

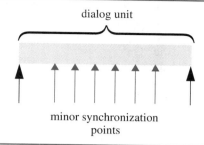

assures the sender that the dialog unit has arrived at where it is finally supposed to be. If an error occurs before acknowledgment, the sender may resynchronize or retransmit data starting from the most recent synchronization point. Retaining copies of the dialog unit is the sender's responsibility. However, once a dialog unit has been acknowledged, the sender may delete it and free the buffer space.

Minor synchronization points are similar to major ones. The sender may refine the dialog unit by inserting them. Figure 1.30 shows the placement of minor synchronization points. The user may resynchronize to a minor synchronization point within the current dialog unit. Minor synchronization points are not acknowledged, which reduces overhead. On the other hand, the sender cannot free the space used to buffer the dialog units. (Can you guess why?)

**Activities**: The user may place another structure on the data by defining a unit of work called an **activity**. Figure 1.31 shows that an activity consists of one or more dialog units. Activities are separate, independent units much like the dialogs and, as with dialog units, must be defined.

One way to think of an activity is as a series of requests that must be processed on an all-or-nothing basis. For example, suppose you work in the catalog order

**FIGURE 1.31    Session Activity**

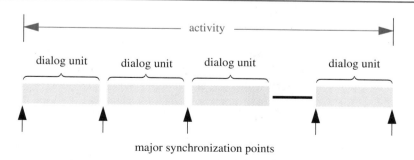

department of a retail store. When a customer calls in an order, the information you enter from a PC is transmitted across a network to the company's main computer. Suppose you have just entered the customer's account number. Since many databases lock records during accesses, the customer's account is now locked. Now suppose the PC stops working, perhaps because someone accidentally unplugs it. When it is running again, you try to resume by accessing the customer's account, but you get a message stating the account is locked. (It is like locking yourself out of the house and leaving your keys inside.)

To avoid such an occurrence, the session layer user can request the **quarantining** of a series of commands or messages transmitted on a network. The receiving session layer puts them all in a buffer before processing any of them. Since the messages are not processed immediately, the scenario just described does not occur. When you enter the account number, the session layer saves it. The customer's account is not accessed and hence not locked.

The sending session layer marks the beginning and end of an activity with special commands. When the receiving session layer detects the start of an activity it buffers all incoming commands until it sees the end of the activity. Then and only then will it pass the commands to the higher layers where they perform the required task.

## PRESENTATION LAYER

Computer networking would be much simpler if all computers spoke the same language. We are not talking here about languages such as Pascal, C, Ada, or COBOL. We refer to the way in which a computer represents the entity we call information.

We must distinguish between information and data, as the difference is important. When we speak of data, we conjure up images of hoards of numbers, hexadecimal dumps, or pages of letters and special symbols. In short, a computer does not store information, it stores data. Information is a meaning we attach to the data. By itself, data is an assortment of bits and bytes and other unmentionable things. Information is a human interpretation of it. A problem exists because different computers have different ways of representing the same information. Thus, it is not enough to define effective data communications. We must define effective communication of information. The **presentation layer** does this.

For example, consider a network that transmits data between two computers (Figure 1.32). One stores information using ASCII and the other uses EBCDIC, which represent two different ways of storing data (Chapter 2 discusses ASCII and EBCDIC further). When the ASCII-based computer says "Hello", the network transmits the ASCII message. The EBCDIC-based computer receives and stores the data. Unfortunately, anyone interpreting it will see it as "   <<!" because of the different interpretation placed on the bits received.

What we really want is communication of information as shown in Figure 1.33. The ASCII version of "HELLO" is transmitted. Because the receiver uses EBCDIC, the data must be converted. In this case, the hex characters '48 45 4C 4C 4F' are transmitted, but 'C8 C5 D3 D3 D6' are received. The two computers have not

FIGURE 1.32    Data Exchange Between Two Computers

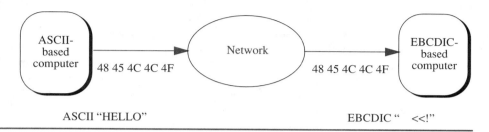

FIGURE 1.33    Information Exchange Between Two Computers

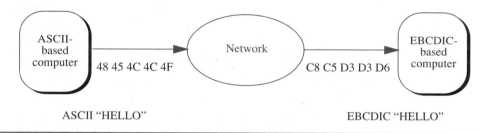

exchanged data; instead, and more important, they have exchanged information in the form of the word "HELLO".

The problem involves more than just code conversion. We also may have problems transmitting numbers. For example, computers may store integers using either a two's complement or a one's complement format. The difference is minor, but it must be considered. In addition, the number of bits used to represent an integer varies. Common formats use 16, 32, 64, or 80 bits. Bits must be added or removed to allow for the different sizes. Sometimes a translation is impossible. For example, the maximum integer in a 16-bit format is 32,767. What happens if a computer that uses 32-bit integers tries to transfer 50,000 to a computer limited to 16-bit integers?

Floating point numbers also present problems. Figure 1.34 shows a common format, although many variations exist. The number of bits used for the mantissa and

FIGURE 1.34    Generic Format for Floating Point Numbers

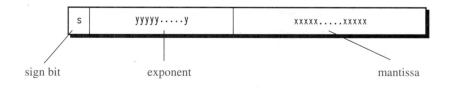

exponent vary. The number of bits may even vary within a machine, since numbers may be either single or double precision. The exponent may also be interpreted in different ways. Sometimes it is a power of 2; in other cases, it is a power of 16. Sometimes the mantissa is not stored in contiguous bits. When one considers the range of differences, it is amazing that computers can share numeric information at all.

The problem increases with more sophisticated data structures such as arrays, records, and linked lists. The presentation layer must consider how the fields of a record are stored. For example, does each one begin on a word boundary or a byte boundary? Where are link fields stored? How many bytes do they occupy? Is a multidimensional array stored by row or by column?

The presentation layer must know the system it serves. It must also know the format of data it receives from other sources. It must ensure the proper transfer of information throughout the network.

Another function of the presentation layer is **data compression**.[*] It is a way to reduce the number of bits while retaining their meaning. If transmission is expensive, compression can lower costs significantly and increase the amount of information that can be sent per unit of time. For example, suppose the data in a large file consists entirely of strings of capital letters. For example, it might be a list of keywords or employees' last names. How many data bits must be transferred? If the characters are EBCDIC, the number is $8*n$, where $n$ is the number of characters. If the presentation layer redefined the code assigning 0 to A, 1 to B, and so on up to 25 to Z, each character of the alphabet can be represented using 5 bits (the fewest number of bits required to store numbers up to 25). Thus, about 38% fewer bits are actually sent. There are many other ways to do data compression, and Section 3.5 discusses them in more detail.

Security is another reason to change the bits (or encrypt them) before sending them. If an unauthorized person intercepts the transmitted message, its encrypted form makes the message unintelligible. To understand its meaning, the data must be decrypted. Chapter 4 deals with the important issue of encryption in detail.

## Application Layer

The **application layer**, the highest layer in the OSI model, communicates with the user and the application programs. It is called the application layer because it contains network applications, which differ from user applications such as payroll or accounting programs, graphic design packages, language translators, or database programs. Typical network applications include electronic mail, file transfer, and virtual terminal protocols (all discussed in Chapter 8) and distributed systems.

Most colleges and major organizations are connected to worldwide networks that allow the exchange of personal or professional messages—**electronic mail**. As

---

[*]The most effective data compression can be done at this level because the most knowledge of the data and its usage is available. However, compression often is done at lower levels instead of or in addition to this level.

an example, many of the comments the author and editor exchanged during production of this book were done by email. The lower layers of the model provide the means of expressing the message and getting it to its destination. The email protocol in the application layer defines the architecture of an electronic mail system. It stores mail in a mailbox (really a file) from which users can organize and read their messages and provide responses.

A **file transfer protocol** also allows users to exchange information, but in a different way. It typically allows a user to connect to a remote system, examine some of its directories and files, and copy them to the user's system. To the user it is almost that simple, except for a few problems. One is file structure. Some files consist of a simple sequence of bytes; others are flat files consisting of a linear sequence of records. Hashed files allow random access to a record through a key field value. Hierarchical files[*] may organize all occurrences of a key field in a tree structure. These differences pose a problem when transferring files.

A **virtual terminal protocol** allows a user at a terminal to connect to a remote computer across a computer network. Once connected, the user interacts as though the computer were on-site. Allowing access to different computers from different terminals presents problems because of the variety of equipment and software. One problem is that software often is written with specific equipment in mind. Full screen text editors are examples. The editor displays text on a screen and allows the user to move the cursor and make changes. The displayed number of rows and columns, however, varies from one terminal to another. Commands to move the cursor, delete, and insert text require control sequences that also vary by terminal. Perhaps you have noticed that different terminals have different keyboards. Other examples include software that depends on screen formats for input. Often layouts provide a simple uncluttered view of a user's options. Spacing, tabs, and highlighting help the user work with the software. Again, such features are terminal dependent.

**Distributed systems** are another growing application of computer networks. A distributed system allows many devices to run the same software and to access common resources. Example resources include workstations, file servers, mainframes, and printers (Figure 1.35). In a true distributed system, a user logs on and has no knowledge of the underlying structure. The user requests a particular resource and gets it without knowing or caring where it came from or on what kind of workstation he or she is using to get it. The distributed system hides the details.

Distributed systems present many challenges. Suppose a user requests a file by name. A problem is that different systems use different rules for naming files. How can we make these rules transparent to the user and still adhere to what a particular computer requires? Often the files exist on different computers. How does the distributed system know where to look for a requested file? Since different computers are used, how does the distributed system handle the problem of duplicate file

---

[*] Be sure to distinguish between a file's structure and its implementation. For example, a file may be hierarchical, but there are many implementations of a hierarchical structure.

FIGURE 1.35    **Distributed System**

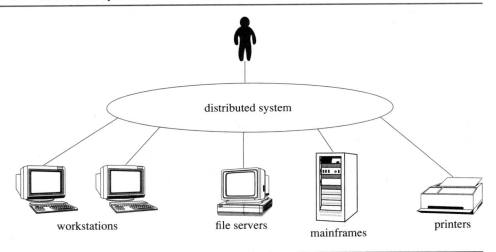

names? The problems of a true distributed system are many, and references 11, 12, 13, 14, 15, and 16 address some of them.

## SUMMARY

This section has described each of the seven layers of the OSI protocol model. Each layer defines communication protocols of computer networks and insulates the layer above from the details of the one below. Together, they insulate the user from bit-level details of data communications. If fully implemented, they also allow communication between incompatible devices.

The lowest three layers deal primarily with network communications. The physical layer sends and receives bit streams without regard to meaning. It does not know what the data means or even if it is correct. The physical layer also contains connection strategies. Circuit switching creates and maintains dedicated lines between nodes. Message switching routes messages through the network. There are no dedicated lines connecting nodes. Packet switching divides a message into packets for independent routing.

The data link layer provides error detection for the physical layer. Error detection techniques include parity bits and other detection or correction codes. Some can detect single-bit errors only; others can detect when noise destroys many bits. The data link layer also contains contention strategies. Collision detection allows simultaneous transmission by multiple devices, but detects any resulting collision. Each device then waits a random amount of time before retransmitting. With token passing, a token moves among the network nodes. A node can transmit only when it has the token.

The highest of the bottom three layers is the network layer. It contains routing strategies. Algorithms can determine the cheapest route between two nodes and each node knows its successor on a route. But because the cheapest route may vary with time as network conditions change, adaptive routing strategies may be used to detect changes in the network and alter routes accordingly.

The top four layers service the user. The lowest one is the transport layer. It provides buffering, multiplexing, and connection management. Connection management ensures that delayed messages do not compromise requests to establish or release connections.

The session layer manages dialogs between users. In half-duplex communication, the session layer keeps track of who can speak and who must listen. It also allows the definition of synchronization points that protect against a failure at a higher layer. Data between major synchronization points must be buffered to permit recovery. This layer also allows the quarantining of requests when a sequence of requests must be processed on an all-or-nothing basis.

The presentation layer accounts for differences in data representation. It allows two systems to exchange information even though they may have different ways of storing it. It can also compress data to decrease the number of transmitted bits. One technique is a Huffman code that assigns short bit patterns to frequently used characters, and longer ones to the less frequently used characters. The presentation layer also implements encryption and decryption.

The last and highest layer is the application layer, which contains user services such as electronic mail, file transfer software, and virtual terminals. It communicates directly with the user or application program.

## 1.5    The Future of Data Communications

We have invested time discussing the history of communications and current technologies and models. The next logical question is: Where do we go from here? In other words, what can we expect to see in the future? Exotic and fantastic predictions are being made, but they probably are no more fantastic than today's realities appeared to people a few decades ago. To them, the concept of spacecraft circling the earth transmitting television pictures and telephone conversations was science fiction. The prospect that light could be used to transmit picture and sound was fantasy. Certainly the very idea that computers could actually "talk" to each other was absurd and maybe a little scary to people who saw too many movies about computers taking control of the world.

The fact is that much of what we will see in the future already exists. It's just that many products that are technologically feasible are not always economically feasible on a large scale. So we return to the question: What can we look forward to? Here are some possibilities.

- **Electronic telephone directories**: The telephone will be replaced by a communications terminal. France already has done so, as have a few test cities in the United States. One of the terminal's functions will be the same as the telephone. Another function will allow callers to access telephone databases. They will enter someone's name and address, and the terminal will display the phone number for that person. Callers also will be able to enter a product or service and get a list of businesses that provide it—electronic yellow pages.

The terminal also will transmit and receive video images. The main obstacle to this technology has been the tremendous amount of information transmitting a quality image requires. With the increasing capacities of optical fibers and satellites, we now have the ability to do this. Bringing it into everyone's home, however, is not yet economically feasible.

- **Portable telephones**: Bring your telephone with you wherever you go. This idea is not futuristic, as cellular telephones are already quite common. Many people use them for business or status reasons, and an increasing number of people are finding other good reasons to have them. Imagine having your car break down at 2:00 A.M. on a deserted highway 10 miles from the nearest telephone booth. Eventually, telephone booths may be seen only in the Smithsonian. With portable telephones will come portable fax machines. If you are late for a business meeting because you are stuck in rush-hour traffic, you will be able to fax your notes or sales charts to your office from your car.

- **Electronic mail**: Wide area networks already allow electronic mail (email) to be exchanged worldwide. But again, this technology is used primarily by companies, government agencies, and universities. Most people at home cannot use it unless they have a modem or some other means to communicate with a computer that is connected to a wide area network. It is not economically feasible, and many people probably don't care to use it or do not want to change lifelong habits of writing letters by hand. To them, sending greeting cards, anniversary cards, or sympathy cards electronically would not carry the same emotional content as a Hallmark card. On the other hand, information services such as Prodigy, CompuServe, MCI-Mail, and others are attracting a growing number of subscribers.

- **All-digital telephone system**: This is a little tough to describe without getting into the differences between analog and digital signals, as Chapter 2 does. For now, just think of it as communicating using the same signal types a computer uses. Most people do not care whether their phone calls are carried by an analog or digital signal. If someone calls and tells me I won the lottery, I am certainly not going to ask whether the phone call is analog or digital. All-digital systems will have definite impacts, however. For example, digital signals can carry information to the destination telephone. As your telephone rings, the telephone number of the caller is displayed on a communications terminal. You can use this information to decide whether or not to answer the telephone. A professional such as a doctor, lawyer, or broker might use software to key the incoming telephone number to a client or patient database, which would be displayed before the phone is answered. The 911 emergency system can quickly display the number of an incoherent person or small child.[*] Displaying the caller's number also would reduce the number of obscene phone calls.

---

[*] Emergency systems already have the ability to determine the source of incoming calls, but an all-digital system would improve the process.

One drawback to this system is lack of privacy. Many people have unlisted phone numbers and should not have their numbers displayed whenever they make a call. The system will need to determine when a number should be displayed. All-digital systems do exist and standards are being developed for an eventual worldwide digital communication system. This standard, the integrated services digital network (ISDN), is discussed in Chapter 8.

- **Electronic media access**: Currently we have to go to our favorite video store to rent a tape or to the library to borrow a book or look something up in an encyclopedia. Someday your television can be a two-way communications device. You will be able to use it to access a library of movies, specials, or documentaries and view them at your convenience. Similarly, you will be able to access books electronically from a library. Electronic access probably will not replace the practice of settling down at night with a good book, but it will be useful to those who want factual information such as that found in an encyclopedia or government document.

- **Videoconferencing**: Every day millions of people spend part (often too much) of their day in meetings. Sometimes they must travel long distances at significant cost to attend meetings. Videoconferencing allows people in different locations to see and hear each other in a real-time setting. They are able to converse and display charts as if they were all in the same room. Until recently, videoconferencing has not been economical because of the enormous amount of information multiple video images require. However, advances in desktop video technology, high resolution graphics, PC applications, and new standards (Reference 17) have changed the field. Once considered a luxury for only the largest corporations, videoconferencing is now accessible to a wide variety of businesses (Reference 18 and 19). Some people predict that full-motion video will someday be available at the desktop of any network user (Reference 20), although such a development certainly would necessitate significant changes in LANs and networks in general.

- **Three-dimensional imaging**: Video images are two dimensional. The old "3-D" movies were accomplished by showing two different images of the same thing and then giving viewers special glasses. Each lens filtered out one of the images so that each eye received a slightly different image. The brain interpreted these signals differently, giving the perspective of what we call distance. Someday your television may be replaced by a holographic box in which real three-dimensional images are displayed. This development probably will not occur in the near future. Consider how long it has taken for high-definition television (HDTV) to get off the ground. It will be even longer before people embrace the technology to the point where they will scrap their old televisions and buy new ones.

But why stop at images? People weren't content to stop at voice transmissions. They had to figure out a way to send two-dimensional video images, then three-dimensional images. What about transmitting actual objects or, in the extreme case, people? Sound like science fiction? Of course it is, as anyone who has ever watched "Star Trek" knows. But so were all these other technologies at one time. Transmitting physical objects would be the ultimate in data communication.

- **Electronic locators**: Another seemingly sci-fi device allows people to wear a badge that tells a central computer their exact location. Similar devices are used today. For example, some trucking firms have installed transmitters in all of their trucks. The transmitter sends signals to a satellite, which forwards them to a company's computer and allows dispatchers to determine the truck's location. The accuracy of these systems can place a truck within a couple of miles anywhere in the country.

  Some people believe that similar devices eventually will be installed in automobiles. The car could have a small video display showing a state road map. Using the satellite tracking system, it could also display a blinking "you are here" mark showing the current location of your car. Such a system would be useful for someone lost on a lonely country road. Similar systems might be even more useful as part of a boat's navigation system on open waters.

- **Voice communications**: Currently, most data communication originates with computer devices such as terminals, scanners, display screens, or disk drives. Sophisticated processors now can be taught to recognize speech patterns. This would be of great service to physically impaired people, who could control a wheelchair or a robot arm by talking to it. A similar device already allows an individual to program a VCR using voice commands.

- **Mind communications**: Can a computer read a person's mind? Before you scoff at the question, remember that each person produces a brain-wave pattern that is unique and detectable by an electroencephalograph. This author once saw a documentary in which a test person was connected to such a device while watching the projected image of a ball being moved up, down, left, and right while brain-wave patterns were recorded for later reference. Next, the person looked at the ball projected on the screen and attempted to move it himself by "thinking" one of the four directions. The brain-wave patterns generated by this exercise were compared with those stored, and commands were given by a computer to move the projected ball image in the correct direction. It worked! Can a computer read a person's mind? You be the judge.

Communications technologies will present many challenges. Perhaps the most significant ones relate to privacy and security. The tremendous amounts of information traveling through the air will invite unscrupulous people to attempt illegal reception and transmissions. How do you prevent people from getting things they should not see or have not paid for? How can you prevent people from disrupting a television network transmission and sending their own messages? These are not hypothetical situations; they have happened.

What about different governmental policies on the transmission and exchange of information? We cannot set up checkpoints at national borders to restrict or filter information. Should we restrict and filter information? If so, who defines the policies on what information is appropriate? How do we distinguish that from censorship?

The challenges are many, and we must be prepared to meet them. First, we must understand them and the technology that creates them. It is time to begin.

# Review Questions

1.  What is the difference between contention and collision?

2.  Name five standards-making agencies and at least one standard for which each is responsible.

3.  What is a switchboard?

4.  List five communications applications and how they might be used.

5.  What is an open system?

6.  List five ways to organize a local area network.

7.  What is a de facto standard? Give an example of one.

8.  What is meant by a layered protocol? Why are protocols layered?

9.  Match the functions in the table with the OSI layer that performs them.

| OSI LAYER | FUNCTION |
| --- | --- |
| Physical | activity definition |
| Data link | bracketing |
| Network | buffering |
| Transport | contention |
| Session | data compression |
| Presentation | definition of a signal's electrical characteristics |
| Application | dialog management |
| | electronic mail |
| | encryption/decryption |
| | error detection |
| | establishing and releasing a connection |
| | file transfers |
| | format conversion |
| | multiplexing |
| | quarantining |
| | remote job entry |
| | routing |
| | switching |
| | synchronization |
| | token passing |

10.  Distinguish between even and odd parity.

11.  Distinguish between message and packet switching.

12.  What are the major differences between a two-way handshake and a three-way handshake protocol?

13. Are the following statements TRUE or FALSE? Why?

   a. The first computer was developed to aid in establishing communications systems.

   b. Telstar was a satellite designed to transmit television and telephone signals across the Atlantic Ocean.

   c. An open system is one that allows free access to a variety of computing and information services.

   d. A computer network can connect many types of storage devices even if they store information in different formats.

   e. Two pairs of devices can communicate simultaneously along a common bus if each pair is at opposite ends of the bus.

   f. A fully connected LAN topology is most common because it allows direct transfer of information between any two devices.

   g. Standards eliminate the inconsistencies between computing devices.

   h. The seven-layer OSI model would, if fully implemented, allow any two computing devices to communicate as long as there is a way to physically transfer the information between them.

   i. Layered protocols allow lower layers to be implemented independent of the higher layers and vice versa.

   j. Datagrams are better than virtual circuits at dealing with congestion in networks.

   k. Establishment of an OSI transport requires only that one side make the connection request and the other side acknowledge it.

14. Which network topologies allow token passing?

15. Which of the OSI model layers deal primarily with network operations?

16. Distinguish between upward and downward multiplexing.

17. Discuss the merits and drawbacks of having a caller's telephone number displayed on a viewing screen whenever the telephone rings.

18. What is the difference between the communication of data and the communication of information?

# Exercises

1. Make a sketch outlining the LAN topology at your school or place of business.

2. Which of the applications listed in Section 1.1 have you used? Why have you used them?

3. What types of devices are connected to the LAN at your school or place of business? Are they likely to be found in other LANs? Why or why not?

4. Suppose a bidirectional token ring network connects eight devices numbered 1 through 8 in clockwise order. What device failures would prevent device #1 from sending messages to device #4?

5. Suppose the network in the previous exercise had $n$ devices. Is it possible for two devices to fail and for all the remaining devices to still be able to communicate? If so, under what conditions can this situation occur?

6. In Figure 1.20, list four routes through which A can communicate with F. How many are there all together (assume a route does not pass through a node more than once)?

7. Consider the following frames

```
011010001010001 x
100111000101101 x
100001100011000 x
```

Suppose x is the parity bit. What must x be to establish even parity? Odd parity?

8. Argue that if exactly two bits are altered during a transmission, simple parity checking will not detect the error.

9. In general, when will simple parity checking detect an error? When will errors go undetected?

10. What is the reason for using sequence numbers in the three-way handshake protocol?

11. Give examples of videoconferencing that your school or place of business has used.

12. What aspect of data communication will have the most significant impact on your personal or professional life?

13. Section 1.5 described an example in which a person gave a computer commands to move an image of a ball simply by thinking up, down, left, or right. One can argue correctly that this is a long way from reading a person's mind. How would you respond to that argument?

14. How many direct connections would there be in a fully connected topology containing $n$ nodes?

## REFERENCES

1. Silver, G. A. and M. L. Silver. *Data Communications for Business,* 2nd ed. Boston: Boyd & Fraser, 1991.

2. Fitzgerald, J. *Business Data Communications: Basic Concepts, Security, and Design,* 3rd ed. New York: Wiley, 1990.

3. Rowe, S. H. *Business Telecommunications,* 2nd ed. New York: Macmillan, 1991.

4. Stallings. W. *Business Data Communications,* New York: Macmillan, 1990.

5. Sherman, K. *Data Communications: A User's Guide,* 3rd ed. Englewood Cliffs, NJ: Prentice-Hall, 1990.

6. Quarterman, J. S. *The Matrix: Computer Networks and Conferencing Systems Worldwide.* Bedford, MA: Digital Press, 1990.

7. Tanenbaum, A. S. *Computer Networks,* 2nd ed. Englewood Cliffs, NJ: Prentice-Hall, 1988.

8. Spragins, J. D., J. L. Hammond, and K. Pawlikowski, *Telecommunications Protocols and Design* , Reading MA: Addison Wesley, 1991.

9. Tomlinson, R. S. "Selecting Sequence Numbers." *Proceedings of the ACM SIGCOMM/SIGOPS Interprocess Communications Workshop* (1975), 11–23.

10. Stallings, W. *Data and Computer Communications,* 4th ed. New York: Macmillan, 1994.

11. Coulouris, G. F. and J. Dollimore. *Distributed Systems: Concepts and Design.* Reading, MA: Addison-Wesley, 1988.

12. Satyanarayanan, M. "Scalable, Secure, and Highly Available Distributed File Access." *Computer,* vol. 23, no. 5 (May 1990), 9–22.

13. Champine, G., D. Geer, and W. Ruh. "Project Athena as a Distributed Computer System." *Computer,* vol. 23, no. 9 (September 1990), 40–51.

14. Tanenbaum, A. S. et al. "Experiences with the Amoeba Distributed Operating System." *Communications of the ACM,* no. 12. (December 1990), 46–63.

15. Levy, E. and A. Silberschatz. "Distributed File Systems: Concepts and Examples." *Computing Surveys,* vol. 22, no. 4 (December 1990), 321–74.

16. Cheriton, D. "The V Distributed System." *Communications of the ACM,* no. 3 (March 1988), 314–33.

17. Richardson, S.,"Videoconferencing: The Bigger (and Better) Picture." *Data Communications,* vol. 21, no. 9 (June 1992), 103–11.

18. Johnson, J. T. "Videoconferencing: Not Just Talking Heads." *Data Communications,* vol. 20, no. 15 (November 1991), 66–8.

19. Johnson, J. T. "A New Look for Videoconferencing Services." *Data Communications,* vol. 22, no. 8 (May 1993), 67–72.

20. Tobagi, F. A. "Multimedia: The Challenge Behind the Vision." *Data Communications,* vol. 22, no. 2. (January 1993), 61–6.

# CHAPTER 2

## TRANSMISSION FUNDAMENTALS

This chapter covers the basics of communication. It begins with discussions of the various media used to transmit data and then addresses the issue of why there are different ways to transmit data. In other words, what are their advantages and disadvantages?

Many factors help determine the best way to connect communication devices:

- Cost of a connection
- Amount of information that can be transmitted per unit of time
- Immunity to outside interference
- Susceptibility to unauthorized "listening"
- Logistics (how you connect a printer to a mainframe differs depending on whether the printer is on a different floor in the same building or in a different building across a 12-lane highway)

Once devices are connected, you might think the hardest part is done and the devices can easily communicate. Unfortunately, this is not correct. One major problem is in the way information is presented. For example, two people stand face to face talking to each other. If they speak the same language, communication usually (but not always!) occurs. If they speak different languages and neither understands the other's language, communication usually does not occur. Different computers may not represent data the same way. The resulting problems must be dealt with by communications protocols. Section 2.2 discusses some of the standard ways to represent data. Even if two devices represent data the same way, problems still may occur. We must consider the way in which data are transmitted. For example, computers transmit data using **digital signals**, sequences of specified voltage levels. Graphically they are often represented as a square wave (Figure 2.1a). In this figure the horizontal axis represents time and the vertical axis represents the voltage level. The alternating high and low voltage levels constitute the sequence over a period of time.

FIGURE 2.1    **Analog and Digital Signals**

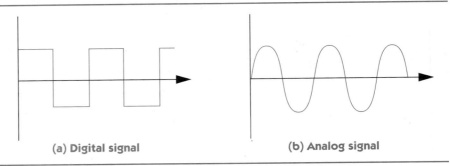

(a) Digital signal            (b) Analog signal

Computers sometimes communicate over telephone lines using **analog signals**, which are formed by continuously varying voltage levels. They are most often represented by their characteristic sine wave (Figure 2.1b). Now we have another problem: Digital and analog signals transmit data in different ways. As a result, if a computer is going to communicate over an analog phone line, we need to find a way to convert signals of one type to signals of another and back again.

Section 2.4 discusses analog and digital signals. It presents their limitations and reports on two famous results that specify limits on the amount of data that can be transmitted per unit of time. Section 2.5 describes modulation and demodulation techniques. Finally, Section 2.6 covers modems, common devices used for modulation and demodulation. It also covers intelligent modems and standards.

## 2.1    Communications Media

There are three types of transmission media, each with many variations. The first is a conductive metal such as copper or iron. We will show how an electric current traveling along a wire can be used to transmit data. The second medium is a transparent glass or plastic strand that transmits data using light waves. The third requires no physical connection at all and relies on electromagnetic waves such as those found in noncable television and radio broadcasts.

One factor to consider in a discussion of communications media is cost. For example, wires, cables, and strands all have different manufacturing costs. In addition, devices to which they attach have various costs.

Another factor to consider is the amount of data each communications medium can transmit per unit of time. Two measures are important: **data rate** and **bandwidth**. The **data rate** is a measure of the number of bits that can be transmitted per unit of time. The typical unit of measure is bits per second (bps). Depending on the medium and the application, data rates commonly range from a few hundred bps to billions of bps.

Before defining bandwidth, let us take a closer look at what a signal is. Many analog signals, for example, exhibit the sine wave pattern of Figure 2.2. It is an example of a **periodic signal**, which means it repeats a pattern or cycle continuously. The **period** of a signal is the time required for it to complete 1 cycle. The signal in Figure 2.2 has a period of *p*. A signal's **frequency**, *f*, is the number of cycles through which the signal can oscillate in a second. The unit of measurement is cycles per second or **Hertz (Hz)**. For example, suppose *p* from Figure 2.2 was 0.5 microsecond (μsec). Since 0.5 μsec is the same as $0.5*10^{-6}$ second, the signal's frequency is $1/(.5*10^{-6})$ or 2,000,000 Hz. The frequency and period are related by

$$f = \frac{1}{p}.$$

A given transmission medium can accommodate signals within a given frequency range. The **bandwidth** is equal to the difference between the highest and lowest frequencies that may be transmitted. For example, a telephone signal can handle frequencies between 300 Hz and 3300 Hz, giving it a bandwidth of 3000 Hz. In terms of audible sounds, this means that very high or low pitched sound cannot pass through the telephone system. Most human speech falls within this range and consequently is easily recognizable. The loss of high- and low-frequency sounds, however, will cause a problem for someone wanting to listen to and appreciate the New York Philharmonic over the telephone.

Sometimes the term bandwidth is used when referring to the amount of data that can be transmitted. Technically, bandwidth and data rates are different, but there is an important relationship between them. This complex relationship will be explored in more detail in Section 2.4.

To transmit data between two devices there must be a way for a signal to travel between them. Typically, this requires either a physical connection or the ability to use electromagnetic waves such as those used by radio and television. This section discusses several ways to make physical connections: twisted wire pair, coaxial cable, and optical fiber. It also discusses "wireless communications" using microwave and satellite transmission.

**FIGURE 2.2    Periodic Signal**

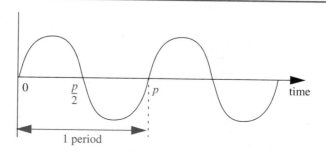

## CONDUCTIVE METAL

**Twisted Pair**    One of the oldest transmission media is conducting metal which was used to transmit information as early as 1837, when Samuel Morse invented the telegraph. Basically, it is a circuit consisting of a power source, a switch, and a sensor (Figure 2.3). The switch, at location *A*, can be opened or closed manually, thus controlling whether current flows. A sensor, at location *B*, detects current and creates the clicking sound with which you are probably familiar from TV and movie Westerns. Figure 2.3 shows a telegraph system allowing transmission in just one direction. Other designs exist that allow transmissions in both directions (Reference 1). Opening and closing the switch in different patterns controls the frequency and duration of signals sent to location B. The familiar Morse code, which we present in Section 2.2, associates data with different signal patterns.

Copper wire probably is the most common way to connect devices. Copper is used because of its electrical conductive properties. That is, electricity flows through copper with less resistance than many other materials. In addition, copper is more resistant to corrosion than other conducting metals such as iron, a property that makes it a good choice in places where it is exposed to moisture or humidity.

One of the most common uses of copper is in the **twisted pair** in which two insulated copper wires are twisted around each other. The insulation prevents the copper in each wire from making contact and thus short-circuiting the circuit. Since straight copper wires tend to act as antennas and pick up extraneous signals, the twisting helps reduce the amount of outside interference. It also reduces the interference the wires would otherwise have on each other.

Twisted pairs often are bundled together and wrapped in a protective coating. Each pair has a different twist length, reducing the interference between them (crosstalk). The protective coating allows the bundled cable to be buried. For a long time, this medium was the primary mode of telephone communications and is still common in connecting a home telephone to a nearby telephone exchange. It is also common in connecting low-speed devices such as computer terminals to a high-speed network.

FIGURE 2.3     **One-Way Telegraph System**

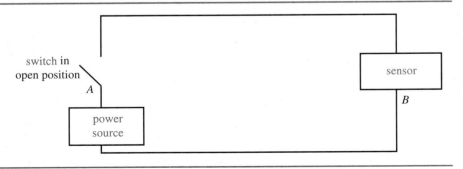

FIGURE 2.4     **Two Points Connected Using a Repeater**

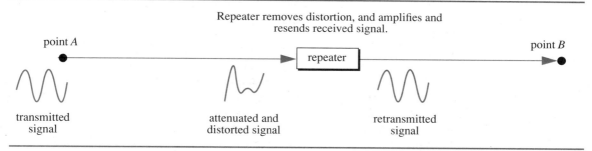

Even though copper is a good conductor, electrical resistance still occurs, and a signal transmitted over a copper wire may eventually distort and lose strength (attenuates). In practice, this means there is a limit on the twisted pair's length before the transmitted signal becomes distorted beyond recognition.

If the wire must connect two points separated by a long distance, a repeater must be inserted between the two points (Figure 2.4). A repeater is a device that intercepts a transmitted signal before it has distorted and attenuated too badly and then amplifies the signal and retransmits it. With repeaters, there is no limit on how far a signal can be transmitted.

A twisted pair has a bandwidth of up to 250 kHz (1 kHz = 1000 Hz) for analog signals. Digital signal data rates vary with distance. For example, a twisted pair can achieve a 10 Mbps (1 Mbps = 1,000,000 bps) data rate, but only for distances of about 300 feet. It can maintain a 2400 bps rate for up to 10 miles.

**Coaxial Cable**     Another common medium is **coaxial cable** (Figure 2.5), consisting of four components. First is the innermost conductor, a copper or aluminum

FIGURE 2.5     **Coaxial Cable**

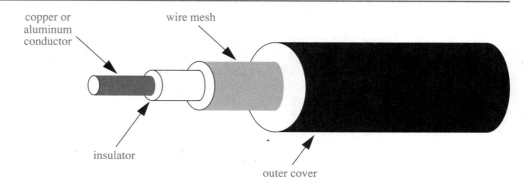

wire core. As with the twisted pair, the core carries the signal. An insulation layer surrounds the core and prevents the conductor from making contact with the third layer, typically a tightly wound wire mesh.* The wire mesh acts as a shield, protecting the core from electromagnetic interference. It also protects the core from hungry rodents looking for a free meal. The last layer is what you see on the cables connecting your VCR to your television set, a plastic protective cover.

The wire mesh shield provides excellent protection from extraneous electrical signals. Consequently, coaxial cable has a bandwidth of about 500 MHz (1 MHz = 1,000,000 Hz) and can achieve data rates of up to 500 Mbps.† However, because the primary mode of transmission is still an electrical signal through a metal conductor, the repeater spacing is about the same as with twisted pair. Also, coaxial cable is more expensive than twisted pair.

Coaxial cable typically transmits information in either a **baseband mode** or a **broadband mode**. In baseband mode, the cable's bandwidth is devoted to a single stream of data. Thus, the high bandwidth capability allows high data rates over a cable. This is typical in local area networks where only one data stream is present at any time. With broadband, the bandwidth is divided into ranges. Each range typically carries separate coded information, which allows the transmission of multiple data streams over the same cable simultaneously. Special equipment is used to combine the signals at the source and separate them at the end. Cable television is an example of multiple signals (one for each channel) traveling a single section of cable. We will further discuss combining signals in Section 3.3 under multiplexing.

## OPTICAL FIBER

A problem with both twisted pair and coaxial cable is that electric signals are susceptible to interference coming from sources such as electric motors, lightning strikes, and other wires. We will see in Section 2.4 that this interference limits the amount of data that can be transmitted. But there is another problem as well: Wherever there is an electric signal, there is also the possibility of a spark. In communications lines, amperage is low so the sparks are not dangerous to people, at least not directly. However, if inflammable chemicals are nearby, such as may be found in a chemical plant, a small spark could prove hazardous. Is there an alternative to electric signals?

One alternative is **optical fiber.** It uses light, not electricity, to transmit information. Telephone companies make widespread use of optical fiber, especially for long distance service. It is impervious to electrical noise and has the capacity to transmit enormous amounts of information. In addition, optical fibers are very thin (compared to cables), which allows many of them to be bundled together using the same

---

*Sometimes a solid metal conductor is used instead of a mesh on cables that do not need much flexibility.

† Actual data rates in practice may vary with distances.

amount of space old-fashioned cables require. For those faced with the task of routing them through conduits, above ceilings, or between walls this is a big advantage.

Optical fibers are becoming more common in computer networks. High-capacity CDs and increased integration of computers and video imaging are generating a need for networks with high bandwidth capabilities. Section 6.3 discusses fiber distributed data interface (FDDI), a standard for fiber networks. Reference 5 discusses the economics of installing optical fiber in a variety of cases.

The principles that make optical fiber viable are grounded in physics, specifically optics and electromagnetic wave theory. We do not intend to go into a detailed discussion of these topics, but we feel it is important to cover some of the basics so you will have an idea of how it works.

To begin, consider a light source directed toward some surface (Figure 2.6). The surface represents a boundary between two media such as air and water. Let $\alpha$ be the angle at which the light wave intersects the boundary. Some of the light will reflect back at an angle $\alpha$ with the plane and some will cross the boundary into the other medium. This is **refraction**. However, the angle the direction of light makes with the boundary changes. In other words, if $\beta$ is the angle at which the light wave travels from the boundary, $\beta \neq \alpha$. Next you might ask whether $\beta$ is larger or smaller than $\alpha$. If you did, congratulations. That's a good question.

If $\beta > \alpha$ (as it is in Figure 2.6), we say the second medium has a higher optical density than the first (as water has a higher density than air). However, if the first medium has a higher optical density, then $\beta < \alpha$. Refraction explains why a lens in a pair of eyeglasses will distort the normal view, or why objects under water appear distorted if viewed from above the surface. The light reflected off the objects we see is distorted, making them look different.

The relation between $\beta$ and $\alpha$ is of interest. Physicists use a measure known as the **index of refraction** to describe it. It is defined by

$$\frac{\cos(\alpha)}{\cos(\beta)}$$

**FIGURE 2.6    Light Refraction and Reflection**

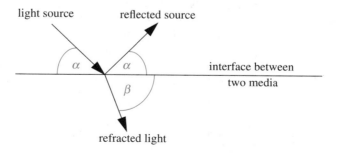

Thus, an index of refraction less (greater) than 1 means light is traveling into a less (more) optically dense medium. Remember, angles $\beta$ and $\alpha$ are between 0° and 90° so that $\cos(\alpha) < \cos(\beta)$ means $\alpha > \beta$, and vice versa.

Another interesting phenomenon occurs when the index of refraction is less than 1 ($\alpha > \beta$). When $\alpha$ is less than a certain critical angle, there is no refracted light. In other words, all the light is reflected. This is what makes fiber optics work.

The three main components to a fiber optic filament are the core, the cladding, and a protective cover. The core is made from very pure glass or plastic material. The cladding surrounds the core. It is also glass or plastic but is optically less dense than the core. How pure is the core? As we will see, an optical fiber works by allowing light to travel through the core. In some cases the fiber is up to 20 miles long. Since light travels from end to end we can think of the core as 20 miles thick. Thus, imagine a block of glass so pure that a chunk 20 miles thick is nearly transparent.

Next question: How does light enter the fiber? A light source such as a **light emitting diode (LED)** or a laser is placed at one end of the fiber. Each is a device that responds to an electric charge to produce a pulse of light typically near the infrared frequency of $10^{14}$ Hz. The laser produces a very pure* and narrow beam. It also has a higher power output, allowing the light to propagate farther than that produced by an LED. The LED produces less concentrated light consisting of many wavelengths. LEDs are less expensive and generally last longer. Lasers normally are used where a high data rate is needed over a long distance, such as in long distance telephone lines.

The light source emits short but rapid pulses of light that enter the core at different angles. Light that hits the core/cladding boundary at less than the critical angle is totally reflected back into the core, where it eventually hits the boundary on the opposite side of the core. Since the angle of reflection is the same, it again is totally reflected back into the core. The effect is that the light bounces from boundary to boundary as it propagates down the core. Eventually, the light exits the core and is detected by a sensor. Light that hits the boundary at an angle greater than the critical one is partly refracted into the cladding and absorbed by the protective cover. This prevents light from leaking out and being absorbed by other nearby fibers.

There is a potential problem with light propagating down a core. Typically, the core is fairly thick (relative to a wavelength of light) and thus allows the light to enter it at many places and many different angles. Some of the light essentially goes down the center of the core, but some hits the boundary at different angles (Figure 2.7). The study of electromagnetic waves (specifically Maxwell's Equations) tells us that some of the reflecting rays interfere with each other. Consequently, there is a finite number of angles at which the rays reflect and propagate the length of the

---

*Light often consists of many wavelengths, or colors, as indicated by the fact that light passing through a prism is divided into its component rainbow colors. A laser can produce "pure" light, or light consisting of very few wavelengths.

FIGURE 2.7     **Step Index Multimode Fiber**

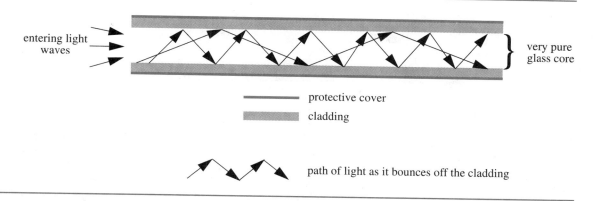

fiber. Each angle defines a path or a mode. Fiber that transmits light this way is called **step index multimode fiber**.

Light that reflects at larger angles reflects more often and travels a greater distance than light that reflects at smaller angles. Consequently, it takes a bit longer to get to the other end of the fiber. This phenomenon is called **modal dispersion**. Imagine many people racing down a hallway. Some are running down the center, and others, who are blindfolded, are bouncing off the walls. We know who will win that race.

Modal dispersion is a problem if the fiber is too long. Light from one pulse (reflecting at small angles) could actually catch up with light emitted from a previous pulse (reflecting at larger angles), thus eliminating the gap in between. The sensors no longer see pulses of light; they see a steady stream of light rays, and any information that was coded in the pulses is destroyed.

One way to address the problem of modal disperson is to use a **graded index multimode fiber**. It makes use of another phenomenon related to the fact that the speed of light depends on the medium through which it travels: Specifically, light travels faster through less optically dense media.

A graded index multimode fiber (Figure 2.8) also has a core, cladding, and protective cover. The difference is that the boundary between core and cladding is not sharply defined. In other words, moving out radially from the core, the material becomes gradually less dense. Consequently, as light travels radially outward it begins to bend back toward the center, eventually reflecting back. Because the material also becomes less dense, the light travels faster. The net result is that although some light travels a greater distance, it travels faster, and modal dispersion is reduced.

Another way to deal with modal dispersion is to eliminate it. "How?" you may ask. Earlier we stated that there are a finite number of modes for light to propagate. The exact number depends on the core's diameter and the light's wavelength. Specifically, reducing the core's diameter decreases the number of angles at which light

FIGURE 2.8    **Graded Index Multimode Fiber**

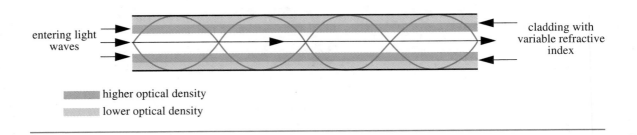

entering light waves

cladding with variable refractive index

higher optical density
lower optical density

can strike the boundary. Consequently, it also reduces the number of modes. If we reduce the diameter enough, the fiber has only one mode. Cleverly, this is called **single mode fiber** (Figure 2.9).

How far must we reduce the diameter? Another principle of physics relates the ability to reflect an electromagnetic wave (such as light) to the size of the reflector. Specifically, it tells us that to reflect a light ray in the manner we have described, the reflector must be larger than the wavelength of the reflected light. Since the reflector here is wrapped around the core, its size depends on the core's diameter. The relationship between frequency and wavelength states

$$\text{wavelength} = \frac{\text{speed of light}}{\text{frequency}}$$

Since light traveling through optical fibers has a frequency of approximately $10^{14}$ Hz, its wavelength evaluates to approximately $2*10^{-6}$ meters, or 2 microns (1 micron = $10^{-6}$ meters). Because of this, single mode fibers typically have a diameter measured in microns (typically 4–8), very thin indeed (many fibers are as thin as a human hair). Its small diameter makes the fiber more fragile and difficult to splice. Consequently, it is most often used in long-distance trunk lines, applications where handling and splicing are minimal.

Optical fiber technology has many advantages over conducting metal:

* It can transmit data more quickly.

* It has very low resistance. Thus, signals can travel farther without repeaters. For example, repeaters may be placed up to 30 miles apart; cable requires them every 2.3 miles.

FIGURE 2.9    **Single Mode Fiber**

entering light waves

- It is unaffected by electromagnetic interference, as the signals are transmitted by light.
- It has very high resistance to the environmental elements such as humidity. This property makes it well-suited for coastal areas.

On the other hand, current computers are electronic devices, so the use of optical fiber requires the conversion of electrical signals to light rays and vice versa. This process adds an extra level of complexity. In addition, optical fibers are more difficult than copper wire to tap into or splice together. Components can be added relatively easily to a copper bus by tapping into it, but much more care is necessary when tapping into a glass fiber.

### WIRELESS COMMUNICATIONS

All modes of communication using conductive metal or optical fiber have one thing in common: Communicating devices must be connected physically. Physical connection is sufficient for many applications such as connecting PCs in an office or connecting them to a mainframe within the same building. It is acceptable for short distances, but expensive and difficult to maintain for long distances. Imagine a coaxial cable connected to NASA flight control headquarters hanging out the back end of the space shuttle or a cable hanging between two towers in New York and London!

In many occasions, a physical connection is not practical or even possible. Suppose participants in a proposed network are in two different buildings separated by an 8-lane highway. Stringing a cable over the highway or disrupting traffic to lay underground cable probably will not meet with approval by city planners. The network participants need a way to communicate without a physical connection; that is, wireless communications.

Wireless transmissions involve **electromagnetic waves**. As they are a significant part of a physics course, we will not attempt a thorough discussion of them. For our purpose, it is sufficient to say they are oscillating electromagnetic radiation caused by inducing a current in a transmitting antenna. The waves then travel through the air or free space where they may be sensed by a receiving antenna. This is how free radio and TV transmit signals.

Figure 2.10 shows the electromagnetic wave spectrum. The radio waves are used for both radio and television transmissions. For example, television **VHF (very high frequency)** broadcasts range from 30 MHz to 300 MHz, and **UHF (ultra high frequency)** broadcasts range from 300 MHz to 3 GHz.* Radio waves also are used for AM and FM radio, ham radio, cellular telephones, and shortwave radio. Each of these communications is assigned a frequency band by the Federal Communications Commission (FCC). Some properties of electromagnetic radiation are important to

---

*MHz is MegaHertz, or $10^6$ Hz. GHz is GigaHertz, or $10^9$ Hz.

FIGURE 2.10    **Electromagnetic Waves**

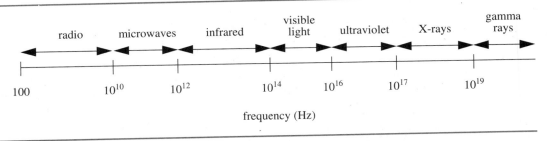

communications. One is a previously stated relation between the wavelength and frequency:

$$\text{wavelength} = \frac{\text{speed of light}}{\text{frequency}}$$

Consequently, high-frequency waves have short wavelengths and vice versa. Table 2.1 shows some actual values.

Physics tells us that low-frequency waves, when broadcast from the ground, tend to reflect off the upper levels of the atmosphere with little loss. By bouncing back and forth between the atmosphere and the ground, such signals can travel far, following the curvature of the earth. Shortwave (between 3 and 30 MHz) radios, for example, have been known to receive signals from halfway around the world. Higher-frequency signals tend to reflect with more loss and typically do not travel as far (as measured across the earth's surface).

Low-frequency waves also require a very long antenna. Perhaps some of you remember a controversy in the 1970s and 1980s that involved an attempt by the Navy to install a large (over 50 miles long) antenna in the upper peninsula of Michigan. Its purpose was submarine communication using **extra low frequency** (ELF) signals in the less than 300 Hz range. The controversy over **Project ELF** centered around potential health risks of people exposed to such electromagnetic radiation.

TABLE 2.1    **Wavelength as a Function of Frequency**

| FREQUENCY (Hz) | APPROXIMATE WAVELENGTH (METERS) |
|---|---|
| $10^2$ | $3*10^6$ |
| $10^4$ | $3*10^4$ |
| $10^6$ | 300 |
| $10^8$ | 3 |
| $10^{10}$ | 0.03 |
| $10^{12}$ | 0.0003 |

Even today, there is much concern over potential health risks due to radiation caused by devices such as power lines and computer terminals (Reference 2).

Two types of wireless communication are particularly important: microwave and satellite transmissions.

**Microwave Transmissions**      Microwave transmissions typically occur between two ground stations. Two properties of microwave transmission place restrictions on its use. First, microwaves travel in a straight line and will not follow the earth's curvature as some lower-frequency waves will. Second, atmospheric conditions and solid objects interfere with microwaves. For example, they cannot travel through buildings.

A typical mechanism for transmitting and receiving microwave transmissions uses the **parabolic dish reflector** (Figure 2.11). No doubt you have seen them in backyards (for receiving satellite signals for television), on top of buildings, or mounted on a tower in the middle of nowhere (Figure 2.12). The last are commonly used for telephone communications.

Parabolic dishes use a well known but probably forgotten fact from precalculus mathematics. Given a parabolic curve, draw a straight line perpendicular to a line tangent to the vertex. This is the line of symmetry. All lines parallel to the line of symmetry reflect off the curve and intersect in a common point called the focus. Figure 2.11 shows how this is applicable to receiving transmissions. The actual dish is not the receiver, just a reflector. Because it has a parabolic shape, incoming signals are reflected and will intersect at the focus. Placing the actual receiver there allows the signals to be received accurately. (As a side note, parabolic reflectors are used to illustrate the whispering phenomenon at museums. Two parabolic dishes are placed at opposite ends of the room facing each other. A person at the focal point of one speaks softly, and the voice is reflected directly to the other one. A second person listening at its focal point hears the first one's voice.)

**FIGURE 2.11**    **Parabolic Dish Receiving Signals**

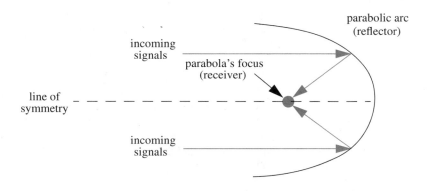

FIGURE 2.12    **Microwave Transmission Tower** (courtesy of AT&T Archives)

Another type of antenna is the **horn antenna** (Figure 2.13). Transmitting antennas are often this type. (Figure 2.12 shows both horn and parabolic dish antennae.) The horn antenna consists of a cylindrical tube called a **waveguide**. It acts to guide the waves and transmit them directly into a concave reflector. The reflector's shape is designed to reflect the microwaves in a narrow beam. The beam travels across an unobstructed region and is eventually received by another antenna. The next time you take a leisurely drive in the countryside, look around and you may see both types of antenna mounted on towers. (But, don't look too long; there are other cars on the road!)

Because there must be a direct line of sight between the transmitter and receiver, there is a limit on how far apart they can be. The limit depends on the tower's height, the earth's curvature, and the type of terrain in between. For example, antennae on tall towers separated by flat land can cover long distances, typically 20–30 miles, although higher towers or towers constructed on a hilltop can increase the distance. In some cases, antennae are separated by short distances within city limits. However, there will be a problem if someone constructs a building directly in the line of sight.

FIGURE 2.13    **Horn Antenna**

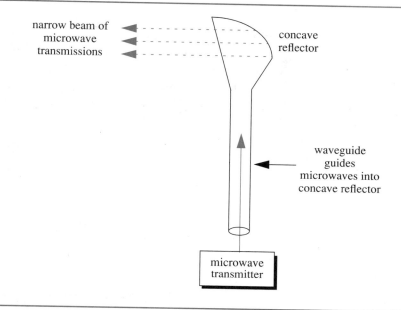

narrow beam of
microwave
transmissions

concave
reflector

waveguide
guides
microwaves into
concave reflector

microwave
transmitter

If transmissions must travel a long distance, several repeater towers may be placed in between (Figure 2.14). One antenna transmits to its neighbor, which in turn transmits to its neighbor. Proceeding this way allows transmissions between sites whose line of sight cuts through the earth.

**Satellite Transmission**    Primarily, satellite transmission is microwave transmission in which one of the stations is a satellite orbiting the earth (Figure 2.15). It is certainly one of the more common means of communication today. Applications include telephone, television, news services, weather reporting, and military use.

Many of you probably have heard of Arthur C. Clarke. He is best known as a science fiction author whose many novels include the Space Odyssey Trilogy. Few people know that Clarke is a physicist who, in 1945, wrote about the possibility of using satellites in space for worldwide communication (Reference 3). In 1945 this idea was science fiction; today, it is common science. At the time, Clarke did not believe that satellite communications would be economically or technically feasible until the 21st century (Reference 4). Instead, it took just 20 years and the invention of the transistor for satellite communications to become a reality.

It began with a historic event on October 4, 1957, an event that shook American society and political leaders. On that day, the then-Soviet Union launched the Sputnik satellite. The Sputnik entered a low earth orbit (560 miles high) and sent electronic "beeps" to the ground. As it moved across the sky, the ground station had

FIGURE 2.14    **Microwave Towers Used as Repeaters**

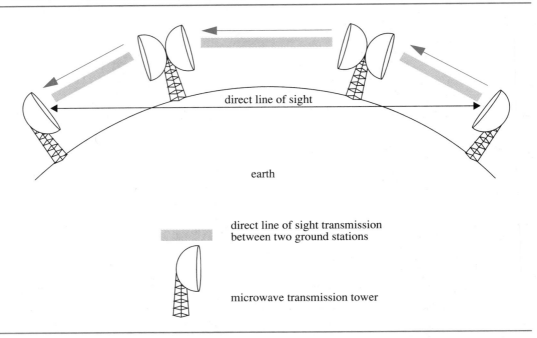

direct line of sight

earth

direct line of sight transmission
between two ground stations

microwave transmission tower

FIGURE 2.15    **Satellite Communications**

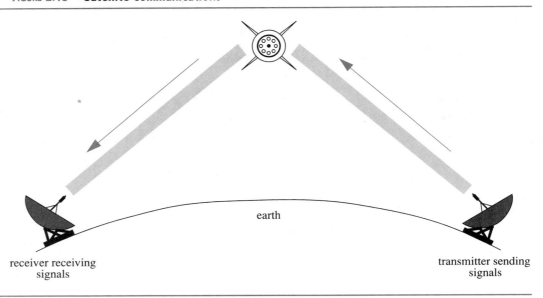

earth

receiver receiving
signals

transmitter sending
signals

to rotate its antenna to track it. By today's standards it was not sophisticated, but then it was truly remarkable because it showed that communication between the earth and an object in space was possible.

Because the satellite moved across the sky, communication was possible for only a short time. As it dropped below the horizon, communication ceased until it later appeared above the other horizon. Such a situation is inappropriate for many of today's applications. Imagine cable TV or a telephone conversation being interrupted every time the satellite dropped below the horizon! (Of course, if it could be synchronized to occur at the start of each commercial, perhaps the concept *would* have merit.)

One solution to this problem would be a series of satellites. They would be arranged so that when one disappeared below the horizon, another would appear to take its place. However, depending on the orbital height, many dozens of satellites circling the earth would be required. Another and better solution would be to have a satellite that remains in a fixed position.

Satellite orbits are predictable using mathematical models based on Kepler's laws of planetary motion. The idea is fairly simple. Given a height, a certain velocity is needed to keep an object in orbit. Higher velocities will send the object out of orbit and into space. Lower velocities will be insufficient to counteract gravitational force and the object will fall. In other words, given a height, the orbital velocity is determined. Kepler's third law relates the time to revolve around a planet to the height of an orbit.

Specifically, suppose the period $P$ of a satellite is the time it takes to rotate around another planetary body. Kepler's third law says

$$P^2 = K \cdot D^3$$

where $D$ is the distance between the satellite and the planet's center and $K$ is a constant depending on gravitational forces. In other words, higher orbits (larger $D$) mean a longer period.

A logical question is: At what orbital height will a satellite have a 24 hour period? According to Kepler's law, the answer is 22,300 miles above the equator, considerably higher than the Sputnik traveled. The answer has great significance. Since the earth takes 24 hours to rotate on its axis, an orbiting satellite at that height appears stationary to a ground observer. This is called a **geosynchronous orbit**. If the observer were a transmitter or receiver, it could remain in a fixed position. It need not be rotated and communications need not be interrupted.

The Sputnik and many early satellites were in much lower orbits. Technology simply did not provide rocket engines powerful enough to boost them into higher orbits. Consequently, they rotated around the earth in less than 24 hours, which is why they appear to move across the sky when observed from the surface. Today, powerful rockets boost communication satellites much higher into geosynchronous orbits. Three equally spaced satellites at 22,300 miles above the equator can cover almost the entire earth's surface (Figure 2.16), except some polar regions.

Lower orbits do have advantages. Applications such as military surveillance require that a satellite not remain in a fixed position. A lower orbit also allows the satellite to move relative to the earth's surface and scan different areas.

FIGURE 2.16    **Satellites in Geosynchronous Orbit Above the Equator**

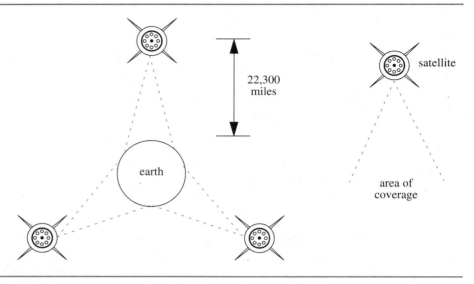

Satellite communication is straightforward. A transmitter sends a signal to a satellite, which relays the signal back down to earth to a different location (Figure 2.15). Satellite communications are now commonly used to transmit telephone and television signals. Many people have their own receivers for cable television reception. In some locations it is difficult to drive through the countryside and not see a satellite receiving dish in someone's backyard.

Satellites commonly transmit using signals in the 4–6 GHz (microwave) range. Upward and downward transmissions (also known as **uplinking** and **downlinking**) use different frequencies so a receiver can distinguish a transmitted signal from a reflected one. Signals reflected by the earth or the atmosphere will always have a different frequency than one legitimately sent from another source.

Some satellites transmit and receive in the 12–14 GHz range. As Section 2.4 will show, higher frequencies will allow more information to be sent per unit of time. The main problem with higher frequencies is that atmospheric conditions such as rain or moisture cause more interference. The problem becomes worse if the ground station is farther away (measured across the earth's surface) and the signal must travel through more atmosphere (Figure 2.17). This problem can be corrected by boosting the power of a signal or by designing more sophisticated receivers to filter out noise. But technology must advance to the point where it becomes cost effective. We can expect future satellites to transmit and receive at much higher frequencies.

Some satellites transmit a signal that can be received anywhere on earth as long as there is a direct line-of-sight path. This type of broadcasting is useful for telephone and television transmission, in which the receivers are widely dispersed. Other applications, such as for military uses, must restrict geographic areas that can

FIGURE 2.17    **Atmospheric Interference as a Function of Angle of Transmission**

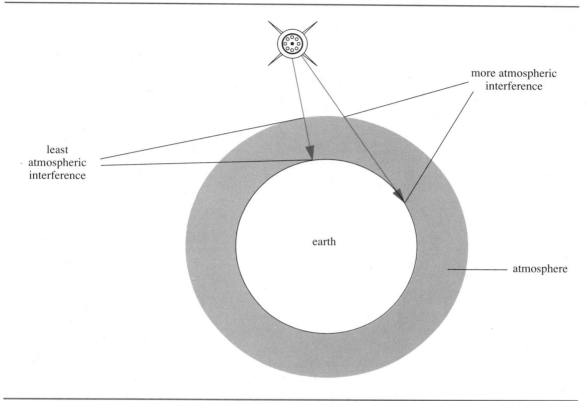

receive signals. Special antennae that provide **beam shaping** allow a signal to be concentrated in a smaller area such as a city. The future will provide **spot beam antennae**, which will allow transmissions to a single site.

Currently, there are many hundreds of satellites orbiting the planet providing communications for different applications. Many of them receive signals in the 4–6 GHz range, so how can a satellite discriminate signals that were not meant for it? For example, suppose ground stations 1 and 2 send to satellites 1 and 2, respectively, using the same frequency (Figure 2.18). The area the signal covers depends on the angle of signal dispersion. If two satellites are too close or the angle of dispersion is too large, both satellites receive both signals. Consequently, neither can tell which signal to ignore.

If the dispersion angles are smaller and satellites are sufficiently far apart, however, no two satellites will receive signals from more than one station (Figure 2.19). The Federal Communications Commission (FCC) defines U.S. satellite positions. For example, it has defined positions at 2° increments between 67° and 143° west longitude for U.S. communications. This is closer together than the previous

FIGURE 2.18    **Satellite Receiving More than One Signal**

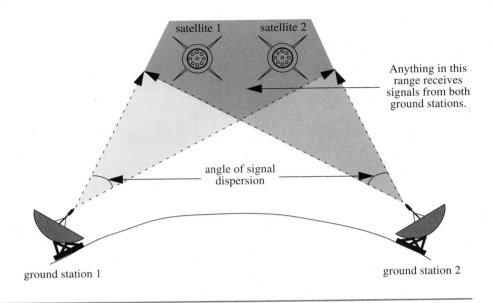

4° separation allowed. Greater needs require more satellites, which must be placed closer together. As a result, ground stations must have smaller dispersion angles for transmitted signals.

Satellite communications have created problems. For example, how do you prevent unauthorized reception of signals? For that matter, how do you define unauthorized reception of a signal that travels through the public airwaves? Legalities are not often clear cut. For example, there have been different views on whether it is legal to receive cable television's pay channels such as HBO using backyard satellite dishes. Cable companies claim they lose revenue by such access. Dish owners claim the signals travel through public air space, and anyone should be able to receive them as they would any television signal.

Perhaps worse, how do you prevent unauthorized transmission via satellite? There have been instances of intruders sending harmless messages via satellite. But what about an intrusion that disrupts communications? Considering how many applications rely on satellite communications, this could be disastrous. In many cases, satellite signals are scrambled or encrypted to make the signal unintelligible to unauthorized receivers. Chapter 4 deals with encryption and security in more detail.

Not all satellites are for telephones, weather forecasting, and military applications. Many private industries see satellites as an alternative to the telephone system, especially where a need exists for data transmission over a long distance. Using the

FIGURE 2.19    **Satellite Receiving One Signal**

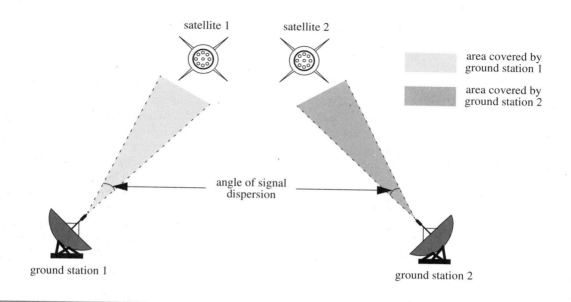

phone system and going through many switches makes data transfer less reliable, and heavy usage may cause longer response times. The solution may be the **very small aperture terminal** (**VSAT**) system, developed in the 1980s. A VSAT system commonly connects a central location with many remote ones. For example, the central location may contain a large database to which many regional offices or users need access. Communication between two sites is via a satellite and allows the use of small antenna dishes (approximately 5 to 6 feet) that can be placed to allow easy access to the central location.

VSAT equipment may connect directly to user equipment such as workstations or controllers. Many applications rely on VSAT systems, especially those that require high data rates for short periods of time. Examples include the National Weather Service, news services, credit card verifications, automatic tellers, car rental agencies, and others (References 4, 5, and 6).

One of the more interesting recent developments is the **wireless LAN**, a system that allows PCs and other typical LAN devices to communicate without a physical connection. It promises many uses where cabling is impractical or for people who rarely stay in one spot. For example, medical personnel could use a laptop computer connected to a wireless LAN as they visit patients in their rooms (Reference 7). Executives might use a wireless LAN to access information during important meetings.

As of this writing there are no formal standards governing the use of wireless LANs. Thus, existing wireless LANs have been designed piecemeal. However, the

FCC is working to assign part of the radio frequency for wireless LAN use, and the IEEE is working on an 802.11 access control standard (Reference 8). Projections currently call for the ability to make LAN resources available to a PC located anywhere in a building or on a university campus.

Three ways to transmit over a wireless LAN include spread spectrum radio, narrowband radio, and infrared light. **Spread spectrum radio** involves sending a radio signal over a broad frequency spectrum. It results in a secure transmission since only devices that know how the signal was constructed can receive and decode it. However, it tends to have a lower data rate than the other two methods. **Narrowband radio** transmission uses a single radio frequency and has a higher data rate. **Infrared light** transmission uses light waves in the infrared range and has the highest data rate. Its major disadvantage is that since light cannot penetrate non-transparent solid objects it requires a direct line-of-sight transmission. In other words, walls get in the way with infrared transmission but not with radio transmission. Reference 8 discusses these three methods in more detail and, along with Reference 9, lists some of the products available.

Despite the lack of a formal standard, wireless LANs are finding applications. Reference 10 describes a couple of them. One of interest is a wireless LAN installed at Edwards Air Force Base. This system uses a combination of optical fiber and microwave transmissions to connect test facilities and laboratories over 30 miles of desert. Their need to test-fire rockets required equipment that had to be isolated. Connecting devices using optical fiber over the rough desert terrain would have been an expensive venture, and the alternative use of microwave links has proved to be very reliable.

## Summary

This section has covered many different transmission media. You might ask, "Which one is best?" The answer is not easy. In data communications, newer technologies do not necessarily make older ones obsolete. Indeed, development of fiber optics and satellite communications have not obviated the need for twisted pair or cable. Each medium has a place in the communications world. Table 2.2 compares the media discussed here.

## 2.2 Communication Services and Devices

### Telephone System

Of all the inventions in the past century, the telephone certainly has had one of the most profound effects on our lives. The ability to call almost anywhere in the world by specifying (dialing) a few numbers is absolutely incredible. But the telephone is more than just voice communications among friends and relatives; it is becoming indispensable to businesses using it for computer communications. The ability to transfer information across a computer network or by fax is now commonplace.

TABLE 2.2 **Comparison of Transmission Media**

|  | TWISTED PAIR | COAXIAL CABLE | OPTICAL FIBER | MICROWAVE | SATELLITE |
|---|---|---|---|---|---|
| **Data rate** | Varies depending on wire length and thickness. Typical rate is 1–2 Mbps for 1 mile. May go 10 miles at a data rate of 2.4 Kbps. | 10 Mbps is quite common. | Often 400–500 Mbps, but rates in the Gbps range have been achieved. | 200–300 Mbps. | 1–2 Mbps, but the development of higher-frequency communication will increase this rate. |
| **Susceptibility to interference** | Electrical interference from nearby wires or motors. | Shielding eliminates much of the electrical interference. | Immune to electrical interference. | Solid objects cause interference. Needs direct line-of-sight between both ends. | Interference caused by atmospheric conditions. Becomes worse at higher frequencies. |
| **Distance** | Depends on thickness and data rate. Typical use is up to 1 mile. Longer distances possible at lower data rates. | 2–3 miles. | 20–30 miles. | 20–30 miles, but depends on height of antenna and terrain between both ends. | Worldwide. |
| **Typical uses** | Useful where space is limited or where high data rates are not needed such as behind a wall leading to a terminal. | Often used as the primary communication medium in a computer network. | Commonly used in long distance phone lines. Also becoming popular as the primary communication medium in a computer network (Ref. 19). | Typically used where laying a cable is not practical; e.g., telephone service in sparsely populated areas, data communication between two sites in a metropolitan area. Some potential in LAN connection (Ref. 20). | Worldwide communication. Applications include phone, military, weather, and television. |

TABLE 2.2    (*cont.*)

|  | TWISTED PAIR | COAXIAL CABLE | OPTICAL FIBER | MICROWAVE | SATELLITE |
|---|---|---|---|---|---|
| **Comments** | Can be shielded to allow higher data rates at longer distances. | New devices can be attached easily. Also easy to splice. | Difficult to splice. Adding new devices is difficult. | New construction between the two sites will cause problems. | Difficult to prevent unauthorized reception. Also a delay due to long distances traveled. |

Note: 1 Kbps = $2^{10}$ bits per second ≈ 1000 bits per second
      1 Mbps = $2^{20}$ bits per second ≈ 1 million bits per second
      1 Gbps = $2^{30}$ bits per second ≈ 1 billion bits per second

The telephone works by converting sound into electrical energy (Figure 2.20). What we perceive as sound is caused by small fluctuations in air pressure (sound waves). The waves travel through the air causing some objects to vibrate. The same principle causes old windows or light fixtures to rattle during a thunderstorm. It also allows us to hear as the waves cause our eardrum to vibrate and send signals to the brain.

The telephone mouthpiece consists of a chamber filled with carbon granules (Figure 2.20). Two electrical contacts are connected to the chamber. As you speak into the mouthpiece, the sound waves cause a diaphragm covering the chamber to vibrate. As it vibrates it exerts varying pressure on the carbon granules. Higher pressure causes

FIGURE 2.20    **Converting Sound Waves to Electric Signals**

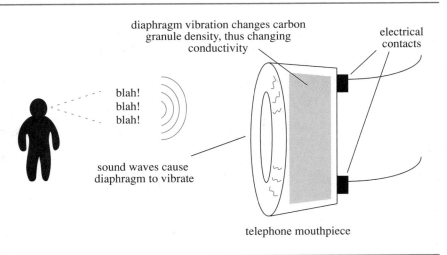

diaphragm vibration changes carbon granule density, thus changing conductivity

electrical contacts

blah!
blah!
blah!

sound waves cause diaphragm to vibrate

telephone mouthpiece

them to be compacted more closely, which in turn, causes them to be a better conductor of electricity. Less pressure has the opposite effect. The net result is that varying amounts of electricity caused by the sound are conducted. On the receiving end the electricity activates a voice coil causing an attached speaker to vibrate. The vibrating speaker causes changes in air pressure, which we interpret as sound.

To place a phone call, the caller enters a sequence of digits by dialing or touching buttons. Each digit sends a code to a local exchange office, which interprets the sequence and determines the destination. If there is an available route to the destination and the phone is not busy, two signals are sent. The first goes to the destination and causes the phone to ring. The second goes to the source and alerts the caller that the phone is now ringing.

Since the signals are separate, it is interesting to note that a caller does not actually hear the phone ringing. In fact, because of delays in the circuits you might not hear the ring until after it occurs. Perhaps you have had the experience of having someone answer your call before you heard a ring. Common perception is that it is caused by gremlins in the line or the mystical ability of the phone system. Now you know that it happens only because someone answered the phone before the second signal got back to you.

The code for each digit depends on whether you have tone or pulse dialing. With **tone dialing**, each digit sends a tone consisting of a unique pair of frequencies. With **pulse dialing**, each digit generates from 1 to 10 pulses. Each pulse actually corresponds to opening and closing a circuit similar to depressing the "hook." In fact, if your fingers are fast enough, you can actually dial a number by rapidly depressing the hook the proper number of times for each digit.

**Call Routing**    The way in which phone calls are routed is an amazing feat of engineering. Remember, we are discussing a network connecting many millions of users. The first part of this network is the **local loop**. It consists of phones connected by copper wires running along the familiar telephone pole or in underground cables to a **local exchange**.* The local exchange contains switching logic and determines where to route a call. If the call is to a phone with the same exchange (first 3 digits of the number) the connection can be made directly to the destination. Otherwise the routing strategy depends on the call's destination.

Figure 2.21 shows the major components (centers) of the telephone office. The class 1 regional centers are the fewest in number and cover the largest areas (typically multistate regions). Classes 2, 3, 4, and 5 are increasingly more numerous and cover smaller areas. Those covering the largest areas are owned by long distance carriers, and others are owned by local companies. Table 2.3 summarizes this information. We will provide a brief discussion of the roles these centers play in the complex system of routing phone calls. For more detailed information, consult references 11, 12, 13, 14, and 1.

---

*Other terms used in place of local exchange include the end office, central office, or class 5 office.

FIGURE 2.21    **Telephone Network**

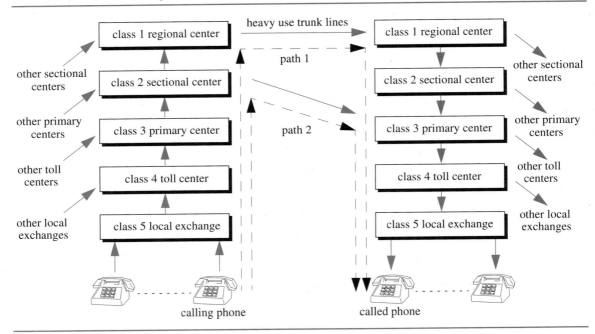

Class 1 centers connect to many class 2 centers. Similarly, class 2 centers connect to many class 3 centers, and so on. At the top of the hierarchy, class 1 centers are connected by high-capacity **trunk** lines, which are capable of transmitting many phone conversations simultaneously. In general, any two phones can connect by going up the hierarchy from the local exchange to the regional center, across a trunk to another regional center, and back down to the proper local exchange (path 1 in Figure 2.21). This is not always the best route, however. Ideally, we would like a call to go through as few centers as possible. The extreme would be to have a direct connection between every pair of phones on this network but, of course, this is unreal-

TABLE 2.3    **Major Centers in Telephone Network**

| CENTER | OWNER | AREA COVERED |
|---|---|---|
| class 1 regional center | long distance carrier | multistate |
| class 2 sectional center | long distance carrier | statewide |
| class 3 primary center | local company or long distance carrier | metropolitan |
| class 4 toll center | local company | one or more cities |
| class 5 local exchange | local company | neighborhood |

istic. In some cases, there may be many phone calls between one sectional center and another primary center. In such cases, it is useful to place another high-capacity trunk line between them as a shortcut to bypass some of the centers and provide alternate routes (path 2 in Figure 2.21).

There are many trunk lines connecting different classes of centers. These connections, driven largely by the traffic between two areas, provide many alternate routes. In the unlikely event all routes are operating at peak capacity, the call will not go through and the caller will receive a busy signal. However, current state-of-the-art hardware and software make this event highly unlikely.

**Private Branch Exchange**    In addition to the public telephone system there are also private telephone systems, called **private branch exchanges (PBX)**. Other common names are private automatic branch exchange (PABX) and computer branch exchange (CBX). A PBX is a computer designed to route telephone calls within a company or organization. This system is especially useful for larger organizations whose many employees must be able to contact one another. A PBX gives the organization complete control over its voice and data communications facilities rather than relying on the telephone company for support. As you might expect, there are advantages and disadvantages. The organization must pay for the hardware, software, and personnel to maintain it. On the other hand, if the company is large enough and its needs great enough, this may be a cost-effective way of establishing communications.

But a PBX is more than just a telephone system. When a PBX is installed, wires connect every office, conference room, or any location where a telephone may be used. Consequently, designers often elect to install additional wire pairs, cable, or optical fibers. The intent is to make them available for data traffic between computers or peripherals. In many cases, the additional wiring is installed even though there is no immediate need for data traffic. The extra cost of installing some redundant wiring is far below the cost for another installation in the future.

The PBX performs many of the same functions as a local area network (LAN), but there are important differences between them. For example, a local area network typically has a broadcast ability. This means one device can send a message to all or a group of devices connected to the network. A PBX typically is used for point-to-point communication. On the other hand, a PBX can define a circuit between communicating devices, something not typical of a LAN. This is an advantage if you need to exchange large amounts of data quickly between two devices. A detailed discussion of a PBX and its comparison with a LAN is beyond the purpose or scope of this book. If you are interested, references 15, 11, and 1 contain detailed discussions of a PBX and its comparison with LANs. Reference 16 surveys some of the uses people are finding for PBXs.

**Integrated Services Digital Network**    The telephone system is still very much dependent on analog signals for communications. Digital technology has provided significant advances in the telephone system with fiber optics and digital switches, but one part of the telephone network is still very much analog: the last mile, or the pair of wires that runs from the local exchange to the user's premises. Since the telephone was (and still is) used mainly for voice communications, this setup made sense, but it is rapidly changing. Every year digital communications make up a larger portion of the telephone system traffic.

A completely digital worldwide communications system called the **integrated services digital network (ISDN)** is emerging. Instead of just a telephone, you would also have a video screen. Some people believe ISDN is the future for worldwide public communications. If fully implemented, it would provide a whole new range of services. For example, because the signals are digital, incoming signals that cause the phone to ring could contain the name and phone number of the caller. This would be an advantage to doctors, brokers, or anyone who deals with clients. They could see the information displayed on a screen and even access the client's file from a database before answering the phone. It would also benefit the 911 emergency service by displaying the name of a caller who might be unable to speak.* Furthermore, it would certainly discourage obscene or nuisance phone calls. It is analogous to saying, "Hello my name is————and I am going to make an obscene call." On the negative side, additional measures would have to be taken to provide privacy for those with unlisted phone numbers.

With ISDN, the telephone book would become obsolete. Instead the information in it would be stored in a database accessible through your telephone. Looking up telephone numbers becomes a database search similar to those done at a library or at a bank. Furthermore, any changes in a phone number would be available immediately.

The technology for such a system exists, so why don't we have it? The answer, in a single word, is "cost." Many millions of private and business telephones would be affected. In addition, long distance carriers and local services each have their own ISDN interface definitions. Getting everyone together will take time and effort (and money), and justifying the cost is difficult. For those with computers or terminals at home with data transfer needs, a strong case can be made. But what about Aunt Martha or Uncle Morris, who primarily use the telephone to reach out and call friends and family? What will a digital system mean to them, especially if they have never used a computer?

The ISDN system raises many concerns. We will devote much more space to them and to the ISDN architecture in Chapter 8. Reference 17 contains a detailed treatment of this topic, and reference 18 discusses the connection between a PBX and ISDN.

**Cellular Phones**     No doubt many of you have seen another technological development embraced by many, the **cellular telephone** (Figure 2.22). It is also known as a **car telephone** or **cellular radio**. Primarily, it allows its user to communicate over the telephone system when he or she is in a car. The term "cellular" pertains to the

---

*911 emergency services already have the ability to trace an incoming call, but ISDN would probably make the system easier and cheaper to use.

**FIGURE 2.22** **Cellular Telephone** (courtesy of AT&T Archives)

way a geographic area is divided to allow communications. It is divided into multiple regions or cells (Figure 2.23), each of which has a reception and transmission station. A **network switching office** (**NSO**) has a computer that controls all the cells and connects them to the telephone system.

The cellular phone is actually a two-way radio capable of communicating with a cell station. The boundaries between cells are not as well defined as Figure 2.23 indicates. Near the cell boundaries the cellular phone is potentially within range of several stations. Each of the stations continuously transmits, so a phone can determine which is closest by determining which signal is strongest. When a call is made from a cellular phone, the phone communicates with the closest station (Figure 2.24). The station in turn communicates with the NSO, which is capable of interfacing with the regular telephone system.

Receiving a call is a little more complex, as there is no way to know which cell the cellular phone is in. However, each cellular phone, just like any phone, has a unique identification number. When it is called, the NSO transmits it to all the cell stations under its control. Each station then broadcasts the number. Since the cellular phone is continuously monitoring broadcasts, it hears its ID broadcast and responds.

FIGURE 2.23    **Cellular Grid**

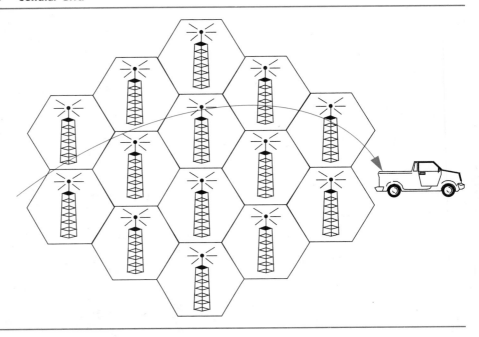

FIGURE 2.24    **Cellular Phone Communication**

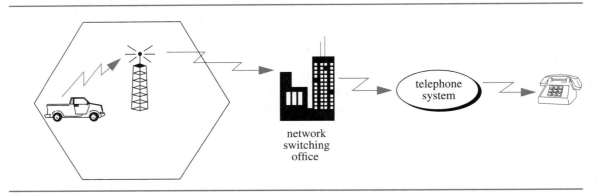

The station, hearing the response, relays the response to the NSO, which completes the connection.

A potential problem exists when a vehicle moves into an adjacent cell. The station with which it is communicating eventually will be out of range. The NSO monitors signals received from cell stations, and if it detects that a signal is becoming weak, it can reassign communication to another cell. The assignment occurs quickly so there is no noticeable interruption for voice communications. If the phone is being used for data transmission, however, there may be some loss.

Using the cell phone for data communications conjures up an image of someone racing down the highway in the driver's seat with a PC or fax machine in their lap. Certainly if you do this or know someone who does, please let me know so I can stay off the road. But some data transfer on the highway is not as bizarre as it sounds initially. For example, an ambulance has a legitimate need for data transfer when it sends an accident victim's vital signs to the hospital.

**Fax Machines**     Another device that became popular during the late 1980s is the **facsimile machine (fax)** (Figure 2.25). Capable of transmitting drawings, letters, or diagrams over the phone in a matter of seconds, it has become an indispensable device for many.

Fax machines are based on a principle similar to that used to display an image on a PC's video screen, on a television set, or in a photograph. The images that appear to be lines and colors are nothing more than dots, but they are too small to be seen individually unless you put your nose against the screen and look very closely.

FIGURE 2.25    **Fax Machine** (courtesy of AT&T Archives)

A fax machine works by taking a picture of the image to be sent and converting it to a binary format. You enter a sheet of paper into the fax much as you would a copier. The sheet is divided into many dots, each representing a portion of the paper. We call this a **bit map** representation, as each dot may be stored as 1 bit of data. Each dot is black or white (binary 0 or 1), depending on what is on that part of the paper. The dots then are transmitted as binary data and reassembled at the other end. For example, Figure 2.26 shows how the letters in the word "Hello" may be represented using a bit map. For simplicity, we have shown only a few large dots; a typical bit map may use 200 dots per inch. More dots provide better quality transmissions. Fewer dots give a "grainy" look to the received image.

Most fax machines do not simply take a picture and transmit the resulting dots. Proceeding that way would require long transmission times for simple documents. For example, suppose a fax recognizes 200 dots per inch. A little arithmetic shows that there are 200 x 200, or 40,000 dots for one square inch. But a typical sheet of paper measures $8\frac{1}{2}$ by 11 inches, or 93.5 square inches. At 40,000 dots per square inch, a typical sheet requires 40,000 x 93.5, or 3,740,000 dots. Using a typical transmission rate of 9.6 K bits per second, we need 3,740,000/9.6 K, or over 6 minutes to send the image on one sheet of paper.

Your first reaction might be, "I have used a fax machine and it didn't take nearly that long." Well, you are correct. Most fax machines will not take that long because they use **data compression**. Rather than sending each dot individually, the fax groups the dots and defines an equivalent binary representation for the group using fewer bits. For example, suppose a part of the image has 800 black dots in succession. Instead of sending 800 black dots, you might send 1 black dot preceded by the number 800. Since 800 has a binary representation of 1100100000 (10 bits), the transmission requires 11 bits (don't forget 1 bit for the dot). Clearly, this is a significant reduction. Certainly there are other ways to compress data. Chapter 3 discusses compression in more detail.

## 2.3  Codes

The previous section described common transmission media and some of their characteristics. Whether the medium uses light, electricity, or microwaves, we must answer

FIGURE 2.26    **Bit Map Representation of "Hello"**

perhaps the most basic of all communications questions: How is information coded in a format suitable for transmission? This and the next two sections answer this question.

Since most data communication is between computers and peripheral devices, we start with the basics of computer storage. Computers are digital devices; they operate by opening and closing tiny electrical switches programmed on a chip. This is obviously an oversimplification, but it is not our intent to discuss computer and CPU architecture. Rather, we take the view that regardless of implementation, all the switches are in one of two states: open or closed. Symbolically, we represent these **bits** the smallest units of information a computer can store, by 0 or 1.

By themselves, bits are not particularly useful, as each can store only two distinct pieces of information. Grouping them, however, allows for many combinations of 0s and 1s. For example, grouping two bits allows $2^2 = 4$ unique combinations (00, 01, 10, and 11). A group of three allows $2^3 = 8$ combinations. They are formed by taking each of the four previous combinations and appending either a 0 or a 1. In general, a group of $n$ bits allows $2^n$ combinations. (Can you prove this?) Grouping bits, therefore, allows you to associate certain combinations with specific items such as characters or numbers. We call this association a **code**. There is nothing difficult about a code. Anybody can define a code any way they want. The trick is to get others to use the same code. If you get enough people to use it, you can ask IEEE or CCITT to make it a standard.

Many codes exist. One of the more annoying problems in communications is to establish communications between devices that recognize different codes. It is as frustrating as trying to converse with someone who does not speak your language. To make life in communications a little easier some standard codes have been devised. But just to make sure that life doesn't get too easy and manufacturers get too complacent, there are different, incompatible standards! (One of the more profound statements in the field of communications is, "The only problem with standards is that there are so many of them.")

The code you use depends on the type of data you are storing. Codes used to represent integers and real numbers vary widely and depend on the computer architecture. Typical codes can be found in almost any book on computer organization (such as Reference 21). We will focus strictly on character codes.

## ASCII Code

The most widely accepted code is the **American Standard Code for Information Interchange (ASCII)**. It is a 7-bit code that assigns a unique combination to every keyboard character and to some special functions. It is used on most, if not all, PCs and many other computers. Each code corresponds to a printable or unprintable character. Printable characters include letters, digits, and special punctuation such as commas, brackets, and question marks. "Unprintable" does not mean those that are banned from newspapers, televisions, or personalized license plates. Rather, it corresponds to codes that indicate a special function such as a line feed, tab, or carriage return.

Table 2.4 shows characters and their ASCII codes written in both a binary and hexadecimal format. For example, the letter 'M' has the ASCII code of 1001101.

TABLE 2.4      **ASCII Codes**

| BINARY | HEX | CHAR | BINARY | HEX | CHAR | BINARY | HEX | CHAR | BINARY | HEX | CHAR |
|--------|-----|------|--------|-----|------|--------|-----|------|--------|-----|------|
| 0000000 | 00 | NUL | 0100000 | 20 | SP | 1000000 | 40 | @ | 1100000 | 60 | ` |
| 0000001 | 01 | SOH | 0100001 | 21 | ! | 1000001 | 41 | A | 1100001 | 61 | a |
| 0000010 | 02 | STX | 0100010 | 22 | " | 1000010 | 42 | B | 1100010 | 62 | b |
| 0000011 | 03 | ETX | 0100011 | 23 | # | 1000011 | 43 | C | 1100011 | 63 | c |
| 0000100 | 04 | EOT | 0100100 | 24 | $ | 1000100 | 44 | D | 1100100 | 64 | d |
| 0000101 | 05 | ENQ | 0100101 | 25 | % | 1000101 | 45 | E | 1100101 | 65 | e |
| 0000110 | 06 | ACK | 0100110 | 26 | & | 1000110 | 46 | F | 1100110 | 66 | f |
| 0000111 | 07 | BEL | 0100111 | 27 | ' | 1000111 | 47 | G | 1100111 | 67 | g |
| 0001000 | 08 | BS | 0101000 | 28 | ( | 1001000 | 48 | H | 1101000 | 68 | h |
| 0001001 | 09 | HT | 0101001 | 29 | ) | 1001001 | 49 | I | 1101001 | 69 | i |
| 0001010 | 0A | LF | 0101010 | 2A | * | 1001010 | 4A | J | 1101010 | 6A | j |
| 0001011 | 0B | VT | 0101011 | 2B | + | 1001011 | 4B | K | 1101011 | 6B | k |
| 0001100 | 0C | FF | 0101100 | 2C | , | 1001100 | 4C | L | 1101100 | 6C | l |
| 0001101 | 0D | CR | 0101101 | 2D | - | 1001101 | 4D | M | 1101101 | 6D | m |
| 0001110 | 0E | SO | 0101110 | 2E | . | 1001110 | 4E | N | 1101110 | 6E | n |
| 0001111 | 0F | SI | 0101111 | 2F | / | 1001111 | 4F | O | 1101111 | 6F | o |
| 0010000 | 10 | DLE | 0110000 | 30 | 0 | 1010000 | 50 | P | 1110000 | 70 | p |
| 0010001 | 11 | DC1 | 0110001 | 31 | 1 | 1010001 | 51 | Q | 1110001 | 71 | q |
| 0010010 | 12 | DC2 | 0110010 | 32 | 2 | 1010010 | 52 | R | 1110010 | 72 | r |
| 0010011 | 13 | DC3 | 0110011 | 33 | 3 | 1010011 | 53 | S | 1110011 | 73 | s |
| 0010100 | 14 | DC4 | 0110100 | 34 | 4 | 1010100 | 54 | T | 1110100 | 74 | t |
| 0010101 | 15 | NAK | 0110101 | 35 | 5 | 1010101 | 55 | U | 1110101 | 75 | u |
| 0010110 | 16 | SYN | 0110110 | 36 | 6 | 1010110 | 56 | V | 1110110 | 76 | v |
| 0010111 | 17 | ETB | 0110111 | 37 | 7 | 1010111 | 57 | W | 1110111 | 77 | w |
| 0011000 | 18 | CAN | 0111000 | 38 | 8 | 1011000 | 58 | X | 1111000 | 78 | x |
| 0011001 | 19 | EM | 0111001 | 39 | 9 | 1011001 | 59 | Y | 1111001 | 79 | y |
| 0011010 | 1A | SUB | 0111010 | 3A | : | 1011010 | 5A | Z | 1111010 | 7A | z |
| 0011011 | 1B | ESC | 0111011 | 3B | ; | 1011011 | 5B | [ | 1111011 | 7B | { |
| 0011100 | 1C | FS | 0111100 | 3C | < | 1011100 | 5C | \ | 1111100 | 7C | | |
| 0011101 | 1D | GS | 0111101 | 3D | = | 1011101 | 5D | ] | 1111101 | 7D | } |
| 0011110 | 1E | RS | 0111110 | 3E | > | 1011110 | 5E | ^ | 1111110 | 7E | ~ |
| 0011111 | 1F | US | 0111111 | 3F | ? | 1011111 | 5F | _ | 1111111 | 7F | DEL |

Using hexadecimal notation allows us to group the bits as 100-1101 and write the code as 4D. Please note that the use of D here has no relation to the character 'D'. It is simply the hexadecimal notation for the four bits 1101.

FIGURE 2.27   **Transmitting an ASCII-Coded Message**

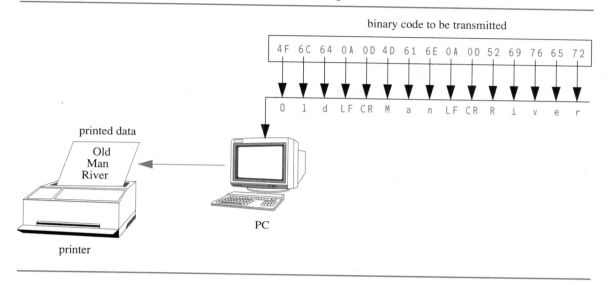

To illustrate how a transmission may work, suppose a computer sends the data in Figure 2.27 to a printer that recognizes ASCII codes. Assume the codes are sent leftmost one first. As the printer receives each code, it analyzes it and takes some action. Thus, receiving the codes 4F, 6C, and 64 causes it to print the characters 'O', 'l', and 'd'. The next two codes, 0A and 0D, correspond to unprintable characters. Table 2.4 shows them as LF (line feed) and CR (carriage return), respectively. When the printer receives 0A it prints nothing but activates the mechanisms to advance to the next line. The code 0D causes the print mechanism to return to its leftmost position. At this point, subsequent printable characters appear on the new line beginning in the leftmost column (Figure 2.27).

Other control characters besides LF and CR are described in Table 2.5. We will discuss a few of them further in Section 5.5. We also note that some control characters vary depending on equipment and systems. We intend this information to be instructional and anyone wishing to write communications software should consult the appropriate manuals for an exact description of each control character.

TABLE 2.5   **ASCII Control Characters**

**ACK**   Acknowledgment indicates an acknowledgment for a transmission sent previously. Chapter 5 discusses the concept of acknowledgments more thoroughly.

**BEL**   **Bel**l causes the receiving device (usually a CRT or terminal) to emit an audible sound usually heard as a "beep." This signal is commonly used to attract the user's attention when special messages are sent or when something significant is about to happen (Figure 2.28).

TABLE 2.5    *(cont.)*

| | |
|---|---|
| **BS** | Back Space causes the print mechanism or cursor to move backward one position. This can be used to print two characters in one position (useful for underlining) or to print a character in bold face (print the same character twice in the same position). On a CRT it replaces the first character with the second one. |
| **CAN** | Cancel causes previously submitted data to be canceled. |
| **CR** | Carriage Return causes the print mechanism or cursor to return to the leftmost print position. NOTE: This character is independent of a line feed. |
| **DC1, DC2, DC3, DC4** | Device Controls correspond to special functions or features dependent on the device. For example, DC1 and DC3 sometimes correspond to **X-ON** and **X-OFF** characters generated by the **control-Q** and **control-S** keyboard sequences. If a device's buffers are filling up, it can send an X-OFF character to the sender, causing it to stop sending. Sending an X-ON causes transmission to continue.[a] |
| **DLE** | Data Link Escape acts as a toggle switch causing the device to interpret subsequently received characters differently. |
| **EM** | End of Medium indicates the physical end of a storage medium. |
| **ENQ** | Enquire is used to request that a remote station identify itself. |
| **EOT** | End of Transmission indicates the end of a transmission. |
| **ESC** | Escape causes one or more subsequent characters to be interpreted differently. For example, sending the escape code followed by the codes for the characters '[', '2', and 'J' to a VT100 terminal will clear the screen. |
| **ETB** | End of Transmission Block indicates the end of a block of data. |
| **ETX** | End of Text indicates end of text transmission. Used in conjunction with STX |
| **FF** | Form Feed used with special forms or screens. It causes the print mechanism or cursor to advance to the beginning of the next form or screen. |
| **FS, GS, RS, US** | Used as separators. First letter indicates what is being separated (**F**ile, **G**roup, **R**ecord, or **U**nit). |
| **HT** | Horizontal Tab causes the cursor or print mechanism to advance to the next selected tab stop. |
| **LF** | Line Feed advances to the next line. |
| **NAK** | Negative **Acknowledgment** indicates that an expected transmission was not received or was received incorrectly. |
| **NUL** | Null is used as a filler (occupy space where there is no data) in a partially filled record. |
| **SI** | Shift In indicates that subsequent character codes correspond to characters in the standard set (e.g., ASCII). Used in conjunction with SO. |
| **SO** | Shift Out indicates that subsequent character codes correspond to nonstandard characters. It can be used to go beyond the ASCII character set without defining additional codes. Used in conjunction with SI. |

**SOH**    Start **of H**eading indicates beginning of a header containing information about a transmission. It may contain an address, length of message, or data used for error checking.

**SP**    **Sp**ace (blank) character. Blanks are not an absence of data, but are legitimate characters in their own right.

**STX**    **Start** of **T**ext indicates the beginning of text transmission. Used in conjunction with ETX.

**SUB**    **Sub**stitute character is used in place of a character that may have been damaged during transmission.

**SYN**    **Syn**chronous character is used to synchronize transmissions.

**VT**    **V**ertical **T**ab causes the cursor or print mechanism to advance to the next preassigned print line.

---

*    A student's first exposure to X-ON and X-OFF often occurs by accident. For example, suppose you enter a command to a terminal to print a file (such as one containing machine language) containing unprintable characters. The file's contents are incorrectly interpreted as ASCII-coded characters. If one of the codes corresponds to an X-OFF character, the terminal interprets it to stop sending characters. Consequently, anything the user types is not transmitted, which causes the terminal to "freeze up."

---

**FIGURE 2.28    Significant Event Requiring Use of BEL Character**

## EBCDIC CODE

The second most common code is the Extended Binary Coded Decimal Interchange Code (EBCDIC), used primarily on IBM mainframes and peripherals. It is an 8-bit code, thus allowing up to 256 different characters. Like the ASCII code, there are printable and unprintable characters. Table 2.6 shows the EBCDIC codes (both binary and hexadecimal format) and associated characters. In this case, the letter 'M' has the EBCDIC code of 11010100. As before, hexadecimal notation allows us to group the bits as 1101-0100 and write the code as D4.

As many of the control characters are similar to the ASCII ones, we will not provide another complete description of them here. If you need to know their specific functions, consult a technical manual for the appropriate device.

## BAUDOT, MORSE, AND BCD CODES

The ASCII and EBCDIC codes are the most common in computer communications. You will encounter them most of the time. To be complete, however, we should mention the Baudot, Morse, and binary coded decimal (BCD) codes

The oldest is the **Morse code**. Developed by Samuel Morse in 1838, it was used in telegraph communications. Table 2.7 shows the code as a sequence of dots and dashes. A unique aspect of this system is that the letter codes have varying lengths; for example, the letter 'E' corresponds to a single dot and the letter 'H' has four dots. The varied code length allows messages to be sent quickly. In the original telegraph, an individual sent a message by tapping a switch to open and close the circuit. For example, suppose each letter's code length is 5 (a code length of 4 would allow only $2^4 = 16$ possible combinations). The time it takes to send a message is proportional to five times the number of letters in the message. If some of the letters required fewer taps, the telegrapher could send the message more quickly. To take the greatest advantage of a varying length code, the most common letters were assigned short codes. This method helped reduce the average code length.* To illustrate, consider sending the alphabet. A code length of 5 for each 26 character requires 130 taps to send the message. Using the Morse code, the same transmission requires only 82 taps.

The code developed by Jean-Marie-Emile Baudot was dubbed, not surprisingly, the **Baudot code** It uses 5 bits for each character and letter (see Table 2.7). Originally designed for the French telegraph it is still used today in telegraph and telex communications.

The observant reader might notice that a 5-bit code allows $2^5 = 32$ possible combinations—but that there are 36 letters and digits (not to mention other symbols not listed in Table 2.7). If you carefully scrutinize the table you can see some duplicate codes. For example, the digit 1 and the letter Q have the same code. In fact, each digit's code duplicates that of some letter. (Can you find them?)

---

*Some modern codes also have variable lengths, which significantly affects transmission costs. Chapter 3 discusses them in more detail.

TABLE 2.6 **EBCDIC Codes (00 through 7F)**

| BINARY | HEX | CHAR | BINARY | HEX | CHAR | BINARY | HEX | CHAR | BINARY | HEX | CHAR |
|--------|-----|------|--------|-----|------|--------|-----|------|--------|-----|------|
| 00000000 | 00 | NUL | 00100000 | 20 | DS | 00100000 | 40 | SP | 01100000 | 60 | − |
| 00000001 | 01 | SOH | 00100001 | 21 | SOS | 00100001 | 41 | | 01100001 | 61 | / |
| 00000010 | 02 | STX | 00100010 | 22 | FS | 00100010 | 42 | | 01100010 | 62 | |
| 00000011 | 03 | ETX | 00100011 | 23 | | 00100011 | 43 | | 01100011 | 63 | |
| 00000100 | 04 | PF | 00100100 | 24 | BYP | 00100100 | 44 | | 01100100 | 64 | |
| 00000101 | 05 | HT | 00100101 | 25 | LF | 00100101 | 45 | | 01100101 | 65 | |
| 00000110 | 06 | LC | 00100110 | 26 | EOB | 00100110 | 46 | | 01100110 | 66 | |
| 00000111 | 07 | DEL | 00100111 | 27 | ESC | 00100111 | 47 | | 01100111 | 67 | |
| 00001000 | 08 | | 00101000 | 28 | | 00101000 | 48 | | 01101000 | 68 | |
| 00001001 | 09 | | 00101001 | 29 | | 00101001 | 49 | | 01101001 | 69 | |
| 00001010 | 0A | SMM | 00101010 | 2A | SM | 00101010 | 4A | ¢ | 01101010 | 6A | |
| 00001011 | 0B | VT | 00101011 | 2B | | 00101011 | 4B | . | 01101011 | 6B | , |
| 00001100 | 0C | FF | 00101100 | 2C | | 00101100 | 4C | < | 01101100 | 6C | % |
| 00001101 | 0D | CR | 00101101 | 2D | ENQ | 00101101 | 4D | ( | 01101101 | 6D | _ |
| 00001110 | 0E | SO | 00101110 | 2E | ACK | 00101110 | 4E | + | 01101110 | 6E | > |
| 00001111 | 0F | SI | 00101111 | 2F | BEL | 00101111 | 4F | \| | 01101111 | 6F | ? |
| 00010000 | 10 | DLE | 00110000 | 30 | | 01010000 | 50 | & | 01110000 | 70 | |
| 00010001 | 11 | DC1 | 00110001 | 31 | | 01010001 | 51 | | 01110001 | 71 | |
| 00010010 | 12 | DC2 | 00110010 | 32 | SYN | 01010010 | 52 | | 01110010 | 72 | |
| 00010011 | 13 | DC3 | 00110011 | 33 | | 01010011 | 53 | | 01110011 | 73 | |
| 00010100 | 14 | RES | 00110100 | 34 | PN | 01010100 | 54 | | 01110100 | 74 | |
| 00010101 | 15 | NL | 00110101 | 35 | RS | 01010101 | 55 | | 01110101 | 75 | |
| 00010110 | 16 | BS | 00110110 | 36 | UC | 01010110 | 56 | | 01110110 | 76 | |
| 00010111 | 17 | IL | 00110111 | 37 | EOT | 01010111 | 57 | | 01110111 | 77 | |
| 00011000 | 18 | CAN | 00111000 | 38 | | 01011000 | 58 | | 01111000 | 78 | |
| 00011001 | 19 | EM | 00111001 | 39 | | 01011001 | 59 | | 01111001 | 79 | |
| 00011010 | 1A | CC | 00111010 | 3A | | 01011010 | 5A | ! | 01111010 | 7A | : |
| 00011011 | 1B | | 00111011 | 3B | | 01011011 | 5B | $ | 01111011 | 7B | # |
| 00011100 | 1C | IFS | 00111100 | 3C | DC4 | 01011100 | 5C | * | 01111100 | 7C | @ |
| 00011101 | 1D | IGS | 00111101 | 3D | NAK | 01011101 | 5D | ) | 01111101 | 7D | ' |
| 00011110 | 1E | IRS | 00111110 | 3E | | 01011110 | 5E | ; | 01111110 | 7E | = |
| 00011111 | 1F | IUS | 00111111 | 3F | SUB | 01011111 | 5F | ¬ | 01111111 | 7F | " |

(Table 2.6 continues)

The obvious question is "How can we tell a digit from a letter?" The answer is by using the same principle that allows a keyboard key to represent two different characters. On a keyboard, the shift key allows the same key to generate the code for one of two characters. The Baudot code assigns the 5-bit codes 11111 (shift down)

TABLE 2.6     **EBCDIC Codes (80 through** FF**)**

| BINARY | HEX | CHAR | BINARY | HEX | CHAR | BINARY | HEX | CHAR | BINARY | HEX | CHAR |
|---|---|---|---|---|---|---|---|---|---|---|---|
| 10000000 | 80 | | 10100000 | A0 | | 11000000 | C0 | { | 11100000 | E0 | \ |
| 10000001 | 81 | a | 10100001 | A1 | | 11000001 | C1 | A | 11100001 | E1 | |
| 10000010 | 82 | b | 10100010 | A2 | s | 11000010 | C2 | B | 11100010 | E2 | S |
| 10000011 | 83 | c | 10100011 | A3 | t | 11000011 | C3 | C | 11100011 | E3 | T |
| 10000100 | 84 | d | 10100100 | A4 | u | 11000100 | C4 | D | 11100100 | E4 | U |
| 10000101 | 85 | e | 10100101 | A5 | v | 11000101 | C5 | E | 11100101 | E5 | V |
| 10000110 | 86 | f | 10100110 | A6 | w | 11000110 | C6 | F | 11100110 | E6 | W |
| 10000111 | 87 | g | 10100111 | A7 | x | 11000111 | C7 | G | 11100111 | E7 | X |
| 10001000 | 88 | h | 10101000 | A8 | y | 11001000 | C8 | H | 11101000 | E8 | Y |
| 10001001 | 89 | i | 10101001 | A9 | z | 11001001 | C9 | I | 11101001 | E9 | Z |
| 10001010 | 8A | | 10101010 | AA | | 11001010 | CA | | 11101010 | EA | |
| 10001011 | 8B | | 10101011 | AB | | 11001011 | CB | | 11101011 | EB | |
| 10001100 | 8C | | 10101100 | AC | | 11001100 | CC | | 11101100 | EC | |
| 10001101 | 8D | | 10101101 | AD | | 11001101 | CD | | 11101101 | ED | |
| 10001110 | 8E | | 10101110 | AE | | 11001110 | CE | | 11101110 | EE | |
| 10001111 | 8F | | 10101111 | AF | | 11001111 | CF | | 11101111 | EF | |
| 10010000 | 90 | | 10110000 | B0 | | 11010000 | D0 | } | 11110000 | F0 | 0 |
| 10010001 | 91 | j | 10110001 | B1 | | 11010001 | D1 | J | 11110001 | F1 | 1 |
| 10010010 | 92 | k | 10110010 | B2 | | 11010010 | D2 | K | 11110010 | F2 | 2 |
| 10010011 | 93 | l | 10110011 | B3 | | 11010011 | D3 | L | 11110011 | F3 | 3 |
| 10010100 | 94 | m | 10110100 | B4 | | 11010100 | D4 | M | 11110100 | F4 | 4 |
| 10010101 | 95 | n | 10110101 | B5 | | 11010101 | D5 | N | 11110101 | F5 | 5 |
| 10010110 | 96 | o | 10110110 | B6 | | 11010110 | D6 | O | 11110110 | F6 | 6 |
| 10010111 | 97 | p | 10110111 | B7 | | 11010111 | D7 | P | 11110111 | F7 | 7 |
| 10011000 | 98 | q | 10111000 | B8 | | 11011000 | 8D | Q | 11111000 | F8 | 8 |
| 10011001 | 99 | r | 10111001 | B9 | | 11011001 | D9 | R | 11111001 | F9 | 9 |
| 10011010 | 9A | | 10111010 | BA | | 11011010 | DA | | 11111010 | FA | \| |
| 10011011 | 9B | | 10111011 | BB | | 11011011 | DB | | 11111011 | FB | |
| 10011100 | 9C | | 10111100 | BC | | 11011100 | DC | | 11111100 | FC | |
| 10011101 | 9D | | 10111101 | BD | | 11011101 | DD | | 11111101 | FD | |
| 10011110 | 9E | | 10111110 | BE | | 11011110 | DE | | 11111110 | FE | |
| 10011111 | 9F | | 10111111 | BF | | 11011111 | DF | | 11111111 | FF | |

and 11011 (shift up) to determine how to interpret subsequent 5-bit codes. Upon receiving a shift down, the receiving device interprets all subsequent codes as letters. The interpretation continues until a shift up is received. Then all subsequent codes are interpreted as digits and other special symbols. Thus, sending the message "ABC123" requires the following Baudot code (read from left to right):

```
11111      00011     11001     01110     11011     10111     10011     00001
shift down   A         B         C      shift up     1         2         3
```

The last code we discuss is the **binary coded decimal (BCD)** code, common in many early IBM mainframe computers. One of the reasons for it was to facilitate the entry and subsequent computation of numeric data. For example, if a programmer wanted to enter the number 4385, he or she had to punch the digits '4', '3', '8', and '5' on a punched card. (Remember, we are talking about the dinosaur age of computers.) Each digit then was read by a card reader.

Instead of combining the codes for each digit and creating one representation for the precise numeric equivalent, each digit was stored using the BCD code shown in Table 2.7. This method was considered easy and efficient, especially when there was a lot of data input. The processing unit was then able to do arithmetic between numbers stored in that format. For compatibility reasons, many architectures still support computations between numbers stored in a BCD format. As computer technology evolved and new applications were found, there was a greater need to store

TABLE 2.7    **Baudot, Morse, and BCD Codes**

| CHARACTER | BAUDOT CODE | MORSE CODE | BCD CODE | CHARACTER | BAUDOT CODE | MORSE CODE | BCD CODE |
|---|---|---|---|---|---|---|---|
| A | 00011 | . – | 110001 | S | 00101 | . . . | 010010 |
| B | 11001 | – . . . | 110010 | T | 10000 | – | 010011 |
| C | 01110 | – . – . | 110011 | U | 00111 | . . – | 010100 |
| D | 01001 | – . . | 110100 | V | 11110 | . . . – | 010101 |
| E | 00001 | . | 110101 | W | 10011 | . – – | 010110 |
| F | 01101 | . . – . | 110110 | X | 11101 | – . . – | 010111 |
| G | 11010 | – – . | 110111 | Y | 10101 | – . – – | 011000 |
| H | 10100 | . . . . | 111000 | Z | 10001 | – – . . | 011001 |
| I | 00110 | . . | 111001 | 0 | 10110 | – – – – – | 001010 |
| J | 01011 | . – – – | 100001 | 1 | 10111 | . – – – – | 000001 |
| K | 01111 | – . – | 100010 | 2 | 10011 | . . – – – | 000010 |
| L | 10010 | . – . . | 100011 | 3 | 00001 | . . . – – | 000011 |
| M | 11100 | – – | 100100 | 4 | 01010 | . . . . – | 000100 |
| N | 01100 | – . | 100101 | 5 | 10000 | . . . . . | 000101 |
| O | 11000 | – – – | 100110 | 6 | 10101 | – . . . . | 000110 |
| P | 10110 | . – – . | 100111 | 7 | 00111 | – – . . . | 000111 |
| Q | 10111 | – – . – | 101000 | 8 | 00110 | – – – . . | 001000 |
| R | 01010 | . – . | 101001 | 9 | 11000 | – – – – . | 001001 |

non-numeric data. Consequently, the BCD code was expanded to include other characters. Technically, the expanded code is called the **binary coded decimal interchange code (BCDIC)**.

## 2.4   Analog and Digital Signals

At this point we have covered two primary areas of data transmission: the medium and the symbolic representation of data. Now it is time to combine them. In other words, now that we know how data may be stored symbolically, how does that relate to electrical signals, microwaves, or light waves? The next logical step is to relate physical signals to the symbolic representation of data. More simply put, what does a 0 or a 1 actually look like as it travels through a wire, optical fiber, or space?

The answer depends in part on whether we use analog or digital signals. Remember, an analog signal is a continuously varying signal oscillating between two values. A digital signal has a constant value for a short time and then changes to a different value. Figure 2.1 shows the difference. Concepts of frequency, bandwidth, and periodicity discussed in Section 2.1 apply to both signal types.

### DIGITAL ENCODING SCHEMES

There is a natural connection between digital signals and digitally encoded data. Data stored digitally is represented by a sequence of 0s and 1s. Since digital signals can alternate between two constant values, we simply associate 0 with one value and 1 with the other. The actual values used are not important here. With electrical signals, they are sometimes equal but opposite in sign. To keep the discussion general, we will refer to them as "high voltage" and "low voltage."

**NRZ Encoding**      Perhaps the simplest encoding scheme is the **Non-Return-to-Zero (NRZ)**. A 0 is transmitted by raising the voltage level to high and a 1 is transmitted using a low voltage. Thus, any sequence of 0s and 1s is transmitted by alternating appropriately between high and low. The name NRZ refers to the fact the voltage level stays constant (i.e., does not return to 0) during the time a bit is transmitted. Figure 2.29 shows the NRZ transmission of the binary string 10100110.

NRZ coding is simple, but it has a problem. Look at the transmission in Figure 2.30. What is being transmitted? Your answer should be "a sequence of 0s." Well, that's true, but how many zeros? To this, you should respond that it depends on the duration of 1 bit. Now suppose we tell you that graphically, the duration corresponds to a line 1 millimeter long. All you have to do is measure the length of the line and convert to millimeters. This will tell you the number of 1-millimeter segments there are and, consequently, the number of 0-bits. In theory this method works, but in practice it may not. Suppose one person used a ruler and constructed one thousand 1-millimeter line segments end-to-end. How long is the resulting line? The answer should be one meter, but imprecisions in taking measurements and actually drawing the lines will probably result in a line close to but not exactly one meter long. Thus,

FIGURE 2.29    **NRZ Encoding**

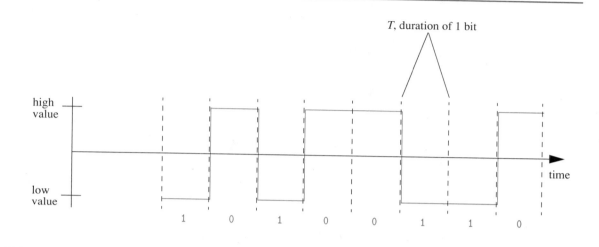

a second person measuring the line will conclude there are slightly more or less than one thousand segments. Even if the first person was lucky and measured accurately, imprecisions in the second person's measurements will cause a discrepancy.

What does this have to do with data transmissions? When a device transmits a digital signal for one bit, it generates a constant signal for a certain duration, say $T$. An internal clock defines the timing. The receiving device must know the duration of the signal so it can sample the signal every $T$ units. It also has an internal clock defining the timing. So all that is needed is to make sure both clocks use the same $T$.

Next question: Do all the clocks in your house have the same time down to the last second? Mine don't. Unfortunately, any physical device is subject to design limitations and imperfections. There will almost certainly be very small differences

FIGURE 2.30    **NRZ Encoding of a Sequence of 0s**

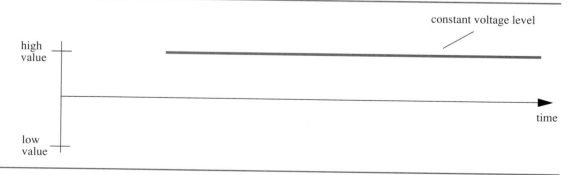

between the clocks that cause one's signal sampling to drift from the other's transmission. It is similar to synchronizing two clocks on New Year's Day, only to find that by the year's end, they differ slightly. Similarly, musicians in an orchestra may all start playing at the same time with the same tempo, but unless they watch the conductor and listen to each other, their tempos may begin to drift. It won't take much timing drift to destroy the piece, making it sound as though it were played by the author and his colleagues.

Communicating devices need some mechanism to make sure their timing does not vary, much like the conductor makes sure the musicians stay synchronized. With a constant signal, there is no synchronizing mechanism. However, if the signal changes, the changes can be used to keep the devices synchronized. Some schemes force signal changes for that reason.

**Manchester Encoding**     The **Manchester code** uses signal changes to keep the sending and receiving devices synchronized. Some call it a **self-synchronizing code**. To avoid the situation of Figure 2.30, it distinguishes between a 0 and 1 by changing the voltage. Specifically, it represents a 1 by a change from high to low and a 0 by a change from low to high. Figure 2.31 shows the Manchester encoded transmission of the bit string 10100110. As the figure shows, the signal will never be held constant for a time longer than a single bit interval. Even for a sequence of 0s or 1s, the signal will change in the middle of each interval. This change allows the receiving device's clock to remain consistent with the sending device's clock.

A disadvantage in Manchester encoding is that twice the bandwidth is needed. That is, the signals must change twice as frequently as with NRZ encoding.

A variation of this method is called **differential Manchester encoding**. Like Manchester encoding, there is always a signal change in the middle of each bit

FIGURE 2.31    **Manchester Encoding**

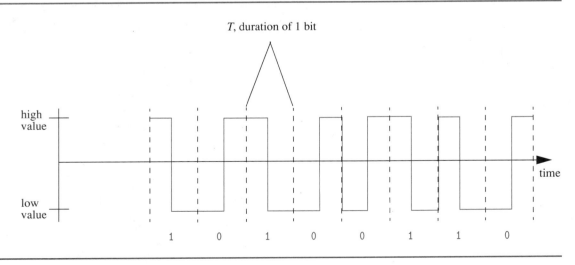

$T$, duration of 1 bit

high value

low value

time

1    0    1    0    0    1    1    0

FIGURE 2.32    **Differential Manchester Encoding**

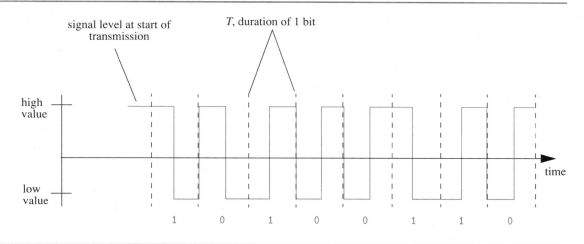

interval. The difference is in what happens at the beginning of the interval. A 0 causes the signal to change at the start of the interval. A 1 causes the signal to remain where it was at the end of the previous interval. Thus, a 0 may go from low to high or high to low depending on the initial value of the signal. Figure 2.32 shows the differential Manchester encoding for the bit string 10100110. In this case, 0s and 1s are distinguished by whether there is a change in the signal at the beginning of the interval. Detecting changes is often more reliable, especially when there is noise in the channel. It is also useful when someone reverses connecting wires, which reverses high and low values. (Now, you might ask who in their right minds would switch the two connecting wires. There are several possible answers. First is someone in a hurry. Second is someone who just made an honest mistake. It happens!) With differential encoding you don't have to mark the wires to indicate which has the high voltage and this, in turn, makes the wire less expensive.

## ANALOG SIGNALS

Dealing with analog signals adds complexity to data communications. One problem is that digital computers are incompatible with analog transmission media. As much of the telephone system is analog, and analog is a major medium for computer communications, the problem must be dealt with. That is, we need a device that converts a digital signal to an analog one (**modulation**) and another that converts an analog signal to digital (**demodulation**). A modem (short for modulation/demodulation) does both. The next two sections discuss the functions and standards of modems. Here we provide an important theoretical foundation for analog signals.

To start, we will define an analog signal more carefully. Earlier we stated that an analog signal is a continuously varying signal between two values, and we used a diagram similar to Figure 2.33 to illustrate. This is certainly true, but it is far from a complete description. The signal in Figure 2.33a may be represented mathematically by a simple trigonometric function $y = \sin(t)$. In other words, Figure 2.33a is the graph of $y = \sin(t)$. But we can alter sine functions in many ways and thus affect the resulting signal. In general, an analog signal is characterized by its frequency, amplitude, and phase shift.

If the signal varies with time and repeats a pattern continuously, the **period** is the time it takes to complete the pattern once. Such a function is periodic. In Figure 2.33a, the period is $2\pi$. However, by changing the function to $y = \sin(Nt)$, we change the period to $2\pi/N$ (Figure 2.33b). To see this, as $t$ goes from 0 to $2\pi/N$, the sine

**FIGURE 2.33    Analog Signals**

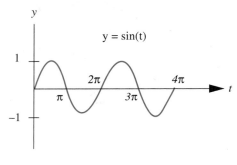

**(a) Period $2\pi$**

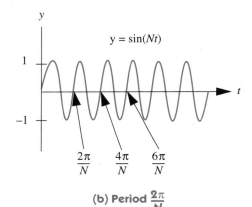

**(b) Period $\dfrac{2\pi}{N}$**

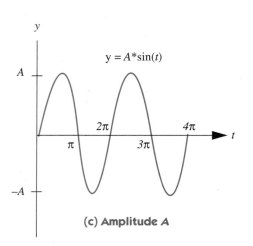

**(c) Amplitude $A$**

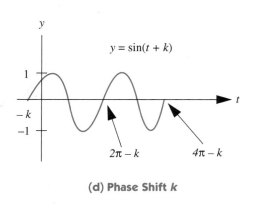

**(d) Phase Shift $k$**

function's argument ($Nt$) goes from 0 to $2\pi$. In general, if $N > 1$, the period is smaller than $2\pi$. If $N < 1$, the period is bigger than $2\pi$.

The period is related to the **frequency**, the number of times the signal oscillates per unit of time. Its units of measurement are cycles per second or, equivalently, Hertz (Hz). Specifically, if $f$ is the frequency and $p$ is the period then

$$f = \frac{1}{p}.$$

Thus, the signal of Figure 2.33b has a frequency of $N/2\pi$.

The **amplitude** defines the values between which the signal oscillates. Since $y = \sin(t)$ oscillates between 1 and $-1$, then $y = A*\sin(t)$ oscillates between $A$ and $-A$ (Figure 2.33c).

The last way to change a signal is through a **phase shift**. Graphically, this is a horizontal shift in the graph of a sine function. In general, we can achieve a horizontal shift by adding or subtracting from the argument. For example, if $k > 0$, the graph of $y = \sin(t + k)$ (Figure 2.33d) is that of Figure 2.33a shifted to the left $k$ units. This is easily verified by evaluating both functions at different values of $t$.

**Fourier's Result**    We now see that an analog signal is more complex than a simple sine wave (graph of a sine function). In general, its amplitude, frequency, and phase shift can all vary with time and thus create very complex functions. Perhaps the most familiar example of an analog signal is the one produced by speaking into the telephone (Figure 2.34). As you speak, you vary the sounds you make in order to form words. Your voice also gets louder or softer depending on whether you are having an argument with your boss or speaking to your fiancé. Speaking louder or softer or in a higher or lower pitch creates sound that translates to electrical analog signals. The amplitude reflects the volume and the frequency reflects the pitch. (At this point, there is no simple sound equivalent corresponding to a phase shift.) The result is a very complex combination of signals that represents your voice.

FIGURE 2.34    **Sound Creating an Analog Signal**

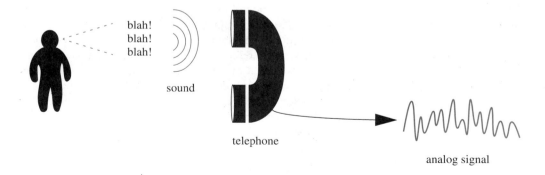

The problem now is how to transmit complex signals. There are infinitely many ways to vary the amplitude, frequency, and phase shift. Furthermore, electrical engineering tells us that different signals can experience different amounts of distortion. How do engineers design hardware to do the job? Do they design different hardware and transmission media for different signal types? Do the functions that represent different analog signals require separate analysis?

The answer to the last two questions is no. A famous mathematician, Jean Baptiste Fourier, developed a theory stating that any periodic function can be expressed as an infinite sum of sine functions of varying amplitude, frequency, and phase shift. The sum is called a **Fourier series**. Its importance is that no matter how complex periodic functions are, they all consist of the same components.

In more mathematical terms, suppose $s(t)$ is a periodic function with period $P$. One form for Fourier's results states that

$$s(t) = \frac{a_0}{2} + \sum_{i=1}^{\infty} \left[ a_i * \cos\left( \frac{2\pi it}{P} \right) + b_i * \sin\left( \frac{2\pi it}{P} \right) \right]$$

(There are other forms, but this suits our needs here.)

The coefficients $a_i$, $i = 0, 1, 2, \ldots$ and $b_i$, $i = 1, 2, 3, \ldots$ are determined using

$$a_i = \frac{2}{P} \int_{-P/2}^{P/2} s(t) * \cos\left( \frac{2\pi it}{P} \right) dt \quad \text{for } i = 0, 1, 2, 3, \ldots\ldots$$

and

$$b_i = \frac{2}{P} \int_{-P/2}^{P/2} s(t) * \sin\left( \frac{2\pi it}{P} \right) dt \quad \text{for } i = 1, 2, 3, \ldots\ldots$$

A rationale or derivation of these equations is far beyond the goals of this book. We simply present them for the purposes of explaining the limitations of different communications media. If you are interested, you can find a more complete description of the Fourier series in references 11, 22, and 23. What is important to us is that Fourier analysis tells us that every periodic signal is a sum of analog signals with different frequencies and amplitudes. We conclude from this that the ability to send and analyze an analog signal depends on the range of frequencies (bandwidth) the medium is capable of handling.

Consider an example. Let $s(t)$ be defined by

$$s(t) = \begin{cases} 1 \text{ for } 0\pi \leq t < \pi;\ 2\pi \leq t < 3\pi;\ 4\pi \leq t < 5\pi;\ \text{etc.} \\ -1 \text{ for } \pi \leq t < 2\pi;\ 3\pi \leq t < 4\pi;\ 5\pi \leq t < 6\pi;\ \text{etc.} \end{cases}$$

Figure 2.35a shows its graph. Since it is periodic (with a period of $2\pi$), we can write it as a Fourier series. In this case all constants $a_i$, for $i \geq 0$, are all 0. Constants $b_i$ are defined by

$$b_i = \begin{cases} 0 \text{ if } i \text{ is even} \\ \dfrac{4}{\pi i} \text{ if } i \text{ is odd} \end{cases}$$

FIGURE 2.35    **Fourier Approximations**

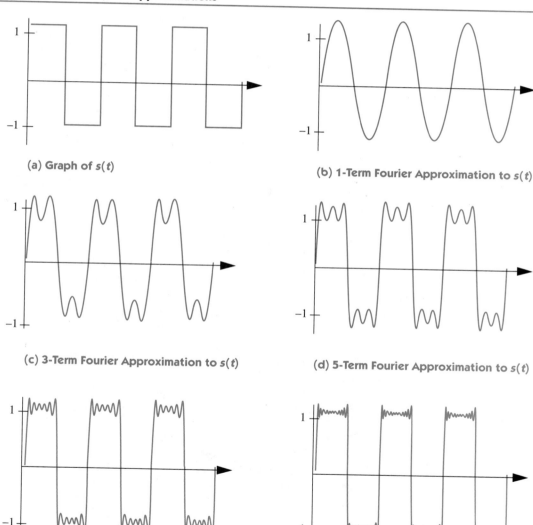

(a) Graph of $s(t)$

(b) 1-Term Fourier Approximation to $s(t)$

(c) 3-Term Fourier Approximation to $s(t)$

(d) 5-Term Fourier Approximation to $s(t)$

(e) 11-Term Fourier Approximation to $s(t)$

(f) 21-Term Fourier Approximation to $s(t)$

We have used calculus to determine these values and will not duplicate the calculations here. If you are familiar with integration techniques, you should verify the results. If not, don't worry about it.

The bottom line is that we can write the periodic function as

$$s(t) = \sum_{i = 1 \text{ and } i \text{ odd}}^{\infty} \frac{4}{\pi i} \sin(it)$$

Calculating an infinite sum is likely to take some time (probably more than you are willing and able to do). The best we can hope to do is to approximate the function using a finite number of terms—but we must accept the tradeoffs. We can get an approximation very quickly using few terms. Unfortunately, the approximation is not very accurate. Of course, we can easily improve the approximation by using more terms, which gives us better accuracy but takes more effort. Figures 2.35b through 2.35f show the graph of the approximation using 1, 3, 5, 11, and 21 terms. As the figures show, using just a few terms creates an approximation that barely resembles the original function. However, as we use more terms, the graph becomes flatter over each interval and the jumps between 1 and –1 occur more quickly.

**Applications of Fourier's Results**     Again you might ask, "So what?" Well, Fourier's results are essential to the study of communications. Transmitting a complex analog signal over a medium with a limited bandwidth is the same as approximating the function using some of the Fourier series terms. We can use this principle to explain why, for example, listening to someone's CD player over a telephone is different from listening to it in person.

High-fidelity equipment is capable of producing sounds within a bandwidth of several tens of thousands of Hz. (Actual bandwidth, of course, depends on the equipment.) It can produce sounds ranging from about 30 Hz (cycles per second) to 20,000–30,000 Hz. The telephone, on the other hand, can transmit signals between approximately 300 Hz and 3300 Hz. Consequently, the original signal loses its very low and very high frequency components. The audible effect is that low bass and high treble sounds are lost, and the result is a less than clear sound. Fourier's results also explain why a person's voice never sounds exactly the same over the phone as in person. However, in this case, a normal voice does not have the range of sounds that an instrument has; that is, most of the voice frequencies are within the bandwidth of a telephone. Thus, although there is some loss of tonal quality, enough is saved to understand completely what is being said.

Fourier's results also are used in defining hardware. For example, a **filter** will block certain frequencies while allowing others to pass. Filters have a wide range of applications. For example, an equalizer attached to a stereo can be adjusted to bring out certain tones in music. If we want to highlight bass sounds or accentuate higher pitched sounds such as soprano voices or a flute on the high end of the music scale, we can set the equalizer to vary the frequencies blocked by the filter.

Another example is in cable television. A bewildered consumer may wonder how a television can receive as many as 100 channels. The answer lies in the ability to view a complex signal as many simple ones. Each channel is assigned a certain range of frequencies, and a signal defining the sound and pictures is created using frequencies within that range. The physical cable transmits one signal consisting of the sum of signals from all channels. This process, **multiplexing**, is discussed in more detail in Chapter 3. Selecting a channel on a television simply allows frequencies within a certain range to pass. Television circuits analyze them and produce sounds and pictures.

## DATA RATE

**Nyquist Theorem and Noiseless Channels**      The next step in the discussion of signals is to relate them to data transfer. Computer networks now use all forms of transmission for this purpose. Furthermore, as the needs and capacities continue to grow, fundamental questions must be asked. For example: Given a particular media, how much data can be transferred? The **data rate** is used to describe a medium's capacity and is measured in bits per second (bps). An important result in communications theory relates the data rate to the bandwidth. Simply put, a higher bandwidth medium is capable of a higher data rate. The relation between them is so strong that many people often use the terms interchangeably.

Before describing the relation, let's make sure we understand the mechanism behind data transfer. Figure 2.36 illustrates the main components. Basically, a transmitter sends a signal representing data. The receiver "listens" to the medium and creates data based on the signal it receives.

Let's take a close look at the signal. The data to be transferred can be divided into parts, each represented by a bit string $b_1 b_2 \ldots b_n$. The transmitter alternately analyzes each string and transmits a signal component uniquely determined by the bit values. Once the component is sent the transmitter gets another bit string and repeats the process. The different signal components make up the actual transmitted signal. The frequency with which the components change is the **baud rate**.

Precisely how the transmitter determines each component is the topic of the next section and is not important here. If you would like something more concrete

FIGURE 2.36      **Sending Data via Signals**

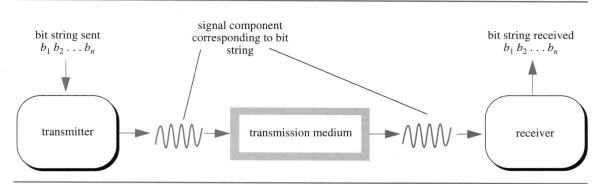

for now, just think of a unique signal amplitude for each bit combination. For example, the signal components may have up to $2^n$ different amplitudes, one for each unique combination of values for $b_1 b_2 \ldots b_n$.

At the receiving end, the process is reversed. The receiver alternately samples the incoming signal and generates a bit string. The bit string, of course, depends on the sample. For this to work, the receiver must be able to sample with a frequency equal to the baud rate. (If it samples less frequently than components can change, some can go unsampled, and the result is lost data.)

Consequently, the data rate depends on two things: the frequency with which a component can change (baud rate) and $n$, the number of bits in the string. Many people often use the terms baud rate and data rate interchangeably. Based on our discussion, we now see that this idea is not correct. In fact,

$$\text{data rate} = \text{baud rate} * n$$

This would seem to imply that one can always increase the data rate by increasing either the baud rate or $n$. This is true, but only up to a point. Some classic results put an upper bound on the data rate.

The first result is surprisingly old, dating back to the 1920s, when Harry Nyquist developed his classic theory. Reference 23 provides a formal treatment. We will not prove it here, but we will state it and explain its importance to data communications. First, Nyquist showed that if $f$ is the maximum frequency the medium can transmit, the receiver can completely reconstruct a signal by sampling it $2*f$ times per second. (We interject here that he assumed absolutely no noise or distortion altered the signal. That is, he assumed a perfectly noiseless channel. We discuss noisy channels shortly.) Another way to say this is that the receiver can reconstruct the signal by sampling it at intervals of $1/(2*f)$ second or twice each period (remember, one period $= 1/f$). For example, if the maximum frequency is 4000 Hz, the receiver need only sample the signal 8000 times per second. In other words, the signal can be recovered completely by sampling it every 1/8000th of a second.

Now, suppose the transmitter changed the signals at intervals of $1/(2*f)$. In other words the baud rate is $2*f$. We then have the results of the Nyquist theorem, which states

$$\text{data rate} = \text{baud rate} * n = 2*f*n$$

Some books state the Nyquist theorem using the number of different signal components instead of $n$. In other words, if $B$ is the number of different components then

$$B = 2^n$$

or, equivalently

$$n = \log_2 (B).$$

In such cases, we can write

$$\text{data rate} = 2*f*\log_2 (B).$$

Table 2.8 summarizes some results assuming a maximum frequency of 3300 Hz, the approximate upper limit for the telephone system.

TABLE 2.8    **Results of Nyquist's Theorem for a Maximum Frequency of 3300 Hz**

| $n$, NUMBER OF BITS PER SIGNAL COMPONENT | $B$, NUMBER OF SIGNAL COMPONENTS | MAXIMUM DATA RATE |
|---|---|---|
| 1 | 2 | 6600 bps |
| 2 | 4 | 13200 bps |
| 3 | 8 | 19800 bps |
| 4 | 16 | 26400 bps |

**Noisy Channels**    So far, this information seems to imply there is no upper bound for the data rate given the maximum frequency. Unfortunately, this is not true for two reasons. First, more signal components mean subtler changes among them. For example, suppose a signal's amplitude must be less than or equal to 5 volts and that each component is determined by amplitude only. If we used two components defined by $2\frac{1}{2}$ and 5 volts, the signals differ by $2\frac{1}{2}$ volts. However, using 16 signal components requires a difference of about $\frac{1}{3}$ volts between adjacent amplitudes. The receiver must be more sophisticated (and more expensive) to be able to detect smaller differences. If the differences become too small, we eventually exceed the ability of a device to even detect them.

The second reason occurs because many channels are subject to **noise**, which means a transmitted signal can be distorted. If the distortion is too large the receiver cannot reconstruct the signal. For example, consider the digital signal in Figure 2.37a. (We use a digital signal simply because it is easier to illustrate. A similar discussion can certainly be made for analog signals.) The transmitter sends two signals,

FIGURE 2.37    **Effect of Noise on Digital Signal**

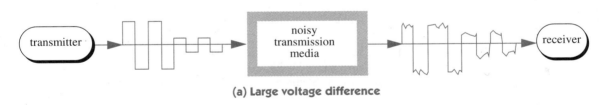

**(a) Large voltage difference**

**(b) Small voltage difference**

each of which oscillates between two voltage levels. However, the transmitted signal is subjected to some noise and the received signal differs from it. The distortion is not too great, so the received signal still pretty clearly defines two voltage levels. Thus, it would not be too difficult to reconstruct them.

Figure 2.37b shows a similar situation, except in this case the original two voltage levels differ by less. Now when noise occurs the two distorted signals overlap voltage levels and it is difficult, if not impossible, to reconstruct the original signal from the received one.

**Shannon's Result**    We have learned that noise can alter and possibly destroy information. Whether the information can be reconstructed depends on how powerful the noise is. For example, a little static electricity is not going to do much to transmissions from a 50,000-watt radio transmitting tower. However, a lightning strike can do amazing things to computer communications. The difference, of course, is the strength of the noise relative to that of the transmitted signal.

Electrical engineers use a parameter called the **signal-to-noise ratio** to quantify how much noise there is in the presence of a signal. We define it as $S/N$ where $S$ is the signal power and $N$ is the noise power. You may also recognize it as a specification on audio equipment to measure clarity of sound. A large ratio means a clear signal; a small one indicates more distortion. In high-fidelity equipment, high signal-to-noise ratios indicate a higher quality sound (although in some cases the improved quality may be measurable but not audible). Because $S$ is usually much larger than $N$, the ratio is often scaled down logarithmically and expressed as

$$B = \log_{10} \left( \frac{S}{N} \right) \text{Bels}$$

Here, Bel is the unit of measurement. So, for example, if $S$ is 10 times as large as $N$ ($S = 10*N$), then $B = \log_{10} ((10*N)/N) = \log_{10} (10) = 1$ Bel. Similarly, $S = 100*N$ yields 2 Bels, $S = 1000*N$ yields 3 Bels, and so on.

Perhaps a more familiar term is the **decibel (dB)** We define it as $1dB = 0.1$ Bel. To better understand what this means in terms of $S$ and $N$, let's look at another example. Consider a rating of 25 dB. It is equivalent to 2.5 Bels and means $B = \log_{10} (S/N) = 2.5$. This, in turn, forces $S/N$ to be $10^{2.5}$ or, equivalently, $S = 10^{2.5}*N = 100\sqrt{10}*N \approx 316*N$.

In the 1940s, Claude Shannon went beyond Nyquist's results and considered noisy channels. He related the maximum data rate not only to the frequency, but also to the signal-to-noise ratio. Specifically, he showed that

$$\text{data rate} = \text{bandwidth}*\log_2 (1 + \frac{S}{N}) \text{ bps}$$

The formula states that a higher bandwidth and signal-to-noise ratio allow a higher data rate. If the noise power increases, however, the allowable data rate decreases. The idea behind this is that if the signal-to-noise ratio is too small, noise can render two different signals indistinguishable.

Again, we illustrate with an example showing the practical upper limit for data transfer over telephone lines. The telephone system has a bandwidth of approximately 3000 Hz and a signal-to-noise ratio of about 30 dB. The latter implies $S = 1000*N$. Using these values in Shannon's result yields

$$\text{data rate} = \text{bandwidth} * \log_2 (1 + \frac{S}{N}) = 3000*\log_2 (1 + 1000) \text{ bps}$$

$$\approx 3000*9.97 \text{ bps}$$

$$\approx 29,901 \text{ bps}$$

As a final note, we stress that this is not just a theoretical result with little bearing on network users and consumers. In particular, it has a very real implication for modem users. During the 1980s 2400 bps and 9600 bps modems became common. Higher rate modems were available but rather expensive. The 1990s will certainly see faster modems at an affordable price, but, according to Shannon's result, if you are going to wait for modems with a data rate capacity over 30,000 bps, your wait will be a long one. If your needs exceed 30,000 bps, you will have to wait until the telephone increases the signal-to-noise ratio for all its voice grade equipment (not likely) or seek another communications media such as fiber, cable, or satellite.*

## 2.5    Modulation and Demodulation

The previous section described transmission using analog and digital signals. If either analog or digital signals were used exclusively, communications would be simplified and this section would not be needed. In reality, there is a wide mix of analog devices communicating using digital signals and digital devices communicating using analog signals. Furthermore, there are good reasons not to convert everything to either digital or analog.

For example, by now you know that computers are digital devices. In fact, most computer communications such as terminal-to-computer or computer-to-disk transmissions use digital signals. In addition, most local area networks rely entirely on digital signals. So where do analog signals enter the picture? The answer is remote communications. Many people use PCs in their home to communicate with a computer at work. PCs also allow access to bulletin boards, stock quotations, and airline reservations systems. In most cases there is no direct connection such as a local area network. The physical connection uses existing hardware found in the telephone system. However, since the telephone is an analog device, the PC cannot communicate with it directly.

The solution to this problem is a device that converts a PC's digital signals to analog signals: a **modem** (short for modulation/demodulation). It fits between a PC and the telephone (Figure 2.38). The PC sends a digital signal out its modem port, where the modem intercepts it and converts (modulates) it to an analog signal. From

---

*Actually, there is a way to exceed the theoretical limit using data compression. Section 2.6 mentions this briefly, and Chapter 3 discusses compression techniques.

there it goes through the telephone system and is treated as any voice signal. The process is reversed at the receiving end or for any signal destined for the PC. The analog signal comes through the phone line and into the modem, and the modem converts it to a digital signal and sends it to the PC via the modem port.

The most common example of analog devices communicating using digital signals is the telephone system. Section 2.1 described how voice sounds are converted to analog signals. In the old days of the telephone system the analog signals were transmitted over wire or cable to the receiving telephone, where they were converted into sound. Today's fiber technology has changed completely the way a voice is transmitted. Perhaps you have seen television commercials describing how optical fibers carry thousands of telephone conversations. Since optical fibers transmit digital signals, a device called a **codec** (short for coder/decoder) translates the analog voice signal into a digital equivalent (Figure 2.39). The digital signal is then transmitted. At some point it is converted back to an analog signal so it can be converted to sound by the telephone's receiver.

The purpose of this section is to explain how digital signals are converted to analog and vice versa. We will cover digital-to-analog and analog-to-digital conversion methods. Section 2.6 will discuss modem operations and modem standards.

FIGURE 2.38    **Computer Data Transmitted over Telephone Lines**

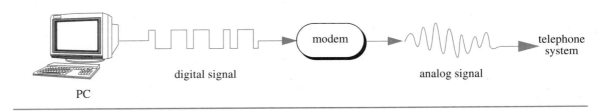

FIGURE 2.39    **Voice Information Transmitted Digitally**

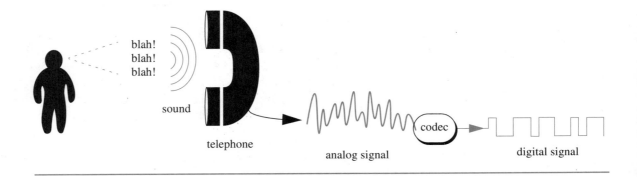

FIGURE 2.40    **Frequency Shift Keying (2 Frequencies), 1 Bit per Baud**

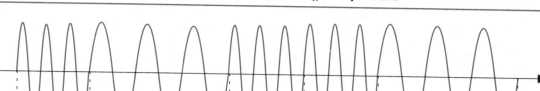

## DIGITAL-TO-ANALOG CONVERSION

Converting a digital signal to an analog one is not difficult. Basically, all you need to do is assign a group of one or more bit values to a particular analog signal. The previous section described three ways to vary an analog signal: by frequency, amplitude, and phase shift.

The first method, **frequency shift keying (FSK)**, sometimes called **frequency modulation (FM)**, assigns a digital 0 to one analog frequency and a 1 to another. For example, if 0 corresponds to a higher frequency and 1 to a lower one, Figure 2.40 shows the analog signal resulting from the bit string 01001. For each bit, the modem transmits a signal of the appropriate frequency for a specified period of time. The period, and hence the number of cycles, varies. (Section 2.6 gives some specifics for particular modems.) The fact that Figure 2.40 shows three cycles per period has no significance yet. We simply drew that many cycles to show the frequency.

Using only two frequencies means that each signal change sends one bit of data. This is a case in which the baud rate (how often a signal can change) and bit rate are the same. Alternative forms of frequency modulation could use more frequencies. For example, since two bits can have one of four combinations, we could assign each pair to one of four frequencies. Thus, each frequency change conveys two bits of data; that is, the bit rate is twice the baud rate.

In general, $n$ bits can have one of $2^n$ combinations, and each can be assigned to one of $2^n$ frequencies. In this case, the bit rate is $n$ times the baud rate.

**Amplitude shift keying (ASK)**, sometimes called **amplitude modulation (AM)** is similar to frequency shift keying. The difference, as you might suspect, is that each bit group is assigned to an analog signal of a given magnitude. Also, as with FSK, a bit group may have one, two, or more bits, again defining a relation between the bit rate and baud rate.

To illustrate, suppose we designate four magnitudes as $A_1, A_2, A_3$, and $A_4$. Using these designations, Table 2.9 shows how two bits are associated with each magnitude. Figure 2.41 shows the analog signal for the bit string 00110110. In this case,

TABLE 2.9    **Signal Association for Amplitude Modulation**

| BIT VALUES | AMPLITUDE OF GENERATED SIGNAL |
|---|---|
| 00 | $A_1$ |
| 01 | $A_2$ |
| 10 | $A_3$ |
| 11 | $A_4$ |

the bit rate is twice the baud rate. Each of the two bits (starting from the leftmost ones) defines a signal with the appropriate magnitude. As with frequency shift keying, the signal is transmitted for a fixed period of time.

**Phase shift keying (PSK)**, sometimes called **phase modulation (PM)**, is similar to the previous techniques. The signals differ by phase shift instead of frequency or amplitude. Typically, a signal's phase shift is measured relative to the previous signal. In such cases, the term **differential phase shift keying (DPSK)** is often used. Also, as before, $n$ bits can be assigned a signal having one of $2^n$ phase shifts, giving a technique where the bit rate is $n$ times the baud rate.

Any of these simple techniques can be used with any number of different signals. More signals means a greater bit rate with a given baud rate. The problem is that a higher bit rate requires more signals and thus reduces the differences among them. As the previous section discussed, this creates difficulties as we need equipment that can differentiate between signals whose frequencies, magnitudes, or phase

FIGURE 2.41    **Amplitude Shift Keying (4 Amplitudes), 2 Bits per Baud**

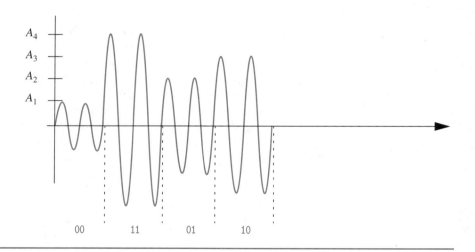

TABLE 2.10 **Signal Association for Quadrature Amplitude Modulation**

| BIT VALUES | AMPLITUDE OF GENERATED SIGNAL | PHASE SHIFT OF GENERATED SIGNAL |
|---|---|---|
| 000 | $A_1$ | 0 |
| 001 | $A_2$ | 0 |
| 010 | $A_1$ | $1/(4f)$ |
| 011 | $A_2$ | $1/(4f)$ |
| 100 | $A_1$ | $2/(4f)$ |
| 101 | $A_2$ | $2/(4f)$ |
| 110 | $A_1$ | $3/(4f)$ |
| 111 | $A_2$ | $3/(4f)$ |

shifts differ by just a little. In addition, noise may distort signals so that differences between two signals may be unmeasurable.

One common approach is to use a combination of frequencies, amplitudes, or phase shifts, which allows us to use a larger group of legitimate signals while maintaining larger differences among them. One common technique is **quadrature amplitude modulation (QAM)**, in which a group of bits is assigned a signal defined by its amplitude and phase shift.*

For example, suppose we use two different amplitudes and four different phase shifts. Combining them allows us to define 8 different signals. Table 2.10 shows the relation between three-bit values and the signal. We define the amplitudes as $A_1$ and $A_2$ and the phase shifts as 0, $1/(4f)$, $2/(4f)$, and $3/(4f)$ where $f$ is the frequency. The shifts correspond to 1/4, $2/4f$, and $3/4f$ of a period, respectively.

Figure 2.42 shows the changing signal due to the transmission of the bit string 001-010-100-011-101-000-011-110. (The hyphens are inserted for readability only and are not part of the transmission.) To understand why the signal looks this way, let's proceed very carefully. The first three bits, 001, define a signal with amplitude $A_2$ and phase shift 0. Consequently, as discussed in the previous section, the signal starts at 0 volts and oscillates between $A_2$ and $-A_2$. As before, the number of cycles

---

*An electrical engineer may disagree with this definition. Quadrature amplitude modulated signals are created by adding two analog signals with the same frequency. One signal corresponds to a sine function and the other to a cosine. (Sine and cosine functions differ by a 90° angle, hence the term quadrature.) This means the signal has the form $C*\sin(x) + D*\cos(x)$. Variable $x$ varies with time depending on the signal's frequency, and $C$ and $D$ depend on the initial signal.

However, trigonometry shows $C*\sin(x) + D*\cos(x)$ may also be written as $A*\sin(x + P)$ where $A = \sqrt{C^2 + D^2}$ and $P = \text{Arcsin}(C/\sqrt{C^2 + D^2})$. Thus, for our purposes, we can think of the signal as one with a varying amplitude and phase shift.

FIGURE 2.42    Quadrature Amplitude Modulation (2 Amplitudes and 4 phases), 3 Bits per Baud

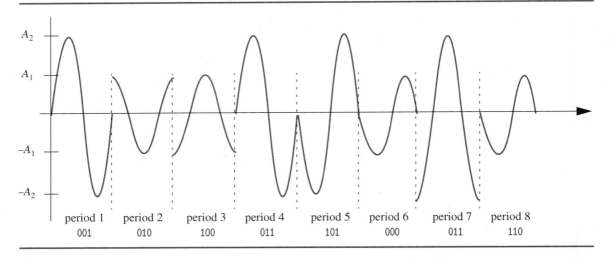

| period 1 | period 2 | period 3 | period 4 | period 5 | period 6 | period 7 | period 8 |
|----------|----------|----------|----------|----------|----------|----------|----------|
| 001 | 010 | 100 | 011 | 101 | 000 | 011 | 110 |

FIGURE 2.43    Effect of Phase Shift on a Signal

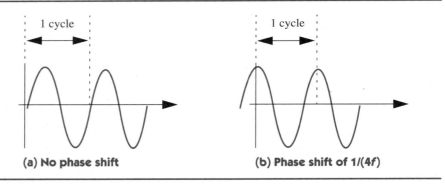

(a) No phase shift              (b) Phase shift of 1/(4*f*)

depends on the frequency and the length of time the signal is transmitted. We have drawn one cycle for convenience.

The next three bits, 010, define a signal with amplitude $A_1$ and phase shift $1/(4f)$. Thus, as Figure 2.42 shows, the signal oscillates between $A_1$ and $-A_1$. Now, with no phase shift the signal would start at 0 and increase to $A_1$. However, as the previous section discussed, a positive phase shift corresponds to a left horizontal shift in the graph. To help illustrate, Figure 2.43 shows (a) a graph with no phase shift and (b) one with a phase shift of $1/(4f)$.

To understand the graph in Figure 2.43b recall that $p = 1/(4f)$ where $p$ is the period. This means $1/(4f)$ corresponds to one fourth of a period, and the graph in Figure 2.43b is that of Figure 2.43a shifted left one fourth of a period. Therefore, it can be viewed as starting at its maximum, decreasing to its minimum, and rising again to its maximum. In effect, we can view the first one fourth of a period, the part where it goes from 0 to its maximum, as being cut out. This is exactly what the second period in Figure 2.42 shows.

The third set of three bits, 100, defines a signal with amplitude $A_1$ and phase shift $2/(4f)$. Before we explain its effect, examine the signal at the end of the second period. It is currently at its maximum of $A_1$. Now if there were no phase shift the signal would just continue starting at $A_1$ and decrease to $-A_1$. But a phase shift of $2/(4f)$ means that half of a period is eliminated. Since the previous signal ended at its maximum, half of a period corresponds to that part of the signal that decreases from $A_1$ to $-A_1$. Consequently the signal begins at its minimum value at the start of the third period.

Now let's provide a general description of how to generate a signal from a three-bit group. The signal generated by a three-bit group depends on where the previous signal ends. The phase shift is relative to that ending point. Table 2.11 defines the new signal as a function of the phase shift and position of the previous signal. Keep in mind that the minimum or maximum in the first column refers to that of the previous signal, whereas the minimum or maximum in the second through fifth columns refer to the maximum of the current signal.

Let's show how to apply this table in defining the signal over the fourth period in Figure 2.42. The position of the previous signal (in period 3) is at its minimum. Moreover, the bits 011 define a signal of amplitude $A_2$ and phase shift $1/(4f)$. Thus the signal is defined by the bottom row of the third column: It starts at 0 and increases to its maximum of $A_2$, just as the figure shows.

Note that a three-bit value will not always define the same signal. For example, periods 4 and 7 both correspond to 011, but the signals are different. Of course, they both have the same amplitude. However, the phase shift is relative to where the previous signal ended. As a result, even though the phase shifts are both $1/(4f)$, the two signals start at different values. Another observation worth noting is that the same signal in two different periods may correspond to different bit values. For example, periods 6 and 8 have the same signal but the bits are different. (Why?)

Other ways to modulate using combinations of amplitude, frequency, and phase shift are presented in Section 2.6 during its discussion of modem standards.

As the previous section discussed, higher bit rates can be achieved by associating more bits per baud and using more signal definitions. However, recall that

**TABLE 2.11    Rules for Signal Definition Using Quadrature Amplitude Modulation**

| POSITION OF PREVIOUS SIGNAL | NO PHASE SHIFT | $\frac{1}{4}$ PERIOD PHASE SHIFT | $\frac{2}{4}$ PERIOD PHASE SHIFT | $\frac{3}{4}$ PERIOD PHASE SHIFT |
|---|---|---|---|---|
| at 0, increasing | start at 0, increase | start at maximum | start at 0, decrease | start at minimum |
| at maximum | start at maximum | start at 0, decrease | start at minimum | start at 0, increase |
| at 0, decreasing | start at 0, decrease | start at minimum | start at 0, increase | start at maximum |
| at minimum | start at minimum | start at 0, increase | start at maximum | start at 0, decrease |

using more signals reduces the differences among them and increases the probability that a small amount of noise can make one signal look like another. If this happens, the receiving modem interprets the signal incorrectly and sends the wrong bits to its device.

One method of dealing with incorrect transmissions is, **Trellis coded modulation (TCM)**, which uses correction mechanisms. It adds extra bits to a group in such a way that only certain bit combinations are valid. The expanded groups then define a signal using a modulation technique similar to QAM. The signals are defined in such a way that if noise makes one look like another, the distorted one defines an invalid bit sequence. As a result, the receiver knows the received signal was incorrect.

We will not provide a detailed discussion of TCM at this point, but Chapter 5 will discuss error detection and correction methods in detail. We do note that TCM is a standard in some modems with high bit rates.

## ANALOG-TO-DIGITAL CONVERSION

Some analog-to-digital conversions are nothing more than the reverse of what we have just discussed. The modem examines incoming signals for amplitudes, frequencies, and phase shifts and generates digital signals accordingly. These analog signals have constant characteristics, at least over short intervals. What about analog signals whose characteristics change continually? The most obvious example may be analog signals produced by a sound such as a voice. They are more complex than those generated by digital data and require alternative conversion techniques.

One approach to digitizing an analog signal is **pulse amplitude modulation (PAM)**. In this simple process an analog signal is sampled at regular intervals and then a pulse with amplitude equal to that of the sampled signal is generated. Figure 2.44 shows the result of sampling at regular intervals.

On one hand, PAM generated signals look digital, but because a pulse may have any amplitude the signal has analog characteristics. One way to make the pulses truly digital is to assign amplitudes from a predefined set to the sampled signals.

FIGURE 2.44    **Pulse Amplitude Modulation**

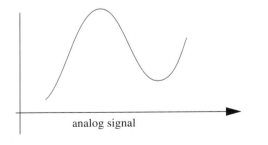

analog signal

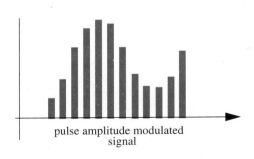

pulse amplitude modulated
signal

FIGURE 2.45    **Pulse Code Modulation**

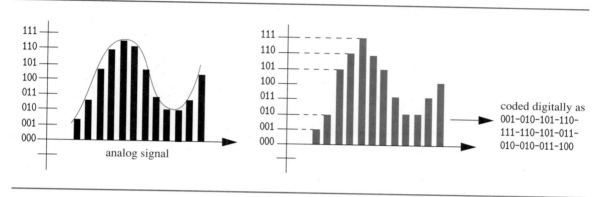

coded digitally as
001-010-101-110-
111-110-101-011-
010-010-011-100

This process is called **pulse code modulation (PCM)**. For example, suppose we divide the amplitude range into a set of $2^n$ amplitudes and associate an $n$-bit binary number with each one. Figure 2.45 shows a division into 8 values ($n = 3$).

As before, we sample the analog signal periodically. But this time we choose one of $2^n$ amplitudes that most closely matches the sample's amplitude. We then encode the pulse using the corresponding bit sequence. The bit sequence can then be transmitted using whatever digital transmission is in use. By sampling at regular intervals at a rate of $s$ per second, we achieve a bit rate of $n*s$ bits per second. Figure 2.45 shows the process. The first sample corresponds to 001, the second to 010, and so on.

At the receiving end the bit string is divided into groups of $n$ bits and the analog signal is reconstructed. The accuracy of the reconstruction depends on two things. The first is the sampling frequency $s$. Sampling at a frequency less than that of the signal can cause some oscillations to be missed completely (Figure 2.46). Consequently, the reconstructed signal can be a poor approximation to the original one. Thus we must sample frequently enough to preserve all the characteristics of the original signal. It would seem, therefore, that more samples are better. This is true, but only up to a point. Recall the Nyquist result from the previous section. It stated that sampling a signal at a rate twice its frequency is sufficient to preserve the signal's information. Now we have a nice application for the Nyquist result. If the original signal's maximum frequency is $f$, anything larger than $s = 2*f$ will not provide a better approximation than with $s = 2*f$.

The second factor that affects accuracy is the number of amplitudes from which to choose. Figure 2.45 showed just 8 amplitudes for simplicity. With relatively large differences between the sampled signal and the pulse, the reconstructed signal becomes distorted. Reducing differences between adjacent pulse amplitudes helps reduce it.

One more note: Higher sampling frequencies and more pulse amplitudes create higher quality transmissions, but at a price. Each produces more bits per second, requiring a higher bit rate, which costs more.

FIGURE 2.46    **Sampling at Too Low a Frequency**

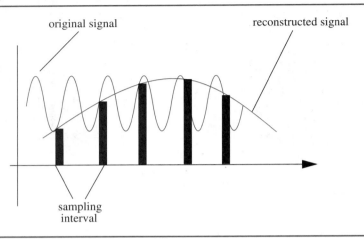

original signal

reconstructed signal

sampling
interval

There are several common applications of PCM. One is the digitizing of voice signals over long distance telephone lines. A worldwide standard makes 8000 samples per second and uses 8 bits per sample. In accordance with the Nyquist result, this frequency represents a little more than twice the maximum voice frequency your telephone can handle. It also requires a bit rate of 8*8000, or approximately 64K bps.*

Another application is in **compact disc (CD)** technology. The music on a CD is coded optically in a digital format using PCM. To preserve the high quality of sound, however, PCM coding requires a higher frequency and more bits per pulse. Actual values depend on specific equipment. For example, we checked the owner's manual of a CD player and found the following technical specifications:

Sampling frequency: 44.1 kHz

D-A conversion: 16-bit linear

The D-A, as you might guess, refers to digital-analog. Sixteen bits allows approximately 64,000 sample amplitudes. The sampling frequency of approximately 44,000 samples per second is slightly more than twice the listed frequency response range of 2–20,000 Hz. The term "linear" means the pulse amplitudes are distributed evenly[†].

---

*In practice, optical fibers used by long distance carriers have much higher bit rates because they are capable of carrying many phone conversations simultaneously by multiplexing. Section 3.3 discusses this in more detail.

[†] In some cases, such as in telephone systems, the amplitudes are not distributed evenly. There are more pulse amplitudes in a range where values are more likely to occur. This uneven distribution, called companding, can improve voice quality without using more bits for each sample.

There are other modulation techniques, but we will not elaborate here. For example, pulse duration modulation varies the duration of equal amplitude pulses to code information. Differential pulse code modulation measures differences in consecutive samples. Delta modulation is a variation on differential pulse code modulation that uses just 1 bit per sample. For more information on these and other modulation techniques, consult Reference 11.

## 2.6    Modems and Modem Standards

Now that we have discussed how to communicate via telephone line, you may think that we are done, and that all you need is a modem to connect to the telephone system to communicate with anything else using a modem connection. Well, you might as well say, "I just bought a computer and now I can do wonderful things with it."

In the early 1980s, when PCs (often advertised as "home computers") first became available, a lot of people rushed to be among the first to have access to these new and powerful tools. However, many overlooked one, small detail. They had to learn how to use software. This was not an easy task for the novice (it wasn't always an easy task for the professional either).

In addition, many people who did manage to learn software found that their friends and colleagues bought different computers and learned different software. This made sharing and communicating next to impossible. The key words that apply to modems as well are "software" and "compatibility." Figure 2.47 shows a modem connected to a PC. The modulation techniques we have described show how digital

FIGURE 2.47    **Modem Connected to a PC** (reproduced by permission of Hayes Microcomputer Products, Inc.)

signals are changed to analog. But to get the signals to the modem in the first place, and to retrieve digital signals the modem creates from telephone signals, we need software.

Now suppose you have software and attach the PC to the modem. When it receives analog signals it must know how they were modulated. Likewise, when it modulates, it must use a scheme the modem at the receiving end can understand. If the two modems do not understand the same modulation schemes they will not communicate. We need compatibility to do this.

Fortunately, the standards to which modem manufacturers adhere define bit rate, baud rate, and the modulation scheme. The best known standards, defined by CCITT, typically are identified by "V.xx," where "xx" is an identifying number. There are also AT&T or Bell modems very similar to certain CCITT standards.

We will describe a couple of standards in detail and provide a list of the most popular standards. The CCITT V.21 modem modulates using frequency shift keying. One bit defines the frequency, consequently its bit rate and baud rate are the same (300, very slow by today's standards).

The frequency assignment depends on whether the modem has originated (**originate mode**) or received (**answer mode**) a call. If the modem is in originate mode it sends a 0 using 980 Hz and a 1 using 1180 Hz. In answer mode, a 0 corresponds to 1650 Hz and a 1 to 1850 Hz. Using two sets of frequency allows full duplex communication (discussed in Section 3.1). For now, it means that data can be transmitted in both directions at the same time.

Since the baud rate is 300, the signal's duration is $1/300 \approx .0033$ second. In the early days of communications, the relatively long duration made the signal less susceptible to noise. If some of it was distorted, there was enough left to be recognized by the unsophisticated (by today's standards) modems. Today's more sophisticated devices can use much shorter durations, thus increasing both baud and bit rate.

The AT&T 103 modem works similarly. It uses 1070 Hz for a 0-bit and 1270 for a 1-bit in originate mode and 2025 Hz for a 0-bit and 2225 for a 1-bit in answer mode.

Another standard is the V.22 modem. It uses phase shift keying associating two bits with each phase shift. It has a baud rate of 600 and a bit rate of 1200. Frequency and amplitude are constant.

## SIGNAL CONSTELLATION

Modems that modulate by changing the phase shift and amplitude have a **signal constellation**, a diagram that uses points plotted on a coordinate system to define all legitimate signal changes. Figure 2.48 shows how to interpret one point. It is quantified by its length (distance from the origin) and the angle it makes with the horizontal axis. Recall from the previous section that length and angle (phase shift) are defined by variables $C$ and $D$, amplitudes of the sine and cosine function that create the QAM signal. Each point defines a legitimate signal change. The signal's amplitude corresponds to the point's distance from the origin, and the phase shift corresponds to the angle with the horizontal.

FIGURE 2.48   **Quantifying a Point on a Signal Constellation**

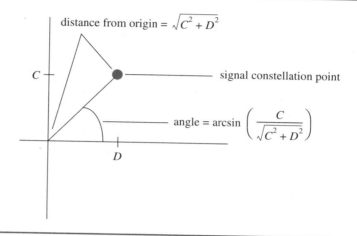

In general, angles on a signal constellation measure between 0° and 360°. Previously, however, we defined phase shifts as a fraction of a period ranging between 0 and 1 period. To interpret the signal constellation correctly, we define a linear relationship between the angles in the constellation and the fraction of a period. Specifically, an angle of $x°$ corresponds to $x/360$ of a period. So, for example, an angle of 90° corresponds to $90/360 = 1/4$ of a period.

Using this interpretation, Figure 2.49 shows the signal constellation for a V.22 modem. It shows four points all the same distance from the origin, which means the amplitude does not change with the signal. These four points also make angles of 0°, 90°, 180°, and 270° with the horizontal axis. Therefore, legitimate phase shifts are none, one-fourth, one-half, and three-fourths of a period.

A more complex standard is the V.22bis standard. Figure 2.48 also shows its signal constellation of 16 points. The standard calls for 600 baud and 4 bits per baud, giving a data rate of 2400 bps. If you look carefully at the signal constellation you see there are 3 different amplitudes and 12 possible phase shifts. These figures should provide 36 combinations, but only 16 are used. The restriction is due to error detection mechanisms, to be discussed shortly.

The last signal constellation in Figure 2.49 corresponds to the V.32 standard. It is a 32-point constellation, using 2400 baud and 5 bits per baud. However, the data rate is 4*2400 = 9600 bps. The extra bit per baud occurs because the standard uses Trellis coded modulation, an error correction modulation scheme that transmits extra bits.

By looking at these signal constellations (and others), you might notice they have one thing in common. The points all seem to be spaced evenly. This is not just to create pretty constellation pictures. Modems, like grumpy people who have no appreciation for art, don't care what the picture looks like. The fact remains that

FIGURE 2.49    **Signal Constellations**

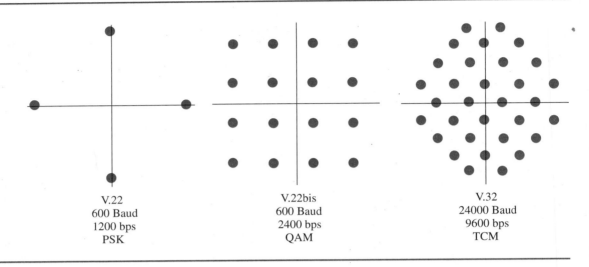

| V.22 | V.22bis | V.32 |
| 600 Baud | 600 Baud | 24000 Baud |
| 1200 bps | 2400 bps | 9600 bps |
| PSK | QAM | TCM |

FIGURE 2.50    **Distortion of Signal Constellation Points**

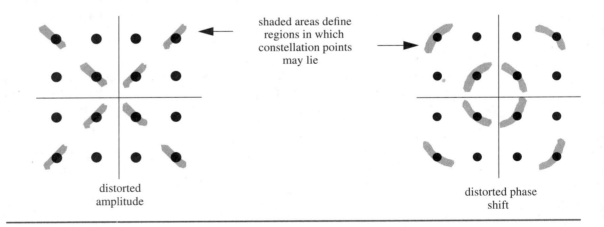

shaded areas define
regions in which
constellation points
may lie

distorted
amplitude

distorted phase
shift

most communications occur over noisy lines. To say that two signals differ by a 45° phase or that one's amplitude is twice the other is legitimate only in the absence of noise. The truth is, the phases may differ by 45° ± x° where x corresponds to noise. Similarly, a signal's amplitude will actually be measured as A ± y where y corresponds to noise.

Figure 2.50 shows the effect of some noise on a signal constellation. A change in amplitude moves a constellation point farther from or closer to the origin. As a result, the point for the actual signal may be anywhere in the figure's shaded region. Similarly, a distorted phase shift can cause the point to move along a small circular arc. Worse yet, noise does not discriminate. Either type of distortion can occur independent of the other. The result is that the constellation point for a distorted signal may be anywhere within a circular region of where it should be.

If the initial points are separated enough and the noise is small enough, the noisy regions do not overlap. Consequently, a modem can recognize a distorted signal. However, if the noise is such that the regions overlap, then communication is impaired. If the point for a distorted signal lies in the intersection of two shaded regions, the modem cannot tell which one it should be in (Figure 2.51).

As you probably expect, there are many other modem standards. They vary in baud rate, bits per baud, and modulation technique. Table 2.12 summarizes some of them. We must also note that many modems adhere to several standards. This is useful when communicating with a site that implements several of them. Typically, the modem can dial, exchange protocols, and then choose automatically the appropriate standard. These **autobaud modems** are convenient because users do not have to remember which phone number corresponds to which standard. They also allow users to communicate using any of several standards with the same modem and PC. Users can determine the standards by looking at the technical specifications in the owner's manual. There is a section specifying the data encoding mechanism at several data rates. For example, the Smartmodem 9600, manufactured by Hayes Microcomputer Products, Inc., will communicate at 300 bps (V.21), 1200 bps (V.22), 2400 bps (V.22bis), or 4800 or 9600 bps (V.32).

References 22, 24, 25, 26, and 27 contain descriptions of some of the standards expected to be popular in the 1990s and some of the products that use them. For example, the V.42bis standard uses data compression, a technique that reduces the number of bits used to store information. Reducing the number of bits before transmission allows more information to be sent per unit of time. The result is a per-

**FIGURE 2.51    Interpreting Constellation Points for a Distorted Signal**

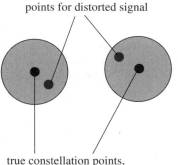
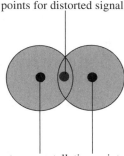

points for distorted signal

points for distorted signal

true constellation points, nonoverlapping noise ranges

true constellation points, overlapping noise ranges

TABLE 2.12    **Some Modem Standards**

| STANDARD | BAUD RATE | BIT RATE (BPS) | MODULATION TECHNIQUE |
|---|---|---|---|
| V.21/Bell 103 | 300 | 300 | FSK |
| V.22/Bell 212 | 600 | 600 or 1200 | PSK |
| V.22bis | 600 | 1200 or 2400 | QAM |
| V.23 | 1200 | 1200 | FSK |
| V.26 | 1200 | 2400 | PSK |
| V.26bis | 1200 | 1200 or 2400 | PSK |
| V.26ter | 1200 | 1200 or 2400 | PSK |
| V.27 | 1600 | 4800 | PSK |
| V.27bis | 1200 or 1600 | 2400 or 4800 | PSK |
| V.27ter | 1200 or 1600 | 2400 or 4800 | PSK |
| V.29 | 2400 | 4800 or 9600 | PSK or QAM |
| V.32 | 2400 | 4800 or 9600 | QAM or TCM |
| V.32bis | 2400 | 14400 | TCM |
| V.32terbo | 2400 | 19200 | TCM |
| V.33 | 2400 | 14400 | QAM |

ceived increase in the data rate, allowing rates in excess of the theoretical maximum mentioned in Section 2.4. Chapter 3 will discuss compression techniques.

Yet another standard under development is the V.fast standard, which, depending on the baud rate, would use up to 768 points in the signal constellation. As of this writing, CCITT had not assigned a number. Reference 24 refers to it as V.fast. Some are estimating it will achieve a raw bit rate of approximately 24,000 bps. If used with V.42bis compression, perceived data rates could approach 100,000 bps. Clearly, much is being done in modem standards.

## INTELLIGENT (HAYES COMPATIBLE) MODEMS

We end our discussion of modems by discussing the **intelligent modem**, or **Hayes compatible modem**. As we have discussed, modems modulate and demodulate signals. However, almost every modem on the market does more. With appropriate software, a user can enter commands directing the modem to take certain actions such as dialing or answering the phone. Such intelligent modems have a processor to carry out these functions.

Hayes Microcomputer Products, Inc., developed a modem that has become commonplace. The Hayes modems are designed to respond to a set of instructions called AT commands. Using appropriate software, the user enters the letters AT followed by the command. Each command consists of one or more letters followed by parameters. Two common parameters are the D and T commands. The letter D represents dial and instructs the modem to dial the number that follows the command.

The letter T indicates the modem should use tone dialing (as with push-button) as opposed to pulse dialing (as with rotary dials). To illustrate, a user wanting the modem to dial the number 555-1234 from a touch tone phone would enter the command ATDT5551234.

In some cases, when dialing from within an organization, you must first enter 9, wait for another dial tone, and dial the number. How will a modem respond to this need? If it simply dials the numbers before the second dial tone, it may try to connect to an operator's recorded message saying, "Your phone call cannot be completed . . . ." In some cases, you can instruct the modem to pause by including a comma ',' as part of the command. For example, if you must dial 9, wait, and then dial 555-1234, the appropriate command would be ATDT9,5551234.

Table 2.13 lists some common modem commands. Note that commands can be listed consecutively to form command strings such as the one described previously. We intend this as a general overview and not as a complete command list. You should certainly consult your modem's manual for proper operation.

TABLE 2.13    **Example Modem Commands**

| COMMAND | FUNCTION |
|---|---|
| A | Put modem in answer mode. The modem will go off-line (i.e., answer a call) when it detects an incoming signal. |
| AT | Stands for Attention code. Precedes most commands. |
| B | Use CCITT V.22bis standard to communicate at 1200 baud. |
| D | Dial the following number. |
| E0, E1 | Enables (E1) or disables (E0) echo printing of characters sent to the modem from the terminal. |
| H | Put modem "on hook"; that is, hang up. |
| H1 | Put modem "off hook." |
| Ln | Adjust speaker volume according to value of $n$. |
| P | Use pulse dialing. This is typical for rotary dial telephones. Typically appears following the $D$ command |
| Q0, Q1 | Enables (Q0) or disables (Q1) returning result codes. |
| Sn | Display contents of register $n$ on terminal. |
| Sn=x | Store value of $x$ in register $n$. |
| T | Use tone dialing. Typically appears following the D command. |
| V0, V1 | After receiving a command, a modem returns a result code. It may be displayed as digits (V0) or as words (V1). |
| W | Wait an amount of time specified by a register value. This can be used where you must wait for a dial tone. |
| Xn | Different values of $n$ select a set of options for dialing and connect messages. For example, after the connection is made, you will see a message stating "CONNECT" or "CONNECT 2400," with the latter specifying the data rate at which the modem will operate. You can also specify whether to wait for a dial tone before dialing or to recognize a busy signal. |

The commands of Table 2.13 can be entered from a PC using appropriate software. Some software also allows you to write several commands on a file. The files may be called **scripts** or **macros**, and they allow the user to execute the commands on a file many times without having to type them each time. This is useful in cases where you frequently dial up the same line and go through the same logon procedures.

A last item worth mentioning is the use of modems in which a call waiting feature is available. Call waiting means that you hear an audible click if you are on the telephone and someone else is trying to call. The audible click is actually a brief, but temporary, disconnection. However, some modems will actually disconnect (go on hook) if this happens, thus terminating your connection. Others will not react to brief, temporary interruptions. Of course, if data is being transmitted during the interruption, some of it will be lost. Certainly it is something you want to be aware of when you use a modem. In many cases call waiting can be disabled by entering *70 on your phone before calling.

## 2.7  Summary

This chapter dealt mainly with communications media and equipment, applications, and communications theory. Primary communications media include twisted pair, coaxial cable, fiber optics, and microwave and satellite transmission. Electrically conducting media such as twisted pair and cable are cheaper than fiber and easier to tap into. However, they have smaller bandwidths and are subject to electrical interference.

Microwaves and satellites communicate through free space. That is, they require no physical connection. Satellites offer worldwide communications, and microwaves provide communication across distances where physical connections are impossible or impractical. The data rates depend on the transmission frequencies. Higher frequencies provide higher rates but are subject to more interference in the atmosphere.

Communication applications include VSAT (very small aperture terminal) systems, the telephone system, PBXs (private branch exchanges), ISDN (integrated services digital network), cellular phones, and fax machines. VSAT uses satellite technology and allows a viable alternative to the telephone system for many businesses and industries. The telephone system connects the largest number of people. For many years it was used primarily for voice communications, but each year finds more people using it for data communications. In fact, many organizations install a private system called a PBX for both voice and data. For many, it is a viable and economical alternative to the telephone system. For internal company communication, many PBXs bypass the central office but still have trunks to the interexchange telephone system.

Cellular telephones have provided telephone users freedom from a physical connection. An area is divided into regions or cells, each of which has a transmitter capable of communicating with the telephone system. The cellular telephone then communicates with a transmitter within the cell. ISDN defines what many believe is the future of worldwide communications. When operational, it will replace the conventional analog signaling mechanisms of the telephone with completely digital ones. It will transform the home telephone into a computer terminal that can be used for voice or data communications. The fax machine has combined the two technologies of copying and transmissions. Like a copier, it reproduces images on paper. However, it reproduces them electronically and transmits them through the telephone system. The fax on the other end receives the signals and recreates the original image.

To transmit data we need to use a code, a mechanism that associates bit strings to certain information. The most common codes are ASCII (American standard code for information interchange) and EBCDIC (extended binary coded decimal interchange code). Each associates a bit string with each keyboard character and many special control functions. Other codes of importance are the Baudot, Morse, and BCD (binary coded decimal).

The next step is to determine what kind of digital or analog signal will define a 0 or 1 bit. Digital encoding schemes include NRZ (non-return-to-zero), Manchester, and Differential Manchester. NRZ assigns a fixed voltage level to a 0 and another to a 1. Both Manchester schemes (also called self-clocking codes) distinguish between a 0 and 1 by either a high-to-low or low-to-high voltage transition.

Analog signals convey information by changing amplitudes, frequencies, or phase shifts. In general, the number of bits per change depends on the number of allowable changes. Consequently, the data rate depends on the baud rate. The Nyquist result and the sampling theorem together show that over a noiseless channel the data rate = $2*f*\log_2(B)$. Here, $f$ is the maximum frequency and $B$ is the number of different signals.

Claude Shannon extended the result to include noisy channels. His famous result states that the data rate = bandwidth$*\log_2(1+S/N)$. Here, $S$ and $N$ are the signal and noise power respectively. This result puts a theoretical limit on the data rate over any noisy channel.

A significant amount of communication involves connecting digital devices using analog signals and connecting analog devices using digital signals. Consequently, there is a need to study modulation and demodulation techniques. Digital to analog conversions often require changing an analog signal in response to a group of bits. Typical changes affect the amplitude (amplitude shift keying), frequency (frequency shift keying), or the phase shift (phase shift keying). Another technique known as quadrature amplitude modulation uses combinations of these changes.

One way to convert from analog back to digital is to simply reverse these processes. However, if the original signal is a complex analog signal such as voice we need a different mechanism. One approach called PCM (pulse code modulation) samples an analog signal at regular intervals. It then associates a bit string with each sample and transmits it. On the receiving end the bits are received and the analog signal reconstructed.

Modems are perhaps the most familiar modulation/demodulation devices. They are used to connect digital devices such as a PC and a computer via the telephone system. Modems use different modulation techniques, which are defined by standards. Two devices can communicate only if the modems on each end recognize the same standard. Most modems are also small special-purpose computers. They can respond to commands a user, with the help of appropriate software, enters at a terminal. These intelligent or Hayes compatible modems are commonplace.

Data communication is a dynamic field of study. Researchers are continually increasing the data rates of different media and reducing their costs to make them technologically and economically feasible for more people than ever before.

# Review Questions

1. List five transmission media and rank them in order of data rate capability.

2. Distinguish between a digital and an analog signal.

3. Distinguish between data rate and bandwidth.

4. What three components completely describe an analog signal?

5. How are a signal's period and frequency related?

6. Distinguish between baseband and broadband modes.

7. Define the index of refraction.

8. What is the difference between a laser and LED in optical fiber communications?

9. List three modes for optical fiber communication and compare them.

10. Are the following statements TRUE or FALSE? Why?

    • Direct microwave transmission can happen between any two surface points on earth.
    • Satellite transmission requires a stationary communication satellite.
    • Thicker optical fiber allows a higher data rate.
    • Satellite transmission rates are limited only by the limitation of equipment to send and receive high frequency signals.
    • Local area networks do not require a physical connection among their components.
    • Satellite communications are practical only for the largest companies and agencies.
    • A Fax machine scans a page and transmits text information one character at a time.
    • Light can travel through optical fiber at different speeds.
    • Visible light and electromagnetic waves are the same.
    • Optical fibers have a hollow center through which light passes and reflects off a reflective surface surrounding it.

11. Distinguish between a horn and a parabolic dish antenna.

12. List the five major components of the telephone system.

13. Describe how a cellular telephone works.

14. What is a very small aperture terminal system?

15. Which transmissions are susceptible to interference?

16. What is a periodic signal?

17. Why are the wires in a twisted pair twisted (as opposed to using parallel wires)?

18. What is the purpose of the cladding in optical fiber communications?

19. What was the Sputnik?

20. What is a private branch exchange?

21. What is the difference between a printable character and a control character?

22. What is the difference between the ASCII and the EBCDIC codes?

23. The Baudot code for the character '0' (zero) is the same as that for the character 'P'. How can that be?

24. Distinguish among NRZ, Manchester, and Differential Manchester digital encoding.

25. With all the precision equipment currently available, why does a long run of 0s or 1s present a problem when using an encoding scheme such as NRZ?

26. What baud rate is required to realize a 10 Mbps data rate using NRZ encoding? Using Manchester encoding?

27. Distinguish between the Nyquist and the Shannon results.

28. Define signal-to-noise ratio.

29. Suppose a transmission were free of noise. Does this imply that there is no limit on the maximum data rate that can be achieved with current equipment?

30. Given the proliferation of computing equipment using telephone lines, why is the telephone's bandwidth only approximately 3000 Hz?

31. Shannon's result relates data rates and bandwidth in the presence of noise. However, the amount of noise varies with the medium and source. How does Shannon's result account for it?

32. What does a modem allow you to do with a PC?

33. What is the difference between modulation and demodulation?

34. Distinguish among frequency modulation, amplitude modulation, and phase modulation.

35. What is quadrature amplitude modulation?

36. Distinguish between pulse code modulation and pulse amplitude modulation.

37. Why are there so many different modem standards?

**38.** What is a signal constellation?

**39.** What is an intelligent modem?

**40.** If a modem supports several different standards, how does it know which one to use when you connect to another computer over a telephone line?

# Exercises

**1.** If a satellite's orbital height is fixed, why is it not possible to change the time required to orbit the earth by changing the speed of the satellite?

**2.** Suppose a company is trying to establish communications between several sites in different parts of a large city. Would microwave links be a good idea? Why or why not?

**3.** Digital signals can be translated to analog signals by using relatively simple techniques such as varying the amplitude or frequency between two specified values. What is the advantage of using more complex schemes such as QAM?

**4.** Write a program that prompts its user with a message and a bell sound to input a number and echo print it.

**5.** Write a program that reads a character string and prints it on the screen moving the cursor from right to left rather than the usual left to right orientation.

**6.** Write a program that clears the screen.

**7.** What is the Baudot code for the character string 'SDG564FSDH65'?

**8.** Table 2.4 shows ASCII codes for 0 through 9. Why is there not an ASCII code for 10?

**9.** Draw the digital signals for the bit string 0010100010 using each of the NRZ, Manchester, and differential Manchester digital encoding techniques. Assume the signal is "high" prior to receipt of the first bit.

**10.** What is the bit string associated with the following Manchester encoded signal? What is the bit string if it is a differential Manchester encoded signal?

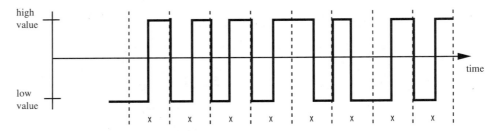

11.   Draw analog signals corresponding to the following functions.

- $y = \sin(t)$
- $y = \sin(2t)$
- $y = 4\sin(2t)$
- $y = 2\sin(2t + \pi/2)$
- $y = 3\sin(t)$
- $y = \sin(t + \pi/4)$
- $y = \sin(2t - \pi/2)$

12.   Assume the maximum analog frequency of a medium is 6000 Hz. According to the Nyquist result, what are the maximum data rates for schemes that use 1, 2, 3, and 4 bits per signal component?

13.   According to Nyquist, what frequency is necessary to support a data rate of 30,000 bps using only one bit per signal component? Three bits per signal component?

14.   In your own words, what is the significance of Shannon's result?

15.   What is the actual signal power (relative to the noise power) if the signal-to-noise ratio is given as 60 decibels?

16.   What is the decibel rating if the signal power is twice the noise power?

17.   Assume the maximum analog bandwidth of a medium is 6000 Hz. According to the Shannon result, what is the maximum data rate if the signal-to-noise ratio is 40 decibels? 60 decibels?

18.   According to Shannon, what bandwidth is necessary to support a data rate of 30,000 bps assuming a signal-to-noise ratio of 40 decibels? What bandwidth is necessary if the number of decibels is doubled?

19.   Suppose you want to achieve a data rate of 64,000 bps using a maximum bandwidth of 10,000 Hz. What is the minimum allowable signal-to-noise ratio?

20.   Can a phase shift of one period be used to distinguish signals?

21.   Using QAM, is it possible for the exact same signal in two different periods to correspond to different bit values?

22.   Using QAM, do the same bits always correspond to the same analog signals?

23.   Draw the QAM analog signal (*carefully*) that transmits the following bit string:

001011010101101010110

Assume the current analog signal is established as shown here. You need draw only one complete cycle for each modulation change.

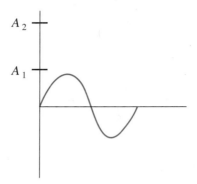

**24.**   Suppose a modem uses quadrature amplitude modulation described by Table 2.10. What bit sequence corresponds to the following signal (starting with the second time period)?

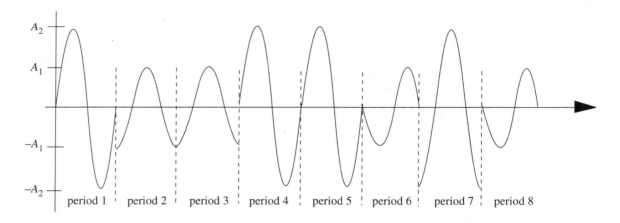

**25.**   Design a QAM technique that uses up to 8 phase shifts and 2 amplitudes. How many bits per baud are there?

**26.**   Assume a QAM technique has up to $m$ phase shifts and $n$ amplitudes. How many bits per baud are there?

**27.**   Why don't modems use PCM techniques?

**28.**   If you have a CD player, examine its technical specifications and relate them to the discussions on PCM.

**29.** Why can't professionals design modems with arbitrarily high baud rates and thus realize unlimited data rates?

**30.** If you have a modem, check to see which standards it supports.

**31.** Draw the signal constellation for a modem that uses the QAM defined by Table 2.10. Draw another one for the QAM techniques described by Exercise 25.

**32.** Describe the signal changes (i.e., specify the amplitude and phase changes) associated with the signal constellations in Figure 2.49.

**33.** How many bits correspond to one signal component using the V.21 standard? What is the duration for one signal component?

**34.** Repeat Exercise 33 for the V.32 standard.

## REFERENCES

1. Sherman, K. *Data Communications: A User's Guide*, 3rd ed. Englewood Cliffs, NJ: Prentice-Hall, 1990.

2. Brodeur, P. *Currents of Death*. New York: Simon and Schuster, 1989.

3. Clarke, A. C. "Extra-Terrestrial Relays: Can Rocket Stations Give World-Wide Radion Coverage?" *Wireless World* (October 1945).

4. Hudson, H. *Communication Satellites*. New York: Free Press, 1990.

5. Politi, C. and J. Stein. "VSATs Give Corporate Networks a Lift." *Data Communications*, vol. 20, no. 2 (February 1991), 89–94.

6. Roussel, A. "VSAT Service Crosses the Border." *Data Communications*, vol. 22, no. 7 (May 1993), 73–8.

7. Saunders, S. "Wireless LAN Users: Take a Hike." *Data Communications*, vol. 22, no. 10 (July 1993), 49–50.

8. Saunders, S. "Wireless LANs: Closer to Cutting the Cord." *Data Communications*, vol. 22, no. 5 (March 1993), 59–64.

9. Dryden, P. "Wireless Technology Keeps Mobile Workers in Touch." *LAN Times*, vol. 10, no. 12 (June 1993), 1, 104–5.

10. Didio, L. "Microwave LAN Links Rocket Test Site." *LAN Times*, vol. 9, no. 20 (October 1992), 1, 102–4.

11. Black, U. *Data Networks Concept, Theory, and Practice*. Englewood Cliffs, NJ: Prentice-Hall, 1989.

12. Chorafas, D. N. *Telephony: Today and Tomorrow*. Englewood Cliffs, NJ: Prentice-Hall, 1984.

13. Pierce, J. R. *Signals: The Telephone and Beyond.* San Francisco: Freeman and Company, 1981.

14. Wasserman, N. *From Invention to Innovation: Long Distance Telephone Transmissions at the Turn of the Century.* Baltimore: Johns Hopkins University Press, 1985.

15. Rowe, S. H. *Business Telecommunications*, 2nd ed. New York: Macmillan, 1991.

16. Mulqueen, J. "Users Rate PBXs." *Data Communications*, vol. 20, no. 7 (June 1991), 77–82.

17. Stallings, W. *ISDN and Broadband ISDN*, 2nd ed. New York: Macmillan, 1992.

18. Mier, E. "Appraising PBXs with an Eye toward ISDN." *Data Communications*, vol. 19, no. 6 (May 1990), 105–12.

19. Head, J. "Fiber Optics in the '90s: Fact and Fiction." *Data Communications*, vol. 19, no. 12 (September 1990), 55–7.

20. Theodore, D. "LAN Interconnect Takes to the Airwaves." *Data Communications*, vol. 20 no. 9 (July 1991), 83–9.

21. Stallings, W. *Computer Organization and Architecture,* 3rd ed. New York: Macmillan, 1993.

22. Taub, H. and D. Schilling. *Principles of Communications Systems*, New York: McGraw-Hill, 1971.

23. Walrand, J. *Communications Networks: A First Course.* Boston: Richard D. Irwin, 1991.

24. Krechmer, K. "Modems 1991: Renewed, Revitalized, Ready." *Data Communications*, vol. 20, no. 7 (June 1991), 85–110.

25. Johnson, J. T. "Modem in the Middle: Sizing up V.32terbo." *Data Communications*, vol. 22, no. 6 (April 1993), 57–61.

26. Johnson, J. T. "V.32bis: The Modem in the Middle." *Data Communications*, vol. 21, no. 3 (February 1992), 87–92.

# CHAPTER 3

# DATA COMMUNICATION

Chapter 2 discussed transmission fundamentals and the specific mechanisms required to transmit information. This chapter goes one step farther and discusses communication. You might ask, "What is the difference between transmission and communication?"

To answer, consider an analogy of human speech. We could discuss the mechanisms behind speech—how the vocal chords contract and expand to allow air to exit our lungs and form sound and how the mouth manipulates these sounds to form what we call speech. But this is a long way from communicating. The words that come out must be organized to make sense. If they come out too quickly or too slowly, the speaker will not be understood. If many people speak simultaneously, no one is understood. If someone speaks a language you don't understand, communication is lost. If a sentence contains missing words or phrases (such as might occur when speaking in a second language), some meaning may be lost.

Electronic communication has similar problems. The receiver must know how message bits are organized to understand the message. The receiver must know how quickly they arrive to interpret the message. What happens if many people try to use a common medium simultaneously, as often occurs in a local area network (LAN)? Are there ways to transmit fewer bits and preserve the meaning of a message (presumably to save on transmission costs)?

This chapter discusses these topics. Section 3.1 discusses ways of communicating using serial, parallel, synchronous, and asynchronous transmission. It also contrasts one-way and two-way communications. The best way to ensure that devices send and receive in compatible ways is to adhere to standards. Section 3.2 discusses standards such as RS-232 and RS-449, which are commonly used to connect devices.

Sections 3.3 and 3.4 discuss ways that allow many messages to be transmitted on a single transmission medium. They discuss multiplexing and contention strategies common to LANs and the airwaves. Section 3.5 covers various data compression

**135**

methods, which reduce transmission costs by transmitting fewer bits without losing any information.

## 3.1 Transmission Modes

A transmission mode defines the way in which a bit group goes from one device to another. It also defines whether bits may travel in both directions simultaneously or whether devices must take turns sending and receiving.

### SERIAL AND PARALLEL TRANSMISSION

The first distinction we make is between serial and parallel transmission. **Parallel transmission** means that a group of bits is transmitted simultaneously by using a separate line (wire) for each bit (Figure 3.1a). Typically, the lines are bundled in a cable. Parallel transmissions are common especially where the distance between the two devices is short. For example, a PC-to-printer connection up to 25 feet is considered a safe distance. The most common examples are communication between a computer and peripheral devices. Other examples include communication among a CPU, memory modules, and device controllers.

Parallel transmission loses its advantage over longer distances. First, using multiple lines over long distances is more expensive than using a single one. Second, transmitting over longer distances requires thicker wires to reduce signal degradation. Bundling them into a single cable becomes unwieldy. A third problem involves the time required to transmit bits. Over a short distance, bits sent simultaneously will be received almost simultaneously. Over a long distance, however, wire resistance may cause the bits to drift a little and arrive at slightly different times, which can create problems at the receiving end.

FIGURE 3.1     **Parallel and Serial Transmission**

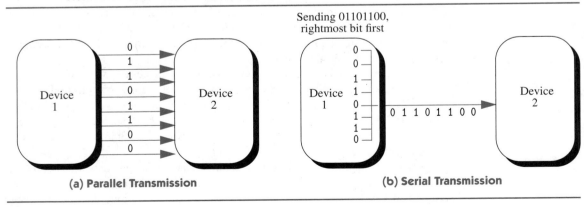

(a) Parallel Transmission          (b) Serial Transmission

**Serial transmission** provides an alternative to parallel transmission (Figure 3.1b). Using just one line, it transmits all the bits along it one after another. It is cheaper and more reliable than parallel transmission over long distances. It is also slower because the bits are sent one at a time.

The sending and receiving devices have an additional complexity. The sender must determine the order in which the bits are sent. For example, when sending 8 bits from one byte the sender must determine whether the high-order or low-order bits are sent first. Similarly, the receiver must know where to place the first-received bit within the destination byte. It may seem like a trivial issue, but different architectures may number the bits in a byte differently and if the protocols do not agree on how to order the bits the information will be transmitted incorrectly.

## Asynchronous and Synchronous Transmission

There are two ways to provide serial communication: asynchronous and synchronous transmission. **Asynchronous transmission** means that bits are divided into small groups (usually bytes) and sent independently. The sender can send the groups at any time and the receiver never knows when they will arrive (somewhat like a visit from a long-lost relative!).

One common example is using a terminal to communicate with a computer. Pressing a key containing a letter, number, or special character sends an 8-bit ASCII code.[*] The terminal sends the codes at any time, depending on how well or fast you type. Internally, the hardware must be able to accept a typed character at any time. (We should note that not all keyboard entries are transmitted asynchronously. Some intelligent terminals can buffer entries and transmit an entire line or screen to the computer. This is synchronous transmission, which we discuss shortly.)

Terminal input is not the only example of asynchronous transmission. In some cases, data is sent to a line printer one byte at a time. Asynchronous transmission is typical of **byte oriented I/O**, an operating systems term meaning that data is transferred a byte at a time.

There is a potential problem with asynchronous transmission. Remember that the receiver does not know when data will arrive until it gets there. By the time it detects it and can react, the first bit has come and gone. It is similar to someone coming up behind you unexpectedly and starting to talk. By the time you react and start listening, the first few words are missed. Consequently, each asynchronous transmission is preceded by a start bit (Figure 3.2). It alerts the receiver to the fact that data is arriving. This gives the receiver time to respond and accept and buffer the data bits. At the end of the transmission, a stop bit indicates the transmission's end. By convention an idle line (one that is transmitting no data) actually carries a

---

[*] We haven't forgotten that we defined the ASCII code as a 7-bit code. However, in many cases the 8th bit is used for parity checking. We will discuss this in Chapter 4. Even without parity, you can think of a 7-bit code as an 8-bit code in which the leading bit is always 0. Since most memory consists of 8-bit bytes, this is the simplest way to store a 7-bit code.

FIGURE 3.2    **Asynchronous Transmission**

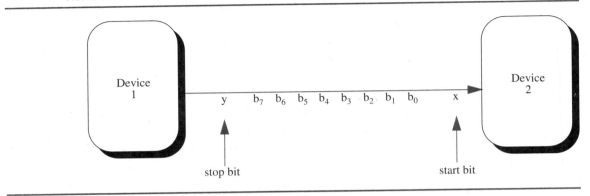

signal defining a binary 1. The start bit then causes the signal to change, corresponding to a 0. The remaining bits cause the signal to change depending on bit values. Finally the stop bit brings the signal back to the equivalent of a 1, where it stays until the next start bit arrives.

For example, suppose you enter the digits 321 at a terminal. Using an 8-bit extended ASCII code (with a leading 0) defines the following bits to be sent:

```
00110001 for the digit 1
00110010 for the digit 2
00110011 for the digit 3
```

Suppose we send each digit (left most bit first) separately using NRZ coding. Figure 3.3 shows the transmitted signal. In each case the start bit raises the signal alerting the receiver that other bits will follow. When they have all arrived for that digit, the stop bit lowers the signal. It remains low until the next start bit raises it.

Asynchronous transmission is designed for use with slow devices such as keyboards and some printers. It also has a high overhead. In the example above two extra bits are transmitted for every 8. This represents a 25% increase in the total transmission load. For slow devices that transmit little data, this is a small problem. However, for fast devices that transfer a lot of data, a 25% increase in load is significant.

With **synchronous transmission** much larger bit groups are sent. Instead of sending many characters separately, each with its own start and stop bit, they are grouped together and then transmitted as a whole. We call this group a **data frame** or **frame**.

The precise organization of a data frame varies with the protocol, discussed in Chapter 5. Data frames do have many common characteristics. Figure 3.4 shows the organization of a generic data frame. Again, the orientation is rightmost bits first.

The first part of the frame contains SYN characters, unique bit patterns that alert the receiver that a frame is arriving. A syn character is similar to the start bit discussed previously except that here, the pattern also ensures the receiver's sampling rate and the consistency of the rate at which the bits arrive.

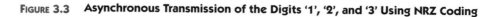

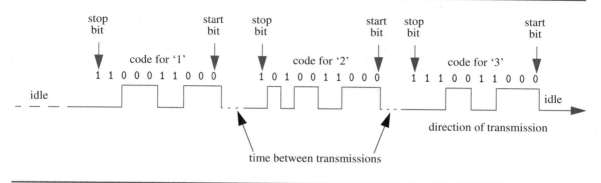

Next are control bits, which may include the following elements:

- Source address specifying where the frame originated.
- Destination address specifying where the frame should go. This is important in networks where a frame may go through several nodes to get to its destination. Each intermediate node uses the destination to determine where to route it. Chapter 7 discusses routing further.
- Actual number of data bytes.
- Sequence number. This is useful when many frames are sent and, for some reason, arrive out of order. The receiver uses the sequence numbers to reassemble them. Chapter 5 discusses this further.
- Frame type, distinguished by some protocols. Chapter 5 discusses some of these.

FIGURE 3.4    **Synchronous Transmission**

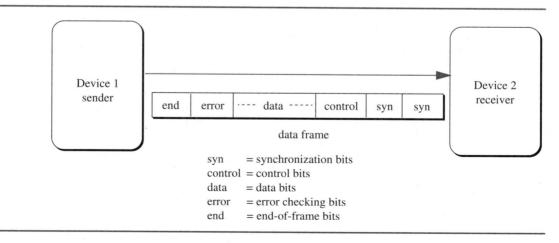

The data bits define the information being sent. There are no start and stop bits between the characters. The error checking bits are used to detect or correct transmission errors. We know from Chapter 2 that electrical interference can distort signals. But how does the receiver know when this happens? Typically, the sender transmits extra bits that depend on the data. If the data is altered the extra bits are not consistent with the data. Chapter 4 discusses error detection and correction techniques.

The last part of the frame is an end-of-frame marker. Like the SYN characters, it is a unique bit string indicating that no more bits are arriving (at least until the start of the next frame).

Synchronous transmission generally is much faster than asynchronous. The receiver does not start and stop for each character. Once it detects the SYN characters, it receives all the others as quickly as they arrive. In addition, there is less overhead. For example, a typical frame may have 500 bytes (4000 bits) of data containing 100 bits of overhead (specifics will vary). In this case, the added bits mean a 2.5% increase in the total bits transferred. Compare that with the 25% increase with asynchronous transmission.

It should be noted that as the number of data bits increases, the percentage of overhead bits decreases. On the other hand, larger data fields require larger buffers in which to store them, putting a limit on the size of a frame. In addition, larger frames occupy a transmission medium for a longer uninterrupted amount of time. In an extreme case, this could cause excessive waiting by other users.

A third transmission mode we mention briefly is **isochronous transmission**. Like asynchronous, characters are not transmitted contiguously; that is, there may be gaps between them. The gaps are not arbitrary, however. The gap is equal to the amount of time needed to send an integral number of characters. That is, if $T$ is the time required to send one character, the time between consecutive characters will be $n*T$, where $n$ is some integer.

In your readings you may encounter the term **bisync**. It is not a transmission mode in the same sense as asynchronous or synchronous. It is an acronym for binary synchronous communication, sometimes abbreviated as BSC, and is a protocol IBM introduced in the 1960s for synchronous communication between a computer and terminals. We will discuss it in Chapter 5.

## SIMPLEX, HALF-DUPLEX, AND FULL-DUPLEX COMMUNICATIONS

So far this chapter has dealt with ways to transmit information from one device to another, with a definite distinction between sender and receiver. This is an example of **simplex communications** (Figure 3.5). That is, communication goes only in one direction. The many examples include airport monitors, printers, television sets, or you talking with an unsympathetic professor about a bad grade.

Other applications require a greater flexibility in which a device can both send and receive. The methods vary. Some use **half-duplex communications** in which both devices can send and receive, but they must alternate. It is used in two-way radios, some modems, and some peripheral devices. For example, the previously mentioned bisync protocol is half duplex.

FIGURE 3.5    **Simplex, Half-Duplex, and Full-Duplex Communication**

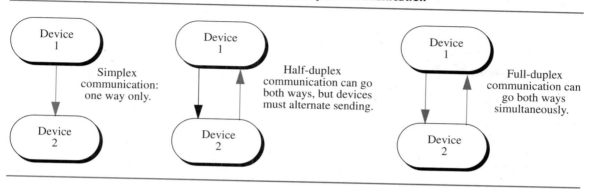

The most flexible method is **full-duplex communications**. Here a device can send and receive simultaneously. When a device is sending over one line it may be receiving on another. Many computer terminals use full-duplex communications. This is evidenced by the ability to continue typing at the same time that information is being printed on the screen. Many modems are also full duplex.

Two-way communication becomes complex, especially over networks. Protocols must be used to make sure information is received correctly and in an orderly manner and to allow devices to communicate efficiently. Discussions of these issues will be covered in the next two chapters.

## 3.2  Interface Standards

Chapter 2 and the previous section described several ways to transmit information. One might conclude that as long as two devices use the same mechanisms to send and receive, they can communicate. Communication does not necessarily occur, however. If two people speak at the same time, neither listening to the other, they are not communicating. Common sense dictates that in order to communicate, they must take turns listening and speaking. Orderly discussions require that rules (protocols) be established that recognize an individual wanting to speak. Communications among devices must be guided similarly by protocols. Sending modulated signals to a device does no good if the device is not prepared to sense the signals and interpret them.

Figure 3.6 shows a typical arrangement of connected devices. The acronym **DCE** means **data circuit-terminating equipment**, and **DTE** means **data terminal equipment**. The DTE (a PC, for example) does not connect to a network directly. It communicates through a DCE (a modem, for example). We call the connection between the DTE and DCE the **DTE-DCE interface**. This section focuses on DTE-DCE interface standards.

FIGURE 3.6    **DTE-DCE Interface**

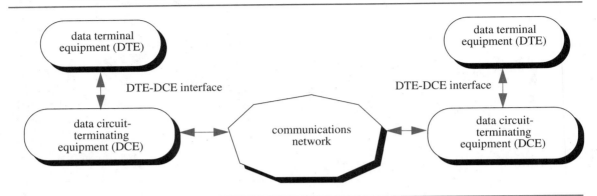

## RS-232 INTERFACE

One well-known standard is the **RS-232 standard**. It was developed by the Electronic Industries Association (EIA) in the early 1960s and has been revised several times. Probably the most common version, developed in the late 1960s, is known as RS-232-C. The technical level of detail differentiating the versions is beyond the scope of this text, but we will discuss the RS-232-C standard.[*]

The most obvious (visible) aspect of the standard is the number of lines (25) between the DTE and DCE. If the standard is fully implemented, the DTE and DCE are connected by a 25-line cable (sometimes called a DB-25 cable) connected to each device using a 25-pin connector (Figure 3.7). Each line has a specific function in establishing communication between the devices. Table 3.1 summarizes them and specifies the signal direction (i.e., whether the line is used to transmit from the DCE to the DTE or vice versa). The table also contains the EIA designation (circuit code) for each line.

FIGURE 3.7    **RS-232 Connector**

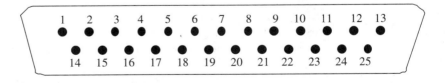

---

[*] Some years ago the EIA decided to replace the 'RS' designation with 'EIA'. Consequently, the standard is properly called the EIA-232 standard. However, because of its popularity and the fact that old habits die hard, the 'RS' designation is still commonly used.

TABLE 3.1    **RS-232-C Circuit Definitions**

| Circuit Code | Line # | Signal direction | Function |
|---|---|---|---|
| AA | 1 | | Protective ground. It is connected to the equipment frame and sometimes to external grounds. |
| AB | 7 | | Electrical ground. All signal voltages are measured relative to this ground. |
| BA | 2 | DTE to DCE | Transmit data (TD). DTE transmits data to the DCE on this circuit. |
| BB | 3 | DCE to DTE | Receive data (RD). DTE receives data from the DCE on this circuit. |
| CA | 4 | DTE to DCE | Request to send (RTS). DTE uses this circuit to request permission from the DCE before it can transmit data. |
| CB | 5 | DCE to DTE | Clear to send (CTS). The DCE uses this circuit to give the DTE permission to transmit data. |
| CC | 6 | DCE to DTE | Data set ready (DSR). A signal on this line indicates the DCE has connected to a communications medium and is ready to operate. For example, if the DCE is a modem, this circuit indicates whether it is off-hook. |
| CD | 20 | DTE to DCE | Data terminal ready (DTR). A signal on this line indicates the DTE is ready to transmit or receive. It can be used to signal a modem when to connect to a communications channel. |
| CE | 22 | DCE to DTE | Ring indicator. Indicates the DCE is receiving a ringing signal (e.g., when a modem receives a call) from the communications channel. |
| CF | 8 | DCE to DTE | Data carrier detect (DCD). Indicates the DCE is receiving a carrier signal that meets "suitability criteria" from the communications network. Essentially, this means the DCE understands the incoming signal. |
| CG | 21 | DCE to DTE | Signal quality detector. Indicates whether there is a high probability the incoming signal is error free. |
| CH/CI | 23 | DTE to DCE or DCE to DTE | Data signal rate selector/indicator. Where two signal rates are possible from the DTE to the DCE, this line specifies which is used. |
| DA | 24 | DTE to DCE | Transmitter signal element timing. Provides clock signals to DCE used for timing in signal generation. |
| DB | 15 | DCE to DTE | Transmitter signal element timing. Similar to DA, except the DCE provides timing signals to the DTE for the signals the DTE sends. |
| DD | 17 | DCE to DTE | Receiver signal element timing. Similar to DA, except the DCE provides timing signals to the DTE for the signals the DCE sends. |
| SBA | 14 | DTE to DCE | Secondary transmitted data. Same as BA except it uses a secondary channel. |
| SBB | 16 | DCE to DTE | Secondary received data. Same as BB except it uses a secondary channel. |

*(continues)*

Table 3.1    *(cont.)*

| Circuit Code | Line # | Signal direction | Function |
|---|---|---|---|
| SCA | 19 | DTE to DCE | Secondary request to send. Same as CA except it uses a secondary channel. |
| SCB | 13 | DCE to DTE | Secondary clear to send. Same as CB except it uses a secondary channel. |
| SCF | 12 | DCE to DTE | Secondary data carrier detect. Same as CF except it uses a secondary channel. |
| RL | 21 | DTE to DCE | Remote loopback. For testing, instructs DCE to return transmitted signals. |
| LL | 18 | DTE to DCE | Local loopback. Instructs local DCE to return transmitted signal. |
| TM | 25 | DCE to DTE | Test mode. Indicates DCE is in a test mode. |

Figure 3.8    **Sending and Receiving over an RS-232 Connection**

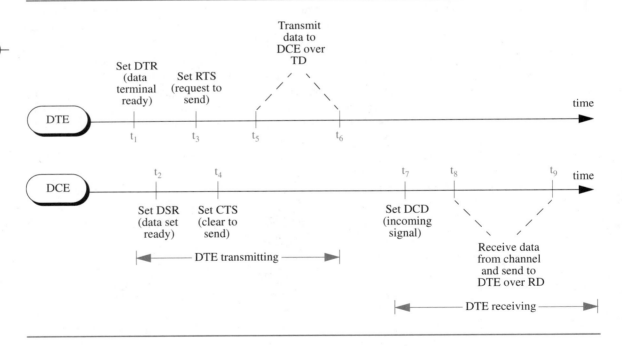

We will not provide a thorough discussion of every connection, but we will describe the role some of the circuits play in a typical DTE-DCE connection. If you would like a more detailed description, consult a reference such as 1 or 2.

Suppose the DTE is a PC and the DCE is a modem. Chapter 2 discussed how a modem communicates with the analog world, so we now focus on the exchange between it and the PC. The first six circuits primarily are used to establish an exchange that ensures that neither device will send data when the other is not expecting it. Figure 3.8 shows the exchange that occurs over a period of time.

Since the DCE interfaces to a network on behalf of the DTE, it must know when the DTE is ready. The DTE does this by asserting (sending a signal) DTR circuit number 20 (time $t_1$ in Figure 3.8). The DCE senses the signal and responds by connecting (if it has not already done so) to the network. Once the DCE has connected and is also ready, it asserts DSR circuit number 6 (time $t_2$). Effectively, the DCE acknowledges the DTE's state of readiness and declares it also is ready.

Once they are both ready, the DTE requests permission to transmit data to the DCE by asserting RTS circuit 4 (time $t_3$). This circuit also controls the direction of flow in half-duplex communications. On sensing RTS, the DCE enters a "transmit mode," meaning it is ready to transmit data over the network. It then responds by asserting the CTS circuit number 5 (time $t_4$). Finally, the DTE sends data over TD circuit number 2 (between times $t_5$ and $t_6$).

When the DCE detects an incoming signal from a network it recognizes it asserts DCD circuit number 8 (time $t_7$). As the signals come in, the DCE sends them to the DTE using RD circuit number 3. In some cases, if the DCE is a modem, it has lights on its front that show whenever certain lines are asserted. This signal provides the user with a chance to "see" what is actually occurring. In most cases, however, the lights flash so rapidly that it is difficult to distinguish on from off.

## RS-232 SUBSETS

If you look at the back of a PC or terminal you might notice that something seems inconsistent with our previous discussion. The connectors to the RS-232 ports do not have 25 pins. Remember that we have discussed the RS-232 standard. Whether a vendor chooses to implement the full standard is another matter. The fact is, many interfaces include only a subset of the RS-232 definitions.

To illustrate, many PC-to-modem connections use a cable with a 25-pin connector at one end and an 8- or 9-pin connector on the other. It sounds a bit like plugging a 3-pronged plug into a 2-hole socket, but there is a reason for the difference. For versatility, many modems comply with the complete standard. However, many users do not need to use the full range of RS-232 abilities. Primarily they need to communicate much as we have described in the most recent example. Consequently, modem ports generally require an 8- or 9-pin connector using the 7 circuits described in the most recent example plus one or both grounds. This decision usually is driven by economics: Why implement (and pay for) the full range of abilities when there is little chance you will ever use them? Cables with different connectors on each end connect only needed circuits. The extra lines on the modem side are not connected to the PC.

One drawback to the RS-232 standard is its limited bandwidth and distance. It is typically used for transmissions of 20,000 bits per second (bps) over a distance of up to 50 feet. In some cases, such as situations with little interference, longer distances are possible, but in those cases there are other standards, which we discuss shortly.

## NULL MODEMS

Sometimes, you may want to allow two devices such as PCs to communicate directly; that is, with no network nor DCEs between them. In such cases, your first reaction might be to connect their RS-232 ports with a cable and let the protocols do their job. After all, they both send and receive from the RS-232 ports. Using a simple cable, however, connects the same pins on each side. For example, the cable would connect pin 2 of each DTE. The problem is that both pins try to send over the same line. The first DTE sends data and the second receives it over line 2. Since the second DTE expects to receive data over line 3, the direct connection will not work. Similarly, since the cable connects pin 3 on each end, both expect to receive on the same circuit, but neither sends over it.

One solution to this problem is to connect the DTEs but cross some circuits. Figure 3.9 shows one way to do this using a **null modem**. A null modem may be either a cable connecting different pins on each connector or a device that simply crosses connections using existing cables. Either way, the result is the same. The null modem in Figure 3.9 connects pin 2 on one end to pin 3 on the other end. Consequently, when the DTE sends data using pin 2, it is routed to pin 3 on the other end, where it is received correctly.

FIGURE 3.9    **Null Modem**

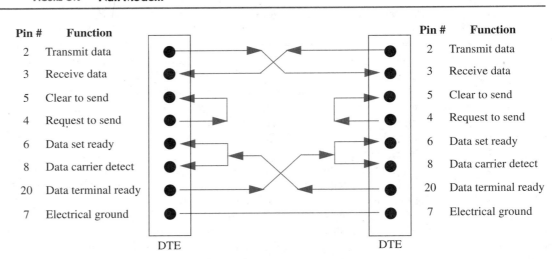

The null modem of Figure 3.9 also connects pin 4 and 5 of the same DTE. The reason for this is found in the example discussed previously. When a DTE wants to transmit, it must request permission and wait for a clear-to-send signal from the DCE. Since there is no DCE, the null modem routes a request-to-send signal (pin 4) back to pin 5. The DTE, sensing its own signal on pin 5, is fooled into "thinking" the DCE has responded with the clear-to-send message.

The other cross connections make sure each DTE is ready before any transmissions occur. As described previously, the DTE asserts the DTR line 20 when it is ready, expecting the DCE to respond by asserting DSR line 6. Here one DTE's line 20 is routed to the other's line 6, so that when each DTE signals it is ready the other receives that signal. Again, this fools the DTE into "thinking" its DCE has connected to a network and is also ready.

Figure 3.9 shows just one example of the many variations of null modems. They vary depending on device requirements and how much of the full RS-232 protocol they use. For other variations, see references 3 and 4.

## RS-449 Interface

As mentioned previously, the RS-232 standard was limited in bandwidth and distance. Another standard, **RS-449** (sometimes referred to as EIA 449), was designed to replace it and increase both distance and bandwidth. The RS-449 standard, unlike RS-232, differentiates between operational and electrical specifications. That is, RS-449 defines pin functions, but relies on one of two other standards, RS-422 or RS-423, for the electrical standards. We will discuss these standards shortly.

RS-449 defines a 37-pin connection and looks a lot like the one in Figure 3.7, except that it has more pins. Many of the circuit functions are similar to those of RS-232, and it also provides new ones for modem testing. Table 3.2 lists the circuits and their functions. The left set of columns in the table defines circuits that have similar counterparts in RS-232; the right columns define new functions. Describing each function in detail is beyond this book's goals; if you are interested in more detail consult references 1 and 3.

The two electrical standards, **RS-422** and **RS-423**, correspond to **balanced circuits** and **unbalanced circuits**, respectively. An unbalanced circuit uses one line for signal transmission and a common ground. Thus, signal voltage levels are relative to that ground. A balanced circuit uses two lines for signal transmission. The transmitting device sends equal but opposite signals over each line. Balanced signals are less susceptible to noise and allow higher transmission rates over longer distances.

Figure 3.10 shows why balanced signals are more reliable. We have seen that a signal is partly determined by its voltage level. With an unbalanced signal the level is the difference between it and the ground. If noise occurs, the level can change and the signal may be interpreted incorrectly. With a balanced signal the lines have equal but opposite signals. In this case, the important measure is the difference between them, not an individual signal's level. The rationale is that if noise does occur it will affect both signals equally. The difference between them is still the same. Since the

TABLE 3.2　**RS-449 Circuit Definitions**

| CIRCUIT CODE | PIN # | SIGNAL DIRECTION | FUNCTION | CIRCUIT CODE | PIN # | SIGNAL DIRECTION | FUNCTION |
|---|---|---|---|---|---|---|---|
| | 1 | | Shield | IS | 28 | DTE to DCE | Terminal in service |
| SG | 19 | | Signal ground | LL | 10 | DTE to DCE | Local loopback |
| SD | 4, 22 | DTE to DCE | Send data | NS | 34 | DTE to DCE | New signal |
| RD | 6, 24 | DCE to DTE | Receive data | RC | 20 | DCE to DTE | Receive common |
| RS | 7, 25 | DTE to DCE | Request to send | RL | 14 | DTE to DCE | Remote loopback |
| CS | 9, 27 | DCE to DTE | Clear to send | SB | 36 | DCE to DTE | Standby indicator |
| DM | 11, 29 | DCE to DTE | Data mode | SC | 37 | DTE to DCE | Send common |
| TR | 12, 30 | DTE to DCE | Terminal ready | F | 16 | DTE to DCE | Select frequency |
| IC | 15 | DCE to DTE | Incoming call | SS | 32 | DTE to DCE | Select standby |
| RR | 13, 31 | DCE to DTE | Receiver ready | TM | 18 | DCE to DTE | Test mode |
| SQ | 33 | DCE to DTE | Signal quality | | | | |
| SR | 16 | DTE to DCE | Signal rate selector | | | | |
| SI | 2 | DCE to DTE | Signaling rate indicator | | | | |
| TT | 17, 35 | DTE to DCE | Terminal timing | | | | |
| ST | 5, 23 | DCE to DTE | Send timing | | | | |
| RT | 8, 26 | DCE to DTE | Receive timing | | | | |

receiving device measures only the difference between the signals, the noise hasn't destroyed the information the difference represents.

This principle is similar to that used in providing homes with 220-volt circuits. Contrary to what some might believe, the current's voltage is not actually doubled.

FIGURE 3.10　**Effect of Noise on Balanced and Unbalanced Signals**

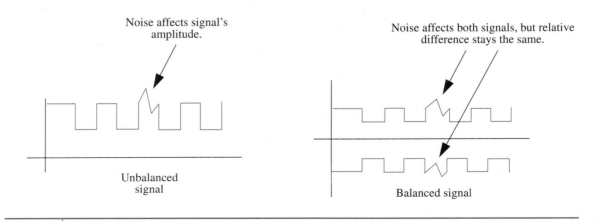

Noise affects signal's amplitude.

Unbalanced signal

Noise affects both signals, but relative difference stays the same.

Balanced signal

The 110-volt circuit uses two wires, one carrying 110 volts of electricity and the other a ground. With a 220-volt circuit, both lines carry an equal but opposite electric current (they differ in phase shift by 180°). The difference is 220 volts. (This principle also explains why birds can sit on high-voltage lines without being electrocuted. As long as they don't touch anything connected to the ground the voltage difference between their toes is 0).

RS-449 using a balanced signal can transmit up to 10 Mbps over short distances (about 40 feet). Lowering the data rate to 100 Kbps allows transmission up to about 4000 ft. Using an unbalanced circuit, the data rate is limited to 100 Kbps at 40 feet. It also allows for communications up to 4000 feet, but only at a data rate of 1200 bps.

RS-449 also allows for an optional 9-pin connector. The shield, signal ground, send, and receive are pins 1,5, 9, and 6, respectively. It also defines a secondary data channel sending and receiving over circuits 3 and 4. The last three pins are for secondary channel control defining a request to send, clear to send, and receiver ready as pins 7, 8, and 2.

## X.21 Interface

The **X.21** interface standard is defined by CCITT. It uses a 15-pin connector and, like RS-449, allows balanced (electrical standard X.27) and unbalanced (X.26 standard) circuits. There are a couple of significant differences between X.21 and the RS standards. The first is that X.21 was defined as a digital signaling interface. Experts agree that analog communications systems eventually will be replaced by entirely digital ones. Some see X.21 as an interim standard to ISDN (integrated services digital network). We will discuss ISDN, which some see as the future of worldwide communications, in Chapter 8.

The second difference involves how control information is exchanged. The RS standards define specific circuits for control functions. More control requires more circuits, thus making connections more inconvenient. The principle behind X.21 is to put more logic circuits (intelligence) in the DTE and DCE that can interpret control sequences and reduce the number of connecting circuits.

Table 3.3 shows the X.21 circuit definitions for a balanced circuit. The DTE uses just two circuits (T and C) to transmit to the DCE. Similarly, the DCE uses two (R and I). The other circuits are used for timing signals in synchronous communications. With fewer circuits for transmission, more logic is needed to interpret the signals they carry. Typically, T and R are used to transmit bit strings, and C and I are in an ON (binary 0s) or OFF (binary 1s) state. Consequently, T and R are used for signaling and sending data and control information.

The signals on T, C, R, and I define the states (status) for the DTE and DCE. CCITT defines many different states for X.21, but we will not elaborate on all of them here. (references 3, 5, and 6 provide more detail.) We will, however, illustrate how the protocol works for a simple connection.

Figure 3.11 illustrates the signal exchange sequence as the DTE and DCE exchange information. To start, when both DTE and DCE are idle, the C and I circuits are both OFF and the T and R circuits transmit binary 1s. When the DTE wants to connect to a remote DTE, it begins sending 0s over T and sets C to ON (time $t_1$ in Figure

TABLE 3.3    **X.21 Interface Standard for Balanced Circuit**

| CIRCUIT CODE | PIN # | SIGNAL DIRECTION | FUNCTION |
|---|---|---|---|
| | 1 | | Shield |
| G | 8 | | Signal ground |
| T | 2, 9 | DTE to DCE | Transmit data or control information |
| R | 4, 11 | DCE to DTE | Receive data or control information |
| C | 3, 10 | DTE to DCE | Control |
| I | 5, 12 | DCE to DTE | Indication |
| S | 6, 13 | DCE to DTE | Signal element timing |
| B | 7, 14 | DCE to DTE | Byte timing |

3.11). The DCE, sensing the change, responds by sending a sequence of '+' characters over R (time $t_2$). This is analogous to picking up the handset on a telephone and having the local switching office respond by transmitting the dial tone back to your phone.

If you were placing a phone call your next step would be to dial the number. The DTE responds similarly by transmitting control and data information over T

FIGURE 3.11    **Sending and Receiving over an X.21 Connection**

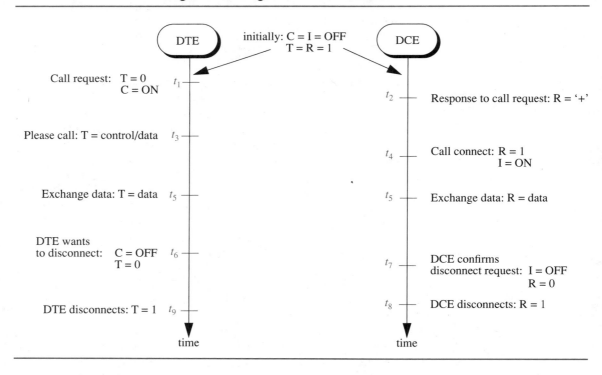

(time $t_3$). This provides the DCE with necessary information, such as an address, to establish communications with a remote DTE via the network. As the DCE is trying to make the connection it sends a series of SYN characters over R. When the connection is established the DCE informs the DTE by sending 1s over R and setting I to ON (time $t_4$).

At this point (time $t_5$), the DTE and DCE can exchange data, with the DTE using the T circuit and the DCE using R. Eventually, the DTE will decide to terminate its activities. It indicates its intention to the DCE by transmitting 0s over T and setting C to OFF (time $t_6$). The DCE confirms the intention by transmitting 0s over R and setting I to OFF (time $t_7$). Finally, the DCE disconnects by transmitting 1s over R (time $t_8$), and the DTE disconnects by transmitting 1s over T (time $t_9$). This brings both devices to the idle state with which we began this example.

There are many other interface standards, but describing them all is far beyond the scope of this text. (Reference 2 lists approximately 100 such standards.) We have described some of the most common or well known standards here and will describe a couple of others later (X.25 network interface in Chapter 7 and ISDN in Chapter 8).

## 3.3    Multiplexing

When it comes to data transmissions, it should not be hard to convince you that higher data rates are better. If you have ever upgraded to a faster PC, disk drive, or modem, you no doubt found that the faster response times helped you work more efficiently. Remember when the first $3\frac{1}{2}$ inch drives first became available? The ability to get a file in just a couple of seconds was a wonderful improvement over the $5\frac{1}{4}$ inch drives. And with the hard disk drives today, we now have to find ways to amuse ourselves while waiting for anything on a $3\frac{1}{2}$ inch disk.

The same is true of networks and communications: Faster is generally better. Speed does have its drawbacks, however. First, it is expensive, and second it has a point of diminishing returns. That is, after a certain point many users can't make use of the increased speed. For example, a common bit rate over networks is 10 Mbps. Many PC applications simply do not have the volume of data necessary to make use of that speed. Even if they did, many DTE-DCE interfaces don't provide data rates anywhere near 10 Mbps (remember the limits on the RS-232 interface from the previous section).

One response is to not worry about developing very high speed networks as most users cannot utilize their full potential. This solution has a serious flaw, however. Suppose the network shown in Figure 3.12 supports a data rate of 9600 bps (for simplicity, the DCEs are not shown). If the only activity involves two PCs communicating at that rate, the network serves it purpose. However, if several hundred PCs need to communicate with one another, the 9600 bps limit will create quite a bottleneck. Increasing the data rate will reduce it.

A good analogy is a major freeway system in a large city during rush hour. If traffic moves at 15 mph, the lines on entrance ramps will grow very long. If traffic

FIGURE 3.12    **Many Users Communicating over a Network**

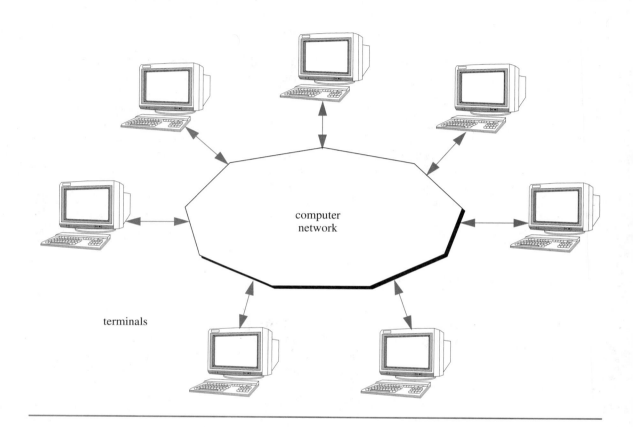

moves at a normal speed of 55 mph, the cars will not wait as long to enter the freeway.

A second response to the problems of higher data rates is to develop high-speed networks, but somehow reduce the cost of connecting to them. In Figure 3.12, there is a cost for each PC connection. Figure 3.13 shows a common alternative using a **multiplexer** (sometimes called **mux** to minimize transmission from the larynx and movement of muscles in and around the vocal cavity known as the mouth). It is a device that routes transmissions from multiple sources to a single destination. In Figure 3.13, the sources are PCs and the destination is the network. The multiplexer also routes transmissions in the reverse direction, from the network to any of the PCs.

In general, a multiplexer's output line to the network has a much higher data rate than any of the input lines from the PCs. This way it can utilize the network's high data rate and, by providing a single connection for multiple users, cut the cost per connection.

FIGURE 3.13    **Multiplexing Low-Speed Devices**

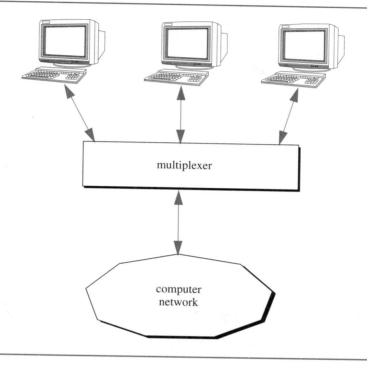

This description of multiplexing is just one of several depending on the signal types and the activity of the units connected to it. Next, we will describe specific multiplexing methods and provide an example used in long distance telephone communications.

## FREQUENCY DIVISION MULTIPLEXING (FDM)

Frequency division multiplexing (FDM) is used with analog signals. Perhaps its most common use is in television and radio transmission. A multiplexer accepts analog signals from multiple sources, each of which has a specified bandwidth. The signals then are combined into another more complex signal with a much larger bandwidth. The resulting signal is transmitted over some medium to its destination, where another mux extracts and separates the individual components.

This method of multiplexing involves several steps. First, the available bandwidth of the transmission medium is divided into separate ranges or **channels**. For example, the bandwidth for broadcast television (54 MHz–806 MHz) is divided into 68 channels of 6 MHz each. VHF channels 2–13 correspond to 6 MHz bands, between 54 MHz. and 215 MHz. UHF channels 14–69 correspond to 6 MHz bands between 470 MHz and 806 MHz. Each channel corresponds to one of the multi-plexer's input signals.

Next, a **carrier signal** is defined for each channel. It is changed (**modulated**) by the corresponding input signal to create another signal (**modulated signal**). There are several ways to do this. For example, Figure 3.14 illustrates **amplitude modulation**. The carrier signal has a specified frequency typically centered in a channel's bandwidth. Its amplitude is changed to alternate between values depending on the other signal's maximum and minimum values.

A complete understanding of amplitude modulation requires some knowledge of the mathematical representation of wave forms and Fourier series. Consequently, a detailed explanation is beyond the scope of this text. If you want a more rigorous discussion, references 3 and 7 have them. We can, however, illustrate the process using a simple example.

Consider an analog signal corresponding to the formula $f(t) = [\sin(2\pi t)/4] + 0.5$. Figure 3.15 shows its graph between $t = 0$ and $t = 2$. Suppose the carrier signal corresponds to $g(t) = \sin(10*2\pi t)$. Figure 3.15 does not show the graph of $g(t)$ but, if drawn, its graph would oscillate 20 times between 1 and $-1$ as $t$ ranged from 0 to 2. Multiplying $f(t)$ and $g(t)$ generates the modulated signal shown in Figure 3.15.

In general, signals have much higher frequencies and correspond to complex sums of sine functions. Still, the process of amplitude modulation remains essentially the same as in the example. Other modulation techniques are **frequency modulation** and **phase modulation**. As you might expect, frequency modulation alters the frequency of the carrier depending on the input signal, and phase modulation alters the signal's phase shift. Again, references 3 and 7 contain more rigorous discussions.

In the last step of frequency division multiplexing, the modulated signals from all the inputs are combined into a single more complex analog signal (Figure 3.16).

FIGURE 3.14     **Amplitude Modulation**

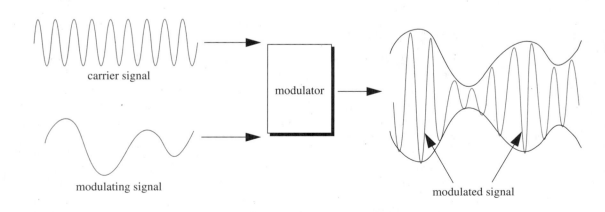

FIGURE 3.15    **Graphs of Modulated Signal**

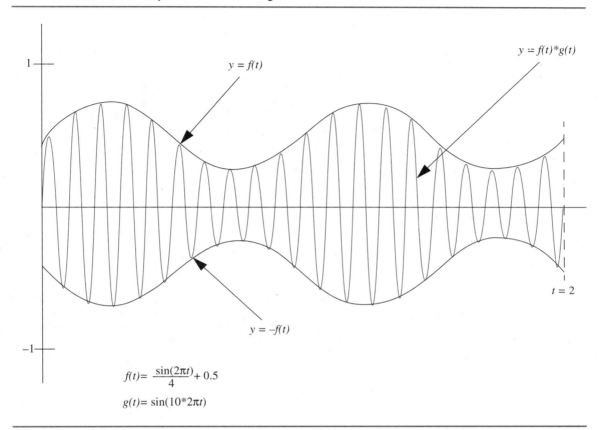

$$f(t) = \frac{\sin(2\pi t)}{4} + 0.5$$

$$g(t) = \sin(10 * 2\pi t)$$

Its frequencies lie within the ranges of all the channels. The channels themselves are separated by **guard bands** (unused parts of the frequency range) in order to prevent interference between adjacent channels. The resulting signal is transmitted and another multiplexer receives it. It then uses **bandpass filters** to extract the individual modulated signals. Finally, the signals are demodulated and the original signals restored. In applications such as television and radio, the channel or frequency selectors specify which of the original signals is converted to sound and picture.

## TIME DIVISION MULTIPLEXING (TDM)

In time division multiplexing (TDM) many input signals are combined and transmitted together, as with FDM. TDM is used with digital signals, however. As a result, in contrast to FDM, which combines them into a single more complex signal, TDM keeps the signals physically distinct but logically packages them together.

FIGURE 3.16        **Frequency Division Multiplexing**

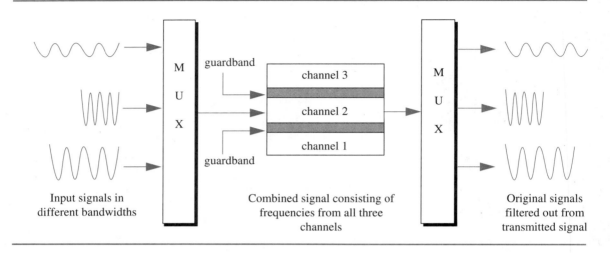

Input signals in different bandwidths

Combined signal consisting of frequencies from all three channels

Original signals filtered out from transmitted signal

Figure 3.17 illustrates TDM. Suppose $A_i$, $B_i$, $C_i$, and $D_i$ ($i = 1, 2, 3, \ldots$) represent bit streams from distinct sources. A few bits from each source are buffered temporarily in the multiplexer. The multiplexer scans each buffer, storing the bits from each in a frame, and then sends the frame. As it does so, it begins building a new

FIGURE 3.17        **Time Division Multiplexing**

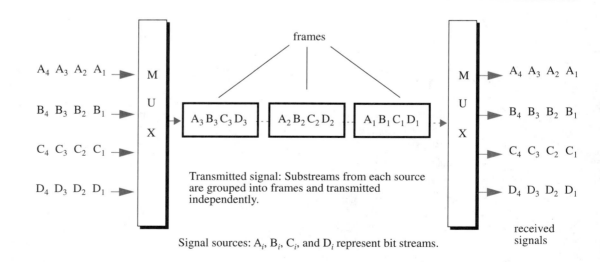

Transmitted signal: Substreams from each source are grouped into frames and transmitted independently.

Signal sources: $A_i$, $B_i$, $C_i$, and $D_i$ represent bit streams.

frame by again scanning the input buffers for new data that has arrived. If the timing is right it will construct a new frame just in time to transmit it immediately following the previous one. This process keeps the output line active and makes full use of its capacity.

In Figure 3.17 the bits $A_1$, $B_1$, $C_1$, and $D_1$ are buffered separately. The multiplexer packages them into a single frame and transmits it. It then follows by gathering $A_2$, $B_2$, $C_2$, and $D_2$ and sending another frame. The process continues as long as the sources are providing bit streams.

The multiplexer's design depends in part on the input and output transmission rates. For example, if source bits from the combined inputs arrive faster than the previous frame can be sent, frames are generated more quickly than they can be discarded. If the multiplexer has no capacity to store the extra frames they are lost. We must not supply the multiplexer with information faster than it can release it. On the other hand, if the source bits arrive too slowly, the previous frame will have been sent and the multiplexer has to wait for enough bits to arrive to form a new one. During this time the output line is idle and the multiplexer is not using it to its fullest capacity.

The optimal situation is when the global input rate (sum of rates from each source) equals the output rate. Suppose $r_i$ is the input rate from the $i$th source and $r_{output}$ is the multiplexer's transmission rate. Mathematically, we express this as $\sum_{i=1}^{n} r_i = r_{output}$. For example, if data from 10 sources arrived at a rate of 9.6 Kbps, the multiplexer should be able to send them at a rate of 96 Kbps. (We describe an alternative shortly.)

Another part of the multiplexer's design is the size of the frame components. One design defines $A_i$, $B_i$, $C_i$, and $D_i$ as 8 bits or 1 byte. In this case it is called a **byte multiplexer**. In other cases, $A_i$, $B_i$, $C_i$, and $D_i$ are larger, containing many bytes (block). In this case, strangely enough, it is called a block multiplexer.

## STATISTICAL MULTIPLEXERS

Previously, we stated that an optimal design requires that the sum of input rates equals the output rate. However, sometimes this is not practical. In the previous example, we assumed that bits were arriving from each source continuously, but in many cases they arrive in bursts with periods of inactivity in between. This is especially true when the sources are terminals and the user alternates between thinking and typing. It is also true for an intelligent terminal where a user enters a screenful of data locally and sends the entire screen. There is a delay as the user enters another screenful of data.

In such cases there are two approaches for multiplexing the data. The first is to design the multiplexer to skip empty buffers and leave part of the frame vacant. For example, in Figure 3.17 suppose the third source was inactive. That is, $C_1$, $C_2$, $C_3$, and $C_4$ do not exist. Each frame would have space reserved for those bits, but would not contain any meaningful information. This has the advantage of keeping all the frames the same size and simplifying the protocols. The obvious disadvantage is that useless information occupies the transmission medium and thus wastes bandwidth.

Another approach is to have the multiplexer scan the buffers and create a variable-size frame depending on how many buffers contain data. We call this a **statistical multiplexer**. Some also use the term **concentrator.**[*]

Figure 3.18 shows how this works. Here all sources are active, but not at the same time. The symbol $\emptyset$ indicates no information has arrived from a source. Initially bit streams $A_1$ and $C_1$ are buffered, but the others are empty due to inactivity at the sources. Therefore, the multiplexer puts $A_1$ and $C_1$ into a frame and sends it on its way. In the meantime $A_2$ and $C_2$, along with $B_1$, arrive. The multiplexer puts them together in another, larger frame and sends it. At this point there is inactivity from the C source, but the D source becomes active. Now $A_3$, $B_2$, and $D_1$ arrive. As before, the multiplexer puts them in a frame and sends it. This process continues as long as any of the inputs are active.

A complication with this approach is that sources are no longer assigned a fixed position in the frame. For example, in Figure 3.17 bits from each source always occupied the same positions in a frame. In Figure 3.18, this is not so. For example, bits from source B sometimes occupied the 2nd or 3rd (counting from the right) positions. In such cases the frame format is more complex and requires additional

FIGURE 3.18     **Statistical Time Division Multiplexing**

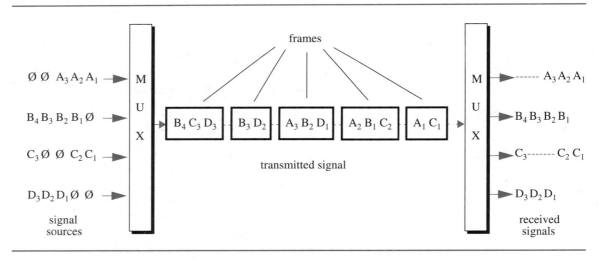

---

[*] Strictly speaking, the two terms are different. A concentrator is a more intelligent statistical multiplexer that allows us to do other things such as verify, acknowledge, and compress data. These are topics we discuss in Section 3.5 and in Chapters 4 and 5. The actual definitions often depend on whom you talk to. We will not make a distinction here. In fact, sometimes the term **asynchronous time division multiplexer** is used.

information such as destination addresses. The receiving multiplexer must have additional logic to seek out the addresses and route the information in the correct direction.

As defined, a statistical multiplexer may not fully use its output capacity. In the extreme case, if no sources are active there are no transmissions. The probability that none are active depends on how many sources there are. An astute observer may notice that we could connect additional sources to decrease this probability and keep the output line busier. If this happens, then $\sum_{i=1}^{n} r_i > r_{output}$. That is, the input capacity of the multiplexer is now larger than its output capacity.

Having a higher input rate is not necessarily a problem. Remember, $r_i$ represents the capacity of the $i$th source, not its actual rate. If it is inactive, the actual bit rate is 0. The design assumes that although the sum of input rates is larger than $r_{output}$ the sources are not all active at the same time. The ideal is where the combined input rate from active sources is equal to $r_{output}$. Since activity depends on the user, it is hard to predict and the ideal is difficult to achieve. There will be times when the combined input rate from active sources is smaller or even larger than $r_{output}$. In the latter case, additional logic and buffers must be designed in order to accommodate temporary surges in data. This is one reason they are sometimes called concentrators: They concentrate additional data for brief periods.

An analysis of statistical multiplexers can be difficult because of the random way in which the sources send data. Many questions must be asked. How frequently will the combined input rates exceed the output rate? How often will all sources be busy? How large must the internal buffers be to handle temporary surges? How long are the delays when surges occur? One approach to the analysis is the use of queuing theory, a field of mathematics that defines models for studying events such as waiting in lines (queues) for events to occur. It can be applied to many areas including communications systems in which input streams may arrive in random patterns. In such cases the events are the transmissions over the output lines. References 3, 7, 8, and 9 contain introductory discussions of queuing theory.

## T-1 CARRIER

We close this section with a discussion of a multiplexing standard used in long distance communications. Much of what we think of as the "telephone system" was designed to transmit digitized voice signals over high-speed media such as optical fiber or microwaves. In fact, AT&T developed a complex hierarchy of communications systems used to multiplex voice signals and transmit them all over the United States. The system is also used in other countries such as Canada and Japan. Still other countries use a similar but different system defined by CCITT standards.

This system uses **time division multiplexing** to combine many voice channels into one frame. Of the many ways to do this, one approach uses T-1 transmission and DS-1 signaling. The designations T-1 and DS-1 refer to the circuit and signal respectively. For example, Figure 3.19 shows a DS-1 frame in which voice data is

FIGURE 3.19    **DS-1 Frame**

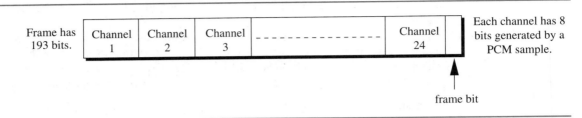

digitized using pulse code modulation (discussed in Chapter 2). It contains 193 bits divided into 24 slots (one for each channel) of 8 bits each. This leaves one extra bit called a framing bit, which is used for synchronizing.

Figure 3.20 shows how a T-1 carrier system works. Eight-bit voice samples are taken from each of 24 channels at a rate of 8000 per second. Each sample then occupies one slot in the DS-1 frame. According to the Nyquist theorem from Chapter 2, this is sufficient to maintain all the information in the original voice analog signal. Consecutive samples are stored in different DS-1 frames. The voice messages are thus transmitted using many DS-1 frames to another multiplexer. This one extracts the bits from each slot and routes them to their appropriate destination, where they eventually are converted back to analog signals. The result is converted into the original sound of the person's voice.

What is the bit rate of the T-1 carrier system? Each 8-bit slot is generated at a rate of 8000 per second for a rate of 64 Kbps. To support this speed, T-1 must transmit a DS-1 frame every 1/8000 of a second, or 8000 frames per second. In other words, it must transmit 8000*193 bits each second for a data rate of 1.544 Mbps. This rate is fast by some standards but pales when compared to the capabilities of optical fibers or microwaves. Consequently, there are other carrier and signal designations with more channels and faster bit rates. Table 3.4 summarizes some of them. A common approach is to multiplex signals from a low-speed carrier into a high-speed one. For example, the T-3 carrier could multiplex 7 DS-2 frames, 14 DS-1C frames or 28 DS-1 frames, giving it the ability to carry 672 channels in each frame.

TABLE 3.4    **North American Communication Carriers**

| CARRIER | FRAME FORMAT | NUMBER OF CHANNELS | DATA RATE IN MBPS |
|---------|--------------|--------------------|-------------------|
| T-1 | DS-1 | 24 | 1.544 |
| T-1c | DS-1C | 48 | 3.152 |
| T-2 | DS-2 | 96 | 6.312 |
| T-3 | DS-3 | 672 | 44.376 |
| T-4 | DS-4 | 4032 | 274.176 |

**FIGURE 3.20    T-1 Carrier System**

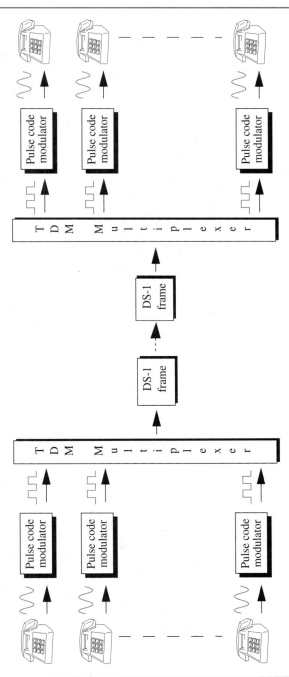

Voice data is not the only type that can be transmitted. Many companies lease phone lines to transfer digital information between computers. In fact, the principle behind the fax machine is to convert images on paper to digital signals and transmit them over telephone lines.

As a final note, we mention that the number of channels in each system can be increased by using different modulation techniques. Pulse code modulation digitizes voice information at a rate of 64 Kbps. **Adaptive differential pulse code modulation** digitizes voice information at 32 Kbps, which allows each of the carrier systems to support twice as many channels as listed in Table 3.4.

## 3.4   Contention Protocols

Multiplexing (particularly TDM) goes a long way toward making a medium available to many users, but it is not enough. To route all users through a multiplexer onto a medium is unrealistic for two reasons. First, there may be too many users for a single multiplexer. Second, the logistics may prohibit a user from using a particular multiplexer.

A highway system provides a nice analogy. Interstate highway 94 connects Chicago and Seattle. In Chicago, many interchanges (the automobile's multiplexer) allow a driver access to the highway. But what if someone in Fargo, North Dakota, wants access to the highway in order to drive to Seattle? Would we expect her to first drive to Chicago, some 600 miles in the wrong direction? Of course not. She simply uses another access point to the interstate.

Communications media are similar. The multiplexer provides access for many users to one access point, but a large network requires many access points, just as the interstate highway system does. Access to the medium from many entry points is called **contention**. It is controlled with a **contention protocol**. Figure 3.21 shows

FIGURE **3.21**   **No Contention Protocol**

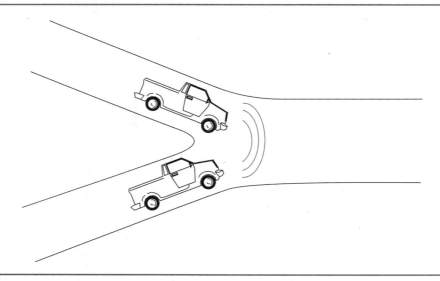

FIGURE 3.22    **Stop and Go Access Protocol**

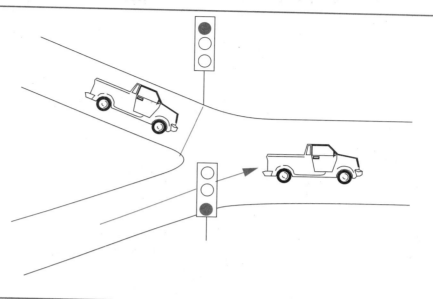

what happens with no contention protocol in the highway system. Vehicles enter randomly and collisions occur periodically. At best they are unpleasant; at worst they are fatal. Fortunately, the highway system is not set up this way (although, with some drivers, you'd never know it). Figure 3.22 shows a common and simple contention strategy for traffic. This stop and go protocol uses traffic lights to control access. As long as motorists abide by the protocol they can avoid the situation shown in Figure 3.21. We assume that unless you are from a remote area in the Himalayas you are familiar with the details of this protocol and we won't discuss it further.

Communications require some protocol to ensure that transmitted data reaches its destination. This section explores some of the protocols used. Perhaps not surprisingly, there are many options depending on the actual medium, the amount of traffic, and the sophistication of the needs (which has a direct correlation to cost).

## ALOHA PROTOCOLS

One of the earliest contention protocols was developed in an area quite different from the remote area of the Himalayas. **The Aloha Protocol** was developed at the University of Hawaii in the early 1970s. We also call it **pure Aloha** in contrast to another protocol we discuss shortly. The Aloha system was designed to establish communication among the islands using a packet radio system. The word "packet" or "frame"* refers to the information broadcast during a single transmission. Terminals

---

* Depending on the protocol, the term "packet" or "frame" may be used to indicate the contents of a single transmission. For now we continue to use the term "frame."

FIGURE 3.23    Aloha System

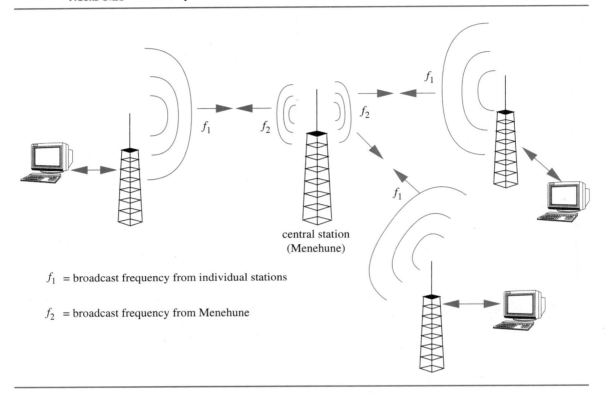

$f_1$ = broadcast frequency from individual stations

$f_2$ = broadcast frequency from Menehune

(Figure 3.23) were connected to a radio channel, which in turn broadcast information from the terminal to a central facility called the Menehune. Stations broadcast frames at the same frequency. Consequently, the medium (the air space) was truly shared. Any attempt to broadcast two different frames simultaneously using the same frequency disrupted both signals. The end result, of course, was that neither transmission was successful.

The Aloha protocol worked on a very simple principle. Essentially, it allowed for any station to broadcast at any time. If two signals collided, so be it. Each station would simply wait a random time and try again. The highway analogy would be to enter the freeway with your eyes closed. If you have a collision, get a new car and try again. Although it would be an expensive protocol for traffic control, it worked well for the Aloha system.

Collisions were detected quite easily. When the Menehune received a frame it sent an acknowledgment. It used a different frequency so as not to interfere with incoming signals. If a station received an acknowledgment, it concluded that its frame was transmitted successfully. If not, it assumed a collision occurred and waited to send again. Because each station waited a random time, the chance that they waited the same time was reduced. In turn this reduced the chances of a second collision. If they did collide a second time (perhaps even with another station) the same rules applied. Wait a random amount of time and try again.

In this type of situation, collisions occur not only when two stations send simultaneously. They occur if two transmissions overlap even by the smallest amount. It does not matter if all or part of the frame is destroyed. It's like receiving a telephone call and hearing "I've got good news for you. You have just $%^#$%" If the "$%^#$%" represents static you don't know if you won the lottery, received an inheritance, or were elected to political office (good news?). What's lost is gone, and conventional wisdom dictates the entire frame be sent again.

The advantage to the Aloha protocol is its simplicity. It works very well if there are not many transmissions, but if a station broadcasts more frequently or there are more stations, the protocol is less effective. In either case, more collisions occur—just as they do on heavily traveled roads.

When we are faced with increased transmissions, what can we do to decrease the collisions? First, let us analyze a little more closely how collisions occur. As stated, a collision occurs if any part of two transmissions overlaps. Suppose that $T$ is time required for one transmission and that two stations must transmit. The total time required for both stations to do so is $2T$.

Next, consider an arbitrary interval of time $2T$. Unless one station begins its transmission at the start of the interval, completing both transmissions before the end of the interval is impossible. (Why?) Consequently, allowing a station to transmit at arbitrary times can waste time up to $2T$.

As an alternative, suppose we divide time into intervals (slots) of $T$ units each and require each station to begin each transmission at the beginning of a slot. In other words, even if a station is ready to send in the middle of a slot, it must wait until the start of the next one (Figure 3.24b). This way, the only way a collision

**FIGURE 3.24    Transmission Using Pure Aloha and Slotted Aloha**

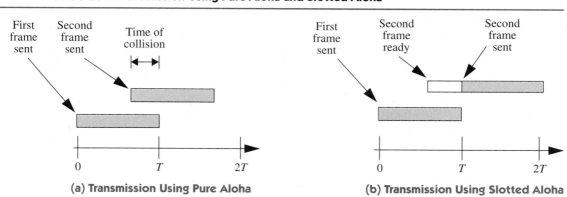

**(a) Transmission Using Pure Aloha**              **(b) Transmission Using Slotted Aloha**

occurs is when both stations become ready in the same slot. Contrast this to the previous scenario (3.24a), where a collision occurs if the second station transmits when the frame is ready.

Requiring a station to transmit at the beginning of a time slot is the **slotted Aloha protocol**. According to the previous discussion, it would seem to perform better than the pure Aloha protocol. In fact, a rigorous analysis of both protocols shows that the slotted Aloha protocol does perform better. A detailed description of the analysis here is beyond our goals, but we will summarize the findings and interpret them. More rigorous discussions are found in references 7, 3, 10, 4, and 11.

Intuitively, we know there is a relationship between the number of frames sent and the number sent successfully. A mathematical model can be created that, under certain assumptions, defines the relationship as follows:

Let $G$ represent the traffic measured as the average number of frames generated per slot. Let $S$ be the success rate measured as the average number of frames sent successfully per slot. ($e$ is the mathematical constant 2.718 . . .) The relationship between $G$ and $S$ for both pure and slotted Aloha is

$$S = Ge^{-2G} \text{ (pure Aloha)}$$
$$S = Ge^{-G} \text{ (slotted Aloha)}$$

Your next logical question is probably "So what! What does it mean?" For an answer, look at the graphs in Figure 3.25. The vertical axis represents $S$ and the horizontal one represents $G$. Values for $S$ range from 0 to 1. Since we have chosen the slot time to equal that required to send one frame, $S$ can be no larger.

FIGURE 3.25     **Success Rate for Slotted and Pure Aloha Protocols**

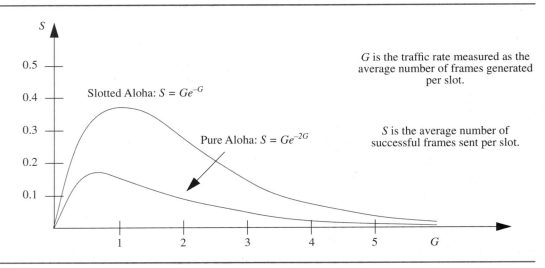

First note that both graphs have the same basic shape. If $G$ is small, so is $S$. This makes sense since few frames will be sent successfully if there are only a few frames generated. As $G$ increases so does $S$, up to a point. More transmissions mean more successfully sent frames, until they start colliding. At that point, which corresponds to the high point on each graph, the success rate decreases. As $G$ continues to increase, $S$ approaches 0. This corresponds to the situation in which there are so many frames, they are almost always colliding. It becomes a rare event when a frame gets through without colliding.

The model shows how the pure and slotted Aloha protocols compare. Differential calculus shows how to calculate the maximum value in each case. If you are familiar with the details, just take the derivative of each function with respect to $G$ and equate with 0. In any case, the maximum for slotted Aloha occurs at $G = 1$ for which $S = 1/e \approx 0.368$. In other words, the best rate of successful transmissions is approximately .368 frames per slot time. Another way to say it is that about 37% of the time will be spent on successful transmissions. The rest will be on collisions or idle time.

For pure Aloha, the maximum occurs at $G = 0.5$ for which $S = 1/2e \approx 0.184$. Again, this means that approximately 18% of the time is spent on successful transmissions.

At first it may seem strange that slotted Aloha generally won't provide a better success rate. Providing not much more than a frame every 3 slots seems like underachieving. But a critical assumption the models make is that frames become ready randomly. There is no intent to coordinate transmissions beyond waiting until the beginning of the next slot. As the model shows, this important assumption degrades performance.

Another question might be, "Should we try to coordinate transmissions in order to achieve better efficiency?" In general, the answer is "no." If you were at a PC connected to a network, you would probably find it inconvenient to coordinate your network access with others. Most users want access on demand and expect the protocols and hardware to provide good response.

## CARRIER SENSE MULTIPLE ACCESS (CSMA)

An observant person might ask, "Couldn't we improve on the success rate if the stations listened to the medium[*] for existing transmissions before sending its own?" They certainly have the capability to determine when frames are in transit. Why not hold a frame until another has finished? This way a station would not destroy a frame currently being sent, and the success rate should improve.

The idea of listening makes sense and is used in many networks today such as Ethernet (actually Ethernet uses a variation of it that we describe later). We call this

---

[*] Although the Aloha system was developed for packet radio, we use the term "medium" in a very general sense. Unless otherwise specified, it may be air space, fiber, cable, or twisted pair.

approach **Carrier Sense Multiple Access (CSMA)**. In general, the protocol is described simply. If a station has a frame to send it does the following:

1.  Listen to the medium for any activity.

2.  If there is no activity, transmit; otherwise wait.

Does this system eliminate collisions? It will eliminate some but not all. A collision still can occur if two (or more) stations want to transmit at nearly the same time. If there is currently no activity both conclude that it is safe to send and do so. The result, of course, is a collision. However, such collisions generally are less common because there is a very small time delay between when a station detects no activity and when its transmitted frame reaches other stations. In order for a collision to occur, another station must decide to transmit within this period of time. Since the interval is small, so is the probability the second station will send a frame in that interval.

But collisions still can occur, and variations on CSMA try to improve efficiency by reducing the number of them. With one type, **p-persistent CSMA**, the station continues to monitor an active medium. When it becomes quiet, the station transmits with probability $p$ ($0 \leq p \leq 1$). Otherwise it waits for one time slot (probability of $1 - p$). Note that if $p = 1$ the station always transmits when the medium is quiet. If $p = 0$ it always waits. With **non-persistent CSMA**, the station does not continue to monitor the medium. It simply waits one time slot and again checks for activity. At this point it transmits if the medium is idle; otherwise it waits another time slot.

Collisions still can be a problem, especially with p-persistent CSMA. If two stations want to transmit at nearly the same time and the medium is idle, a collision occurs. Although collisions for this reason may not be common they occur in other ways. For example, consider the case where $p = 1$. If two (or more) stations become ready while another is transmitting, both wait. But since $p = 1$, both stations send when the first is done and their frames collide. As more stations transmit this scenario occurs more frequently and collisions become more of a problem.

One way to reduce the frequency of collisions is to lower the probability a station will send when a previous one is done. For example, suppose two stations using a 0.5-persistent protocol are waiting. When the medium is idle, each sends with a probability of 0.5. Thus, four events occur with equal probability:

*   They both transmit immediately.
*   They both wait.
*   The first sends and the second waits.
*   The second sends and the first waits.

Rather than a certain collision, there is a 0.5 probability that one will be able to send the beginning of the next slot. (Note, however, that there is also a 0.25 probability that neither sends. This is another type of inefficiency we will discuss shortly.)

Figure 3.26 shows the success rates of various p-persistent protocols. As before, we have not developed the equations, but we do consider the results and what they mean. However, if you are interested in their derivation, see Reference 16.

$$S_{\text{non-persistent}} = \frac{G}{1+G}$$

$$S_{\text{p-persistent}} = \frac{Ge^{-G}(1+pGx)}{G+e^{-G}}$$

$$\text{where } x = \sum_{k=0}^{\infty} \frac{(1-p)^k G^k}{(1-(1-p)^{k+1})!}$$

FIGURE 3.26   **Success Rate of CSMA and Aloha Protocols**

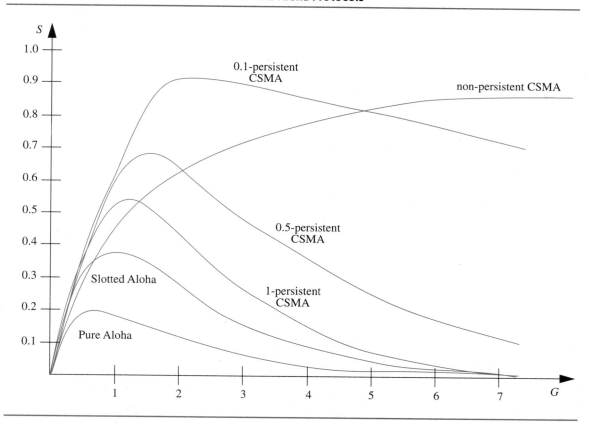

In general, smaller values of $p$ result in fewer collisions. However, the number of waiting stations increases and causes a proportionate increase in the chances no one will send at all. Still, as the number of stations increases the traffic goes up. The probability that at least two will send simultaneously increases, and eventually collisions become a problem again.

With non-persistent CSMA no station waits for the medium to be idle. Instead, each checks periodically and waits one time slot if it is busy. Thus, the only times collisions occur is when two stations detect a quiet medium at nearly the same time. As Figure 3.26 shows, the success rate increases with $G$ and for large values of $G$ is much better than that of persistent or Aloha protocols.

The success rate is only one statistic and can be misleading, however. As we defined it, the success rate is impressive, but it isn't achieved until there is a glut of frames that stations want to send. For example, the model's equations show that a success rate of 0.9 is achieved when $G = 9$. In other words, 90% of the time is spent sending frames only when they are generated at a rate of 9 per slot. This is a rate that exceeds the medium's capacity by a factor of 9. In this case we have other problems far exceeding those caused by the protocol. The stations are saturating the medium, thus causing delays.

A good analogy here is a bank that hires only one teller on its busiest days. Customers wait about 45 minutes to make a deposit and complain to the manager. The manager responds by stating the teller is busy most of the time and there is no problem. It's now time to take your money and hide it in your mattress.

For smaller values of $G$, the persistent protocols have higher success rates because idle time is more of a problem for the non-persistent protocols. If a station detects another transmitting it waits a full slot. If the transmission ends well before that time, the medium is unnecessarily idle. For lighter traffic, the non-persistent is not aggressive enough.

## COLLISION DETECTION

Another way to improve the success rates is to reduce the time during which collisions occur. Previously, when a station had a frame, it sent the whole thing and concluded that a collision occurred when it did not get responses. The problem is that the medium is unusable for others during the time the frame is colliding. Is there some way to have a station monitor the medium to listen for collisions? If so, it could stop transmissions immediately and decrease the time that signals are colliding.

Figure 3.27 illustrates. In Figure 3.27a, the time of collision spans from the transmission of the first frame to the end of the second one. The wasted time could extend up to two time slots. In Figure 3.27b both stations stop transmitting when the collision occurs. Typically each will send a jamming signal (a type of electronic scream) to ensure that all stations know a collision has occurred. In this case, the time spans only part of a slot and the time to send a short jamming signal.

Such a protocol exists and is commonly used with CSMA. We call it **carrier sense multiple access with collision detection (CSMA/CD)**. CSMA/CD typically is used with one of the persistence algorithms. We summarize it as follows:

- If a medium is busy, the station waits per the persistence algorithm.
- If the medium is quiet the station transmits the frame and it continues to listen.
- If it detects a collision it immediately stops transmitting and sends a short jamming signal.
- After a collision it waits a random amount of time before trying to send again.

The last step is important to reduce the chances that two frames will collide a second time. There is certainly no point in two stations waiting the same amount of time just to have their frames collide again.

Two issues that surface in a discussion of collision detection are frame size and transmission distance. If frames are too large, one station can monopolize the medium. On the other hand, collision detection requires that frames be at least a minimum size so that a station can detect a collision before it finishes sending the frame. If it detects a collision after the frame is sent, it does not know if its frame was involved. The frame may have reached its destination and two others collided. You might respond by suggesting that we could use the method described previously that looks for an acknowledgment. We could, but we would defeat the reason for collision detection in the first place: to avoid sending the entire frame before a collision occurs.

Next question: How small should a frame be? The answer depends on the maximum time it takes to detect a collision. Sometimes a collision is detected almost

FIGURE 3.27 **Collision With and Without Detection**

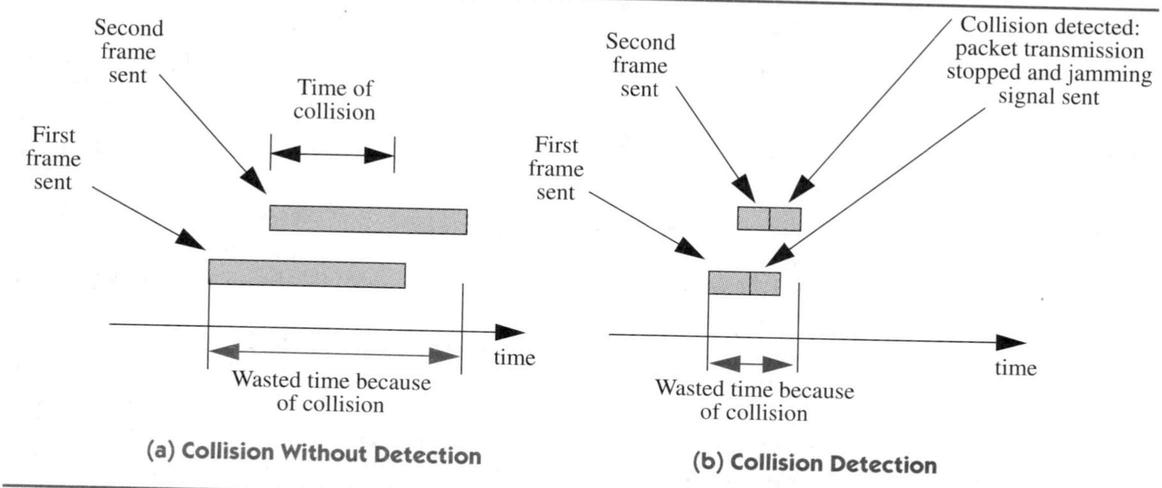

(a) **Collision Without Detection**

(b) **Collision Detection**

immediately. In other cases, the signal may travel a very long distance only to meet another signal. Even then the noise from the collision must travel back to the sending station. Consequently, in the worst case, the time to detect a collision is twice the time it takes a signal to span the longest distance covered by the medium.

As an example, suppose the following:

- A station sends frames over a coax cable at a rate of 10 Mbps.
- The largest distance between two stations on the cable is 2 km.
- A signal propagates along a cable at a rate of 200 m/μsec (meters per micro-second).

In the worst case, the frame travels 2 km (taking 10 μsec) before it collides with another. The corrupted signal then travels 2 km back to the sending station. The round trip takes a total of 20 μsec. Thus, a frame should require at least 20 μsec to send. A data rate of 10 Mbps is the same as putting out 10 bits per μsec; therefore, it could put out 200 bits in 20 μsec. This would mean that the frame should be at least 200 bits, or 200/8 = 25 bytes long. Chapter 6 discusses specific networks and protocols, and we will see that they do indeed specify minimum frame sizes.

The other problem in collision detection is distance. For example, listening and collision detection do not work well for satellite networks, in which the time required for a frame to travel from ground to satellite and back is approximately one quarter of a second. That may not sound like much, but in a world measured in microseconds it is a very long time. If a ground station listened for satellite transmission it could detect only what was sent one quarter of a second ago. Consequently, it may hear nothing when in reality someone else's frame is speeding up to the satellite on a collision course with anything that might be sent.

A strong advantage of the protocols discussed so far is that the protocol need not be changed when new stations are added. A station need not have knowledge of any other particular station. The ability to add new stations without changing the protocol makes growth easier. A significant disadvantage, however, is the fact that collisions do occur. We have argued that the protocols can work well, yet there is no theoretical limit on the number of collisions that can occur. There is always a small chance that unusual delays will occur. For most applications a periodic delay is not serious, but they can be disastrous in real-time applications such as chemical and nuclear plants, air traffic control systems, or factory automation.

In some cases after collisions occur the wait times are not completely random. One common technique defines the wait time as an integral multiple of a slot time. The number of slot times must be limited so a station does not wait excessively long.

Defining the limits is not easy, however. For example, if the limit were large, random waits may also be large and cause excessive idle time. On the other hand, the larger number of slot times from which to choose lessens the chance that two or more stations will choose the same and collide again. If the limit were fairly small, colliding stations will not wait long, but with fewer slot times to choose from the chances for a second collision increase.

A technique called **binary exponential backoff** varies the limit. It works in the following way:

- If a station's frame collides for the first time, wait 0 or 1 time slot (chosen randomly) before trying again.
- If it collides a second time, wait 0, 1, 2, or 3 slots (again, chosen randomly).
- After a third collision, wait anywhere from 0 to 7 slots.
- In general, after $n$ collision, wait anywhere from 0 to $2^n-1$ slots if $n \leq 10$. If $n > 10$ wait between 0 and 1024 ($2^{10}$) slots.
- After 16 collisions, give up. There is probably an error somewhere and the inability to transmit the frame is reported to the controlling computer. In this case, other software must investigate so it may determine the problem.

This approach clearly tries to minimize excessive waits by keeping the number of possible time slots small. After all, if two stations collide there is a 50% chance they will succeed on the next try (assuming that no other stations are sending).

If many stations collide, however, the chances are very small that even one will be successful on the next try. The successful one would have to choose either 0 or 1 slot with all the others making the other choice. By increasing the number of possible slots after each collision, the chances of colliding again decrease exponentially. The only time a large number of slots is possible is when all previous attempts have failed. In this case, long waits by some may be the only solution.

## TOKEN PASSING

The previous protocols took a somewhat anarchistic approach to sending signals by allowing stations to send whenever they wanted. A logical question at this point is whether there is some way stations can agree in advance about who sends when. In other words, is there some way they can take turns?

**Token Ring**    The difficulty with many networks is that no central control or authority makes such decisions. Still, there is a way for all participating stations to agree on a protocol for taking turns: **token passing**, a common protocol used in office environments in **token ring** networks. In a token ring network (Figure 3.28), the stations are commonly PCs connected circularly to a wire or fiber medium. An **interface card (IC)** connects each to the network and contains the hardware and logic allowing a PC to communicate with the network.

The contention protocol here is an orderly one compared to the "send when you can" protocols discussed previously. The devices in a token ring execute a protocol allowing them to take turns sending. The process involves a specially formatted frame called a token. It contains bit codes the IC recognizes and circles the ring visiting each IC. According to the protocol, a PC can send when its IC has the token.[*]

---

[*] In some situations this is not true. Chapter 6 provides a complete discussion of the token ring protocol.

FIGURE 3.28     **Token Ring Network**

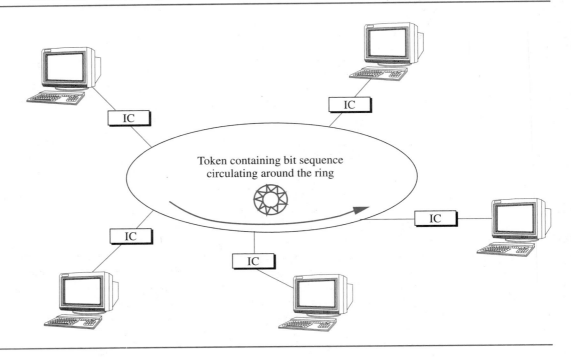

Chapter 6 describes exactly how stations exchange frames. In general, the concept is as follows. When a station receives the token one of two things occurs. If it has nothing to send it simply sends the token on to its neighbor. If it does have something to send it inserts the data and the destination address into the token. It also changes some control bits identifying the token as a **data frame** (one containing information). Proceeding this way allows the token to visit each station and pick up data when it is available. (It's a lot like an electronic Federal Express traveling around picking up and dropping off frames.)

When a station receives a frame it examines the control bits. If they indicate the frame contains no data, the station proceeds as before according to whether it has data to send. If the frame contains data, the station examines the destination address. If it is destined for some other station it just routes it to its neighbor. Otherwise the station copies the information and sends it to the PC. It then puts the frame back onto the ring. Eventually the frame returns to the sending station, which removes it and puts the token or another frame back onto the ring. Proceeding this way, the data eventually reaches its destination.

Token ring operations can be expanded to include prioritization and a reservation system that allows a station to reserve a token that already has data for future use. We will discuss these operations in Section 6.3.

**Slotted Ring**     Our description so far allows only one data frame per token. Thus a station will not send data until it receives an empty token. This fairly simple approach can have drawbacks, as Figure 3.29 shows.

Suppose station *A* wants to send many frames to station *C*. When it gets the token it inserts the first frame in it and routes it to its neighbor, station *B*. Station *B*, following the prescribed protocol, sends the frame to its neighbor. Eventually

FIGURE 3.29     **One Station Sending Many Frames**

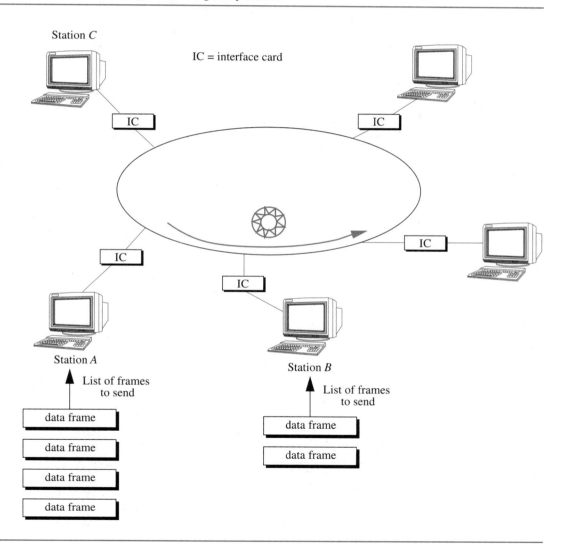

the frame gets back to station *A*. At this point, station *A* could send another frame.

Proceeding in this manner allows *A* to send all its frames without giving *B* a chance. With its transmissions delayed, station *B* sees the ring as slow and unresponsive. What can be done? One approach allows *B* to reserve a token as it passes by. We will explain this method in Chapter 6 when we discuss the IEEE token ring standard in detail.

Another approach is to use a slotted ring. It is also called the Cambridge ring as much of its development was done at the University of Cambridge. A slotted ring is much like a token ring except that it contains several rotating tokens or slots. As before, slots may be empty or contain data. The protocol for sending is similar to that of the token ring: A station must wait for a free slot. In contrast however, a station may not send any other frames until the slot that carried its previous data frame returns. This allows other free slots to pass it by and visit other stations picking up their data frames.

The slotted ring is more suited to rings with a long distance around the ring's perimeter to accommodate the many slots. For example, we stated previously that a signal propagates along a cable at about 200 m/μsec. Suppose the ring supports a data rate of 10 Mbps or 10 bits every μsec. This means that one bit travels 20 meters before the next one is put on the ring; in other words, 1 bit occupies 20 meters of the ring. Since more frames mean more bits occupying the ring, large rings are needed unless there are delays at each station caused by temporary storage of bits.

Rings have another advantage similar to that of the protocols discussed earlier. New stations can be added easily. When a station sends a frame to its neighbor it does not know if it has been added recently or has been there a long time. Consequently, stations need not be notified of changing neighbors.

One disadvantage is that one station can "hog" the token. In addition, a break in the link between two consecutive stations can bring the entire network down since the token cannot circulate. Another problem occurs if an IC fails while it is sending a token onto the ring. The result is an incomplete and invalid token circulating the ring. Stations looking for the proper token format are waiting for something that is not on the ring. Yet another problem occurs if, for some reason, the station responsible for removing a frame fails. Every station passes the frame to its neighbor and the frame circulates forever. The abundance of token ring networks suggests that these problems all have solutions. We will present some solutions when we cover higher layer-protocols in Chapter 6.

**Token Bus**     The token bus network has applications in assembly line and factory automation environments. Physically, it looks like a common bus (Figure 3.30), but it communicates using a principle similar to that in the token ring. All of the stations are numbered and a token is passed among them in order of number. The highest numbered station passes the token to the lowest numbered one. The numbering scheme organizes the stations into a logical ring independent of their physical locations on the bus. That is, two stations numbered consecutively need not be physically adjacent.

As with a token ring, the station with the token transmits. Because the stations are not connected physically in a ring, a station can transmit to any other directly. As with the previous protocols, the bus interface examines the addresses of transmitted frames and reads the frames destined for it.

The strongest proponents of the token bus were people interested in factory automation. The common bus structure allowed computer-controlled devices to be positioned along an assembly line. However, these proponents were uncomfortable with CSMA/CD approaches because there was no theoretical limit on the number of collisions that could occur and, consequently, no theoretical limit on frame delays. For obvious reasons they wanted to ensure that when a large piece of machinery came rolling down the assembly line, the computer-controlled devices would be ready to receive them.

Token bus protocols have one difficulty we have not yet encountered. A new station cannot be added as simply as with the previous protocols. Here, a station sends a token to its neighbor via the common bus and since all stations sense the bus the station must know who or where its neighbor is. (No isolationism here.) Consequently, adding or deleting stations does require some additional work to be done to inform appropriate stations of the change. A discussion of this process requires some knowledge of higher-level protocols. We will revisit this topic more fully in Chapter 6.

FIGURE 3.30    **Token Bus Network**

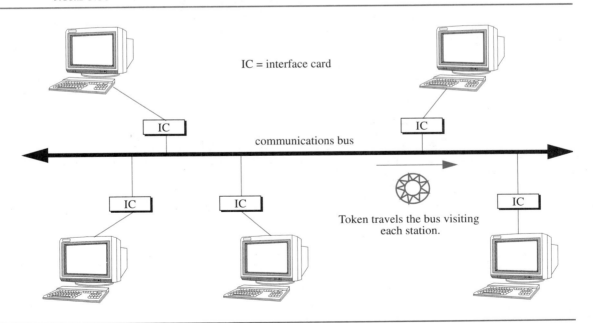

TABLE 3.5     **Summary of Contention Protocols**

| PROTOCOL | SIGNIFICANCE | ADVANTAGES | DISADVANTAGES |
|---|---|---|---|
| Aloha | Variations are useful in satellite communications where listening is not practical because of the time delay. | Simple approach. | Potential delays as stations may not know its frame has collided until well after it is sent. |
| P-persistent | Combined with CSMA/CD, a popular choice for the Ethernet and for a network. | Tends to decrease the chances of an idle medium. | May have excessive collisions under heavy traffic, wasting bandwidth of the medium. |
| Non-persistent | According to the model the success rate does not decrease under heavy loads. | Reduces the number of collisions, especially under heavy loads. | Transmission medium may be idle even when there are stations wanting to send something. |
| CSMA/CD | Combined with 1-persistence, it is commonly used with Ethernet. | Reduces the time of a collision. | No theoretical upper bound on the time it takes to transmit a frame successfully. |
| Token ring | Especially popular protocol used in office and business environments. | Simple interface as a station can only send to and receive from a neighbor. Upper bound on the time a station must wait before getting the token. | A malfunction at one station can destroy a token or break the ring, thus affecting the entire network. |
| Token bus | Originally favored by many interested in factory automation. | Upper bound on the time a station must wait before getting the token. | More difficult to add or delete a new station since its logical neighbors must be told of a change. |

## SUMMARY OF PROTOCOLS

The contention protocols we have discussed in this section represent some of the most popular and important ones. We have summarized them in Table 3.5. Other protocols do exist. If you are interested in them, see references 3 and 6.

## 3.5   Data Compression

With so many new applications requiring electronic communications there is an obvious trend to build faster and less costly ways of sending data. Chapter 2 mentioned some of the current areas of research such as optical fiber, higher frequency microwaves, and faster modems. All have their place and will certainly contribute to the field.

Some applications, however, cannot wait for these new developments. Their demand has forced people to look for other ways to communicate quickly and cheaply. For example, consider one of the more significant developments of the 1980s, the fax machine. Chapter 2 described how the fax machine divides a sheet of paper into dots depending on the image on it. A typical fax uses 40,000 dots per square inch resulting in nearly 4 million dots per page. Using a 9.6 Kbps modem would require over 6 minutes to transmit. If you have ever used a fax machine you know it does not take that long.

Another example is color television signals. What we see as motion on a TV screen is actually a display of 30 pictures (frames) per second (the same principle behind motion pictures). Furthermore, each picture actually consists of approximately 200,000 dots or **pixels** (picture elements), each with different intensities of the primary colors of blue, green, and red. Various combinations allow the generation of different colors in the spectrum. This means a TV signal for one frame has to have information on the intensity of each primary color for each pixel. Since a signal carries 30 frames per second it would need a digital transmission capability of over 100 Mbps and, according to the Nyquist theorem, require a signal bandwidth well above the 6 MHz currently allocated to each channel.

Both examples show that there are ways to get around the physical limits of different media. But how? The answer is **data compression**, a way to reduce the number of bits during transmission while retaining the meaning of the transmitted frame. It decreases both cost and time to send. Data compression has found uses in a variety of areas such as fax machines and the V.42 modem standards. It is also used in disk storage, and many software vendors compress programs on disks in order to use fewer disks.

The next logical question is, "How do you eliminate bits and still maintain necessary information?" For example, suppose the data in a large file consists entirely of strings of capital letters. How many data bits must be transferred? If the characters are stored as 8-bit ASCII codes, the number is $8*n$, where $n$ is the number of characters. However, if the information to be sent consists of upper case letters only, we do not need the full 8-bit ASCII code. Can we devise a code that represents just capital letters? Yes! Table 3.6 shows a 5-bit code using the numbers 0 through 25.

**TABLE 3.6     Alternative Code for Capital Letters**

| LETTER | CODE |
|:------:|:----:|
| A | 00000 |
| B | 00001 |
| C | 00010 |
| D | 00011 |
| : | : |
| : | : |
| X | 10111 |
| Y | 11000 |
| Z | 11001 |

Using this table, the sending station can substitute each 5-bit code for the original 8-bit one. The receiving station can convert back. The result is that the information was sent and the number of data bits transferred is $5*n$—a 37.5% reduction.

Again, many questions pop up (won't they ever stop?). What if there are control characters? What about lower case letters? What if the data are not letters? These are valid questions and must be addressed. Table 3.6 is a very simple method of compression not suitable for many applications. Its main purpose is to show what compression is and what it can do. There are many other ways to compress data.

## HUFFMAN CODE

The ASCII code and the code in Table 3.6 have one thing in common. All characters use the same number of bits. The **Huffman code** (Reference 12) varies the number according to the frequency with which a character appears. Such a code is also called a **frequency dependent code**. It assigns shorter codes to characters that appear more often, such as vowels and 'L', 'R', 'S', 'N', and 'T'. (The frequency factor is why they are worth less in a *Scrabble* game and, except for the vowels, which are not worth any money, are often chosen on the game show "Wheel of Fortune.") Thus, fewer bits are needed to transmit them.

For example, suppose Table 3.7 shows the frequencies (percentage of time they appear) of characters in a data file. To keep the example manageable we assume just 5 characters. If you want, you can do a similar example with all 26 letters.

Table 3.8 shows a Huffman code for these characters. Note that we say "a" Huffman code since, as we will show, it is not unique. We will show how to develop this code shortly.

Next, suppose the bit stream 01110001110110110111 was Huffman coded. If the leftmost bits were transmitted first, how do you interpret it? Fixed length codes have an advantage. Within a transmission, we always know where one character ends and the next one begins. For example, in the transmission of ASCII-coded characters, every set of 8 data bits defines a new character. This is not true of Huffman codes, so how do we interpret the Huffman-coded bit stream? How do we know where one letter ends and the next one begins?

TABLE 3.7    **Frequencies for the Letters 'A' through 'E'**

| LETTER | FREQUENCY |
|--------|-----------|
| A | 25% |
| B | 15% |
| C | 10% |
| D | 20% |
| E | 30% |

TABLE 3.8    **Huffman Code for the Letters 'A' through 'E'**

| LETTER | CODE |
|:------:|:----:|
| A | 01 |
| B | 110 |
| C | 111 |
| D | 10 |
| E | 00 |

The answer lies in a property of Huffman codes called the **prefix property**. That is, the code for any character never appears as the prefix of another code. For example, the Huffman code for 'A' is 01, so no other code starts with a 01.

Figure 3.31 shows how to interpret a Huffman-coded string. As bits are received, a station builds a substring by concatenating them. It stops when the substring corresponds to a coded character. In the example of Figure 3.31, it stops after forming the substring 01 meaning that 'A' is the first character sent. To find the second character, it discards the current substring and starts building a new one with the next bit received. Again, it stops when the substring corresponds to a coded character. In this case, the next three bits 110 correspond to the character 'B'. Note that the substring does not match any Huffman code until all 3 bits are received. This is a consequence of the prefix property. The station continues this approach until all bits have been received. The data in Figure 3.31 consists of the character string "ABEC-ADBC."

**Huffman algorithm**: The following steps show how to create a Huffman code.

- To each character associate a binary tree consisting of just one node. To each tree, assign the character's frequency, which we call the tree's weight.

- Look for the two lightest-weight trees. If there are more than two, choose among them randomly. Merge the two into a single tree with a new root node whose left and right subtrees are the two we chose. Assign the sum of weights of the merged trees as the weight of the new tree.

- Repeat the previous step until just one tree is left.

FIGURE 3.31    **Receiving and Interpreting a Huffman-Coded Message**

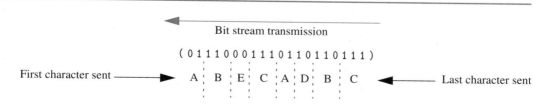

When completed, each of the original nodes is a leaf in the final binary tree. As with any binary tree, there is a unique path from the root to a leaf. For each leaf, the path to it defines the Huffman code. It is determined by assigning a 0 each time a left child pointer is followed and a 1 for each right child pointer.

Figure 3.32 (parts a through e) shows the construction of the Huffman code in Table 3.8. Figure 3.32a shows the 5 single-node trees with their weights. The trees for 'B' and 'C' have the smallest weights, so we merge them to give the results of Figure 3.32b. For the second merge there are two possibilities: merge the new tree with 'D' or merge 'A' with 'D'. In this case we arbitrarily chose the first, and

FIGURE 3.32     **Merging Huffman Trees**

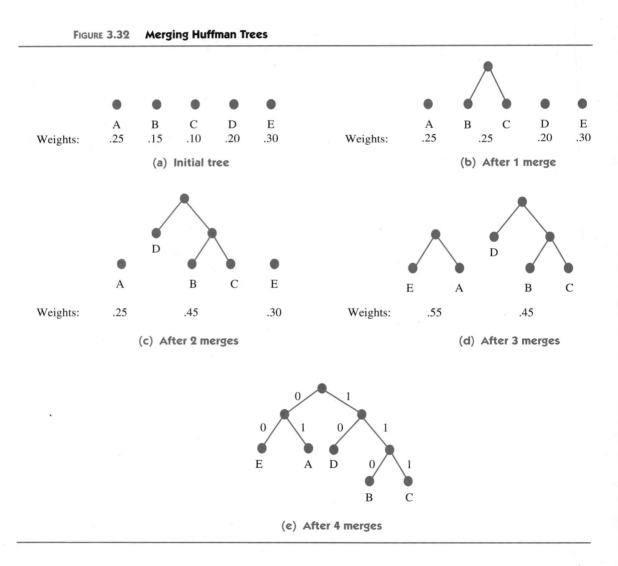

Figure 3.32c shows the result. Proceeding this way eventually gives the tree in Figure 3.32e. In it we see each left or right child pointer assigned a 0 or a 1. Following the pointers to a leaf node gives the Huffman code for the associated character. For example, following a left child (0) pointer and then a right child (1) pointer gets us to the leaf node for 'A'. This is consistent with the Huffman code of 01 for the letter 'A'.

## RUN LENGTH ENCODING

Huffman codes do reduce the number of bits to send, but they also require that frequency values be known. As described, they also assume that bits are grouped into characters or some other repeatable units. Many items that travel the communications media, including binary (machine code) files, fax data, and video signals do not fall into that category.

The fax, for example, transfers bits corresponding to light and dark space on a sheet of paper. It does not transfer the characters directly. Consequently, there is a need for a more general technique that can compress arbitrary bit strings. One approach, called **run length encoding**, uses a simple and perhaps obvious approach: It analyzes bit strings looking for long runs of a 0 or 1. Instead of sending all the bits, it sends only how many are in the run.

This technique is especially useful for fax transmission. If you were to examine closely the space in which a character is typed, potentially up to 70–80% is white space. The exact amount, of course, depends on the font and character. The actual dark spots from typed characters make up very little of a fax transmission. For example, note the amount of white space in a magnified representation of a lower-case 'f' within one print position.

**Runs of the same bit:** There are a couple of ways to implement run length encoding. The first is especially useful in binary streams where the same bit appears in most of the runs. In a fax example consisting primarily of characters there will be many long runs of 0s (assuming a light spot corresponds to a 0). This approach just transmits the length of each run as a fixed-length binary integer. The receiving station receives each length and generates the proper number of bits in the run, inserting the other bit in between.

For example, suppose 4 bits are used to represent the run length. Consider the bit stream of Figure 3.33a. Figure 3.33b shows the compressed stream that is sent. The original stream starts with 14 zeroes, so the first 4 bits in the compressed stream are 1110 (binary 14). The next 4 bits in the compressed stream are 1001 (binary 9 for the second run of nine 0s). After the second run there are two consecutive 1s. However,

FIGURE 3.33     **Stream Prior to Compression and Run Length Encoded Stream**

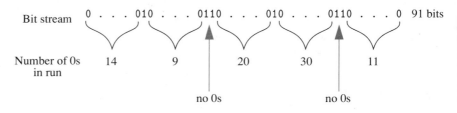

(a) **Stream prior to compression**

| Run lengths (binary) | 1110 | 1001 | 0000 | 1111 | 0101 | 1111 | 1111 | 0000 | 0000 | 1011 | 40 bits |
|---|---|---|---|---|---|---|---|---|---|---|---|
| Run lengths (decimal) | 14 | 9 | 0 | 15 | 5 | 15 | 15 | 0 | 0 | 11 | |

(b) **Run length encoded stream**

this approach sees them as two distinct 1s separated by a run of no 0s. Consequently, the third group of 4 bits is 0000.

The fourth run has 20 zeroes. Unfortunately, 20 cannot be expressed using 4 bits. In this case, the run length is expressed using a second 4-bit group. The two 4-bit numbers are then added to determine the run length. In Figure 3.33b, the 1111 (binary 15) and 0101 (binary 5) determine a run length of 20.

If the run length is too large to be expressed as a sum of two 4-bit numbers, the method uses as many 4-bit groups as necessary. The receiving station must know that a group of all 1s means the next group corresponds to the same run. Thus, it continues summing the group values and stops after it receives something other than all 1s. Consequently, the run of length 30 is represented by 1111, 1111, and 0000. In this case the 0s are needed to tell the station the run stops at thirty 0s.

How would the compressed stream differ if the stream in Figure 3.33a started with a 1? Similar to the case for two consecutive 1s, the method considers the stream to actually start with a run of no 0s. Thus, the first 4 bits sent would be 0000.

This technique is best suited where there are many long 0 runs. As the 1-bits increase in frequency, the technique becomes less efficient. In fact, you might try to construct a stream where this approach actually generates a longer bit stream.

**Runs with different characters**: Knowing that the same bit is involved simplifies matters since we only need to send the run length. But what about cases with runs of different bits or even characters? In such cases, your first response is probably correct: Send the actual character along with the run length. For example, the character string

HHHHHHHUFFFFFFFFFFFFFFFFFYYYYYYYYYYYYYYYYYYYYYDGGGGGGGGGGG

might actually be sent as the alternating set of numbers and characters 7, H, 1, U, 14, F, 20, Y, 1, D, 11, and G.

## RELATIVE ENCODING

The two compression techniques already discussed have their applications, but in certain cases neither provides much help. A common example is in video transmissions, where images may be very complex in contrast to the black/white transmission of a fax or a text file. Except perhaps for test patterns that appear before a station goes on the air, little in a video picture is repetitive. Consequently, neither of the previous methods offers much hope of compressing the signals for a picture.

Although a single video image contains little repetition, there is a lot of repetition over several images. Remember, a typical television signal sends 30 pictures per second. Furthermore, each picture generally varies only slightly from the previous one. Over the course of a fraction of a second not much action occurs. Therefore, rather than trying to treat each frame as a separate entity and compress it, we might think about how much a frame differs from the previous one. Encoding that information and sending it has potential when the differences are small. This method is called: **relative encoding** or **differential encoding**.

The principle is fairly straightforward. The first frame is sent and stored in a receiver's buffer. The sender then compares the second frame with the first, encodes the differences, and sends them in a frame format. The receiver gets the frame and applies the differences to the frame it has, thus creating the second frame the sender had. It stores the second frame in a buffer and continues the process for each new frame.

Figure 3.34 shows how it works. Here we represent a frame using a 2-dimensional array of integers. We put no interpretation on their meaning; they're just easier to draw than video signals. The first frame contains a set of integers, and the second differs very little from the first.

The figure shows another two dimensional array below the second frame containing 0s, 1s, and –1s. A 0 in any position means the element in that position of the frame is the same as that in the same position in the previous frame. A nonzero value indicates what the change is. So a 1 means the element in that frame position is one larger than the one in the same position in the previous frame. A minus one means it is one smaller. Certainly values other than 1 and –1 can be used. The point is that the frames to be sent contain long runs of 0s, making them candidates for run length encoding.

## LEMPEL-ZIV ENCODING

With run length encoding we compressed by looking for runs of a character or a bit. The idea is to reduce repetitious or redundant transmissions. But not all redundancy

FIGURE 3.34    **Relative Encoding**

```
5 7 6 2 8 6 6 3 5 6          5 7 6 2 8 6 6 3 5 6          5 7 6 2 8 6 6 3 5 6
6 5 7 5 5 6 3 2 4 7          6 5 7 6 5 6 3 2 3 7          6 5 8 6 5 6 3 3 3 7
8 4 6 8 5 6 4 8 8 5          8 4 6 8 5 6 4 8 8 5          8 4 6 8 5 6 4 8 8 5
5 1 2 9 8 6 5 5 6 6          5 1 3 9 8 6 5 5 7 6          5 1 3 9 7 6 5 5 8 6
5 5 2 9 9 6 8 9 5 1          5 5 2 9 9 6 8 9 5 1          5 5 2 9 9 6 8 9 5 1
```

First frame                  Second frame                 Third frame


```
                             0 0 0 0 0 0 0 0 0 0          0 0 0 0 0 0 0 0 0 0
                             0 0 0 1 0 0 0 0 –1 0         0 0 1 0 0 0 0 1 0 0
                             0 0 0 0 0 0 0 0 0 0          0 0 0 0 0 0 0 0 0 0
                             0 0 1 0 0 0 0 0 1 0          0 0 0 0 –1 0 0 0 1 0
                             0 0 0 0 0 0 0 0 0 0          0 0 0 0 0 0 0 0 0 0
```

Transmitted frame is the          Transmitted frame is the
encoded differences between       encoded differences between
the first and second frames.      the second and third frames.

occurs in the form of single bit or character repetitions. In some cases, entire words or phrases may be repeated. This is especially true with large text files such as manuscripts. An author's writing style is often characterized by a choice of words or phrases that may be repeated frequently.

The **Lempel-Ziv encoding** method looks for often-repeated strings and stores them just once. It then replaces multiple occurrences with a pointer to the original and a value indicating its length. This is one of the basic principles behind database management strategies: Store one piece of information in just one place and reference it through pointers. This technique is used by the UNIX compress command and the DOS ARC utility.

For example, consider the following writing sample (Reference 13):

> The tropical rain fell in drenching sheets, hammering the corrugated roof of the clinic building, roaring down the metal gutters, splashing on the ground in a torrent.

Several letter sequences are repeated. Ignoring case sensitivity, some of them are 'the ', 'ren', 'ing '. Note the first and third sequences contain a space. Figure 3.35 shows the result of replacing duplicate occurrences with a pointer to the original and a byte count. For example, the string 'ing ' appears in the word "drenching." It also appears in the words "hammering" and "roaring." Consequently, the figure shows an arrow followed by a 4 (character count) where this string would otherwise appear. Note that the string 'ing' (no space) appears at the end of 'building'. The comma prevents the use of the space but the 'ing' portion can still be replaced by a pointer followed by a 3.

FIGURE 3.35    **Lempel-Ziv Encoding**

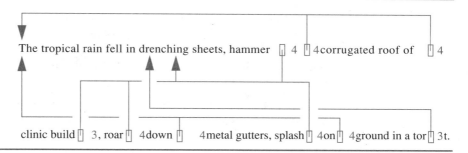

The string in Figure 3.35 did not compress the original by much, but you can't expect much repetition in a single sentence. With longer text and longer repetitions the compression improves.

It is worth noting that the overhead cost of looking for all these repetitions is rather high and could offset any savings by compressing a single transmission. But high overhead does not make the technique worthless. Compression techniques can be used to decrease the data for long-term storage on a disk or tape, and some operating systems have commands (such as UNIX "compress") that do just that. It not only saves disk space (which is cheap anyway) but is advantageous if the compressed file is accessed frequently by a file server in a distributed system or network.

### SUMMARY OF COMPRESSION TECHNIQUES

The compression techniques discussed here are representative of schemes in actual use, but they by no means represent the entire spectrum of techniques. References 4, 6, 7, and 14 mention others and reference 15 is devoted completely to compression techniques (and is good reading for anyone seriously interested in the topic). Remember that compression techniques are designed for different types of transmissions. Table 3.9 gives a brief summary of transmission types for which each technique is best suited.

TABLE 3.9    **Summary of Compression Techniques**

| COMPRESSION TECHNIQUE | HOW IT COMPRESSES |
| --- | --- |
| Huffman code | Uses short bit patterns for more frequently used letters and longer ones for less frequently used letters. |
| Run length encoding | Looks for long runs of a particular bit or character. |
| Relative encoding | Looks for small differences between consecutive frames. |
| Lempel-Ziv encoding | Looks for repeated occurrences of strings. |

## 3.6   Summary

This chapter dealt with data communication, which we see is a step above data transmission. It is one thing to send signals over some medium, but it is quite another to communicate effectively. We must be aware of the information inherent in the data and the measures necessary to make sure it reaches its destination. The chapter covered the following important topics:

- **Parallel and serial transmission**. Parallel transmission sends bits simultaneously using several lines; serial transmission sends them in sequence using a single line.

- **Synchronous and asynchronous transmission**. Asynchronous transmission sends each byte separately with a start and stop bit before and after the byte. Synchronous transmission groups bytes into a frame format and sends the entire frame.

- **Simplex, half-duplex, and full-duplex communication**. Simplex communication is one way only. Half-duplex communication allows two-way communication, but the sending and receiving stations must alternate. Full-duplex communication allows both stations to send simultaneously.

- **Interface protocols**. The RS-232 protocol connecting a DCE and DTE is probably the most well known. It defines circuit definitions and rules both devices must follow to communicate with each other. The RS-449 protocol was designed to improve on the RS-232 protocol by allowing faster data rates over longer distances. Because of its popularity, however, the RS-232 is still used frequently. The X.21 interface was designed for digital interfaces. Compared to the RS standards, it uses fewer lines between the DTE and DCE but requires more logic to interpret the exchanged signals.

- **Multiplexing**. Many applications do not need the full power of a high-speed network, or the cost often makes separate connections prohibitive. A multiplexer can interface between several devices and a single network connection. Frequency division multiplexers combine analog signals from different channels into a single analog signal. Time division multiplexers put bit streams from different sources into a single frame of fixed length. Statistical multiplexers also combine bit streams into a single frame, but vary the frame size depending on which sources are sending data.

- **Contention protocols**. Since a network is meant to service many users it must allow them all to communicate. This means making decisions when two or more users want to send simultaneously. One approach, the Aloha protocol, was designed for packet radio communication in the Hawaiian Islands. If two frames overlap, they collide. When the sending station hears no acknowledgment, it sends again. Slotted Aloha is similar, but requires that each station send only at the start of predefined time slots.

  CSMA took Aloha one step farther by listening to the medium before sending. It would send only if there was no traffic. If there was traffic its next step depended on which variation was used. With p-persistent CSMA, the station continued to monitor the medium. When the medium became quiet, there was a probability of $p$ the station would send. With non-persistent CSMA, the station did not monitor the medium. It just waited a random number of slot times and tried again. The last variation, CSMA/CD, used collision detection technique to stop sending if a station detected a collision. The intent was to decrease the amount of time during which frames collide.

Another protocol, token passing, is used in two types of networks, token ring and token bus networks. In both types, a special frame called a token circulates among the stations. A station can send only when it has the token. A token ring station is organized physically in a ring and token bus stations communicate via a common bus.

- **Data compression**. One goal of data communications is to send information faster and more cheaply. One solution is to reduce the number of bits sent. The Huffman algorithm does this by assigning shorter codes to more frequently occurring symbols. Run length encoding replaces long runs of a character or bit by the length of the run. Relative encoding measures the difference between successive frames and sends it. The Lempel-Ziv algorithm replaces redundant character sequences by a pointer to the original sequence and a count stating how many characters appear.

# Review Questions

1. Distinguish between serial and parallel communications.

2. Distinguish between synchronous and asynchronous communications.

3. List typical fields in a data frame and what they contain.

4. Distinguish among simplex, half-duplex, and full-duplex communications.

5. How does full-duplex communication prevent signals traveling in opposite directions from colliding?

6. Are the following statements TRUE or FALSE? Why?

   - Parallel and serial communications require different types of cables.
   - A PC normally connects directly to a network.
   - An RS-232 interface requires a 25-pin connector.
   - Two compatible PCs can communicate by installing a cable between each one's RS-232 port.
   - Devices using an RS-232 interface can automatically communicate.
   - Frequency division multiplexing is a form of parallel communications.
   - Time division multiplexing applies only to digital communications.

- A time division multiplexer allows its combined input capability to exceed its output capability.
- The non-persistent protocols outperform the persistent protocols in all cases.
- 1-persistent is optimal among the p-persistent protocols because a station never waits voluntarily, thus wasting time.

7. Distinguish between a DTE and DCE.

8. What is a null modem?

9. In Figure 3.9, why is each DTE pin 20 connected to the other's pin 8?

10. In Figure 3.9, why are each DTE's pins 4 and 5 connected?

11. Distinguish between a balanced and an unbalanced circuit.

12. Distinguish between frequency division multiplexing and time division multiplexing.

13. What is a multiplexer?

14. What is a channel?

15. Distinguish among a carrier signal, a modulating signal, and a modulated signal.

16. What is a primary motivation for using a multiplexer?

17. Why does a DS-1 frame field have eight bits for each channel?

18. What are guard bands?

19. What is a contention protocol?

20. Describe the Aloha protocol, listing its advantages and disadvantages.

21. Distinguish between slotted and pure Aloha.

22. What is the difference between 0-persistent CSMA and non-persistent CSMA?

23. Why does collision detection improve the performance of CSMA?

24. Why does the performance of persistent protocols degrade as $G$ increases, whereas the reverse is true of a non-persistent protocol?

25. What is the binary exponential backoff algorithm?

26. What is a token?

27. What is a slotted ring?

28. Distinguish between token ring and token bus networks.

29. Distinguish between data and information.

30. What is a Huffman code?

31. What is the Huffman code's prefix property?

32. What is a frequency dependent code?

33. What does run length encoding mean?

34. What is relative encoding?

35. What is Lempel-Ziv encoding?

# Exercises

1. Why does asynchronous communications require additional start and stop bits? What is wrong with letting the first bit in a transmission act as a start bit and the last one act as a stop bit?

2. Since parallel communications transmits bits simultaneously, why not design parallel communications with an arbitrarily large number of parallel lines to decrease transmission time?

3. What is a minimal set of circuits required to establish a full-duplex communication over an RS-232 Interface?

4. Why must the DTE assert a RTS (request to send) circuit before sending to the DCE, but the DCE is not required to assert any request to send line prior to sending to the DTE?

5. Some null modems connect a DTE's pin 20 to its own pins 5 and 6. What purpose does this serve?

6. Some null modems connect a DTE's pin 4 to its own pin 5 and to the other's pin 8. What purpose does this serve?

7. RS-449 was designed to replace RS-232 and, in fact, can do anything RS-232 can. Yet, RS-232 remains a dominant standard. Why do you suppose this is true?

8. If you have a PC or access to a terminal that has an RS-232 interface, check the manual to determine what circuits are used.

9. Write a program to produce the graph of a modulating signal and a modulated signal similar to those of Figure 3.15.

10. Suppose five devices are connected to a statistical time division multiplexer (similar to the situation in Figure 3.18) and that each produces output as shown here. Construct the frame that it sends.

```
Device 1: . . . . Ø A₃ Ø A₂ A₁
Device 2: . . . . B₄ B₃ Ø B₂ B₁
Device 3: . . . . Ø C₂ Ø Ø C₁
```

```
Device 4: . . . . D₅ D₄ D₃ D₂ D₁
Device 5: . . . . Ø Ø E₂ Ø E₁
```

11. What is the purpose of adding 0.5 to the sine function to form $f(t)$ in Figure 3.15? That is, what happens if that term is eliminated?

12. Discuss the significance of the graphs in Figure 3.25.

13. Comment on the following statement:

> With 1-persistent CSMA a waiting station always transmits when the medium is clear. Why not change the protocol so that when a medium is clear the station waits the amount of time it would take for another station's transmission to reach it? If it is still clear, then transmit. This should decrease the chances of two waiting stations colliding.

14. Comment on the usefulness of a 0-persistent CSMA.

15. Suppose three stations using a 0.5-persistent protocol are waiting for an idle medium.

    • What is the probability of a collision when the medium clears?
    • What is the probability of a successful transmission when the medium clears?
    • What is the probability that no station will send anything when the medium clears?

16. Repeat Exercise 15, but assume the stations use a 0.25-persistent protocol.

17. Suppose two stations using CSMA/CD and the binary exponential backoff algorithm have just sent transmissions that have collided.

    • What is the probability they will collide again during the next time slot?
    • What is the probability both stations will transmit successfully during the next two time slots?
    • What is the probability they will collide two more times? Three more times?

18. Suppose three stations using CSMA/CD and the binary exponential backoff algorithm have just sent transmissions that have all collided.

    • What is the probability they will all collide again during the next time slot?
    • What is the probability all three stations will transmit successfully during the next three time slots?
    • What is the probability any two will collide during the next time slot?

19. Suppose the binary exponential backoff algorithm is altered so that a station will always wait 0 or 1 time slots regardless of how many collisions have occurred. How is the effectiveness changed?

20. Suppose the binary exponential backoff algorithm is altered so that a station will always wait anywhere between 0 and $2^n - 1$ time slots regardless of how many collisions have occurred. How is the effectiveness changed?

21. Can you devise a 4-bit code similar to that in Table 3.6?

22. Devise a Huffman code for letters whose frequency of occurrence is in the following table.

| LETTER | FREQUENCY |
|--------|-----------|
| A | 15% |
| B | 25% |
| C | 20% |
| D | 10% |
| E | 10% |
| F | 20% |

Without constructing them, how many different Huffman codes could you create?

23. Compress the following bit stream using run length encoding. Use 5 bits to code each run length. Parenthesized expressions indicate runs.

1 (33 zeroes) 1 (25 zeroes) 1 1 1 (44 zeroes) 1 (2 zeroes) 1 (45 zeroes)

Express the length of the compressed stream as a percentage of the original.

24. With run length encoding, how many 0s must appear in a run before the code actually compresses?

25. Give an example of a situation in which run length encoding would perform better (worse) than a Huffman code.

26. Apply the Lempel-Ziv encoding scheme to the text below. Consider only strings with 3 or more characters.

With so many new applications requiring electronic communications there is an obvious trend to build faster and less costly ways of sending data.

27. Comment on the following statement:

In an era of megabit and gigabit transmissions, compression schemes will save only the smallest fractions of a second. Therefore, the time saving is not worth the additional overhead of compressing bits.

28. Use the Huffman code from Table 3.8 and interpret the following bit stream (starting from the leftmost bit).

110011100100010001110110

**29.** Which of the following are Huffman codes? Why?

| CHARACTER | CODE | CHARACTER | CODE | CHARACTER | CODE |
|-----------|------|-----------|------|-----------|------|
| A | 01 | A | 10 | A | 1 |
| B | 001 | B | 001 | B | 01 |
| C | 10 | C | 11 | C | 000 |
| D | 110 | D | 101 | D | 001 |
| E | 010 | E | 000 | E | 0001 |

## REFERENCES

1. Black, U. *Data Networks Concept, Theory, and Practice.* Englewood Cliffs, NJ: Prentice-Hall, 1989.

2. Sherman, K. *Data Communications: A User's Guide,* 3rd ed. Englewood Cliffs, NJ: Prentice-Hall, 1990.

3. Stallings, W. *Data and Computer Communications,* 4th ed. New York: Macmillan, 1994.

4. Russel, D. *The Principles of Computer Networking.* Cambridge University Press, 1989.

5. Moshos, G. *Data Communications: Principles and Problems.* St. Paul, MN: West, 1989.

6. Tanenbaum, A. S. *Computer Networks,* 2nd ed. Englewood Cliffs, NJ: Prentice-Hall, 1988.

7. Walrand, J. *Communications Networks: A First Course.* Boston: Richard D. Irwin, 1991.

8. Chu, W.,"Asynchronous Time-Division Multiplexing Systems." In *Computer Communication Networks,* ed. Abramson and Kuo. Englewood Cliffs, NJ: Prentice-Hall, 1973.

9. Martin, J. *Systems Analysis for Data Transmission.* Englewood Cliffs, NJ: Prentice-Hall, 1972.

10. Roberts, L. "ALOHA Packet System With and Without Alots and Capture." *Computer Communications Review,* April 1975.

11. Mitrani, I. *Modeling of Computer and Communication Systems.* London: Cambridge University Press, 1987.

12. Huffman, D. "A Method for the Construction of Minimum Redundancy Codes." IRE Proceedings, vol. 40 (September, 1952), 1098–1101.

13. Crichton, M. *Jurassic Park.* New York: Ballantine Books, 1990.

14. Lucky, R. W. *Silicon Dreams: Information, Man, and Machines.* New York: St. Martins Press, 1989.

15. Nelson, M. *The Data Compression Book.* Redwood City, CA: M & T Books, 1991.

16. Kleinrock, L. and F. Tobagi. "Random Access Techniques for Data Transmission over Packet-switched Radio Channels," AFIPS Conference Proceedings, Vol. 44 (1975), 187.

# CHAPTER 4

# DATA SECURITY AND INTEGRITY

## 4.1 Introduction

Chapters 2 and 3 dealt with many of the mechanisms necessary to transmit information. All of these methods, no matter how sophisticated, are not sufficient to guarantee effective and safe communications. Consider an example in which you receive the following message via electronic mail:

"I heard from your brothel in New Orleans. Plan to meet there tomorrow."

Your reactions could be anything from confusion to shock to terror. What if your spouse got the message first? There was no way for your spouse to know that the message should have read:

"I heard from your brother in New Orleans. Plan to meet there tomorrow."

What happened? The person sending the message is not a practical joker. He or she actually sent the innocuous message. The problem was in the message transmission. The letter 'r' from the word "brother" was ASCII coded as 1110010. Unfortunately, some electrical interference changed the middle four bits 1001 to 0110, and the received bit string was 1101100, the code for the letter 'l'.

I think we would all agree that a system that allows altered messages to be delivered is less than desirable. But the fact is that errors do occur. Any message transmitted electronically is susceptible to interference. Sunspots, electrical storms, power fluctuations or a digger hitting a cable with a shovel can do amazing and unpredictable things to transmissions. We simply cannot allow shuttle astronauts to receive incorrect navigational instructions or Swiss banks to deposit a million dollars more than they should (unless it's into my account!). Any communications system must deliver accurate messages.

The ability to detect when a transmission has been changed is called **error detection**. In most cases, when errors are detected the message is discarded, the sender is notified, and the message is sent again. We will discuss protocols that do this in Chapter 5. In other cases when an error is detected it may actually be fixed without a second transmission. This is called **error correction**. The sender never knows the message was damaged and subsequently fixed. The bottom line is that the message eventually is delivered correctly.

Integrity is not enough, however. Another issue is security. When you go to the bank, you don't normally show your deposit slips and balances to the person standing in line with you. For the same reasons, electronic funds transfers between banks must be secure so that unauthorized people cannot get access to your financial arrangements. Not just banks, but many other communications systems as well must be secure. Ideally, they should provide easy access to authorized people and no access to unauthorized people. But how can you have security when information is sent over microwaves and satellites? The information travels freely through the air, and unauthorized reception is virtually impossible to enforce. Even with cable it may be difficult to prevent someone from finding an isolated spot in a closet or basement and tapping into the cable.

One common approach to secure transmissions, strangely enough, does not worry about unauthorized reception. Why worry about what you cannot prevent? Instead, this approach alters (encrypts) messages so that even if they are intercepted by unauthorized people they are not intelligible. Encryption is common in cable television (CATV) transmission. Anyone with CATV can receive the premium movie stations, but the signals are scrambled so that viewing is impossible. If you pay your local cable company the appropriate fees they will unscramble the signals for you or give you a device that does so. Only then may you watch all the available movies.

In this chapter, we deal with the issues of integrity and security. Sections 4.2 through 4.4 discuss different ways to detect and correct transmission errors. They show that some techniques are implemented easily but are not very effective whereas other, more complex techniques are very effective. Effectiveness at the expense of simplicity is an almost universal tradeoff.

Sections 4.5 and 4.6 present different ways of encrypting information and some of the issues surrounding encryption standards. True to the universal tradeoff just mentioned, some simple encryption schemes are not very secure and some theoretically difficult ones are very secure. We finish the chapter by discussing some of the most serious threats to computer and communications security: worms, viruses, and hackers. We will describe them and discuss some common approaches to battling them.

## 4.2 Parity Checking

Most error detection techniques require sending additional bits whose values depend on the data that is sent. Thus, if the data is changed the additional bit values no longer correspond to the new data (at least in theory). Probably the most common approach is parity checking, which involves counting all the 1-bits in the data and adding one more bit to make the total number of 1-bits even (**even parity**) or odd

(**odd parity**). The extra bit is called the **parity bit**. We will base our discussions on an even parity and leave it to the reader to construct similar discussions with odd parity.

To illustrate, suppose the number of 1-bits in the data is odd. By defining the parity bit as 1 the total number of 1-bits is now even. Similarly, if the number of 1-bits in the data is already even, the parity bit is 0. Consider the bit streams in Figure 4.1. The first one has four 1-bits. Therefore, its parity bit is 0. The second one has five 1-bits, so its parity bit is 1.

### Parity Checking Analysis

Parity checking will detect any single-bit error. The parity bit is transmitted with the data bits and the receiver checks the parity. If the receiver finds an odd number of 1-bits, an error has occurred. Single-bit errors are very rare, however. For example, suppose an error occurred because of a brief power surge or static electricity whose duration is a hundredth of a second. In human terms, a hundredth of a second is barely noticeable. But if the data rate is 19.2 Kbps (kilobits per second), 192 bits may be affected in that hundredth of a second. When many bits are damaged we call this a **burst error**.

How does parity checking work for arbitrary burst errors? Suppose two bits change during transmission. If they were both 0, they change to 1. Two extra 1s still make the total number of 1-bits even. Similarly, if they were both 1 they both change to 0 and there are two fewer 1-bits, but still an even number. If they were opposite values and both change, they are still opposite. This time the number of 1-bits remains the same. The bottom line is that parity checks do not detect double-bit errors.

In general, if an odd number of bits change, parity checking will detect the error. If an even number of bits change, parity checking will not detect the error. The conclusion is that parity checks will catch about 50% of burst errors, and a 50% accuracy rate is not good for a communications network.

Does this make the discussion of parity checks useless? The answer is no, for two reasons. First, some computer memory organizations store the bits from a byte or word on different chips. Thus when the word is accessed the bits travel different paths. In such cases the malfunction of one path can cause a single-bit error. Such

---

FIGURE 4.1    **Detecting Single Bit Errors Using Parity Checking**

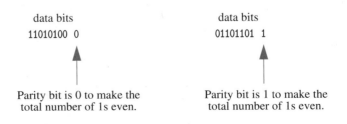

data bits
11010100  0

data bits
01101101  1

Parity bit is 0 to make the
total number of 1s even.

Parity bit is 1 to make the
total number of 1s even.

architectures often use additional memory chips for parity bits. (The details are beyond the scope of this text, but Reference 1 discusses this topic.) The second reason is that parity checking is the basis for other, more sophisticated detection techniques, discussed in this and the next sections.

## DOUBLE BIT ERROR DETECTION

Since a single parity check will detect any single-bit error you might guess that extra parity checks can detect multiple errors. They can, up to a point. For example, suppose we wanted to detect double-bit errors. One approach is to use two parity checks, one for the odd-numbered bits and one for the even-numbered bits. Figure 4.2 shows how to do this. In that case, one parity bit is used for positions 1, 3, 5, and 7 and the other for positions 2, 4, 6, and 8. Consequently, if any single bit or any two consecutive bits are changed, one or both parity checks fail.

You might respond by asking what happens if two even- (or odd-) numbered bits change. The answer is simple: It doesn't work. Even though this method provides a little more error checking than single-parity checks it still won't detect all errors. It is possible to define additional parity checks to account for different combinations of errors, but the choice of which positions to check becomes more difficult. In addition, the number of parity bits increases, resulting in more transmission overhead. Nevertheless, one error correction method does use this approach; we will discuss it in Section 4.4.

## BURST ERROR DETECTION

Trying to detect errors in arbitrary positions (burst errors) certainly can be difficult. But perhaps we are approaching this problem the wrong way. Earlier we stated that some computer memory organizations store bits from a byte in separate chips. The bits travel different paths and the byte is assembled afterward. We can use this idea in com-

**FIGURE 4.2    Detecting Consecutive Double-Bit Errors Using Parity Checking**

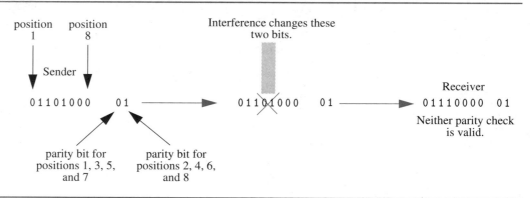

FIGURE 4.3    **Detecting Burst Errors Using Parity Bits**

| | | | | | | |
|---|---|---|---|---|---|---|
| Sender | | | | Receiver | | |
| Row (frame) number | Parity bit for one row | | | Row number | | Parity bit for one row |
| 1 | 01101 | 1 | | 1 | 01101 | 1 |
| 2 | 10001 | 0 | | 2 | 10001 | 0 |
| 3 | 01110 | 1 | | 3 | 01100 | 1* |
| 4 | 11001 | 1 | | 4 | 11001 | 1 |
| 5 | 01010 | 0 | Burst error occurs and destroys column four, making it all zeroes. | 5 | 01000 | 0* |
| 6 | 10111 | 0 | | 6 | 10101 | 0* |
| 7 | 01100 | 0 | | 7 | 01100 | 0 |
| 8 | 00111 | 1 | | 8 | 00101 | 1* |
| 9 | 10011 | 1 | | 9 | 10001 | 1* |
| 10 | 11000 | 0 | | 10 | 11000 | 0 |
| Column number | 12345 | 6 | | Column number | 12345 | 6 |

\* Parity bit is not correct

munications as well. Frequently, messages (especially long ones) are divided into smaller, more manageable units called **frames**. Rather than sending all bits from one frame together we can send them separately. Transmitting just one bit of information is not very efficient, however. It is analogous to writing a letter, cutting out the words and stuffing them into separate envelopes, and mailing them. On the other hand, if there are many frames to send perhaps we can transmit many bits together but just one from each frame. The sender has to disassemble them and the receiver reassemble them.

Figure 4.3 illustrates this principle. Create a two-dimensional bit array in which each row corresponds to one frame. The first column contains the first bits from each frame, the second column contains the second bits from each frame, and so on. The figure shows ten frames of 5 bits each. Next we construct a single-parity bit for each frame, which gives us an extra column. Now instead of sending each frame with its parity bit, we send each column separately. In Figure 4.3 we would send six columns consisting of 10 bits each.

Now suppose a burst error occurs and interferes with one transmission. At the most, one bit from each original data frame is actually changed, and the parity checks will detect them. In Figure 4.3 column 4 was damaged, making all the bits 0.* The receiver performed the parity checks and found that five of them failed.

---

*Note that a burst error does not necessarily change every bit. The bits in a transmission may or may not be damaged. In this example some of the 0's were present in the original frame; some were not. The point is that the receiver has no way of knowing which ones are correct.

Now it does not know which column is the culprit so it will request a retransmission of all the columns.

This method will guarantee error detection for any single burst error whose duration is less than the time to send one column. But what about burst errors affecting two or more columns? Let's consider the case for two columns. Earlier we said that parity checks will not detect a case in which two bits actually change. Therefore, the only way a burst error affecting two columns can go undetected is when either two bits or no bits are actually changed in each row. In other words, the error must actually change the same bits in each of the two columns.

What are the odds of this happening? Suppose columns i and j were affected by burst errors. Suppose the bits from column i are affected randomly (i.e., there is no predictable pattern of which ones actually change). Now consider any bit from column j. It either changed or it didn't (pretty conclusive, right?). Therefore there is a 1/2 probability the same thing happened to it that happened to the corresponding bit in column i. If there are $n$ bits in a column, there is a probability of $(1/2)^n$ that either two or no bits are changed in each row and the error goes undetected.

For large $n$, most burst errors that affect two different columns will be detected. For example, if $n = 20$ the probability the errors will not be detected is $(1/2)^{20} = 1/1048576$. This corresponds to a success rate of about 99.9999%. As the number of affected columns increases, the chances that all parity checks are successful become even more remote.

A major disadvantage of this approach is the assembling and reassembling of the frames, which causes quite a bit of overhead. Fortunately, there is another method that is theoretically more difficult to understand, but has an efficient implementation and is very accurate.

## 4.3  Cyclic Redundancy Checks (CRC)

In the previous section we saw that parity checking by itself is not very reliable. However, if we combine frames into two-dimensional bit arrays and send them one column at a time, parity checking can be very reliable. A problem with this approach is that an error is not detected until after all the columns are sent. Consequently, the receiver does not know which columns are incorrect. Thus there is no choice but to retransmit all the columns—a lot of extra work for a single error. The problem is compounded if another error occurs as the columns are being sent the second time.

Is there a way to send a frame and determine immediately whether there was an error? In this section we discuss a method called cyclic redundancy check that does exactly that. We also show that it is a very reliable method and can be implemented efficiently.

CRC is a rather unusual but clever method that does error checking via polynomial division. Your first reaction is probably, "What does polynomial division have to do with transmitting bit strings?" The answer is that the method interprets each bit string as a polynomial. In general, it interprets the bit string

$$b_{n-1} b_{n-2} b_{n-3} \ldots . b_2 b_1 b_0$$

as the polynomial

$$b_{n-1} x^{n-1} + b_{n-2} x^{n-2} + b_{n-3} x^{n-3} + \ldots + b_2 x^2 + b_1 x + b_0$$

For example, the bit string 10010101110 is interpreted as

$$x^{10} + x^7 + x^5 + x^3 + x^2 + x^1$$

Since each $b_i$ is either 0 or 1, we just write $x^i$ when $b_i$ is 1 and do not write any term when $b_i$ is 0.

We outline the CRC method below. We also assume all computations are done modulo 2.

- Given a bit string, append several 0s to the end of it (we will specify how many and why later) and call it $B$. Let $B(x)$ be the polynomial corresponding to $B$.

- Divide $B(x)$ by some agreed-on polynomial $G(x)$ (**generator polynomial**) and determine the remainder $R(x)$.

- Define $T(x) = B(x) - R(x)$. Later we will show that $T(x)/G(x)$ generates a zero-remainder and that the subtracting can be done by replacing the previously appended 0-bits with the bit string corresponding to $R(x)$.

- Transmit $T$, the bit string corresponding to $T(x)$.

- Let $T'$ represent the bit stream the receiver gets and $T'(x)$ the associated polynomial. The receiver divides $T'(x)$ by $G(x)$. If there is a 0-remainder the receiver concludes $T = T'$ and no error occurred. Otherwise, the receiver concludes an error occurred and requests a retransmission.

Before you throw your hands up in despair, we agree that questions need answering. Why do we perform each of these steps? Is there any validity to the receiver's conclusion after dividing $T(x)$ by $G(x)$? How accurate is this method? Must a sender and receiver go through all this work each time a frame is sent? However, we cannot answer these questions until we have covered a few preliminaries. We assume you have some knowledge of polynomials and polynomial operations using real numbers, but we will provide a brief summary of modulo 2 division of polynomials.

## POLYNOMIAL DIVISION

Figure 4.4 shows an example of polynomial division $T(x)/G(x)$ where

$$T(x) = x^{10} + x^9 + x^7 + x^5 + x^4$$

and

$$G(x) = x^4 + x^3 + 1$$

FIGURE 4.4    Calculation of $(x^{10} + x^9 + x^7 + x^5 + x^4) / (x^4 + x^3 + 1)$

$$
\require{enclose}
\begin{array}{r}
x^6 \qquad\quad + x^3 \quad + x \\[2pt]
x^4 + x^3 + 1 \enclose{longdiv}{x^{10} + x^9 \qquad + x^7 \qquad + x^5 + x^4} \\[2pt]
\underline{x^{10} + x^9 \qquad + x^6} \\[2pt]
x^7 + x^6 + x^5 + x^4 \\[2pt]
\underline{x^7 + x^6 \qquad\quad + x^3} \\[2pt]
x^5 + x^4 + x^3 \\[2pt]
\underline{x^5 + x^4 \qquad + x} \\[2pt]
x^3 \quad + x \qquad \text{remainder}
\end{array}
$$

This is just like polynomial division from an algebra course except that the calculations use modulo 2 arithmetic. Modulo 2 addition and subtraction are defined by

$$0 + 0 = 0; \; 1 + 0 = 1; \; 0 + 1 = 1; \; 1 + 1 = 0$$

and

$$0 - 0 = 0; \; 1 - 0 = 1; \; 0 - 1 = 1; \; 1 - 1 = 0$$

Note that modulo 2 addition and subtraction are the same as and, in fact, correspond to the exclusive-or operation. This is an important fact we use later when we discuss CRC implementation.

Figure 4.5 shows the same division using synthetic division. You might recall from the same algebra class that it is a shortcut that uses only the coefficients of the polynomials (in this case, bit strings). Remembering to use zeroes where there are no polynomial terms, the coefficient list for $x^{10} + x^9 + x^7 + x^5 + x^4$ is 11010110000 and for $x^4 + x^3 + 1$ is 11001.

## How CRC Works

Let's now describe how CRC works. Suppose we want to send the bit string 1101011, and the generator polynomial is $G(x) = x^4 + x^3 + 1$. (We will discuss some criteria for choosing $G(x)$ later.)

FIGURE 4.5    **Synthetic Division of $(x^{10} + x^9 + x^7 + x^5 + x^4) / (x^4 + x^3 + 1)$**

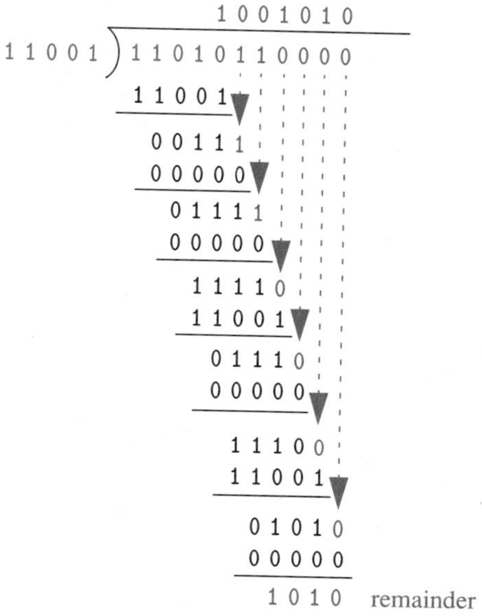

```
                              1 0 0 1 0 1 0
            1 1 0 0 1 ) 1 1 0 1 0 1 1 0 0 0 0
                        1 1 0 0 1
                        ─────────
                          0 0 1 1 1
                          0 0 0 0 0
                          ─────────
                            0 1 1 1 1
                            0 0 0 0 0
                            ─────────
                              1 1 1 1 0
                              1 1 0 0 1
                              ─────────
                                0 1 1 1 0
                                0 0 0 0 0
                                ─────────
                                  1 1 1 0 0
                                  1 1 0 0 1
                                  ─────────
                                    0 1 0 1 0
                                    0 0 0 0 0
                                    ─────────
                                      1 0 1 0    remainder
```

**Step 1**: Append 0's to the end of the string. The number of 0's is the same as the degree of the generator polynomial (in this case, 4). Thus the string becomes 11010110000.

**Step 2**: Divide $B(x)$ by $G(x)$. Figures 4.4 and 4.5 show the result for this example, giving a remainder of $R(x) = x^3 + x$ or its bit string equivalent of 1010. Note that we can write this algebraically as

$$\frac{B(x)}{G(x)} = Q(x) + \frac{R(x)}{G(x)}$$

where $Q(x)$ represents the quotient.
Equivalently, we can write

$$B(x) = G(x){*}Q(x) + R(x).$$

**Step 3**: Define $T(x) = B(x) - R(x)$. Since the subtraction takes the difference of coefficients of like terms, we calculate the difference by subtracting the bit strings associated with each polynomial. In this case, we have

| | |
|---:|:---|
| 11010110000 | bit string $B$ |
| - 1010 | bit string $R$ |
| 11010111010 | bit string $T$ |

Note that the string $T$ is actually the same as string $B$ with the appended 0s replaced by $R$. Another important fact, as shown by Figure 4.6, is that if we divide $T(x)$ by $G(x)$ the remainder is 0.* The sender then transmits the string $T$.

**Step 4**: If the string $T$ arrives without damage, dividing by $G(x)$ will yield a 0 remainder. But suppose that during transmission string $T$ is damaged. For example, suppose that four bits in the middle changed to 0 and the string arrives as 11000001010. The receiver synthetically divides it by $G(x)$ and the remainder is not 0 (Figure 4.7). Since the remainder is not 0, the receiver concludes that an error has occurred. (Note: This is not the same as saying that dividing a damaged string by $G(x)$ will always yield a non-zero remainder. It can happen, but if $G(x)$ is chosen wisely it occurs only rarely. We will discuss this topic next.)

## ANALYSIS OF CRC

The mechanisms of CRC are fairly straightforward. The question we have yet to answer is whether the method is any good. Will the receiver always be able to detect a

FIGURE 4.6   **Dividing $T(x)$ by $G(x)$**

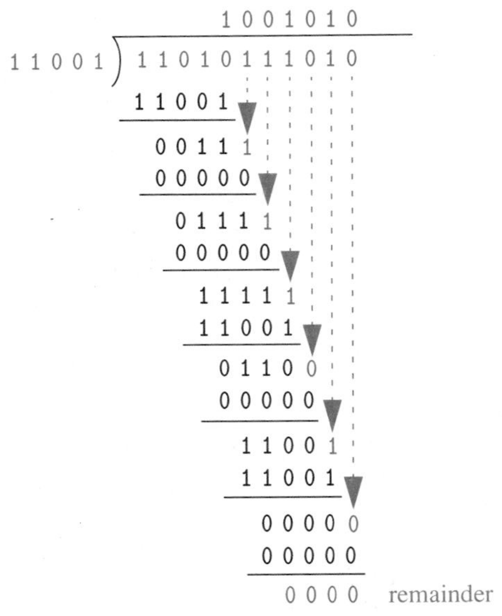

---

*There is an analogy using integers that says if $p$ and $q$ are integers and $r$ is the integer remainder obtained by dividing $p$ by $q$, then $p - r$ is evenly divisible by $q$. For example, 8/3 generates a remainder of 2 and $8 - 2$ is evenly divisible by 3.

FIGURE 4.7    **Division of Received Polynomial by** $G(x)$

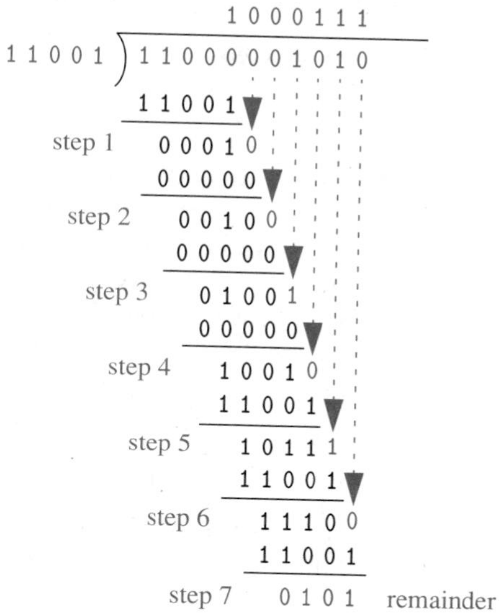

```
                                      1 0 0 0 1 1 1
                        1 1 0 0 1 ) 1 1 0 0 0 0 0 1 0 1 0
                                    1 1 0 0 1
            step 1         0 0 0 1 0
                           0 0 0 0 0
            step 2         0 0 1 0 0
                           0 0 0 0 0
            step 3         0 1 0 0 1
                           0 0 0 0 0
            step 4         1 0 0 1 0
                           1 1 0 0 1
            step 5         1 0 1 1 1
                           1 1 0 0 1
            step 6         1 1 1 0 0
                           1 1 0 0 1
            step 7         0 1 0 1     remainder
```

damaged frame? We relied on the proposition that a damaged frame means that dividing by $G(x)$ yields a non-zero remainder. But is this always true? Is it possible to change the bit string $T$ in such a way that dividing by $G(x)$ does give a zero remainder?

A complete and detailed proof requires knowledge of factorization properties of polynomial rings (a field in abstract mathematics), and we will not provide one here. Instead, we will provide a brief discussion to give some sense of why it works. To begin, let's specify more accurately what we are looking for. Changing the bits in $T$ is analogous to adding some unknown polynomial to $T(x)$. Thus, if $T'$ represents the received string and $T'(x)$ the associated polynomial, then $T'(x) = T(x) + E(x)$, where $E(x)$ is unknown to the receiver of $T'$. In the previous example,

string T = 11010111010 corresponds to

$$T(x) = x^{10} + x^9 + x^7 + x^5 + x^4 + x^3 + x;$$

string E = 00010110000 corresponds to $E(x) = x^7 + x^5 + x^4;$

string T' = 11000001010 corresponds to $T'(x) = x^{10} + x^9 + x^3 + x.$

Don't forget the addition is done using the exclusive-or operation. So, for example, adding the $x^7$ terms from $E(x)$ and $T(x)$ yields $x^7 + x^7 = (1+1)*x^7 = 0$.

The question we must answer, therefore, is: When will $(T(x) + E(x))/G(x)$ generate a zero remainder? Since $(T(x) + E(x))/G(x) = T(x)/G(x) + E(x)/G(x)$ and the first term has a zero remainder, the latter term determines the remainder. Therefore, the question can be reformulated: For what polynomials $E(x)$ will $E(x)/G(x)$ have a zero remainder?

We can now make the following statement:

**Undetected transmission errors correspond to errors for which $G(x)$ is a factor of $E(x)$.**

The next question is, "Under what conditions is $G(x)$ a factor of $E(x)$?" Let's examine the simplest case first, where just one bit in $T$ changes. In this case $E(x)$ is just one term, $x^k$ for some integer $k$. The only way $G(x)$ can be a factor of $x^k$ is if $G(x)$ is $x$ raised to some power. So as long as we choose $G(x)$ with at least two terms it won't happen. Thus CRC will detect all single-bit errors.

Next, consider a burst error of length $k \le r =$ degree $G(x)$.* Suppose $T(x)$ is represented by

$$t_n\, t_{n-1} \cdots \underbrace{t_{i+k-1}\, t_{i+k-2} \cdots t_i}_{k \text{ affected bits}}\, t_{i-1} \cdots t_1\, t_0$$

and $t_{i+k-1}$ and $t_i$ are the first and last bits to be damaged. The bits in between have been damaged arbitrarily. This means that

$$E(x) = x^{i+k-1} + \ldots + x^i = x^i * (x^{k-1} + \ldots + 1)$$

Therefore,

$$\frac{E(x)}{G(x)} = \frac{x^i * (x^{k-1} + \ldots + 1)}{G(x)}$$

Now, suppose we chose $G(x)$ so that $x$ is not a factor of $G(x)$. Consequently, $G(x)$ and the $x^i$ from the previous fraction have no common factors. Thus, if $G(x)$ is a factor of the numerator then it must in fact be a factor of $(x^{k-1} + \ldots + 1)$. Remember, however, that since we chose $k \le r$ then $k - 1 < r$, and $G(x)$ cannot be a factor of a polynomial having a smaller degree.

We therefore draw the following conclusion:

**If $x$ is not a factor of $G(x)$, then all burst errors having length smaller than or equal to the degree of $G(x)$ are detected.**

Consider next a burst error of any length in which an odd number of bits is affected. Since $E(x)$ has a term for each damaged bit, it contains an odd number of terms. Therefore, $E(1)$ (exclusive-or of an odd number of 1's) evaluates to 1. On the other hand, suppose that $x + 1$ is a factor of $G(x)$. We can therefore write $G(x) = (x + 1) * H(x)$, where $H(x)$ is some expression.

---

*The degree of a polynomial is its highest power of $x$.

Now look at what happens if we assume an undetected error occurs. Recall that an undetected error means that $G(x)$ is a factor of $E(x)$. This means that $E(x) = G(x)*K(x)$, where $K(x)$ is the other factor of $E(x)$. Replacing $G(x)$ with $(x + 1)*H(x)$ yields $E(x) = (x +1)*H(x)*K(x)$. Now, if this equation is evaluated at $x = 1$, the $x +1$ factor makes $E(1)$ evaluate to 0. This is in direct contrast to the previous claim that $E(1)$ evaluates to 1.

Clearly both cannot occur. If we maintain our assumption that $x + 1$ is a factor of $G(x)$, then the other assumption of an undetected error damaging an odd number of bits cannot happen. In other words:

**If $x + 1$ is a factor of $G(x)$, then all burst errors damaging an odd number of bits are detected.**

The last case we consider is a burst error with length > degree $G(x)$. From our previous discussion we have

$$\frac{E(x)}{G(x)} = \frac{x^i*(x^{k-1} + \ldots + 1)}{G(x)}$$

But this time since we assume that $k-1 \geq r =$ degree $G(x)$, it is possible that $G(x)$ is a factor of $(x^{k-1} + \ldots + 1)$. The question is, what are the chances this will happen? Let's first consider $k-1 = r$. Since the degree of $G(x)$ is also $r$, then $G(x)$ is a factor of $(x^r + \ldots + 1)$ means that $G(x) = (x^r + \ldots + 1)$. Now the terms between $x^r$ and 1 define which bits are actually damaged. Since there are $r - 1$ such terms there are $2^{r-1}$ possible combinations of damaged bits. If we assume all combinations can occur with equal probability, there is a probability of $1/2^{r-1}$ the combination matches the terms of $G(x)$ exactly. In other words, the probability of an error going undetected is $1/2^{r-1}$.

The case for $k-1 > r$ is more complex and we do not discuss it here. However, it can be shown that the probability of an undetected error is $1/2^r$. References 2 and 3 provide a more rigorous analysis of error detection codes.

CRC is widely used in local area networks (LANs), where there are standard polynomials for $G(x)$ such as:

CRC-12:        $x^{12} + x^{11} + x^3 + x^2 + x + 1$

CRC-16:        $x^{16} + x^{15} + x^2 + 1$

CRC-CCITT:  $x^{16} + x^{12} + x^5 + 1$

CRC-32:        $x^{32} + x^{26} + x^{23} + x^{22} + x^{16} + x^{12} + x^{11} + x^{10} + x^8 + x^7 + x^5 + x^4 + x^2$
                        $+ x + 1$

In general, CRC is very effective if $G(x)$ is chosen properly. Specifically, $G(x)$ should be chosen so that $x$ is not a factor but $x + 1$ is a factor. In this case, CRC detects the following errors:

- all burst errors of length $r <$ degree $G(x)$

- all burst errors affecting an odd number of bits

- all burst errors of length $= r + 1$ with probability $(2^{r-1} - 1)/2^{r-1}$
- all burst errors of length $> r + 1$ with probability $(2^r - 1)/2^r$ (The CRC-32 polynomial will detect all burst errors of length $> 33$ with probability $(2^{32} - 1)/2^{32}$. This is equivalent to 99.99999998% accuracy rate. Not bad!)

## CRC IMPLEMENTATION USING CIRCULAR SHIFTS

Finding an accurate error detection method is half the battle. The other half is finding a way to implement it efficiently. Considering the nearly countless number of frames that travel across networks, an efficient implementation is essential.

Having learned about CRC, your first reaction might be to write a program to do polynomial division. However, during the time it takes to run such a program, several other frames will probably arrive. As we take the time to verify each of those, even more will arrive and a real bottleneck will occur. It's like having the cashier at a grocery store call for a price check on every item in your cart. Meanwhile, the customers behind you start making nasty remarks, and the Eskimo pies in your cart are melting!

Can we divide two polynomials and get the remainder quickly? Do we even need to go through a complete division when all we really need is the remainder? The quotient was never used. Let's take a close look at Figure 4.7, which showed the synthetic division. The entire process can be visualized as nothing more than a sequence of shifts and exclusive-or operations between the divisor and parts of the dividend.

One widely used CRC implementation uses a circuit constructed depending on the generator polynomial $G(x)$. Since there are standard polynomials, these circuits can be mass produced. The circuit contains a **shift register** and does exclusive-or operations according to the following rules:

- Interpret $G(x) = b_r x^r + b_{r-1} x^{r-1} + \ldots + b_2 x^2 + b_1 x + b_0$ where $b_i$ is either 0 or 1, $i = 0, \ldots r$. The number of bit positions in the register is $r$. The rightmost position corresponds to $b_0$ and the leftmost to $b_{r-1} x^{r-1}$.
- An exclusive-or circuit lies to the right of any position for which the associated value of $b_i$ is 1.
- A bit string enters the register one bit at a time starting with the rightmost position.
- As new bits enter, each bit in the register is shifted left one position. Each bit goes through exclusive-or circuits where they exist, forming one operand in the exclusive-or operation.
- The bit in the leftmost position is routed to each of the exclusive-or circuits, forming the second operand in each exclusive-or operation.

Figure 4.8 shows the register and exclusive-or circuits for the polynomial $G(x) = x^4 + x^3 + 1$. Note the exclusive-or symbol to the right of the positions corresponding to $x^3$ and 1, and none to the right of the positions corresponding to the missing terms $x^2$ and $x$. Initially, the register contains all 0s.

FIGURE 4.8   **Division Using Circular Shifts**

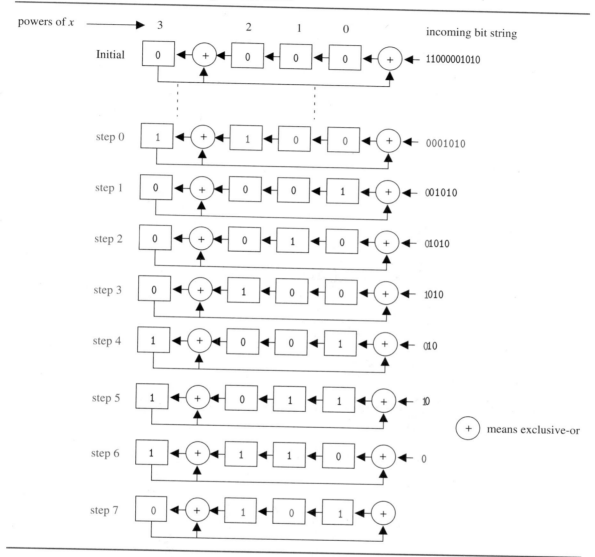

This figure shows the same computations as in Figure 4.7. At step 0, the first bit of the incoming string (dividend from Figure 4.7) has been shifted to the leftmost register position. At step 1, the leftmost bit is routed to each exclusive-or and everything else shifted left. Note that the register's contents are exactly the same as the result of the first exclusive-or operation from step 1 in Figure 4.7.

Each step defines the same process of shifting left and doing exclusive-or operations. The register's contents at each step are always the same as the results of similarly labeled steps from Figure 4.7. By the time the bits from the incoming string have all been moved into the register, the register's contents are the remainder (Step 7 in Figures 4.7 and 4.8).

Error detection using CRC is an accurate and widely used method. It can also be implemented efficiently requiring time proportional to the string's length. The standard generator polynomials allow the entire method to be designed into hardware (chips), thus further enhancing its efficiency.

## 4.4   Hamming Codes

As stated previously, when errors are detected there are typically two choices: resend the original frame or fix the damaged frame. The latter choice requires a method to not only detect an error but also to determine precisely which bits were affected. The simple parity checks could not do this.

### SINGLE-BIT ERROR CORRECTION

A method developed by R. W. Hamming involves creating special code words from data to be sent. The Hamming code requires the insertion of multiple parity bits in the bit string before sending. The parity bits check the parity in strategic locations. The idea is that if bits are altered, their positions determine a unique combination of parity check errors. When a frame is sent the receiver recalculates the parity checks. If any fail, the combination of failures tells the receiver which bits were affected. The receiver then can set the bits to their correct values. This technique is quite common for memory addressing and transferring bits from registers to RAM and back.

Let's illustrate how a Hamming code works for the simplest case, the detection and correction of any single-bit error. Suppose that frames consist of 8 bits. Label them as $m_1 m_2 m_3 m_4 m_5 m_6 m_7 m_8$. The next step is to define parity bits for parity checks in select positions. The logical questions are "How many parity checks do we use?" and "Which positions does each one check?"

If we use one parity check, it will either fail or succeed. From this we can conclude that an error either occurs or does not occur. It says nothing about where an error might be. If we use two parity checks one of four things can happen: They both fail; they both succeed; the first fails and the second succeeds; the second fails and the first succeeds. These four cases might be used to convey four events: no error or a bit error in one of three positions. Since there are more than three bit positions, two checks are not enough.

In general, if $n$ parity checks are used, there are $2^n$ possible combinations of failures and successes. We must associate each bit position with a unique combination to allow the receiver to analyze the parity checks and conclude where an error occurred (if one occurred). However, in order to account for every bit position we

**TABLE 4.1**    **Number of Combinations of Parity Successes and Failures as a Function of** *n*

| *n* (NUMBER OF PARITY CHECKS) | NUMBER OF BITS SENT | $2^n$ (NUMBER OF COMBINATIONS OF POSSIBLE PARITY SUCCESSES AND FAILURES) |
|:---:|:---:|:---:|
| 1 | 9 | 2 |
| 2 | 10 | 4 |
| 3 | 11 | 8 |
| 4 | 12 | 16 |

need $n$ so that $2^n$ is larger than the number of bits sent. We also must remember that each additional parity check requires another bit to be sent.

Table 4.1 shows the relationship between $n$ and the number of bits sent, assuming we start with an 8-bit frame. As it shows, if we use 4 parity checks there are 16 possible combinations of parity successes and failures. The 4 additional parity bits with the 8 original bits mean 12 bits are actually sent. Thus, 13 events are possible: There is no error or there is a single-bit error in one of 12 positions.

The next step is to associate a combination with a unique event. To do this, construct 4 parity bits $p_1$, $p_2$, $p_3$, and $p_4$ and insert them into the frame as shown in Figure 4.9. Each parity bit establishes even parity for selected positions listed in the figure. The next questions are "Why put the parity bits in those positions?" and "How did we determine the positions for each parity check?"

To answer these questions, let's make an observation about the positions in each parity check. The first parity check involves all the odd-numbered positions. These

**FIGURE 4.9**    **Hamming Code for Single-Bit Error Correction**

Data to send:     $m_1$   $m_2$   $m_3$   $m_4$   $m_5$   $m_6$   $m_7$   $m_8$

Hamming code:     $p_1$   $p_2$   $m_1$   $p_3$   $m_2$   $m_3$   $m_4$   $p_4$   $m_5$   $m_6$   $m_7$   $m_8$

    Bit position 1                        Bit position 12

$p_1$    even parity for positions 1, 3, 5, 7, 9, 11

$p_2$    even parity for positions 2, 3, 6, 7, 10, 11

$p_3$    even parity for positions 4, 5, 6, 7, 12

$p_4$    even parity for positions 8, 9, 10, 11, 12

positions, if written in binary, all have 1 as the least significant digit. If you write the positions covered by the second parity check in binary, they all have 1 as the second least significant digit. Similarly, the positions covered by the third and fourth parity checks have 1 as the third and fourth least significant digit, respectively.

How does this help us? Create a 4-bit binary number $b_4 b_3 b_2 b_1$ where $b_i = 0$ if parity check for $p_i$ succeeds and $b_i = 1$ otherwise ($i = 1, 2, 3,$ or 4). Table 4.2 shows the relationship among erroneous bit positions, invalid parity checks, and the 4-bit number. As the table shows, the 4-bit binary number and the erroneous bit position coincide.

When a receiver gets a transmitted frame it performs each of the parity checks. The combination of failures and successes then determines whether there was no error or in which position an error occurred. Once the receiver knows where the error occurred, it changes the bit value in that position and the error is corrected.

To illustrate, consider the example in Figure 4.10. Here we see the initial frame 0 1 1 0 0 1 1 1 and the Hamming code 0 1 0 1 1 1 0 1 0 1 1 1 to be transmitted. You should go through the computations to convince yourself that the parity bits establish even parity in the correct positions.

Figure 4.11 shows the received frame 0 1 0 1 0 1 0 1 0 1 1 1. Now, if we perform each parity check, we see that the checks for $p_1$ and $p_3$ are invalid. That is, there is an odd number of 1-bits in positions 1, 3, 5, 7, 9, and 11, and in positions 4, 5, 6, 7, and 12. Thus, according to Table 4.2, the error is in bit 5. Since bit 5 is 0, the receiver changes it to 1 and the frame is corrected.

## MULTIPLE-BIT ERROR CORRECTION

We can make similar comments about single-bit error correcting codes that we made about single-bit error detection codes. That is, single-bit errors are not common in data communications. One response to this information applies when there are many data frames to send. We can create a Hamming code for each, visualize all the Hamming codes as a two-dimensional bit array, and transmit the array one column at a time. If a single burst error affects no more than one column, no more than one bit in each row is destroyed. The receiver can determine the original data. The second response is to generalize Hamming codes for double- or

---

FIGURE 4.10     **Bit Stream Before Transmission**

| Data: | 0 | 1 | 1 | 0 | 0 | 1 | 1 | 1 |
|---|---|---|---|---|---|---|---|---|
| | $m_1$ | $m_2$ | $m_3$ | $m_4$ | $m_5$ | $m_6$ | $m_7$ | $m_8$ |

| Hamming code: | 0 | 1 | 0 | 1 | 1 | 1 | 0 | 1 | 0 | 1 | 1 | 1 |
|---|---|---|---|---|---|---|---|---|---|---|---|---|
| | $p_1$ | $p_2$ | $m_1$ | $p_3$ | $m_2$ | $m_3$ | $m_4$ | $p_4$ | $m_5$ | $m_6$ | $m_7$ | $m_8$ |

FIGURE 4.11    **Parity Checks of Frame After Transmission**

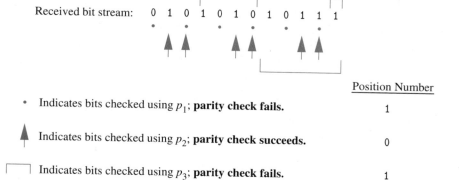

|  |  | Position Number |
|---|---|:---:|
| • | Indicates bits checked using $p_1$; **parity check fails.** | 1 |
| ▲ | Indicates bits checked using $p_2$; **parity check succeeds.** | 0 |
| ⬜ | Indicates bits checked using $p_3$; **parity check fails.** | 1 |
| ⊔ | Indicates bits checked using $p_4$; **parity check succeeds.** | 0 |

Error is in position $0101 = 5$

TABLE 4.2    **Bit Position Errors and Associated Parity Errors**

| ERRONEOUS BIT POSITION | INVALID PARITY CHECKS | $b_4 b_3 b_2 b_1$ |
|:---:|:---:|:---:|
| no error | none | 0000 |
| 1 | $p_1$ | 0001 |
| 2 | $p_2$ | 0010 |
| 3 | $p_1$ and $p_2$ | 0011 |
| 4 | $p_3$ | 0100 |
| 5 | $p_1$ and $p_3$ | 0101 |
| 6 | $p_2$ and $p_3$ | 0110 |
| 7 | $p_1, p_2$ and $p_3$ | 0111 |
| 8 | $p_4$ | 1000 |
| 9 | $p_1$ and $p_4$ | 1001 |
| 10 | $p_2$ and $p_4$ | 1010 |
| 11 | $p_1, p_2$ and $p_4$ | 1011 |
| 12 | $p_3$ and $p_4$ | 1100 |

multiple-bit error correction. Such codes do exist, but we will not discuss them here. The number of extra bits becomes quite large and is used in very specialized cases. If you are interested, references 4 and 5 discuss them.

## COMPARISON OF ERROR DETECTION AND ERROR CORRECTION

Which is better, error detection or error correction? The answer, as you might expect, is that neither is better, at least in a general sense. Correction techniques generally require more overhead and cannot always be justified in applications where errors occur rarely. It is usually much cheaper just to ask for a retransmission. Typically, most computer networks fall into this category.

As errors occur with more frequency, the extra overhead due to increased transmissions becomes a problem. In such cases, it may be cheaper to include additional correction bits rather than clutter the media with excessive redundant transmissions.

Error rate is not the only consideration. Time may be a critical factor. Sending a frame again will take time; how much depends on many factors such as the traffic, data rate, and distance. In most cases, a short delay in receiving an email message or a file from a LAN server is not so bad. A real-time environment, however, where messages must be delivered on time to avoid disaster, cannot afford small delays. Deep space probes, in which signals require many hours to reach their destination, are severely handicapped if a message must be retransmitted, especially when there is a high probability that interference will occur again. Imagine an astronaut saying, "Hello, NASA . . . can't read you. What's that about an impending collision with an alien spacecraft?"

## 4.5    Encryption and Decryption

Error detection and correction methods help prevent people from getting incorrect information. Another potentially dangerous problem is the illegal or unauthorized reception of information. Such cases involve the usual sender and receiver, plus a third party who intercepts a transmission not intended for him or her (Figure 4.12). The worst part is that neither sender nor receiver may be aware of the unauthorized reception until the guilty party has used the intercepted information for some purpose such as blackmail, criminal fraud, or a breach of national security. By then the damage is done. Clearly, if we are going to send sensitive information over some medium we would like some assurance of privacy.

With so much information being broadcast using microwaves and satellites it is virtually impossible to prevent unauthorized reception. Portable antenna dishes can be placed almost anywhere to receive information from a satellite. Even cable systems are susceptible. They frequently run through basements, isolated closets, and under streets. Finding a secluded spot and tapping the cable is not difficult.

As a result, much effort has gone into ways to make information unintelligible to unauthorized receivers. The idea is that even if they do receive the transmission they won't be able to understand its contents. The rendering of information into a different, unintelligible form is called **encryption**. The authorized receiver must be able to understand the information, so he must be able to change the encrypted data

FIGURE 4.12    **Sending Unsecured Messages**

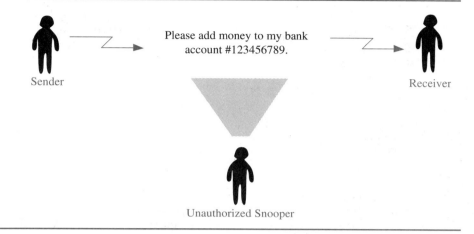

to its original form. We call this **decryption**. We also use the terms **plaintext** for the original message and **ciphertext** for the encrypted one.

Figure 4.13 illustrates the process. The sender uses an **encryption key** (usually some character or numeric constant) to change the plaintext (P) into a ciphertext (C). We write this symbolically as $C = E_k(P)$ where $E$ and $k$ represent the encryption algorithm and key, respectively. If some unauthorized person gets C, its unintelligible form makes it useless. Eventually the receiver gets C and decrypts it to get the original message. We write this symbolically as $P = D_{k'}(C)$, where $D$ and $k'$ represent the decryption algorithm and key. In general, $P = D_{k'}(E_k(P))$. Also, in many cases (but not always) $k=k'$.

As usual, questions arise. How do the encryption and decryption algorithms work? Is an encrypted message really unintelligible to an unauthorized receiver? If an unauthorized receiver knows how the message was encrypted can she decrypt it? Ideally an encrypted message should be impossible to decrypt without knowing the decryption algorithm and key. Unfortunately, most completely secure codes are analogous to unsinkable ships such as the Titanic: As soon as you are sure it is secure someone will prove you wrong.

## Caesar Cipher

One of the earliest and simplest codes replaces each plaintext character with another character. The choice of a replacement depends only on the plaintext character. This method is called a **mono-alphabetic cipher** or **Caesar cipher**, reputedly dating back to the days of Julius Caesar. For example, you might add 1 (the encryption key) to the ASCII code of each character. Thus, A becomes B; B becomes C; and so on. This approach is widely used, occurring in places such as children's television

FIGURE 4.13    **Sending Encrypted Messages**

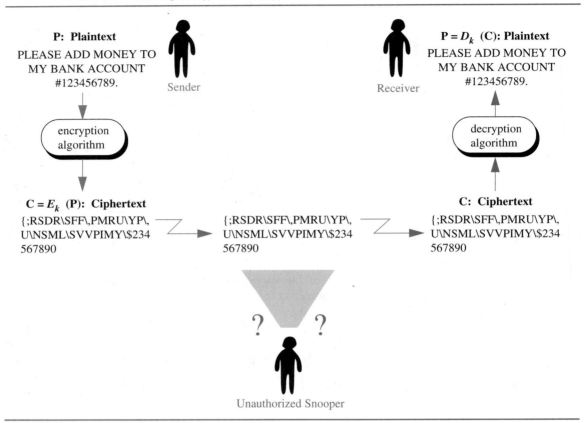

shows, decoder rings, and the backs of cereal boxes. Figure 4.13 used a Caesar cipher. Can you determine the rationale behind the letter substitutions?

The decryption algorithm normally reverses the encryption steps. In the previous example, subtracting 1 from the ASCII codes of each ciphertext character yields the original plaintext character. This is a case in which the encryption and decryption keys are equal. We should point out that the example could have changed the ASCII codes by any constant.

Although they are simple to describe and certainly seem to yield unintelligible messages, Caesar ciphers are rarely used in serious applications. They are relatively easy to decode without knowledge of the original encryption method because the code does nothing to disguise frequently used letters or combinations. For example, the most commonly used letters in English are E, T, O, A, and N. Thus, if a certain letter appears frequently in a ciphertext, there is a high probability it is one of these common letters rather than a Q or Z. This gives a potential code-breaker a place to start.

To illustrate, consider the following ciphertext (from Figure 4.13). Pretend you never saw the plaintext.

{;RSDR\SFF\,PMRU\YP\,U\NSML\SVVPIMY\$234567890

The most common ciphertext characters are \ (7 times), S (4 times), R, P, and M (3 times each). Consequently there is a high probability they are substitutions for E, T, O, A, and N.

The next step would be to try various combinations of the common plaintext characters in place of the ciphertext ones. For example, after several attempts you might come up with the following partially decrypted character string (decrypted characters are the larger ones):

{;EADE\AFF\,ONEU\YO\,U\NANL\AvvOINY\$234567890

To continue, you might further observe that most messages have blanks between the words and that the most common character (\) might represent a blank. You try it and generate

{;EADE AFF ,ONEU YO ,U NANL AvvOINY $234567890

Next you might look at the YO and the AFF and ask how many two-letter words end in the letter O or how many three-letter words begin with A followed by a repeated letter. There are not many, so you might try replacing the Y with a T and the F with a D. Now you have

{;EADE ADD ,ONEU TO ,U NANL AvvOINT $234567890

By making some educated guesses, we have the message half decrypted. It would not be difficult to continue making educated guesses and finish decrypting. (It's really a lot like playing the game "Hangman" or the equivalent television show "Wheel of Fortune.") The important point to emphasize here is that a secure code should not preserve particular letter sequences or the frequency with which letters occur.

## POLY-ALPHABETIC CIPHER

One way to change the frequencies and destroy common sequences is to use a **poly-alphabetic cipher**. Like the mono-alphabetic cipher, it replaces each character with another. The difference is that a given plaintext character is not always replaced with the same ciphertext one. We can choose a replacement depending not only on the actual plaintext character but on its position in the message as well.

An example of a poly-alphabetic cipher is a **Vigenère cipher**. It uses a two-dimensional array of characters (its encryption key) in which each row contains the letters of the alphabet. Figure 4.14 shows an example. The first row (row zero) contains the letters written from A to Z. The second row has the letters written from B to Z followed by A at the end. Each subsequent row is formed by moving each letter from the previous row left one position with the leftmost character being moved to the rightmost position.

FIGURE 4.14    **Key for Vigenère Cipher**

```
row 0:   A B C D E F G H I J K L M N O P Q R S T U V W X Y Z
row 1:   B C D E F G H I J K L M N O P Q R S T U V W X Y Z A
row 2:   C D E F G H I J K L M N O P Q R S T U V W X Y Z A B
row 3:   D E F G H I J K L M N O P Q R S T U V W X Y Z A B C


row 24:  Y Z A B C D E F G H I J K L M N O P Q R S T U V W X
row 25:  Z A B C D E F G H I J K L M N O P Q R S T U V W X Y
```

To replace a letter, let $i$ be its relative position (first position is relative position zero) in the message and $j$ its relative position in the alphabet. Let $V$ be the array. Replace the letter with the one in $V[(i \bmod 26), j]$. Figure 4.15 shows a procedure written in partial C code that does this assuming the plaintext letters are all upper case.* For example, suppose the word THE appears three times in a message beginning in positions 25, 54, and 104. Table 4.3 shows the required calculations and the substituted ciphertext letters. As the table shows, the three occurrences of the word THE encrypt to SHF, VKI, and TIG.

FIGURE 4.15    **Encryption Algorithm for Vigenère Cipher**

```
int encrypt(P, C, V)
  char P[];                /* plain text*/
  char C[];                /* cipher text*/
  char V[26] [26];         /* Vigenere cipher key*/

{
  int i, j;

  for i = 0 to end of plaintext
  {
    j = P[i] - 'A' ;        /* relative position of P[i] in the alphabet */
    C[i] = V[i % 26] [j];   /* % is the mod operator in C */
  }
}
```

*It also assumes that the letters correspond to consecutive binary codes such as in the ASCII code.

TABLE **4.3**   **Letter Substitutions Using the Vigenère Cipher**

| PLAINTEXT LETTER | $I$ = RELATIVE POSITION IN MESSAGE | $I$ MOD 26 | $J$ = RELATIVE POSITION IN ALPHABET | CIPHERTEXT LETTER |
|:---:|:---:|:---:|:---:|:---:|
| T | 25 | 25 | 19 | S |
| H | 26 | 0 | 7 | H |
| E | 27 | 1 | 4 | F |
| T | 54 | 2 | 19 | V |
| H | 55 | 3 | 7 | K |
| E | 56 | 4 | 4 | I |
| T | 104 | 0 | 19 | T |
| H | 105 | 1 | 7 | I |
| E | 106 | 2 | 4 | G |

The Vigenère cipher seems to solve the repetition problems, but in fact it has only reduced them. Repetitions and patterns still occur. For example, the two encrypted words SHF and TIG may seem dissimilar, but they are not. Can you see a relation between them? The letters in TIG are the alphabetic successors to the letters in SHF. To a professional trying to break a code this is a very large clue to the encryption method.

In fact, all of the encrypted forms of THE share a similarity. Consider two consecutive letters occupying the same relative positions in each of two encrypted versions of THE. The difference (modulo 26) of their ASCII codes is the same. For example, the differences between the ASCII codes of S and H, T and I, and V and K are all 11. The common differences occur because each row of the matrix in Figure 4.14 is essentially in alphabetic order. The only exception is the transition point from Z to A.

This problem can be fixed by making each row a random permutation of the alphabet, but even that will not be enough, at least for long text. Since there are 26 rows, there are essentially 26 ways to encrypt a letter or a word. In a long message common words may appear several hundred times. With only 26 different ways to encrypt the word repetitions will still occur. They will just be a little harder to find.

Again, you might respond by using even more rows in the matrix, each with a unique permutation of the alphabet, to provide more ways to encrypt words, thus reducing the repetitions. Indeed, 26! (approximately $4*10^{26}$) unique permutations of the alphabet provide many alternatives. In the extreme case we could use a number of rows equal to the length of the message. Here each row is used just once during encryption, thus avoiding any repetition (except for statistically random ones). The problem now, however, is that the encryption key is longer than the message. Communicating it to authorized receivers and storing it securely become problems.

## TRANSPOSITION CIPHER

The **transposition cipher** method rearranges the plaintext letters of a message (rather than substituting ciphertext letters). One way to do this is to store the plaintext characters in a two-dimensional array with $m$ columns. The first $m$ plaintext characters are stored in the array's first row; the second $m$ characters in the second row, and so on. Next we determine a permutation of the numbers 1 through $m$, and write as $p_1, p_2, \ldots, p_m$. The permutation may be random or determined by some secret method. Either way, the final step is to transmit all the characters in column $p_1$, followed by those in column $p_2$, etc. The last set of characters transmitted are those in column $p_m$.

To illustrate, suppose the following message's characters are stored in a two-dimensional array with five columns (Table 4.4).

MISS PIGGY KERMIT ANIMAL AND FOZZIE BEAR

Suppose the column numbers are rearranged as 2, 4, 3, 1, 5. That is, the characters in column 2 are transmitted first, followed by the characters in columns 4, 3, 1, and 5, respectively. Therefore, the transmitted message looks like

IIKTMNZBSGRAL IASGE ADZEMP IIAO   YMN FER

The transmitted message looks nothing like the original, but if the receiver knows the number of columns and the column number permutation, he can easily reconstruct the message. This is done by storing incoming characters in columns in order of the permutation. In the previous example, the incoming characters would be stored in column 2 followed by columns 4, 3, 1, and 5. This is another example in which the decryption algorithm is defined by essentially reversing the steps of the encryption algorithm.

The problem with the transposition cipher is that it is not very secure. For one thing, letter frequencies are preserved. On reception, an unauthorized receiver could analyze the ciphertext and notice the high frequency of common letters. By itself

TABLE 4.4    **Two-Dimensional Array Used for the Transposition Cipher**

| COLUMN NUMBERS | | | | |
|---|---|---|---|---|
| 1 | 2 | 3 | 4 | 5 |
| M | I | S | S | |
| P | I | G | G | Y |
| | K | E | R | M |
| I | T | | A | N |
| I | M | A | L | |
| A | N | D | | F |
| O | Z | Z | I | E |
| | B | E | A | R |

FIGURE 4.16    **Encrypting Using Exclusive-Or Bit Operation**

1101100101001    Plaintext
1001011001010    Encryption key
0100111100011    Ciphertext = plaintext exclusive-or'd with the encryption key
1001011001010    Decryption key (same as the encryption key)
1101100101001    Plaintext = ciphertext exclusive-or'd with the decryption key

this is an indication that letter substitutions were probably not used and that this may be a transposition cipher. The next step in breaking the code would be to group the characters and store them in different columns. The receiver would not try column arrangements randomly but would instead try arrangements that yielded commonly used sequences such as THE, ING, or IS in a row. This process would reduce the number of guesses greatly and provide a lot of help and information to the unauthorized but highly motivated receiver.

## BIT-LEVEL CIPHERING

Not all transmissions are character sequences. Consequently, not all encryption methods work by manipulating or substituting characters. Some work at the bit level. One method defines the encryption key as a bit string. The choice is determined randomly and secretly. The bit string to be transmitted is divided into substrings. The length of each is the same as the length of the encryption key. Each substring is then encrypted by computing the exclusive-or between it and the encryption key.

In this case the decryption does not reverse the encryption steps, as in previous methods but instead repeats them. In other words, to decrypt we compute the exclusive-or between the encryption key and each of the encrypted substrings. Here, the encryption and decryption keys are the same.

Figure 4.16 demonstrates that doing the exclusive-or operation twice produces the original string. But does it always work this way? Yes! To see how, let $p_i$ be any plaintext bit and $\oplus$ represent the exclusive-or operation. During the encryption/decryption process $p_i$ is exclusively or'd with either 0 or 1 twice. If it is 0 we have

$$(p_i \oplus 0) \oplus 0 = (p_i) \oplus 0 = p_i$$

If it is 1 we have

$$(p_i \oplus 1) \oplus 1 = p_i \oplus (1 \oplus 1) = p_i \oplus (0) = p_i$$

Either way, performing the exclusive-or twice generates the original bit $p_i$.

The security of this code depends largely on the length of the encryption key. A short key means the original string is divided into many substrings with each encrypted separately. With many substrings, there is a greater chance that repetitions will occur. Since they are encrypted using the same key, the encrypted substrings are also repeated. As before, the repetitions can help an unauthorized receiver trying to break the code.

Using longer encryption keys means longer but fewer substrings. In the extreme case, the length of the encryption key is the same as that of the message to be sent. In this case, each bit is encrypted using a unique bit in the key. If the key's bits are truly random, no patterns will exist in the encrypted string and the code is truly unbreakable without trying every possible decryption key.

This method (where the key length is equal to the original string length) is similar to the poly-alphabetic cipher in which each character was substituted using a unique key. The difference is essentially that between bit or character substitutions. Like the poly-alphabetic cipher, the drawback is the large key that must be communicated to the receiver, thus making the method somewhat unwieldy.

## DATA ENCRYPTION STANDARD

The encryption methods discussed so far are not terribly complex. In fact, when used with short keys they're not even very good because the ciphertext contains many clues that help an unauthorized person break the code. With longer keys, however, the ciphertext becomes more cryptic. In the extreme case, the code is virtually unbreakable. The difficulty is that long keys make implementation more difficult.

There is another approach that keeps the keys short and uses complex procedures to encrypt the data. One such method, the **data encryption standard (DES)**, was developed by IBM in the early 1970s. It was adopted as a standard in 1977 by the U.S. government for all commercial and unclassified information. The logic of this widely used method is built into hardware (VLSI chips) to make it even faster.

The DES divides a message into 64-bit blocks and uses a 56-bit key. It uses a complex combination of transpositions (rearrangement of bits), substitutions (replacing one bit group with another), exclusive-or operations, and a few other processes on each block to eventually produce 64 bits of encrypted data. In all, the 64-bit block goes through 19 successive steps, with the output of each step being input to the next step.

Figure 4.17 shows the primary steps. The first step does a transposition on the 64 data bits and the 56-bit key. The next 16 steps (labeled encryption in the figure) involve many operations, which we will describe shortly. Each step is the same except that it uses a different key derived from the original. The important thing now is that the output from one step is the input to the next. The second-to-last step (swap in the figure) swaps the first 32 bits and the last 32 bits. The last step is another transposition. In fact, it is the reverse of the transposition done in the first step. The result is 64 bits of encrypted data.

Figure 4.18 outlines the primary operations of each of the middle 16 steps. In the figure we represent a bit string with a letter and a numeric subscript. The subscript indicates the number of bits in the string. For example, $K_{56}$ refers to the 56-bit string used as a key, and $X_{48}$ is a 48-bit string resulting from some intermediate operation. When reading through the ensuing discussion, remember that even though we use the symbol $X$ throughout the figure, it represents different strings at

FIGURE 4.17    **Outline of the DES**

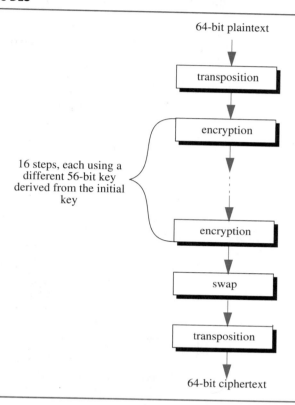

each stage. This method seems more sensible than using different names for each operation.

First, DES divides $C_{64}$ (the 64 bits being encrypted) in half. The first 32 bits are $L_{32}$ and the remaining 32 bits are $R_{32}$. Next, it expands $R_{32}$ to a 48-bit string by transposing some of the bits and duplicating others. We label the result as $R_{48}$ to reinforce the fact that it is determined completely from $R_{32}$. The algorithm also changes the 56-bit key by dividing it in half and doing a circular bit-shift on each half. The number of bits shifted depends on which of the 16 steps the algorithm is in. The point is that each step uses a different key. After the shifts the key is transposed. The result is labeled $K_{56}$.

Next, the algorithm does an exclusive-or operation between $R_{48}$ and the first 48 bits of $K_{56}$. The result is labeled $X_{48}$. Next, $X_{48}$ is divided into eight 6-bit groups ($X_6$.) Each 6-bit group goes through a substitution algorithm and is replaced by a 4-bit group $X_4$. The resulting eight 4-bit groups are then combined and subjected to another transposition, giving another 32-bit group ($X\s\do6(32)$). The algorithm then does an exclusive-or operation between this string and $L_{32}$. Again, we call the result

FIGURE 4.18    One of 16 Encryption Steps of the DES

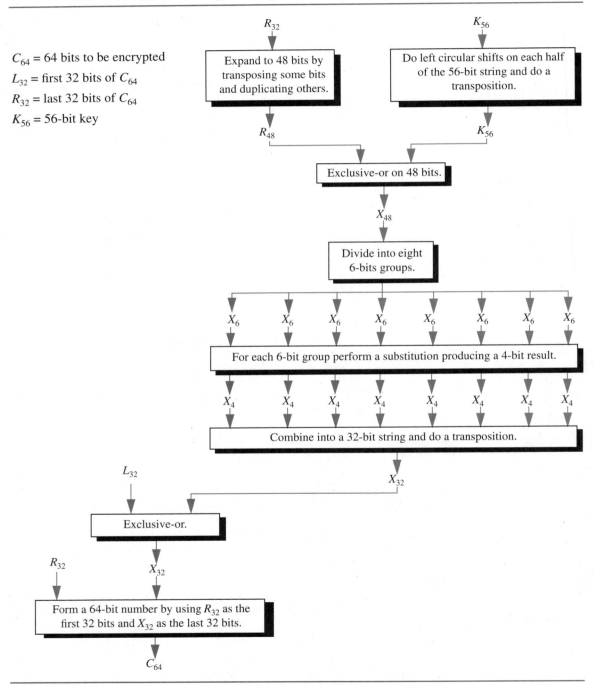

$C_{64}$ = 64 bits to be encrypted

$L_{32}$ = first 32 bits of $C_{64}$

$R_{32}$ = last 32 bits of $C_{64}$

$K_{56}$ = 56-bit key

$X_{32}$. Finally, the algorithm creates a 64-bit string by using $R_{32}$ as the first 32 bits and $X_{32}$ as the last 32 bits.

Confusing? Well, it is supposed to be. IBM's intent was not to design a method everyone understands easily. The idea was to design a method that consists of many convoluted steps and is virtually impossible to reproduce without prior knowledge of the encryption key.

This entire process is done 16 times. Each time, the input is the result of the previous step and a different key is used. We have left out many details such as how the transpositions are done or how the 6-bit groups are substituted with 4-bit groups. Some of these details are not difficult. For example, the following C procedure does a transposition of the elements of array $b$.

```
void transposition(b, t);

sometype b[N];          /* array of elements to be transposed */

int t[N];               /* contains the numbers from 0 to N-1 in random order */

{

    sometype temp [N];   /* temporary storage for elements in b */

    int i;               /* used for subscripting */


    for (i=0; i<N; i++)   /* copy elements into temporary storage */

        temp[i] = b[i];

    for (i=0; i<N; i++)   /* as i increases, t[i] is used to get elements randomly from */

        b[i] = temp[t[i]];  /* positions in array temp */

}
```

The details of making substitutions depend largely on the substitution rules, which we won't discuss here. If you are interested, Reference 6 contains Pascal procedures describing all the details of the DES algorithm.

Without doubt, the algorithm is complex, as it consists of many convoluted steps. On the other hand, when the DES algorithm is complete, a 64-bit string has been replaced with another 64-bit string, making it essentially a substitution cipher—although we admit that the rules for the substitution are obscure.

The standardization of the DES has been controversial (Ref. 7). One argument is that despite the complexity the DES isn't secure enough. Indeed, when IBM researchers began working on the problem they used a 128-bit key. But, at the request of the National Security Agency (NSA), it was reduced to 56 bits. Furthermore, the reasons behind the reduction to 56 bits haven't been made public. You might ask, "So what?" What's the difference between using a 56-bit key and a 128-bit key?

The difference is in how an unauthorized receiver might try to break the code. The DES was designed so that the decryption algorithm uses the same key as the encryption algorithm and uses the same steps, but in reverse. An unauthorized receiver can break the code simply by trying the decryption algorithm with every possible key. Of course, with $2^{56} \approx 7*10^{16}$ possible key values, that will take awhile. On the other hand, the development of faster processors and massive parallel processor systems allows computers to make computations a lot faster than they once could. Consequently, this number is not as big as it used to be and to some is uncomfortably small.

Another factor contributing to the controversy is that some people feel the rationale behind substitutions in the DES algorithm was never fully explained. The fear is that there may be something in the substitution that could compromise the cipher's integrity. These factors have led to speculation that the NSA was uncomfortable with a code that even it would have trouble breaking. Remember, with the widespread use of electronic mail, the availability of DES chips, and the emergence of digital voice transmission, there is a lot of DES-encrypted information. The inability to decrypt when necessary must make NSA officials just a bit jittery. To make matters worse, there have been reports that the government has tried to suppress research or publication dealing with more secure ciphers (Reference 8).

## KEY DISTRIBUTION AND PROTECTION

All of the methods discussed so far use a decryption key that is derivable from (or equal to) the encryption key. Consequently, the best encryption method in the world is no good if the key cannot be kept secret. Therefore, we face another problem: How does the sender communicate the key to the receiver (key distribution)? Your first suggestion might be for the sender simply to send the key. But, as before, what if an unauthorized receiver gets it? Encrypt it, you might say, but what method should the sender use? How does the sender communicate that method's key to the receiver? This does not solve the problem; it merely redefines it.

Maintaining a key's secrecy is not an easy task, but there are options. For example, the two persons communicating could meet in some clandestine location (such as a local McDonald's restaurant) and agree on a key. But sometimes logistics do not allow such meetings (or maybe the principal parties are vegetarians). Another option would be to transport a key under armed guard. This conjures up images of people with attaché cases handcuffed to their wrists surrounded by people with bent noses and their hands hidden inside their suit coats.

**Merkle's Puzzles**     Such options exist, no doubt, but there are other more academic solutions. One technique, described in Reference 9, involves the use of puzzles. A **puzzle** is an encrypted message containing a potential encryption key, an identifying number, and a predefined pattern. In order for a sender and a receiver to agree on an encryption key the following steps occur:

1.  The sender sends *n* puzzles, each encrypted with a separate key. The receiver does not know the encryption key and must break the code as any unauthorized receiver would. Typically the encryption key is not too large to allow the receiver to attack the code by brute force if necessary.

2.  The receiver chooses a puzzle randomly and breaks the code. The receiver knows when the code is broken because of the pattern inserted into the puzzle.

3.  The receiver extracts the encryption key from that puzzle and sends a message back specifying the ID of the puzzle he has broken.

4.  The sender receives the puzzle ID and assumes the receiver solved the puzzle and got the key in it. Both sender and receiver can now communicate using the agreed-on encryption key.

You might wonder, if the intended receiver can get a key this way, why can't an unauthorized one? The reason is that the intended receiver chooses randomly which puzzle to solve. The unauthorized receiver does not know which puzzle is chosen and is left with few choices other than to try to solve all $n$ puzzles. If $n$ is large, however, solving all the puzzles will take a lot of time (more time than this person has, we hope). Meanwhile, the sender and receiver communicate while the eavesdropper is trying to solve the right puzzle.

**Shamir's Method**    Another method of key distribution, Shamir's method is used in a different scenario. Suppose the information to be encrypted is so sensitive that no one person can be trusted to send or receive it. We want to store the key in such a way that at least $k$ people must be present to determine it. We further assume that any $k$ people with appropriate clearance will suffice. That is, we impose no requirement that any particular person or persons be present.

Storing the key in any one spot will not work, as this violates the condition that $k$ people must be present. We could divide the key into $k$ distinct pieces and distribute the pieces. If each person gets one piece we have a constraint on who may be present (only those with mutually distinct pieces). If we give several pieces to any person, fewer than $k-1$ persons have the remaining pieces, which violates the condition that at least $k$ persons must be present.

Shamir's method (Reference 10) is a clever one based on polynomial interpolation. Specifically, suppose that $p(x) = a_0 + a_1x + a_2x^2 + \ldots + a_{k-1}x^{k-1}$ is a polynomial of degree $k-1$. Suppose also that $(x_1,y_1), (x_2,y_2), \ldots, (x_k,y_k)$ are known points on the graph of $p(x)$ and that $x_i \neq x_j$ whenever $i \neq j$. Then these $k$ points determine the polynomial $p(x)$ uniquely and from them we can determine the values of $a_0, a_1, \ldots,$ and $a_{k-1}$.

In Shamir's method the polynomial $p(x)$ is constructed so that one of the coefficients (say $a_0$) is the encryption key. Each person who is cleared to send or receive information is given precisely one data point on the graph of $p(x)$, making sure that no two data points have the same $x$-coordinate. Any group of $k$ persons can provide $k$ unique data points. All of the data points allow them to determine the polynomial and consequently the key.

If there are fewer than $k$ people, there are not enough data points to determine the polynomial uniquely. Even so, a small group of subversives could pool their data points and determine relationships among the $a_i$, which could yield hints to the key's value. Shamir's method avoids this possibility by doing all the computations using modular arithmetic.

## 4.6    Public Key Encryption

All of the previous encryption methods share one feature. If an unauthorized receiver intercepts the ciphertext and, for some reason, knows the encryption algorithm and key ($E_k$), then the decryption method ($D_{k'}$) is easy to determine. For example, if the ciphertext for a Caesar cipher was determined by adding $k$ to the ASCII codes of the plaintext, we simply decrypt by subtracting $k$ from the ASCII codes of the ciphertext. Similarly, if we know the key for the Vigenère cipher, it is a simple matter to decrypt the ciphertext. You should convince yourself that we can make similar comments about the other methods discussed so far.

It certainly seems reasonable that knowing $E_k$ makes decryption trivial. Like many other reasonable things, however, it is not true. In 1976, Diffie and Hellman (Ref. 11) proposed the use of encryption methods for which the decryption algorithm and key are not determined easily even when both the encryption method and key are known. The rationale is that if an unauthorized person knows the encryption algorithm and key, that knowledge is of no use in helping him or her decrypt the ciphertext.

There is another advantage to such methods. Suppose someone needs to get secret messages from many sources (Figure 4.19). Rather than having each source use a different encryption method, they can all use the same one, $E_k$. Only the receiver knows the decryption method $D_{k'}$. In fact, $E_k$ could be made public. Since $D_{k'}$ cannot be derived from that knowledge, there is no danger. Even different senders cannot decrypt others' messages despite the fact they use the same encryption method.

Such systems are called **public key cryptosystems**. Typical uses include a bank receiving sensitive financial requests from many customers or a military command

**FIGURE 4.19    Multiple Senders Using the Same Encryption Method**

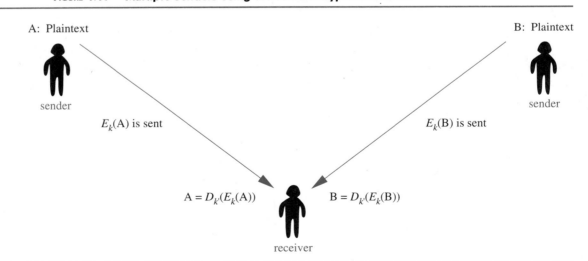

center receiving reports from various locations. It also is being used in networking software such as Novell's NetWare 4.0 (Reference 12).

## RSA ALGORITHM

The RSA algorithm (named after its developers, Rivest, Shamir, and Adleman), described in Reference 13, uses modular arithmetic and the factorization of very large numbers. The ciphertext is surprisingly easy to calculate and very difficult to break, even when $E_k$ is known.

To describe how this method works, we consider messages consisting of capital letters only. However, the method can be generalized to include a larger character set. The following steps describe the RSA encryption algorithm and include an example to illustrate the steps.

1.  Assign a simple code to the letters, such as 1 through 26 for A through Z, respectively.

2.  Choose $n$ to be the product of two large prime numbers $p$ and $q$. (A prime number has no factors except itself and 1.) In practice, a large prime number consists of 200 or more digits. However, we will conserve space and energy by using $n = p*q = 11*7 = 77$.

3.  Find a number $k$ that is relatively prime to $(p-1)*(q-1)$. Two numbers are relatively prime if they have no common factors except 1. In our example, we choose $k = 7$ which is relatively prime to $(p-1)*(q-1) = 10*6 = 60$. The number $k$ is the encryption key.
    You might ask, Can we always find a number $k$ with this property? The answer is yes. A well-known result in number theory proves it.

4.  Divide the message into components. In general, each component will contain many letters to avoid repeated components. However, for our example, we will have just one letter per component. If the message is "HELLO," the components are H, E, L, L, and O.

5.  For each component, concatenate all the binary codes of each letter in the component and interpret the resulting bit string as an integer. Here, each component has just one letter. So, the integers are 8, 5, 12, 12, and 15 (the numbers assigned to the letters originally).

6.  Encrypt the message by raising each number to the power of $k$. However, do all arithmetic modulo $n$. In our example, this requires the following computations:

    $8^7$modulo 77; $5^7$modulo 77; $12^7$modulo 77; $12^7$modulo 77; $15^7$modulo 77

    The results are the encrypted message. Here the calculations evaluate to 57, 47, 12, 12, and 71, respectively. (We will show how to make this calculation shortly.) Note that here the two 12's indicate a repeated letter. This is a consequence having 1 letter per component. If a component contains several letters, repetitions like this are avoided.

The receiver gets the encrypted message 57, 47, 12, 12, and 71. How does she decrypt it? The following steps show the decryption method and continues the example to illustrate each step.

1.  Find a value $k'$ for which $k*k' - 1 = 0$ modulo $(p - 1)*(q - 1)$. This means that $k*k' - 1$ is evenly divisible by $(p - 1)*(p - 1)$. The value for $k'$ is the decryption key. In this example $(p - 1)*(q - 1) = 60$, and $k' = 43$ works nicely. That is, $7*43 - 1 = 300$ is divisible by 60.

    Again, you might ask, Can a value $k'$ always be found? Yes! Again, famous results in number theory by Euler and Fermat prove this.

2.  Raise each encrypted number from step 6 to the power $k'$, and do the arithmetic modulo n. The results are the original component numbers from step 5. In our example, this requires the following calculations.

$57^{43}$ modulo 77; $47^{43}$ modulo 77; $12^{43}$ modulo 77; $12^{43}$ modulo 77; $71^{43}$ modulo 77

The results are the original numbers: 8, 5, 12, 12, and 15.

Using previous notation $E_k(x) = x^k$ modulo $n$ and $D_k(y) = y^{k'}$ modulo $n$, we have $D_{k'}(E_k(x)) = (x^k)^{k'}$ modulo $n$. As long as $k$ and $k'$ are chosen as described $(x^k)^{k'}$ modulo $n$ evaluates to $x$. Once again, verification of this lies in the work of number theorists.

The encryption and decryption algorithms are surprisingly simple. Both involve exponentiation and modular arithmetic. But there is a potential problem: How do you calculate the exact modular value of a number like $71^{43}$? This particular number evaluates to approximately $10^{79}$ and is actually very small compared to numbers that occur in practice. It certainly seems to be an intimidating calculation. We are interested only in modular arithmetic, however, so we can take some shortcuts that allow you to do this on any calculator. Let's illustrate by calculating $71^{43}$ modulo 77.

The first step is to write the exponent as a sum of powers of 2. Doing this, we get

$$71^{43} = 71^{32+8+2+1} = 71^{32}*71^8*71^2*71^1 \qquad \text{Equation 4.1}$$

Now $71^2 = 5041 = 36$ modulo 77. Again, this means 5041 and 36 have the same integer remainder on dividing by 77. Since Equation 4.1 requires only the modular value, we can replace $71^2$ by 36. Furthermore, we can write $71^8$ as $(71^2)^4$. Again since we need only the modular value this is the same as $36^4$. Similarly, the modular equivalent of $71^{32}$ is $(71^2)^{16}$ or $36^{16}$. Therefore, Equation 4.1 reduces to

$$71^{43} = 36^{16}*36^4*36*71 \text{ modulo } 77 \qquad \text{Equation 4.2}$$

As you can see, we have reduced the necessary calculations significantly. But we can go farther. Proceeding in a similar fashion we have $36^2 = 1296 = 64$ modulo 77. Consequently, we can write $36^4 = (36^2)^2 = 64^2$ modulo 77 and $36^{16} = (36^2)^8 = 64^8$ modulo 77.

Now Equation 4.2 reduces to

$$71^{43} = 64^8 *64^2*36*71 \text{ modulo } 77 \qquad \text{Equation 4.3}$$

Of course, we can continue the process to get

$$71^{43} = 64^8 * 64^2 * 36 * 71 \text{ modulo } 77$$
$$= 15^4 * 15 * 36 * 71 \text{ modulo } 77$$
$$= 71^2 * 15 * 36 * 71 \text{ modulo } 77$$
$$= 36 * 15 * 36 * 71 \text{ modulo } 77$$
$$= 15 \text{ modulo } 77$$

There's no calculation here that cannot be verified by any calculator.

The RSA algorithm is relatively easy to implement, but is it secure? The encryption algorithm requires $n$ and $k$ and the decryption algorithm requires $n$ and $k'$. Now, suppose you intercept an encrypted message and that you know $n$ and $k$. It doesn't seem like it should be difficult to determine $k'$. But, remember, $k'$ is chosen so that $k*k' - 1 = 0$ modulo $(p - 1)*(q - 1)$. Therefore, all you need to do is find $p$ and $q$, the factors of $n$. But if $n$ is very large, say on the order of 200 digits, this is very difficult (or at least very time consuming) to do.

## DIGITAL SIGNATURES

Another interesting use for public key cryptosystems is in **verification**. For example, when you make a withdrawal from a bank you must fill out a form and sign it. Your signature verifies your identity. If you later claim you never made the withdrawal the bank can produce the form with your signature. Of course, you can always claim the signature was forged and sue the bank. If the case goes to court the bank can produce a handwriting expert who can verify the signature is yours. Consequently, you will lose the suit and the bank's loan officers will probably not approve your request for a mortgage on your new house.

But consider a slightly different scenario. You send a request electronically to your Swiss bank account to transfer a large sum of money to your ex-spouse's account. What can the bank do if you later claim you never made the request, especially since your ex-spouse took the money and moved to Bolivia? There is no signature on file for a handwriting expert to analyze. The bank might respond by stating a password had to be entered to authorize the request and only you knew the password. Of course, the bank's computers also have the password somewhere to verify it when you enter it. You might claim that someone got the password from the bank's records and the bank is at fault for not providing proper protection.

Is there a way for the bank to prove it was not at fault and to verify it was you who made the request? Figure 4.20 illustrates the general problem. Someone sends a message, receives a response, and then claims he never sent it. Can the receiver verify the claim is false? Verifying the identity of a sender is called **authentication**.

One method of authentication is to use a **digital signature**. Essentially, it involves encrypting a message in a way that only the sender would know. More specifically, it uses an encryption key only the sender knows. It is similar to a password except that passwords are also stored in the receiver's files for verification. The encryption key is nowhere except in the sender's possession. The sender

FIGURE 4.20     **Sender Denying Sending a Message**

might claim someone stole it, but since the receiver has no record of the key, the receiver is not at fault. It's like losing the key to your home. Ultimately, you are responsible.

Figure 4.21 shows how to send encrypted messages containing a digital signature. It uses two pairs of public key encryption/decryption methods. We label them $(E_k, D_{k'})$ and $(E_j, D_{j'})$, where the public keys are $j$ and $k$ and the private keys are $k'$ (known only to the sender) and $j'$ (known only to the receiver). Furthermore, the pairs should have the following properties:

$$E_k(D_{k'}(P)) = D_{k'}(E_k(P)) = P \text{ and } E_j(D_{j'}(P)) = D_{j'}(E_j(P)) = P.$$

We have already stated an encryption followed by a decryption yields the original message, but we also require the reverse to be true. That is, decrypting first and then encrypting also yields the original.

Suppose the sender wants to send an encrypted message and identify himself. If P is the plaintext message, the sender calculates $E_j(D_{k'}(P))$ and sends it.* The receiver applies $D_{j'}$ to the message. Since $D_{j'}$ and $E_j$ are inverse operations, the result is $D_{k'}(P)$.† The receiver stores $D_{k'}(P)$ in the event the sender eventually denies

---

*Sometimes the sender may apply $D_{k'}$ only to his signature or ID and then encrypt everything. This is faster than altering the entire message twice, especially if the message is long.

† If just the sender's ID was altered the first time, the receiver now has the plaintext and the ID altered by $D_{k'}$.

FIGURE 4.21    **Sending a Message Using a Digital Signature**

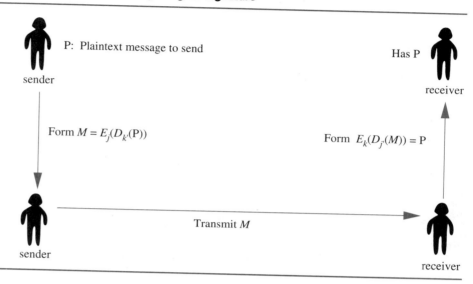

P: Plaintext message to send

Has P

sender

receiver

Form $M = E_j(D_{k'}(P))$

Form $E_k(D_j(M)) = P$

Transmit $M$

sender

receiver

sending the message. Next it applies $E_k$ giving $E_k(D_{k'}(P)) = P$ and the message is received.

Now suppose the sender denies sending the message. To authenticate the sender's identity, the receiver supplies both $D_{k'}(P)$ and P to an arbiter (someone who must decide who is lying). The arbiter applies $E_k$ (the public key encryption method) to $D_{k'}(P)$ and gets P. This shows the message P is derived from $D_{k'}(P)$. Furthermore, since $D_{k'}(P)$ was determined using a private key not derivable from $E_k$, the arbiter concludes that $D_{k'}(P)$ could have been constructed only by someone with knowledge of the private key $k'$. Since the sender is the only person with that knowledge, the sender is guilty as charged.

The ability to authenticate messages is certainly important in an age of electronic transfers of and access to so much information. Use of public key cryptosystems (or any encryption scheme) to authenticate is only one approach, and it has disadvantages. For example, by some standards these systems are considered slow (Reference 14). Another problem is that some algorithms are subject to patents and licenses, which has implications for overall security. Some research is being conducted into designing authentication methods that do not use encryption algorithms, but instead use a type of hash function. For further discussion, see Reference 14.

## SUMMARY OF ENCRYPTION METHODS

Table 4.5 provides a brief summary of the encryption methods discussed in Sections 4.5 and 4.6.

TABLE 4.5        **Summary of Encryption Methods**

| METHOD | RELATIONSHIP BETWEEN ENCRYPTION AND DECRYPTION KEYS | COMMENTS |
|---|---|---|
| Caesar cipher | They are same. If we add $k$ to the plaintext, we subtract $k$ from the ciphertext. | Each plaintext character is replaced with a ciphertext character. All occurrences of a character combination translate to the same ciphertext. |
| Poly-alphabetic cipher | They are the same. | Replaces a plaintext character with a ciphertext character. Replacement character depends on plaintext character's position in the message. Larger keys reduce the frequency of letter combinations in the ciphertext, but it becomes more unwieldy. |
| Transposition cipher | They are the same. | Makes no attempt to disguise the plaintext letters. This method can provide clues to someone trying to break the code. |
| Bit-level cipher | They are the same. | Performs exclusive-or operations between a key and message segments. Short keys allow some letter combinations to be encrypted the same way. Longer keys do not, but they become unwieldy. |
| DES | They are the same. | Uses a complex collection of transpositions, substitutions, and exclusive-or operations to disguise the translation process. Still, it defaults to a substitution cipher for 64-bit segments. |
| RSA algorithm | They are related by some well-known results in number theory. | Encrypts by raising numbers to powers that depend on large prime numbers. Determining the decryption key, even when the encryption key is known, requires the factoring of very large numbers, which can take a very long time. |

## 4.7   Viruses, Worms, and Hacking

Up to now we have considered the integrity and security of data as it travels along some medium. We answered questions about detecting data that has been damaged and disguising data so unauthorized persons cannot understand it. Other serious threats to the security and integrity of information are computer **viruses** and **worms**.

Strictly speaking, viruses and worms may be less of a computer network problem and more of an operating system or human behavior problem. Although networks certainly facilitate the spread of some viruses, just being connected to one does not mean viruses are going to jump into your computer and eat your disks. In fact, two main reasons that viruses and worms exist are security holes in operating systems and careless behavior by PC users.

On the other hand, network connections are not without danger, as victims of the Internet worm incident (discussed shortly) can testify. Access to electronic bulletin boards and connectivity among computers all over the world make the existence of worms and viruses a serious problem. Consequently, a chapter on security must at least discuss them and their capabilities.

## INFECTING FILES

A virus is a collection of instructions attached to an executable file that does something the executable file was not designed to do. On MS-DOS machines, a virus commonly attaches to a file with the .EXE or .COM extension. On a Macintosh, a file's resource fork typically is infected. When a virus attaches to a file, we say the file is infected. Worms are a lot like viruses, but they usually appear as a separate program. Like a virus, they are an intrusion to the system and are potentially damaging to the system's security.

Figure 4.22 shows one way to differentiate between an infected and an uninfected file. There are other ways and, if interested, you should consult references 15 and 16. The uninfected file contains executable code that runs when it is referenced. In an infected file, however, the virus has placed a branch command to the virus's code. When the user calls on the infected file to do some task the branch command transfers control to the virus code first. The virus does its deed and executes another branch to begin the requested task. As far as the user is concerned, the requested task

**FIGURE 4.22    Virus on an Executable File**

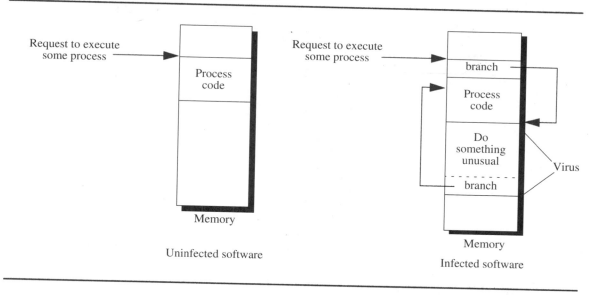

is done. Unless the virus performed an obvious task such as erasing the hard disk the user may not know the virus exists.

What is a virus capable of doing? Unfortunately, just about anything. A virus may do "harmless" tasks such as displaying Christmas trees on your PC during the holiday season.* It may be very destructive and erase your hard disk or destroy your file system. In these cases the effects usually can be minimized, but only if you have backups! If not, you're in serious trouble.

The worst viruses do not cause massive destruction immediately. Instead, they are very subtle, making small (and usually unnoticeable) changes in files as they run. Over a period of time the small changes compound and eventually are noticed. By that time the information has been corrupted. Worse yet, if you made backups diligently they also may be infected. Restoring the pre-infected files may be difficult.

How does the virus attach itself to an executable file? The first step is to bring an infected file into your computer and run it. Once it runs the attached virus can infect files in different ways. For example, it might probe your file system looking for other executable files (Figure 4.23). With a little knowledge of a file system this is not difficult. Whenever it finds an executable file the virus can execute instructions to duplicate itself and store the copy on the file, as in Figure 4.22.

FIGURE 4.23   **Virus Duplicating Itself**

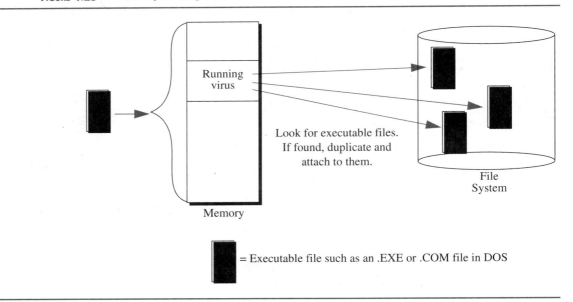

Running virus

Look for executable files. If found, duplicate and attach to them.

File System

Memory

= Executable file such as an .EXE or .COM file in DOS

---

*Some "harmless" viruses may actually do a great deal of harm, even if they do not explicitly destroy or damage existing information. We will see a few examples shortly.

Such viruses can be detected more easily than others. The process of seeking executable files and changing them requires extra disk I/O. Consequently, if you notice a lot of disk activity when you do a simple task, be suspicious. On the other hand, it's very easy to be preoccupied with what you are doing and not even notice the hardware. If the virus is subtle and infects only a few files, you may not notice the extra activity, especially with a fast hard drive.

## MEMORY RESIDENT VIRUSES

Rather than scanning the disk's file system, the virus may copy itself into memory and wait for an executable file to be stored in memory. When a file enters, the virus attacks it. Picking the files off one by one as they enter memory is a much more subtle type of attack—not unlike a sly predator hiding and waiting for its prey to arrive unsuspecting, only to become the predator's next meal.

But how does a memory resident virus become activated? It is still a program and cannot be activated until it is called. On PCs some viruses take advantage of the MS-DOS **interrupt mechanism**. Typically BIOS and DOS service routines are located via an **interrupt table** or **interrupt vector**. The interrupt table is a collection of addresses to service routines. When a user requires a service or when some asynchronous event occurs that needs action, DOS locates the required service by finding its address in the table and begins executing the program at that location. A memory resident virus will change the interrupt table to create addresses that locate the virus instead (Figure 4.24). Consequently, when an interrupt occurs the routine located via the table's address is called. In this case, it is the virus that does its deed. As before, it may try to disguise what it did by calling the intended service routine, making the user think everything is progressing normally.

## VIRUS SOURCES

Where do viruses come from? Initially they are created by individuals who for whatever reason try to invade a system. Whether it is done as a prank or as an unprincipled and malicious act of destruction is usually of no consequence. What's destroyed is destroyed and reasons are of no value to the victim.

Like any biological virus, computer viruses are spread by sharing. We saw how a file can become infected. Consider what happens if an infected file is copied to a disk and the disk is inserted in another computer. When the infected file is run, the other computer's files can become infected. If any of those are copied to a disk and transported to yet another computer, the virus spreads further. Obviously you want to be very careful where you get software.

The growing use of networks and communications has compounded the problem. What happens if an infected file gets into an electronic bulletin board, commercial software, or a network file server? The virus now has the potential to spread to thousands of users in a short period of time. The growth rate of the virus can stagger the imagination.

FIGURE 4.24    **Memory Resident Virus**

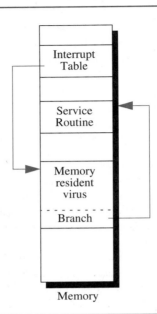

THE INTERNET WORM

Don't infer from this discussion that bulletin boards, networks, and commercially distributed software are a haven for viral infections. Reputable bulletin board operators and vendors go through great effort to make sure their software is not infected. Still, in this business there are no guarantees. In 1988 there was an incident (16) in which a commercial software package contained a virus that displayed a peace message and then erased itself. This is an example of a "harmless" virus doing damage. It may be harmless in the sense that it neither destroys files nor steals valuable information. The vendor, however, will have to rebuild its damaged reputation and restore confidence in its consumers. The company could lose business, which in turn can force layoffs. To a vendor and its employees, such incidents are far from harmless.

Given that viruses are unavoidable, how can you deal with them? As with most illnesses, prevention is your best bet. Many virus detection packages are available. Sometimes a virus detection package scans any disk inserted into a drive looking for viruses. If it detects one it sounds a warning and, in some cases where the disk is a floppy, ejects it. The user then can request the package to remove the virus or can replace all the infected files with uninfected backups (making sure they are uninfected).

## THE INTERNET WORM

One of the more famous instances of intrusion was the **Internet worm**. Several interesting and accessible articles describe the worm, its effects, and how it worked. For detailed accounts see references 17, 18, 19, and 20.

In November 1988 a Cornell graduate student released a worm into the Internet, a worldwide collection of wide area networks running the TCP/IP protocol.* It invaded thousands of Sun 3 and VAX computers running variants of the 4 BSD UNIX operating system. This worm was of the so-called harmless variety; it did not damage any information or give away any of the secret passwords it uncovered.

On the other hand, it was a serious breach of security. It replicated quickly throughout the Internet, clogging communications and forcing many systems to be shut down. It also forced many experts to spend days tracking the source of the problem and cleaning up after it. It caused an FBI investigation to determine whether there was a violation of the 1986 Computer Fraud and Abuse Act and resulted in an indictment of the perpetrator. The case went to court, and a federal jury found the defendant guilty. The defendant was sentenced to three year's probation, fined $10,000, and ordered to do 400 hours of community service (21). So much for harmless worms! (Computer worms and viruses are federal crimes and in most cases will be investigated by the FBI. Federal laws are stricter than most state laws.)

The worm itself was written in C and attacked UNIX systems through flaws in the software. It used several techniques, each of which is described in reference 17. In one approach it used a utility called *fingerd* that allows one user to obtain information about other users. The *fingerd* program is designed to accept a single line of input from a remote site (a request) and send back output corresponding to the request (Figure 4.25). The flaw that was exploited was that the *fingerd* program's input command (C language *gets* command) did not check for buffer overflow. Consequently, a worm running on a remote machine connected to the *fingerd* program

FIGURE 4.25    **The *fingerd* Utility**

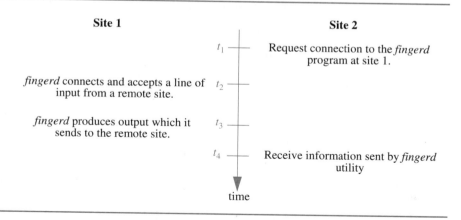

*We will discuss the Internet, wide area networks, and the TCP/IP protocol in Chapter 7. Specific knowledge of what they are and how they work is not needed for this discussion. The important fact here is that thousands of computers worldwide are interconnected.

and sent a specially constructed message that overflowed the *fingerd* program input buffer.

Figure 4.26 shows what happened. The transmitted message overflowed the input buffer and overwrote parts of the system stack. However, the stack contains a return address (of the calling procedure) to be referenced when *fingerd* is done. Because of the overflow this address was changed to point to some instructions stored in the buffer. Consequently, when *fingerd* finished, control returned to the "program" located by the new return address. This "program" effectively replaced *fingerd* with the UNIX shell (interface or command interpreter). The result was that the worm was now connected to the shell. From that point the worm communicated with the shell and eventually sent a copy of itself, thus infecting the new machine. The worm then proceeded to inspect system files looking for connections to other machines it could infect.

It also attacked a password file trying to decipher user passwords. Deciphering a password allowed the worm to attack other computers where that user had accounts. An interesting note here is that the passwords were all stored in encrypted form using the DES. In theory, deciphering the passwords without the key is next to impossible. The worm took a rather straightforward approach, however. It simply guessed passwords, encrypted them, and looked for matches. In theory, the number of possible passwords is huge, making this an impractical method of seeking passwords. However, the worm used words from an on-line dictionary and in many cases found matches. In some cases, over 50 percent of the passwords were uncovered (Reference 17). The moral of this story is don't use passwords commonly found in a dictionary.

## COMPUTER HACKERS

Widespread connectivity has opened many doors for another security threat, the computer hacker. Basically, a hacker is someone who writes programs just for the

---

FIGURE 4.26    **Intruding into the System**

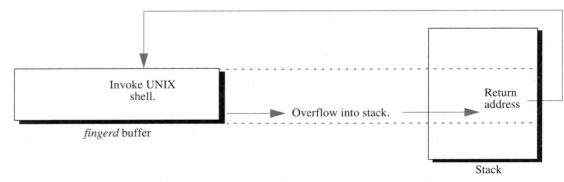

sheer enjoyment of writing them. Some people see hackers as unprincipled people who try to gain unauthorized access to a computer system, often by exploiting security holes in operating systems and determining user passwords.

Why do unprincipled hackers do what they do? That's tough to answer. Some people believe that most hackers see breaking into a system as a challenge or a game. They often do not realize the consequences of their actions. To them, looking at private information does not carry the same stigma as intruding on the privacy of a person's home. This does not necessarily make them less dangerous, however. Some people believe the perpetrator of the Internet worm did not have malicious intent since the worm did not try to destroy information. Nevertheless, its effect was far-reaching and very disruptive. People who hack with the sole purpose of stealing or altering information do exist. They often accept the risk of getting caught or perhaps do not even care. Reference 22 discusses the motives of some hackers and suggests that there are some very dangerous people doing the hacking.

The existence of widespread networks has created the potential for more severe and potentially dangerous problems (Reference 23). For example, one hacking incident described in references 24 and 25 received widespread publicity. It started with a 75-cent accounting error at Lawrence Berkeley Laboratory (LBL) in August 1986 and led to the arrest of a West German hacker. The hacker attacked many computers on MILNET (a military production network) and passed information to the KGB, the secret police of the former Soviet Union. In 1990 a West German court convicted him of espionage for the KGB.

References 24 and 25 provide fascinating reading. They detail the activities of many people as they monitored the intruder's efforts and eventually tracked him to his West German location. They characterized the intruder as not particularly resourceful but very persistent using primitive attack methods such as guessing passwords. As with the Internet worm, many of his attacks were successful simply because of the widespread use of common words used as passwords.

## 4.8    Summary

This chapter dealt primarily with two topics: the security and integrity of transmitted information. Integrity means making sure that information that is received is the same as that which is sent. Security means making sure only authorized people get access to transmitted information.

Sections 4.2 through 4.4 dealt with two approaches to integrity. The first approach is to develop methods to detect damaged transmissions and simply ask for a retransmission when they occur. Two methods were discussed.

- **Parity bits**. This method is geared primarily for single-bit error detection, as it is only 50% accurate for burst errors. However, it can be useful when bits are transmitted separately such as in some computer memory architectures or if single bits from many messages are grouped and sent. It also is the foundation of an error correction technique.

- **Cyclic redundancy checks**. This method is based on the theory of polynomial division. Bit strings are interpreted as polynomials. CRC bits are created so that a message divided by a generator polynomial yields a zero remainder. Dividing a received message by the generator polynomial and checking the remainder yields a very high probability that errors are detected. This method is commonly used and is implemented easily using circular shift circuits and a register. Certain polynomials have been declared as standards.

The second approach to integrity involves detecting and correcting errors. This is most useful when a retransmission is too costly or violates time constraints. The Hamming code establishes a collection of parity bits for strategic positions. If any single-bit error occurs, the position will affect a unique combination of parity checks. This not only allows the error's detection but also provides its position. Knowing its position subsequently allows the bit to be corrected.

Sections 4.5 and 4.6 discussed encryption as a security method. The idea is to disguise information so that even if it does fall into the wrong hands it cannot be understood. The tricky part of encryption is to determine a method so that an unauthorized receiver cannot analyze the ciphertext and reverse the encryption process (decrypt). Several methods were discussed:

- **Caesar cipher**. This method substitutes one character for another. It preserves common letter sequences and is relatively easy to break.

- **Poly-alphabetic cipher**. Like the Caesar cipher one character is substituted for another. The difference is that the substitution choice for a common character would vary depending on the letter's position in the message.

- **Transposition cipher**. This method makes no attempt to disguise the characters but instead rearranges them.

- **Exclusive-or bit operations**. The key is a bit string. An exclusive-or operation between it and parts of the message encrypts the message.

- **Data Encryption Standard (DES)**. This method is essentially a substitution cipher, but the rules for the substitution follow many convoluted steps, thus making the process difficult to reverse without knowing the encryption steps. The method is controversial, as some feel the National Security Agency weakened the standard from the original proposal. The speculation was that the NSA did not want an encryption method it would have trouble breaking.

- **RSA algorithm**. This method is an example of a public key cryptosystem that encrypts by treating a bit string as a number and raising it to a very large power using modular arithmetic. It is also unique among the methods discussed in that the decryption key (private key) is very difficult to determine even when the encryption key (public key) is known.

Other issues involving encryption such as key distribution and digital signatures were discussed. Key distribution means communicating keys in a secure way. One method, Merkle's puzzles, involves sending many encrypted messages (each with a different key) and having the receiver choose one randomly, break the code, and determine the key. Another, Shamir's method, involves using a key as part of a polynomial expression. Then, points that the polynomial's graph pass through are distributed. To determine the key, a minimal number of people are needed to provide enough points to determine the original polynomial.

Digital signatures are a way of authenticating the author of an encrypted message. The idea is to encrypt using a private key and decrypt using a public one. If the author later disputes ownership of the message, the receiver can provide both the received ciphertext and the plaintext. Since the private key is known only to the author then only the author could have sent the message.

The last topics on security were viruses, worms, and hackers. Viruses are programs that attach themselves to other programs. What they do varies and can be very destructive. Like viruses, worms represent invasions into a system, but they are not actually part of another program, as viruses are. Computer hackers are individuals who attempt to break through a system's security. They may try to steal private information or plant viruses or worms in order to do damage. Two rather famous cases of intrusion were the Internet worm which invaded thousands of computers on the Internet, and the West German programmer who attacked computers on MILNET and sold information to the former KGB.

## Review Questions

1. What is a parity bit?

2. Distinguish between even and odd parity.

3. Distinguish between error correction and error detection.

4. What is a burst error?

5. Are the following statements TRUE or FALSE? Why?

   - It is not unusual to lose a bit or two during a transmission.
   - Although an accurate technique, CRC is time-consuming because it requires a lot of overhead.
   - A generator polynomial can be chosen arbitrarily as long as both sender and receiver know it.
   - CRC will detect a burst error of arbitrary length as long as the number of bits affected is odd.
   - Error correction codes are more efficient than error detection codes since they obviate the need for retransmissions.
   - The Caesar cipher has no real value where serious security is needed.
   - Public key encryption allows different people to use the same encryption key even when they are not supposed to know what another person is sending.

- The most serious viruses destroy a lot of data very quickly.
- Viruses that do not destroy information or otherwise compromise a computer system are harmless.

**6.** What is a cyclic redundancy check?

**7.** Under what conditions will CRC detect the following errors?

- single-bit errors
- double-bit errors
- burst errors of length less than or equal to the degree of the generator polynomial
- burst errors of length greater than the degree of the generator polynomial

**8.** What conditions should a generator polynomial satisfy? Why?

**9.** Classify the errors that a CRC method will always detect.

**10.** Classify errors that a CRC method will not detect.

**11.** What is a shift register?

**12.** What is a Hamming code?

**13.** Distinguish between encryption and decryption.

**14.** Distinguish between ciphertext and plaintext.

**15.** What is a Caesar cipher?

**16.** Distinguish between a mono-alphabetic and a poly-alphabetic cipher.

**17.** What is a Vigenère cipher?

**18.** What is a transposition cipher?

**19.** If the encryption key is long enough encryption techniques such as bit-level ciphering are truly unbreakable. Why aren't they used more?

**20.** What is the Digital Encryption Standard (DES)?

**21.** What was the controversy surrounding DES?

**22.** What are Merkle's puzzles?

**23.** What is Shamir's method for key distribution?

**24.** How does public key encryption differ from regular encryption?

**25.** What is a digital signature?

**26.** What are the main features of the RSA algorithm?

**27.** What makes the RSA algorithm so difficult to break?

**28.** Distinguish between a virus and a worm.

**29.** What is an "infected file"?

30. List some ways you can help prevent the spread of computer viruses.

31. What is the UNIX *fingerd* utility?

32. What is a memory resident virus?

33. What was the Internet worm?

# Exercises

1. Construct an argument showing that simple parity checking detects errors only when an odd number of bits change.

2. Consider the double parity check approach in Section 4.2. What can you say about its effectiveness with a burst error of length $n$?

3. Suppose some static of duration 0.01 second affects the communication line for a 14400 bps modem. How many bits could be affected?

4. Consider the error detection technique described by Figure 4.3. What is the probability that two distinct burst errors will go undetected? Assume each burst error has duration less than the time to send one column.

5. Why is $0 - 1 = 1$ using modulo 2 subtraction?

6. What polynomial corresponds to the following bit string?

   0110010011010110

7. Calculate the remainder of the following division using the methods described by Figure 4.4 and 4.5:

$$\frac{x^{12} + x^{10} + x^7 + x^6 + x^5 + x^3 + x^2}{x^7 + x^4 + x^2 + 1}$$

8. Suppose you want to transmit the data 100111001 and the generator polynomial is $x^6 + x^3 + 1$. What bit string is actually sent?

9. Draw the circular shift register and exclusive-or circuits for the CRC-12 and CRC-16 standard polynomial.

10. Calculate the remainder of the following division using circular shifts:

$$\frac{x^{12} + x^{10} + x^7 + x^6 + x^5 + x^3 + x^2}{x^7 + x^4 + x^2 + 1}$$

11. Investigate the documentation for the LAN at your university or company and determine what method of error detection (if any) is used.

12. Suppose the generator polynomial had the term $x$ as a factor. Give an example of an undetected error.

13. Suppose we want to devise a single-bit error correcting Hamming code for a 16-bit data string. How many parity bits are needed? How about for a 32-bit data string?

14. The following 12-bit Hamming-coded (single-bit correction) string was received. What ASCII-coded letter is it?

110111110010

15. Construct Hamming codes for each of the characters 'A', '0', and '{'.

16. Assume a sender has the following data frames:

| FRAME NUMBER | DATA |
|---|---|
| 1 | 0 1 1 0 1 0 0 1 |
| 2 | 1 0 1 0 1 0 1 1 |
| 3 | 1 0 0 1 1 1 0 0 |
| 4 | 0 1 0 1 1 1 0 0 |

Suppose the sender constructs a Hamming code for each frame, forms a two-dimensional bit array, and sends it one column at a time. What does the receiver get if an error makes the fifth column all 0s? Apply error correction methods to the received data and correct it.

17. Develop a Hamming code capable of correcting any single-bit errors and detecting double-bit errors for an 8-bit data string.

18. Suppose the four-bit number $b_4\, b_3\, b_2\, b_1$ described by Table 4.2 forms a number exceeding 12. What does that mean?

19. Write a computer program to take 8 bits of data and create the 12-bit Hamming code.

20. How were the letter substitutions in Figure 4.13 determined?

21. Write a program to encrypt and decrypt using a Caesar cipher. The program should request the encryption key as input.

22. The following message was encrypted using a Caesar cipher. What is the original message?

fcvceqoowpkecvkqpucpfeqorwvgtpgvyqtmu

23. Write a decryption algorithm to decrypt ciphertext created by the encryption algorithm in Figure 4.15.

24. Consider the transposition cipher applied to Table 4.4. What is the transmitted message if the columns are rearranged as 5, 1, 4, 2, and 3?

25. Write a program to accept a binary string and a binary key. It should then use the key to encrypt the string using bit-level ciphering.

26. Consider the bit string 00101101010100001111110100101101 and the key 10110. Use the key to encrypt and then decrypt the string using bit-level ciphering.

27. Suppose that the rows (except row 0) in the key of Figure 4.14 are rearranged so that the ASCII codes of the first letters in two consecutive rows differ by 3 (instead of the current 1) modulo 26. Use the resulting key to encrypt the message

    TIME FLIES LIKE AN ARROW FRUIT FLIES LIKE A BANANA*

28. Repeat the encryption process of the message "HELLO" discussed in Section 4.6 using a different encryption key but with the same value for $n$.

29. Suppose you intercepted the following encrypted message:

    20 5 21 3 49 4 49 3 4 15

    You also know the encryption key is $k = 7$ and it was determined using $n = 55$. Decrypt this message. Assume 'A' through 'Z' were initially coded using 1 through 26 and a blank was initially coded using 27.

30. Calculate $95^{91}$ modulo 121.

## REFERENCES

1. Stallings, W. *Computer Organization and Architecture,* 3rd ed. New York: Macmillan, 1993.

2. Peterson, W. W. and E. J. Weldon. *Error Correcting Codes,* 2nd ed. Cambridge, MA: MIT Press, 1972.

3. Moshos, G. *Data Communications: Principles and Problems.* St. Paul, MN: West, 1989.

4. Kohavi, Z. *Switching and Finite Automata Theory,* 2nd ed. New York: McGraw-Hill, 1978.

5. Hamming, R. W. *Coding and Information Theory.* Englewood Cliffs, NJ: Prentice-Hall, 1980.

6. Tanenbaum, A. S. *Computer Networks* 2nd ed. Englewood Cliffs, NJ: Prentice-Hall, 1988.

7. Kolata, G. B. "Computer Encryption and the National Security Agency Connection." *Science,* vol. 197 (July 1977), 438–40.

*Apologies to Groucho Marx.

8.  Shapely, D. and G. B. Kolata. "Cryptology: Scientists Puzzle over Threat to Open Research, Publication." *Science*, vol. 197 (September 1977), 1345–9.

9.  Merkle, R. C. "Secure Communications Over an Insecure Channel." *Communications of the ACM*, vol. 21, no 4 (April 1978), 294–9.

10. Shamir, A. "How to Share a Secret." *Communications of the ACM*, vol. 22, no 11 (November 1979), 612–3.

11. Diffie, W. and M. E. Hellman. "New Directions in Cryptography." *IEEE Transactions on Information Theory*, November 1967, 644–54.

12. Ruiz, B. and J. Herron. "Netware 4.0: A Directory to the Enterprise." *Data Communications*, vol. 21, no. 13 (September 21, 1992), 53–60.

13. Rivest, R. L., A. Shamir, and L. Adleman. "On a Method for Obtaining Digital Signatures and Public Key Cryptosystems." *Communications of the ACM*, vol. 21 no. 2 (February 1978), 120–6.

14. Tsudik, G. "Message Authentication with One-Way Hash Functions." *Computer Communication Review*, vol. 22, no. 5 (October 1992), 29–38.

15. Spafford, E., K. Heaphy, and D. Ferbrache. "A Computer Virus Primer." Article 20 in *Computers Under Attack: Intruders, Worms, and Viruses*, ed. Peter Denning. Reading, MA: Addison-Wesley, 1990.

16. Fites, P., P. Johnston, and M. Kratz. *The Computer Virus Crisis*. New York: Van Nostrand Reinhold, 1989.

17. Spafford, E.. "The Internet Worm: Crisis and Aftermath." *Communications of the ACM*, vol. 32, no. 6 (June 1989), 678–87.

18. Rochlis, J. and M. Eichin. "With Microscope and Tweezers: The Worm from MIT's Perspective." *Communications of the ACM*, vol. 32, no. 6 (June 1989), 689–98.

19. Seeley D. "Password Cracking: A Game of Wits." *Communications of the ACM*, vol. 32, no. 6 (June 1989),700–3.

20. Denning, P., ed. *Computers Under Attack: Intruders, Worms, and Viruses*. Reading, MA: Addison-Wesley, 1990.

21. Montz, L. "The Worm Case: From Indictment to Verdict." Article 15 in *Computers Under Attack: Intruders, Worms, and Viruses*, ed. Peter Denning. Reading, MA: Addison-Wesley, 1990.

22. Landreth, B. and H. Rheingold. *Out of the Inner Circle: A Hacker's Guide to Computer Security*, Bellevue, WA: Microsoft Press, 1987.

23. National Research Council. *Computers at Risk*. Washington, DC:National Academy Press, 1991.

24. Stoll, C. "Stalking the Wily Hacker." *Communications of the ACM*, vol. 31, no. 5 (May 1988), 484–97.

25. Stoll, C. *The Cuckoo's Egg: Tracking a Spy Through the Maze of Computer Espionage*. New York: Doubleday, 1989.

26. Denning, D. and F. Drake. "A Dialog on Hacking and Security." Article 25 in *Computers Under Attack: Intruders, Worms, and Viruses*, ed. Peter Denning. Reading, MA: Addison-Wesley, 1990.

# CHAPTER 5

# PROTOCOL CONCEPTS

## 5.1 Introduction

Almost everything we have discussed so far has dealt with a single transmission from a sender to a receiver. Whether we discussed digital or analog signals, compression, contention, security, or integrity, the discussion was generally aimed at a single transmission or frame. Most communications are more complex than that. The following issues also should be considered:

- What if the transmitted message is very long? Examples include large data files or a copy of a speech given at a political rally. Treating the entire message as a single transmission entity monopolizes the medium. This is fine for the sender but not so good for anyone else waiting to transmit.

- How do we react to damaged transmissions? In the previous chapter we stated that the receiver simply requests a retransmission. But how does the receiver do this? Does the sender's protocol depend entirely on the receiver's ability to notify him of damaged frames? Should the sender conclude that a frame arrived correctly if the receiver sends no such request? What happens if the receiver's request for a second transmission is itself damaged or lost?

- What if the sending and receiving computers work at different speeds? For example, you might download a data file from a Cray to a 286-based PC. Or perhaps the receiver is busier than the sender. In general, how do you prevent a sender from overwhelming a receiver with more data than the receiver can handle?

- What happens if a sender's frame gets lost? For example, the damaged part of a frame may include the receiver's address. If so, the frame will never be delivered. We know the receiver can detect damaged frames. But what happens if a receiver gets nothing? Does it mean a frame was lost or that nothing was sent? How does the receiver distinguish between the two?

- In our previous examples, the distinction between sender and receiver was sharp. What if both want to send and receive simultaneously? It's a lot like talking and listening at the same time. We all do it on occasion but some of what we hear is lost. We do not want our receivers to lose information.

This chapter discusses two important functions necessary to establish and maintain effective communications: error control and flow control. **Error control** defines how a station checks frames for errors and what it does if it finds them. Sections 4.2 and 4.3 discussed ways of detecting errors but did not address what happened afterward. A common approach is for the receiving station to send a message to the sending station indicating that an error occurred. What the sending station does next varies, and we discuss several protocols. The message is effectively a request to resend the frame, so this type of error control is also often called **automatic repeat request (ARQ)**.

**Flow control** defines the way in which many frames are sent and tracked and how the stations do error control. It determines when frames can be sent, when they cannot be sent, and when they should be sent a second time. In general, flow control protocols ensure that *all* of the related frames arrive at their destination accurately and in order.

As with any topic, protocols range from simple to complex. Section 5.2 discusses relatively simple flow control protocols. The protocols range from sending one frame at a time (stop and wait) to sending all of them at once (unrestricted flow). This section also discusses the use of special signals or specific byte values to indicate when to send data. The latter is analogous to a traffic signal regulating traffic flow onto a highway. As long as the light is green, traffic can enter the highway. But when the highway traffic reaches a certain saturation point the light turns red, halting any additional flow onto the highway.

Section 5.3 defines a more complex approach that numbers the frames and sends only a few at a time. The sender then waits for acknowledgment before sending more. The go-back-n protocol discussed in Section 5.3 assumes that frames arrive in the same order in which they were sent. The selective repeat protocol also discussed in Section 5.3 allows for cases in which frames might be delayed and delivered out of order.

Discussing protocols and how they work is one thing. Verifying that they are correct is quite another. For simple algorithms, verification is often easy, but the complex ones require some special tools. Section 5.4 discusses some verification tools such as Petri nets and finite state models. Its orientation is more theoretical, and it may be skipped without loss of continuity.

The final two sections take a practical approach and discuss actual protocols in use today. Section 5.5 discusses data link protocols such as synchronous data link control (SDLC) and high-level data link control (HDLC). Section 5.6 discusses Kermit, a popular file transfer protocol.

## 5.2    Basic Flow Control

### SIGNALING

This section introduces relatively elementary approaches to flow control useful in simple communication systems. The first approach, signaling, is straightforward

(Figure 5.1). The sender transmits data as long as the receiver is able to receive it. The receiver may not be able to receive data all the time, however. For example, the buffers that hold received data may be filling up, or the receiver may not be ready if it is doing other things. In such cases, the receiver sends a signal to the sender. On receipt of the signal, the sender stops transmitting. The protocol also allows for another signal to be sent when the receiver is again ready to receive more data. This approach is analogous to a nonproductive argument in which one person says,"Stop! I don't want to hear any more."

## DTE-DCE Flow Control

Section 3.2 discussed one way to signal readiness to send and receive data over an RS-232 interface. It involved sending signals over specified lines (DTR and DSR) to indicate a state of readiness. When the DTE wanted to send to the DCE, it sent another signal (RTS) requesting to send. It then waited for a clear-to send signal (CTS) before transmitting. The details are in Section 3.2 so we won't rehash old material here.

**X-ON/X-OFF**    The RS-232 interface was complex in that it required separate lines for separate signals. Another approach is to send the signal as part of the trans-

**FIGURE 5.1    Flow Control Using Signaling**

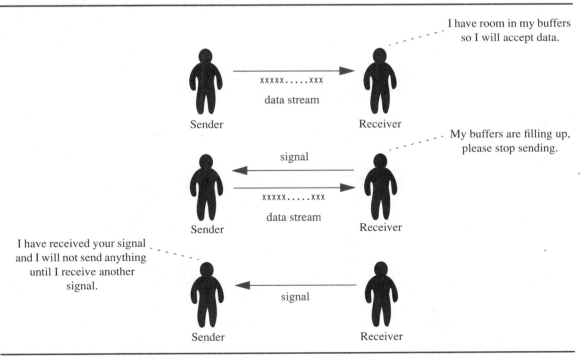

I have room in my buffers so I will accept data.

data stream

Sender                    Receiver

My buffers are filling up, please stop sending.

signal

data stream

Sender                    Receiver

I have received your signal and I will not send anything until I receive another signal.

signal

Sender                    Receiver

mitted data. This is called **inband signaling**. In this case, the receiver has to analyze the incoming data looking for any special signals to which it must respond.

The ASCII character set defines two control characters for flow control (see Table 2.4 in Section 2.2). Symbolically, they are DC3 (ASCII code 19) and DC1 (ASCII code 17), also called X-OFF and X-ON, respectively.[*] It is commonly used for flow control between a terminal and mainframe. Figure 5.2 shows how it works.

The figure assumes full-duplex communications so there is no distinction between a sender and receiver. Stations *A* and *B* both send to and receive from each other. If *A*'s buffers are starting to fill up it can respond by inserting the X-OFF character into the data it is sending to *B*. When the X-OFF character arrives, *B* sees it and stops transmitting its data to *A*. (Note, however, that *A* is still sending to *B*.) If *A* has more room in the buffers later, *A* can send the X-ON character to *B*, which signals *B* that it is permissible to resume transmitting.

When one station sends the X-OFF character, it continues to receive data for a short time because of a small delay between the time the X-OFF character is sent and the time the other station can respond to it. Consequently, a station usually will send when data in its buffers exceeds some threshold value.

Your first exposure to this protocol may have been by accident. For example, a common activity in a programming class is to list text files on the screen. Occasionally, through a mistake or inattention, you might try to list a binary file such as an executable file. The result usually is the appearance of strange characters on the screen, some beeping noises, and random cursor movement. In some cases, the terminal becomes unresponsive to further keyboard entries. That is, the keyboard "freezes up" on you. Since most bytes in a binary file do not correspond to printable characters the terminal often responds to their contents in unexpected ways such as line feed, vertical tab, or horizontal tab codes that cause the cursor to move randomly. They may also contain the BEL code (hexadecimal code 07), causing the

**FIGURE 5.2    Flow Control Using Inband Signaling**

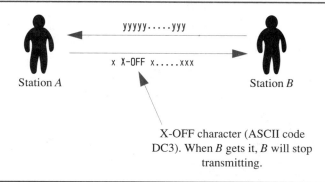

---

[*] They also correspond to the control-S and control-Q keyboard sequences.

beeping sound. (This should destroy popular belief that the beeps are a warning that the terminal is about to self-destruct.)

The "freezing up" problem occurs if one of the file's bytes contains an X-OFF character. Because the terminal received the X-OFF character, it responded by stopping transmission back to the computer. Thus, if you make subsequent keyboard entries they are not sent, and the terminal freezes up. Solutions range from turning off the terminal or entering a local mode at the terminal and clearing communications. The latter is done on DEC terminals.

Another common use of this protocol occurs when printing a large file on the screen. To prevent information from scrolling off the screen you can enter a control-S (hold the control key and enter S) from the keyboard to freeze the screen. Control-S sends an X-OFF character, which stops the transmission of the file. Later, having read what you wanted, you can enter control-Q, which sends the X-ON character, and allows the file's transmission to resume.

### FRAME-ORIENTED CONTROL

Protocols such as X-ON/X-OFF are byte oriented and are typical of asynchronous communications (Section 3.1). That is, transmission can start and pause at any given byte. Synchronous communications (Section 3.1) are frame oriented and require more organization. Information is sent and retrieved in larger pieces, not as a byte stream. Because a station must be able to buffer all the bytes in a frame it receives, different protocols are used to restrict the number of frames that can be sent. How the restrictions are applied, of course, varies.

Another consideration is that those who send and receive information usually do not care about the frames and their structure. Indeed, if you send a file from a PC to a mainframe over a modem you do not want to be bothered with these details. You simply want to enter a command to send a file and have the software worry about the details. Consequently, most protocols divide the information to be sent into frames of the appropriate format and send them. Figure 5.3 illustrates how this is done in a typical case.

Someone or something that we call a **patron** has information it must send to another. The patron typically is a user or a higher layer in a multilayer protocol. The sender gets enough information (a **packet**) from the patron to put into one frame and transmits the frame. The receiver gets the frame, extracts the packet, and gives it to the patron that it serves. This process is repeated using as many frames as needed to transmit all the information.

Typically, the sender, receiver, and patrons of Figure 5.3 define consecutive layers in some communications software. This is typical of the interaction between the data link (sender and receiver) and network layer (patron) in the OSI model. Flow control also exists in higher-layer protocols such as TCP/IP and is part of IBM's SNA architecture. (We describe each of these later in this book.) At this point where the sender, receiver, and patron exist is not important. Flow control exists in different models and in different layers. However, it is important to realize that flow

FIGURE 5.3    **Sending and Receiving Between Patrons**

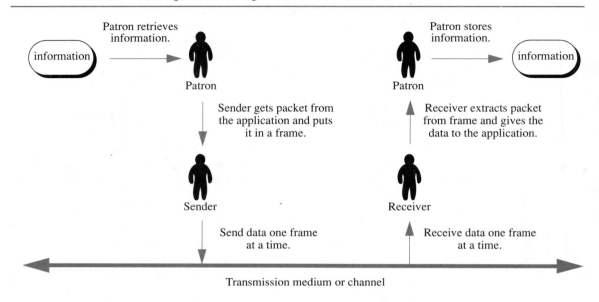

control typically is part of the interaction between two consecutive layers in some protocol.

**Unrestricted Protocol**    The easiest protocol, unrestricted protocol, assumes the receiver either has an unlimited capacity to receive frames or uses them fast enough so that buffer space is always available. Figure 5.4 shows the sender and re-

FIGURE 5.4    **Unrestricted Flow Control**

```
void send_data;                          void receive_data;
{                                        {
   while there are packets to send           while there are frames to receive
   {                                         {
      get packet from the patron;               wait for frame to arrive;
      put packet into a frame;                  receive(frame);
      send(frame);                              Extract packet from the frame;
   }                                            Give packet to the patron;
}                                            }
                                         }
              Sender code                              Receiver code
```

ceiver logic written in partial C code.[*] The sender and receiver use primitive calls *send* and *receive*. Typically, they are calls to a layer below the sender and receiver that take care of details required to transmit the frame or retrieve it.

The sender executes a loop repeatedly as long as there is information to send. With each pass of the loop it gets a packet from its patron, puts it into a frame, and sends the frame. It sends frames repeatedly and makes no effort to limit the number it sends. The receiver also executes a loop repeatedly. We assume the receiver is always capable of receiving a frame. With each pass through the loop the receiver waits (i.e., exists in a suspended or wait state) until a frame arrives. The arrival causes the receiver to wake up and receive the frame. It extracts the packet and passes it to its patron and then goes back into a wait state until another frame arrives.

This approach does not consider any of the problems we have discussed previously. There is no attempt to check for damaged, lost, or delayed frames or to control the number of frames sent. It assumes that every frame will arrive without damage and in the order sent. It is much like our dependence on the Post Office when we mail letters.

**Stop and Wait Protocol**    This protocol differs from the previous one in two ways. First, every time the receiver gets a frame it sends an **acknowledgment** back to the sender. The acknowledgment is another frame specifying whether the received frame was damaged. Second, after sending a frame the sender waits for an acknowledgment before sending another frame. Thus rather than sending all the frames in rapid sequence, this protocol sends one, waits for an acknowledgment, sends another, waits for an acknowledgment, and so on. We call this the **stop and wait protocol**. In some ways it represents the opposite extreme of the previous method. Where the unrestricted protocol sent the maximum number of frames per unit of time, this one sends the minimum number.

Figure 5.5 outlines the sender's and receiver's protocol. The receiver protocol is similar to the unrestricted one. It consists of an infinite loop in which it waits for a frame to arrive. When a frame arrives, the receiver checks it for damage. Whether it uses CRC or some form of parity checking discussed in Chapter 4 is not relevant at this level of the discussion. The important thing is that it can detect a damaged frame.

If the frame was not damaged, the receiver defines an *error* field in a record structure called *ack* as 0. It proceeds to extract the packet from the frame and give it to the patron. If the frame was damaged the *error* field of *ack* is set to 1. It does not extract a packet from the frame and the patron gets nothing. In any case, the receiver sends the acknowledgment back to the sender. Since the *error* field specifies the status of the received frame, the sender can respond accordingly.

The sender executes a loop repeatedly, sending frames and waiting for acknowledgments. Prior to sending a frame, the sender must decide whether it

---

[*] We make no attempt to write syntactically correct C code. We will combine C syntax with informal statements to convey the program's meaning without a lot of language detail. A good exercise is to modify all the protocols we discuss into syntactically and logically correct programs.

FIGURE 5.5	**Stop and Wait Flow Control**

```
void send_data;                          void receive_data;
{                                        {
  damaged=0;                               while there are packets to receive
  while there are packets to send          {
  {                                          Wait for frame to arrive;
    if (!damaged)                            receive(frame);
         /* !0 is the same as true in C */   Examine frame for transmission error;
    {                                        if no transmission error
      Get packet from the patron;            {
      Put packet into a frame;                 ack.error=0;
    }                                          Extract packet from the frame;
    send(frame);                               Give packet to the patron;
    Wait for acknowledgment to arrive;       }
    receive(ack);                            else
    if ack.error                               ack.error=1;
      damaged=1;                             send(ack);
    else                                   }
      damaged=0;                         }
  }
}
            Sender code                              Receiver code
```

should send a new one or resend the old one. It does this through a local variable called *damaged* whose value indicates the status of the most recently sent frame (1 means the frame was damaged, 0 means it was not). Initially, it is 0. At the beginning of the loop, the sender checks *damaged*. If it is 0, the sender gets a new packet from the patron, puts it into a frame, and sends it. If *damaged* is 1, the sender sends the current frame (the one it sent earlier). Either way, it waits for an acknowledgment after sending the frame. When the acknowledgment arrives, the sender checks the *error* field, which the receiver defined. If the error field indicates the previous frame was damaged, the sender defines *damaged* = 1. Thus, the next time through the loop, the sender does not get new data from the patron but resends the frame. If *damaged* = 0, the sender gets a new packet in the next pass and sends it.

As we have described it, stop and wait seems preferable to the unrestricted protocol. Still, it has some shortcomings:

- If the sender's frame is lost, the receiver never sends an acknowledgment, and the sender will wait forever.
- If the receiver's acknowledgment is lost, the same thing happens.

- If the acknowledgment is damaged, the sender may draw the wrong conclusion and make the protocol fail.

- The sender certainly does not overwhelm the receiver with too many frames, but perhaps it has gone to the other extreme. Both sender and receiver do a lot of waiting. It's analogous to a teacher giving an assignment one question at a time. The student takes the question home, works on it, brings it back to school, gives it to the teacher, waits for the teacher to grade it, gets another question, and does the same thing all over again. In some cases it would be far more efficient to take all the questions home, finish them, and return them the next day.

These observations need responses, and the next two sections provide them. Before discussing more complex protocols, however, let's introduce the notion of protocol efficiency.

## PROTOCOL EFFICIENCY

We can measure efficiency in several ways. For example, how much buffer space does the protocol require? With the stop and wait protocol there is never more than one frame being sent at a time, so a buffer capacity of one frame is sufficient. With the unrestricted protocol they may arrive faster than the receiver can formally receive them. Therefore, they must be stored in the interim. The number stored depends on how fast they arrive and how quickly the receiver can dispense them. In any case, the stop and wait protocol requires less space and can be considered more efficient from that perspective.

Another measure of efficiency is **channel utilization**. What percentage of the time is the channel transferring data frames? Channel utilization is complex as it depends on several factors such as the distance between the sender and receiver, signal speed over the channel, the bit rate, frame size, and the amount of time needed to construct and send a frame.

Let's illustrate with an example. Assume the following definitions, with the numbers in parentheses to be used in the example:

$R$ = transmission rate (10 Mbps or 10 bits per μsec).

$S$ = signal speed (200 meters per μsec).

$D$ = distance between the sender and receiver (200 meters).

$T$ = time to create one frame (1 μsec).

$F$ = number of bits in a frame (200).

$N$ = number of data bits in a frame (160).

$A$ = number of bits in an acknowledgment (40).

We begin by determining the amount of time needed to construct and send a frame (Figure 5.6). Assume the sender begins at time zero. The sender will have gotten in-

FIGURE 5.6     **Time Required to Send a Frame to a Receiver**

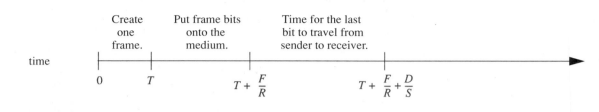

formation and put it into a frame at time $T$. The next step is to transmit the frame (put its bits on the channel). Since $R$ is the data rate, then $1/R$ is the time needed to transmit 1 bit. Therefore, $F/R$ is the time needed to transmit one frame. The total time used so far is $T + F/R$.

Once the sender has transmitted the frame, the bits require time to travel through the channel to the receiver. The travel time is $D/S$. Thus, after the last bit is transmitted, it requires another $D/S$ time units to reach the receiver. Therefore, the receiver receives the last bit at time $= T + F/R + D/S$. Note that the amount of time a frame is in transit is $F/R + D/S$.

For the stop and wait protocol the receiver must send an acknowledgment. A similar argument shows that the time required for the sender to receive the acknowledgment is $T + A/R + D/S$.[*]

Next question: How much time elapses between sending two data frames? With the unrestricted protocol, the sender starts building the next frame as soon as it has transmitted the last bit from the previous one. With stop and wait, the sender must wait for each acknowledgment. Therefore, the elapsed time between sending two consecutive frames is:

$$\text{time} = T + \frac{F}{R} \quad \text{for the unrestricted protocol} \qquad \textbf{Equation 5.1}$$

and

$$\text{time} = \left( T + \frac{F}{R} + \frac{D}{S} \right) + \left( T + \frac{A}{R} + \frac{D}{S} \right)$$

$$= 2 * \left( T + \frac{D}{S} \right) + \frac{F + A}{R} \quad \text{for the stop and wait protocol} \qquad \textbf{Equation 5.2}$$

---

[*] Strictly speaking the amount of time needed for the receiver to construct the acknowledgement frame is different from $T$. However, specifics depend on CPU speed, efficiency of compiled code, and software scheduling. To simplify matters, we just assume both the sender and receiver can construct a frame in the same amount of time.

Previously, we stated that the amount of time a data frame is actually in transit is $F/R + D/S$. Thus, if we define $P$ as the percentage of time during which frame bits occupy the channel, then we have:

$$P \text{ (unrestricted protocol)} = 100 * \frac{\dfrac{F}{R}}{T + \dfrac{F}{R}}$$                          **Equation 5.3**

$$= 100 * \frac{\dfrac{200 \text{ bits}}{10 \text{ bits/}\mu\text{sec}}}{1\mu\text{sec} + \dfrac{200 \text{ bits}}{10 \text{ bits/}\mu\text{sec}}}$$

$$\approx 95\%$$

and

$$P \text{(stop and wait protocol)} = 100 * \frac{\dfrac{F}{R} + \dfrac{D}{S}}{2 * \left( T + \dfrac{D}{S} \right) + \dfrac{F + A}{R}}$$                          **Equation 5.4**

$$= 100 * \frac{\dfrac{200 \text{ bits}}{10 \text{ bits/}\mu\text{sec}} + \dfrac{200 \text{ meters}}{200 \text{ meters/}\mu\text{sec}}}{2 * \left( 1\mu\text{sec} + \dfrac{200 \text{ meters}}{200 \text{ meters/}\mu\text{sec}} \right) + \dfrac{200 \text{ bits} + 40 \text{ bits}}{10 \text{ bits/}\mu\text{sec}}}$$

$$\approx 75\%$$

Thus, if we measure efficiency solely by channel utilization, the unrestricted protocol is more efficient.

Another useful measure is the **effective data rate**. It is the actual number of data bits (as opposed to the maximum number of bits or capacity) sent per unit of time. To calculate the effective data rate, we divide the number of data bits ($N$) sent by the elapsed time between sending two frames. Continuing with our example, we have the following:

$$\text{effective data rate (unrestricted protocol)} = \frac{N}{T + \dfrac{F}{R}}$$                          **Equation 5.5**

$$= \frac{160 \text{ bits}}{1 \ \mu\text{sec} + \dfrac{200 \text{ bits}}{10 \text{ bits/}\mu\text{sec}}}$$

$$\approx 7.6 \text{ bits/}\mu\text{sec} = 7.6 \text{ Mbps}$$

effective data rate (stop and wait protocol) $= \dfrac{N}{2*\left(T + \dfrac{D}{S}\right) + \dfrac{F + A}{R}}$    **Equation 5.6**

$$= \dfrac{160 \text{ bits}}{2*\left(1 \ \mu\sec + \dfrac{200 \text{ meters}}{200 \text{ meters}/\mu\sec}\right) + \dfrac{200 \text{ bits} + 40 \text{ bits}}{10 \text{ bits}/\mu\sec}}$$

$\approx 5.7 \text{ bits}/\mu\sec = 5.7 \text{ Mbps}.$

It is important to note that raw bit rate capacity does not guarantee that much data will be moved. In this example, the stop and wait protocol realizes only about 57% of the channel's actual capacity. The effective data rate depends very much on the protocols, frame sizes, distance traveled, and so on. For example, increasing the frame size will increase the effective data rates (assuming there is a proportionate increase in the frame's data bits). This may not be obvious from the previous equations, but try it and see what happens. Can you determine what effect increases in the other variables will have on the effective data rate?

These measures provide only part of the total picture, and we make no claim that unrestricted protocol is better just because its effective data rates and channel utilization are higher. Other factors to consider are the users the protocols serve, amount of data to transfer, and the fact that the channel will be used by others. The fact is that these two protocols represent two extremes (send everything at once and send one frame at a time), and some commonly used protocols fall somewhere in between. The next two sections discuss two of them.

## 5.3    Sliding Window Protocols

The previous protocols work reasonably well if the number of frames and the distance between stations is not large. If the number of frames becomes large, the unrestricted protocol can flood the channel and overwhelm the receiver. Equation 5.6 shows what happens with the stop and wait protocol if the distance increases. The $D$ in the denominator forces the effective data rate to decrease. In theory, choosing $D$ large enough makes the rate arbitrarily small.

Since communications often occur over large distances and involve large amounts of data, alternative protocols are needed. One approach is a compromise between the unrestricted and stop and wait protocols called a sliding window protocol. It numbers the frames to be sent and defines a **window** as a subset of consecutive frames. If the window contains $i$ frames numbered starting with $w$ ($w$ and $i$ are integers), then the following statements are true (Figure 5.7):

- Every frame numbered less than $w$ has been sent and acknowledged.
- No frame numbered greater than or equal to $w + i$ has been sent.
- Any frame in the window has been sent but may not yet have been acknowledged. Those not yet acknowledged are **outstanding frames**.

FIGURE 5.7    **A Sliding Window Protocol**

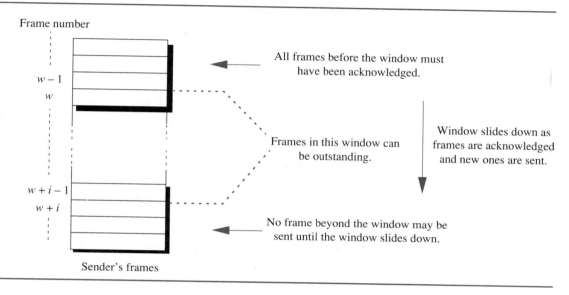

Initially, the window contains frames starting with frame 0. As the patron provides packets, the window expands to include new frames, which then are sent. A limit on the window's size, however, limits the number of outstanding frames. When the limit is reached, the sender takes no more packets from the patron. As outstanding frames are acknowledged, the window shrinks to exclude acknowledged frames. Subsequent to this the window again can expand to include more new frames to send.

As the window changes the previous conditions must always be met and the window always contains frames numbered consecutively. For example, if frame $w + 1$ is acknowledged but frame $w$ is not, the window will not change until frame $w$ is acknowledged. Even if every frame was acknowledged except frame $w$, the window will not change. Frames are excluded from the window in the same order in which they were included.

This approach is a compromise because it allows multiple (but not necessarily all) frames to send before receiving acknowledgments for each. The maximum window size defines the number of frames that may be outstanding. If the window size is 1, we have essentially the stop and wait protocol. If the window size is greater than the total number of frames, we have essentially the unrestricted protocol. Adjusting the window size can help control the traffic on a network and change the buffering requirements.

There are two common implementations of a sliding window protocol. The go-back-n protocol requires frames to be received in the same order they are sent.[*] The selective repeat protocol does not. Go-back-n is simpler as the receiver rejects every frame except the one it is supposed to receive. Selective repeat requires the receiver to be able to hold onto frames received out of order before passing them on to a higher layer in the correct order.

### FRAME FORMAT

With these protocols we drop a previous assumption and eliminate the sharp distinction between sender and receiver. That is, we assume a more realistic model in which two stations ($A$ and $B$) are sending to (and receiving from) each other (Figure 5.8). This is a conversational or full-duplex mode of communication. Thus the protocol must be able to not only send frames but receive them as well.

Let's review briefly what a frame actually contains. Figure 5.9 shows typical fields. We will see some specific formats in Sections 5.5 and 5.6. The frame fields are as follows:

- **Source address**. This is the address of the station sending the frame. It is often needed so a station receiving a frame knows where to send an acknowledgment.

- **Destination address**. This is the address where the frame should be sent. It is needed so a station can determine which frames are destined for it.

- **Frame number**. Each frame has a sequence number starting with 0. If this field has $K$ bits, the largest number is $2^K - 1$. More than $2^K$ frames cause complications, which we discuss shortly.

- **Ack**. The integer value of this frame is the number of a frame being acknowledged. Note that because a station both sends and receives, it can avoid sending a separate acknowledgment by including the acknowledgment in a data frame. This is called **piggybacking**.

- **Type of frame**. This field specifies the type of frame. For example, a data frame has type "data." However, there may be occasion to acknowledge a frame sepa-

FIGURE 5.8    **Two-Way Communication Between Stations A and B**

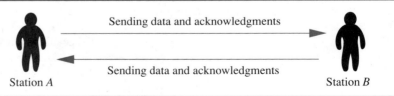

Station A — Sending data and acknowledgments → Station B

Station A ← Sending data and acknowledgments — Station B

---

[*] The reason frames can arrive out of order varies. It is a lot like the Post Office. The letter you mailed on Monday will probably arrive before the one you mail on Tuesday, but don't bet your retirement pension on it. Heavy traffic, hardware or software failures, and damaged frames can all contribute to delaying or even losing a frame.

FIGURE 5.9    **Typical Frame Format**

| Source | Destination | Number | Ack | Type | ...Data... | CRC |
|--------|-------------|--------|-----|------|------------|-----|

rately. Piggybacking can be used only when there is data to send; without data, the protocol uses separate acknowledgments using a frame of type "ack." We also use a type **"nak"** for **negative acknowledgment** for problem situations. For example, the protocol sends a nak frame when a received frame is damaged or if the wrong one has arrived. In either case, the protocol is letting the other station know something went wrong.

- **Data.** This represents the information in a data frame.
- **CRC.** This corresponds to the bits used for error checking (Section 4.3).

## GO-BACK-N PROTOCOL

The go-back-n protocol has several identifying features:

- Frame numbers must lie between 0 and $2^K - 1$ ($K$ = number of bits in the number field), inclusive. If there are more than $2^K$ frames, frame numbers are duplicated. For example, suppose $K = 6$ and there are more than 64 frames to send. Frames 0 through 63 are numbered 0 through 63. However, frames 64 through 127 are also numbered 0 through 63. In general, frames are all numbered consecutively modulo $2^K$. We will see that this feature puts restrictions on the window size in order to allow the stations to correctly interpret the frame numbers.

  This also requires a slight adjustment in how we define a window. We still require that the window contain frames numbered [*] consecutively. However, we now consider 0 as the next frame number after $2^K - 1$. For example, if $K = 6$ then frames numbered 62, 63, 0, 1, 2, etc. are consecutive modulo $2^6 = 64$.

- The receiving station always expects to receive frames in order (modulo $2^K$) of frame number. If it receives one out of order, it ignores the frame and sends a nak for the frame it expected. It then waits until the correct one arrives.

- If a frame arrives and is damaged, the receiving station ignores it and sends a nak for it.

- A receiving station does not acknowledge each received frame explicitly. If a sending station receives an acknowledgment for frame $j$ and later receives one

---

[*] From this point when we refer to a frame number, we mean the value that appears in the number field of the frame.

for frame $k$ $(k > j)$, it assumes all frames between $j$ and $k$ have been received correctly. This reduces the number of acknowledgments and lessens network traffic. Of course, the station sending the acknowledgments must make sure the assumption is valid.

- A station uses the piggyback approach whenever possible to acknowledge the most recently received frame. However, if no data frames are sent during a period of time, the station sends a separate acknowledgment frame. An **ack timer** is set whenever a data frame arrives. The ack timer counts down and stops only when the station sends something. The rationale is that when a data frame arrives it should be acknowledged within a period of time defined by the ack timer. If there are no outgoing frames the timer continues to count down to 0. If the timer reaches 0 (expires), the station sends a separate acknowledgment frame in lieu of the piggyback acknowledgment. If the station sends a frame as the timer counts down, the timer stops because an acknowledgment goes with the frame.

- The sending station buffers the packets from all frames in the window in the event it has to resend them. Packets are removed from the buffer as they are acknowledged.

- If a station does not receive an acknowledgment for a period of time, it assumes something went wrong and one or more outstanding frames did not reach their destination. It then uses a **frame timer**, one for each frame, which is set whenever a data frame is sent. The frame timer counts down and stops only when the associated frame is acknowledged. If the frame timer expires, the protocol resends every frame in the window.

  The rationale for sending all outstanding frames is that the receiving station rejects any frame with the wrong number. If the receiving station got the first frame in the window, the sending station should have received an acknowledgment. Not getting one, the sending station assumes something happened to it. It also reasons that since the receiving station did not get the first frame, it would have rejected all subsequent frames. Thus, all frames must be present. If there are $n$ frames, it goes back to the beginning of the window to resend them. Hence the term go-back-n.

How many frames can the sending protocol have outstanding at one time? In other words, what is the maximum window size? If frames are numbered between 0 and $2^K - 1$, the window size can be no larger than $2^K$. If it were, there would be more than $2^K$ frames outstanding. Consequently, there will be two different outstanding frames with the same number. When the sending station receives an acknowledgment for that number, it has no way of telling which of the two frames is actually being acknowledged. For example, suppose $K = 3$ and the first nine frames are outstanding. The first eight frames are numbered 0 through 7. The last one is numbered 0. If the sending station receives an acknowledgment for frame 0, it does not know if it corresponds to the first or the last frame.

From this, we conclude that the window size must be less than or equal to $2^K$. However, if the window size is equal to $2^K$, an unfortunate sequence of events still can make the protocol fail. Suppose $K = 3$, and consider the events shown in Figure

5.10. Assume both stations have been exchanging frames prior to time $t_1$. At time $t_1$ station $A$ sends frames 0 through 7 to station $B$. Station $B$ receives each of them in the correct order and at time $t_2$ sends an acknowledgment for the most recent one received, number 7. Unfortunately, this acknowledgment gets lost because of a hardware or software error somewhere.

Station $B$ has no way of knowing the acknowledgment was lost and is waiting for the frame after frame 7 (frame 0). Station $A$, on the other hand, does not receive the acknowledgment and does not know whether the frames arrived or not. Following the protocol, it resends frames 0 through 7 at time $t_3$. At time $t_4$ station $B$ receives frame 0. The problem is that this frame 0 is a duplicate of the previous frame 0. But station B is expecting a new frame 0 and has no way of knowing it has received a duplicate. It therefore accepts the duplicate as a new frame, and the protocol fails.

The problem occurs because two consecutive windows contain the same frame numbers. Station $B$ had no way of knowing which window frame 0 was in. Reducing the window size by 1 corrects this problem. Figure 5.11 shows what happens if similar events happen with the reduced window size. Here, station $A$ sends frames 0 through 6 at time $t_1$ and station $B$ receives them all. At time $t_2$ station $B$ acknowledges frame 6 and the acknowledgment gets lost. The difference now is that station $B$ is expecting to receive frame 7. When station $A$ resends frames 0 through 6

**FIGURE 5.10   Protocol Failure When Window Size Equals $2^K$**

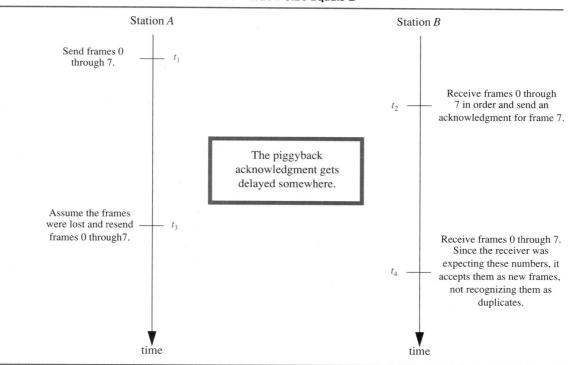

FIGURE 5.11    **Protocol Success When Window Size Equals $2^K - 1$**

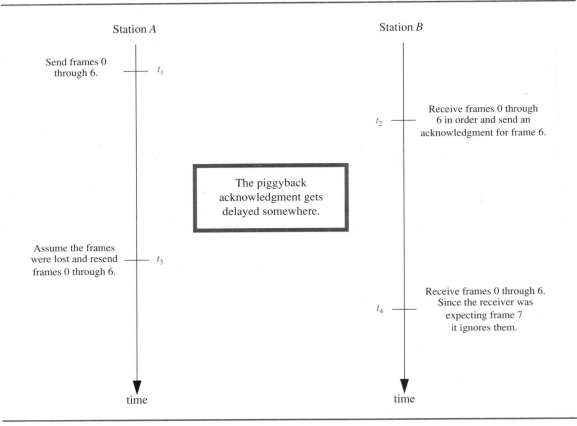

Station *A*                                        Station *B*

Send frames 0
through 6.          $t_1$

                                                   Receive frames 0 through
                                        $t_2$        6 in order and send an
                                                   acknowledgment for frame 6.

The piggyback
acknowledgment gets
delayed somewhere.

Assume the frames
were lost and resend   $t_3$
frames 0 through 6.

                                                   Receive frames 0 through 6.
                                                   Since the receiver was
                                        $t_4$        expecting frame 7
                                                   it ignores them.

time                                               time

(at time $t_3$), they arrive at *B* at time $t_4$. Since they are not what *B* is expecting, *B* ignores them. Eventually *B* sends another acknowledgment which *A* receives (we hope).[*] Station *A* advances its window to include frame 7 and the protocol continues. From this, we conclude that the window size must be strictly less than $2^K$ or the go-back-n protocol can fail.

We are finally ready to present a more detailed description of the go-back-n protocol. Figure 5.12 shows a partially coded C program containing the logic and variable names. Figure 5.7 should also help you understand the use of protocol variables

---

[*] We have not yet explained how we know *B* sends another acknowledgement. When we discuss specifics of the algorithm we will describe how the protocol guarantees the acknowledgment.

FIGURE 5.12    **Go-back-n Protocol**

```
#define MAX=2ᴷ;                           /* K = number of bits in the frame.number field */
#define N=MAX-1;                          /* N is the maximum window size and largest frame
                                             number */
#define increment(x) x=(x+1) % MAX;       /* Increment x modulo MAX */
void go_back_N;
{
    int w=0;                              /* First position in the window */
    int i=0;                              /* Current size of window */
    int last=N;                           /* Frame number of last data frame received */
    packettype buffer[N];                 /* Packet buffers */
    while (the earth rotates on its axis)
    {
        wait for an event;
        if (event is "packet from patron") && (i<N)
        {                                 /* If frame fits in the window, send it */
            get packet from the patron and store in buffer[(w+i) % MAX] ;
            construct frame with frame.ack=last, frame.type=data, and frame.number=(w+i) % MAX;
            send frame;
            reset frametimer(frame.number); /* Define timer for expected ack of this frame*/
            stop acktimer;                /* Stop ack timer since an ack is piggybacked */
            i++;                          /* Increase window size by 1 */
            continue;                     /* Skip to the end of the while loop */
        }
        if (event is "expired acktimer")
        {                                 /* No frames have been sent in a while. Send a
                                             special ack frame */
            Construct and send a frame with frame.type=ack and frame.ack=last;
            continue;
        }
        if (event is "expired frametimer")
        {                                 /* Have not received an ack in a while; resend all
                                             frames in the window */
            for (j=w; j is "between" w and (w+i-1) % MAX; increment(j) )
            {
                construct and send a data frame as before with packet from buffer[j];
                reset frametimer(j);      /* Start timer for expected ack of this frame* */
            }
            stop acktimer;                /* Stop ack timer; an ack is piggybacked */
            continue;
        }
```

```
              if (event is "damaged frame arrives")
      {
        Construct a frame with frame.type=nak and frame.ack=last and send it;
        stop acktimer;                /* Stop ack timer; an ack is being sent */
        continue;
      }
      if (event is "undamaged frame arrives")
      {                                     /* Remove all frames  between  w and frame.ack from
                                               window */
        receive(frame);
        for (j=w; j is "between" w and frame.ack; increment(j) )
        {
          i--;
          stop frametimer(j);         /* Stop frame timer; the ack has been received */
        }
        w=(frame.ack+1) % MAX;
        if (frame.type==data) && (frame.number==((last+1) % MAX))
            {                         /* If data frame is received in sequence, pass it to
                                         the patron */
                                      /* Ignore any frame received out of sequence */
          increment(last);
          extract packet from the frame and give it to the patron;
          if acktimer not active then
              reset acktimer;         /* Start ack timer for the frame being accepted */
          continue;
        }
        if (frame.type == nak)
        {                             /* resend all buffered packets */
          for (j=w; j is "between" w and (w+i-1) % MAX; increment(j) )
          {
            construct and send a data frame as before with packet from buffer[j];
            reset frametimer(j);      /* Start timer for expected ack of this frame*/
          }
          stop acktimer;             /* Stop ack timer; an ack is piggybacked */
          continue;
        }
          if (frame.type==date) && (frame.number!=(last+1) % MAX)
          {                           /* Send a nak for the frame that was expected */
            construct and send a frame with the frame.type=nak and frame.ack=last;
            stop acktimer;           /* Stop ack timer; an ack is piggybacked */
        }
      }                               /* end of "undamaged frame arrives" event */
    }                                 /* end of while loop */
  }                                   /* end of go_back_N */
```

*w* and *i*. As before, we make no attempt to be syntactically correct or worry about whether the code compiles correctly. The intent is to describe how the protocol works without becoming mired in language-specific details. The important thing to remember is that *both* stations are running a copy of the algorithm as they exchange frames. That is, each station responds to events that correspond to it sending and receiving frames. Read the following discussion and algorithm carefully and slowly; the algorithm is complex.

The algorithm consists of a loop controlled by a condition that should remain for a very long time. If this condition becomes false, protocol failure is of little consequence by comparison. As the algorithm loops, it responds to events as they occur. If multiple events have occurred during one pass of a loop, the algorithm chooses one randomly and responds to it. We do not care how it chooses. That is system dependent. Presumably it will respond to the other events with subsequent passes of the loop.

With each pass through the loop, the station waits for an event to occur. The five events and the protocol's responses are:

1. The patron has delivered a packet. If the window size (*i*) is its maximum value (*N*), nothing happens and the event remains pending until the window size decreases. If the window size is less than *N*, the protocol builds a data frame containing the packet. It also defines a piggyback acknowledgment of the last frame sent (frame.ack = *last*) and specifies the frame number (frame.number = ($w + i$) % MAX where MAX = $2^K$). The expression ($w + i$) % MAX also defines which buffer the packet is stored in. After buffering the packet and sending the frame, it increments the window size by one (*i++*) and resets the corresponding frame timer. It also stops the ack timer.

   The ack timer, as explained previously, detects long periods of time during which no frames are sent. Since one is sent, the ack timer is stopped. The frame timer is to detect a long period of time during which the specified frame is not acknowledged. By resetting a timer,[*] we begin the countdown.

2. An ack timer has expired. When no data frames are sent, the other station does not receive any piggybacked acknowledgments. In order to keep the other station aware of what the current station is receiving, the protocol sends a special acknowledgment frame when the ack timer expires. Its sole purpose is to acknowledge the most recently received frame (frame.ack = last).

3. A frame timer has expired. If the protocol has not received an acknowledgment in a while, something may have gone wrong. Perhaps the acknowledgments were lost or the frames in the current window were lost. Since the protocol does not know which, it assumes the worst and resends all the frames in the window

---

[*] How timers are implemented is not pertinent to our discussion. There could be an internal interrupting clock or the protocol could just build a list of records for each timer, time-stamp each record, and check the list periodically. We leave the details to someone who is willing to implement the protocol as a programming exercise.

("between"[*] buffer slots $w$ and $(w + i - 1)$ % MAX). It also resets each of the frame timers in order to provide enough time for the newly sent frames to get to their destinations and an acknowledgment to return before assuming another error occurred. Last, it stops the ack timer since a piggybacked acknowledgment is also being sent.

4.   A damaged frame arrives. A damaged frame is ignored. If the damaged frame was the expected one, the protocol eventually will ignore all subsequently numbered frames. The protocol therefore must notify the other station that a problem occurred so it can resend all of its buffered frames. The protocol does this by sending a frame of type "nak." The station also acks the last frame it did receive correctly and stops the ack timer.

5.   An undamaged frame arrives. This is the most complex part of the protocol. The first thing the protocol does is receive the frame. Then it checks the piggyback acknowledgment and removes all frames that have been acknowledged from the window. It does this by decreasing the window size by one for each frame "between" $w$ and frame.ack. It also stops the frame timers for the acknowledged frames. It then redefines the beginning of the window ($w$) to locate the first frame not acknowledged (frame.ack + 1) % MAX.

If the frame contains data, the protocol determines whether it has the expected number, ( (*last* + 1) % MAX). Remember, the variable *last* represents the most recently received frame. Thus, the number after it is the one expected. If the received frame is the expected one, the protocol extracts the packet and gives it to the patron. It also increments the value of *last*, thus remembering the new frame most recently received. Then it sets the ack timer, defining the time during which it should send an acknowledgment.

If the frame is a nak frame, the protocol resends all frames in the window as it did with the expired frame timer event. If the frame is a data frame, but not the one expected, the protocol ignores it but sends a nak frame.

## SELECTIVE REPEAT PROTOCOL

The go-back-n protocol works well especially over reliable channels. When frames are rarely lost, damaged, or delayed, the assumption that they arrive in the order they were sent is usually valid. In the few cases where there is a problem, little time is lost by resending all outstanding frames. As the reliability decreases, however, the overhead of resending all frames in a window when just one is damaged or arrives out of order becomes excessive. A logical question to ask is this: Why not allow the receiving station to receive frames out of order and sort them

---

[*] We define "between" $w$ and $(w + i - 1)$ % MAX in a modulo MAX sense. If $w \le (w + i - 1)$ % MAX, "between" has its conventional meaning. If $w \ge (w + i - 1)$ % MAX, "between" includes those numbers from $w$ through MAX − 1 and 0 through $(w + i - 1)$ % MAX. For example, suppose MAX = 16. If $w = 3$ and $(w + i - 1)$ %16 = 12, "between" means values from 3 through 12, inclusive. If w = 12 and $(w + i - 1)$ % 16 = 3, "between" means values 12, 13, 14, 15, 0, 1, 2, and 3.

when they all arrive? This question is answered by another sliding window protocol called **selective repeat**.

The selective repeat protocol is similar to go-back-n in the following ways:

- Frame formats are similar and frames are numbered using a $K$-bit field (Figure 5.9).
- The sender has a window defining the maximum number of outstanding frames.
- It uses piggybacked acknowledgments where possible and does not acknowledge every frame explicitly. If a frame is acknowledged the sending station assumes all prior ones have also been received.
- The protocol uses naks for damaged frames and frames received out of order.
- It uses timers to send special acknowledgment frames during periods of low traffic and to resend frames that have not been acknowledged for a while.

The similarities end here. Probably the most apparent difference is that the selective repeat protocol defines two windows, one each for the sending and receiving parts of the protocol (Figure 5.13). Thus, each station using a selective repeat protocol has both a sending and a receiving window. The sending window is the same as for the go-back-n protocol. It defines which frames may be outstanding.

The receiving window defines which frames can be received. As with the sending window, frames in the receiving window are numbered consecutively (modulo $2^K$ where $K$ = number of bits used for the frame number). Thus, the receiving station is not required to receive frames in order. A frame arriving out of order can be received as long as it is in the window. However, you will recall that part of the protocol's responsibility is to deliver packets to its patron in the proper

FIGURE 5.13 **Sending and Receiving Windows for Selective Repeat Protocol**

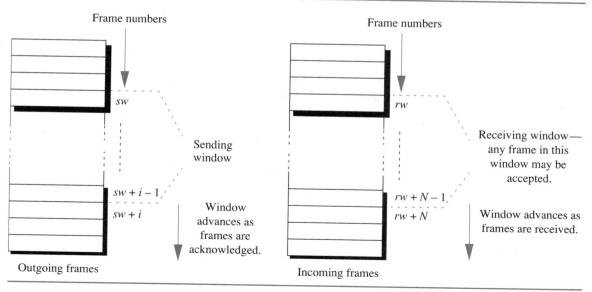

order. Thus the protocol needs a buffer for each frame in the window. Out-of-order frames are buffered until their predecessors arrive. Then the protocol can deliver them in the correct order.

Other differences between selective repeat and go-back-n are listed here, along with the protocols' responses:

- If an arriving frame is in the receiving window, it is buffered. However, it is not given to the patron until all of its predecessors (within the window limits) have also arrived. Thus, whenever a frame is buffered, the protocol checks the window slots prior to the new arrival. If they all contain packets the protocol delivers them to the patron and advances the window.

- Whenever an out-of-order frame is received, the protocol sends a nak for the frame it was expecting. The rationale is that an out-of-order frame signals that something may have happened to the one expected frame. The nak notifies the sender of a possible loss. Remember, though, that as long as the received frame is in the window, it is still accepted.

- If a frame timer expires, only the timed-out frame is resent. With go-back-n, all outstanding frames were resent. With selective repeat, the receiving station may have received the other frames, and unless they also time out, there is no need to resend them.

- If the protocol receives a nak, it resends just the frame specified by the nak. Go-back-n resent all outstanding frames. The rationale for sending just one frame is the same used for a frame timer expiration.

- A piggyback acknowledgment doesn't necessarily acknowledge the frame most recently received. Instead, it acknowledges the frame immediately prior to the one at the beginning of the receiver's window. The rationale is that acknowledging the most recently received frame does not allow the sending station to conclude that prior frames have also been received. Remember, the most recent frame may have arrived out of order. Effectively that would force an acknowledgment for each frame. Acknowledging the last frame to be excluded from the receiving window allows the sending station to conclude that prior frames have also been excluded from the window and thus received. Again, the result is fewer overall acknowledgments.

With the go-back-n algorithm we saw that there were constraints on the window size. Specifically, the window size had to be strictly less than $2^K$ or the protocol could fail with certain events. Constraints also exist with the selective repeat protocol. Suppose the maximum sending window size and receiving window size are equal. In that case, the constraint is that both must be less than or equal to one-half of $2^K$ ($2^{K-1}$).

To see what can happen otherwise, let's consider a couple of examples. In both examples we will use $K = 3$ so that $2^K = 8$. In the first example, suppose the sending window meets the constraint and has a maximum size of 4. But consider what happens if the receiving window is larger, say 5 (Figure 5.14).

At time $t_1$ station $A$ sends the maximum number of frames, frames 0 through 3. Since station $B$ has a window size of 5, it can accept any frame numbered between 0

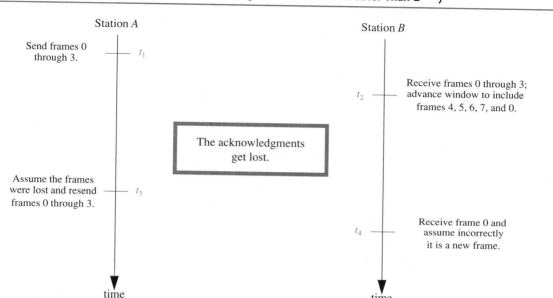

**FIGURE 5.14    Protocol Failure: Receiving Window Size is Greater Than $2^{K-1}$)**

and 4, inclusive. At time $t_2$, $B$ receives frames 0 through 3. Since they are in the window, they are accepted and passed to the patron. $B$ then advances its window to include frames 4, 5, 6, 7, and 0.

Meanwhile, the acknowledgments that $B$ sends are lost. Eventually $A$ gets tired of waiting and assumes something went wrong. Consequently, as dictated by the protocol, $A$ resends frames 0 through 3 (time $t_3$). Since frame 0 is in the receiving window, $B$ accepts it (time $t_4$) not realizing it is a duplicate of the previous frame 0. The protocol fails.

Similar problems can occur if the receiving window size meets the constraint but the sending window does not. For example, suppose this time that $A$'s window size is 5 and $B$'s window size is 4 (Figure 5.15). At time $t_1$ $A$ sends frames 0 through 4. Since $B$'s window size is 4 it can accept only frames 0 through 3. But suppose frame 4 was delayed because it met an attractive frame going the other way and "did lunch" before arriving. Meanwhile frames 0 through 3 arrive and are accepted (time $t_2$). $B$ advances its window to include frames 4 through 7.

When frame 4 eventually arrives, it is within the new window and is accepted. The window advances again and now includes frames 5, 6, 7, and 0. At this point $B$ sends something to $A$ with the acknowledgments piggybacked. The same mysterious gremlin that ate the previous acknowledgments is insatiable and gets another one. Again, $A$ gets tired of waiting and resends frames 0 through 4 (time $t_3$). The frames finally get through (the gremlin is resting from its lunch) and since frame 0 is within

FIGURE 5.15     **Protocol Failure: Sending Window Size is Greater Than $2^{K-1}$**

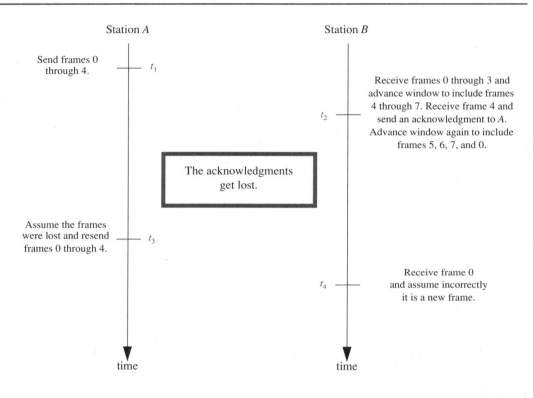

the receiving window, it is accepted (time $t_4$). Again, $B$ does not recognize that it is a duplicate of the previous frame 0, and the protocol fails.

Each of these problems can be corrected by making both window sizes equal to 4. In fact, these problems could have been eliminated by using window sizes of 5 and 3 instead of 5 and 4 (or 3 and 5 instead of 4 and 5). The problem occurs when the receiving window advances to the point of including new frame numbers still in the sending window. This can happen when the two sizes sum to a value larger than $2^K$ (the number of distinct frame numbers). By reducing the window sizes so that this won't happen we eliminate that type of problem. Typically, the window sizes are the same ($2^{K-1}$).

Figure 5.16 contains a partially C-coded algorithm for the selective repeat protocol. It is designed similar to the go-back-n protocol in that it loops continuously, responding to events as they occur. Both sending and receiving windows have size $N = 2^{K-1}$.

**FIGURE 5.16    Selective Repeat Protocol**

```
#define MAX=2^K;                    /* K = number of bits in the frame.number field */
#define N=MAX/2;                     /* N = maximum sending window size, actual receiving
                                        window size, and number of buffers */
#define increment(x) x=(x+1) % MAX;  /* Increment x modulo N */
#define decrement(x) (x==0 ? MAX-1 : x-1)/* Decrement x modulo N */
void selective_repeat;
{
  int frame_no=0;                    /* Maintain frame numbers of outgoing frames */
  int sw=0;                          /* First position in sender's window */
  int rw=0;                          /* First position in receiver's window */
  int i=0;                           /* Current size of sender's window */
  packettype sbuffer[N];             /* Sender's packet buffers */
  packettype rbuffer[N];             /* Receiver's packet buffers */
  int status[N];                     /* Status of frame in receiving window. 1 means it
                                        arrived, 0 means it has not */
  while (Hades does not freeze over)
  {
    wait for an event;
    if (event is "packet from patron") && (i<N)
    {                                /* If frame fits in window, send
                                        it */
      Get packet from the patron and store it in sbuffer[(sw+i) % N];
      construct frame with frame.ack=decrement(rw), frame.type=data, and
         frame.number=frame_no;
      send frame;
      increment(frame_no);           /* Define number of next outgoing frame */
      reset frametimer(frame.number); /* Start timer for expected ack of this frame */
      stop acktimer;                 /* Stop ack timer; an ack is piggybacked */
      i++;                           /* Increase sending window size by 1 */
      continue;                      /* Skip to the end of the while loop */
    }
    if (event is "expired acktimer")
    {                                /* No frames have been sent in a while. Send a special
                                        ack frame */
      Construct and send a frame with frame.type=ack and frame.ack=decrement(rw);
      continue;
    }
    if (event is "expired frametimer")
    {                                /* Have not received an ack in a while; resend
                                        frame */
      fn = frame number corresponding to the timer;
      construct and send as before a data frame with packet from sbuffer[fn % N];
```

```
        reset frametimer(fn);           /* Start timer for expected ack of this frame */
        stop acktimer;                  /* Stop ack timer; an ack is being sent */
        continue;
    }
    if (event is "damaged frame arrives")
    {
        Construct a frame with frame.type=nak and with frame.ack=decrement(rw); send it;
        stop acktimer;                        /* Stop ack timer; an ack is being sent */
        continue;
    }
    if (event is "undamaged frame arrives")
    {                                     /* Remove all frames "between" sw and frame.ack from
                                             sender's window */
        receive(frame);
        for (j=sw; j is "between" sw and frame.ack; increment(j) )
        {
          i--;
          stop frametimer(j);            /* Stop frame timer; the ack has been received */
        }
        sw=(frame.ack+1) % MAX;


    if (frame.type==data) && (frame.number != rw)
    {
        construct a frame with frame.type=nak and frame.ack=decrement(rw) and send it;
        stop acktimer;                   /* Stop ack timer; an ack is being sent */
    }
    if (frame.type==data) && (frame.number is in the receiving window) &&
       (status[frame.number % N]==0)
    {                                          /* If data frame is in the window and has not yet
                                                  arrived, buffer it */
        extract packet from the frame and put in rbuffer[frame.number % N];
        status[frame.number % N]=1;
        for(;status[rw % N]==1; increment(rw) )
        {                                      /* Give received packets stored in consecutive
                                                  window slots to the patron */
        extract packet from rbuffer[rw % N] and give to patron;
        status[rw % N]=0;
        }
        reset acktimer;                  /* Start ack timer for frames being accepted */
    }
    if (frame.type == nak) && ( framenum = (frame.ack+1) % MAX is in the sending window)
    {                                          /* Resend the frame the receiving station expected
                                                  to receive */
```

```
        construct and send a frame with packet from sbuffer[framenum % N];
        reset frametimer(framenum % N);   /* Start timer for expected ack of this frame */
        stop acktimer;                    /* stop ack timer; an ack is being piggybacked */
        continue;
      }
    }
  }
}
```

The algorithm has a few additional variables that the go-back-n algorithm does not have. In addition to the sending buffer (*sbuffer*) there is a receiving buffer (*rbuffer*). Since each window size is $N$, both buffers are defined as packet arrays with $N$ elements. This generates another difference from the go-back-n algorithm. With go-back-n the packets are stored in buffer slots subscripted by the frame number. Here there are twice as many frame numbers as buffer slots. To avoid using an excessive number of buffers, the buffer subscript is equal to the frame number modulo $N$.

Another variable not present in the previous algorithm is the status array. Since arriving frames can be buffered in random order, we use the status array to determine whether a buffer slot is empty. A value of status[$i$] = 1 means buffer number $i$ contains a packet. A value of 0 means it does not.

As the algorithm loops continuously it responds to events. We list the events and the protocol's response here. Because of the similarities to the go-back-n protocol, we will not discuss each step in detail. We will concentrate only on those parts that differ from go-back-n.

1.  The patron has delivered a packet. The protocol responds much as the go-back-n protocol does. If the sending window size is its maximum value, nothing happens. Otherwise it buffers the packet, builds a frame, and sends it. It also piggybacks an acknowledgment for the frame prior to the one in the beginning of the receiving window (frame.ack=decrement(rw)). The macro named "decrement" subtracts 1 modulo $2^K$. Unlike the "increment" macro, it does not change the variable passed to it.

2.  An ack timer has expired. The protocol sends an ack frame acknowledging the frame prior to the one in the beginning of the receiving window.

3.  A frame timer has expired. Instead of resending every outstanding frame, the protocol sends only the frame corresponding to the expired timer. How the frame is determined depends on how the timers are implemented. As before, there could be an interrupt mechanism identifying the frame number or some list containing time values and frame numbers.

4. A damaged frame arrives. The protocol sends a nak frame containing an acknowledgment for the frame prior to the one in the beginning of the receiving window.

5. An undamaged frame arrives. After receiving the frame the protocol removes all frames that have been acknowledged from the window. If the frame contains data, the protocol checks to see if it arrived in order. In other words, is the frame number equal to the number corresponding to the beginning of the receiving window? If not, a nak frame is sent back.

   Next, the protocol checks two more conditions: Is the received frame in the window, and has its packet not yet been buffered? The packet may have been buffered already if the frame arrived previously, but an ack was late in getting back to the sending station. In that case the frame would have timed out and the protocol would have sent it again. By checking the value of status[frame.number % $N$] we avoid the extra work of extracting a packet that is already buffered.

   If both conditions are met, the packet is extracted and stored in the buffer. Next, the protocol determines whether it can advance the receiving window and deliver packets to the patron. It does this by checking consecutive positions in the status array. It stops when it finds the first empty window slot.

   Finally, if the frame is a nak frame, the protocol examines the value in frame.ack. When a nak is sent, the frame.ack field contains the number of the frame prior to the one in the beginning of the receiving window. This means something happened and the receiving protocol did not get the frame it expected ((frame.ack+1) % MAX). If this frame is still in the sending window, the protocol must send it. (Can you construct a scenario in which this frame is not in the sending window?)

## SLIDING WINDOW PROTOCOL EFFICIENCY

Section 5.2 analyzed the unrestricted and stop and wait protocols and showed that the protocol can affect the amount of actual data transmitted per unit of time (effective data rate). We saw that the effective data rate also depended on raw bit rate, distance between stations, frame size, and other factors. A full-fledged analysis for sliding window protocols is much more difficult because other factors contribute to the effective data rate. Such factors include the rate at which frames are lost or damaged, timer values used to determine when special ack frames are sent, and the number of data frames in the reverse direction carrying piggybacked acknowledgments.

We will provide an analysis for sliding window protocols under certain assumptions. Specifically, we will assume that lost or damaged frames do not happen. We also assume consistent traffic in both directions to make the most use of piggybacked acknowledgments. The latter assumption allows us to ignore ack timers because they won't be used. If you are interested in a more complete analysis of sliding window protocols, see references 1 and 2.

All things being equal, a sliding window's effective data rate should lie between that of the unrestricted and stop and wait protocols. But what effective rate can we expect from the sliding window protocols? How does the window size affect it?

Recall from Section 5.2 the following definitions and values used in the examples:

$R$ = transmission rate (10 Mbps or 10 bits per μsec).

$S$ = signal speed (200 meters per μsec).

$D$ = distance between the sender and receiver (200 meters).

$T$ = time to create one frame (1 μsec).

$F$ = number of bits in a frame (200).

$N$ = number of data bits in a frame (160).

$A$ = number of bits in an acknowledgment (40).

Let's add one definition to that list: $W$ = window size (4 frames).

To begin, we observe that two cases can occur with a sliding window protocol. The first is that the sender's window never reaches its maximum size. This will happen when the first acknowledgment arrives before all the frames in the window are sent. Once this happens, and assuming there are no delays at the other end, the sender never has to wait for an acknowledgent. In other words, old frames are removed from the window as fast as new ones are added to it. In effect, the sending protocol behaves just like the unrestricted protocol.

In the second case, when all $W$ frames have been sent and the first acknowledgment has not yet arrived (Figure 5.17), the protocol must wait for it. When it does arrive the protocol then can send the next frame. If the acknowledgments arrive at the same rate that data frames are sent, other $W$ frames are sent before the protocol must wait again. In other words, the protocol sends $W$ frames, waits for the first acknowledgment, sends $W$ more frames, waits for an acknowledgment, and so on. This protocol now resembles stop and wait. However, instead of sending and waiting for individual frames, it sends and waits for a window full of frames.

Mathematically, these two cases can be distinguished by comparing the time to send $W$ frames with the time to send one frame and receive an acknowledgment. From Equation 5.1, the time to build and send one frame is $T + F/R$. Thus, the time to build and send $W$ frames is $W*(T + F/R)$. From Equation 5.2, the time to send a frame and receive an acknowledgment (assuming the acknowledgment comes back right away) is $2*(T + D/S) + (F + A)/R = 2*(T + D/S) + 2F/R = 2*(T + D/S + F/R)$. In this equation we substituted $F$ for $A$ because acknowledgments arrive piggybacked on data frames (of size $F$) instead of via separate ack frames (of size $A$).

Consequently we have:

Case 1 (unrestricted protocol): $W*\left(T + \dfrac{F}{R}\right) > 2*\left(T + \dfrac{D}{S} + \dfrac{F}{R}\right)$;

Case 2 (window-oriented stop and wait): $W*\left(T + \dfrac{F}{R}\right) > 2*\left(T + \dfrac{D}{S} + \dfrac{F}{R}\right)$;

FIGURE 5.17    **Sending All Windowed Frame and Waiting**

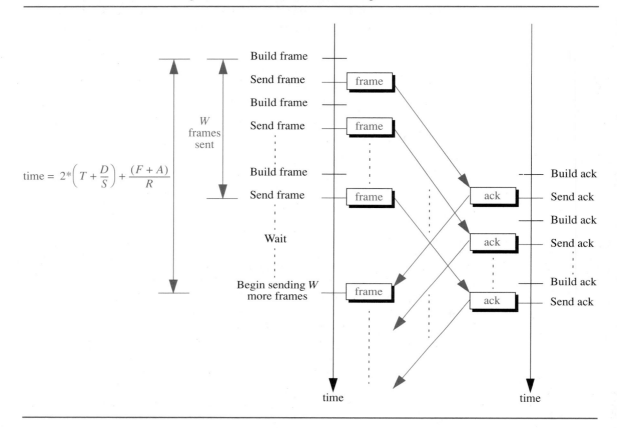

In the first case we have, from Equation 5.5,

$$\text{effective data rate} = \frac{N}{T + \dfrac{F}{R}} \quad \text{(unrestricted version)}$$

Because our sample values satisfy the condition of Case 1, the effective data rate evaluates to

$$\frac{160 \text{ bits}}{1 \ \mu\text{sec} + \dfrac{200 \text{ bits}}{10 \text{ bits}/\mu\text{sec}}} \approx 7.6 \text{ bits}/\mu\text{sec} = 7.6 \text{ Mbps.}$$

The effective data rate for Case 2 is derived from Equation 5.6. This equation was derived under the assumption that just one frame was sent. As we now send $W$

TABLE 5.1     **Comparison of Flow Control Protocols**

|                        | STOP AND WAIT PROTOCOL | UNRESTRICTED PROTOCOL | GO-BACK-N PROTOCOL | SELECTIVE REPEAT PROTOCOL |
|------------------------|------------------------|-----------------------|--------------------|---------------------------|
| Sending window size    | one frame              | unlimited number of frames | less than $2^K$ | less than or equal to $2^K$ — receiving window size |
| Receiving window size  | one frame              | unlimited number of frames | one frame | less than or equal to $2^K$ — sending window size |

frames in the same amount of time, we replace $N$ with $W*N$. Remembering to replace $A$ with $F$, we have

$$\text{effective data rate} = \frac{W*N}{2*\left(T + \dfrac{D}{S}\right) + \dfrac{2F}{R}} \text{ (window-oriented stop and wait version).}$$

Since our sample values do not satisfy the condition of Case 2, using them in this equation would yield a nonsensical value. If we increase the distance ($D$) from 200 meters to 5,000 meters, however, the values will satisfy the condition of Case 2. Using these values, we have

$$\text{effective data rate} = \frac{4*160 \text{ bits}}{2*\left(1\,\mu\sec + \dfrac{5000 \text{ meters}}{200 \text{ meters}/\mu\sec}\right) + \dfrac{2*200 \text{ bits}}{10 \text{ bits}/\mu\sec}}$$

$$\approx 6.96 \text{ bits}/\mu\sec = 6.96 \text{ Mbps for the stop and wait protocol.}$$

### SUMMARY OF PROTOCOLS

We have discussed four flow control protocols: stop and wait, unrestricted, go-back-n, and selective repeat. In some ways (excluding timers, acks, and naks) they can all be viewed as variations of a sliding window protocol (Table 5.1). For example, go-back-n is essentially selective repeat in which the receiving window has just one frame. In stop and wait, both windows have just one frame. The unrestricted protocol has unlimited frame sizes.

## 5.4     Protocol Correctness

In the previous sections we have presented some protocols and the conditions under which they seem to work correctly. Note that we say "seem to work." This uncertainty is necessary because we have not proved that they do work. Providing formal proof or verification that a protocol works is very difficult, and we leave such formal methods to courses in software engineering or advanced courses in protocol design. In this section we introduce two basic tools of verification.

## FINITE STATE MACHINES

Much of what we perceive to be continuous or analog is, in fact, a collection of separate or discrete events. Perhaps the most common example is a motion picture. As we munch popcorn, sip sodas, or stretch our arms and yawn we view the action on the screen as a flowing or continuous movement. In reality, it is a rapid display of still pictures shown through a projector. This view allows us to see a movie in a new way as a collection of individual pictures. It is not the most desirable way to watch some of the classics, but it is precisely the way movie personnel such as special effects technicians must see a movie. They see a sequence of pictures to be spliced, cut, and altered to create the proper effect.

Computer algorithms also can be viewed as a sequence of "pictures." The computers that run them are digital devices. Their actions are controlled and synchronized by internal clocks and driven by the programs they run. Each clock pulse defines a new set of internal values, and, for a brief period (length of a clock pulse) nothing changes. In a sense, the entire architecture is frozen in time and the collection of internal values defines a picture or the **machine state**. With the next clock pulse they change, defining a new machine state. This process continues repeatedly, defining a sequence of machine states.

Similarly, we can view an algorithm as a sequence of states. Each state is defined in part by the values of program variables at an instant in time. In theory, we can categorize (list) all possible states and the events that cause a change from one state to another. The term **finite state machine** (sometimes finite state model) corresponds to this categorization. An event that causes a change of state is called a **state transition**.

Viewing an algorithm in this discrete way allows us to represent it through a directed graph called a **state transition diagram (STD).** Recall that a directed graph consists of a set of vertices and edges. Each vertex represents a state and usually is represented visually by a dot or circle. Each edge is an ordered pair of vertices and usually is represented visually by an arrow from the first vertex to the second. Through graph theory we can analyze the state transition diagram and draw conclusions with regard to the reachability of certain states or possible sequences of events (transitions).

Figure 5.18 shows a state transition diagram. It has six different states, and the arrows show the possible transitions. For example, if the system is currently in state $S_1$, three different events could occur, one causing the system to move to state $S_2$, the others causing it to move to state $S_4$ or $S_5$.

By analyzing the graph we can draw conclusions about the system it represents. For example, note that there are no edges pointing to $S_1$. This means there are no transitions to state $S_1$. If this graph represented an algorithm designed to respond to events, this observation could mean a flaw in the algorithm's logic. That is, the algorithm does not respond to any event that puts the system into state $S_1$. If this is in contrast to what we know about the system, we have detected a flaw.

FIGURE 5.18    **General State Transition Diagram**

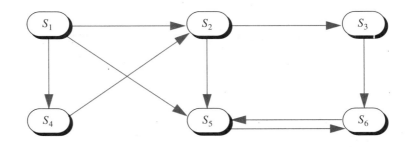

This graph shows another potential problem. Suppose an event occurs that causes a transition to state $S_5$. It can respond only to events that cause it to move to state $S_6$. Once there, it can only go back to state $S_5$. In other words, once this model progresses to state $S_5$ or $S_6$, it will remain in one of those two states forever. This might correspond to an infinite loop or a deadlock (waiting for an event that will never happen). As before, this most likely represents a flaw in our algorithm.

**STD for a Simplified Go-back-n Protocol**    How can we apply this diagram to an actual protocol? First consider the go-back-n protocol with a sender window size of 1 and a one-bit frame number field. Assume that no timeouts or transmission errors occur, all data goes in one direction only (sender to receiver), and the receiver acknowledges each frame received. Essentially, it is the stop and wait protocol with frame numbers. The folllowing events occur:

- Send frame 0.
- Receive frame 0; send ack 0.
- Receive ack 0; send frame 1.
- Receive frame 1; send ack 1.
- Receive ack 1; send frame 0.

We can associate 4 distinct states with this protocol. They are labeled by ordered pairs $(x,y)$ in Figure 5.19. The value of $x$ is either 0 or 1 depending on the ack number the sender is waiting for. Similarly, $y$ is either 0 or 1 depending on the frame number the receiver is waiting for. Thus, state $(0,0)$ means the sender has sent frame 0 and is expecting its acknowledgment. It also means the receiver is waiting for frame 0.

The arrival of frame 0 is an event that causes a transition from state $(0,0)$ to $(0,1)$. The receiver has received frame 0, sent its acknowledgment, and is now waiting for frame 1. However, the sender is still waiting for an acknowledgment to frame 0. When that acknowledgment arrives the sender accepts it, sends frame 1 next and begins waiting for its acknowledgment. This is state $(1,1)$ as the receiver is still waiting for frame 1. The sending and receiving of frames and acknowledgments continues and the states in Figure 5.19 occur in clockwise order.

FIGURE 5.19    **STD for a Stop and Wait Protocol With Frame Numbers**

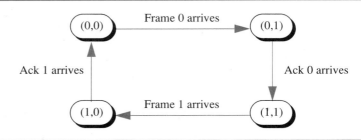

An observant reader might ask: Aren't there really more states associated with this protocol? For example, there is a period of time after the sender receives the acknowledgment but before it sends its next frame. Shouldn't there be a state for which the sender is waiting for the patron to provide a packet? Yes! In fact, we could go to the extreme and define a state corresponding to the execution of each step in the algorithm. But does it pay to do so?

Defining states is an important design issue. Ideally, we would like to define states that represent significant steps in a system's evolution and not worry about insignificant or trivial differences. But determining what is significant is often difficult and depends a great deal on what is being modeled. There are often many levels of refinements to which we can subject an STD. We will give an example showing how to do a refinement and how an STD can locate flaws in a system. Our purpose here, however, is only to introduce the concepts, and we will not provide elaborate STDs. If you are interested in more detail or a higher level of discussion, references 1, 2, 3, and 4 can provide it.

**STD for a Faulty Go-back-n**    Consider the previous version of the go-back-n protocol. This time we assume a window size of 2, which, according to Section 5.3, can fail. To help, Figure 5.20 shows the algorithm with the restrictions (e.g., the sender receives only acks or naks, the receiver receives only data, and frame numbers alternate between 0 and 1).

Figure 5.21 represents a first approximation to an STD showing some states and state transitions. In this case, we categorize each state by what the sender or receiver is waiting for. Specifically, we represent each state by an ordered triple $(a, b, c)$ defined as follows:

- If the sender is waiting for an ack to frame 0 then $a = Y$. Otherwise, $a = N$.
- If the sender is waiting for an ack to frame 1 then $b = Y$. Otherwise, $b = N$.
- If the receiver is waiting for frame 0 then $c = 0$. Otherwise $c = 1$.

For example, suppose the model is in state (N, N, 0). The sender is expecting no acks and the receiver is waiting for frame 0. If the sender sends frame 0 the model moves to state (Y, N, 0). The sender now expects an ack for frame 0. While in this state, two other events can happen. The first is that the sender sends frame 1, in which case the model moves to state (Y, Y, 0). The other event is that frame 0 arrives

FIGURE 5.20    **Go-back-n Protocol for One-Way Data Transfer (Window Size = 2)**

```
void send_data;                                void receive_data;
{                                              {
#define increment(x) x=(x==0 ? 1 : 0);         #define increment(x) x=(x==0 ? 1 : 0);
int w=0;                                       int last=-1;
int i=0;                                       while there are packets to receive
packettype buffer[2];                          {
while there are packets to send                  wait for an event;
{                                                if (event is "damaged frame arrives")
  wait for an event;                             {
  if(event is "packet from patron") && (i<2)       Construct a frame with frame.type=nak and
  {                                                   frame.ack=last and send it;
    get packet from the patron and store in          stop acktimer;
      buffer[(w+i) % 2];                             continue;
    construct and send frame with                  }
      frame.number=(w+i) % 2;                      if (event is "undamaged frame arrives")
    reset frametimer(frame.number);              {
    i++;                                           receive(frame);
    continue;                                      if (frame.number != last)
  }                                                {
  if (event is "expired frametimer")                 increment(last);
  {                                                  extract packet from the frame and give it to the patron;
    resend one or both frames in window;             if acktimer not active then reset acktimer;
    reset one or both frametimers;                   continue;
    continue;                                      }
  }                                                if (frame.number == last)
  if (event is "undamaged frame arrives")          {
  {                                                  construct and send a frame with the
    receive(frame);                                    frame.type=nak and frame.ack=last;
    remove any acknowledged frames from window;      stop acktimer;
    decrement i by number of frames removed;       }
    stop frametimers for acknowledged frames;      if (event is "expired acktimer")
    w=(frame.ack+1) % 2;                          {
    if (frame.type == nak)                           Construct and send a frame with frame.type=ack and
    {                                                  frame.ack=last;
      resend frames in the window;                   continue;
      reset frametimers;                           }
    }                                            }
  }
}
}
```

Sender code                                    Receiver code

FIGURE 5.21     First Approximation STD for Go-back-n (Window Size = 2)

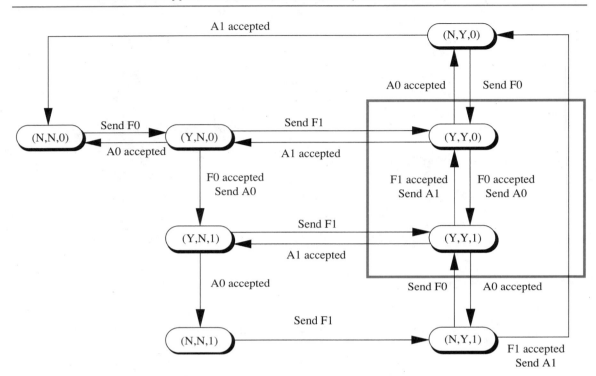

and is accepted and the receiver sends an ack. In this case the receiver now waits for the next frame and the state is (Y, N, 1).

You should take the time to follow some arrows and understand why the states change as shown. As you do so, you might find some anomalous events. For example, consider the following two ways to move from state (N, N, 0) to state (Y, Y, 0):

1. Send frames F0 and F1.
2. Send F0; F0 accepted and A0 sent; Send F1; F1 accepted and A1 sent.

In the first case just one event can happen next: F0 arrives and is accepted. The other events shown (A0 and A1 accepted) cannot happen because neither acknowledgment has been sent yet. Similar reasoning shows that in the second case the only event that can occur next is that A0 or A1 is accepted. F0 cannot arrive because it has already done so. (We will assume that frames do not clone themselves as they travel, resulting in an invasion of an army of frames.) The point is that Figure 5.21 does not distinguish between cases 1 and 2 and shows events that may be impossible depending on how a state was reached.

The problem is that we have not refined our state definitions to accurately portray the system. One solution is to refine the state definitions to include the frames actually in transit, which will allow us to distinguish between the two cases (and others). It will also create additional states and state transitions and make the diagram more complex.

Figure 5.22 shows a partial refinement of the STD's boxed-in region from Figure 5.21. This refinement also shows how the STD can locate flaws in our design. We have further defined each state by specifying not only what the stations are waiting for but what is actually in transit. We represent this by adding an ordered pair $(x,y)$ to each state. Variable $x$ defines which frames are actually in transit (0 for frame 0, 1 for frame 1, B for both, and N for neither). Similarly, $y$ specifies which acknowledgment is in transit. For example, state (Y, Y, 0) : (B, N) means the sender is waiting for an acknowledgment to frames 0 and 1 and that these frames are still in transit. The receiver is waiting for frame 0 and there are no acknowledgments in transit. We have also included additional events that cause state changes. (There are other events we have not shown, but these are sufficient for our needs.)

We next show how this refined model can expose a problem. Recall from your data structures course that a path through a graph is a list of nodes where every two adjacent nodes in the list are connected by an edge. In an STD, a path defines a sequence of events. The graph of Figure 5.22 shows a path (actually a cycle) in which both (Y, Y, 0) and (Y, Y, 1) appear. Consider what happens if we follow the cycle repeatedly. This defines a sequence of events that causes the receiver to alternately expect and receive frames 0 and 1. However, none of the events corresponds

FIGURE 5.22    **Partial Refinement of STD from Figure 5.21**

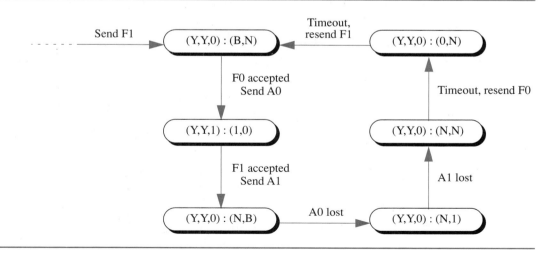

to sending new frames (just resending old ones). This means the receiver repeatedly accepts new frames even though no new ones are being sent. That is, the receiver is accepting old frames as if they are new, just as we discussed in Section 5.3.

In general, STDs can be used to trace sequences of events and intermediate states. If a path exhibits state changes that should not occur given the events, there is a flaw in the model.

## PETRI NETS

Like a finite state model, a Petri net uses a graph to represent states and transitions, but the way it does so is different. A Petri net consists of four parts:

1. **Places**. Represented visually by circles, places correspond to part of a state. This is one difference from the finite state model. Each vertex of an STD represents a complete state; with a Petri net we may need several places to represent the complete state. We'll see an example shortly.

2. **Transitions**. Represented visually by a short horizontal or vertical line, transitions show movement between places.

3. **Arrows**. Arrows connect a place to a transition or vice versa. A place at the source of the arrow is called the **input place** of the transition to which the arrow points. Any place pointed to by the arrow is the **output place** of the transition at the arrow's source.

4. **Tokens**. Tokens, represented by heavy dots inside places, collectively define the current state of the system.

A Petri net can be represented by a graph. A graph vertex may be either a place or a transition, and an edge is an arrow. With STDs, state transitions are defined by moving from one vertex to another along an edge. With Petri nets, they are defined by the way tokens move from one place to another. Thus, the next step is to define the rules by which tokens can move:

- A transition is **enabled** if each of its input places contains a token.
- Any enabled transition can **fire**. That is, tokens are removed from each of the input places and tokens are stored in each of the output places. After firing, there may be more or fewer tokens, depending on the number of input places and output places.
- One transition fires at a time. If several transitions are enabled, however, the choice of transition is indeterminate. For our purposes, this means the choice is made arbitrarily. Because firing transitions will correspond to real events, we do not want rules to dictate the order in which they occur.

Part (a) of Figure 5.23 shows a Petri net just before firing. There are two transitions T1 and T2, but only T1 is enabled (all of its input places have tokens). Part b shows the Petri net after firing. The tokens are removed from each input place of T1. Next a token is put into each of the output places of T1. Other tokens in places associated with a different transition remain where they are.

FIGURE 5.23    **Petri Net Before and After Firing**

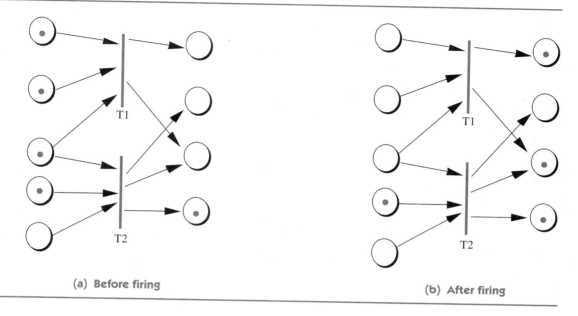

(a) **Before firing**                              (b) **After firing**

Next, let's see how we can use a Petri net to model a protocol. The one we will use is the go-back-n protocol of Figure 5.20, changed to use a window of size 1. Figure 5.24 shows part of the Petri net for it. As before, we have left out some parts of the Petri net to simplify the diagram and our discussion.

Instead of trying to describe the state of the system in one vertex, we divide the system into its parts and represent the state of each. In this case, the system consists of a sender, receiver, and channel between them. Thus, the system state depends on what the sender and receiver are waiting for and what is on the channel, just as with our previously refined STD. Specifically, the sender has two states, each represented by a place. The sender is waiting for an acknowledgment for frame 0 (Wait for A0) or for frame 1 (Wait for A1). The receiver also has two states: waiting for frame 0 (F0) or frame 1 (F1). The four places in the middle correspond to what is on the channel. F0 and F1 are places corresponding to frame 0 or 1 being transmitted. A0 and A1 correspond to the acknowledgments for frame 0 or 1 being transmitted.

The tokens in Figure 5.24 show the current state of the system. The sender has sent frame 0, which is currently on the channel. The receiver is waiting for it and the sender is waiting for an acknowledgment of it.

Next let's consider the transitions. Transitions correspond to events that can occur, and their input places correspond to states that must exist before the event can occur. For example, look at the first transition for the sender labeled "Receive A1, Send F0." It has two input places, "Wait for A1" for the sender and "A1" for the channel. A firing of this transition means the sender has received an ack for frame 1

FIGURE 5.24    **Partial Petri Net for Go-back-n with Sender Window Size = 1**

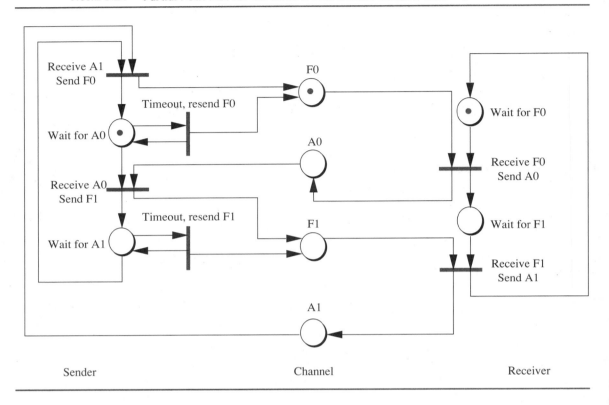

and has sent the next frame, F0. However, for this to occur the sender must be waiting for A1, and A1 must be on the way. Thus for the transition to fire, tokens must be in these two input places. We can make similar arguments about the other transitions for the sender and the receiver.

This Petri net also has two timeout transitions. Each has one input place corresponding to the sender waiting for an ack. For example, suppose the sender is waiting for A0 (token in that place). The corresponding timeout transition is enabled. This does not mean it will fire, however. It means it could fire. If a frame timer expires, the timeout transition fires. If that happens, the token is removed from the input place and others are placed in the two output places. One of them is the F0 place for the channel, indicating frame 0 is being sent. The other output place is the same as the input place, meaning the sender is again waiting for A0.

Confused? Let's trace token movement for a sequence of typical events. Parts (a) through (d) of Figure 5.25 show Petri nets corresponding to successive transition firings. Places, transition, and arrows are as in Figure 5.24, but we have eliminated the labels to simplify the diagram. The token placement in Figure 5.25a is the same as in Figure 5.24. The sender is waiting for A0, the receiver is waiting for F0, and F0 is on the channel. Together they define the system state. At this point two transitions are enabled (marked with *): the first timeout transition for the sender and the transition for the receiver labeled (from Figure 5.24) "Receive F0, Send A0."

Suppose the latter transition fires. The tokens are removed from the two input places and new ones put into places as shown in Figure 5.25b. The system is in a new state. The sender is still waiting for A0, which is now on the channel. The

**FIGURE 5.25    Firing Sequence for Normal Exchange of Frames and Acknowledgments**

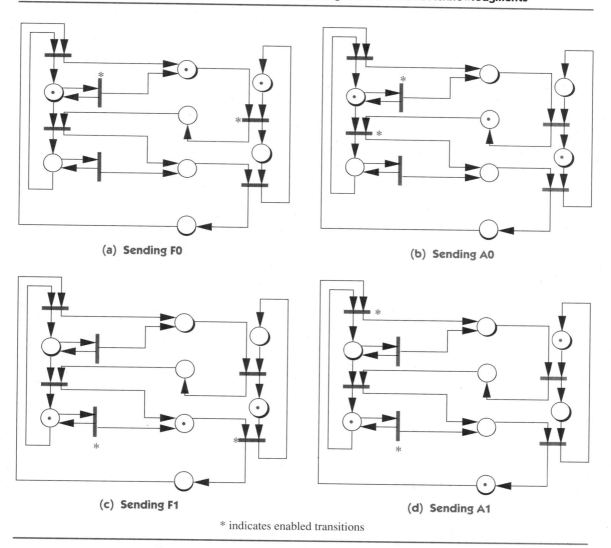

(a) Sending F0

(b) Sending A0

(c) Sending F1

(d) Sending A1

* indicates enabled transitions

receiver is now waiting for F1. Again, two transitions in Figure 5.25b are enabled. They are the timeout and the reception of A0. Again, the latter transition fires, and the tokens are moved to their positions in Figure 5.25c. Again the system is in a new state. The sender has sent F1, which is on the channel, and is waiting for A1. Meanwhile the receiver is still waiting for F1. If the receiver gets the frame, the tokens move to their positions in Figure 5.25d. The sender is still waiting for A0, which is on its way, and the receiver is waiting for F0. If the acknowledgment arrives the Petri net changes again and token placement is as in Figure 5.25a. Thus, if frames and acknowledgments are communicated without error these four Petri nets describe the changing system states.

Earlier we stated that the Petri net of Figure 5.24 does not include transitions for every possible event. For example, there is always a token in one of the channel's places implying there is always something on the channel. This, of course, is not true. A token on the channel could get lost or destroyed, resulting in a state in which the sender and receiver both are waiting but nothing is on the channel (something our Petri net doesn't show). This state is fixed easily by making each of the channel's places an input place for a new transition labeled "lost." None of these transitions would have an output place. Thus, whenever something is on the channel one of these transitions is enabled. If it fires the token is removed from the input place. With no output place, that token disappears. Eventually a timeout transition would fire and place a token into one of the places again.

Another way we could refine the Petri net is to divide the sender's transitions into two separate ones. In our model, when the sender gets an ack it immediately sends out the next frame. We assume there are always frames to send and that may not be the case. We could define new sender places corresponding to situations in which the sender has to wait for a packet from its patron. We encourage you to consider some of the cases and redraw the Petri nets (see questions at the end of the chapter).

As with STDs, Petri nets can be analyzed to look for protocol errors. For example, if tokens could never reach certain places, certain states could not be represented by the Petri net. If they are known to be possible, our model would be in error. Another error would be indicated if tokens moved through certain places without landing in places in between. For example, suppose a sequence of firings resulted in Petri nets in which a token moves alternately between the receiver's places in Figure 5.24. If, in these same Petri nets, one of the sender's places never gets a token, an error exists because the Petri nets indicate the receiver is getting frames but the sender is not sending them.

If you are interested in further study or other examples of Petri nets, see references 1,2, and 5.

## 5.5   Data Link Control Protocols

We have discussed general concepts of flow control and the maintenance of data frame exchange. Now it is time to present some specific protocols. Those we present here are called data link control protocols because they are found in or are similar to protocols in the OSI data link layer. Their primary responsibility is to manage and control the flow of frames between two stations.

## HIGH-LEVEL DATA LINK CONTROL (HDLC)

HDLC is a **bit oriented protocol** that supports both half-duplex and full-duplex communications. (We discussed half duplex and full duplex in Section 3.1.) By "bit oriented" we mean that the protocol treats frames as bit streams. In other words, it does not recognize or interpret byte values as some protocols discussed previously (such as X-ON/X-OFF) do. Defined by ISO, HDLC is used worldwide.

Three types of stations run the HDLC protocol:

- **Primary station** (sometimes called the **host station** or **control station**). It manages data flow by issuing commands to other stations and acting on their responses. We will see some examples later in this section. It also may establish and manage connections with multiple stations.

- **Secondary station** (sometimes called the **target station** or **guest station**). It responds to commands issued by a primary station. Furthermore, it can respond to just one primary station at a time. It does not issue commands to other stations (although it can send data).

- **Combined station**. As the name implies, it can act as both primary and secondary station. It can issue commands to and respond to commands from another combined station.

Stations running HDLC can communicate in one of three modes:

- **Normal response mode (NRM)**. In NRM, the primary station controls the communication. That is, the secondary station can send only when the primary station instructs or allows it to do so. This operational mode is common in two configurations. In a **point-to-point link** (Figure 5.26a) the primary station communicates with a single secondary station. In a **multipoint link** (sometimes called a **multidrop link**), the primary station can communicate with several secondary stations (see Figure 5.26b). Of course, it must manage and keep separate the different sessions it maintains with each of them.

- **Asynchronous response mode (ARM)**. Like NRM, ARM involves communication between a primary station and one or more secondary stations. Here, however, the secondary station is more independent. Specifically, it can send data or control information to the primary station without explicit instructions or permission to do so. However, it cannot send commands. The responsibility for establishing, maintaining, and eventually ending the connection still resides with the primary station. This mode is most common in the point-to-point links of Figure 5.26a.

- **Asynchronous balanced mode (ABM)**. ABM is used in configurations connecting combined stations (Figure 5.26c). Either station can send data, control information, or commands. This is typical in connections between two computers and in the X.25 interface standard (discussed in Chapter 7).

FIGURE 5.26    **HDLC Configurations**

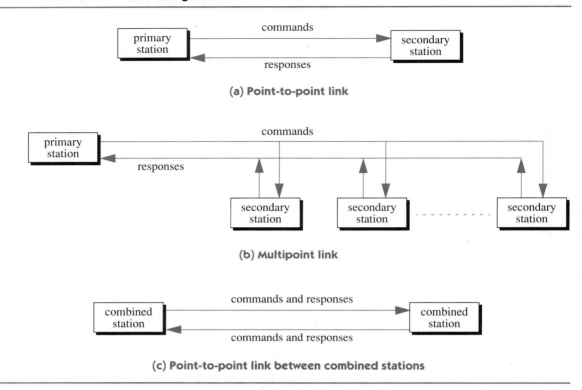

**(a) Point-to-point link**

**(b) Multipoint link**

**(c) Point-to-point link between combined stations**

**Frame Format**    HDLC frames are similar to the general formats discussed previously. Figure 5.27 shows the frame format. Some of the fields can occur in one of two sizes. The smaller size defines a **standard format** and the larger an **extended format**. Which format is used must be decided when the link is established.

There are three different types of frames. They differ in the contents of the control field and whether the frame actually contains data. We will first discuss the fields common to all types and then differentiate among them.

FIGURE 5.27    **HDLC Frame Format**

number of bits:

| 8 | 8 or 16 | 8 or 16 | variable | 16 or 32 | 8 |
|---|---|---|---|---|---|
| Flag | Address | Control | - - - - - Data - - - - - | FCS | Flag |

The **flag field** marks the beginning and end of each frame and contains the special bit pattern 01111110. A station receiving this pattern knows an HDLC frame is on its way. Since the frame size may vary, the station examines arriving bits looking for this pattern to detect the frame's end. This pattern presents a problem: Since the protocol is bit oriented, the data fields (and others, as well) can consist of arbitrary bit patterns. If the flag pattern exists in another field, won't the station interpret it incorrectly as the end of the frame? We certainly do not want to constrain the data to disallow certain bit patterns from appearing.

Fortunately, this problem has a relatively easy solution called **bit stuffing**. The sending station monitors the bits between the flags before they are sent. If it detects five consecutive 1s (Figure 5.28), it inserts (stuffs) an extra 0 after the fifth 1. This breaks any potential flag pattern and prevents it from being sent. Now the data is no longer correct so the receiving station must correct it. Whenever five consecutive 1s are followed by a 0, it assumes the 0 was stuffed and removes it. Since the flag field is not subjected to bit stuffing by the sending station, it is the only place where the flag pattern can appear.

The **address field** is self-explanatory. It has 8 bits for the standard format and 16 bits for the extended. The extended format allows a greater number of stations to

FIGURE 5.28     **Bit Stuffing**

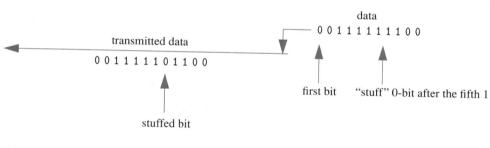

(a) **More than five consecutive 1's**

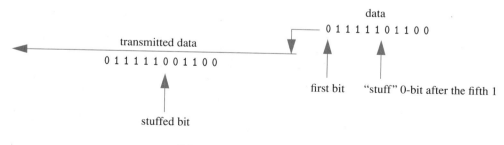

(b) **Five consecutive 1's**

be identified. If a primary station sends the frame, the address field defines the identity of the secondary station where the frame is being sent. This is necessary in multipoint configurations where there are several secondary stations. If a secondary station is sending the frame, the address field contains the sender's identity. As there is only one primary station and secondary stations do not send to each other, the destination address is not needed. The source address is needed to let the primary station know where a frame originates.

In some cases the field may contain a **group address** or **broadcast address** (all 1s). A frame with a group address is accepted by all secondary stations in a predefined group. One with a broadcast address is accepted by every secondary station with whom the primary station has established a link.

The **data field** contains the data, and its length is variable. We will see that in some cases there is no data and this field does not exist. The (**frame check sequence**) **FCS** is used for CRC error detection. The field may be 16 (standard format) or 32 (extended format) bits long. Most common is a 16-bit field defined as described in Section 4.3 using the CRC polynomial $x^{16} + x^{12} + x^5 + 1$.

The **control field** is 8 (standard format) or 16 (extended format) bits long and is used to send status information or issue commands. Its contents depend on the frame's type. The three types are information frame, supervisory frame, and unnumbered frame. Figure 5.29 shows the format for each using the standard format. With

FIGURE 5.29    **Control Fields for HDLC Frames**

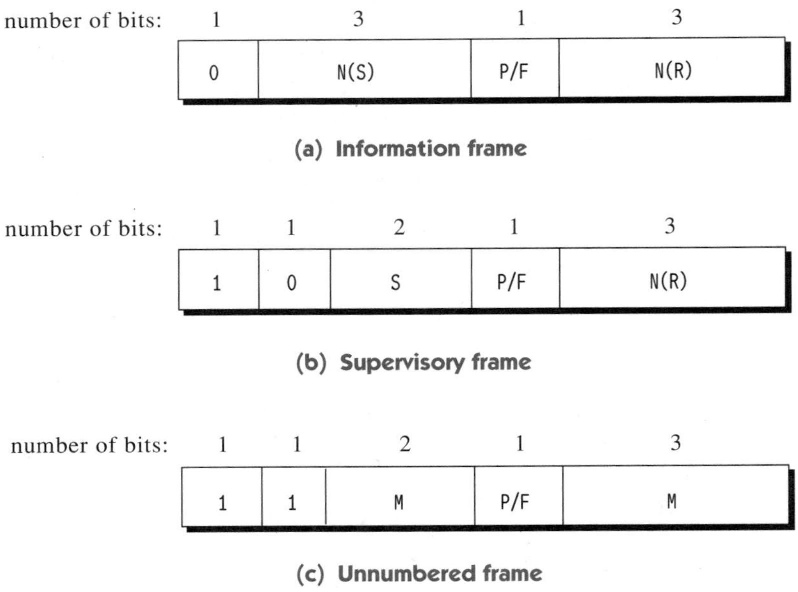

| number of bits: | 1 | 3 | 1 | 3 |
|---|---|---|---|---|
| | 0 | N(S) | P/F | N(R) |

(a) **Information frame**

| number of bits: | 1 | 1 | 2 | 1 | 3 |
|---|---|---|---|---|---|
| | 1 | 0 | S | P/F | N(R) |

(b) **Supervisory frame**

| number of bits: | 1 | 1 | 2 | 1 | 3 |
|---|---|---|---|---|---|
| | 1 | 1 | M | P/F | M |

(c) **Unnumbered frame**

the extended format, the fields are larger or the frame contains unused bits the differences are not important here.

The first one or two bits define the frame type. As Figure 5.29 shows, an information frame always starts with 0; a supervisory frame always starts with 10; and an unnumbered frame always starts with 11. These definitions allow the receiving stations to determine the type of an arriving frame.

**Information frames** are used primarily to transfer information (data field of Figure 5.27) using either the go-back-n or the selective repeat sliding window protocols. The fields N(R) and N(S) are similar to what we previously called frame.ack and frame.number, respectively. Specifically, N(R) (number of received frame) is a piggyback acknowledgment indicating that all frames up to N(R) − 1 have been received. Equivalently, the station is currently expecting a frame numbered N(R). Similarly, N(S) is the number of the frame being sent. The fields N(R) and N(S) are either 3 bits (standard frame) or 7 bits (extended frame) long. Consequently, frame numbers and arithmetic such as N(R) − 1 are modulo 8 ($2^3$) or modulo 128 ($2^7$).

The P/F bit stands for poll/final bit. Its meaning depends on whether the frame is being sent by a primary (poll bit) or secondary station (final bit). The primary station can request a response from a secondary station by sending it a frame with the P bit set to 1. For example, the primary station may want to know if the secondary station has any data to send or may request its status with regard to some ongoing process. In any case, the secondary station is expected to respond (we'll see some examples shortly). When sent by a secondary station, the F bit indicates the current frame is the last in a sequence of frames.

**Supervisory frames** are used by either station to indicate its status or to nak frames received incorrectly. The N(R) and P/F bits do the same thing as in information frames. The differences are in the 2-bit S field, which is defined as follows:

• **RR: Receive ready** (00). When a station wants to indicate it is ready and able to receive information it sends an RR frame. The RR frame is also used to acknowledge received frames periodically when there is no outgoing data (recall the discussion of ack timers in Section 5.3).

• **REJ: Reject** (01). This is similar to the naks discussed using the go-back-n protocol. It requests that the other station resend all outstanding frames starting with the one whose number is specified by N(R). This can occur if a frame arrives out of order or damaged.

• **RNR: Receive not ready** (10). If a station's buffers are filling or it detects an error on its side of the link, it can stop the flow of incoming frames by sending an RNR frame.

• **SREJ: Selective reject** (11). This is similar to the naks discussed using the selective repeat protocol. It requests that the other station resend the frame whose number is specified by N(R).

Whereas the information and supervisory frames control and manage the transfer of frames, the **unnumbered frames** establish how the protocol will proceed. For example, we stated previously that HDLC can use go-back-n or selective repeat, it can use different frame sizes, and it can communicate in one of three modes. How do the stations decide when to do what?

Part (c) of Figure 5.29 shows the unnumbered frame format. The two fields marked M together define five flags whose values define the communication protocol. A primary station sends commands and a secondary station responds to commands by setting these flags appropriately. Table 5.2 lists some of the possible commands and responses that can be coded in an unnumbered frame.

TABLE 5.2    **HDLC Unnumbered Frame Functions**

| FUNCTION (C=COMMAND; R=RESPONSE) | MEANING |
|---|---|
| SNRM: Set normal response mode (C) | Communicate using normal response mode and standard frame format. |
| SNRME: Set normal response mode extended (C) | Communicate using normal response mode and extended frame format. |
| SARM: Set asynchronous response mode (C) | Communicate using asynchronous response mode and standard frame format. |
| SARME: Set asynchronous response mode extended (C) | Communicate using asynchronous response mode and extended frame format. |
| SABM: Set asynchronous balanced mode (C) | Communicate using asynchronous balanced mode and standard frame format. |
| SABME: Set asynchronous balanced mode extended (C) | Communicate using asynchronous balanced mode and extended frame format. |
| DISC: Disconnect (C) | Initiates a disconnection between the two stations. The disconnection is completed when the other station responds with a UA function (see below). |
| RSET: Reset (C) | Each station tracks the values of $N(R)$ and $N(S)$ as frames come and go. If an error occurs (say at a higher level than HDLC), the data link control may have to reinitialize the frame exchange. RSET resets the tracked values of $N(R)$ and $N(S)$ to a previously established value. |
| SIM: Set initialization mode (C) | Instructs the other station to initialize its data link control functions. |
| UP: Unnumbered poll (C) | A poll (request) to get status information from a specified station. |
| UI: Unnumbered information (C or R) | Used to send status information. Typically sent following a UP or SIM. |
| XID: Exchange identification (C or R) | Allows two stations to exchange their identification and status. |
| RIM: Request initialization mode (R) | Request from a secondary station that the primary station send SIM. |
| RD: Request disconnect (R) | Request from a secondary station that the primary station initiate a disconnect by sending a DISC frame. |

| DM: | Disconnect mode (R) | Tells the primary station that the secondary station is not operational (i.e., in a disconnect mode). |
|---|---|---|
| UA: | Unnumbered acknowledgment (R) | Used to acknowledge previously sent commands such as a set mode or disconnect. |
| TEST: | Test (C or R) | Request to the other station to send a test response. The sending station may put something in the data field for the receiving station to return to test the link. |
| FRMR: | Frame reject (R) | Used to indicate an arriving frame was rejected. The REJ function rejects frames that are damaged or received out of order. FRMR is used if, for example, a control field is defined incorrectly or a frame that was never sent is acknowledged. |

**HDLC Example**    The following example describes the process of establishing a link, exchanging frames, and terminating the link. Figure 5.30 shows a possible sequence of exchanges between two stations, A (primary station) and B (secondary station). We will assume a go-back-n protocol so that the receiving windows have 1 frame. Vertical arrows represent passing time. Slanted arrows between them indicate the sending of frames and their direction. Text at the arrow's source specifies the frame's contents. Text at the arrow's end specifies what happened when the frame arrived. To simplify the figure, no text appears in cases where the frame was accepted without error.

To begin, Figure 5.30a shows how a connection might be established. Station B starts by sending an unnumbered frame with the function RIM. This is a request that the primary station (A) send an unnumbered frame with function code SIM. When B receives the SIM it begins its initialization procedure as mentioned previously and acknowledges receipt of the SIM by sending another unnumbered frame with function UA. When A receives UA it knows that B is initializing. In this case, A decides the response mode will be ARM and sends another unnumbered frame with that function. When B receives the frame, it again acknowledges by sending another UA frame. When A receives the acknowledgment the stations are ready to communicate.

Figure 5.30b shows an example exchange of frames. Since the response mode is ARM, A and B both begin sending. B sends its first two frames with frame numbers $N(S) = 0$ and 1. In both cases, $N(R)$ is 0. Since B has not received anything yet, it is expecting the first frame (number 0). Meanwhile, A sends its first three frames with numbers $N(S) = 0$, 1, and 2. In the first two frames, $N(R) = 0$ because A has not received anything yet. However, A receives a frame from B after it sends its second frame. Consequently, with the third frame, A sets $N(R) = 1$, thus acknowledging its receipt of frame 0.

Next, suppose the second frame that A sends arrives damaged. B sends a supervisory frame containing the function code REJ and $N(R) = 1$. This frame does two things: It acknowledges that B received frame 0 from A and states that an error occurred and that A should resend everything beginning with frame 1. Meanwhile, B

FIGURE 5.30    **Communicating Using HDLC**

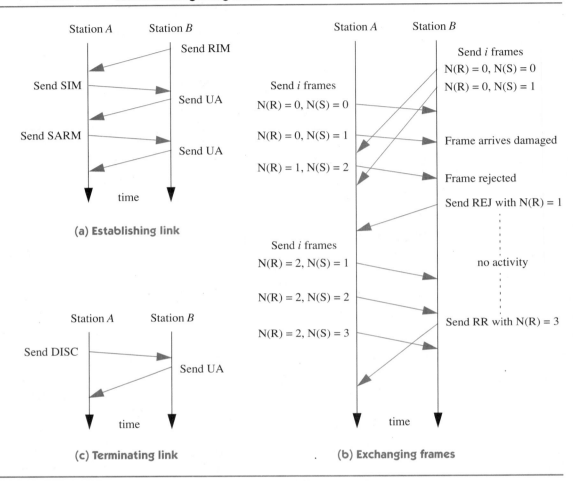

(a) **Establishing link**

(c) **Terminating link**

(b) **Exchanging frames**

is still expecting frame 1 so when the next frame arrives, *B* rejects it as being out of order.

Eventually, *A* receives the REJ frame and resends frames beginning with the specified number. If it has three frames to send they contain N(S) = 1, 2, and 3. Note that N(R) is now 2 in each of these frames. This is because while we were discussing what *B* did with the damaged frame, *A* received another (its second) *i* frame. These three frames eventually reach *B*. However, *B* has entered a period of inactivity and cannot piggyback any acknowledgments. Consequently, between the arrival of frames 1 and 2, its timer expires. It sends a supervisory frame with function code RR, which reaffirms that *B* is still ready to accept frames and acknowledges the receipt of frame number 2 (sets N(R) = 3). Using RR here is a lot like listening on the telephone to your eccentric aunt complain about her neighbors. You hold the phone by your ear while you make a batch of cookies and respond every five minutes or so with a "Yes, Aunt Mabel."

Frame exchanges like this occur until both stations have finished sending. Station A decides it is time to disconnect by sending an unnumbered frame with function code DISC (Figure 5.30c). When B receives the frame, it acknowledges it by sending a UA frame. When A receives the acknowledgment, it knows both sides have agreed to disconnect and it terminates the link. (Don't hang up on Aunt Mabel without her consent; you might be in her will!)

**Other Bit-Oriented Protocols**     HDLC is not the only bit-oriented protocol. Several others are very similar to HDLC. Some are actually modified subsets of HDLC, and others provide some additional functions. In general, their frame formats and function codes differ little from the previous discussions. Therefore, we will not discuss each in detail, but will mention them and where they are used. If you are interested in the detailed differences between them and HDLC, references 6 and 7 provide more in-depth discussions. The other protocols are:

- **Synchronous data link control (SDLC)**. HDLC was derived from SDLC, which was developed by IBM in the early 1970s. IBM had submitted SDLC to the ISO for acceptance. ISO modified it and renamed it HDLC. Effectively, SDLC is IBM's equivalent to HDLC. (If you sit on the other side of the fence, HDLC is ISO's equivalent to SDLC). SDLC uses go-back-n and is part of IBM's Systems Network Architecture (SNA), discussed in Chapter 8. It is typically used in IBM terminal-to-computer communications.

- **Advanced data communications control procedure (ADCCP)**. IBM also submitted SDLC to ANSI for acceptance. As all good standards organizations do, they modified it and renamed it ADCCP.

- **Link access protocols (LAP)**. There are several link access protocols. The CCITT adopted and modified HDLC for use in its X.25 network interface standard (discussed in Chapter 7). Originally it was labeled LAP, but subsequently was changed to **LAPB** (B for balanced). It allows devices to be connected to packet-switched networks. A variation on LAPB is LAPD, the link control for the Integrated Services Digital Network (ISDN). ISDN is an entirely digital communication system being defined by CCITT. It is designed to eventually replace the telephone system. LAPD allows devices to communicate over the ISDN D-channel (discussed in Chapter 8).

- **Logical link control (LLC)**. LLC (an IEEE standard) is also similar to HDLC but is used in local area networks (LAN). It allows LANs to connect to other LANs and to wide area networks.

## BINARY SYNCHRONOUS COMMUNICATIONS (BSC) PROTOCOL

The binary synchronous control protocol, often referred to as the **BSC** or **bisync protocol**, was made popular by IBM. It is used with synchronous, half-duplex communications and uses a stop and wait flow control. As with the previous protocols, it can be used in point-to-point or multipoint connections. It is perhaps most typical in multipoint connections where the primary station is a CPU and the secondary ones are terminals. It is older than the bit-oriented protocols we have discussed, but it is still used in enough applications to warrant its discussion.

Unlike the previously discussed protocols BSC is **byte oriented.** That is, the stations interpret frames as a sequence of control and data bytes. Byte values can be interpreted using either the ASCII or EBCDIC character sets.[*] BSC uses several different frame formats. Figure 5.31 shows three typical ones, a control frame format and two data frame formats. We discuss the control frame first and then discuss the difference between the transparent and nontransparent data frames shortly. In each case, the frame starts with two **SYN characters**. Primarily, they alert the receiving station that a frame is arriving. The bit patterns also allow the station to synchronize byte acceptance with the rate at which the bytes are arriving. Two SYN characters are used to make sure the receiving station has sufficient time to synchronize.

The SYN bytes are followed by one or more control bytes. In a control frame (Figure 5.31c), the control bytes constitute the bulk of the information transmitted. Control information is similar to what we have discussed previously. It can acknowledge frames received correctly, nak those received incorrectly, or request a response from another station. We will discuss a few of them in detail. Table 5.3 provides a short summary of typical control characters and their function.

FIGURE 5.31     **BSC Frame Formats**

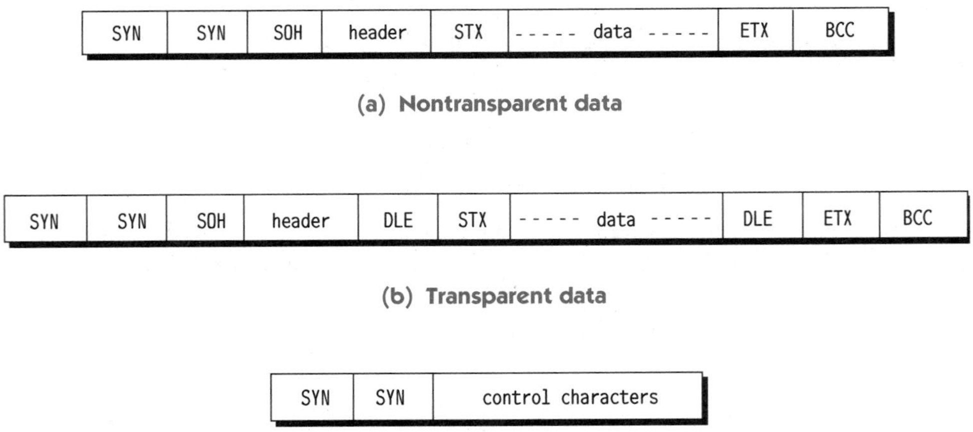

(a) **Nontransparent data**

(b) **Transparent data**

(c) **Control frame**

---

[*] It may be interesting to note that BSC can also be used with a lesser-known 6-bit code called Transcode.

TABLE 5.3    **BSC Control Characters**

| BSC CHARACTER | MEANING |
| --- | --- |
| ACK: **ACK**nowledge | Verifies that a block of data was received correctly. Since BSC is a half-duplex, stop and wait protocol, ACK also tells the sender that it may send the next frame. |
| DLE: **D**ata **L**ink **E**scape | Typically used with STX. The DLE/STX sequence specifies that all successive bytes, including control bytes up to a DLE/ETX or DLE/ETB sequence, are to be treated as data. Afterward, any control character is interpreted accordingly. |
| ENQ: **ENQ**uiry | Requests a response from another station. Responding stations might send a data frame or an ACK or NAK depending on their status. |
| EOT: **E**nd **O**f **T**ransmission | Indicates end of transmission and tells the stations they may disconnect. |
| ETB: **E**nd of **T**ransmission **B**lock | If a message requires many frames, ETB indicates the end of an intermediate frame. |
| ETX: **E**nd of **T**e**X**t | Indicates the end of the last frame in a multiframe message or the end of a frame in a single-frame message |
| NAK: **N**egative **A**c**K**nowledgment. | Indicates the previous frame was received incorrectly. |
| NUL: **NUL**l | Used as a filler character where frames must be a minimal length. |
| SOH: **S**tart **O**f **H**eader | Indicates the start of header information in the frame. |
| STX: **S**tart of **T**e**X**t | Indicates the start of data within the frame. |
| SYN: **SYN**chronous idle | Two SYN characters are at the start of each frame alerting the station of an arriving frame. |

In a data frame, the first control byte is SOH (start of header). It tells the receiving station that successive bytes in the arriving frame contain header information. Header information will vary, but typically contains the identity or address of the sending or receiving stations. For example, a destination identifier is needed when a primary station is sending something over a multipoint line and a receiving identifier is needed when a primary station is receiving something from it.

The header information is followed by an STX character (Figure 5.31a) or a DLE-STX combination (Figure 5.31b). In the first case, STX indicates the start of text. This means that successive bytes represent data. However, since the number of data bytes can vary, the protocol needs a way to specify the end of them. It does this by using the ETX (end of text) character. Thus, a receiving station receives and accepts the bytes as data until it encounters ETX.

In some cases an ETB character (Table 5.3) is used in place of ETX. For example, suppose a sending station needs to send a message that will not fit into one data frame. The obvious solution is to send multiple frames. But now, the receiving station needs to know not only the end of the data in a frame, but also which frame contains the last of the data. In the first and successive blocks the sender inserts an ETB (end of transmission block) character in place of ETX. In the last block it uses ETX.

For applications in which the data consist of printable character codes this is a simple way to indicate its end. But what about binary files whose data consist of bytes with random bit patterns? What happens if a frame's data contains an ETB or ETX character (Figure 5.32)? What is to prevent the receiving station from interpreting it as a control byte and missing the remaining data? A station using the BSC protocol handles this by preceding the STX character with a **DLE character**. The DLE, which stands for **data link escape**, acts like a toggle switch. When the receiving station sees the DLE-STX pair, it disables any checking for control bytes such as ETX or ETB. Moreover, the checking remains disabled until the receiving station encounters another DLE character. Once this DLE is encountered, the receiving station enables its checking for ETX or STX characters.

At first glance it may seem we have not solved any problems. What if the data contain a DLE character? The protocol gets around this problem by disguising DLE characters in its data. Figure 5.33 shows how. A sending station examines the characters it sends as data. Whenever there is a DLE character, it inserts an extra DLE character. This process is called **byte stuffing** and is similar to bit stuffing discussed previously; it just operates on a different level. Thus, when a receiving station encounters a DLE it looks for a second one following immediately. If it finds one, it knows the second one is bogus and accepts the first as data. If not, it knows the DLE is not data and enables control character checking. Data delimited this way are called **transparent data**. That is, the data field's contents are transparent to the receiving station. Data delimited with STX and ETX (or ETB) only are **nontransparent data**.

FIGURE 5.32    **Encountering Control Bytes in Data**

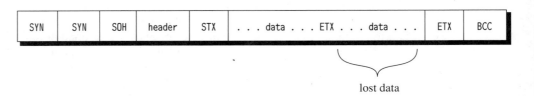

FIGURE 5.33    **Byte Stuffing**

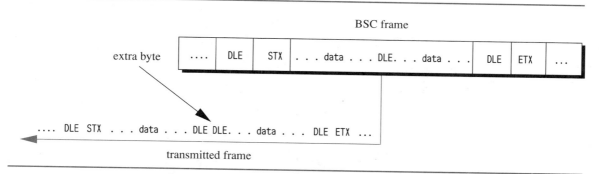

The last character from the formats shown in Figure 5.31 is **BCC, block check character**. It is used in BSC's error checking method. The BCC field's contents depend on which error checking method is used. If the protocol uses the CRC check, BCC will correspond to the CRC-16 polynomial (see Section 4.3). In other cases, BSC uses a **longitudinal redundancy check**. This method visualizes the frame as a two-dimensional bit array where each row represents one byte. For each column a parity bit is determined from the bits in that column and is stored in the BCC field.

**Frame Exchange**: Because BSC is a half-duplex protocol using stop and wait flow control, the process of sending and acknowledging frames is simplified. Figure 5.34 shows a typical sequence of events. Station *A* (primary station) sends an ENQ control frame to *B*. Since ENQ frames request a response, station *B* sends an acknowledgment. After *A* receives the acknowledgment, *A* and *B* exchange a sequence of data frames and acknowledgments. If *B* receives a frame correctly it

FIGURE 5.34    **Frame Exchange**

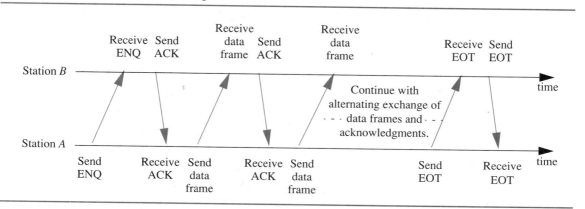

TABLE 5.4    **Comparison of BSC and HDLC Protocols**

| HDLC | BSC |
|------|-----|
| Full duplex | Half duplex |
| ARQ with go-back-n or selective repeat flow control | ARQ with stop and wait flow control |
| Bit-oriented protocol | Byte-oriented protocol |
| Code independent | Requires ASCII, EBCDIC, or Transcode |
| One frame format specifying three frame types | Multiple frame formats |
| Achieves data transparency through bit stuffing | Achieves data transparency through byte (DLE) stuffing |
| Bit flags delimit frames | SYN , ETX, and ETB characters delimit frames |
| Uses control field for control information | Uses control frames for control information |

sends a control frame containing the ACK control character. When *A* receives it, the ACK character indicates the previous frame has been received. Consequently, *A* sends the next one. This exchange continues as long as *A* has frames to send. When *A* has no more data to send it sends an EOT frame. *B* responds by sending its own EOT frame. When *A* receives it the connection between the two is terminated.

Naturally there are provisions for responding to damaged frames or for using timers to check for lost frames. But since these methods do not differ significantly from what we have discussed previously, we will not duplicate the discussions.

### SUMMARY: DATA LINK PROTOCOLS

HDLC (and its many variations) and BSC represent two of the most common data link protocols. Table 5.4 summarizes the main differences between them.

## 5.6    Case Study: Kermit

We finish this chapter by describing Kermit, a popular file transfer protocol. By now, we have covered enough material to describe adequately how a specific protocol runs. We choose Kermit because it is available in all the major platforms such as UNIX, DOS, Macintosh, and VAX. We describe only the aspects of Kermit that relate to what we have discussed thus far. If you are interested in an in-depth study, Reference 8 does a thorough and understandable job.

Kermit was written at Columbia University in the early 1980s in response to a growing demand to transfer mainframe files to a new and emerging technological wonder, the floppy disk. Kermit is unique in that it is not proprietary software. In other words, it doesn't cost anything. It is exchanged freely and is widely available. Its availablity has allowed many people to study it and make suggestions for improving it. Consequently, Kermit has grown and appears in many versions.

Because there are so many versions the features we discuss here may or may not be true for your version. We intend this discussion to be general and to relate to the topics we have discussed previously. For complete details you should consult the documentation at your site.

The name Kermit probably seems familiar. Indeed, Kermit is named after one of the late Jim Henson's Muppet characters. According to daCruz (Reference 8), the name Kermit was chosen because the Muppet frog is "a pleasant, unassuming sort of character" and the protocol designers liked the association. To justify its use they tried to think of a phrase for which Kermit was an acronym. After failing in their attempt, they decided to use the name anyway and requested (and got) permission from Henson Associates, Inc. to do so.

To transfer a file between two computers, each must run a copy of Kermit. Figure 5.35 shows the general approach involving a PC and a remote computer connected by a phone line and modem. The PC's user runs some communication software to log on to the remote machine. Once logged on, he or she calls Kermit by entering its name. The user then enters the command "Receive myfile." At this point, the Kermit running on the remote computer is waiting for a file to arrive. The boldface characters in the figure indicate system prompts (which will vary with the system).

Next, the user calls Kermit from the local PC and then enters the command "Send datafile." This activates the PC's Kermit. At this point, the user's interaction

**FIGURE 5.35**     **Kermit File Transfer**

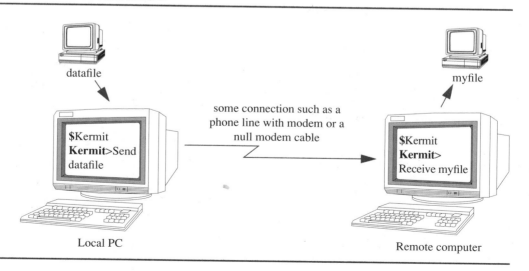

is done and Kermit does the rest. It looks for a file named "datafile" on the local PC and divides it into packets, the number depending on the size of the file and a packet. The PC Kermit constructs and sends frames through the modem and phone lines using the techniques, standards, and protocols described in Chapters 2 through 5. When the frames arrive at the remote computer, its Kermit receives them. If there are no errors, it extracts the packets and creates a file named "myfile." Once all the packets have been reassembled, the PC's Kermit informs the user the file transfer was successful.

From the user's perspective, the transfer was almost trivial. Two commands on each end were enough to do the job. But each of the topics discussed in the previous four chapters must be addressed somewhere, making the transfer far from trivial.

**Frame Format**        Kermit is a byte-oriented protocol. As with BSC, the Kermit frame consists of a sequence of bytes. Each byte's placement in the frame determines its meaning. Figure 5.36 shows the frame format and, as you might expect, it differs little from what we have discussed previously. It contains the ASCII SOH character, a frame number, and data. It also contains the number of bytes or length of a frame. This differs from previous protocols in which variable length frames were terminated by a special character. With Kermit, the receiving station finds the frame's end by counting the number of bytes and comparing with the length field.

Each frame also contains an error checking field. Error checking may be done using the CRC method or checksums. The checksum method computes a modular sum of frame bytes treated as integers. The sum is stored and sent with the frame. The receiving station recalculates the sum and compares it with the stored sum. Any discrepancy indicates an error.

Finally, each frame has a type field represented by a character. Kermit's frame types are similar to previously discussed types. Table 5.5 summarizes some of them. A complete list is found in reference 8.

## PROTOCOL

Kermit was written as a half-duplex (but will support full-duplex), stop and wait[*] protocol for a point-to-point connection. The station (*A*) that sends the first file starts by sending an initiation frame (type S) to the other station (*B*). As specified in Table

FIGURE 5.36    **Kermit Frame Format**

| SOH | Length | Number | Type | ... data ... | ErrorCheck |
|-----|--------|--------|------|--------------|------------|

[*] Newer versions of Kermit do support a sliding window protocol.

**TABLE 5.5    Kermit Frame Types**

| FRAME TYPE | MEANING |
|---|---|
| B | Break transmission. Indicates the two communicating stations should disconnect. |
| D | Data frame. |
| E | Error. Indicates a fatal error has occurred and the data field specifies the error. |
| F | File header. Contains the name of the file that will be sent. |
| G | Generic command. The data field contains one of a number of commands and optional parameters that can be sent to the other station. |
| N | Negative acknowledgment. |
| S | Send initiation. Sent to the receiving Kermit. It indicates a file will be coming soon and contains parameters (discussed shortly) used in the protocol. |
| Y | Acknowledgment frame. Used to acknowledge both data and control frames. |
| Z | End of file frame. Indicates that all frames for the file have been sent. |

5.4, this frame informs the receiving station that it will be receiving frames. The S frame and its eventual acknowledgment contain parameters on which the stations must agree in order for the protocol to work correctly if *A* and *B* exchange several files. The S frame contains parameters such as:

- **The longest frame that *A* expects to get.** This prevents *B* from sending *A* more than it can handle.

- **Timeout period.** This specifies how long *B* should wait for a frame before a timeout occurs.

- **Control prefix character.** If a file's data includes certain control characters, sending them can have unexpected effects if a device such as a modem intercepts and interprets them. To avoid misinterpretation of data, Kermit replaces a control character with two printable characters. The first is an agreed-on prefix such as the character #. *A* must tell *B* which prefix character to use so that *A* can recognize it.

    The second character is obtained by adding 64 to the control character's code, thus making it a printable character (see Table 2.4 in Section 2.2). For example, if the control characters X-ON and X-OFF appeared as data they would be sent as the two-letter sequences #Q and #S, respectively. When *B* receives a two-character sequence starting with #, it discards the # and subtracts 64 from the second character. (What do you think happens if # was actually part of the original data?)

- **Eighth-bit prefix character.** Many versions of Kermit are written to transfer seven-bit ASCII text files. However, the seven-bit codes are often stored in eight-bit bytes with the eighth bit 0. In such cases, an eighth bit is replaced by a parity bit determined from the other seven. When the file arrives, a 0-bit replaces the parity bit. A problem can occur when binary files are sent because all eight bits in a byte are meaningful. If the eighth bit is replaced with a parity bit then it is lost for good and the protocol fails.

One option for dealing with binary files is to use an eighth-bit prefix character. If the eighth bit in a byte is 1, the seven remaining bits are sent with parity. However, the sending Kermit will insert the agreed-on prefix character (such as an &) prior to it. If the eighth bit is 0 then no eighth-bit prefix is sent. When the receiving Kermit sees the & character, it removes it and concludes the eighth bit of the next byte is a 1. Otherwise it concludes the eighth bit is 0.

• **Run-length encoding prefix.** In Section 3.5, we discussed run length encoding, a data compression method that replaces long strings of a character with a single occurrence of it preceded by the number of times it occurs. Kermit also can provide run length encoding. However, the receiving Kermit must be able to determine when it receives a run length encoded string. For example, suppose it receives two consecutive bytes 0000 0111 (binary 7) and 0100 0001 (ASCII code for A). Are these data, or do they represent a run length encoded string? To differentiate the two cases, the sending Kermit inserts a special prefix (such as ~) prior to a run length encoded string. Thus, when the receiving Kermit sees the character ~, it concludes the following characters define a run length encoded string.

Figure 5.37 shows a typical exchange of Kermit frames. Station *A* starts by sending an S frame containing the previous information. *B* responds by sending a Y frame (acknowledgment). The Y frame may also contain the previous information. This exchange allows each station to inform the other what it expects. Next, *A* sends an F frame specifying the name of the file it will send. Again, *B* responds by acknowledging the F frame by sending another Y frame. Sending data frames proceeds as described in previous sections, with *B* acknowledging the ones it receives correctly and sending naks (N frames) when it receives a damaged frame or times out. When the last frame has been sent, *A* sends a Z frame indicating the entire file has been sent. Again, *B* responds with an acknowledgment. Finally, if there is no more work to be done, *A* sends a *B* frame indicating its intention to disconnect. *B* acknowledges it and the disconnection occurs.

**Commands**    Many people who use Kermit do not know how it works. In many cases they do not want or need to know. However, they do need to know how to interact with it to perform necessary tasks. We finish this section by discussing some of the more common commands to which Kermit responds. Remember, this description is general, and all commands may not be available on every Kermit. Reference 8 lists approximately 100 commands; to completely cover each one in detail, spelling out where they are used, is far beyond our scope here. However, Table 5.6 lists some of the commands that relate to previous discussions.

FIGURE 5.37 **Kermit Protocol to Send a File**

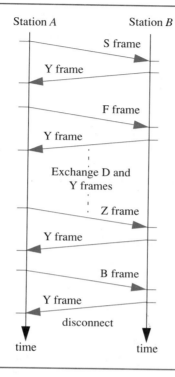

S - send initiation frame
Y - acknowledgment frame
F - file header frame
D - data frame
Z - end of file frame
B - break transmission

TABLE 5.6 **Some Kermit Commands**

| COMMAND | FUNCTION |
| --- | --- |
| clear | Clears buffers and removes deadlocks caused if each station sends the other an X-OFF character. |
| get | Request (usually to a file server) for a specified file. It differs from receive, which assumes the other station has issued a send command independent of the receive. The get command requests that the server send it. |
| receive | Tells Kermit to wait for a file that will be arriving. If the command specifies a file name, the incoming file will be stored under that name. If not, the file will be stored under the name specified in the file header (F frame). It is expected that a file has been (or will be) sent, otherwise the wait is very long. |
| send | Tells Kermit to send one or more files to the other station. It is expected the other station can receive it. |

| set baud | Defines the baud rate. |
|---|---|
| set block-check | Specifies how error checking will be performed. As stated previously, the choices are a checksum or cyclic redundancy check. |
| set delay | Defines how much time Kermit waits before sending the first frame in response to a send command. This is needed when a user is running two Kermits and enters a send command. He or she needs time to get to the other Kermit to enter the receive command before frames start arriving. |
| set duplex | Specifies whether the connection is half or full duplex. |
| set parity | Establishes how and if parity is used. Choices are ODD (for odd parity), EVEN (for even parity), MARK (parity bit always 1), SPACE (parity bit always 0), NONE (no parity, all eight bits are data). It is essential that both Kermits use the same method. |
| set receive | Used to establish previously discussed parameters such as the maximum frame length and prefix characters for incoming frames. |
| set send | Used to establish previously discussed parameters such as the maximum frame length and prefix characters for outgoing frames. The parameters can be changed by a "send receive" command entered at the other Kermit. |
| set timer | Used to enable or disable the timeout mechanism. |
| set window | Allows Kermit to use a sliding window protocol (go-back-N) instead of the typical stop and wait to improve overall efficiency. A parameter for this command specifies the window size (between 0 and 31). |
| set {send or receive} packet-length | Changes the default frame[*] size to send or receive. The default maximum is 94, but an extended version of Kermit allows frame sizes up to 9000. |
| set {send or receive} timeout | Specifies how long a station should wait for a frame before responding with a negative acknowledgment. |

* Typical Kermit terminology uses the term *packet* where we have used *frame*. Some books interchange the two terms freely and others make a very careful distinction between them. The reader should be careful with this terminology.

---

Kermit is included here primarily because of its widespread use, but the reader should not conclude that it is the only file transfer protocol. There are others, such as XMODEM, XMODEM-CRC, XMODEM-1K, WXMODEM, YMODEM, and ZMODEM. The differences among them, including frame sizes and formats, error checking methods, and control characters used, are not huge. On the other hand, as anyone who has ever written a program knows, even the smallest differences can make protocols incompatible. If you are interested in further distinctions, Reference 9 has a short discussion of each protocol.

## 5.7  Summary

In previous chapters we discussed details necessary for the transmission of a single frame, but Chapter 5 considered multiple frames. Specifically, it discussed protocols that deal with the following issues:

- Tracking multiple frames and their acknowledgments.
- Responding to frames that arrive damaged.
- Responding when a frame or acknowledgment never arrives or arrives late.

Several protocols were discussed. The unrestricted protocol simply sends all frames and assumes the receiver has enough buffer space to handle them. It also assumes that all frames arrive correctly. The stop and wait protocol sends one frame at a time, waiting for an acknowledgment to each. These two represent extremes in protocol design.

A sliding window protocol represents a compromise between the two extremes. It defines a window for the sending station containing frames that can be sent but not yet acknowledged. Adjusting the window size can make it behave more like an unrestricted or a stop and wait protocol. We discussed two different sliding window protocols. The go-back-n protocol requires that the receiving station accept all frames in the order they are sent. If one arrives out of order, the receiving station does not accept it and the sending station must resend it. The selective repeat protocol defines a window for the receiving station. The receiving station then can accept any frame in its window. It buffers them and eventually delivers them in order to its patron.

Both sliding window protocols respond to frames that arrive damaged or out of order by sending negative acknowledgments (naks). A station receiving a nak must resend frames. Under the go-back-n protocol it resends all outstanding frames, but under the selective repeat protocol it resends only the nak'd frame. Each protocol also relies on timers so that if an acknowledgment is not received within a period of time, the station assumes one or more frames are lost and resends them.

With both sliding window protocols there are restrictions on the window size. Generally, with the go-back-n protocol if there are $2^K$ distinct frame numbers, the sender's window must have fewer than $2^K$ frames. With selective repeat, the sum of the sender's and receiver's windows must not exceed $2^K$. Violating these restrictions does not mean the protocol will fail, but it does mean the protocol is subject to failure if a certain sequence of events occurs.

The algorithms are complex, and providing a formal mathematical proof is outside the scope of this text. However, Section 5.4 introduced two tools that can be used for verification: state transition diagrams and Petri nets. Both use directed graphs to represent the states and state transitions of a system, but they differ in the way they do so. State transition diagrams use nodes for states and edges for state transitions. The execution of an algorithm thus can be equated to defining paths through the state transition diagram. Petri nets are more complex. They use places, transitions, arrows, and tokens. The collection of tokens corresponding to places defines the state of the system. Tokens move from place to place subject to rules that allow transitions to fire. In both cases, the models can be analyzed to detect anomalies that can occur.

Sections 5.5 and 5.6 discussed specific examples of flow control protocols used in practice. The three main protocols discussed were HDLC, BSC, and Kermit.

HDLC is an example of a bit-oriented protocol. That is, its frames are treated as bit streams. It is defined by the ISO for point-to-point or multipoint connections, is used for half- and full-duplex communications, and can use either the go-back-n or selective repeat protocol. It defines different frame types and uses them to exchange data, commands, or control information.

BSC is a byte-oriented protocol; the frames are treated as byte streams. It also is used in point-to-point or multipoint connections, but is typically used with half-duplex communication and uses a stop and wait protocol. Like HDLC, it defines different frame types to exchange data, commands, and control information.

Kermit is a popular file transfer protocol written at Columbia University and is a public domain program (i.e., distributed without charge). Kermit is a byte-oriented protocol used primarily in point-to-point connections. Depending on the version, it can run in half- or full-duplex modes and can use either a stop and wait or sliding window protocol.

All three of these protocols (and many others) represent different ways to do the same thing. In all cases, the stations exchange frames according to specified rules. They differ in those rules and the types of frames they recognize. Because of these differences, two or more stations must run the same protocols in order to communicate. If either station is unaware of what the other is sending it, communication is impossible.

# Review Questions

1. What is automatic repeat request error control?

2. What is flow control?

3. What are X-ON and X-OFF characters?

4. What is an unrestricted flow control?

5. What is stop and wait flow control?

6. Are the following TRUE or FALSE? Why?

   a. Unrestricted flow control generally has a better channel utilization than the stop and wait flow control.

   b. Unrestricted flow control really amounts to no flow control.

   c. Unrestricted and stop and wait flow control are special cases of a sliding window protocol.

d.   Sliding window protocols can work with any size window.

e.   The go-back-n algorithm will resend several frames even if just one fails to arrive at its destination.

f.   For the selective repeat protocol, the receiving window size is independent of the sending window size.

g.   Petri nets and finite state machines represent two different ways to accomplish the same thing.

h.   HDLC is a byte-oriented protocol.

i.   HDLC can use either a selective repeat or go-back-n protocol.

j.   Kermit is a half-duplex byte-oriented protocol.

7.   Distinguish between bit rate and effective data rate.

8.   Define two measures of transmission efficiency.

9.   What important role does an acknowledgment play in a flow control protocol?

10.   What is a sliding window flow control protocol?

11.   What is a piggybacked acknowledgment?

12.   Why are frames numbered modularly rather than being allowed to increase as large as needed?

13.   List typical fields in a data frame.

14.   Distinguish between a frame timer and an ack timer.

15.   What purpose does the window size play in a sliding window flow control protocol?

16.   Distinguish among an ack, a nak, and a data frame.

17.   What are the major differences between the go-back-n and selective repeat protocols?

18.   What is the constraint on the sending window size for the selective repeat protocol?

19.   For the selective repeat protocol, what is the relationship between the sending and receiving window size?

20.   What is a finite state machine (or model)?

21.   What is a state transition diagram?

22.   What is a Petri net?

23.   Define the terms *place, transition, arrow,* and *token* as applied to Petri nets.

24.   What does it mean when a transition "fires"?

25.   Distinguish between a byte-oriented and a bit-oriented protocol.

26.   What are the three communication modes of HDLC? Describe each one.

27. What is bit stuffing and why is it necessary?

28. Distinguish among a primary station, secondary station, and combined station.

29. Distinguish among the main HDLC frame types.

30. Define the four status types a supervisory frame can indicate.

31. What is a broadcast address?

32. List other protocols similar to HDLC and each one's sponsoring organization.

33. List the main differences between HDLC and BSC protocols.

34. What is a SYN character?

35. What is a data link escape?

36. Distinguish between transparent and nontransparent data.

37. What is byte stuffing?

38. Distinguish among end of transmission, end of transmission block, and end of text characters.

39. What is Kermit?

40. List some of the Kermit frame types.

41. What is a control prefix character?

42. What is an eighth-bit prefix character?

43. What is a run length encoding prefix?

# Exercises

1. What happens if *A* and *B* from Figure 5.2 both insert X-OFF characters into their data streams?

2. With the X-ON/X-OFF protocol, why does one station send X-OFF before the buffers are full instead of waiting until they are full?

3. Modify the unrestricted protocol in Figure 5.4 to reflect the following changes:

   a. The sender has a fixed number of frames to send.

   b. A frame could be damaged.

4. What are effective data rates for the unrestricted protocol and stop and wait protocol given the following values:

   $R$ = capacity (16 Mbps).
   $S$ = signal speed (200) meters per µsec.

$D$ = distance between the sender and receiver (200 meters).

$T$ = time to create one frame (2 μsec).

$F$ = number of bits in a frame (500).

$N$ = number of data bits in a frame (450).

$A$ = number of bits in an acknowledgement (80).

5. For each variable (except signal speed and the number of data bits) in Exercise 4, how will an increase in its value affect the effective data rate for both the unrestricted and stop and wait protocols? For each case, give credence to your answer by doubling the value from that in Exercise 4 and calculating the effective data rate.

6. The scenario in Figure 5.10 shows one way the go-back-n protocol can fail if the window size equals the maximum number of sequence numbers. Describe another way the protocol can fail under the same assumption.

7. Consider the go-back-n algorithm of Figure 5.12 with a window size of 7. Describe the actions of both sending and receiving protocols, specifying variable values and buffer contents, in the following cases. What is the current state of each protocol after responding to the events specified?

   a. Station $A$ sends frames 0 through 6. Station $B$ receives them in order, but frame 4 was damaged.

   b. Station $A$ sends frames 0 through 6 and station $B$ receives them in order. Station $B$ sends one data frame to $A$ (which $A$ receives correctly) after receiving frame 4 but before receiving frame 5.

   c. Same scenario as in (b) but the data frame sent to $A$ is damaged.

   d. Station $A$ has 12 frames to send to $B$, but $B$ has nothing to send to $A$.

8. How could the go-back-n algorithm of Figure 5.12 fail under each of the following conditions:

   a. Remove the check for "expired acktimer."

   b. Remove the check for "expired frametimer."

   c. Remove the check for condition ($i < N$) in the first "if statement" in the main loop.

   d. Remove the statement "w = (frame.ack+1) % MAX" from the code under the last event check.

9. Reproduce the scenarios of Figures 5.14 and 5.15 with both window sizes equal to 4 and show the protocol does not fail.

10. Consider the selective repeat algorithm of Figure 5.16 with window sizes of 4. Describe the actions of both sending and receiving protocols, specifying variable

values and buffer contents, in the following cases. What is the current state of each protocol after responding to the events specified?

a. Station *A* sends frames 0 through 3. All except frame 2 arrive. Frame 2 is lost.

b. Station *A* sends frames 0 through 3. They arrive at *B* in the order 0, 1, 3, 2.

c. Station *A* sends frames 0 through 3. Station *B* receives frames 0 and 1 and sends a piggyback acknowledgment, which *A* receives.

d. Same scenario as in (c), but the acknowledgment gets lost.

11. Consider the selective repeat protocol of Figure 5.16. Construct a scenario in which the condition frame.type==nak, but the second condition following it does not hold.

12. How could the selective repeat algorithm of Figure 5.16 fail under each of the following conditions:

a. Remove the check for "expired acktimer."

b. Remove the check for "expired frametimer."

c. Remove the check for condition ($i < N$) in the first "if statement" in the main loop.

d. Remove the statement "sw = (frame.ack+1) % MAX" from the code under the last event check.

13. Consider the analysis of the sliding window protocol in Section 5.3 and assume the following values:

$R$ = transmission rate (10 Mbps or 10 bits per μsec).
$S$ = signal speed (200 meters per μsec).
$D$ = distance between the sender and receiver (unknown).
$T$ = time to create one frame (1 μsec).
$F$ = number of bits in a frame (200).
$N$ = number of data bits in a frame (160).
$W$ = window size (4 frames).

At what distance will the first acknowledgment arrive precisely when the last frame in the window is sent? What is the effective data rate?

14. Consider your answer to Exercise 13. What happens to the effective data rate if the window size increases? Decreases?

15. Repeat Exercise 14 for each of the other parameters.

16. Consider the state transition diagram of Figure 5.21. Why is there no state transition from (Y, N, 1) to (Y, N, 0)?

17. Expand the boxed-in area of Figure 5.21 to include the states (Y, N, 0) and (Y, N, 1) and refine, resulting in an expansion of Figure 5.22.

18. Consider the Petri net of Figure 5.24. Consider the case that a sender receives an ack but may not have the next frame to send. That is, it must wait for the patron to give it a packet. What does the new Petri net look like?

19. Draw the sequence of Petri nets (similar to those in Figure 5.25) for the following sequence of events:

   a. Send F0.

   b. Timeout, resend F0.

   c. Receiver gets F0 and sends A0.

   d. Sender gets A0 and sends F1.

   e. Timeout, resend F1.

20. A timeout could occur after the receiver gets a frame and sends the ack but before the sender gets the ack. Thus the sender would resend a frame the receiver is not expecting. Modify the Petri net of Figure 5.24 to account for this possibility.

21. What is the transmitted binary string after bit stuffing the following (leftmost bit first):

   01011111101111101111111101111

22. Redraw Figure 5.30b, but assume that $B$ sends SREJ (instead of REJ) when it detects the error.

23. Redraw Figure 5.30b, but assume that $B$ has sent four information frames, which arrived at $A$ before $A$ sent the second batch of frames. Also assume $B$'s third frame is damaged in transit.

24. Section 5.5 described byte stuffing by inserting an extra DLE character whenever DLE occurs in data. The intent was to avoid misinterpreting a "data DLE" from a "control DLE." Why can't we achieve the same effect simply by using STX prior to data bytes, and if ETX or ETB occurs in the data, just insert an extra one?

25. Write a program that does byte stuffing on a character string. Write a complementary one that accepts a byte-stuffed character string and removes the stuffed bytes.

26. Section 5.6 discusses sending an S frame containing the specification of various prefixes such as a #, &, or ~. This was done to identify certain encoding schemes. But what happens if any of these characters is part of a file's data? What prevents the receiving station from interpreting it as a particular prefix? (Hint: We have faced similar problems previously.)

**27.**   Refer to the discussion of prefix characters in Section 5.6 and code the following strings.

   **a.**   text string "AJKKKKKKKKKKDK"

   **b.**   binary string 01011010 01011010 10010110 01011001 10011010.

## REFERENCES

1. Tanenbaum, A. S. *Computer Networks*, 2nd ed. Englewood Cliffs, NJ: Prentice-Hall, 1988.

2. Walrand, J. *Communications Networks: A First Course*, Boston: Richard D. Irwin, 1991.

3. Lin, F., P. Chu, and M. Liu. "Protocol Verification Using Reachability Analysis: The State Space Explosion Problem and Relief Strategies," *Proceedings of the ACM SIGCOMM 1987 Workshop*, 1987, 126–35.

4. Russel, D. *The Principles of Computer Networking*. Cambridge University Press, 1989.

5. Peterson, J. *Petri Net Theory and the Modeling of Systems*. Englewood Cliffs, NJ: Prentice-Hall, 1981.

6. Halsall, F. *Data Communications, Computer Networks and Open Systems*, 3rd ed. Reading, MA: Addison-Wesley, 1992.

7. Black, U. *Data Networks: Concepts, Theory, and Practice*. Englewood Cliffs, NJ: Prentice-Hall, 1989.

8. da Cruz, F. *Kermit: A File Transfer Protocol*. Bedford, MA: Digital Press, 1987.

9. Fitzgerald, J. *Business Data Communications*, 3rd ed. New York: Wiley, 1990.

# CHAPTER 6

## LOCAL AREA NETWORKING

### 6.1 Network Topologies

Up to this point we have focused on communication between two stations and, with the exception of multiplexing and contention in Sections 3.3 and 3.4, have not considered the larger picture of connecting many stations. This chapter and the next discuss different connection strategies and the protocols needed to maintain communication among many stations. This chapter deals with local area networks (LANs) protocols, and Chapter 7 deals with wide area networks (WANs). The differences between "local" and "wide" are partly in the geographic area covered as well as protocols. LANs typically connect PCs, printers, and file servers located in a building or cluster of buildings. By contrast, WANs connect devices located throughout a city, state, country, and even the world.

We begin with a discussion of the different LAN topologies (configurations) shown in Figure 6.1. Perhaps the two most common topologies are the bus and ring. In a **bus topology** (Figure 6.1a) a single communication line, typically coaxial cable or optical fiber, represents the primary medium. It is sometimes called the network's backbone. Any station wanting to send to another does so over the backbone. Only one station may send at a time, however. In a **ring topology** (Figure 6.1b), all the stations are arranged in a ring, with each station connected directly only to its two neighbors. If a station wants to send to another, the message must pass through all of the stations in between (either clockwise or counterclockwise). It's a little like neighborhood gossip that spreads from neighbor to neighbor.

Other topologies are the star topology and a fully connected topology. In a **star topology** (Figure 6.1c) one station (often a mainframe or file server) is a logical communication center for all others. Any two communicating stations must go through it. Finally, a **fully connected topology** (Figure 6.1d) connects every pair of stations directly. Fully connected topologies represent an extreme case and are

FIGURE 6.1    Network Topologies

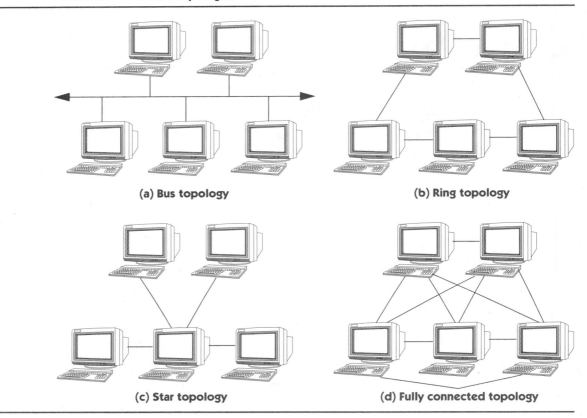

(a) Bus topology

(b) Ring topology

(c) Star topology

(d) Fully connected topology

rarely used in practice (except perhaps in small isolated cases). Therefore we will not discuss them further.

An advantage of the bus topology is its simplicity. The backbone may run through one or more buildings with feeder lines going to specific offices or classrooms (Figure 6.2) and connecting to PCs. It may run the length of an assembly line connecting devices necessary for the assembly of a product such as an automobile. Because of the linear organization, adding new stations or removing old ones[*] is relatively easy. A disadvantage of the linear organization is that only one station can send at a time. With many applications this limitation poses no problem. However, as the number of transmissions increases, serious bottlenecks can occur. You might

---

[*] Be cautious of this statement. Insertion and deletion of stations depends on more than topology. Two very different protocols, Ethernet and token bus, both use the linear organization. We will see that the way in which stations are added and deleted is very different.

FIGURE 6.2    **Bus Topology Connecting Multiple Buildings**

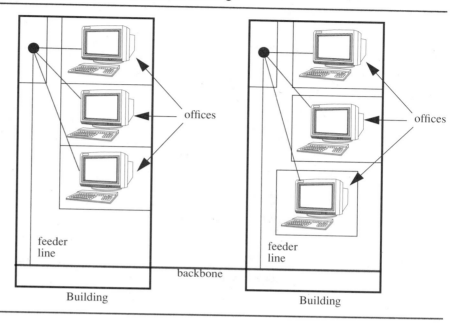

want to refresh your memory by reviewing the discussion of contention protocols in Section 3.4.

Ring topologies allow multiple stations to send using one or more tokens that circulate the ring. Recall from Section 3.4 that a token is a special frame and a station in possession of it may send. The most common ring networks use just one token but some protocols have provisions for more. Ring topologies are common in office environments where multiple PCs must communicate among themselves or with a file server or shared printer.

Sections 6.2 through 6.4 discuss three standards for bus and ring networks: the Ethernet, token ring network, and token bus network. The discussions cover the protocols used to control and maintain the integrity of the network. We will see that the differences among these standards go far beyond the diagrams we have drawn so far.

As the need to communicate increases, the bus and ring topologies become less effective. Greater needs usually require more flexibility than these topologies can provide. As the number of frames increases, the LANs become saturated and performance degrades. Recall again from Section 3.4 how too many frames affect efficiency.

One way to avoid serious bottlenecks is to use more LANs, thus reducing the number of stations per LAN. This solution helps maintain performance at an acceptable level. However, dividing all the stations into multiple LANs raises the question, Which stations are assigned to which LANs? A corollary to Murphy's law states that no matter how you group them, two stations on two different LANs will need to

FIGURE 6.3    **Interconnecting Networks**

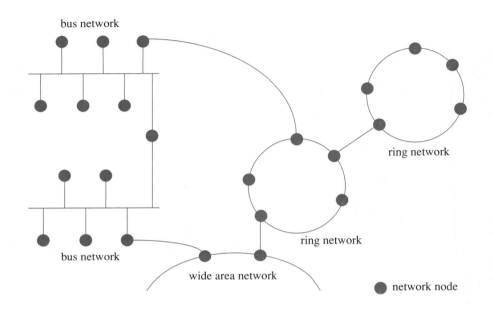

bus network

ring network

ring network

bus network

wide area network

● network node

communicate. Consequently, we must provide some way for communication across LANs. This invariably leads to connecting networks in a manner similar to that in Figure 6.3. The figure shows two bus and two ring networks. Any two stations on a LAN communicate using the LAN's protocols. In addition, connections between LANs allow cross communications. Locating the proper stations across LANs can be tricky. Section 6.5 discusses methods of connecting LANs and the protocols that allow inter-LAN communication.

After studying various LAN protocols you realize that a lot of software is necessary to make them function. There are two ways to get such software: Write it or buy it. Since most people buy it, we present a case study of one of the more popular network software products, Novell Netware. We chose this package because it is popular and because books are available for anyone wanting more information.

## 6.2   Ethernet: IEEE Standard 802.3

The Ethernet has a bus topology. Stations contend for the backbone using a form of the CSMA/DC contention protocol (Section 3.4). It is commonly used to connect PCs, workstations, printers, file servers, and even mainframes. Part of the Ethernet's history dates back to 1973. In his Ph.D. thesis, Robert Metcalfe described much of his research of LAN technology. After graduation, he joined the Xerox Corporation and worked with a group that eventually implemented what became known as the Ethernet. The Ethernet is named after the ether, the imaginary substance that many once believed occupied all of space and was the medium through which light waves propagated.

Later, the concepts of the Ethernet were written up and proposed to the IEEE as a standard for LANs. The proposal had the backing of Xerox, Intel, and DEC. The IEEE eventually adopted it as a standard, and it is now referred to as IEEE standard 802.3. It is worth noting that two other proposals were made to IEEE at about the same time. One was backed by General Motors and the other by IBM. With such influential organizations promoting particular standards, IEEE officials no doubt had difficulties deciding which of the three was most appropriate for a LAN standard. They compromised and made all three LAN standards. The other two standards, 802.5 and 802.4 are the subjects of the next two sections.

## RELATION TO OSI

To fully understand the IEEE 802.3 standard, it is important to understand where it fits in a layered design and how it relates to other topics we have discussed thus far. Recall from Section 1.4 the seven-layer OSI reference model. Network operations typically are defined by the lowest three layers: the physical, data link, and network layers. The data link layer performs services for the network layer and assumes the existence of the physical layer. Specifically, the data link layer is responsible for the accurate communication between two nodes in a network. This involves frame formats, error checking, and flow control, all of which we have discussed so far. In general, however, these topics are independent of the network topology. For example, error-checking algorithms do not care whether a frame was sent via bus or ring.

As a result, the data link layer is further divided into two sublayers, the **logical link control (LLC)** and the **medium access control (MAC)** (Figure 6.4). LLC handles logical links between the stations while MAC controls access to the transmission medium. The LLC is also a standard (IEEE 802.2) and is based on the HDLC protocol discussed in Section 5.5. Primarily the LLC provides service to the network layer and calls on the MAC for specific tasks.

The IEEE 802.3 standard is a MAC protocol. You will see that the token ring and token bus standards discussed in the next two sections are also MAC protocols. Again, we see how the layering of software allows different lower-level protocols with the same higher-level ones. Many of the topics we have discussed are independent of the network topology which gives them a great deal of flexibility and marketability.

## ETHERNET COMPONENTS

Figure 6.5 shows a typical connection between a PC and an Ethernet backbone. Although we use the example of a PC you should remember that other devices also can be connected to the backbone. The backbone is typically a coaxial cable, although

FIGURE 6.4    **Data Link Layer Refinement**

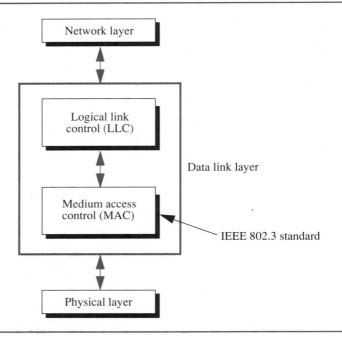

FIGURE 6.5    **Typical Ethernet Connection**

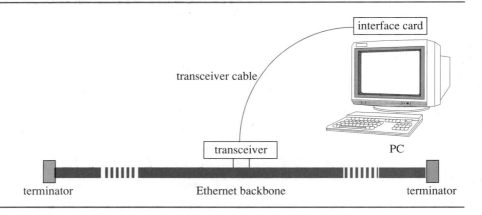

optical fiber is quite common. Electronic terminators are placed at both ends of the backbone. They prevent electronic echoing of signals back and forth through the cable, which creates false signals and causes confusion. It's a little like calling a radio talk show and listening to yourself as you talk. Your voice is usually delayed in order to avoid broadcasting nasty words. Thus, speaking and hearing your delayed words can be disorienting.

A PC can connect to the backbone, but it requires some hardware. First, a **transceiver** clamps onto the cable and taps into the cable's conducting core. Its primary function is to create an interface between the PC and the backbone. One of its functions is to transmit bits onto the cable using CSMA/CD contention, which allows it to determine when there is information moving along the cable and to detect collisions when they occur. The tranceiver communicates with the PC using a **transceiver cable**. The cable consists of five twisted pairs. Two are used to send data and control information to the PC. Two more are used for receiving data and control information. The fifth pair can be used to connect to a power source and ground. Some transceivers can communicate with multiple devices, thus taking on the characteristics of a multiplexer.

The transceiver cable connects to the PC through an **interface card** (or board) installed in the PC. The interface card contains the logic necessary to buffer data and move it between the transceiver cable and the PC's memory. It also does error checking, creates frames, and determines when to retransmit after collisions occur. The interface card is used to relieve the PC's processor from these tasks and allow the processor to attend to typical PC activities.

To put things in perspective, let's describe and sequence the activities required for a PC to send data to another PC. The steps are as follows:

1.  The sending PC executes network software that routes a packet of information from the PC's memory through its internal bus to the interface card.

2.  The interface card receives the packet and creates the correct frame format. It then waits for a signal from the transceiver, which is monitoring the backbone waiting for a chance to send.

3.  When the transceiver detects a quiet backbone it signals the card, which then sends the frame to the transceiver. The transceiver transmits the bits onto the backbone, listening for any collisions. If none occur, it assumes the transmission was successful. If a collision does occur, the transceiver notifies the interface card. The interface card executes the binary exponential backoff algorithm of Section 3.4 to determine when it should try again. If collisions continue to occur it will signal the network software, which will provide the user with an error message or execute some algorithm in response to the error.

4.  The transceiver at the receiving end monitors backbone traffic. When it detects a frame destined for it, it copies the bits from the backbone and sends them to the interface card in the receiving PC.

5.  The interface card does a CRC error check and signals the PC that a packet has arrived.

6.  The PC executes network software and determines whether the packet can be accepted according to the algorithms discussed in Chapter 5. If it can, the PC moves the information from the card to memory to await further processing. If not, the network software responds according to the protocols at the next higher layer.

## CABLE SPECIFICATIONS

The IEEE 802.3 standard defines limits such as the maximum backbone length, the number of stations that can connect to it, and the data rates. There are five specifications depending on the type of cable used. Table 6.1 lists the cable types and some specifications for each one.[*] All use Manchester encoding except 10 BROAD 36, which uses differential phase shift keying (recall Section 2.5).

The original proposal defined the 10 BASE 5 cable, a 50 ohm, 10 millimeter diameter coaxial cable. However, in order to allow cheaper LANs more suited to PC environments, the 10 BASE 2 cable was added to the standard. The smaller diameter allowed the cable to bend more easily, an important feature when trying to route cable around corners and into cabinets. It was also cheaper and has been dubbed "Cheapernet." The additional flexibility allows a different connection than that shown in Figure 6.5. The thicker 10-mm cable typically runs through basements or under floors. The transceiver cable then is used to connect PCs located in different areas. The thinner, more flexible 10 BASE 2 cable can be routed directly to individual PCs, thus eliminating the transceiver and transceiver cable. Done this way, all the interfacing electronics and logic can be combined into a **medium attachment unit (MAU)** and installed in the PC. This method also helps reduce the cost of the LAN. A drawback of 10 BASE 2 is that the thinner cable has more electronic resistance and cannot span as long a distance.

Another addition to IEEE 802.3 is the 10 BROAD 36, which uses broadband transmissions rather than the baseband transmissions of 10 BASE 5 and 10 BASE 2. It uses a 75 ohm coax cable such as that used with cable television. The 1 BASE 5 and 10 BASE T types both use unshielded twisted pair instead of cable. With 1 BASE 5, the data rate is decreased to 1 Mbps between stations up to 500 meters

TABLE 6.1    Cable Types for IEEE 802.3

| CABLE TYPE | BACKBONE | MAXIMUM DISTANCE BETWEEN STATIONS (METERS) | DATA RATE |
|---|---|---|---|
| 10 BASE 5 | 50 ohm coax cable, 10 mm diameter | 500 | 10 Mbps |
| 10 BASE 2 (Cheapernet) | 50 ohm coax cable, 5 mm diameter | 185 | 10 Mbps |
| 10 BROAD 36 | 75 ohm coax cable | 3600 | 10 Mbps |
| 1 BASE 5 | Unshielded twisted pair | 250 | 1 Mbps |
| 10 BASE-T | Unshielded twisted pair | 100 | 10 Mbps |

[*] Although we list current IEEE specifications, don't be misled into thinking an Ethernet will never be more than a 10 Mbps LAN. In fact, IEEE has begun work on a new standard that would allow Ethernet LANs to communicate at data rates up to 100 Mbps (Reference 1).

apart. The 10 BASE T maintains the 10 Mbps data rate but reduces the maximum distance between stations to 100 meters.

Physically, both 1 BASE 5 and 10 BASE T are star topologies (1 BASE 5 is commonly referred to as **StarLAN** , but both behave like a bus topology logically. That is, all the stations are connected to a central hub. A sending station transmits to the hub, which regenerates the signal and broadcasts it to all the stations. Thus, every station sees each transmission, just as in the bus topology. Collisions occur when the hub receives two transmissions simultaneously. Then it broadcasts a special signal alerting the stations that a collision has occurred.

These last two configurations have several advantages. First, they are useful in buildings where the physical configuration is not conducive to linear connection. In addition, they allow networks to be implemented using existing wiring, which is often installed when office buildings are built. Finally, the centralized communications control simplifies diagnostics and testing.

There are other differences among the five versions of IEEE 802.3, but the level of detail is beyond this book's goals. If you are interested, Reference 2 provides more detail.

The maximum distances between stations[*] listed in Table 6.1 impose limits on a backbone's length or the length of the twisted pair connected to a central hub. These limits are necessary because signals degrade as they propagate along the cable. But what can you do if, for example, the total distance spanned by a 10 BASE 5 cable exceeds 500 meters?

The 802.3 committee considered this problem and solved it by allowing multiple backbones to be connected. Figure 6.6 shows one way to do this. The 500-meter limit

FIGURE 6.6    **Connecting Two Backbones**

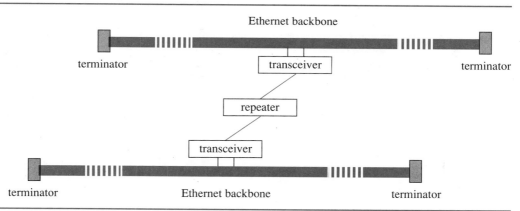

---

[*] Distance is measured along the cable, not as the crow flies. For example, two PCs just a few meters apart may experience problems if connected using several thousand meters of coiled cable. The person responsible may also experience problems during interviews for his or her new job.

is seen as the maximum distance over which an unamplified signal can still be recognized. However, many sites use multiple backbones connected by a **repeater**, a device that receives a signal, amplifies it, and retransmits it. The amplification allows the signals to travel longer distances. In general, the 802.3 standard allows two computers to be separated by no more than four repeaters.[*]

Increasing distance is not the only reason to connect multiple backbones. In a system of many stations with varied needs, a good design may be to isolate the stations with similar needs and allow them to communicate over a single backbone. This design reduces traffic on each backbone and increases efficiency. In another scenario, security may demand that some stations be isolated from others on a separate backbone. Such designs, however, introduce problems not solved by connecting the backbones with a repeater. Section 6.5 discusses some of these problems in more detail.

## FRAME FORMAT

Figure 6.7 shows the Ethernet frame format. As with previous frame formats, there are no surprises. It contains the usual information:

- **Preamble**. A 7-octet[†] pattern consisting of alternating 0s and 1s is used for synchronization. Recall that synchronization establishes the rate at which bits are sampled. It's similar to the late Lawrence Welk's preamble of "uh-one-an-uh-two" to establish the timing and synchronize his band.

- **Start of frame delimiter**. Special pattern 10101011 indicating the start of a frame.

- **Destination address**. If the first bit is 0, this field specifies a specific station. If it is 1, the destination address is a group address and the frame is sent to all stations in some predefined group specified by the address. Each station's interface knows its group address and responds when it sees it. If all bits are 1, the frame is broadcast to all stations.

**FIGURE 6.7    Ethernet Frame Format**

number of octets

| 7 | 1 | 2 or 6 | 2 or 6 | 2 | 46–1500 | | 4 |
|---|---|---|---|---|---|---|---|
| Preamble | Start of frame delimiter | Destination address | Source address | Data field length | Data | Pad | Frame check sequence |

---

[*] In general, there may be many segments in a network. The "four repeater" constraint applies only to the path between two computers.

[†] An octet is really a byte, but since the LLC is a bit-oriented protocol, we can't call eight bits a byte. Instead we call them an octet.

- **Source address**. Specifies where the frame comes from.
- **Data length field**. Number of octets in the combined data and pad fields.
- **Data field**. Self-explanatory.
- **Pad field**. The data field must be at least 46 octets (more about this shortly). If there is not enough data, extra octets are added (padded) to the data to make up the difference.
- **Frame check sequence**. Error checking using 32-bit CRC.

From Figure 6.7, we see an upper and lower limit (from 46 to 1500) on the number of data/pad octets. The upper limit is used to prevent one transmission from monopolizing the medium for too long. The lower limit is to make sure the collision techniques work properly. In Section 3.4 we stated that frame sizes must be a minimum length so a sending station can detect a collision before sending the frame's last bit. The length is determined by the distance a frame travels, a bit's propagation speed, the data rate, and the delays caused by any repeaters. Considering all these factors, the 802.3 standard defines a minimum frame length as 512 bits (64 octets). If all the fields (except the pad) in Figure 6.7 have the smallest number of bytes possible, the total comes to 18 octets. The 46 pad bytes then make up the difference.

## EFFICIENCY

We now address one measure of the efficiency of the 802.3 standard. As we have stated previously in this text, there are many ways to define efficiency, and we leave more extensive treatments of the topic to references 3,4,5, and 6, The measure we address here defines the average amount of time to make a successful transmission. It should depend on several factors such as the data rate, cable length (including repeaters), frame size, and the number of stations. We will see that this is indeed true.

We begin by dividing time into slots of $T$ units each (there was a similar division in Section 3.4). Typically, $T$ is the maximum amount of time needed to detect a collision and is also the maximum round-trip propagation time between the two farthest points on the network. Figure 6.8 helps show why they are the same. Suppose that station $A$ sends a frame. The frame takes $0.5T$ to reach the farthest point (station $B$). Suppose that just prior to the frame's arrival, $B$ sends. Remember, the frame has not yet reached $B$, so $B$ still detects an idle medium. Thus, a collision occurs at approximately $0.5T$ after the frame was sent. The collision's noise must propagate back to $A$ before $A$ can detect it, which requires another $0.5T$ for a total time equal to $T$.

What are the chances a station will send a frame successfully during a time slot? It depends on two things, the total number of stations and the probability of a given station sending during the slot. Suppose $N$ is the total number of stations, each of which sends with probability $p_s$ ($0 \le p_s \le 1$) during slot time $T$. Equivalently, a station does not send with probability $1 - p_s$ during $T$.

The probability ($P$) of a frame being sent without collision during a slot time is the probability that one station sends ($p_s$) times the probability all others do not

FIGURE 6.8    Maximum Time to Detect a Collision

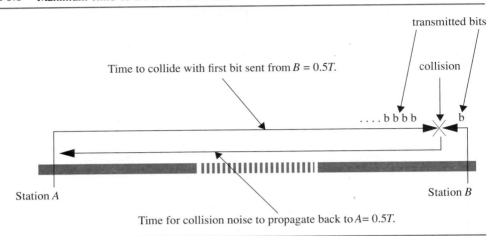

transmitted bits

Time to collide with first bit sent from $B = 0.5T$.

collision

. . . . b b b b          b

Station A

Station B

Time for collision noise to propagate back to $A = 0.5T$.

$((1 - p_s)^{N-1})$ multiplied by $N$ (because any of the $N$ stations could be the one that sends). We therefore write

$$P = N * p_s * (1 - p_s)^{N-1}$$

Equivalently, $1 - P$ is the probability a frame is not sent successfully, due either to a collision or to the fact that no one sent anything.

We would like to know under what conditions the largest number of frames are sent successfully. They can be found by finding the largest value for $P$. Calculus techniques allow us to maximize $P$ by taking its derivative, equating to 0, and solving for $p_s$. We leave the details to those who know calculus, but doing so yields

$$p_s = \frac{1}{N} \quad \text{and} \quad P = \left(1 - \frac{1}{N}\right)^{N-1}$$

This result is of more theoretical than practical[*] interest as a station generally does not know how many others there are and therefore cannot adjust its probability of sending to achieve the maximum. We will, however, use this definition of $P$ in later calculations.

The next question we pose is: How many time slots pass before a frame is sent successfully? We call this the **contention period** ($C$) and express it as a weighted average or a sum of terms, each of which is the product of the number of slots a sta-

---

[*] One must be careful not to infer, however, that anything theoretical is not practical or useful. Theoretical limits or values often are used as benchmarks against which measures are made to estimate efficiency.

tion waits (say, $i$), times the probability of waiting that many slots. Mathematically, we write this as

$$C = \sum_{i=0}^{\infty} (i* \text{ probability of waiting } i \text{ slots})$$

Because the probability a frame is not sent successfully during one time slot is $(1 - P)$, the probability of no successful transmissions for i slots is $(1 - P)^i$. In addition, the probability of waiting $i$ slots followed by a successful transmission is $(1 - P)^i*P$. Therefore, we write

$$C = \sum_{i=0}^{\infty} i*((1-P)^i *P)$$

Evaluating infinite sums is not something we care to do often but, as before, calculus comes to the rescue and allows this equation to be simplified as

$$C = \frac{1-P}{P} = \frac{1}{P} - 1$$

Before we go on, let's stop and reflect: What does this all mean? (No, we haven't changed this into a philosophy text, but a little reflection can benefit computer scientists, too.) First of all, remember that because $P$ is a probability, it lies between 0 and 1. Second, according to this equation, small values (near 0) for $P$ cause a large average contention time, whereas larger values (near 1) make $C$ nearly 0. The ideal would be zero contention, which would mean that each frame is sent successfully during the first time slot. But that is not realistic. We already have stated that the maximum value for $P$ is $P = (1 - 1/N)^{N-1}$. Plugging this into the definition of $C$ yields $C = (1 - 1/N)^{1-N} - 1$.

Next, as $N$ gets large, $P$ approaches the number $1/e \approx 1/2.718$ (another calculus tidbit). Consequently, $C$ approaches $e - 1 \approx 1.718$. Thus, the best average contention period as the number of stations gets large is about 1.7 time slots. Furthermore, this occurs only if the probability of a station sending decreases in proportion to the number of existing stations.

In practice, however, $p_s$ will not depend on the number of stations. A station will try to send what it needs regardless of how many other stations there are. If we repeated the previous analysis with $p_s$ defined as a constant, say $k$, then we would have $P = N*k*(1 - k)^{N-1}$. In this case $P$ approaches 0 as $N$ gets large. Consequently, $C$ approaches $\infty$ as $N$ gets large. The result is very long or unending contention with nothing getting through.

As our last step, we define the **percent utilization** ($U$) as the amount of time spent on transmitting a frame as a percentage of the total time spent on contending and transmitting. Assume the following definitions:

$R$ = transmission rate

$F$ = number of bits in a frame

$T$ = slot time

Since $C$ is the number of contention intervals, then $T*C$ is the contention time. Also, the time required to transmit a frame is $F/R$. Therefore, we can define the percent utilization as

$$U = 100 * \frac{\frac{F}{R}}{\frac{F}{R} + T*C}$$          **Equation 6.1**

Let's consider an example. Consider an 802.3 LAN (10 BASE 5) with 500 stations connected to five 500-meter segments. The data rate is 10 Mbps, and the slot time (defined by the standard) is 51.2 µsec.[*] If all stations transmit with equal probability, what is the channel utilization using a frame size of 512 bytes?

Pertinent variables have the following values:

$F = 512*8 = 4096$ bits

$$\frac{F}{R} = \frac{4096 \text{ bits}}{10 \text{ Mbps}} \approx 0.000410 \text{ seconds or } 410 \text{ µsec}$$

$$C = \left(1 - \frac{1}{N}\right)^{1-N} - 1 = \left(1 - \frac{1}{500}\right)^{1-500} - 1 \approx 1.716$$

$$U = 100 * \frac{410}{410 + 51.2 * 1.716} \approx 82\%$$

What happens if someone tries to exceed the 802.3 limits by adding more stations or increasing the maximum distance between stations? This model provides us with some theoretical limits. Let's consider the case for very large $N$. The best possible scenario causes $C$ to approach $e - 1 \approx 1.718$. Thus the best possible channel utilization is

$$U = 100 * \frac{\frac{F}{R}}{\frac{F}{R} + T*1.718}$$

Simplifying and substituting 51.2 for $T$ and 410 for $F/R$ yields

$$U = 100 * \frac{410}{410 + 51.2 * 1.718} = 82\%$$

---

[*] In this case, the slot time is larger than it would be for a single 2500-meter segment because the standard includes delays at the repeaters.

## 6.3    Token Ring: IEEE Standard 802.5

Token ring LAN is defined by the IEEE standard 802.5. Like the Ethernet, the token ring is a MAC protocol sitting between the logical link control (LLC) and the physical layer in the OSI model. Data rates for token ring networks are typically 4 Mbps, although some older ones may run at 1 Mbps and some newer ones at 16 Mbps. Transmission occurs using the Differential Manchester coding techniques described in Section 2.4.

Stations on a token ring LAN are connected in a ring using an interface card (Figure 6.9). A station can send directly only to its neighbors, and in most cases only to one neighbor (counterclockwise in Figure 6.9). If a station wants to send to another station on the ring, the frame must go through all the intermediate inter-

FIGURE 6.9    **Token Ring Network and Circulating Token**

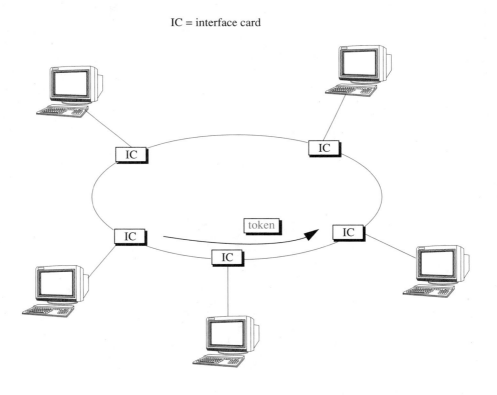

faces. Ring contention is handled through a token (a special frame) that circulates past all the stations. The specifics of claiming tokens and sending frames are involved, and we will discuss them later in this section. For now, we provide a very general and simple description of the process.

When a token arrives at a station one of two things occurs. If a station does not have data to send it routes the token to its neighbor. If a station does have something to send it claims the token, removes it from the ring, and sends a frame in the token's place. The frame then travels along the ring and each station examines its destination address. If the destination address does not match the current station's address, the station routes the frame to its neighbor. If it does match, the destination station copies the frame, sets some status bits in it, and routes the frame to its neighbor. The frame continues along the ring until it eventually arrives at the station that created it. This station removes the frame from the ring, generates a new token, and sends the token back onto the ring.

Two observations can be made almost immediately. The first is that ring contention is more orderly than with the Ethernet. Each station knows when it can send and sends only to its neighbor. An immediate consequence is that there is no wasted bandwidth due to collisions. The second observation is that the failure of one station can cause network failure. Unlike the Ethernet, every station participates in the routing of tokens or data frames. If a station fails it may not route a received token or data frame, thus causing it to disappear from the ring.

The latter problem can be solved by using the configuration in Figure 6.10. Instead of connecting neighboring stations directly, they all communicate through a

FIGURE 6.10     **Token Ring Network Using Wire Center**

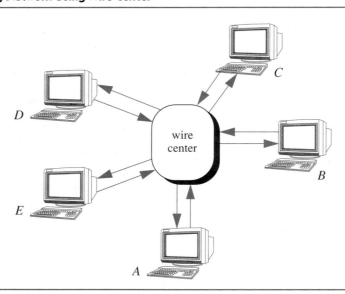

wire center. The configuration resembles a star topology physically, but it is still a ring logically. That is, a station still sends only to its neighbor, but the bits travel through the wire center.

The wire center contains a bypass relay for each station that can respond to current or commands from that station. If a station fails or loses power, the relay bypasses that station. For example, if *A* sends to *C* the frame goes from *A* to the wire center. It then goes to *B*, which routes it back to the center, where it is routed to *C*. If *B* fails the relay causes the frame received from *A* to bypass *B* and go directly to *C*. The wire center is used mainly to improve reliability while preserving the token ring protocol.

On a token ring network, the notion that the token moves from station to station is generally correct, but it does not occur the way you might think. For example, a station does not receive the entire token before passing it on. To illustrate, suppose a token ring network had the following characteristics:

- 20 stations each separated by 10 meters for a total ring length of 200 meters
- Transmission at 4 Mbps, or one bit every 0.25 μsec
- Propagation speed of 200 m/μsec

According to these characteristics, each bit would travel the ring in 1 μsec. But if the bits are sent at a rate of one every 0.25 μsec, no more than 4 bits are ever on the ring at any time. This is a problem because if no stations have anything to send, the token won't even fit on the ring, much less circulate around it. In order to get more bits on the ring, there is a delay at each station allowing it to examine each bit before deciding whether to copy it or repeat it. The delay is typically one bit-time, the time required for one bit to be transmitted. For a 4 Mbps data rate, the bit-time is 0.25 μsec.

In our example, if each station had a one bit-time delay, 24 bits would fit on the ring. As we will see, a token is 24 bits and the ring would accommodate the token. If the number of stations were reduced, however, fewer bits would fit and the token would be too big. Typically, to make the circulating token independent of the number of stations on the ring, one monitor station will have an extra delay to allow all 24 bits to fit on the ring. This monitor station is discussed further under ring maintenance in this section.

## TOKEN AND FRAME FORMATS

We already stated that a token is simply a special frame. Figure 6.11 shows both the token and frame formats. The four fields labeled "destination address," "source address," "data," and "frame check sequence" have the same meanings as those we have discussed in previous sections, so we will not elaborate again. The destination address may be an individual, group, or broadcast address. The data field has no theoretical maximum length, but there is a limit on how long a station can transmit uninterrupted, which puts a practical limit of about 5000 data octets.

Each frame has a **starting delimiter (SD)** and **ending delimiter (ED)** that designate a token's boundaries. SD has the special signal pattern *JK0JK000*. The 0s are

FIGURE 6.11    **Token Ring and Frame Formats**

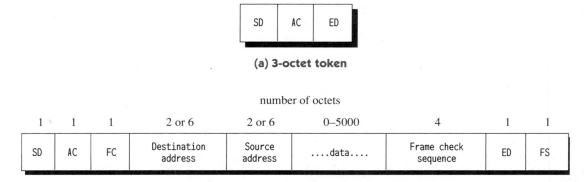

**(a) 3-octet token**

number of octets

| 1 | 1 | 1 | 2 or 6 | 2 or 6 | 0–5000 | 4 | 1 | 1 |
|---|---|---|---|---|---|---|---|---|
| SD | AC | FC | Destination address | Source address | ....data.... | Frame check sequence | ED | FS |

**(b) Variable octet frame**

```
          SD (starting delimiter):  J K 0 J K 0 0 0
               AC (access control):  p p p t m r r
                                     p p p: priority bits
                                           t: token bit
                                           m: monitor bit
                                     r r r: reservation bits
          ED (ending delimiter):  J K 1 J K 1 I E
              FC (frame control):  f f z z z z z z
                                     f: frame type bits
                                     z: control bits
                  FS (frame status):  a c x x a c x x
                                     a: address recognized bit
                                     c: frame copied bit
                                     x: undefined bit
```

binary 0s as defined by the Differential Manchester code. The symbols *J* and *K* correspond to special signals. To understand what they are, recall that the Differential Manchester code defines a signal transition (high to low or low to high) in the middle of each signal interval. The *J* and *K* signals violate that rule. The *J* signal starts out like a 0 but there is no transition in the middle. Similarly, the *K* signal starts out like a 1 and has no transition. Sometimes these signals are referred to as **non-data-*J*** and **non-data-*K***. Because these signals do not conform to the Manchester code for defining bits, they can never appear as part of any information. This makes them useful for indicating special conditions such as the start or end of a frame.

The ending delimiter has the signal pattern *JK*1*JK*1*IE*. The symbols *J* and *K* are the same as in the SD. The 1s are binary 1s. The two remaining bits correspond to an intermediate frame bit (*I*) and an error bit (*E*). As before, a communication between two stations may consist of many frames. Bit $I$ is 0 in the last frame and 1 otherwise. Bit $E$ is set to 1 whenever an error (such as a frame check sequence) is detected.

The second octet in each frame is the **access control** (**AC**). Its bits convey different meanings. The bit labeled $t$ stands for **token bit** and determines the frame type. A token has $t = 0$ and a data frame has $t = 1$, thus allowing a station to determine what it is receiving. The remaining bits deal with ring maintenance and token reservation, discussed later. The third frame octet is the **frame control** (**FC**), which also deals with ring maintenance.

The last octet is the **frame status** (**FS**) and has two copies (in case of errors) each of an **address recognized bit** (bit $a$) and a **frame copied bit** (bit $c$). The sending station initially sets bits $a$ and $c$ to 0. If the destination station is on the ring it sets $a$ to 1, indicating the address has been recognized. If the destination station copies the frame it also sets bit $c$ to 1. Note that the presence of the destination does not automatically mean the frame is copied. Status set at a higher layer (such as LLC) may temporarily prohibit receiving any frames. We have discussed such possibilities in the sections on sliding window protocols.

The frame status field tells the sending station whether the destination station is on the ring and, if it is, whether it copied the frame. If the destination station is there but did not copy the frame, the sending station presumably can try to resend the frame later.

## RESERVING AND CLAIMING TOKENS

The process of capturing tokens and sending data frames at first glance seems relatively simple. Once a station sends a frame and subsequently drains it from the ring, it creates and sends the token to its neighbor, who has the first opportunity to claim the token. Proceeding in this way allows the stations to transmit in the order in which they are connected. This process also puts an upper limit on the length of time a station must wait for a token.[*] But can we override this order? Are there ways to give a station a higher priority and thus allow it to send ahead of others? This certainly would be useful in cases where the token ring services high-priority or real-time devices.

To prioritize and allow stations to capture tokens in a different order, we assume that every station and the circulating token each has a priority. The station's priority is defined locally, and the token's priority is defined by the three **priority bits** in the AC field. A station can claim a token only if its priority is greater than or equal to the token's priority. This forces lower-priority stations to pass available tokens, even if the station has something to send. Only stations with priority higher than or equal to the token's priority can claim the token.

This system raises important questions: Who defines the token's priority? How is it done? Initially, one of the stations sends a token with priority 0. Afterward, the answer lies in the system's **reservation system**, the protocol used to reserve tokens and define priorities.

---

[*] This statement assumes there is a limit on the length of time that a station may possess the token.

Suppose a station receives a token with a higher priority than its own priority (we'll see how this can happen shortly) or receives a data frame. Either way, the station cannot send. However, the station may be able to put in a request (reservation) for the token for the next time it arrives. To do this, a station examines the incoming **reservation bits**. If the value stored there is smaller than the station's priority, it stores its own priority there, thus making the reservation. If the value is larger, the station can make no reservation at this time. Presumably some other station with a higher priority already made a reservation and it cannot be preempted by a lower-priority station. (Indeed, try booking your favorite suite at a five-star hotel when the English Prime Minister has already reserved that floor of the hotel.)

When a station drains a frame and creates a new token, it examines the reservation bits of the incoming frame. If it sees that some station has made a reservation it defines the new token's priority as the reservation value and stores the old priority locally. Afterward, it is designated as a **stacking station**—only it can restore the token to its original priority. Thus, when this token begins to travel the ring, it is claimed by the first station with a higher or equal priority. Lower-priority stations are ignored in favor of the higher-priority ones.

Figure 6.12 shows a pseudo-coded algorithm that describes the priority and reservation system. Each station executes it as frames and tokens arrive. The algorithm is simplified somewhat, as it does not show the receipt of frames destined for a station or deal with a station sending multiple frames. We intend the figure to focus only on making reservations and determining priorities, but it may be expanded as an exercise.

The algorithm refers to a frame's reservation bits and priority bits as **frame.res** and **frame.priority**, respectively. Similar notation is used for a token's bits. Like previous algorithms it is event driven, where the event is the arrival of a frame or token. If a frame arrives, the station determines whether the frame originated there (condition 1) or elsewhere (condition 4). If it originated elsewhere and the current station has a frame to send, it tries to make a reservation. If the station's priority is larger than the contents of frame.res (condition 5), it makes the reservation. If not, it makes no reservation. Either way, it passes the frame to its neighbor.

If the frame originated at the current station it must drain the frame and create a new token. The question that the station must now answer is: "What priority should the new token have? " There are two possible answers.

First, suppose some station with a higher priority than the frame's priority has made a reservation (condition 2). The station gives the token a priority equal to that of the station making the reservation (contents of frame.res). It also defines **token.res** = 0 to give any station a chance to make another reservation. But raising the token's priority is an awesome responsibility. Any station that does this also has the responsibility of lowering it later when the only stations with something to send have a priority lower than the token's priority. At that point the station must recognize a token whose priority it raised and lower it. To achieve this, the station (designated as a **stacking station**) stores the old and new priorities on a stack whenever it raises the priority.

The second answer occurs when the reservation on the incoming frame was made by a station with a smaller priority than the frame's priority. This means that as

FIGURE 6.12    Token Ring Protocol to Reserve and Claim a Token

```
      while (Peter Pan lives in the Never Land)
      {
        wait for an event;
        if (event is "frame arrives")
        {
1         if (frame originated at current station)
          {
            drain frame;
2           if (frame.res > frame.priority)
            {
              create and send token with token.priority = frame.res and token.res = 0;
              put old and new priorities on stacks and designate this station as a stacking station;
              continue;
            } /* end - frame.res > frame.priority */

3           if (current station is stacking station for this frame)
            {
              create and send token with token.priority = max(token.res, stacked priority);
              if token.res is used replace the top of the new priority stack with it;
              if the stacked priority is used, pop it from the old priority stack and discontinue the stacking
                 station designation if that stack is empty;
              continue;
            } /* end - current station is stacking station for this frame */

            create and send token with token.res = frame.res and token.priority = frame.priority;
          } /* end - frame originated at current station */

4         if (frame originated elsewhere)
          {
5           if (there is a frame to send) && (station priority > frame.res)
              store sending priority in frame.res ;
            send frame;
          }
        } /* end - event is "frame arrives" */

        if (event is "token arrives")
        {
6         if (current station is stacking station for this token)
          {
            create token with token.priority = max(token.res, stacked priority);
            if token.res is used replace the top of the new priority stack with it;
```

```
      if the stacked priority is used, pop it from the old priority stack and discontinue the stacking
         station designation if that stack is empty;
   }

7        if (there is a frame to send)
         {
8          if (station priority >= token.priority)
             claim token, create, and send frame;
           else
9            if (station priority > token.res)
               store sending priority in token.res;
         } /* end - frame to send */

      send frame or token;
    } /* end - event is "token arrives" */
  }/* end of while loop */
```

the frame travels the ring, no station that wants to send has a high enough priority to do so. Consequently, the new token's priority must be lowered, but which station has the authority to do so? If the current station did not raise the priority it cannot lower it. Thus, it simply creates a token with the same priority and reservation value as the incoming frame's (last statement under condition 1). Presumably the token will reach the stacking station, which will lower the priority.

However, if the current station is the stacking station (condition 3), it creates a new token with a lower priority. Next question: What is the new priority? The stacking station compares the incoming reservation value with its old stacked priority and chooses the larger value. If the reservation value is larger, this new priority replaces the current priority on the stack. The station is still the stacking station as it has not restored the priority that existed prior to its becoming the stacking station. If the reservation value is not larger, the token gets the stacked priority. The priority is popped from the stack and, if the stack is empty, the station is no longer a stacking station. Note that the stacking station designation is removed only when the old priority stack is empty, as the station could be a stacking station from another priority increase.

Now consider what happens when a token arrives. If the station is a stacking station (condition 6) it proceeds as we have just discussed. Afterward, it determines whether there is a frame to send (condition 7). If so, it compares the token's priority with the station's priority (condition 8). If the station has a high enough priority it claims the token. If not, it compares its priority with the value specified by the reservation bits (condition 9). Again, if it has a high enough priority it makes the reservation. Finally, it sends either the token or the frame (if it created one) to its neighbor.

This discussion is general and describes the major aspects of the priority and reservation system. Now it is time to see an example. Suppose four stations are ready to transmit (Figure 6.13) and that each has just one frame to send. Suppose also that station *C* has just captured the token and is sending its frame. We now apply the algorithm to the situation of Figure 6.13.

To help follow the algorithm, Table 6.2 summarizes what happens at each station as a frame or token travels the ring. The first column lists the steps. The second column indicates the station receiving the frame or token. The third column lists the conditions from Figure 6.12 that are true when the frame or token arrives. The fourth column specifies whether it sends a frame or token. The last two columns specify the priority and reservation value (values 0 through 7) of the outgoing frame or token. We begin the discussion at the point where station *C* has just captured a token and sent its frame.

We pick up the algorithm after *C* sends the frame, so the first line in Table 6.2 corresponds to the arrival of a frame at *D* (step 1). In this case, conditions 4 and 5 are true. That is, the frame did not originate at *D*, *D* has a frame to send, and its priority is higher than that of the incoming frame. As a result, *D* stores its priority (2) in frame.res and passes the frame to its neighbor. When *A* receives the frame (step 2), only condition 4 is true (*A*'s priority is too low). When *B* receives the frame (step 3), it reacts as *D* did previously, increasing frame.res to 5. The frame finally arrives back at *C* (step 4), the originating station, where it is drained from the ring. As conditions 1 and 2 are true, *C* creates and sends a token with priority = 5 and becomes the stacking station. *D* receives the token (step 5) but cannot capture it because the token's priority is too high. However, it does set the reservation value to 2 and sends the token to *A* (step 6). *A*'s priority is too low, so it sends the token to *B* (step 7). Station *B* claims the token (conditions 7 and 8) and sends a frame.

The frame circulates as before and eventually comes back to *B* (step 11). *B* drains the frame and creates a token. Notice now that the token's reservation field

FIGURE 6.13    **Reserving Tokens on a Token Ring**

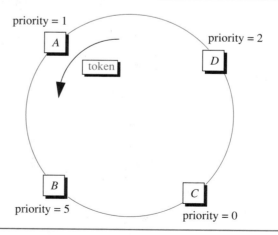

TABLE 6.2          Activities as Token and Frame Travel the Ring

| STEP | ARRIVING AT | CONDITION | STATION SENDS | PRIORITY | RESERVATION |
|------|-------------|-----------|---------------|----------|-------------|
| 1 | D - (frame) | 4 and 5 | Frame | 0 | 2 |
| 2 | A - (frame) | 4 | Frame | 0 | 2 |
| 3 | B - (frame) | 4 and 5 | Frame | 0 | 5 |
| 4 | C - (frame) | 1 and 2 | Token | 5 | 0 |
| 5 | D - (token) | 7 and 9 | Token | 5 | 2 |
| 6 | A - (token) | 7 | Token | 5 | 2 |
| 7 | B - (token) | 7 and 8 | Frame | 5 | 0 |
| 8 | C - (frame) | 4 | Frame | 5 | 0 |
| 9 | D - (frame) | 4 and 5 | Frame | 5 | 2 |
| 10 | A - (frame) | 4 | Frame | 5 | 2 |
| 11 | B - (frame) | 1 | Token | 5 | 2 |
| 12 | C - (token) | 6 | Token | 2 | 2 |
| 13 | D- (token) | 7 and 8 | Frame | 2 | 0 |
| 14 | A - (frame) | 4 and 5 | Frame | 2 | 1 |
| 15 | B - (frame) | 4 | Frame | 2 | 1 |
| 16 | C - (frame) | 4 | Frame | 2 | 1 |
| 17 | D - (frame) | 1 | Token | 2 | 1 |

contains 2 and the priority is 5. Since $B$ was not the stacking station ($C$ was at step 4) it sends a token with the same priority and reservation values as that in the received frame. When $C$ receives the frame (step 12), it sees condition 6 as true and lowers the token's priority to 2. The old priority is still on the stack and $C$ still remains the stacking station. Although the remaining steps are similar to those that already have occurred, you should go through them. Note that Table 6.2 can be expanded to the point where all stations have sent their frames and the token's priority is reduced to 0 again. We leave this as an exercise.

## RING MAINTENANCE

The discussions so far suffice to describe token ring operations as long as nothing goes wrong. This is a dangerous assumption to make, however. Things can and do go wrong; for example:

- A station sends a short frame over a long ring (where the last bit is sent before the first one has come back) and subsequently crashes. It is not able to drain the frame. A frame that is not drained is an **orphan frame**.

- A station receives a frame or token and crashes before it can send it. Now there is no token circulating and the stations waiting to send wait forever.
- Line noise damages a frame. Which station has the responsibility of fixing it?

Some problems can be handled by giving one of the stations a few additional responsibilities and designating it a **monitor station**. For example, to detect an orphan frame a station initially creates a frame with the monitor bit in the access control octet (Figure 6.11) set to 0. When the monitor receives a frame it sets the bit to 1. An orphaned frame is not drained from the ring, causing it to arrive at the monitor a second time with the bit already equal to 1. The monitor drains the frame and generates a new token.

The monitor also can detect a lost token using a built-in timer. The timer is defined depending on the ring's length, number of stations, and maximum frame size. Whenever the monitor sends a frame or token it starts the timer. If the monitor receives no other frame or token before the timer expires it assumes it was lost and generates a new token.

Some problems even the monitor station cannot solve. For example, what if the malfunctioning station is the monitor station? What if a break in the ring causes a lack of tokens? Sending new ones does nothing to correct the problem.

These problems are handled using control frames, as shown in Table 6.3. The control bits in the FC octet (Figure 6.11b) define the frame's function. When a new station enters the ring it sends a **duplicate address test frame** that stores its own address in the destination field. This frame ensures that the station's address is unique among those in the ring. When the frame returns the station checks the address-recognized bit in the frame's status field. If it is 0 there is no other station with that address; if it is 1 the station's address is a duplicate. The station removes itself from the ring and reports the error.

If a new monitor station must be chosen one or more stations submit bids to become the monitor station. The one with the highest address gets the job. The problem is that none of the stations knows which one that is. To determine this each one sends a succession of **claim token (CT) frames**. When a station receives a claim token frame it compares the token's source address with its own. If the token's

**TABLE 6.3    Token Ring Control Frames**

| FRAME TYPE | CONTROL BITS IN FC | MEANING |
|---|---|---|
| Active monitor present | 000101 | Informs stations a monitor is operational and initiates the neighbor identification procedure. |
| Beacon | 000010 | Locates ring faults. |
| Claim token | 000011 | Elects a new monitor. |
| Duplicate address test | 000000 | Checks for duplicate addresses. |
| Purge | 000100 | Clears the ring. |
| Standby monitor present | 000110 | Carries out the neighbor identification procedure. |

source address is larger the station stops sending its own frames and repeats the ones it receives. If the token's source address is smaller the station drains it from the ring and continues to send its own frames. Consequently a CT frame never makes it past another competing station with a higher address and the only CT frames to circumnavigate the ring come from the station with the highest address. When this station receives its own CT frame it considers itself duly elected as monitor station—after a very short campaign and without the help of PAC contributions.

When a station is elected monitor and periodically thereafter, it sends an **active monitor present (AMP) frame** to notify the other stations that there is an active monitor station. If for some reason the monitor malfunctions, no AMP frames are sent. The other stations have timers that expire when they do not detect an AMP frame over a period of time. When this happens they make bids to become the new monitor by sending a CT frame, as discussed previously.

Before a monitor station creates and sends a new token it first sends a **purge frame**. Meanwhile it drains everything it receives including the returning purge frame to make sure the ring is clear before sending a new token or AMP frame.

The **standby monitor present (SMP) frame** is part of the **neighbor identification procedure**. When the monitor sends the AMP frame it sets the *a* bits in the status field equal to 0. The first station receiving it (downstream neighbor) records the source address and sets the *a* bits in the status field to 1 before repeating the frame. That station now knows its immediate upstream neighbor. The *a* bits are set to 1 to inform the other stations in the ring that the arriving frame is not from their immediate neighbor. After receiving the AMP frame from its upstream neighbor the station sends an SMP frame (also with the *a* bits equal to 0). Its downstream neighbor receives the frame, records the source address, sets the *a* bits to 1, and repeats it. After a while it sends its own SMP frame and its downstream neighbor reacts similarly. This cascading effect causes each station to send its own SMP frame to inform its downstream neighbor of its identity. Because the *a* bits are set by the first station receiving each SMP frame, each station can distinguish a frame that its upstream neighbor originated and a frame that the upstream neighbor repeated.

A **beacon frame** is used to inform stations that a problem has occurred and the token-passing protocol has stopped. Previously we stated that each station has a timer to detect an absence of AMP frames. When it happens the station does not know whether the monitor malfunctioned or whether there was a break in the ring. In the latter case, sending a CT frame serves no purpose. Consequently, a station detecting a problem sends a continuous stream of beacon frames containing the address of its upstream neighbor. If they return, the station assumes there is no break (or it has been corrected) and begins sending CT frames as before. If the beacons do not return in a specified amount of time, the station concludes there is a break somewhere and reports the error to a higher layer in the protocol. If the station receives beacons from another station it suspends sending its own and repeats the ones it receives. Eventually, if there is a break, the only station sending beacon frames (Figure 6.14) is the one downstream from the break.

**FIGURE 6.14    Locating a Ring Break**

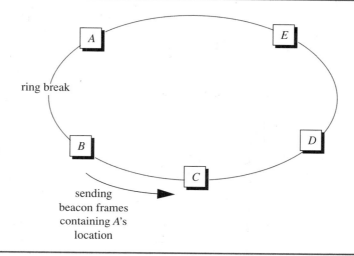

One last function of the monitor is to make sure the token fits on the ring. Previously we discussed the fact that the number of bits that fit on the ring depends on the ring's length and the delays at each station. If both parameters are small, the number of bits that will fit is small. This is not a problem when a frame is being sent as a station can be sending a frame's bits at the same time it is receiving previously sent ones. A circulating token, however, is not drained until it is claimed and it must fit on the ring. The monitor inserts extra delays to allow a full token to occupy the ring and circulate.

## FIBER DISTRIBUTED DATA INTERFACE (FDDI)

The 802.5 token ring networks are common, but the data rates are low by today's standards. Another standard is the **fiber distributed data interface (FDDI)** developed by ANSI. Someone not familiar with the differences among protocols might call it a token ring over fiber. That classification is not entirely correct, but there are many similarities between FDDI and the token ring. For example, both connect stations in a logical ring and both rely on a circulating token to determine which one can send.

Unlike token ring networks, FDDI uses a multimode or single mode optical fiber. The advantages are freedom from electrical disturbances, better security, and faster data rates. FDDI allows a data rate of 100 Mbps over a 200 kilometer ring connecting up to 100 stations. FDDI also connects stations using two rings instead of one. The second ring can be used to send tokens and frames in parallel with the first one (Figure 6.15a). In case of a ring break the rings can be joined to create a single logical ring (Figure 6.15b).

FIGURE 6.15    **Counterrotating Rings**

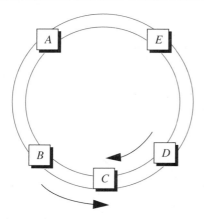

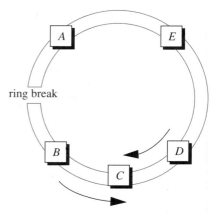

**(a) Counterrotating rings for parallel communication**    **(b) Connecting the ring in case of a break**

Another difference between token ring and FDDI is how a signal is transmitted. Recall that the token ring uses Differential Manchester transmission signals. Its advantage is that it is self-synchronizing. The transition in the middle of each interval, however, means the baud rate must be twice the data rate. For FDDI this would mean that a 200 million baud rate is needed for a 100 Mbps data rate. Instead of requiring such a high baud rate, the approach is to transmit the data bit stream as a sequence of on/off light pulses. The problem with that is that long strings of 0s or 1s mean long constant signals. As we discussed in Section 2.4, this can cause a loss of synchronization.

To lower the baud rate requirement and to maintain a synchronization ability, FDDI uses a **4 of 5 code** in conjunction with an **NRZI (nonreturn to zero invert)** technique. NRZI is similar to NRZ except that the signal remains constant as long as 0s are being sent but changes each time a 1 is sent. Thus a string of 0s still means a constant signal, but a string of 1s causes the signal to change with each 1.

For every four bits of data a 4B/5B encoder creates a 5-bit code, as shown in Table 6.4. Each set of five bits is then transmitted using NRZI. Using this scheme, a signal will change at most five times for each 4 data bits. This means that a 100 Mbps data rate can be achieved using a 125 million baud rate. At the same time, the 4B/5B encoder never codes more than two consecutive binary 0s for data, ensuring that the signal is never constant for long periods. The bottom line is that this method preserves the self-synchronizing ability using a baud rate just 25% higher than the data rate.

Frame and token formats in FDDI are similar to those of the token ring. In fact, comparing Figures 6.16 and 6.11 shows only two differences. First is that each frame or token begins with a preamble. It contains 16 or more idle control signals (80 or more binary 1s). The preamble causes a signal change, with each 1-bit resulting in the signal oscillating at its maximum baud rate. It is used to establish

TABLE 6.4    **4 of 5 Code Definition**

| DATA BITS | ENCODED BITS | CONTROL SYMBOLS | ENCODED BITS |
|---|---|---|---|
| 0000 | 11110 | Halt | 00100 |
| 0001 | 01001 | Idle | 11111 |
| 0010 | 10100 | non-data-J | 11000 |
| 0011 | 10101 | non-data-K | 10001 |
| 0100 | 01010 | Quiet | 00000 |
| 0101 | 01011 | Reset | 00111 |
| 0110 | 01110 | Set | 11001 |
| 0111 | 01111 | Terminate | 01101 |
| 1000 | 10010 | | |
| 1001 | 10011 | | |
| 1010 | 10110 | | |
| 1011 | 10111 | | |
| 1100 | 11010 | | |
| 1101 | 11011 | | |
| 1110 | 11100 | | |
| 1111 | 11101 | | |

synchronization. The other difference is that the access control (AC) field is eliminated in the frame and is replaced by the frame control (FC) field in the token. Some of the bits in these and other fields are different from their counterparts in the token ring, but those differences are not important to our discussion. If you are interested, Reference 2 describes the functions of each bit.

One interesting note is that the elimination of the AC field along with its reservation and priority bits suggests a significant change in claiming tokens. When a station

FIGURE 6.16    **Frame and Token Formats**

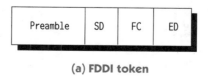

(a) **FDDI token**

| Preamble | SD | FC | Destination address | Source address | ....data.... | Frame check sequence | ED | FS |
|---|---|---|---|---|---|---|---|---|

(b) **FDDI frame**

claims a token it inserts a frame onto the ring, as in the token ring. This time, however, instead of draining the token the sending station reinserts it immediately after the frame. This way the token is always on the ring and any station has the opportunity to insert a frame when the token passes by.

Figure 6.17 illustrates in more detail. Suppose stations *A*, *B*, and *C* have frames frA, frB, and frC to send. When the token reaches *A* (Figure 6.17a), only the token T is on the ring. When *A* gets the token it sends the frame followed by the token (Figure 6.17b). When the frame and token reach *B*, *B* repeats the frame, sends its own, and puts the token back onto the ring (Figure 6.17c). After passing station *C* (Figure 6.17d), the ring contains all three frames followed by the token.

After comparing the token ring with FDDI you might ask, Why doesn't the IEEE standard allow multiple frames in its token ring? There are a couple of ways to answer this. First, for a long time the 4 Mbps data rate with a single token met the user's needs. (It still meets many users' needs; not everyone needs a Cadillac of LANs.) With fiber, however, a single small frame does not make the best use of the increased capacity. For example, sending relatively short frames past 1000 stations over 200 km of fiber means that much of the fiber is idle. It's like building a six-lane highway between two rural communities to be used by occasional tourists and a haywagon. It can be done, but most will agree the cost is not justified—and the haywagon will not reach its destination any faster.

The same is true of fiber. Its increased capacity is best used with a lot of traffic and single small frames do not constitute heavy traffic. Having larger frames or more of them, however, will increase the traffic. In this case using multiple frames is the choice. Still we return to the question: Can't IEEE change the standard? Technically yes, but that defeats the purpose of standards. Standards exist to maintain con-

FIGURE 6.17    **FDDI Ring Contents**

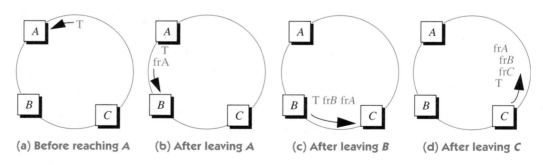

(a) **Before reaching** *A*    (b) **After leaving** *A*    (c) **After leaving** *B*    (d) **After leaving** *C*

| | |
|---|---|
| T: | token |
| frA: | frame sent by *A* |
| frB: | frame sent by *B* |
| frC: | frame sent by *C* |

sistency, and changing them regularly creates inconsistency, which is little different from having no standards at all. But that does not mean new standards cannot be defined to meet growing needs.

Research is being done that would allow 100 Mbps traffic using FDDI specifications over copper. Called CDDI (copper data distributed interface), it would provide a much higher capacity at a much cheaper rate. Reference 7 provides more information on CDDI. Slotted rings are yet another option.

Several comparisons have been made between FDDI and another networking technology, **asynchronous transfer mode** (**ATM**). Both are being promoted as future dominant network technologies. Whereas FDDI was designed as a shared medium LAN, ATM is a very fast packet-switched protocol using small fixed-sized packets optimized for multimedia use. It establishes logical connections similar to X.25, but the short fixed-sized packets allow them to be created and routed using underlying hardware.

Both FDDI and ATM provide very high data rates (measured in the 100 Mbps range), making them especially attractive as alternatives for overcrowded LANs or multimedia applications. Already, many vendors are promising ATM products in the near future (Reference 8). There is some concern that ATM represents a technology whose full potential will not be realized soon and that FDDI, by contrast, is well established. The comparison between the two makes for some interesting reading, and we encourage the reader to investigate references 8, 9, and 10.

## SLOTTED RINGS

A slotted ring (also called a **Cambridge ring** because it was developed at the University of Cambridge) consists of several rotating slots. Slots, similar to tokens, are specially formatted frames that circulate the ring (Figure 6.18). Unlike a token, however, each slot is similar to an empty frame, having 8 bits of space for a destination and source address, 16 bits for data, and some status bits. If an empty slot passes a station that has something to send, the station stores the necessary address and as much data as will fit. If a slot is full the station waits for the first empty slot. When the slot returns the sending station marks the slot as empty by changing one of its status bits. If the station has more data to send it will not use the same slot but will wait for the next empty slot. This forces empty slots onto the ring and prevents one station from monopolizing the slots.

We should note that slotted rings allow many bits to be on the ring simultaneously. Previous discussions showed the number of bits on a ring to be typically small. However, by using longer rings or longer propagation delays at each station, the number of bits on the ring simultaneously can be increased to meet the requirements of multiple slots.

## EFFICIENCY

The discussion on token ring efficiency is mercifully short compared to similar discussions of other protocols. This is because there are no collisions to waste bandwidth and

FIGURE 6.18     **Slotted Ring**

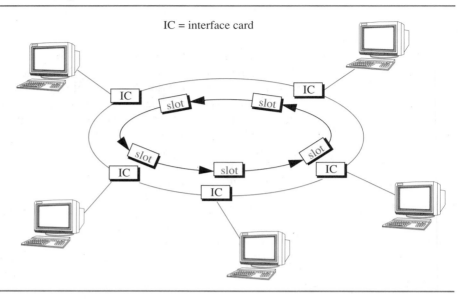

complicate the efficiency. The CSMA/CD contention suffers badly under heavy loads, but token rings achieve very high rates of efficiency. For example, suppose we consider the percent utilization, defined in Section 6.2. Recall that it is the amount of time on an actual successful transmission as a percentage of the total time spent on contending and sending. Here contending means waiting for a free token. To illustrate, assume the worst case of maximum traffic. That is, each station has something to send each time a token arrives. The percent utilization is

$$U \ = \ 100 * \frac{\text{time to send a frame}}{\text{time to send a frame} + \text{time to send a token}}$$

Tokens, however, typically are much smaller than frames and travel much smaller distances (the distance between two stations as opposed to the ring's circumference). This means the time to send a token is very small compared to the time to send a frame. Thus the percent utilization is close to 100%.

This short discussion does not mean there is no basis for further analysis. Indeed there is, but it is not within the scope of this text. If you are interested, references 4 and 11 provide more analysis of the token ring.

## 6.4    Token Bus: IEEE Standard 802.4

The third and last MAC protocol we discuss is the token bus protocol. It combines features of the Ethernet and the token ring protocols. For example, the token bus

operates on the same principle as the token ring. The stations are logically organized into a ring and a token passes among them. A station wanting to send something must wait for the token to arrive. Here, however, the stations communicate
via a common bus as in the Ethernet. For example, Figure 6.19 shows five stations, *A* through *E*, connected to a bus. If the logical order is *A-B-C-D-E*, then *A*
starts by sending a token to *B* along the bus. As with the Ethernet, each station is
capable of receiving it, but the token's destination address specifies which station
gets it. When *B* receives the token it has permission to send a frame. If it has no
frame it sends a token to *C*. Similarly, *C* sends either a token to *D* or a data frame,
and so on.

Generally, a station receives a token from its predecessor and sends a token to
its successor. Another immediate difference between the token bus and token ring is
that token bus stations must know their predecessor and successor. They must know
their successor so they know which destination address to put in the token. The reasons for knowing their predecessor will be discussed later.

Token bus networks have the most support from those involved in factory automation and process control, applications that require real-time processing. The real-
time environments made many people nervous about embracing the 802.3 standard
because there was no theoretical limit on the number of collisions that could occur.
This meant that there was no theoretical limit on the delays one of the network components could experience. With large objects moving down the assembly line, the
possibility of unexpected delays was unacceptable (reminiscent of the old television
gag where pies or pieces of candy are rolling down the assembly line faster than the
worker can pack them). In addition, the token ring did not satisfy their needs. First,
the physical ring is not the best fit for the linear organization of an assembly line.
Second, the point-to-point connections made the system susceptible to disaster if
one of the links failed. Thus, their solution was to use the linear organization to fit
the physical environment but a logical ring order to put an upper limit on the time a
station must wait for a token.

FIGURE 6.19    **Token Bus**

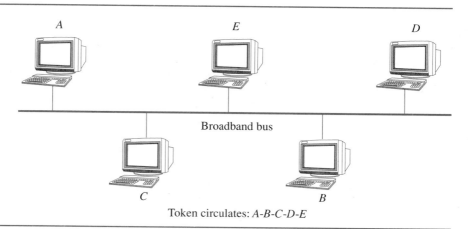

Token circulates: *A-B-C-D-E*

There also are some differences between the bus of the IEEE 802.5 and 802.3 physical layers. The token bus specifies signals to be sent over a baseband cable or a broadband cable like that used for cable television. It allows for three different modulation schemes: continuous FSK (baseband), phase coherent FSK (baseband), and multilevel duobinary AM/PSK (broadband). As these are variations on the modulation schemes discussed in Section 2.5, we will not discuss them further. If you are interested in specifics, you can consult references 2 and 12. Data rates may be as high as 10 Mbps depending on the modulation technique.

Figure 6.20 shows the token bus frame format. All the fields in the frame are similar to similarly named fields discussed previously. The only difference is that there is no special token format. The FC field specifies whether the frame contains data, is a token, or is any of several other control frames we will discuss shortly. Remember, since the tokens are sent along a bus the destination and source addresses must be specified.

## TOKEN BUS OPERATIONS

The linear physical topology coupled with the logical ring organization adds some complexity to the token bus operations. For example, how is a new station added to the station? With token ring it is added between two others and automatically gets the token from its upstream neighbor. In a token bus a predecessor must be determined and notified of its new successor. Similarly, if a station is removed, its predecessor must be informed so it does not send the deleted station any tokens.

How is the logical order determined? Typically, the stations' addresses determine the order, but how do the stations notify each other where they are? How does each one determine who its predecessor and successor are? What makes these questions difficult is that no one station has a global view of anything. Each knows only what it has and what arrives on incoming frames. With no central control the stations must somehow exchange information and come to some consensus about

**FIGURE 6.20     Token Bus Frame Format**

| | | | number of octets | | | | |
|---|---|---|---|---|---|---|---|
| 1 or more | 1 | 1 | 2 or 6 | 2 or 6 | 0—8191 | 4 | 1 |
| Preamble | SD | FC | DA | SA | ....data.... | FCS | ED |

SD:   Start delimiter
FC:   Frame control
DA:   Destination address
SA:   Source address
FCS:  Frame check sequence
ED:   End delimiter

order. It's a bit like an anarchistic society establishing some order without agreeing to any centralized government.

The answers to these questions lie in the different control frames and the rules for using them. Table 6.5 shows the different token bus control frames, their FC fields, and a brief summary of their use.

**Removing Stations**     What happens when a station leaves the ring? Suppose the token passes through three stations in the order $A$, $B$, and $C$. Suppose station $A$ has the token and has nothing to send. It creates a new token addressed to $B$ and sends it. Similarly, if $B$ has nothing to send it sends a token to $C$. Now suppose $B$ leaves or malfunctions and is no longer in the ring. Either way, the result is the same: $A$ sends a token to $B$, but since $B$ no longer exists the token effectively disappears. Meanwhile, $C$ and all subsequent stations wait for a token that will not arrive.

To deal with this problem, whenever $A$ sends a token to its successor $B$, it listens for a response. After $B$ receives the token it sends a token to its successor or a frame (depending on whether it has data to send) containing $B$'s address. Since the frame or token travels along the bus, $A$ can detect it. Thus, $A$ knows its successor received the token. On the other hand, if $A$ detects no response in a reasonable time it suspects a problem. In the event the problem may be transmission interference it sends the token again and listens. If it hears the expected response it concludes the token has been sent successfully.

If it still does not hear a response, it proceeds on the assumption that $B$ is no longer there. The logical thing to do is to send all subsequent tokens to $B$'s successor, but $A$ does not know who it is. To find out, $A$ broadcasts a **who follows frame** specifying $B$ (in the data field) as its current successor. The frame is a request for $B$'s successor to identify itself. Each station is able to examine this frame and

**TABLE 6.5     Token Bus Control Frame Types**

| FRAME TYPE | FC FIELD | FUNCTION |
|---|---|---|
| Claim token | 00000000 | Used in a protocol to establish who gets the token initially or following a recovery. |
| Resolve contention | 00000100 | Used in an arbitration protocol when two or more stations attempt to enter the logical ring simultaneously. |
| Set successor | 00001100 | Used to define a new successor to a specified station. |
| Solicit successor 1 | 00000001 | Used in a protocol that invites certain stations to enter the logical ring. |
| Solicit successor 2 | 00000010 | Same as Solicit successor 1 but pertains to different stations. |
| Token | 00001000 | The holder of this frame has permission to transmit data. |
| Who follows | 00000011 | Used in a protocol to determine a station's successor. |

determine whether it is *B's* successor. One station, in this case *C*, recognizes that it is *B's* successor and responds by sending a **set successor frame** to *A* (whose address was also in the who follows frame). When *A* receives this frame it redefines its successor as *C* and sends the token.

This scenario applies when *B* leaves the ring unexpectedly. If it voluntarily leaves a different protocol is followed. In this case *B* waits for the token and then sends a set successor frame to *A* specifying *C* as *A's* new successor. *A* records the information and *B's* final activity is to send the token to *C*. When the token eventually returns to *A*, *A* sends it to its new successor, *C*.

**Adding Stations**        Adding new stations is a bit more complex. The insertion protocol does not allow a new station to insert itself into the ring. Rather, a new station must wait for an existing station to invite it into the ring. It's like attending a party at a fashionable country club: don't try to get in without an invitation. Periodically (i.e., according to timers) each station sends a **solicit successor 1 frame** specifying its own and its successor's addresses and waits a sufficient time for a station to respond. If none respond, the station assumes no one wants to enter and passes the token to its successor. If there is a station with an address between the two specified ones it may now submit a bid to enter the ring. It does so by sending a set successor frame to the station extending the invitation. That station records its new successor and sends its next token there.

For example, Figure 6.21 shows a token bus containing three stations, *A*, *B*, and *C*. Two new stations, *X* and *Y*, want to enter but have not yet done so. That is, they are physically connected but do not participate in the token passing. Assume the addresses are ordered $A > X > B > C > Y$ and that the token must follow that order. At some point *A* sends a solicit successor 1 frame specifying *A's* and *B's* address. Only *X*'s address is between them, so *X* sends a set successor frame to *A*. *A* recognizes *X* as its new successor and sends all subsequent tokens to *X*.

**FIGURE 6.21    Adding New Stations to a Token Bus**

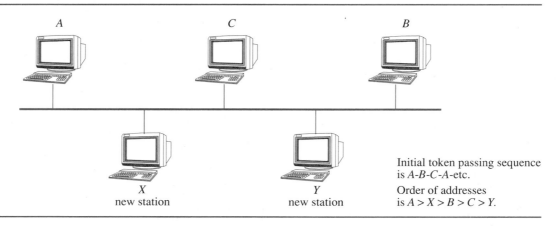

Initial token passing sequence is *A-B-C-A*-etc.

Order of addresses is $A > X > B > C > Y$.

Since the solicit successor 1 frame is an invitation to stations with an address between two given ones, a new station with an address less than or greater than all others will never respond. The **solicit successor 2 frame** is used for those stations. The station with the smallest address sends it periodically specifying the current and successor's addresses (the smallest and largest addresses). Any station with an even smaller or larger address responds as before by sending a set successor frame. In the example of Figure 6.21, station $Y$ cannot enter the ring until station $C$ broadcasts a solicit successor 2 frame. Then $Y$ sends $C$ its set successor frame and enters the ring as $C$'s successor and $A$'s predecessor.

This approach works well when stations enter one at a time. But what happens if two or more stations respond to a solicit successor frame?[*] For example, if the stations of Figure 6.21 were ordered $A > X > Y > B > C$, then both $X$ and $Y$ would respond to a solicit successor frame from $A$. When multiple stations respond their frames collide and the station sending the solicit successor frame hears the noise. It responds by sending a **resolve contention frame**. Each of the colliding stations receives this frame and places itself into one of four groups, depending on the first two bits of its address.

If a station's address begins with 00 it sends another set successor frame immediately. Otherwise it waits 1, 2, or 3 time slots, depending on whether its address begins with 01, 10, or 11, before sending another set successor frame. However, if a waiting station detects a set successor frame on the ring, it stops trying to enter the ring until it receives another invitation. This prioritizes the contending stations and forces some of them to back off from trying to enter.

After sending a resolve contention frame the station again listens. If it receives a set successor frame it proceeds as described previously and allows the station into the ring. However, it could detect another collision (if two or more addresses have the same first two bits), in which case it sends another resolve contention frame and waits. This time the colliding stations place themselves into one of four groups depending on the second pair of bits in their address. As before, a station sends a set successor frame immediately or waits 1, 2, or 3 time slots to do so.

Every time the soliciting station hears a collision it sends another resolve contention frame. Each successive frame causes the colliding stations to use the next pair of address bits to determine their group, thus reducing the number of stations trying to enter. Eventually, only one station's set successor frame will get through, and it will join the ring. The only way collisions will occur with every pair of address bits is if two stations have the same address, which, of course, we don't allow.

**Lost Tokens**     We have discussed how to bring stations into the ring one at a time assuming a previous ring order already has been established. We have discussed what to do if a station due to receive a token malfunctions. But what about a

---

[*] From this point we no longer distinguish between the solicit successor 1 and solicit successor 2 frames.

more difficult question: What happens if the station holding the token malfunctions? For example, suppose station *A* receives the token and sends a frame. Its predecessor detects the frame and concludes the token has been passed successfully. Now suppose station *A* malfunctions after it sends the frame but before it can pass the token to its successor. Station *A* goes down and takes the token with it. All the others are now waiting for a nonexistent token.

The logical solution is for some station to take the initiative and reintroduce a token into the ring. But which one does it? How is that decision reached? Again, the difficulty is caused by the fact that there are many stations waiting and any number of them may take the initiative. There must be a way to resolve the conflicts.

When a station does not receive a token in a reasonable amount of time a timer expires, alerting the station that a token has not arrived. The station responds by sending a **claim token frame**. This is an attempt to notify all other stations that it is trying to claim the token. After sending the frames it listens to the bus for any other such transmissions. If it detects none it concludes it is the only station trying to claim the token. It creates a new token and sends it to its successor. The ring is operational again.

The solution is more complex if several stations' timers expire and they all send claim token frames. In this case they all begin executing a contention resolving algorithm. Each station sending the frame pads the data field (adds bits) to make the total frame length equivalent to 0, 2, 4, or 6 slot times. The first two bits of the station's address determine the frame's length. After sending the frame, the station continues to listen to the bus for another time slot. If another station sends a longer frame, the listening station detects it and drops its claim for the token. The effect is that stations sending shorter claim token frames than other stations give up their claim.

When several stations send equal length frames, if the listening station does not detect another frame it sends another claim token frame whose length depends on the second pair of address bits. Again it listens for at least one slot time and proceeds as just described. If a station sends a third claim token frame it uses the third pair of address bits to determine its length. If necessary, it continues to send claim token frames using subsequent pairs of address bits. The only way two stations could repeatedly send the same length claim token frames is if every pair of address bits is identical. Since this cannot happen (all stations have unique addresses) eventually one station prevails with the longest frame and gets the token.

**Ring Initialization**     All of the previous discussion has assumed that some logical order already existed prior to a particular situation. But what about the initial startup? Remember, each station knows its own address but has no knowledge about other stations. Which one gets the token initially? When a station gets it, to whom does it send the token? In other words, how is the logical ring order determined?

This situation is much like the lost-token situation. Initially, many stations are connected to the ring, but there is no token. Therefore, the logical approach is to proceed as before. Each station goes through the process of sending and resending claim token frames until one station gets it. The difference here is that the station with the token does not know who its successor is and does not know where to send the token. As a result it sends the token to itself. This is not as ludicrous as it seems. Effectively we have just defined a logical ring containing one station whose successor and predecessor are itself. However, the token passing protocol is now in effect, and all the other stations are viewed as new stations waiting to enter the ring. Consequently, the station in the ring eventually sends a solicit successor frame and another station enters the ring. Over a period of time solicit successor frames are sent, thus allowing all of the waiting stations to enter the ring.

### PRIORITIZING FRAMES

The token bus does not prioritize stations and tokens as did the token ring, but it does define priorities for data to be sent. Each station maintains four priorities or service classes numbered 0, 2, 4, and 6. The classes are ordered with class 0 having the lowest priority and class 6 having the highest. As information comes down to the MAC layer from a higher layer, the protocol determines the information's priority. The protocol then creates data frames and stores them in one of four queues (one for each class) the station maintains (Figure 6.22).

When a station gets a token it sends class 6 frames first. If there are none it looks for class 4 frames, then class 2 frames, and finally class 0 frames. A station sends frames in a class until either a timer expires or there are no more frames in that class. Afterward, the station passes the token to its successor or sends frames from the next lowest class.

**FIGURE 6.22**     **Prioritizing Frames**

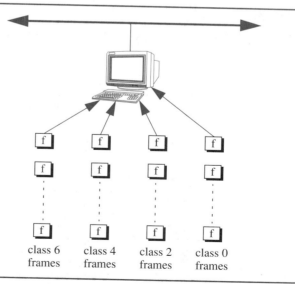

class 6 frames    class 4 frames    class 2 frames    class 0 frames

To control frame transmissions each station maintains two timers: a **token holding timer (THT)** and a **token rotation timer (TRT)**.[*] The THT is the maximum time a station may spend sending class 6 frames. The TRT determines the maximum time for a token to rotate around the ring. It also determines the maximum time allowed for the station to send frames in the lower classes. On receipt of the token a station starts its THT and sends class 6 frames until there are no more or until the THT expires. The station starts its TRT prior to sending the token to its successor. The timer then continues counting while the token travels the logical ring. When the token returns and the station has sent its class 6 frames, the remaining time on the TRT determines how long it has to send any remaining frames. If other stations had little to send the current station has more time sending frames. If other stations send more frames the current one sends fewer. The intent is to minimize delays as the token travels the logical ring.

Figure 6.23 shows pseudo code of the logic behind sending frames. When a token arrives the station starts the THT timer and sends class 6 frames until the THT expires or there are no more class 6 frames. It then sends class 4 frames until the TRT expires or there are no more class 4 frames. It performs similarly for class 2

**FIGURE 6.23    Protocol to Send Frames**

```
while (Horton hears a Who)
{
wait for arriving token;
start THT timer;
while (THT not expired) && (class 6 queue not empty)
    send class 6 frames;
while (TRT not expired) && (class 4 queue not empty)
    send class 4 frames;
while (TRT not expired) && (class 2 queue not empty)
    end class 2 frames;
while (TRT not expired) && (class 0 queue not empty)
    send class 0 frames;
set TRT timer;
send token to successor;
    }       /* end of while loop */
```

[*] Actually, there are three token rotation timers, one for each of classes 0, 2, and 4. To simplify our discussion we assume all three timers are equal and are represented by TRT. If you are interested, Reference 2 discusses the more general case and provides a more detailed analysis.

and class 0 frames. Finally, when the station has finished sending frames it starts the TRT and sends the token to its successor. The TRT continues counting the entire time the token is traveling the ring.

For example, suppose a token circulates among four stations in the order *A-B-C-D*. As the token arrives at *A*, Table 6.6 shows how many frames of each class each station has to send and the time left on each station's TRT. We simplify the example by assuming all frames are the same size and require the same amount of time to send. Suppose timer units are slot times, the time required to send one frame. That is, THT = 6 means a station can send up to six class 6 frames at a time.

When *A* gets the token it sends six class 6 frames and two class 4 frames. It then sets its TRT to 32 before sending the token to *B*. Meanwhile, the time left on *B's, C's,* and *D's* TRTs decreases by 8 (row 1 in Table 6.7). When *B* gets the token it can send only six class 6 frames. At that point both its THT and TRT expire and it sends the token. During this time the others' timers decrease by 6. When *C* gets the token it has 12 units left on its TRT and sends six class 6 tokens and six class 4 frames. Meanwhile, *D's* TRT decreases to 6, and when it gets the token it can send only six class 6 frames. The token returns to *A* and the timers are as shown in row 4 of Table 6.7. The token continues to circulate and if there are no new frames, the remaining rows of Table 6.7 describe the number of frames sent and left along with each station's TRT value.

An important relation between the two timers guarantees a certain amount of high-priority traffic along the bus. Suppose there are *n* stations. If each station spends the full time allowed by the THT sending class 6 frames, the token will take at least *n*\*THT time to circulate the ring once. (For this analysis, ignore the negligible time it takes to send a token to a successor.) In this case, if TRT = *n*\*THT then each station's TRT expires after it sends its class 6 frames. Consequently, it sends nothing below class 6. In other words, class 6 frames get 100% of the bus's bandwidth.

Two conditions allow a station to send lower-priority frames. First is if one or more stations do not send the maximum number of class 6 frames. Second is if TRT > *n*\*THT. The first depends on events beyond a designer's control. Therefore, to guarantee that class 6 frames do not monopolize the bus, we need

TABLE 6.6    **Stations with Frames to Send**

| STATION | NUMBER OF CLASS 6 FRAMES | NUMBER OF CLASS 4 FRAMES | NUMBER OF CLASS 2 FRAMES | NUMBER OF CLASS 0 FRAMES | TIME LEFT ON TRT |
|---------|--------------------------|--------------------------|--------------------------|--------------------------|------------------|
| A | 8 | 4 | 2 | 1 | 8 |
| B | 9 | 4 | 2 | 2 | 14 |
| C | 6 | 7 | 0 | 0 | 26 |
| D | 7 | 8 | 3 | 6 | 32 |

THT = 6
Maximum value in TRT = 32

**TABLE 6.7 Station Information After Receiving Each Token**

| STATION GETTING TOKEN | NUMBER OF FRAMES SENT (NUMBER LEFT), BY CLASS | | | | AMOUNT OF TIME LEFT ON TRT TIMERS PRIOR TO SENDING TOKEN, BY STATION. | | | |
|---|---|---|---|---|---|---|---|---|
| | 6 | 4 | 2 | 0 | A | B | C | D |
| A | 6 (2) | 2 (2) | 0 (2) | 0 (1) | 32 | 6 | 18 | 24 |
| B | 6 (3) | 0 (4) | 0 (2) | 0 (2) | 26 | 32 | 12 | 18 |
| C | 6 (0) | 6 (1) | 0 (0) | 0 (0) | 14 | 20 | 32 | 6 |
| D | 6 (1) | 0 (8) | 0 (3) | 0 (6) | 8 | 14 | 26 | 32 |
| A | 2 (0) | 2 (0) | 2 (0) | 1 (0) | 32 | 7 | 19 | 25 |
| B | 3 (0) | 4 (0) | 0 (2) | 0 (2) | 25 | 32 | 12 | 18 |
| C | 0 (0) | 1 (0) | 0 (0) | 0 (0) | 24 | 31 | 32 | 17 |
| D | 1 (0) | 8 (0) | 3 (0) | 5 (1) | 7 | 14 | 15 | 32 |
| A | no frames to send | | | | 32 | 14 | 15 | 32 |
| B | 0 (0) | 0 (0) | 2 (0) | 2 (0) | 28 | 32 | 11 | 28 |
| C | no frames to send | | | | 28 | 32 | 32 | 28 |
| D | 0 (0) | 0 (0) | 0 (0) | 1 (0) | 27 | 31 | 31 | 32 |

$TRT > n*THT$. Even if each station spends the full time THT allows sending class 6 frames, there will be time left for lower-class frames. Just how much depends on how much larger TRT is.

In general, if all stations have the maximum number of class 6 frames to send, we can guarantee a percentage of bandwidth equal to $100*n*THT/TRT$ for them. For example, if we wanted to guarantee that 75% of the bus's bandwidth is available for class 6 frames, we define $TRT = 4n*THT/3$. Doing so yields $100*n*THT/TRT = 100*n*THT/[(4/3)n*THT] = 100*3/4 = 75\%$. This type of control over the timer adds flexibility to the token bus in order to adapt to real-time situations.

## 6.5 Interconnecting LANs

After reading about three very different standards for local area networks, you may be wondering, doesn't this create confusion and inconsistencies among vendors and users? Let's put it this way: Some things in life are inescapable. Among them are death, taxes, and confusion among network users.

Different networks were designed for different people with very different goals. To assume they are isolated from one another is unrealistic, however. For example, within a large corporation different departments may have specific goals and approaches to their work. Departments of manufacturing, research and development, and marketing are very different. Different factors affect their decisions as they install computer systems or connect to networks. Consequently, they may adopt different and incompatible systems. The departments still must communicate, and if they use incompatible networks they have a problem. This leaves them with two possible solutions. The first is to force them all to adopt a specific network standard. Unfortunately, if the chosen network does not meet the goals and needs of the department then the choice is counterproductive. The second solution is to determine some way for different networks to communicate. Since most people expect computers and networks to be servants rather than masters, the second choice is preferable.

For example, consider the scenario of Figure 6.24 which represents networks used by a large corporation with departments in New York and Texas. Two New York departments and one Texas department each have installed their own LANs. New York stations *A* and *B* access file servers on their respective LANs using protocols we have discussed in previous sections. Texas station *C* does similarly. However, all three stations need access to the other LANs periodically. The two New York networks can be connected directly, but distance prohibits a direct connection with the Texas LAN. Consequently, a larger wide area network[*] is used to connect Texas and New York.

FIGURE 6.24     **Interconnecting Networks**

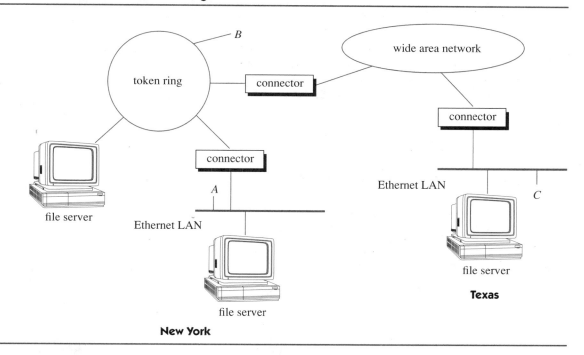

---

[*]The next chapter discusses wide area networks. For now, just think of it as a network spanning a larger distance than a LAN and having different protocols.

The ability to connect networks is certainly not new. There are standards for software and connecting devices, and any computer vendor has many such products to sell. The question is where in the hierarchy of hardware and software these products fit. That is, what do they actually do? Models such as OSI provide several layers of protocols for computer networks. For example, suppose the two New York LANs of Figure 6.24 differ only in the MAC sublayer of the data link layer (Figure 6.4), but the wide area network is different at higher layers. A connection to the wide area network deals with more incompatibilities and is more complex than one connecting the two LANs.

In general, we can connect two identical networks at layer 1, which amounts to little more than an electronic connection to regenerate and repeat signals. We also can connect two totally incompatible networks at the highest layer. Such a connection requires complete knowledge of both protocols and the ability to translate one to another. We also can connect anywhere between the highest and lowest layers, depending on the degree of compatibility between the two networks. This section discusses OSI layer 1 and layer 2 connections.

## LAYER 1 CONNECTIONS

Figure 6.25 shows several networks connected using **repeaters**, devices connecting networks at the physical layer. A repeater accepts a frame's bits from a LAN to which it is connected and buffers them. It then transmits the frame onto the other LAN. It assumes the LANs to which it is connected use the same protocols and same frame formats. A repeater's primary function is to regenerate signals, thereby extending the distance covered by the LAN.

In Figure 6.25 stations *A, B, C,* and *D* are each connected to a different LAN. Each station, however, will see any frame that any other sends. For example, *D* sees everything *A* sends. Whether they accept the frame depends on whom the frame is

FIGURE 6.25    **LANs Connected with a Repeater**

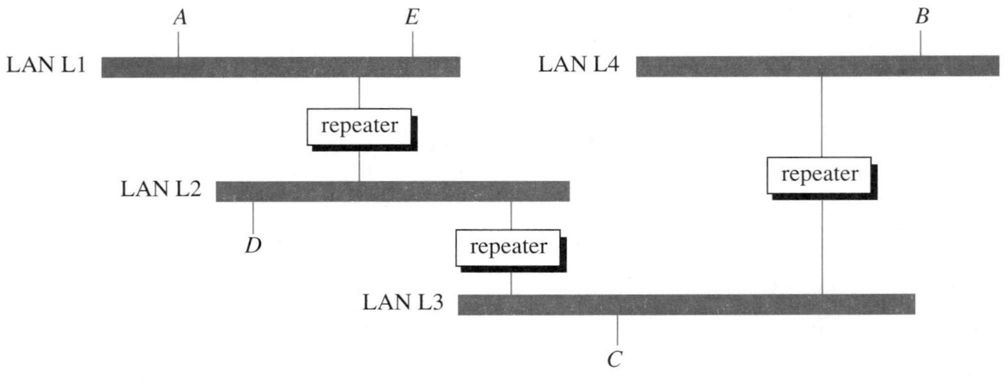

addressed to. The stations have no knowledge of the repeater's existence; as far as they are concerned, they are all connected by a single, but larger, LAN.

Repeaters do present problems, however. One is that more stations can access the medium, which leads to more traffic and can degrade LAN performance. For example, if *A* sends a frame to *E* (both on LAN L1), the repeaters still send the frame to LANs L2, L3, and L4. They have no built-in logic to know that *A* and *E* are on the same LAN and that repeating the frame is pointless. The result, of course, is that none of the other stations can send until station *A* has finished. A second problem is security. Generally, as more people have access to information security is more difficult to implement. If *A* and *E* are exchanging sensitive information, the frames pass by all the other stations and the potential for a security breach increases.

## LAYER 2 CONNECTIONS

Another way to connect LANs is to use a **bridge**, a connector with the ability to execute a subset of a protocol. Typically a bridge is a connector at the OSI layer 2. As such it performs data link functions such as error detection, frame formatting, and frame routing. For example, suppose station *B* sends a frame on LAN L2 in the network configuration of Figure 6.26. Bridge B1 examines the destination address and, if it is destined for any station on LAN L1 (say *A*), accepts the frame and buffers it. (How B1 knows what is on L1 is a major issue that we discuss shortly.) If the frame is destined for a station on one of the other LANs, B1 ignores the frame. Thus, B1 acts like any other station selectively rejecting or accepting frames based on their destination.

If B1 accepts the frame it executes error detection routines to determine whether the frame is correct. If there are no errors it sends the frame over LAN L1.

FIGURE 6.26 **LANs Connected with a Bridge**

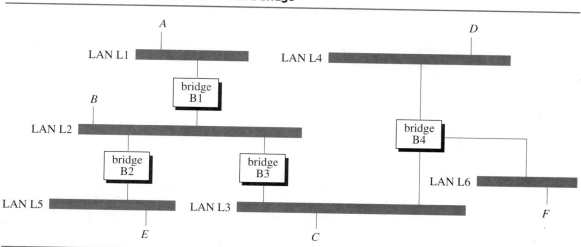

If L1's frame format is the same as L2's, the bridge sends the frame as is. If it is different the bridge must reformat the frame it received into a format consistent with L1's standard. In some cases, reformatting is a simple matter of reorganizing the fields, adding required ones, and dropping unnecessary ones. Unfortunately, as we soon will see, in some cases the reformatting causes other problems, some of which layer 2 protocols cannot handle.

Before discussing bridge design let's pose one last question: What are the reasons for using bridges in the first place? One reason is to enhance efficiency. With repeaters we saw that every frame propagates throughout each LAN, causing a lot of unnecessary traffic. To avoid this possibility a network designer can create a topology in which frequently communicating stations are on the same LAN. For example, each LAN of Figure 6.26 could correspond to a different department in a large company. Thus, stations within a department can communicate with each other, and the bridges do not forward any of the frames onto another LAN. For example, two stations can communicate over L1 at the same time two others communicate over L2. In general, communication within different LANs occurs in parallel, and efficiency is increased.

The bridges also allow interdepartment communications when necessary. Furthermore, the interconnection strategy can be designed depending on the frequency of interdepartment communication. For example, Figure 6.26 shows that LANs L1 and L2 communicate over one bridge whereas communication between LANs L1 and L4 requires three bridges. This makes sense if communication between LANs L1 and L2 are more frequent. The figure also suggests that LANs L3, L4, and L6 communicate among each other equally often, as any two of them can communicate over one bridge.

Security is another reason for using bridges. Because bridges selectively resend frames they can prevent certain frames from propagating throughout the network. This procedure enhances security because some stations never see the transmissions of others. The bridge organization also can reflect different security levels. For example, LAN L1 might connect stations to a file server with the highest priority (one that contains the most sensitive information). LAN L2 might be the second-highest priority LAN, with just one bridge between it and L1. LANs L3 and L5 might have the next-lowest priority, with two bridges between them and L1. In general, each bridge provides an opportunity to block a frame from going to another LAN. Thus, the design can place more bridges between LANs to represent priority differences.

## BRIDGING DIFFERENT TYPES OF LANS

Bridging becomes more difficult when connecting different types of LANs. One problem is that different LANs may have different bit rates. For example, suppose a bridge accepts frames from a fast LAN and sends them to a slower LAN or to one where collisions have occurred. The frames may arrive faster than they can be sent. Consequently, there must be sufficient buffer space in the bridge to allow a backlog of frames. Bridge delays can cause other problems such as timeouts in the flow control protocols. Timers are set to provide a reasonable time for a frame to reach its destination and an acknowledgment to be sent. Delays at bridges can cause excessive time-outs unless the station's network software adjusts them. Now, however, timers depend on interconnection strategies and we lose some of the transparency of the topology.

Frame formatting presents another problem. Recall from the three previous sections (also Figures 6.7, 6.11, and 6.20) that each LAN standard has a different frame format. Therefore, if a bridge connects two different LANs it must also reformat a received frame before resending it. On the surface, reformatting does not seem difficult, as it is primarily a rearrangement of information. Suppose a bridge connects an Ethernet and a token ring LAN, however. Frames on a token ring have a priority; those on an Ethernet do not. Therefore, a frame going from a token ring to an Ethernet loses its priority. Conversely, a frame going from an Ethernet to a token ring must be given a priority; but what? Usually a default is assigned. But what happens if a frame goes from a token ring to an Ethernet and then to another token ring? The frame has an initial priority, loses it when it goes on the Ethernet, and then gets another priority when it reaches the second token ring. There is no guarantee, however, that the initial and ending priorities are the same.

Yet another problem occurs due to the different maximum frame sizes with each LAN protocol. For example, both token ring and token bus may use frames larger than the maximum allowed on an Ethernet. Therefore, a large frame sent to an Ethernet station is not consistent with the Ethernet protocol. There are two possible solutions to this problem. The first is to make each station aware of the different LAN standards that may be encountered when it sends a frame. Then the station's network software can construct frames small enough so they meet the maximum size requirements of any LAN the frame may encounter. Many network packages allow this option. The problem is that each station's protocol now depends on the interconnection topology. Adding new bridges and LANs may require giving each LAN station new parameters. Since a major goal of communication is to create protocols that work regardless of the connection scheme, this is a significant constraint.

The second solution is for the bridge to break large frames into smaller ones. For example, Figure 6.27 shows a 5000-byte frame being sent to an Ethernet. Since the Ethernet does not allow frames above 1518 bytes, the bridge divides the frame into

**FIGURE 6.27    Dividing a Large Frame into Smaller Ones**

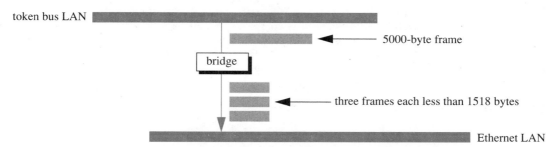

three pieces. The problem with this is that flow control protocols at the data link layer depend on the sending and acknowledging of frames. When a sending station sends a frame it anticipates that the receiving station will or will not receive it. There is no provision for the receiving station to receive what amounts to part of a frame.

The situation is not hopeless, however. Additional logic can be added to the bridge that divides frames and provides for proper acknowledgment of each piece. The logic to do so resides above the data link layer protocol, so the connection between the networks must occur at a higher OSI layer. Devices that achieve this maintain some bridge functions and assume some functions of a **router**.[*] They are called **brouters**.

## BRIDGE ROUTING

For the rest of this section we assume a bridge connects two similar LANs so we can focus on another bridge function: forwarding frames. By itself, forwarding frames is not difficult. The hard question is: How does a bridge know when to accept and forward a frame? For example, suppose bridge B3 in Figure 6.26 detects a frame on LAN L2. If the frame's destination is station A or E, B3 should ignore it. However, suppose the destination is D, C, or F. Station C is on LAN L3, and the only way to get to stations D or F is through L3. Therefore, the bridge must accept the frame and forward it on LAN L3. But how does B3 know that D, C, and F are accessible via L3? Worse yet, what if someone moves F from L6 to L5? How does the bridge know the station is no longer accessible via L3?

These questions may seem trivial at first because you, as the reader, can see the entire network drawn in a diagram. Having a global view of a situation always makes a problem easier. But the bridges do not have this view. They connect two or more LANs and see only what arrives on them. Furthermore, a bridge certainly cannot see what happens on a LAN several bridges away. The process of deciding which frames to forward and to where is called **bridge routing**. We will devote the rest of this section to discussing three approaches to it.

**Fixed Routing Bridges**    One way to route frames is to program each bridge with each station's address and the LAN to which frames destined for that station should be forwarded. That information is then stored in a **routing table** (sometimes called a **forwarding database** or **routing directory**). Where a bridge routes a frame depends on the LAN on which the frame arrives. Each bridge has a routing table for each LAN to which it is connected. When a frame arrives on that LAN the bridge finds the destination address in the appropriate routing table. The table's entry specifies to which LAN the bridge should forward the frame.

To illustrate, Figure 6.28 contains routing tables for the bridges in Figure 6.26. Bridge B1 has two routing tables (Figure 6.28a), one each for LAN L1 and L2. When the bridge detects a frame on L1 it determines the destination address

---

[*] A router connects two networks at the OSI layer 3.

and looks for it in the routing table for L1. If the destination address is one of *B* through *F*, the bridge forwards the frame to L2, the only way to get to those stations. If the destination is *A* the bridge does not forward the frame and the frame stays on L1. Similarly, if the bridge detects a frame from L2 destined for *A* it forwards the frame to L1.

The tables in bridge B3 are similar. The bridge will forward any frame from L2 to L3 that is destined for *C, D,* or *F*. However, if a frame arrives on L2 and is destined for *A, B,* or *E,* the bridge will not forward it. Figure 6.26 shows that those stations cannot be reached by going from L2 to L3. You should read through the other tables and convince yourself that their entries accurately reflect the topology of Figure 6.26.

We call this approach **fixed routing** because we assume the tables' information does not change. In many dynamic network environments, however, this assumption is too restrictive. New stations may be added, old ones removed, and others moved to different locations. Entire LANs may be added or removed. We need correct routing regardless of a station's location and network topology. This will provide the transparency that makes a network easier to use.

FIGURE 6.28    **Routing Tables for Bridges in Figure 6.26**

| SOURCE LAN L1 | | SOURCE LAN L2 | | SOURCE LAN L2 | | SOURCE LAN L5 | |
|---|---|---|---|---|---|---|---|
| DESTINATION | NEXT LAN | DESTINATION | NEXT LAN | DESTINATION | NEXT LAN | DESTINATION | NEXT LAN |
| *A* | -- | *A* | L1 | *A* | -- | *A* | L2 |
| *B* | L2 | *B* | -- | *B* | -- | *B* | L2 |
| *C* | L2 | *C* | -- | *C* | -- | *C* | L2 |
| *D* | L2 | *D* | -- | *D* | -- | *D* | L2 |
| *E* | L2 | *E* | -- | *E* | L5 | *E* | -- |
| *F* | L2 | *F* | -- | *F* | -- | *F* | L2 |

**(a) Bridge B1**        **(b) Bridge B2**

| SOURCE LAN L2 | | SOURCE LAN L3 | | SOURCE LAN L3 | | SOURCE LAN L4 | | SOURCE LAN L6 | |
|---|---|---|---|---|---|---|---|---|---|
| DESTINATION | NEXT LAN | DESTINATION | NEXT LAN | DESTINATION | NEXT LAN | DESTINATION | NEXT LAN | DESTINATION | NEXT LAN |
| *A* | -- | *A* | L2 | *A* | -- | *A* | L3 | *A* | L3 |
| *B* | -- | *B* | L2 | *B* | -- | *B* | L3 | *B* | L3 |
| *C* | L3 | *C* | -- | *C* | -- | *C* | L3 | *C* | L3 |
| *D* | L3 | *D* | -- | *D* | L4 | *D* | -- | *D* | L4 |
| *E* | -- | *E* | L2 | *E* | -- | *E* | L3 | *E* | L3 |
| *F* | L3 | *F* | -- | *F* | L6 | *F* | L6 | *F* | -- |

**(c) Bridge B3**        **(d) Bridge B4**

If we want to use routing tables in a more dynamic environment we have two choices. One is to reprogram the bridges every time someone adds, deletes, or moves a station. In a dynamic environment this approach is not viable, so we are left with the second choice: Determine some way for the bridges to update their routing tables automatically.

**Transparent Bridges**     We call bridges that create and update their own routing tables transparent bridges. They have their own standard (IEEE 802.1d). They are designed so that you can plug them in and have them work immediately regardless of topology and the stations' locations. There is no need to tell them where the stations are. They will determine that automatically and initialize their routing tables. They require no special programming. If a station moves from one LAN to another, each bridge learns this and updates its routing table accordingly. This ability to update its routing table is called route learning or address learning.

**Route Learning**. A bridge learns what to put in its routing table by observing traffic. Whenever it receives a frame it examines the source address. It then knows that the station sending the frame is accessible via the LAN on which the frame just arrived. The bridge examines each of its routing tables looking for the station's address. If a table entry indicates that the station is accessible over a different LAN, the bridge changes the entry specifying the LAN on which the frame arrived. Presumably the station moved to a different LAN.

To illustrate, consider again the routing tables of Figure 6.28 and the LANs of Figure 6.26. Now suppose station D moves from LAN L4 to LAN L1. The routing tables are now incorrect and the only stations able to send to D are those on the same LAN as D. Next, suppose D sends a frame to E on LAN L5. Bridge B1 routes the frame to L2. However, it also examines its routing tables (Figure 6.28a). Since the bridge received a frame from D on L1 it knows that D is in the direction of L1.[*] It therefore changes the fourth entry in each routing table and redefines them as follows:

| SOURCE LAN L1 | | SOURCE LAN L2 | |
|:---:|:---:|:---:|:---:|
| DESTINATION | NEXT LAN | DESTINATION | NEXT LAN |
| A | -- | A | L1 |
| B | L2 | B | -- |
| C | L2 | C | -- |
| D | -- | D | L1 |
| E | L2 | E | -- |
| F | L2 | F | -- |

Bridge B1 now knows not to forward any frame from L1 that is destined for D and to forward any frame from L2 that is destined for D to L1. When bridge B2

---

[*] Note that B1 doesn't necessarily know D is *on* L1. For all it knows the frame may have gone through several bridges before getting to L1. The important thing is that the bridge knows in what direction to forward a frame.

detects $D's$ frame from L2 it updates its tables similarly. In this case B2 realizes $D$ is accessible via L2. However, from B2's perspective this is no different from when $D$ was on L4. As a result, the "updated" values are the same as the original ones.

Some questions still remain. Bridges B1 and B2 learned of $D's$ move only because $D$ sent a frame that B1 and B2 had to forward. Bridges B3 and B4 still do not know of $D's$ move. Must they remain ignorant until $D$ sends something their way? What if $D$ never does? Do they remain in the dark forever? If so, frames sent to $D$ from LANs L3, L4, or L6 will never reach $D$. For that matter, what if $D$ never sent the frame to $E$? Then not even bridges B1 and B2 are aware of $D's$ move and nothing will reach $D$.

So far the discussion has dealt only with changing information. Another issue is how the tables are initialized. What do the bridges do at startup? Fortunately, the 802.1d specifications provide answers. Whenever a bridge updates a routing table entry it includes the time of update. Each bridge also maintains a timer. Whenever the timer expires the bridge examines each routing table entry. If the entry has not been updated since the timer was last set, the bridge removes the entries from the table. The bridge "reasons" that since it has not heard from those stations in a while their locations may not be accurate. Consequently, it maintains no routing information for those stations.

This action appears to make stations inaccessible if they did not move. However, when a bridge receives a frame destined for a station that has no entry in the routing table the bridge uses a **flooding algorithm**. That is, it sends the frame over every LAN to which it is connected except the one on which the frame arrived. This serves two purposes: It guarantees the frame will reach its destination (assuming it exists), and it allows more bridges to see the frame and learn the direction of the sending station. This information keeps their routing tables current.

Consider the previous example in which $D$ moves from L4 to L1 in Figure 6.26 and then sends a frame to $E$. If $E$ has not sent anything for a while, its entries in each bridge are deleted. Therefore, when B1 receives $D's$ frame it notes that there is no entry for $E$ and automatically forwards the frame to L2. Similarly, B2 and B3 also forward the frame to L5 and L3, respectively. Finally, B4 forwards the frame to L4 and L6. The end result is that $E$ gets the frame and each bridge forwards a frame from $D$ and updates its routing table. Consequently, anything sent to $D$ will be forwarded correctly (at least until the next timer expires).

The flooding algorithm also allows bridges to initialize their routing tables. Suppose a LAN is installed and all of the bridges' routing tables are empty. No bridge knows the location of any station. When a bridge receives its first frame from a LAN it sends it along every other LAN to which it is connected. Similarly, bridges on those LANs receive the frame and also forward it using the flooding algorithm. Before long the frame has reached every bridge and every LAN. In particular, the frame has reached its destination and every bridge knows the direction of the sending station.

As more stations send frames the bridges forward them using routing table entries or by flooding. As the frames propagate through the network, the bridges eventually learn the direction of the sending station and can forward frames without using the flooding algorithm.

**Frame Propagation**. The previous approach to designing transparent bridges and route learning worked well with the examples given. However, certain topologies can cause an endless propagation of frames and glut the network. To illustrate, suppose network designers decide to add a second bridge connecting two LANs. Adding a second redundant bridge between two LANs is sometimes used to protect the system in the event of failures. If the first bridge fails the second one is already in place and there is no (or very little) delay caused by the failure. This is particularly useful in real-time systems where delays caused by equipment failure can lead to a disaster.

For example, the simple LAN connection of Figure 6.29 shows two bridges between the same two LANs. Suppose the routing tables are empty and $A$ sends a frame to $B$. Since neither bridge is aware of the other each accepts the frame and forwards it onto LAN L2. Next, bridge B1 sees B2's frame and B2 sees B1's frame on L2. Since neither knows where $B$ is, both bridges accept the frame and forward it onto LAN L1. Again each will see the other's frame and forward it back to L2. Until $B$ identifies its location the frames will be transferred back and forth repeatedly between both LANs.

The situation is made worse if there is a third bridge (B3) connecting the LANs. If $A$ sends one frame along L1 each bridge forwards it to L2, putting three frames on L2. Each bridge sees two of them (one from each of the other two bridges) and forwards them onto L1, putting six frames on L1. Each bridge now sees four frames (two from each of the other two bridges) and forwards them, putting twelve frames back on L2. This process continues, causing an explosion of frames that eventually clogs the system and brings communication to a standstill.

We illustrated the problem with a simple topology showing two bridges between two LANs. The potential for endlessly circulating frames exists in other topologies as well. In particular, two distinct routes between two stations will cause a **loop** in the topology. This means that a frame may leave a LAN via one route only to return via another. Figure 6.30 shows a topology with multiple routes between $A$ and $B$. (We'll see what the costs mean shortly.) In fact, there are at least seven routes if we ignore routes going through the same bridge twice (can you find them?). To

FIGURE 6.29    **Two Bridges Connecting Two LANs**

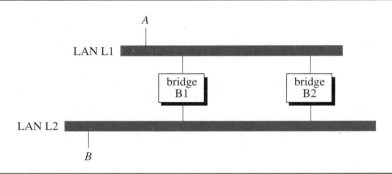

FIGURE 6.30    **Multiple LANs with Loops**

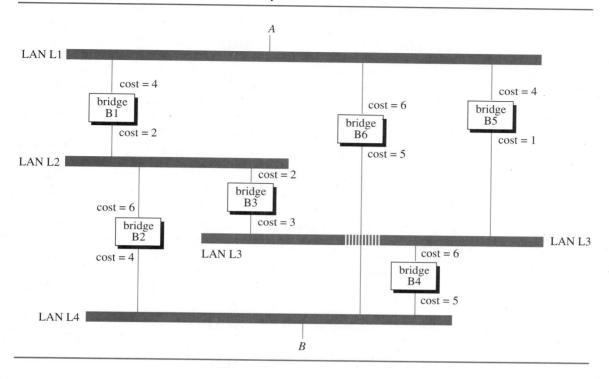

see the magnitude of this problem, suppose $A$ sends $B$ a frame and the bridges use the flooding algorithm. Also consider the route from L1 to L4 through bridges B1 and B2. Bridge B6 will forward the frame back to L1. Bridge B4 will forward the frame to L3. From here B5 forwards it to L1 and B3 forwards it to L2. Next B1 forwards it to L1 and B2 forwards it back to L4, and the process continues. As before, the single frame causes an unending increase in the number of frames moving through the network. If we consider the other routes from L1 to L4, the increase is even more rapid. The number of frames becomes excessive very quickly and the network shuts down.

**Spanning Tree Algorithm.** One approach to this problem is to eliminate the loops by not using certain bridges. We don't disconnect the bridges physically, but we prevent them from forwarding frames. Instead they are used as backups in case another bridge fails. The tricky part is determining which bridges are used and when they should automatically reconfigure if a bridge fails. As usual, we want to let the bridges do the work themselves and make the configuration transparent to the user. One solution calls for the bridges to execute a spanning tree algorithm. A **spanning tree**, a term from data structures, corresponds to a minimal subset of edges taken from a connected graph that connect the graph's vertices. The subset is minimal in that the spanning tree has no loops.[*] For more information on spanning trees, consult a reference on data structures such as reference 13 or 14.

To make the algorithm work, we first associate a cost to each bridge-to-LAN connection, or **bridge port**. It may correspond to a bit rate at which a bridge port can transmit onto a LAN. Typically, lower bit rates mean a higher cost. The cost of sending a frame from one LAN to another is the sum of costs of ports in the route. In some cases, all costs are set to 1 so that the cost of a route is simply the number of bridges in it. Figure 6.30 shows the costs of each bridge port. The cost of sending a frame from L1 to L4 via bridges B1 and B2 is 6, the sum of the costs of going from B1 to L2 (2) plus B2 to L4 (4). Note that the costs associated with the B1-L1 and B2-L2 ports are not included here. They are used for frames going in the other direction.

Next, we visualize the LAN topology as a graph. The LANs and bridges are vertices and the connections between a LAN and a bridge are the edges. Figure 6.31 shows a graphical representation of the topology in Figure 6.30. The figure lists costs for each edge. Remember that as frames move through the graph only costs from a bridge node to a LAN node accrue.

The spanning tree algorithm determines a set of edges that connect all the LAN nodes of Figure 6.31. Remember as we discuss the algorithm that we have the advantage of seeing the entire network topology; the bridges that execute the algo-

FIGURE 6.31     **Graph Representation of the LAN Topology in Figure 6.30**

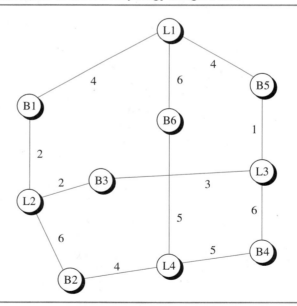

---

[*] In data structure, the term cycle is often used in place of loop.

rithm have no such view. They know only the LANs to which they are connected. This makes the algorithm more complex than it would be if executed by a processor that knows the entire topology.

To begin the spanning tree algorithm, the bridges elect one of their own (true partisan politics) to be a **root bridge**. It is usually the one with the lowest ID, although priorities can be used. Using data structures terminology, the root bridge will be the root of the spanning tree. The bridges elect the root bridge by first sending a series of special frames called **bridge protocol data units** (**BPDU**s) at regular intervals. Each BPDU contains the bridge's ID, the port ID over which the frame was first sent, and the accumulated costs of ports over which it has been received. The latter is the cost of a path from the BPDU's current location back to its source.

When a bridge receives a BPDU it compares the source bridge's ID with its own. If its own ID is larger it knows it will not be the root bridge. It records the sending bridge's ID and the path cost to it, increments the path cost by the cost of the receiving port, and forwards the BPDU through all its other ports. It also stops sending its own BPDUs. If the bridge's ID is smaller than the one that sent the BPDU it will not forward the frame. It reasons that the sending bridge will never be elected so there is no point in forwarding its frames.

Eventually each bridge except the one with the lowest ID will stop sending frames because it knows it will not be the root bridge. The remaining bridge stops forwarding any frames it receives and eventually receives no more. After a time during which it receives no frames it considers itself duly elected as bridge port. It and the other bridges then proceed to the algorithm's next step.

In the second step, each bridge determines its **root port**, the port corresponding to the cheapest path to the root bridge. Since each bridge previously recorded path costs for each BPDU received on each port, it simply looks for the cheapest. Each bridge subsequently will communicate with the root bridge using its root bridge root port.

The last step determines a **designated bridge** for each LAN. This is the bridge that eventually forwards frames from that LAN. The bridges elect a designated bridge by sending BPDUs over each LAN to which they are connected. A bridge will not send a BPDU to a LAN using a previously determined root port. Essentially the root port determines the LAN in the direction of the root bridge. The algorithm now must determine if there are any LANs in any other direction.

Let's examine the activities from the perspective of a specific LAN. The LAN is carrying BPDUs from its bridges requesting to be the designated bridge. Each BPDU contains the cost to the root bridge from the bridge sending the BPDU. When a bridge receives a BPDU it compares the cost in it with its own cost to the root bridge. If its own cost is larger, it knows it will not be the designated bridge and gives up its claim. Eventually the only bridge not seeing a smaller cost becomes the designated bridge for the LAN. In the event there are two or more bridges with the same smaller cost, they use their IDs to break ties. The smallest ID wins.

After selecting designated bridges for each LAN, the spanning tree algorithm is complete. Every LAN is connected to its designated bridge and every bridge can communicate with the root bridge via its root port. This defines a unique path between any two LANs and avoids frame propagation resulting from flooding algorithms.

We now illustrate the spanning tree algorithm with an example. Consider the LAN topology of Figure 6.30 and the associated graph of Figure 6.31. The first step determines the root bridge. If we assume the bridges are numbered in increasing order from B1 through B6 then B1 is elected root bridge.

During the election process each bridge records the cost to the root bridge through each of its ports, and then selects the cheapest one. Figure 6.32 shows the root ports (designated by an arrow) and paths to the root bridge (designated by thicker lines). The path costs are also listed next to the arrows. For example, bridge B2's root port is the one connected to L2. The cheapest path is B2-L2-B1 for a cost of 6. Remember, we only accrue costs from bridges to LANs. B4's root port is the one connected to L3. The path to the root bridge is B4-L3-B3-L2-B1 for a cost of 8. As the figure shows, there are other paths but their costs are higher. You should take some time to understand why the other root ports were chosen as they were.

The last step determines the designated bridge for each LAN. The root ports connect bridges to some LANs, but there may be other LANs not part of the developing connection scheme. For example, in Figure 6.32 there is no root port connected to L4, and we need to determine a bridge to forward information from L4. To do this, bridges B2, B4, and B6 send BPDUs along L4 requesting to be the designated bridge. B4 states that the cost to the root bridge is 8; B2 and B6 indicate their cost to be 6. Consequently, B4 gives up its request because of its higher cost and B6

FIGURE 6.32    **Graph After Determining Root Ports**

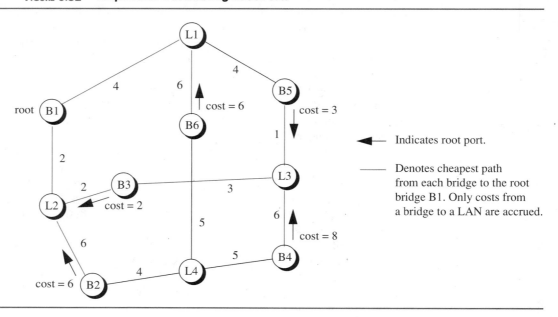

gives up its request because of its higher ID. Thus, B2 becomes the designated bridge for L4. Proceeding similarly, B3 is the designated bridge for L3, and B1 is the designated bridge for L1 and L2 (Figure 6.33).

Figure 6.33 shows the resulting spanning tree and Figure 6.34 relates it to the original network topology. The dotted lines indicate physical but not active connections. The bridges use these connections to send and receive BPDUs but not to forward frames in general. The tree connects all the LANs even though some of the bridges are not used. That is to be expected, however, as the bridges are redundant devices to be used in the event of a failure of another one. As long as no failure occurs, the LANs communicate using the topology of Figure 6.34.

In order to detect a bridge failure and reconfigure the connection scheme, each bridge maintains a timer called a **message age timer**. During the specified time each bridge (even the ones not part of the spanning tree) expects to hear from the root bridge confirming its status as root bridge. When it does it resets the timer. The root bridge, of course, cooperates by sending a **configuration BPDU** periodically to confirm its status. If a bridge malfunctions, one or more bridges do not receive a configuration BPDU and their timers expire. If a bridge other than the root bridge fails, the affected bridges exchange BPDUs to elect a new designated bridge for their LANs. If the root bridge fails they must elect a new root bridge. Either way, they reconfigure the active topology dynamically.

**Source Routing Bridges**. The last approach to forwarding frames on a LAN interconnection puts the burden of routing on the individual stations instead of the

**Figure 6.33    Graph After Determining Designated Bridges**

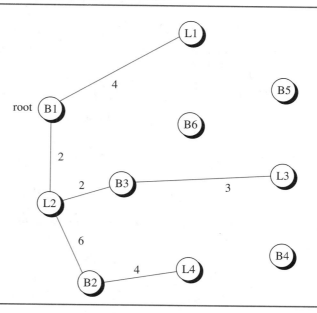

FIGURE 6.34    **Network Topology Showing Active Bridge Connections**

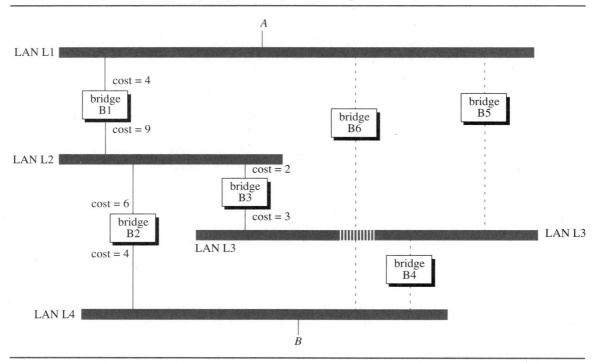

bridges. Specifically, network software at the sending station determines a route to the destination and stores it in the frame (Figure 6.35). The route consists of a sequence of **route designators** each consisting of a LAN and a bridge ID. When a bridge sees a frame it determines whether there is a designator containing its ID and the ID of the LAN carrying the frame. If so, the bridge accepts the frame and forwards it to the LAN specified in the next designator.

FIGURE 6.35    **Partial Frame Format for Source Routing Bridges**

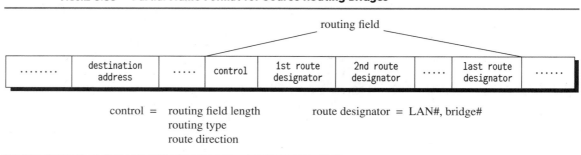

For example, suppose *A* sends *B* (from Figure 6.30) a frame and specifies the route as L1-B5-L3-B4-L4. Both bridges connected to L1 see the frame, but since B5 follows L1 in the sequence only B5 accepts it. B5 then forwards the frame to L3, where bridges B3 and B4 see it. Similarly, since B4 follows L3 in the sequence only B4 accepts the frame. Finally, B4 forwards the frame to L4, where station *B* eventually receives the frame.

At first this may seem like a variation of the fixed routing strategy discussed at the beginning of this section. Each station must be aware of the interconnection strategy and be able to specify a path to any other station. It may seem the only way to do this is to program the topology's structure into each station, which would destroy its ability to reconfigure dynamically. However, this approach does allow a way for each station to learn the location of any other station and to determine the best path.

To determine the path, a station sends a frame to another station, effectively asking, "Where are you?" The receiving station gets the request and responds. When the sending station gets the response it determines the best path. But how does the sending station know where to send the initial request when it does not know the destination? It doesn't. The bridges must help by executing a variation of the flooding algorithm to make sure the request and response are received. The determination of a route to the destination is called **route discovery**.

One way to do this is to send an **all-routes broadcast frame** to the intended destination station. The frame's control field specifies the frame type and notifies the bridges that they should forward the frame onto all available LANs. An exception, of course, is made for the LAN on which the frame arrived. The problem the bridges must solve is the uncontrolled growth of these frames that flooding can produce. To avoid propagation, a station sends an all-routes broadcast frame with the route designator fields empty and the control field's routing field length equal to 0. When a bridge receives the frame it inserts its own and the incoming LAN's IDs to the routing field and increments the routing field length. To avoid forwarding a frame it received previously the bridge examines the existing route designators. It will not forward a frame to a LAN whose ID was part of a route designator of the incoming frame.

When a frame finally arrives at its destination, the routing field contains the route used in getting there. The destination puts this route in the routing field of a **nonbroadcast frame** and sends it back to the source station. It also sets a directional bit in the control field to notify the bridges they should interpret the route designators in reverse order. When a bridge receives a nonbroadcast frame it forwards or drops the frame according to the information in the routing field. When the source station receives all the responses, it chooses which route to use in subsequent transmissions to *B*. Presumably, it would examine the costs (calculated during the broadcast) and choose the cheapest. Alternatively, it could choose the one using the fewest bridges or choose based on bridge IDs.

Figure 6.36 shows an example of an all-routes broadcast from *A* to *B*. *A* sends a frame with no routing information in it. Bridge B1 gets the frame, puts the route designator L1-B1 in it, and forwards it to L2 and to L3. B2 gets it from

FIGURE 6.36    **Sending an All-Routes Broadcast Frame**

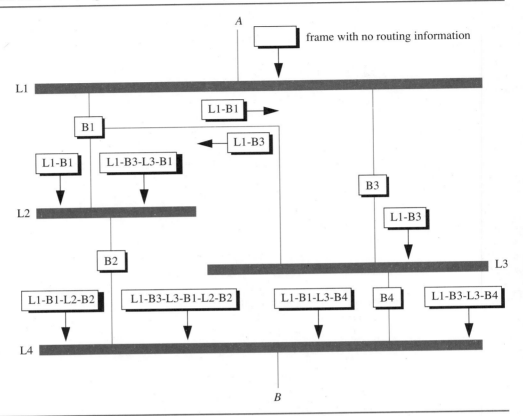

L2, adds the route designator L2-B2, and forwards it to L4, where *B* eventually receives it. Meanwhile, B4 gets the other forwarded frame, adds the designator L3-B4, and forwards it to L4. Station *B* receives that frame as well. Note that B3 also sees the frame on L3 but does not forward it to L1 because L1 is in a route designator.

While all this is happening, B3 also receives the initial frame, adds the designator L1-B3, and forwards it to L3. Both B4 and B1 pick up that frame. B4 forwards it to L4, adding the designator L3-B4, and B1 forwards it to L2, adding the designator L3-B1. Finally, B2 forwards the frame from L2 to L4 and adds the designator L2-B2. Station *B* receives four frames via four different routes. With this approach the destination sends as many frames as it receives. As the number of redundant bridges increases, so does the number of routes and the number of frames on the network.

Another approach to route discovery has the sending station transmit a **single-route broadcast frame**. Like the all-routes broadcast frame, it contains no routing information. This time, instead of broadcasting to all LANs each bridge forwards a frame only through a port that is part of a spanning tree. In this case the destination receives just one request. However, instead of relying on the spanning tree's route the destination station sends an all-routes broadcast frame as its response. The bridges forward the all-routes broadcast frame as before, determining the route as they do so. Eventually the source station receives many responses, one for each route and, as before, can choose the one it wants for subsequent frames. The advantage of this approach is that there are fewer frames traveling from source to destination (although there are just as many going the other way). The disadvantage is that the bridges must determine the spanning tree first.

### SUMMARY

This section has discussed ways to connect LANs together. Layer 1 connections simply repeat what they receive. Layer 2 connections do some error checking and frame reformatting. In some cases, frame reformatting is impossible due to limits on frame size. In those cases, the network software must create frames that meet the limits of any protocol they might encounter, or they pass the frames to higher layers that can divide them.

Most of the section dealt with routing frames across a LAN interconnection. It discussed three types of bridges: fixed routing, transparent, and source routing. Fixed routing is limited because it cannot respond to changing conditions dynamically. The other approaches can change, but they differ in where the changes occur. Table 6.8 summarizes the three approaches.

## 6.6   Case Study: Novell NetWare

Much of this chapter has dealt with local area network standards and internetworking techniques. A logical way to conclude it is to discuss one of the most widely used commercial **network operating systems**: Novell NetWare. Novell NetWare contains the protocols necessary to allow communication among many types of PCs and devices. Most typical are printers; Macintosh computers; and PCs running DOS, Windows, OS/2, or UNIX. It will also run with Ethernet, token ring, and Arcnet protocols.[*] Typical uses allow PC users to access shared printers, data, and software. For example, if all the members of a department use the same word processor for their reports, there is probably no need for each person to have a licensed copy. Another option is to purchase a copy licensed for network use (often cheaper than many individual licenses) and make it available over the network.

Like any commercial product, there are several versions of NetWare. Examples include those written to run on 286 machines (NetWare 286 version 2.x), those

---

[*] The Arcnet is a token passing protocol that uses a star topology. It is not a formally defined standard, but it has hundreds of thousands of users and has been in use for over 15 years.

TABLE 6.8    **Comparison of LAN Bridges**

| | FIXED ROUTING BRIDGES | TRANSPARENT BRIDGES | SOURCE ROUTING BRIDGES |
|---|---|---|---|
| **Ability to reconfigure** | Limited. It is done by reprogramming the bridges with routing information. | High. Bridges maintain information on location of stations. | High. Each station must learn the route to its destination before sending. |
| **Stations' responsibilities** | None. They just send the frames and let the bridges do the work. | None. They just send the frames and let the bridges do the work. | They determine and maintain addresses. |
| **Bridges, requirements** | Routing tables. | Routing tables and the ability to both update them and execute a spanning tree algorithm. | Ability to broadcast or forward, depending on routing designators and ability to execute a spanning tree algorithm. |
| **Routes used** | Determined by designer. | Always along the spanning tree, but not necessarily the cheapest. | Stations can choose the cheapest routes to one another. |
| **Dependence on topology** | Some. Bridges must be programmed, but stations have no need to know. | None. Bridges learn where stations are relative to their ports dynamically and stations have no need to know. | Some. Bridges respond to routing information and spanning tree algorithms, but stations must determine a route to a destination. |

written to make use of 386 and 486 architecture (NetWare 386 version 3.x), and the most recently released NetWare 4.0. With a few notable exceptions we will not distinguish among versions. Most of our discussion relates to version 3.11. For more details see references 15,16,17,18, and 19 which focus on NetWare.

### NetWare Configuration

Figure 6.37 shows a typical network configuration running Novell NetWare. At least one PC is designated as a file server running all of the NetWare protocols and maintaining the network's shared data on one or more disk drives. It also maintains information on NetWare's authorized users, thus providing some security. In some cases it also may act as a bridge or router to another network. Another PC may be designated as a print server. Its job is to allow users to access shared printers. Most of the other devices typically are PCs, often referred to as client PCs, client workstations, or clients.

**File servers** generally allow users on other PCs to access application software or data files. The file server may transfer files to the client PC or, if security allows, alter files as requested by the user. A **print server** manages both requests and printers. It analyzes a print request and determines what type of printer (e.g., what format or model) on which it should be printed. It then stores requests in a queue to await the

FIGURE 6.37    **Novell Network**

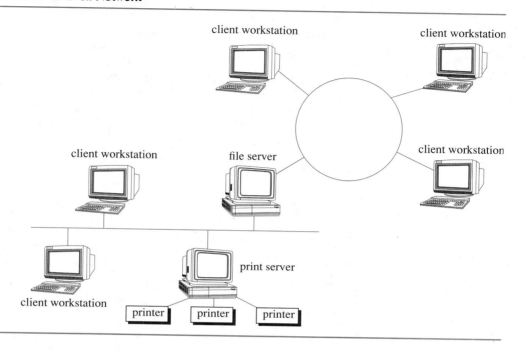

printer. In general, one print server can manage several printers. Conversely, several print servers may have access to a common printer. Consequently, NetWare protocols must allow print servers to access common files. The print server also allows users to examine the queues, request status on queue entries, and even delete them.

The actual number of clients and servers varies in practice. Depending on the licensing agreement, the file server can handle up to 250 different clients. It also has a theoretical capacity to manage up to 4 gigabytes of main memory and up to 32 terabytes (trillion bytes) of disk space with up to 100,000 open files.

There are two types of file servers: a dedicated file server and a nondedicated file server. The **dedicated file server** runs NetWare only and does not run other software such as DOS applications. The **nondedicated file server** can run both applications and NetWare. The latter is useful in small networks as it allows the server to also act as a client, thus adding one to the number of clients. In large networks one extra client is less significant, and a dedicated server handles the larger number of requests more efficiently.

## RUNNING NOVELL NETWARE

To run Novell NetWare one PC must be designated as the file server. Its configuration must meet minimum criteria regarding disk space, internal memory, and other hardware features. Specifics, of course, vary with the implementation; Reference 17 discusses configuration requirements further. The server manages all of the software and data that network users need. It also maintains information on authorized network users and what privileges they have regarding data access.

NetWare's modular design allows users to insert or delete different software modules to best meet their needs. These **NetWare loadable modules (NLMs)** are designed to enhance the network's capabilities. Typical NLMs allow the installation of print servers, utilities to recover damaged files on a file server, drivers for different types of disk drives, and modules that communicate with protocols such as TCP/IP, AppleTalk, and IPX/SPX (discussed later). The NLMs provide greater functionality by allowing diversity among the types of network devices and protocols. Reference 20 provides a nice description of NLMs, addressing how administrators use them to create a proactive environment and how they are different under NetWare's version 4.0.

Each client workstation runs its own operating system (such as DOS) as well as a NetWare shell. The NetWare shell, stored as the file NETx.COM (x stands for the DOS version) on the client, is a command interpreter that accepts commands entered from the workstation (Figure 6.38). It analyzes the request and determines whether it is a DOS request or a NetWare command. If it is a DOS command the shell transfers the command to DOS for processing and does not involve the network.

If the command is a request for a NetWare service, the shell formats and creates a packet according to the definitions of the NetWare core protocol (NCP). NCP defines the procedures the server uses to respond to a client's request. The shell then gives the packet to the internet packet exchange (IPX), a protocol used to establish and maintain connections between network devices. IPX determines

FIGURE 6.38    **NetWare Handling User Requests**

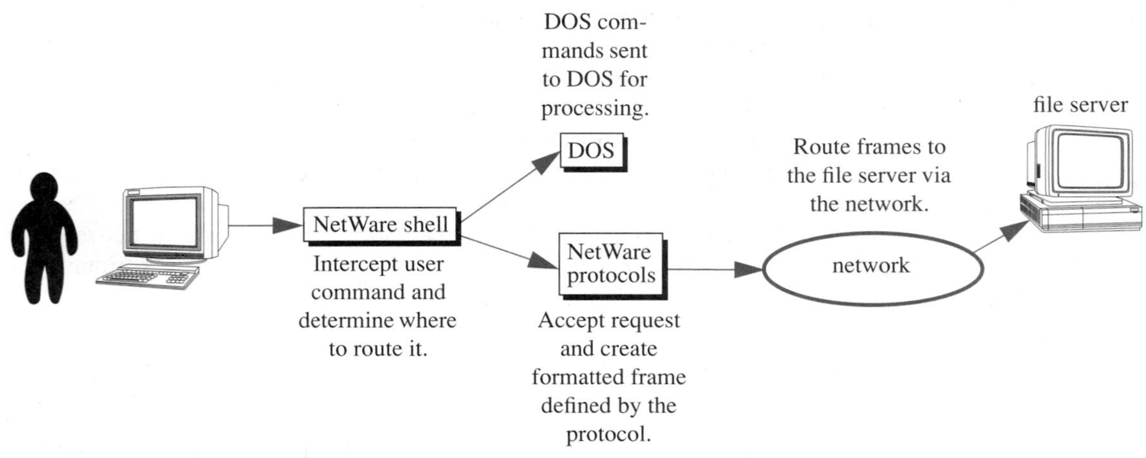

source and destination addresses and attaches them to the packet. When the server receives the packet it extracts the data, determines the request as defined by NCP, and responds accordingly. IPX does not guarantee packet delivery. Another protocol, sequenced packed protocol (SPX), monitors packet transmissions to assure proper delivery. Similar to the protocols of Chapter 5, SPX sends and receives acknowledgments. If it does not receive an expected acknowledgment it will resend the packet.

All packets must eventually pass through a board and onto the actual network. The network driver is the interface that ensures that packets are sent according to the network protocol. Note that the network protocol differs from NetWare protocol. NetWare defines the rules and formats to respond to client's requests. The network protocol, such as token ring or Ethernet, defines how the packets are actually transmitted. Using a network driver builds flexibility into the system and allows IPX to send packets over a variety of different networks.

To give the system even more flexibility, Novell has added another component to its protocol that allows greater interconnectivity among devices running different protocols. The open data-link interface (ODI) allows multiple protocols to send their packets through a single board and network connection. Novell claims the following advantages of using ODI (Reference 21):[*]

- You can expand your network by using multiple protocols (such as IPX/SPX, Appletalk, or TCP/IP as they become available) without adding extra network boards to the workstation.

- You can communicate with a variety of workstations, file servers, and mainframe computers via different protocol stacks without rebooting your workstation.

- You can protect your investment because all protocols written to ODI specification can communicate through any LAN adapter written to ODI specification.

- You can spend less time and money on support. With one LAN driver supporting multiple protocols, you have fewer hardware components to support.

## SECURITY AND INTEGRITY

NetWare provides security in several ways. The first and most obvious is to require users to enter an account number and a password to gain access to the file server. The account number and password are checked against those maintained on the server. If there is no match the user is not allowed to login.

NetWare stores passwords on the server in encrypted form to provide additional protection. NetWare 4.0 has gone a step further by providing authentication using a private/public key cryptographic system (Reference 16). When a user enters a password the client and server proceed in a manner similar to that described in Section 4.6, thus providing a robust process for verification.

---

[*]Reprinted with permission by Novell, Inc.

If the user does login that does not mean he or she has access to all of the server's files. NetWare can grant specific rights to a group of users that allow them to access specific directories and files. They are called **trustee rights** and the user or group is a trustee. NetWare 3.11 maintains trustee rights in a file called a **bindery** on the file server. There are eight different trustee rights:

- **Read**. Open and read a file or execute a program.
- **Write**. Open and write to a file.
- **Create**. Create a file or subdirectory.
- **Erase**. Delete any file or subdirectory.
- **Modify**. Rename a directory or file and/or change its attributes. Typical attributes include whether the file may be copied, deleted, shared, renamed, or open for read only. It does not allow the right to change a file's contents.
- **File Scan**. Get a list of directory files.
- **Access Control**. Change the trustee rights for a file or directory and change the **inherited rights mask** associated with each file or directory when it is created. By default, when trustee rights are given to a directory the trustee also has rights to the files and subdirectories in it. However, the inherited rights mask associated with a file or directory may override the default.
- **Supervisory**. Provide all trustee rights to the file or directory.

NetWare also protects the integrity of information when related updates must be made to several files. For example, suppose a company database maintains a list of its sales personnel and customers. Each salesperson's record contains a reference to one or more customers for which he or she is responsible (Figure 6.39a). If the company loses a customer, not only is the customer's record deleted from the database but any references to it from the salesperson's file also must be deleted. If the customer record was deleted and a network protocol error then prevented the reference to it from being deleted (Figure 6.39b), the database would be inconsistent. To prevent this situation, NetWare provides a **transaction tracking system** (**TTS**) allowing multiple updates to files to be regarded as a single transaction. TTS performs all of the updates or none at all. If it performed some of the updates and a protocol error prevented the others from being done, TTS would restore the affected records to their pretransaction values.

Hardware failures can be devastating, as anyone who has ever experienced a head crash (contact between the disk head and disk) knows. Eventually, all disk drives will fail. In some cases, only the drive mechanism fails, allowing the disk to be removed, and inserted in another drive. In other cases, the disk's directory is damaged but special utilities can often recover the data on it. If the cause is a head crash, however, the disk surface may be destroyed making any recovery impossible.

NetWare provides two ways of reducing such problems (Figure 6.40). Both make duplicates copies of updated data by copying it onto different disks, but they differ in how that is done. **Disk duplexing** uses two different controllers connected

FIGURE 6.39    **Maintaining Consistent Files In NetWare**

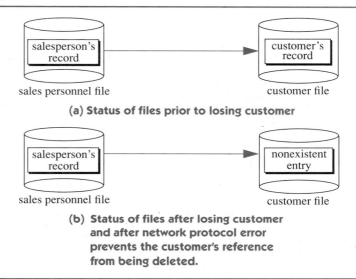

(a) **Status of files prior to losing customer**

(b) **Status of files after losing customer
and after network protocol error
prevents the customer's reference
from being deleted.**

to the server. When the server must make a change, both controllers write the updated data to their respective disks. With **disk mirroring** one controller writes the information on two different disks. Disk duplexing is faster because two controllers are doing the work of one. It is also more reliable. If one controller fails, the other can proceed with required changes. On the other hand, disk mirroring provides a more economical approach.

FIGURE 6.40    **Disk Mirroring and Duplexing**

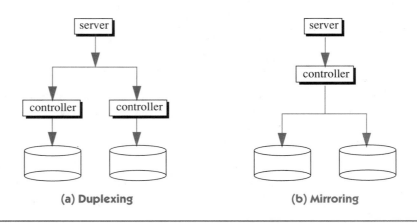

(a) **Duplexing**                    (b) **Mirroring**

## SELECTED NOVELL COMMANDS

Perhaps nothing gives a user a better feel for how software works than a description of the commands he or she uses to interact with it. For this reason we provide a brief description of some of NetWare's more common commands. This is not a complete list, but you may find such a list in any NetWare manual or in Reference 17. We divide NetWare commands into two types. Client commands are those that may be entered from any client or the server. Server commands, or console commands, define high-priority requests typically made by the LAN manager and are entered only from the server's console.

### Client Commands

- ATTACH allows a user to connect to a different file server. The command must specify the server's name and user's ID and password.
- LISTDIR provides a list of the subdirectories within the given directory.
- LOGIN/LOGOUT allows a user to login or logout of the network. The LOGIN command must specify the user's ID and the file server's name if there is more than one. The LOGOUT command may also specify a file server's name if the user wants to logout from just that server. If no parameter is specified NetWare logs the user out of all servers.
- MAP assigns a client's drive letter (DOS prompt) to a directory path on one of the file server's volumes.
- NCOPY copies files.
- NPRINT allows a user to print a file. Parameters include which printer, server, or queue is requested; deleting the file after printing; number of copies to print; and whether a banner page should be printed.
- RIGHTS allows the user to examine the current trustee rights.
- SETPASS allows a user to set a password.
- SEND allows a user to send a one-line message to one or more users logged on to the network.
- SLIST displays a list of all file servers connected to the network.
- TLIST displays trustee information.
- WHOAMI displays information regarding the currently logged in user. It includes the file server name, user name, and login time. If there are multiple servers a display is provided for each one to which the user is connected.

### Server Commands

- BROADCAST sends a message to all users. This can be used to request all users to log off if a manager must bring a server off-line.
- DISABLE LOGIN/ENABLE LOGIN prevents or allows users to login to a server.

- PRINTER provides information about any printers attached to the server. It includes the printer ID, print queues, and printer status.
- PRINTER ADD allows the person entering the command to add new queues and their priorities to the printer.
- QUEUE provides a list of all print queues.

## LOGIN SCRIPTS

One of a network manager's most important functions is to make sure network users have easy access to what they need. The manager must understand that many users are not network literate or need to be. Users accessing LOTUS or dBASE have their own needs and deadlines and may not want to bother with network-specific details or learn NetWare commands to get what they need. Consequently, the network manager must have some way to make network operations transparent to the user.

A common approach is to create login scripts, a collection of commands that are automatically executed each time a user logs into the system. They are similar to MS-DOS's Autoexec.Bat and VMS's Login.Com files. There are two types of login scripts. The **system login script** defines commands that should be done for each user logging in to the system. Examples include assigning a client's drive letter to specific file server directories, displaying messages, and loading specific files into the client workstation. The **user login script** contains commands needed only by a specific user.

Figure 6.41 shows an example of a system login script. All lines starting with REM indicate comments. Line 2 prevents the user from interrupting the login script by entering a "Ctrl C" or "Ctrl Break" sequence, and line 3 suppresses the display of drive maps. Line 4 is a DOS command that defines the user prompt as the name of the current directory followed by the character '>'.

Lines 6, 7, and 9 establish search drives and assign them to specific directories. Search drives define the directories that the operating system searches automatically when the user requests a file not in the current directory. Designated by S1, S2, S3, etc., each drive assignment corresponds to drive letters 'Z', 'Y', 'X', etc. Up to sixteen search drives may be defined. Directories assigned to the search drives have the format "ServerName/Volume:directory-path." The volume is a disk partition, and the directory path has the format "dir1/dir2/dir3 . . ." where dir3 is a subdirectory of dir2 and dir2 is a subdirectory of dir1. Thus line 6 maps drive letter 'Z' to the PUBLIC directory in the SYS volume on the server named ACCT. It is a public-access directory containing NetWare utilities. Line 9 maps drive letter 'X' to the MENUS subdirectory in the APP directory (Figure 6.42). It contains menus used for workstation applications.

The directory of line 7 has different entries in order to accommodate users of different machines, different operating systems, or even different versions of the same operating system. The PUBLIC directory contains different system files dependent on the specific machine and operating system. Line 7 provides access to them. The '%' prior to the entries indicates NetWare identifiers. When executed, they define the type of workstation, and its operating system and version the user is logging in on. This ensures that the user gets the proper files for his or her working environment.

**FIGURE 6.41 System Login Script**

```
REM ** ESTABLISH DOS AND NOVELL CONTROLS **
BREAK OFF
MAP DISPLAY OFF
DOS SET PROMPT="$P$G"
REM ** ESTABLISH SEARCH DRIVES **
MAP S1:=ACCT/SYS:PUBLIC
MAP S2:=ACCT/SYS:PUBLIC/BIN/%MACHINE/%OS/%OS_VERSION
COMPSPEC S2:COMMAND.COM
MAP S3:=ACCT/SYS:APP/MENUS
REM ** DISPLAY GENERAL MESSAGE TO USERS **
FDISPLAY ACCT/SYS:UTIL/MESSAGES/ALL.MSG
REM ** SET UP CUSTOMIZATIONS FOR GROUPS **
IF MEMBER OF "ACCTING" BEGIN
   MAP H:=ACCT/SYS:USERS/ACCTING/%LOGIN_NAME
   FDISPLAY ACCT/SYS:UTIL/MESSAGES/MNG.MSG
END
REM ** SET USERS TO DEFAULT DRIVE H:
DRIVE H:
```

* Reproduced from Michael Palmer and Alvin Rains, *Local Area Networking with Novell Software*, with the permission of South-Western Publishing Co. 

**FIGURE 6.42 Drive Mappings**

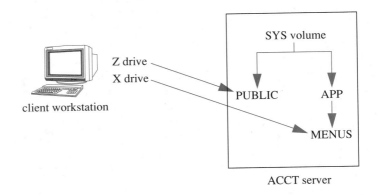

After a user runs applications the DOS command file must be reloaded into the client's memory. Because the server has command files for different operating system versions, it must have some way of knowing which is correct for a particular client. Line 8 provides that information. It specifies S2 as the search drive to locate and reload the command file 'COMMAND.COM'. From line 7 the search drive is mapped to the proper operating system version for the client.

Line 11 displays the contents of the file ALL.MSG in the indicated directory. The network manager can use this file to send messages to any user logging in. This is useful to inform users of any anticipated down times, new network features, or anything of general interest such as who won the weekend football pool. Finally, lines 13 through 18 shows how NetWare defines the working environment for different user groups. If the current user is a member of the "ACCTING" group (the network manager decides who is in what group), the server maps drive H to a particular directory set up for that group. Presumably the directory contains applications or data files frequently needed by members of the "ACCTING" group. The "%LOGIN_NAME" specifier of line 14 contains the user's ID. Line 15 will display any messages intended for anyone in that group, and line 18 sets the current default drive to H:.

User login scripts have the same format as system login scripts. In the former, users can map additional search drives according to their needs. The scripts can display personalized messages to create a more friendly working environment. They also can contain references to executable files that can display menus and request user input. This is especially useful for those who simply want to log in to the network and see their options displayed in menu form. It is the network manager's responsibility to see that all users get what they need and can see their options in a format best suited to those needs. When there are many users with a variety of needs, this is not an easy task.

## NetWare 4.0

Recently Novell released its newest version, NetWare 4.0. It has received significant attention (see references 16,18, and 19) and has been called "a milestone in the LAN industry." It differs significantly from previous NetWare versions in several ways. Rather than storing specific information on specific servers it uses a distributed database. That is, pertinent information to track authorized users and maintain security is distributed across all file servers. Instead of connecting to a specific server the user logs into "the system." NetWare 4.0 also provides authentication based on a public/private key cryptographic system similar to that discussed in Section 4.6. The following list identifies the major features of this version:[*]

- **NetWare Directory Services**: This distributed database directory stores lists of the users, network resources, and access rights on all NetWare servers. Everything is easily accessible by individual users, regardless of their location. All information is replicated on every server, so there is no single point of failure. Users log on to the network, rather than on to a particular server.

---

[*] Preprinted with permission by LAN Times. See Reference 18.

- **Document Imaging**: Novell, working with Kodak Corp., has imbued the core functionality necessary to enable users to transmit images, graphics, and charts across the network. Additional functionality, such as document image-management capabilities, will be available as optional NLMs from third parties (primarily Kodak).

- **Installation Utilities**: These will enable network administrators to perform upgrades in a variety of ways. They can install NetWare 4.0 on a new file server and transfer the data from an existing NetWare 3.x or 2.x server. Or, they can opt to simply upgrade existing servers. Data and binderies are reformatted without requiring backup and restore, although Novell recommends users back up their data.

- **Backward Compatibility**: NetWare 4.0 client software will work with NetWare 2.x and 3.x servers.

- **Increased Memory Protection**: NetWare 4.0 network administrators can elect to run their NLMs in the Intel processor's Ring 0, 1, 2, or 3. Higher rings afford a greater degree of protection — users will no longer live in fear of NLMs conflicting with one another at Ring 0 and crashing the NetWare file server. Arch rival Microsoft Corp. has long contended that NetWare runs faster than its own LAN Manager because it runs in Ring 0.

- **Intelligent File Compression**: This can effectively double available disk space; users can specify which files they want to compress.

- **Increased File Management**: Network administrators can choose from on-line, near on-line, and off-line storage options, such as traditional hard disks, optical disks, and tape. They simply set parameters that determine when files are archived and in which facility they're stored.

- **Foreign-Language Logins**: Users can specify which language their NetWare interface is to display, such as English, French, German, Spanish, or Italian.

- **Software Distribution**: Network administrators can perform automatic software updates from the file server or another system, such as a mainframe or minicomputer.

## 6.7   Summary

The major focus of this chapter has been local area networks, or LANs. The IEEE has defined three very different standards. They are 802.3 CSMA/CD (Ethernet), 802.4 token bus, and 802.5 token ring. Table 6.9 summarizes the major features of each.

Regardless of the LAN standard, there is an upper limit on the number of stations it can handle effectively and the amount of security it can provide. As the need to connect workstations and provide additional security grows, multiple LANs often are connected with bridges. Stations connected to a single LAN can communicate independently of those in a connected LAN. This independence is efficient and provides security. Stations on different LANs can still communicate

TABLE 6.9    **Summary of LAN Standards**

|  | CSMA/CD | TOKEN RING | TOKEN BUS |
|---|---|---|---|
| Maximum delay before sending | none | bounded, depending on distance spanned and number of stations. | bounded, depending on distance spanned and number of stations. |
| Physical topology | linear | ring | linear |
| Logical topology | none | ring | ring |
| Contention | random chance | by token | by token |
| Adding stations | A new station can be added almost anywhere on the cable at any time. | Must be inserted between two specified stations. | Distributed algorithms are needed to add new stations. |
| Performance | Stations often send immediately under light loads, but heavy traffic can reduce the effective data to near 0. | Stations must wait for the token even if no other station is sending. Under heavy loads token passing provides fair access to all stations. | Stations must wait for the token even if no other station is sending. Under heavy loads token passing provides fair access to all stations. |
| Maintenance | no central maintenance. | A designated monitor station performs maintenance. | Distributed algorithms provide maintenance. |

when necessary, however. This puts a burden on bridge design because the bridge must know when to transfer a frame from one LAN to another. Furthermore, if a bridge connects several LANs it must know over which LAN it should send frames.

Section 6.5 discussed three approaches to connecting LANS. Fixed routing bridges must be programmed with each station's location relative to the bridge. Each bridge stores that information in routing tables and routes frames accordingly. Transparent bridges also use routing tables, but they are not programmed. Instead, they learn of a station's location by monitoring the data frames. Source routing bridges put the burden of routing on the sending station, which must determine a route and put it in a frame. The bridges then transmit frames depending on their routing information.

No network can function without a significant amount of software to handle communications. Many proprietary packages exist, but perhaps the most commonly used one is Novell NetWare. Originally designed to connect primarily PCs and printers, it now connects a wide variety of equipment running different protocols. NetWare requires one or more servers to provide other PCs (clients) with application programs or data files. The LAN manager typically designs scripts for the system and the users to make sure the users attach to the proper servers and get what they need without having to learn many network commands. The trend with the latest version is to create a more open system in which client information is stored in a distributed database. This approach further insulates the client from network details. The bottom line, of course, is to make more services available with a minimum amount of hassle by the user.

# Review Questions

1. Distinguish between a local area network and a wide area network.

2. List typical LAN topologies.

3. What is a backbone?

4. What are the two major divisions of the data link layers, and what are their major functions?

5. What is a transceiver?

6. Are the following TRUE or FALSE? Why?

   a. Ethernet is a seven-layer protocol similar to the OSI model.

   b. StarLAN is a physical star topology that behaves like a bus topology.

   c. A high percent utilization for a common bus network is an indication that the network is performing efficiently and meeting the needs of its users.

   d. The pad field in an Ethernet frame is optional.

   e. In a token ring network stations take turns sending frames in order of their arrangement on the ring.

   f. All three LAN protocols allow stations to be prioritized.

   g. Token ring has no central control.

   h. Any station can raise or lower the ring priority in a token ring.

   i. In a token bus LAN the stations' logical order is independent of their physical order.

   j. The biggest problem in routing frames from one LAN protocol to another is reformatting the frames to maintain consistency with the LAN's protocol.

7. Describe each of the 802.3 cable specifications.

8. What is a medium attachment unit (MAU)?

9. Why are repeaters necessary in some networks?

10. Why does an Ethernet frame have a maximum size? Minimum size?

11. What purpose does the token serve in a token ring network?

12. Discuss the content and purpose of each field in the token format.

13. What is a non-data-*J* and non-data-*K* signal?

14. What is a stacking station?

15. What is a monitor station?

16. Describe the purpose of each of the following token ring control frames:

    a. Active monitor present frame

    b. Beacon frame

    c. Claim token frame

    d. Purge frame

    e. Standby monitor present frame

    f. Duplicate address test frame

17. What is the fiber distributed data interface (FDDI)?

18. What is a 4 of 5 code?

19. Distinguish between a slotted ring and a token ring.

20. What is an orphan frame?

21. Distinguish between a token bus and token ring LAN.

22. Describe the purpose of each of the following token bus control frames:

    a. Claim token frame

    b. Resolve contention frame

    c. Set successor frame

    d. Solicit successor 1 frame

    e. Solicit successor 2 frame

    f. Who follows frame

23. Distinguish between a token holding timer and a token rotation timer.

24. Describe how a token bus deals with a lost token.

25. Why does a token bus require a complex initialization procedure?

26. How does a station remove itself from a token bus network?

27. Distinguish between a repeater and a bridge.

28. List major reasons for using bridges between two LANs.

29. What is a routing table?

**30.** Distinguish between a fixed routing bridge and a transparent bridge.

**31.** What is the flooding algorithm and what purpose does it serve?

**32.** What problem can flooding cause when there is a loop in a LAN topology?

**33.** What is a spanning tree within the context of an interconnection of LANs?

**34.** What is a root bridge?

**35.** What is a bridge's root port?

**36.** What purpose does a LAN's designated bridge serve?

**37.** What is a source routing bridge?

**38.** What is a bridge protocol data unit?

**39.** Distinguish between an all-routes broadcast frame and a single-route broadcast frame.

**40.** What is the purpose of Novell NetWare?

**41.** What is a file server?

**42.** Distinguish between a dedicated and a nondedicated file server.

**43.** What are trustee rights?

**44.** Distinguish between disk duplexing and disk mirroring.

**45.** Distinguish between client commands and server commands.

**46.** What is a login script?

## Exercises

**1.** What is the maximum theoretical percent utilization in a 10 Mbps 802.3 LAN (10 BASE 5 cable), with 128 stations connected to five 500-meter segments if the frame size is 128 bytes? 1024 bytes?

**2.** Consider the LAN specifications from Exercise 1. What is the longest time a station might need to detect a collision? if the LAN were just a single 2500-meter segment? Repeat the same calculations as in Exercise 1.

**3.** How many bits can occupy a 500-meter ring containing 50 equally spaced stations (assuming each has a 1-bit delay)? Assume a data rate of 4 Mbps. What about a data rate of 16 Mbps?

**4.** Why do we seemingly complicate the token ring protocol by routing each frame bit or token bit as soon as it is received? Why not just receive all the bits for a token, examine them, and then pass them all to the next station?

5. Consider a 200-meter 4 Mbps token ring containing 20 stations, each transmitting with equal priority. Suppose no station is allowed to transmit more than 5000 data octets before giving up the token. Once a station gives up the token how long will it take (in the worst case) for that station to get the token again?

6. In the discussion on reserving tokens we stated that the station that raises a token's priority has the responsibility to lower it later. Why lower it at all? Why not leave the priority as it is?

7. Finish Table 6.2 to the point where all stations have sent their frames and a token with priority 0 is back on the ring.

8. Repeat the example described by Figure 6.13 and Table 6.2 assuming the token is traveling in a clockwise direction.

9. If a token ring is prioritized, what is the longest time a station may have to wait before it can claim a token?

10. In our discussion of SMP frames, each station receiving one repeated it and later sent its own. Why not have each station that receives an SMP frame drain it from the ring and send its own immediately? That way each station would know its upstream neighbor in the time it takes for one SMP frame to circulate the ring.

11. Consider the algorithm of Figure 6.12. Discuss the effects of removing code associated with each of the following conditions.

    a. Condition 2.

    b. Condition 4.

    c. Condition 7.

12. Why does the token bus protocol use two solicit successor frames instead of just one?

13. Suppose the following stations are trying to get into a token bus network.

    Station V: address = 0011010010
    Station W: address = 0011100110
    Station X: address = 0001100110
    Station Y: address = 0011011000
    Station Z: address = 0011001110

    Suppose station $B$ is station $A$'s successor and that $A$ sends a solicit successor 1 frame. Describe the events that eventually allow the first station into the ring. Which station gets in? Assume $A$'s address is 0011100000 and $B$'s address is 0011000001.

14. Using multiple tokens in a ring can improve performance, but the same is not true for the token bus. Why?

15. Pseudo-code the logic a station uses to claim a token using the claim token frame.

16. Assume the following:

   - There are four stations on a token bus that circulate the token in the order A-B-C-D.
   - THT = 6 and TRT = 32 for each station.
   - Each station has an unending stream of frames in each class to send.
   - The token has just arrived at $A$.

   Describe which frames are sent using the priority mechanism discussed in Section 6.4.

17. Consider an interconnection strategy among LANs in which the most frequently communicating LANs are connected over the fewest bridges. Assume the following LAN pairs must be no more than the specified number of bridges apart. Design an interconnection that uses the fewest number of bridges.

   - One bridge apart: L1 and L5; L2 and L3; L2 and L4.
   - Two (or fewer) bridges apart: L1 and L3; L2 and L5; L1 and L2

18. Build routing tables for the following bridges.

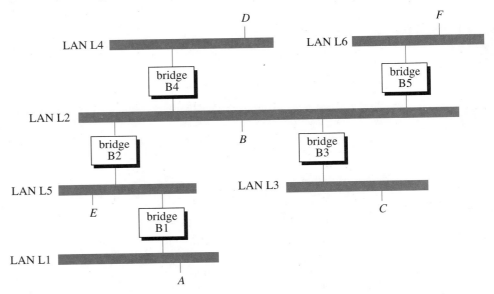

19. Consider the LANs of Figure 6.26 and assume all the routing tables are empty initially. Assume the following events occur in the order listed. Over what LANs are

the specified frames transmitted? Show the routing table entries of each bridge after all frames have been sent.

a.   *A* sends a frame to *F*.

b.   *E* sends a frame to *A*.

c.   *D* sends a frame to *E*.

d.   *C* sends a frame to *B*.

20.   List all routes between *A* and *B* in Figure 6.30. Ignore any route in which a frame goes through the same bridge twice. If we do not ignore those routes how many are there?

21.   Suppose Bridge B1 in Figure 6.30 fails. Execute the spanning tree algorithm and show the new root bridge, cheapest bridge ports, designated bridges, and the resulting enabled bridge connections.

22.   Assume the internetwork of Figure 6.30 is changed so all listed costs are equal. Assuming that the cost of a transmission between two distinct LANs is now the number of bridges through which it must travel, determine the spanning tree.

23.   Suppose *A* sends an all-routes broadcast frame to *B* in Figure 6.30. How many copies of it does *B* receive?

24.   Modify the system login script from Figure 6.41 to account for the following changes:

a.   Define another search drive and assign it to the MENUS1 subdirectory in the APP directory.

b.   Define a working group called ACCTING1 and, for any user in it, map drive G to the ACCTING1 subdirectory in the USERS directory on the SYS volume.

c.   Display a message on the file MSG1.MSG located on the same ACCTING1 subdirectory.

## REFERENCES

1.   Saunders, S. "Ethernet Gears Up for 100 Mbit/s." *Data Communications*, vol. 22, no. 2 (January 1993), 35–9.

2.   Stallings, W. *Handbook of Computer Communications Standards, Vol. 2*, 2nd ed. Howard Sams, 1990.

3.   Schwartz, M. *Telecommunications Networks: Protocols, Modeling, and Analysis.* Reading, MA: Addison-Wesley, 1987.

4.   Walrand, J. *Communications Networks: A First Course.* Boston: Irwin, 1991.

5. Bertsekas, D. and Gallager, R. *Data Networks*. Englewood Cliffs, NJ: Prentice-Hall, 1987.

6. Hammond, J. and O'Reilly, P. *Performance Analysis of Local Computer Networks*. Reading, MA: Addison-Wesley, 1986.

7. Saunders, S. "FDDI Over Copper: Which Cable Works Best?" *Data Communications*, vol. 20, no. 16 (November 1991), 57–64.

8. Hurwicz, M. "FDDI: Not Fastest but Still Fit." *Datamation*, vol. 39, no. 7 (April 1993), 31–4.

9. Tolly, K. "Introduction to FDDI." *Data Communications,* vol. 22, no. 11 (August 1993), 81–6.

10. Saunders, S. "Multimedia Choices: The Three Faces of FDDI." *Data Communications*, vol. 22, no. 10 (July 1993), 53–8.

11. Stallings, W. *Data and Computer Communications*, 4th ed. New York: Macmillan, 1994.

12. Moshos, G. *Data Communications: Principles and Problems*. St. Paul, MN: West, 1989.

13. Tenenbaum, A. M. and M. J. Augenstein. *Data Structures Using Pascal*, 2nd ed. Englewood Cliffs, NJ: Prentice-Hall, 1986.

14. Aho, A. V., J. E. Hopcroft, and J. D. Ullman. *Data Structures and Algorithms*. Reading, MA: Addison-Wesley, 1983.

15. Thompson, M. K. "Netware." *PC Magazine*, vol. 11, no. 11 (June 1992), 328–40

16. Ruiz, B. and J. Herron. "Netware 4.0: A Directory to the Enterprise." *Data Communications*, vol. 21, no. 13 (September 1992), 53–60.

17. Palmer, M. J. and A. L. Rains. *Local Area Networking with Novell Software*. Boston: Boyd & Fraser, 1991.

18. Didio, L. Various articles in *LAN Times,* vol. 9, no. 19 (October 1992).

19. Herron, J. and B. Ruiz. "Netware 4.0: The Work Behind the Network." *Data Communications,* vol. 22, no. 12 (September 1993), 85–92.

20. "Special Report: Network Loadable Modules." *LAN Times*, vol. 10, no. 3 (February 1993), 65–73.

21. Novell, Inc. *Novell NetWare ODI Shell for DOS*. Provo, UT, 1990.

# CHAPTER 7

## WIDE AREA NETWORKS

### 7.1 Introduction

Local area networks (LANs), discussed in Chapter 6, typically cover small geographic areas. They are designed around relatively simple bus or ring topologies. Some networks, however, called wide area networks (WANs), cover much larger areas, sometimes spanning several continents. In those cases, the LAN protocols are inappropriate and new ones must be defined.

Consider again the analogy of a highway system. Many cities have a single major freeway through the center (common bus) or a bypass circling them (ring). If the city is not large, this design handles most highway traffic reasonably well. But what about larger areas such as states or entire countries? It would be unreasonable to have an interstate system consisting of a single highway through America's heartland or circling the country along the coastal areas and the Canadian and Mexican borders. Instead, a complex connection strategy links major highways; bypasses; and state, county, and city roads. It is not reasonable to categorize this type of system as a bus, ring, or even a combination of two. It is much more complex.

Like a national highway system, the topologies of wide area networks are complex, usually somewhere between a simple bus or ring structure and a fully connected one. With more complex topologies come more complex protocols. Collision detection is no longer a viable way to control traffic over so many paths. Similarly, token passing will not work on such a grand scale.

In addition to geographic distance and complexity, there are other differences between LANs and WANs. For example, typical LAN uses include file transfer, electronic mail, and file servers. People use WANs for electronic mail and file transfer, but also for remote logins, an application in which a user in one location logs in to a computer at another. WAN protocols must distinguish among various applications.

Another difference is in routing. Section 6.5 discussed some approaches to routing in LAN interconnections. The more complex WAN topologies require more complex routing strategies. The fact that there are many ways to go from one point to another by itself makes the situation more complex. Anyone who has ever planned a long trip with a detailed map knows the problem of choosing the best route.

To add to the complexity, sometimes a link in a chosen route experiences a failure. What does the network protocol do with all the data traveling that route? In some cases, a route may prove so popular that too much data travels over it. The result is congestion and sometimes failure. Can network protocols avoid such situations? If they can't, what can they do to minimize its effects? To return to our highway analogy, these problems are similar to major road construction preventing traffic flow or excessive traffic on the road to a popular vacation spot during a major holiday. Most of us know these problems well and understand that little can be done short of staying home.

When data is delayed due to failures and congestion it must be stored somewhere while WAN protocols decide what to do with it. Network nodes must be equipped with software and buffers to do this — the equivalent of roadside motels for data.

Management is another problem. LANs are controlled and managed by a single organization or department. If a problem occurs users know whom to call. Some WANs such as the Internet have evolved due mainly to voluntary efforts of universities and government agencies. Consequently, there is no central authority responsible for fixing problems or updating protocols so they do not happen again. Its operations depend on the cooperation of the organizations that use it.

Many WANs evolved by connecting existing networks. Because these networks often used different equipment and different protocols, connecting them was a problem. **Protocol converters**, which define the logic that translates one protocol to another, were used to establish connections.

Chapter 6 discussed some LAN protocol converters called repeaters and bridges. With these methods, the incompatibilities occur at a low level. For example, repeaters, an OSI layer 1 connection, deal primarily with the electrical (or optical) interface (Figure 7.1a), converting one type of signal to another or simply amplifying it. Bridges that work at OSI layer 2 (Figure 7.1b) are needed when frames have different formats or when some logical separation among LANs is needed.

WANs provide a greater variety of networks and incompatibilities. Frame sizes may limit the types of data that can travel among networks. Sometimes frames must be divided to maintain compliance with another network's protocol. Perhaps two networks use different routing strategies. Layer 2 logic cannot deal with these incompatibilities. In such cases, a **router**, a connection at OSI layer 3 (Figure 7.1c), is used to handle the differences. A router knows the differences in the lower 3 layers of both network protocols and translates between them.

In theory, two different networks may differ at any of the OSI layers. The logic required to connect them becomes more complex as the layer where they differ increases. In the extreme case, there may be total incompatibility (up through layer 7). For example, they may use different codes, encryption techniques, or compression

FIGURE 7.1    **OSI Connections**

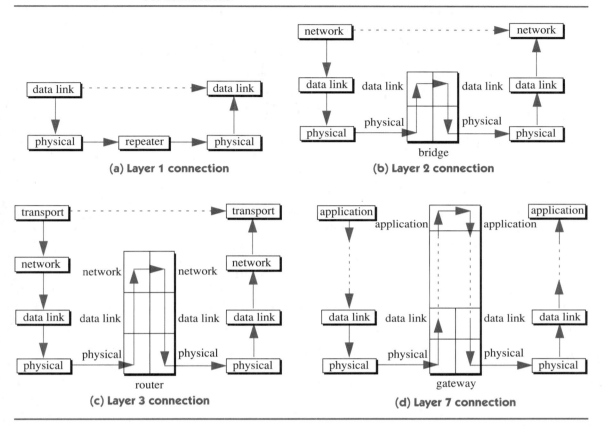

(a) Layer 1 connection

(b) Layer 2 connection

(c) Layer 3 connection

(d) Layer 7 connection

techniques. They may use different rules for establishing and maintaining connections. In such cases, a connection at layer 7 called a **gateway** (Figure 7.1d) converts between protocols.

This chapter discusses some of the issues of WAN design and protocols. For example, Section 7.2 discusses routing, the logic required by network nodes to make sure information gets to its destination. It will present and compare a few common strategies and will address problems, such as congestion, caused by poor routing decisions. Section 7.3 discusses a popular WAN called the packet switched network, one that divides all its information into packets and transmits them individually. This section also discusses the CCITT X.25 protocol, which is commonly used to connect to packet switched networks.

Section 7.4 presents the Internet protocol. Actually, there are two Internet protocols. One is an ISO standard and is part of the network layer in the OSI model. The other is based on an Internet protocol developed by the U.S. Defense Advanced

Research Projects Agency (DARPA).[*] It has been used in the network layer of the ARPANET and is most often used with the **transmission control protocol (TCP)**, a transport protocol discussed in Section 7.5. Together they are known as TCP/IP and form the layer 3 and layer 4 protocols used to connect commercial, research, military, and educational networks. The combined network is accessible to professionals worldwide and is known as the **Internet**.

Section 7.6 concludes this chapter by describing many of the actual networks being used today, including the Internet, ARPANET, and CSnet.

## 7.2   Network Routing

Most people are familiar with the general concept of routing. Essentially it means that if you want to go from point $A$ to point $B$ you have to determine a way to get there. For example, if you live in Winona, Minnesota, and want to drive to Charleston, South Carolina, for your vacation, you will probably spend some time studying road maps to determine the best way to get there. Similarly, if you want to transfer information between computers in those two locations that are connected via a WAN, network protocols must determine how to get it there.

When LANs are organized around a single bus or ring, routing is not a problem. If they are connected with bridges, the bridges make the routing decisions (as explained in Section 6.5). The topologies are not very complex, and the bridges do the routing rather easily.

Figure 7.2 shows a more general network topology. Some stations often communicate directly with more stations than do others. Presumably they represent locations in heavily populated areas or locations with a high volume of information traffic. The stations with fewer connections might have fewer needs or correspond to more remote sites. For example, nodes $A$ and $B$ might represent sites in major metropolitan areas, and nodes $X$ and $Y$ may correspond to locations in remote parts of the country.

Suppose one station wants to communicate with another to which it is not connected directly. Network protocols must find a path that connects them. To make matters more complex, there may be many paths. For example, suppose $X$ sends something to $Y$ in Figure 7.2. Two possible paths are $X$-$A$-$B$-$C$-$D$-$Y$ and $X$-$A$-$Z$-$D$-$Y$. Which is better? The answer typically depends on a comparison of the costs and the time required to send the information over each path.

The comparison is not always straightforward. In Figure 7.2 you might think that the path through $A$, $Z$, and $D$ is better because it is shorter than the other alternative. Shorter is not always better, however, as anyone traveling by car knows. Many people will choose to drive a longer distance if it means using a road that has more lanes, is in better condition, or has more rest stops than a shorter alternative. Even though they drive farther they may reach their destination more quickly and with less difficulty.

---

[*]Recently, DARPA reverted to ARPA, dropping the "Defense" from its name.

FIGURE 7.2    **Generalized Network Topology**

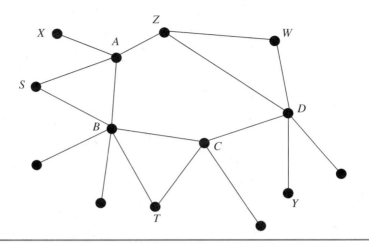

## ROUTING TABLES

Similar to the bridges shown in Section 6.5, network nodes may use **routing tables**. Like those in Section 6.5, routing tables here do not normally specify the entire route. Instead they specify the next node in a route to a specified destination and the cost to get there. For example, consider the network in Figure 7.3, where a cost is associated with the connection between two adjacent nodes. Suppose we want to find the cheapest route, the one that minimizes the sum of the costs of the connections between adjacent nodes in the route. For example, there are several routes from $A$ to $F$ but the cheapest one goes from $A$ to $B$ (cost of 2), $B$ to $E$ (cost of 3), and $E$ to $F$ (cost of 2) for a total route cost of 7.

FIGURE 7.3    **Network and Associated Connection Costs**

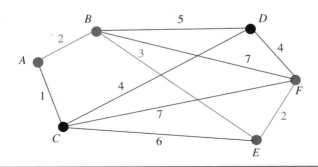

Figure 7.4 shows partial routing tables of nodes *A, B,* and *E.* (We will discuss how these tables are created shortly.) Node *A*'s table indicates that anything destined for node *B, E,* or *F* should be sent directly to *B* where *B*'s routing table will indicate the next node in the cheapest route. Similarly, anything destined for *C* or *D* should be sent to node *C.* From there, *C*'s routing table indicates the next step.

To illustrate, suppose an application at node *A* wants to send data to node *F.* Logic at *A* looks for an entry in its routing table with destination *F.* The entry states that node *B* is the successor on the route, and the network protocol sends the data to *B.* Logic at *B* examines its routing table looking for an entry corresponding to destination *F.* The table's third entry indicates the data should go to node *E* next. Finally, the routing table at node *E* indicates that *F* is the next node on the route.

## TYPES OF ROUTING

Who defines the routing tables and how? The process by which a routing table is defined is called a **routing algorithm.** There are several basic types, and we will discuss four of them: **centralized routing, distributed routing, static routing,** and **adaptive routing.** Then we will discuss in detail some specific routing algorithms.

**Centralized Routing**        Centralized routing means that all interconnection information is generated and maintained at a single central location. That location then broadcasts this information to all network nodes so that each may define its own routing tables. One way to maintain routing information centrally is a routing matrix. It consists of a row and column for each node in the network. A row corresponds to a source node and a column to a destination node. The entry in the position specified by the row and column indicates the first node in the route from the source to the destination. From this entry the entire route can be extracted.

Figure 7.5 shows a routing matrix for the network in Figure 7.3. As before, the routes selected are the cheapest ones. In the case where two routes both have the cheapest cost one is chosen arbitrarily. Consider again the route from *A* to *F.* According to the matrix's first row and sixth column, node *B* is the first one in the

FIGURE 7.4        **Partial Routing Tables for Nodes *A, B,* and *E***

| DESTINATION | NEXT NODE | COST | DESTINATION | NEXT NODE | COST | DESTINATION | NEXT NODE | COST |
|:---:|:---:|:---:|:---:|:---:|:---:|:---:|:---:|:---:|
| B | B | 2 | D | D | 5 | F | F | 2 |
| C | C | 1 | E | E | 3 | | | |
| D | C | 5 | F | E | 5 | | | |
| E | B | 5 | | | | | | |
| F | B | 7 | | | | | | |

| (a) Partial routing table for node *A* | (b) Partial routing table for node *B* | (c) Partial routing table for node *E* |
|:---:|:---:|:---:|

FIGURE 7.5    **Routing Matrix for the Network In Figure 7.3**

|  |  | A | B | C | D | E | F |
|---|---|---|---|---|---|---|---|
|  | A | — | B | C | C | B | B |
|  | B | A | — | A | D | E | E |
| Source Node | C | A | A | — | D | E | F |
|  | D | C | B | C | — | F | F |
|  | E | B | B | C | F | — | F |
|  | F | E | E | C | D | E | — |

cheapest route. The next node is determined by considering the route from $B$ to $F$. Examining the second row and sixth column indicates that node $E$ is next. Finally, the node following $E$ (node $F$) is found in the fifth row and sixth column. Thus, the route is from $A$ to $B$ to $E$ to $F$.

Creating a routing table for a network node requires the row from the matrix corresponding to the node. For example, node $A$'s routing table in Figure 7.4 (minus the cost[*]) is the same as row 1 of the matrix. Similar statements can be made for the other nodes.

**Distributed Routing**    Distributed routing means there is no central control. Each node must determine and maintain its routing information independently. It usually does this by knowing who its neighbors are, calculating the cost to get there, and determining the cost for a neighbor to send data to specific destinations. Each neighbor, in turn, does the same thing. From that information each node can derive its own routing table. This method is more complex, as it requires each node to communicate with each of its neighbors independently.

It is difficult to appreciate the complexity of this approach because examples typically show a global view of a network with its connections and their costs. This overview can bias the way we see the strategy unless we constantly remind ourselves that a node's knowledge of the network is very limited. To illustrate, consider the network shown in Figure 7.6. Assume that each node initially knows only the cost to its neighbor; later it can add to its information base anything its neighbors tell it. For example, $A$ initially knows only that it can send something to $B$ (cost = 1) or to $D$ (cost = 2). It has no knowledge whatsoever that nodes $C$ and $E$ even exist. Other nodes have similar knowledge (or lack of it). However, if neighboring nodes communicate, $A$ learns the identity of $B$'s and $D$'s neighbors and soon learns of nodes $C$ and $E$. By learning of $B$'s and $D$'s costs to get there, and knowing the cost to get to $B$ and $D$, node $A$ can calculate the cost to get to $C$ and $E$. By periodically exchanging information about neighboring nodes, each one learns the identity of

---

[*] We did not include costs in the routing matrix, but it is a simple matter to do so by storing the cost with each node in the matrix.

others in the network and the cheapest paths to them. Shortly we will discuss a specific distributed algorithm to do this.

**Static Routing**    Static routing means that once a node determines its routing table, the node does not change it. In other words, the cheapest path is not dependent on time. There is an underlying assumption that the conditions that led to the table's definition have not changed. This is sometimes a valid assumption as costs often depend on distances and the data rates between intermediate nodes. Except for major equipment upgrades and moving of equipment, these parameters do not change.

**Adaptive Routing**    Static routing works well as long as network conditions do not change. In some networks, however, this is a bad assumption. For example, if the cost of each link depends on network traffic, it is time dependent. Consider the problem of sending packets from node $A$ to node $E$ in the network of Figure 7.6. The optimal route is $A$-$D$-$C$-$E$. Suppose that after node $A$ transmits the packet to node $D$, the $D$-$C$ link and the $D$-$E$ link costs each increases to 10 because of a surge of heavy traffic. The cheapest route from $A$ is now $A$-$B$-$C$-$E$, and the route on which the packet embarked initially is now very expensive. In this case it would actually be cheaper to send the packet back to $A$ and start over again. An **adaptive routing** strategy allows a network node to respond to such changes and update its routing tables accordingly.

There are pitfalls to this system. For example, suppose in our current example $D$ does send the packet back to $A$ and then the cost of the $A$-$B$ link increases to 10. The logical choice would be to send the packet back to $D$. You can now see the problem: Conceivably, the packet could shuttle back and forth among several nodes, never making any progress toward its eventual destination. One technique to avoid this maintains a counter in the packet header that is incremented on each transmission. If the count exceeds some value, the packet receives high priority handling by routing logic at each node. In some cases, it is removed from the network.

In general, adaptive routing is difficult to implement efficiently. Nodes can keep up with changing conditions only by getting reports from other nodes about link

**FIGURE 7.6    Network Example for Distributed Routing**

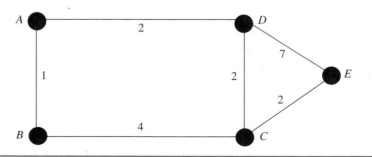

costs. These reports add to network traffic and, in turn, contribute more to the changing conditions. They also take time, so that by the time a node learns of a changing condition, that condition may no longer be in effect.

Table 7.1 gives a brief summary and comparison of the four types of routing.

### DIJKSTRA'S ALGORITHM

**Dijkstra's algorithm**, sometimes called the **shortest path algorithm** or **forward search algorithm**, is a centralized, static algorithm, although it can be made adaptive by executing it periodically. It also requires that a node executing it have information regarding link costs among the network nodes. Several networks such as ARPANET and TYMNET II use this algorithm.

Each node executes Dijkstra's algorithm to determine the cheapest route to each network node. In cases where a route cost is simply the number of intermediate nodes, the cheapest route is also the shortest one. The algorithm is an iterative one building a set of nodes, one by one, with each iteration. Each node in the set has the property that the cheapest route to it from the given node is known.

Figure 7.7 shows an outline of the algorithm. Initially, it defines a set $S$ consisting of just one node $A$, the node executing the algorithm. It then defines a function where, for each node $X$, $Cost(X)$ = the cost of the cheapest route from $A$ to $X$ for which intermediate nodes are in $S$. Initially, since $S$ contains only node $A$, $Cost(X)$ is the cost of a direct link from $A$ to $X$. If there is no such link, $Cost(X)$ is assigned an arbitrarily large number. The function $Prior(X)$ in the algorithm contains the node preceding $X$ in the cheapest route.

The algorithm contains a loop. With each pass it determines a set $W$ consisting of all nodes not in $S$ but with a direct link to something in $S$ (Figure 7.8). It chooses one node $X$ for which $Cost(X) \leq Cost(Y)$ for any other node $Y$ in $W$. It then adds $X$ to

TABLE 7.1    **Types of Routing**

| ROUTING TYPE | ADVANTAGES | DISADVANTAGES |
| --- | --- | --- |
| Centralized routing | Simple method as one location assumes routing control. | The failure of the central location or any links connected to it have a severe effect on providing routing information to network nodes. |
| Distributed routing | Failure of a node or link has a small effect in providing accurate routing information. | Exchange of information is more complex. May also take longer for a node to learn of conditions in remote locations. |
| Static routing | Simple method as nodes do not have to execute routing algorithms repeatedly. | Insensitive to changing conditions. A good route may turn into a very bad one. |
| Adaptive routing | Provides the most current information regarding link costs. | High overhead as nodes must maintain current information. Transmitting information regarding changing conditions adds to network traffic. |

FIGURE 7.7    **Dijkstra's Algorithm**

```
Define S as a set of nodes. Initially S contains node A.

Define Cost(X) as the cost of the cheapest route from A to X using only nodes from S (X
    excepted). Initially, Cost(X) is the cost of the link from A to X. If no such link
    exists, then Cost(X) is an arbitrarily large value (larger than any possible route cost).
    For those nodes linked to A define Prior(X) = A.

do {

    Determine the set of nodes not in S, but connected to a node in S. Call this set W.

    Choose a node X in W for which Cost(X) is a minimum. Add X to the set S.

    For each V not in S, define Cost(V) = minimum {Cost(V), Cost(X)+cost of link connecting X
        to V}. If Cost(V) is changed define Prior(V) = X.

    }

while not all nodes in S.
```

FIGURE 7.8    **Adding Nodes to _S_ Using Dijkstra's Algorithm**

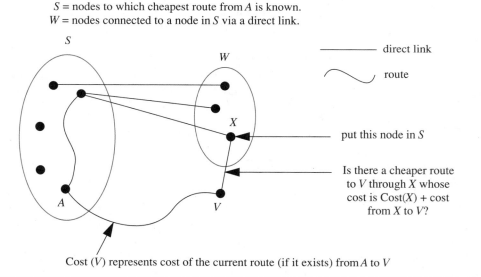

$S$ = nodes to which cheapest route from $A$ is known.
$W$ = nodes connected to a node in $S$ via a direct link.

Cost $(V)$ represents cost of the current route (if it exists) from $A$ to $V$

set $S$ and then updates the cost function Cost($V$) for every $V$ not yet in $S$. It compares
the current Cost($V$) with Cost($X$) plus the cost of any direct link from $X$ to $V$. If the
latter value is smaller, the algorithm redefines Cost($V$) to be that value. The intent is
to determine whether the addition of $X$ to $S$ allows a cheaper route from $A$ to $V$
through nodes in $S$.

The correctness of the algorithm is not obvious, and proof that it is correct exceeds the goals of this text. For a more formal treatment, see Reference 1. We will, however, apply this algorithm to the example network of Figure 7.9. Table 7.2 shows the values the algorithm generates when applied to this network. In step 1, the set $S$ contains only the source node $A$. The only nodes connected to $A$ are $B$ and $C$, and the costs of those edges are 2 and 1, respectively. Consequently, Cost($B$) = 2 and Cost($C$) = 1. Initial values for Cost($D$), Cost($E$), and Cost($F$) are arbitrarily large and designated by $\infty$. Also, Prior($B$) = $A$ and Prior($C$) = $A$. Since the algorithm has not yet found any routes to $D$, $E$, and $F$ the prior function is undefined at those nodes.

As we enter the loop, the set $W$ contains nodes $B$ and $C$, because they are the only ones connected to $A$. Next, since Cost($C$)< Cost($B$), we choose $X = C$ and add it to $S$. The last line in the loop now requires that we examine Cost($V$) for each $V$ not yet in $S$. This consists of nodes $B$, $D$, $E$, and $F$. Since the cost function represents the cheapest path from $A$ through nodes in $S$, we must ask whether the additional node in $S$ provides a cheaper route. In other words, consider any node $V$ not in $S$. If Cost($C$) + cost of the direct link connecting $C$ to $V$ is less than Cost($V$), then the route from $A$ to $C$ followed by the link from $C$ to $V$ represents a cheaper route. Table 7.3 shows the necessary comparisons for each node $V$ not in $S$. For nodes $D$, $E$, and

**FIGURE 7.9    Network and Associated Connection Costs**

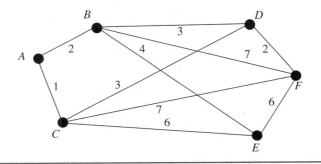

**TABLE 7.2    Values Defined by Dijkstra's Algorithm for the Network in Figure 7.9**

| STEP | S | W | X | COST FUNCTION FOR B | C | D | E | F | PRIOR FUNCTION FOR B | C | D | E | F |
|------|---|---|---|---|---|---|---|---|---|---|---|---|---|
| 1 | {A} | {B, C} | C | 2 | 1 | $\infty$ | $\infty$ | $\infty$ | A | A | — | — | — |
| 2 | {A, C} | {B, D, E, F} | B | 2 | 1 | 4 | 7 | 8 | A | A | C | C | C |
| 3 | {A, B, C} | {D, E, F} | D | 2 | 1 | 4 | 6 | 8 | A | A | C | B | C |
| 4 | {A, B, C, D} | {E, F} | E | 2 | 1 | 4 | 6 | 6 | A | A | C | B | D |
| 5 | {A, B, C, D, E} | {F} | F | 2 | 1 | 4 | 6 | 6 | A | A | C | B | D |

TABLE 7.3    **Cost Comparisons for Dijkstra's Algorithm**

| $V$ | $\text{COST}(V)$ | $\text{COST}(C)$ + COST OF LINK CONNECTING $C$ TO $V$ |
|---|---|---|
| $B$ | 2 | no link from $C$ to $V$ |
| $D$ | $\infty$ | $1 + 3 = 4$ |
| $E$ | $\infty$ | $1 + 6 = 7$ |
| $F$ | $\infty$ | $1 + 7 = 8$ |

$F$, the latter values are smaller, and node $C$ is established as their prior node. The second row of Table 7.2 reflects these changes.

The second pass through the loop proceeds similarly. Node $B$ is added to $S$ because Cost($B$) is smallest among nodes outside of $S$. Furthermore the inclusion of $B$ in $S$ provides a cheaper route to $E$ (through nodes in $S$). Row 3 of Table 7.2 shows how the entries under $E$ change. Node $B$ is the new prior node for $E$, and Cost($E$) is now 6. As an exercise, you should follow the algorithm and verify that rows 4 and 5 in Table 7.2 are correct. When the algorithm finishes, the table's last row shows that the cheapest routes to $B$, $C$, $D$, $E$, and $F$ cost 2, 1, 4, 6, and 6, respectively.

The prior function can be used to recover the actual route. For example, if you want the actual route from $A$ to $F$, Prior($F$) = $D$ specifies that $D$ precedes $F$ on that route. Prior($D$) = $C$ specifies that $C$ precedes $D$, and Prior($C$) = $A$ means $A$ precedes $C$. Thus, the cheapest route from $A$ to $F$ is $A$-$C$-$D$-$F$.

### BELLMAN-FORD ALGORITHMS

Dijkstra's algorithm produced the cheapest path by working forward from a given source. Another approach is to work backward from a desired destination. The **Bellman-Ford algorithm**, sometimes called the **backward search algorithm**, does this. A distributed version of it is used in the Canadian DATAPAC network, Digital Equipment Corporation's DNA, TYMNET I, and the original ARPANET (2,3).

It is based on the following principle. Let Cost($A$, $Z$) be the cost of the cheapest route from node $A$ to $Z$. Suppose $A$ has a direct connection to nodes $B$, $C$, . . . , $D$ (Figure 7.10). Then

$$\text{Cost}(A, Z) = \begin{cases} \text{cost of link from } A \text{ to } B + \text{cost of cheapest route from } B \text{ to } Z \\ \text{cost of link from } A \text{ to } C + \text{cost of cheapest route from } C \text{ to } Z \\ \quad\quad\vdots \\ \text{cost of link from } A \text{ to } D + \text{cost of cheapest route from } D \text{ to } Z \end{cases}$$

According to this principle, node $A$ can determine the cheapest route to $Z$ as long as $A$ knows the cost to each neighbor and each neighbor knows the cheapest route to $Z$. Node $A$ then can perform the preceding calculation and determine the

**FIGURE 7.10    Cheapest Route from A to Z**

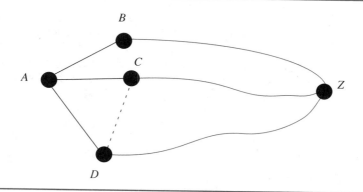

cheapest route. But how does each neighbor know the cheapest route to Z? The answer is in how the algorithm works. There are both centralized and distributed versions of the algorithm (2,4). Having already discussed a centralized algorithm, we will present the distributed version.

As mentioned previously, each node knows only the cost to each neighbor and any information the neighbor can provide. Thus, in the distributed algorithm each node broadcasts what it knows to each of its neighbors. Each node receives new information and updates its routing tables accordingly. As the neighbors continue to broadcast the information periodically, information about each of the network nodes and connections eventually propagates throughout the network. Information coming in to nodes may allow them to discover new nodes and new cheapest paths to other nodes.

To illustrate, we apply the algorithm to the network in Figure 7.11. Each node maintains information on the cheapest route to other nodes. It contains the route's cost and the first node on that route. Initially, each node knows only the cost to get to its neighbor. Table 7.4a shows how this information is stored. Each row corresponds

**FIGURE 7.11    Network for the Bellman-Ford Algorithm**

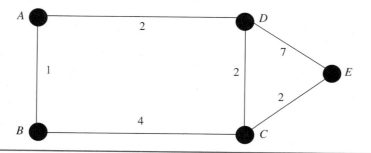

to a source and each column to a destination. Each table entry contains the first node on the route and the route's cost. In Table 7.4a the first node on a route is always the same as the node in the column heading because no routes other than those to neighbors are known yet. This situation will change as the algorithm proceeds, however.

Keep in mind that although this table lists a row and column for each node, each node knows only what is in a row corresponding to it. For example, A knows only that the costs to B and D are 1 and 2, respectively; B knows only that the costs to A and C are, 1 and 4, respectively; and so on. Some nodes may not even know of others' existence. For example, A does not even know nodes C and E exist. B does not know nodes D and E exist; and so on. This is indicated by 'unknown' in the table.

**TABLE 7.4    Three Iterations of the Bell-Ford Algorithm**

|  |  | DESTINATION |  |  |  |  |
|---|---|---|---|---|---|---|
|  |  | A | B | C | D | E |
|  | A | — | (B, 1) | unknown | (D, 2) | unknown |
|  | B | (A, 1) | — | (C, 4) | unknown | unknown |
| Source | C | unknown | (B, 4) | — | (D, 2) | (E, 2) |
|  | D | (A, 2) | unknown | (C, 2) | — | (E, 7) |
|  | E | unknown | unknown | (C, 2) | (D, 7) | — |

**(a) First Iteration**

|  |  | DESTINATION |  |  |  |  |
|---|---|---|---|---|---|---|
|  |  | A | B | C | D | E |
|  | A | — | (B, 1) | (D, 4) | (D, 2) | (D, 9) |
|  | B | (A, 1) | — | (C, 4) | (A, 3) | (C, 6) |
| Source | C | (D, 4) | (B, 4) | — | (D, 2) | (E, 2) |
|  | D | (A, 2) | (A, 3) | (C, 2) | — | (C, 4) |
|  | E | (D, 9) | (C, 6) | (C, 2) | (C, 4) | — |

**(b) Second Iteration**

|  |  | DESTINATION |  |  |  |  |
|---|---|---|---|---|---|---|
|  |  | A | B | C | D | E |
|  | A | — | (B, 1) | (D, 4) | (D, 2) | (D, 6) |
|  | B | (A, 1) | — | (C, 4) | (A, 3) | (C, 6) |
| Source | C | (D, 4) | (B, 4) | — | (D, 2) | (E, 2) |
|  | D | (A, 2) | (A, 3) | (C, 2) | — | (C, 4) |
|  | E | (C, 6) | (C, 6) | (C, 2) | (C, 4) | — |

**(c) Third Iteration**

FIGURE 7.12    **Bellman-Ford Algorithm**

```
For each neighbor insert the entry (neighboring node, link cost) in the current routing
   table.
while network protocols baffle me do
for each neighboring node N do
{
   receive information from N's routing table;
   for each node Z in N's routing table do
     if Z is not in the current routing table
       insert the pair (N, current cost to N + N's cost to Z) in it;
     else
       if the current cost to N + N's cost to Z< current cost to Z
         replace the current cost to Z with the current cost to N + N's cost to Z and
         specify N as the new first node along a route to Z;
}
```

Figure 7.12 contains a pseudo-coded version of the algorithm. Initially, a node stores information about routes to its neighbors in its routing table. The first while loop indicates that the algorithm continually monitors information coming in from its neighbors. Inside the loop a node receives information from each of its neighbors.[*] From each neighbor it learns of nodes to which the neighbor has access and the costs of the associated routes. For each node Z to which a neighbor N has access there are two possibilities:

The current node has no previous knowledge of Z. The current node inserts the entry (N, current cost to N + N's cost to Z) in its routing table. The current node now knows of a route to Z via N.

The current node already has a route to Z. The current node compares the cost of that route with the cost of going to N plus N's cost to Z. If the latter value is smaller the current node has found a cheaper route to Z. It replaces its current cost with the cheaper one and specifies N as the new first node along a route to Z.

Table 7.4b shows how each node's information changes as each of its neighbors tells it what it knows. B tells A it has access to C with a cost of 4. Since A knows it already has access to B with a cost of 1 it concludes it now has access to C with a

---

[*]Although the algorithm depicts an orderly sequence of receptions from each neighbor, it will almost certainly not happen this way. The actual reception of information depends on many real-time events and is very unpredictable. Our main goal is to describe *how* a node responds to that information so the algorithm serves our purposes.

cost of 5 (cost to $B$ plus cost from $B$ to $C$). Similarly, $D$ also tells $A$ it has access to $C$ but with a cost of 2. Node $A$ now concludes that it has access to $C$ via $D$ with a total cost of 4. Since this is cheaper than going through $B$ it inserts the entry $(D, 4)$ in its routing table (Table 7.4b). $D$ also tells $A$ that it has access to $E$ with a cost of 7. Since $A$ knows it has access to $D$ with a cost of 2 it concludes it has access to $E$ with a cost of $7 + 2 = 9$. It then stores the entry $(D, 9)$ in the routing table.

From our view of the network, we know there is a route from $A$ to $E$ through $D$ and $C$ that has a cost of only 6. But remember that we have a unique perspective using information that $A$ does not yet have. Consequently, A does not yet know of this route. Don't let our view bias your interpretation of the algorithm.

Continuing in this way, $B$ receives information from $A$ and $C$ about routes to other nodes.[*] The information from node $A$ tells $B$ there is a route to $D$ with a cost of 3. Similarly, the information from $C$ tells $B$ there is another route to $D$ with a cost of 6 and a route to $E$ with a cost of 6. Assimilating this information and choosing the cheapest routes, row 2 of Table 7.4b shows $B$'s new routing information.

After each node has heard from each neighbor once, Table 7.4b shows each node's routing table. At this point each node knows the best way to get to each neighbor and to each of its neighbor's neighbor. However, it may not yet know of any optimal routes requiring three or more links. Thus, each node goes through another round of gathering information from each neighbor and determining whether there are better routes. For example, $A$ knows from Table 7.4b that the cheapest route to $E$ is via $D$ for a total cost of 9. However, when $A$ hears from $D$ again it learns that $D$ can now get to $E$ with a cost of 4. Therefore, since the link cost from $A$ to $D$ is 2, $A$ now concludes it can get to $E$ via $D$ with a total cost of 6. You should follow all the steps of the algorithm in Figure 7.12 and verify the entries in Table 7.4 b and c.

As long as each node continually applies the algorithm it is adaptive. Depending on the network topology, however, it may react slowly to changes. The reason is that if a link cost changes between two nodes only their immediate neighbors learn of it during one pass of the algorithm. Nodes two links away require up to two passes of the algorithm to learn of the changes, nodes three links away require up to three passes, and so on. In general, news of changing costs can take quite some time propagating through the network.

Another problem is that a node responds only if a neighbor informs it of a shorter path. Consider what happens if the cost of a link in a current shortest path increases or the link itself goes down. There is nothing in the algorithm that invalidates that path. Consequently a node can send packets along what was once, but no longer is, an optimal path.

A solution to this problem is for each node to purge all of its routing tables and rebuild them from scratch periodically. This way the algorithm makes use of more current information. A related issue is the frequency with which a node purges and

---

[*] Exactly what $B$ receives from $A$ depends on whether $A$ sent information before or after it received information from $D$. Since we cannot guarantee the timing we will assume that each node sends what it has at the beginning of each step.

rebuilds its tables. If a node rebuilds tables rarely it is much slower to respond to any degradation in a link. On the other hand, if a node rebuilds tables frequently there is more time during which the tables are being built and may not reflect the best path to a node. Remember, it takes some time for the tables to reflect the network's current conditions, especially at remote nodes. During that time a node routes packets based on incomplete information. If you are interested in a more detailed analysis of this algorithm, refer to references 2 and 4.

## HIERARCHICAL ROUTING

The routing approaches discussed so far have one thing in common: Both are designed to give each node proper routing information. Sometimes, however, there are too many nodes to efficiently provide each one with routing information. Treating each node as an equal participant in a large network generates too much information to share and send throughout the network. An alternative is to have some nodes do the routing for others. One approach is **hierarchical routing**. It has the following features:

- All nodes are divided into groups called **domains**. We can consider a domain to be a separate and independent network.

- Routes between two nodes in a common domain are determined using the domain's or network's protocols.

- Each domain has one or more specially designated nodes called a **router** (sometimes called a **gateway**). They determine routes between domains. Effectively the routers themselves form a network.

- If a domain is large it may consist of multiple subdomains, each of which contains its own router. They determine the routes between subdomains of the same domain.

Suppose node $X$ wants to send a packet to node $Y$. If they are in the same domain the route can be determined using any of the previously discussed techniques. On the other hand suppose they are in different domains (Figure 7.13). Node $X$ sends the packet to router $A$ within its domain. Node $A$ then has the responsibility of determining the best route to node $Y$'s domain (domain 2) and sending the packet. Since node $B$ is a router for domain 2, it receives the packet and then sends it to node $Y$. This approach applies for any pair of nodes from domains 1 and 2. Effectively $A$ is performing necessary routing on behalf of any node in its domain, thus reducing the total number of nodes that must perform such tasks.

We can represent the domain concept using a hierarchical structure (Figure 7.14). All domains correspond to second-level tree nodes under a common root.[*] All network nodes within a domain correspond to third-level tree nodes under the

---

[*] Don't think of the root as an actual network node. It simply means all its dependents (domains) are connected.

FIGURE 7.13        Domains in Hierarchical Routing

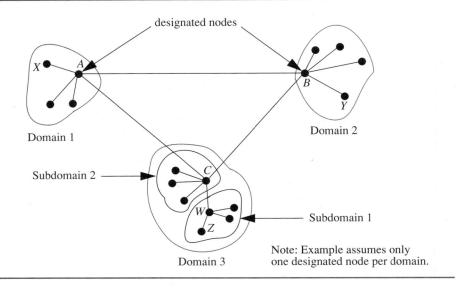

domain. If the domain contains subdomains they also are third-level tree nodes, and any network nodes in them are at the fourth level under the appropriate subdomain.

In general, network routers are defined partly by the hierarchy. Thus, suppose Z in Figure 7.13 wanted to send a packet to X. Since Z is in subdomain 1, it sends the packet to W, the router for Z's subdomain. In turn, W routes across subdomains to C, the router for domain 3. C then routes across domains to A, which finally sends the packet to X.

FIGURE 7.14        Hierarchical Arrangement of Domain Nodes

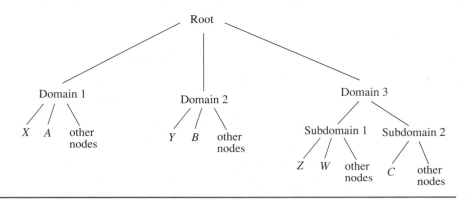

So far we have omitted one detail. For hierarchical routing to work, the sending node specifies the destination's address, including its domain and any subdomains. By including the address, each router determines whether the destination is in the current domain (or subdomain). If it is, the router can deliver the packet. If not, the router must determine the domain to which the packet must go. This is similar to sending letters via the postal system using the typical address format:

> Name
>
> Street address
>
> City, State, ZIP code

Postal workers in Hartford, Connecticut, don't care if a letter is addressed to Jane Smith at 123 Main Street unless the city and state are also specified as Hartford, Connecticut. If the city and state are different, the Hartford postal workers' routing responsibility is to make sure the letter is sent to the appropriate city, where that city's postal workers deliver letters according to address and name. Similarly, a network node specifies an address as a sequence of domain and subdomain specifiers. For example, in Figure 7.13 Node $X$ might send a packet to node $Z$ by addressing it to Z.subdomain-1.domain-3.

The Internet is a network that uses hierarchies in its addressing scheme. An Internet address is a 32-bit address represented as a sequence of four 8-bit numbers separated by dots. For example, the author's Internet address is 143.200.128.3 where each of the four numbers has an 8-bit representation. Each Internet address also consists of two parts: an Internet protocol (IP) network address assigned to a site and a host address. The address given is an example of a **Class B address**,[*] meaning the first 16 bits designate the IP network address (143.200) and the other 16 bits designate the host (128.3).

Some sites may have a single IP network address assigned to them but actually have multiple physical on-site networks (such as token ring and Ethernet). A single address allows a site to expand and develop network applications independent of its connection to Internet. Local management then can use part of the 16-bit host ID (for example, the first octet) to designate a particular physical network. This creates an address hierarchy, with the first two octets designating an IP network, the third octet designating a site's physical network, and the last octet designating the actual destination on that network.

During routing of packets a router first examines the IP network address. If the packet is destined for another site it is routed (using an algorithm discussed later) based solely on that address. Otherwise, the router examines the host ID and extracts, if necessary, the physical address identifier. After that it queues the packet for delivery to its destination along the proper physical network. From there, lower-layer network protocol handles delivery according to the type of network. This process is basically a two-level hierarchical routing technique.

---

[*] Internet also defines Class A addresses (8-bit network address and 24-bit host ID) and Class C addresses (24-bit network address and 8-bit host ID).

The Internet also uses a hierarchy as an administrative mechanism. To an Internet user, an address has the form

user@host.department.institution.domain

where the periods in the address separate the address's components. Using this format ensures unique names across the Internet. The name to the right of the symbol @ generally specifies a computer at the user's destination or site. The rightmost name refers to an Internet domain. A word of caution is needed here! Internet domains are different from domains described previously and do not have any geographic significance. That is, two sites in the same domain may be in the same city or they may be in different countries. These domains are used primarily for administration and not for routing. Table 7.5 lists some common domain names and their meaning.

The other parts of the address format can be almost anything, depending on a particular site. Typically the names identify a site, a department, or a specific computer. For example, UWGB.EDU specifies the University of Wisconsin-Green Bay in the educational domain and NASA.GOV indicates the National Aeronautics and Space Administration in the government domain. If the institution is large enough it may be divided into departments (more subdomains) and host computers within each department. For example, the author's full email address is Shayw@gbms01.uwgb.edu. If we were large enough to warrant separate network connections in different departments, a department identifier could be inserted between "gbms01" and "uwgb." In some cases, when the site is small, it may designate a default computer to receive all incoming messages to obviate the need to specify the computer. In our case, a computer named "gbms01" is the default that allows the author's address to be listed as Shayw@uwgb.edu.

Each host computer runs a protocol called the **domain name server** (**DNS**). It accesses a distributed database used to translate an address of the previous format to the actual 32-bit numeric Internet address. For example, the DNS translates the

TABLE 7.5    **Internet Domains**

| DOMAIN | MEANING |
|---|---|
| COM | Commercial institution |
| EDU | Education institution |
| INT | International organizations |
| GOV | Government agency |
| MIL | Military |
| NET | Administrative centers for other networks |
| ORG | Other organizations |
| country code | e.g., US for the United States or UK for the United Kingdom |

domain name Shayw@gbms01.uwgb.edu to 143.200.128.3. To a typical Internet user the numeric address has no meaning, but to a network router it does.

A significant problem facing the Internet is **address depletion**. The number of Internet users is increasing and depleting the allowable addresses. What happens when the number of users exceeds the number of addresses that can be assigned? Your first response might be to reformat the address structure to allow it to accommodate longer and hence more addresses. Unfortunately, this would require a change to Internet routers and hosts, a very costly solution. Another possibility is address reuse, or allowing addresses in different domains that are not globally unique. Reference 5 has a detailed discussion on this topic.

## ROUTING INFORMATION PROTOCOL (RIP)

How do the routers send each other messages? A common approach used by the Internet is the **routing information protocol** (**RIP**). RIP is the protocol used by the **routed**[*] program developed at the University of California at Berkeley to perform routing on their local networks. Routers that connect multiple networks use RIP to let each other know the shortest route to a specified network. Typically they use a **hop count**, the number of intermediate routers, to measure distance. For example, Figure 7.15 shows several networks connected by routers. The hop count from network N1 to N2 is 1, and the hop count from N1 to N4 is 2, using the shortest route. None of the routers know that yet, however. The algorithm starts when each router sends a message along each of its networks. This message indicates that all of the networks to which the router is connected can be reached in one hop. When routers on that network get the message they know which networks they can reach using two hops. They store this information in their routing tables and periodically broadcast it over the networks. By repeatedly receiving information, storing it, and broadcasting it, each router eventually knows the smallest number of hops to a given network.

FIGURE 7.15    **Routers Connecting Networks**

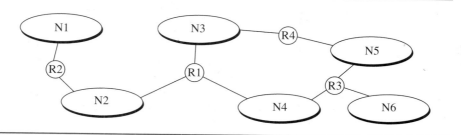

---

[*] Routed is pronounced route-d and was named using UNIX naming conventions.

Let's see how this would work on the network of Figure 7.15. Using RIP, the following events can occur:

1.  R2 sends a message along N2 that it can get to N1 in 1 hop. (It also sends a message along N1 that it can get to N2 in 1 hop.)

2.  Because R1 is connected to N2, it now knows it can get to N1 in two hops and stores that fact in its routing table. Subsequently, R1 broadcasts the following over N4: It can get to N2 and N3 in one hop and to N1 in two hops. (It also broadcasts similar information over N3 and N2.)

3.  R3 receives and stores the information it received over N4 and broadcasts the following over N5 : It can get to N4 and N6 in one hop, N2 and N3 in two hops, and N1 in three hops. It also will broadcast similar information over N4 and N6.

At this point some of the broadcast information becomes redundant. For example, because of R3's broadcast over N5, R4 learns it can get to N2 in three hops. Of course, if it previously received R1's broadcast over N3 it knows it can already get to N2 in two hops. In this case it does not store the most recent information.

What happens if a router or network along a route fails? For example, R4 knows it can get to N2 in two hops, but what if network N3 fails? When a router stores routing information it also starts a timer. When the timer expires it marks the route as invalid. It depends on new routing information to reestablish a route. Of course, the routers must cooperate by sending routing information on a regular basis. Thus, if N3 failed events 1–3 would still occur (except those involving N3). This time when R4 learns that it can get to N2 in three hops it stores that fact because there is no alternative.

## SUMMARY OF ROUTING TECHNIQUES

Table 7.6 provides a brief summary of the routing strategies discussed. They are by no means the only ones, but along with the routing strategies involving LAN bridges in Section 6.5, they represent a significant number of the strategies in use today. For more information on different strategies, Reference 6 probably has the most extensive list.

## CONGESTION AND DEADLOCK

As networks grow larger and accommodate more nodes, routing strategies must deal with an ever-increasing number of packets. The increased demand can put network operations in peril. What happens when one or more network links fail? What happens if the number of packets that must be transmitted exceeds the network's ability to do so? A potentially serious consequence is **congestion** or the excessive buildup of packets at one or more network nodes.

Once again we can draw on the useful analogy of traffic control in an urban area. Highways and roads must be designed with the anticipated amount of traffic in mind. Anyone who has driven in an urban area knows the problem. During rush

TABLE 7.6    **Summary of Routing Strategies**

| DIJKSTRA'S ALGORITHM | BELLMAN-FORD ALGORITHM | HIERARCHICAL ALGORITHM | RIP |
|---|---|---|---|
| Forward learning algorithm best implemented as a central routing strategy. | Backward learning algorithm. Nodes learn from each neighbor the cheapest route to a node and the first node on that route. | Method of dividing nodes into domains. Domain routing protocols do routing within a domain, where routers handle inter-domain routing. | Routing protocol used by domain routers to track the fewest number of hops to a given network domain. |
| Used in ARPANET and TYMNET II. | Used in the Canadian DATAPAC network, Digital Equipment Corporation's DNA, TYMNET I, and the original ARPANET. | Used in Internet. | Developed by UC-Berkeley for its local networks and used in the Internet. |

hour the amount of traffic is excessive and a highway's ability to handle it diminishes. An accident or road construction can put several lanes or an entire stretch of highway out of commission. In either case traffic slows (or stops completely), causing terrible congestion. People in their cars can't reach their destinations. The transportation system has lost its usefulness temporarily.

Similarly, congestion in a network reduces its usefulness. Packets experience longer delays and network users see the network as unresponsive and unable to meet their needs. What can network protocols do in such cases? One option is to do nothing and let congestion disappear naturally. Even in rush hour traffic people eventually get home and the congestion disappears. However, this is not a practical solution for networks. (Many people probably feel it's not a practical solution to highway congestion either.) For one thing, users expect better service, and it should be provided. Second, the congestion might not disappear because it can have a compounding effect. Congestion at one or more nodes hampers the node's ability to receive packets from other nodes. Consequently, those nodes can't get rid of their packets as quickly, and incoming packets begin to accumulate. This can have a chain reaction effect where all nodes begin to experience congestion, making the problem worse.

There are several ways to handle congestion:

**Packet elimination**. If an excessive buildup of packets occurs at a node, eliminate some of them. This reduces the number of outstanding packets waiting for transmission and reduces the network load. The drawback, of course, is that the destroyed packets do not reach their destinations. The problem of lost packets was discussed in Section 5.3. Presumably the sending node's protocol eventually will determine that a packet never reached its destination and will resend it. If the congestion was due to a heavy burst of traffic it may have subsided somewhat when the packet is sent the next time. Destroying packets sounds drastic, but if the congestion is sporadic the network protocols can handle it well and the inconvenience to the unlucky user whose packets are destroyed is minimal. We do not, however, recommend this approach for automobile traffic congestion.

**Flow control**. As Chapter 5 discussed, flow control protocols are designed to control the number of packets sent. However, they are not a true congestion control approach. The problem is that flow control limits the number of packets between two points, whereas congestion often involves packets coming into a node from many sources. Thus, even if nodes regulate the number of packets they send, congestion still can occur if too many nodes are sending them.

You might respond by suggesting that each node regulate its traffic so that even if every node is sending, the total number of packets would still be manageable. The problem is that if many nodes are not sending they are underutilizing the network. Again, you might respond by suggesting that each node reduce its outflow only if it detects other nodes sending. In a large network, however, this is not practical. Many nodes won't even see the packets sent by others. Furthermore, establishing some communication protocol among them would add to the network traffic and compound the problem we are trying to solve.

**Buffer allocation**. This approach can be used with **virtual circuits**. Recall from Section 1.4 that a virtual circuit is an established route between network nodes that is determined before any data packets are actually sent. Once a route is established, protocols at a node on that route can reserve buffers specifically for the virtual circuit. Effectively, the establishment of a virtual circuit notifies participating nodes that packets will be forthcoming and that they should plan for them. If other requests for virtual circuit establishment come to that node it can reject them if insufficient buffer space is available. Network protocols then would have to find a different route for the circuit or notify the source that the request for a virtual circuit has been denied. Section 7.3 discusses virtual circuits further.

**Choke packets**. This approach provides a more dynamic way to deal with congestion. Each node monitors the activity on its outgoing links, tracking the utilization of each. If the utilization of the lines is small the danger of congestion is low. However, an increasing utilization means a larger number of packets are being sent. If the utilization of any line exceeds some specified criterion the node's protocol responds by putting itself into a special warning state. When in the warning state, the node will respond by sending a special choke packet in response to any incoming packet destined for the outgoing line. The choke packet goes to the source of the incoming packet. When the source receives the choke packet it responds by reducing the number of packets it is sending for a specified period of time.

After the period expires, one of two things can happen. If no additional choke packets arrive the node can increase the packet transmission rate to its original value. If more choke packets continue to arrive it will reduce the packet transmission rate even further. By reducing the incoming traffic the original node has a chance to let the utilization of its outgoing lines drop below the threshold to an acceptable level.

In the worst case, congestion can become so severe that nothing moves. Figure 7.16 illustrates this problem. Three nodes, *A*, *B*, and *C* have reached the point where their buffers are full and cannot accept any more nodes. *A*'s packets are all destined for *B* which cannot receive any packets because its buffers are full. Thus *A* cannot send until *B* sends some of its packets and releases buffer space. *B*'s packets are destined for *C* whose buffers are also full. *C*'s packets are destined for *A*, whose buffers are full. In other words, *A* is waiting for *B*'s buffers to clear; *B* is waiting for *C*'s buffers to clear, and *C* is waiting for *A*'s buffers to clear. This situation, in which all nodes are waiting for an event that won't occur, is called **deadlock** (also called **deadly embrace** or **lock-up**).

The case just described is an example of a **store-and-forward deadlock**, so named because nodes store packets while waiting to forward them. Figure 7.17

**FIGURE 7.16**    **Store-and-Forward Deadlock**

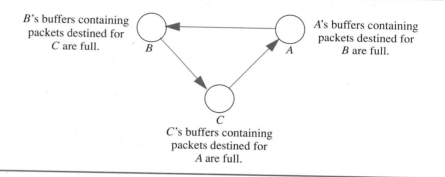

*B*'s buffers containing packets destined for *C* are full.

*A*'s buffers containing packets destined for *B* are full.

*C*'s buffers containing packets destined for *A* are full.

**FIGURE 7.17**    **Reassembly Deadlock**

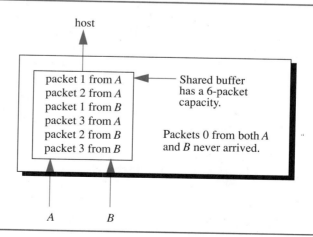

host

packet 1 from *A*
packet 2 from *A*
packet 1 from *B*
packet 3 from *A*
packet 2 from *B*
packet 3 from *B*

Shared buffer has a 6-packet capacity.

Packets 0 from both *A* and *B* never arrived.

*A*          *B*

illustrates another type, **reassembly deadlock**. In this example, the node uses common buffers for incoming packets from different sources (*A* and *B*). It also uses a selective repeat sliding window protocol receiving packets from *A* and *B* destined for the node's host. Recall that the selective repeat protocol allows packets to arrive out of order. The receiver then reassembles them before sending them to the host.

In our example, *A* and *B* both sent a packet 0, neither of which arrived. However, subsequent packets numbered 1 through 3 from both *A* and *B* have arrived. If we assume the buffers are filled, the node cannot accept any more packets. Because both packet 0s are missing, however, the node cannot reassemble them and deliver them in order to the host. Moreover, the node will not accept either packet 0 even if it does arrive. Consequently, the node is placed in a state in which it can neither take action nor respond to an event that would allow it to take action. It is deadlocked.

Reassembly deadlock can be prevented through a handshake establishing a connection between the sending and receiving nodes. The handshake can establish the window size and the receiver can reserve sufficient space and use it only for that connection. Store-and-forward deadlock is a bit more problematic. It can be reduced or even eliminated by using sufficient buffer space, but the problem is knowing just how much buffer space to reserve, especially in datagram services in which packets come and go randomly.

One approach to deadlock is to let it happen and then deal with it. When deadlock occurs the typical response is to discard some packets and release the buffer space. The discarded packets, of course, never reach their destination. This is the price to be paid for breaking the deadlock. Presumably, communication protocols will determine that the packets never arrived and will send them again later. If deadlock occurs rarely, this may be the best way to deal with it.

On the other hand, for a network more susceptible to deadlock it may be less costly to take steps to prevent it from happening or at least decrease its probability of occurrence. Any of the previously mentioned congestion control techniques will decrease the chances of deadlock, but there is still no guarantee deadlock will not occur. Another approach, presented in Reference 7, maintains the number of hops (nodes through which a packet travels) in each packet. When a host first inserts a packet into the network the hop count is 0. As the packet travels through the network each node increments the hop count by one. In addition, each node divides its buffers into distinct groups, each one corresponding to a hop count from 0 up to the maximum expected hops. The node then stores an incoming packet into a buffer depending on the number of hops in the packet, but only if a buffer is available. If not, the packet waits at the preceding node until it is available. Figure 7.18 shows how it works. A host submits a packet initially and the host's node stores the packet in buffer 0. The next node to receive the packet stores it in buffer 1, the next one in buffer 2, and so on.

This method prevents deadlock because a packet always goes to (or waits for) a higher numbered buffer. Another way to state it is that a packet in one buffer will never wait for a lower or equal numbered buffer. Because of this the circular wait condition of Figure 7.16 can never occur. The argument against this approach is that buffers may be underutilized. Preassigning a packet to a buffer prevents its transmission whenever that buffer is occupied. If it is the only buffer occupied the others go unused.

FIGURE 7.18    **Storing Packets Depending on Hop Count**

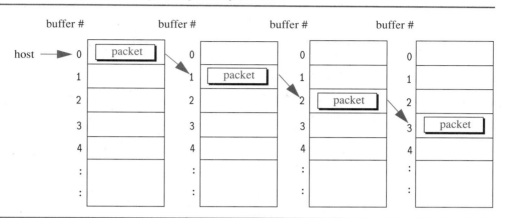

## 7.3    Public Data Networks: The X Series Protocols

In the 1970s many European countries began to develop **public data networks** (networks available to anyone with a need for network services). The problems they faced were different from those in the United States. In the United States, public networks could be developed in large part by leasing existing telephone lines. In Europe this could not be done easily due to problems inherent in traversing communications systems across national boundaries. Thus, instead of developing separate and incompatible standards European countries worked under the auspices of CCITT to develop a single standard. The result is the public data network service interface referred to as the X series of protocols. This section discusses four common protocols: X.25, X.3, X.28, and X.29.

Public data networks are commonly **packet switched networks** represented by the **ubiquitous network cloud** shown in Figure 7.19. They operate by transporting packets submitted at one part of the "cloud" and routing them to their destinations. Typically, switching logic (circuits) at nodes in the network make routing decisions. The previous section focused on this aspect of networks, so we will not discuss it further here. Instead we take the perspective of someone interacting with the network. Packets enter from point *A* and exit at points *B, C,* or *D*. We do not necessarily know (or care) how they get there. Our main focus is to define the logical connection between the source and the destination.

### PACKET SWITCHED NETWORK MODES

**Virtual Circuits**    Packet switched networks typically operate in one of two modes. The first is by a **virtual circuit** between two points. It is somewhat analogous to creating a telephone connection between two people. A device connected to the network requests a connection to a device somewhere else. This request is routed

FIGURE 7.19     **Packet Switched Network**

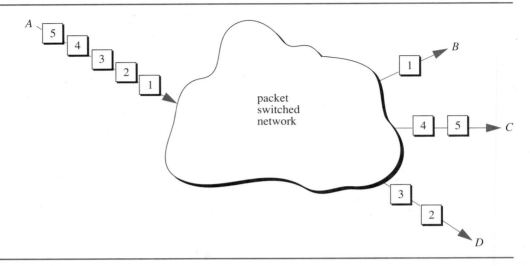

through network nodes, establishing a path between the caller and destination. All subsequent packets sent by the caller follow that same path. (We will discuss the actual process of calling and establishing the connection later in this section.)

The connection is not a physical one, however. The connections between nodes are not dedicated solely to one virtual circuit. In fact, a node and its connection to a neighbor may participate in several virtual circuits. Figure 7.20 shows two overlapping virtual circuits. *A* and *B* have both requested and established connections to *C* and *D*, respectively. The paths begin at different locations but

FIGURE 7.20     **Overlapping Virtual Circuits**

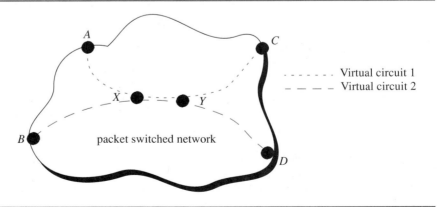

overlap at nodes $X$ and $Y$. $X$ handles packets corresponding to either virtual circuit and routes them to $Y$. $Y$, in turn, routes packets differently depending on the virtual circuit on which they arrive.

Because virtual circuit paths can overlap, each node must be able to determine the virtual circuit corresponding to an incoming packet. As the initial connection request goes through each node, the node assigns a virtual circuit number to it, determines the next node to which it sends the request, and makes an entry in its routing table. The routing table contains each virtual circuit number and the next node along the corresponding path.

Note that each node assigns virtual circuit numbers independently so that one virtual circuit may be identified by different numbers at different nodes. Consequently, each node informs the circuit's preceding node of the virtual circuit number it uses for incoming packets. This allows a preceding node to know the virtual circuit number assigned by the next node and to store it in the packet. Thus, incoming packets contain the number of the virtual circuit coming in to the node. The node's routing logic accesses the routing table entry corresponding to it and sends it to the next node. If the next part of the virtual circuit has a different number the node stores it as well in the packet. For example, Figure 7.21 shows a packet traversing each of the virtual circuits of Figure 7.20. The virtual circuit between $A$ and $C$ is assigned the numbers 1 (by $X$), 5 (by $Y$), and 3 (by $C$). The circuit between $B$ and $D$ is assigned the numbers 2 (by $X$), 3 (by $Y$), and 1 (by $D$).

Table 7.7 shows what relevant entries of $X$'s and $Y$'s routing tables look like. A packet coming in to $X$ from $A$ contains the virtual circuit number 1. $X$'s routing table indicates the next node is $Y$ and it uses 5 as the virtual circuit number. Consequently, $X$ stores 5 into the packet and sends it to $Y$. A packet entering $Y$ from $X$ will contain a virtual circuit number of 5 or 3. If it is 5, $Y$'s routing table indicates $C$ as the next node and an outgoing virtual circuit number of 3. If it is 3, $D$ is the next node and the outgoing virtual circuit number is 1.

FIGURE 7.21    **Sending Packets Along a Virtual Circuit**

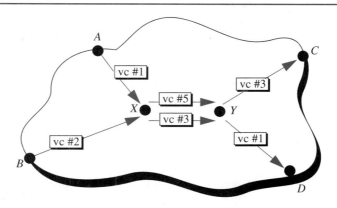

TABLE 7.7    **Routing Tables for Nodes X and Y from Figure 7.20**

| ROUTING TABLE FOR X | | | ROUTING TABLE FOR Y | | |
|---|---|---|---|---|---|
| incoming vc # | outgoing vc # | next node | incoming vc # | outgoing vc # | next node |
| 1 | 5 | Y | 5 | 3 | C |
| 2 | 3 | Y | 3 | 1 | D |

**Datagram Service**    One advantage of virtual circuits is that routing decisions are made just once for each circuit, eliminating the need to make such decisions for each packet. Your first thought might be that this is particularly beneficial when many packets are sent. The opposite may be true, however, because many packets usually means more time has elapsed since the circuit was established. Consequently, the conditions that may have made the current path a good one may no longer be true. That is, conditions may have changed so that the current path takes longer. The result, in that case, is reduced efficiency.

Another option is a **datagram service**. With it each packet contains the source and destination addresses. As packets enter the network, nodes apply routing logic to each node separately. Presumably, this allows each node to route depending on the most current information it has regarding potential paths. Figure 7.22 shows datagrams traversing the network. Packets 1 through 3 enter at A and A routes them to X. Just after packet 3 enters the network, A gets new routing information that indicates Y is now a better choice for packets destined for D. Consequently, it routes packets 4 and 5 to Y.

In theory, all packets may travel different routes and take advantage of the best routes currently available. A disadvantage is that there is no guarantee that packets will arrive at D in the same order they were sent. Consequently, more complex logic is required to reassemble packets at their destination (recall the selective repeat pro-

FIGURE 7.22    **Datagram Service**

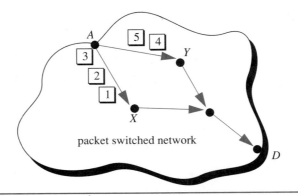

packet switched network

TABLE 7.8     **Comparison of Virtual Circuits and Datagrams**

| VIRTUAL CIRCUIT | DATAGRAM |
| --- | --- |
| Helps prevent congestion. Since a node knows it is part of a virtual circuit it can reserve space for the anticipated arrival of packets. | Unexpected packets make congestion control more difficult. |
| If a virtual circuit is open too long, the current path may not be the best given current network conditions. | Nodes route each packet using the most current information about the network. |
| A routing decision is made just once for each set of packets sent along the virtual circuit. | Separate routing decisions are made for each packet. |
| Packets arrive in the order they were sent. | Packets can arrive out of order requiring the destination to order them. |
| A node failure breaks the virtual circuit connection, causing a loss of packets. | If a node fails packets can be routed around it. |

tocol of Section 5.3). Table 7.8 lists some other advantages and disadvantages of the virtual circuit and the datagram service.

### X.25 PUBLIC DATA NETWORK INTERFACE STANDARD

An important part of working with public data networks is their interface. One widely used interface is the CCITT X.25 standard. Many people use the term "X.25 network" causing some to believe mistakenly that X.25 defines the network protocols. It does not. X.25 defines the protocol between a DTE and a DCE connected to a public data network (Figure 7.23). We note that early versions focused mainly on the asymmetric DTE-DCE relationship. Recent versions have recognized the need for peer-to-peer communications between two DTEs. Consequently, X.25 can be

FIGURE 7.23     **X.25 Public Data Network Interface**

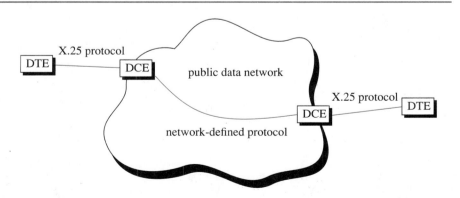

used strictly as a user-network interface or as a user-to-user connection across a public data network. The latter use partially explains why some people refer to public data networks as X.25 networks. The term is technically incorrect, but to those for whom X.25 defines the communication protocol via the network, the misnomer is understandable.

X.25 defines a synchronous transmission analogous to the three lowest layers of the OSI (Figure 7.24). As such, it requires intelligent DTEs capable of creating packets and implementing the protocols. This does not apply to many asynchronous terminals, which we discuss later. The lowest layer of X.25 corresponds to X.21, a standard discussed in Section 3.2. Alternatively, X.25 may use the **X.21bis** standard, which was designed as an interim standard to connect V series modems with public packet switched networks. The X.21 standard was supposed to replace it, but, as with many plans, it did not happen. A more extensive treatment of X.21bis is found in Reference 8. The second layer of X.25 corresponds to the LAPB discussed in Section 5.5. Since we have already discussed the two lower layers, we will focus here on the network layer's packet protocol.

## PACKET FORMAT

The first step is defining the packet format. As with previous protocols, formats vary depending on the type of packet. Figure 7.25 shows two primary formats. The sending network layer defines the packets and gives them to the data link layer. The datalink layer inserts the packet into a LAPB frame format and sends it via the physical layer.

The relevant packet fields are:

- **Flags**. Defines the packet format.
- **Logical group number** and **logical channel number**. Together they define a 12-bit number for a virtual circuit the DTE has established. This allows the DTE to establish up to 4096 virtual circuits.

**FIGURE 7.24    X.25 Protocol Layers**

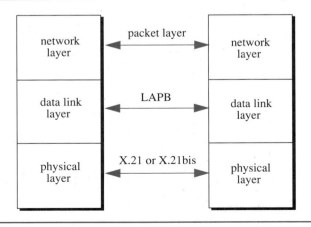

FIGURE 7.25   **X.25 Packet Formats**

number of octets

| 1 | 1 | 1 | variable |
|---|---|---|---|
| flags, logical group number | logical channel number | control | data |

**(a) Data packet**

number of octets

| 1 | 1 | 1 | variable |
|---|---|---|---|
| flags, logical group number | logical channel number | packet type | other information |

**(b) Control packet**

- **Control** (data packet). Contains several subfields such as the send and receive packet counts similar to the N(S) and N(R) fields in HDLC's information frame (Section 5.5). It also contains a bit set in the last of a series of packets to indicate the end of a packet stream.
- **Data** (data packet). Self-explanatory.
- **Packet type** (control packet). There are several packet types, defined in Table 7.9.

**Virtual Calls**   X.25 provides two types of virtual circuits between DTEs. A **permanent virtual circuit** is similar to leasing a telephone line where either DTE can send data without the overhead of making and establishing a call. It is particularly useful when a high volume of data is transferred. A **virtual call**, the second type, requires a call connection protocol to be performed prior to any data transfer.

Figure 7.26 shows the call connection/termination process between two DTEs. (For brevity, we have not shown the DCEs or the network, but don't forget they are there.) The DTE wanting to make a call constructs a call request packet containing the virtual call (or logical channel) number and sends it via its DCE and the network. When the receiving DCE gets the packet it assigns a virtual call number to the request and delivers the packet to the receiving DTE. Note that there is no requirement that the channel numbers be the same at each end. As described previously, they are defined dynamically. If that DTE is willing and able to accept the call it sends a call accepted packet. Once the first DTE receives the call accepted packet the virtual call is established.

Next, the DTEs exchange data and acknowledgment packets in a full-duplex mode, using a flow control similar to that used in HDLC[*] (Section 5.5). When either DTE decides to end the connection (DTE A in Figure 7.26), it creates and sends a

---

[*]There are some subtle but important differences between HDLC and X.25 flow control, but they are not necessary at this level of discussion. References 6 and 9 discuss them further.

TABLE 7.9     **X.25 Packet Types**

| TYPE | FUNCTION |
| --- | --- |
| call request | When a DTE wants to establish a connection (call another DTE) it sends a call request packet. |
| call accepted | If the called DTE accepts the call it acknowledges it by returning a call accepted (or call confirmation) packet. |
| data | Used to transfer high-level protocol data between the DTEs. There are typically up to 128 bytes of data, but handshake protocols may agree to transfer up to 4096 bytes in a packet. |
| clear request | Sent by a node wanting to terminate a virtual circuit. It can also be used by a DTE not wanting to accept a call. A receiving DTE sees it as a **clear indication** packet. |
| clear confirmation | Sent in response to a clear request packet. |
| diagnostic | If a DCE receives a packet containing erroneous codes it may send a diagnostic packet to the DTE, thus indicating a problem. |
| receive ready | A DTE sends a receive ready packet to acknowledge a data packet and to indicate it is able to accept more data packets. It defines network level flow control and is similar to that in HDLC (Section 5.5). |
| receive not ready | A DTE sends a receive not ready packet to acknowledge a data packet and to indicate it cannot accept more data packets until further notice. |
| reject | A DTE sends a reject packet when it does not accept an incoming data packet. |
| reset request | If a protocol error (such as congestion, loss of packet, or failure of a node along the virtual circuit) occurs, a DTE can start over by sending a reset request packet. It eliminates any outstanding packets, recovers buffer space, and reinitializes the sending and receiving packet counts to 0. It does not establish a new virtual circuit between the DTEs; it just reinitializes the current one. In the case of a failed node the two DCEs may have to recreate the virtual circuit. This process is transparent to the DTEs. |
| reset confirmation | Sent to acknowledge a reset request packet. |
| restart request | In the event of a more serious error such as DTE failure or loss of a network connection, a DTE can clear all its virtual circuits with a restart packet. It has the same effect as sending a clear request packet along all current virtual circuits. |
| restart confirmation | Sent to acknowledge a restart request packet. |
| interrupt | Transmission of data packets is subject to flow protocols at the LAPB level. The interrupt packet corresponds to a high-priority packet that bypasses the lower-level flow control constraints. For example, it would not be rejected at the remote DTE due to a full receiving window. It can carry at most 32 bytes of data and is used when data absolutely must get to the remote DTE (sort of like an X.25 Federal Express). Useful if the sending DTE is a terminal and its user has pressed the brake or has entered a control sequence to terminate an activity. |
| interrupt confirmation | A DTE receiving an interrupt packet sends an interrupt confirmation packet in response. X.25 does not allow more than one outstanding interrupt. Thus, once a DTE sends one it cannot send another until it receives a confirmation. |

FIGURE 7.26    **X.25 Virtual Call**

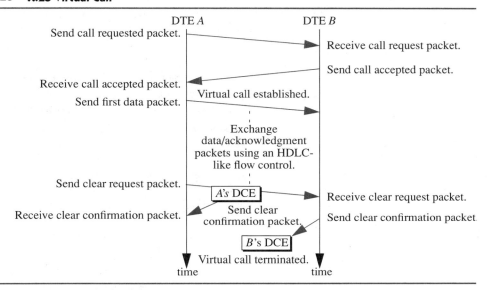

clear request packet. The local DCE responds by doing two things. First, it sends the clear request packet to the remote DTE. Second, it responds to its local DTE by sending it a clear confirmation packet. As far as the local DTE is concerned, the virtual call is terminated and the logical channel number is available for future calls. Eventually, the remote DTE receives the clear request packet. It sees it as a clear indication packet and responds by sending a clear confirmation packet to its DCE. That DCE also clears the channel number, making it available for other calls.

**Limitations of X.25**    Although X.25 is popular, especially in Europe, it has limitations. For example, one of the strongest criticisms is that X.25-based protocols provide only a connection-oriented service. Reference 2 contains the following comments on X.25:[*]

- Standards bodies haven't attempted to make X.25 a complete version of the cited reference model layers. The X.25 packet layer especially is an incomplete implementation of the equivalent reference model layer. A complete network layer includes routing, relaying, flow control, and related protocols within the packet network, but X.25 defines only an interface to a packet network. The undefined aspects are where most of the complexity of the network layer comes in, as all nodes within the packet network must work together to provide these functions.

- X.25's lack of a graceful close, and potential loss of data when errors occur, force higher protocol layers to recover from such losses. No alternate routing

---

[*]Reprinted by permission of Addison-Wesley Publishing Co.

procedures are built into the protocols; virtual circuits are simply cleared under a variety of conditions and responsibility for reestablishing them left to the user, adding to the complexity of upper layers.

- Although X.25 is a standard for interfacing with a packet network, it contains end-to-end features, especially when the D bit[*] is used; interrupt packets are also end-to-end. This makes the distinction between the network layer and the transport layer (supposedly the first end-to-end layer) vague. X.25 contains a few aspects of an ISO transport layer, but it is not (and is not intended to be) a transport layer standard.

- Since X.25 was designed to serve as an interface to packet networks, its primary emphasis has been on remote access rather than on resource sharing (that is, sharing of data and programs by users at remote locations). Although resource sharing is handled primarily by upper layers in the OSI hierarchy, capabilities need to be built into lower layers. Such capabilities have not been built into X.25. For example, although transfer of expedited data such as X.25 interrupt packets is at times essential to get urgent information through quickly, there is no requirement that networks with X.25 interfaces provide special handling for interrupt packets or any type of expedited data service.

- X.25 is poorly suited for some applications of packet networks. An example is packet voice, which cannot tolerate long or (especially) variable delays. Discarding voice packets that suffer excessive delays is far better than delivering them, but X.25 provides no mechanism for doing this, and the packet formats do not provide for a way to label voice packets as different from other types of packets and subject to special handling. Many persons also feel the datagram service dropped from the standard in 1984 will be needed for important applications, especially those involving short interactive data exchanges.

- X.25 was developed for use on public packet data networks using telephone-type facilities. It can be used over other facilities, but cannot necessarily take advantage of their features. For example, it cannot take advantage of possibilities for broadcast communication when geosynchronous communications satellites, packet radio, or local area networks are used.

## TRIPLE X STANDARD FOR NON-X.25 DEVICES

One disadvantage of the X.25 protocol is the need for DTEs that support it. In other words it requires a computer, workstation, or other intelligent device capable of creating and interpreting X.25 packets. These categories leave out the almost countless number of "dumb terminals" or character oriented devices still in use. How can they communicate with devices that support X.25? One approach is to purchase X.25-supported devices and replace the non-X.25 devices. For anyone who must manage a budget, however, this may not be a practical solution.

---

[*] The D-bit is one of the flags preceding the logical group number in the packet format of Figure 7.25. Its setting specifies whether a receiving DTE sends an acknowledgment to the sending DTE.

Fortunately, another solution does exist: a set of protocols defined by the CCITT. They are the **X.3 Packet Assembler/Disassembler(PAD)**, **X.28 PAD-terminal interface**, and **X.29 PAD-host interface** (Figure 7.27). The PAD replaces the DCE as a network interface. It accepts characters from character-oriented devices and assembles them into packets before sending them onto the network. Similarly, it can receive packets from the network, disassemble them, and transmit the data as a character stream to the terminal. The X.28 protocol defines a set of commands the terminal and PAD use to exchange information. Similarly, X.29 defines a communication protocol between the PAD and the remote host.

### X.3 Packet Assembler/Disassembler

A PAD works with dumb terminals, those with no local computing ability. Dumb terminals are little more than electronic typewriters that transfer characters to and from the network. One problem is that many of them work in unique ways. A simple example is the deletion of characters. Most of us are poor typists who make many mistakes, but we usually can correct them by backspacing and deleting unwanted characters. The trouble is that on some terminals you backspace by typing the backspace key. On others you use the 'delete' key, an arrow key (<-), a backslash key (\), or a combination of keys (for example, Ctrl-D or Alt-F). It is like trying to find the windshield wiper, light, and door controls on a car. Somewhere fiends spend their time thinking up new places to put controls and new ways to turn them on or off. Does this unmarked button turn on the lights, open the trunk, lock the doors, or eject you from the seat through the sun roof? All you can do is press it and hope for the best.

The PAD accepts keystrokes used by a particular terminal and translates them into a standard form. For example, suppose two people are using an editor over a network. A person at one terminal may press a left-arrow key, whereas a person at another terminal may press the backspace key. The PAD translates each into the command required by the editor. The editor does not know that two different characters were typed. Similarly, the users do not know their entries were translated. In

FIGURE 7.27    **Triple-X Protocols**

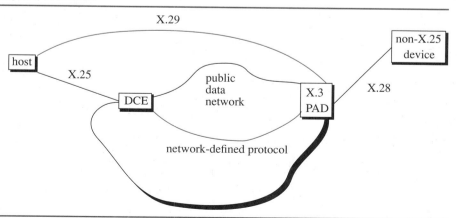

general, a PAD does not route each typed character individually to the network. Instead, it buffers them. At some point, it assembles them into an X.25 packet and transmits it along the network. This is why we use the name "packet assembler."

When data arrives from the network, the process works in reverse. The PAD accepts a packet and disassembles it. It translates control characters into the proper form for a particular terminal. One technique involves creating a **network virtual terminal** (see Section 8.1). The OSI application layer contains software that translates control sequences into standard forms. It converts terminal-specific commands from the user into a form the text editor can understand. Similarly, the text editor can issue cursor movement commands without regard for the type of terminal. The application layer converts them to control a particular type of terminal.

PADs do more than interpret control sequences from terminals and put them into packets. There are 22 parameters that define how a PAD communicates with a DTE. Table 7.10 describes each of them.

**X.28 and X.29 Protocols**    The PAD is the heart of the communications protocol between character-oriented DTEs and remote hosts over an X.25 network. In addition to assembling and disassembling packets, its parameters specify how and when to perform certain functions. In order to provide flexibility we must have the capability to request that it perform those functions and to alter its parameters. Two other protocols, X.28 and X.29, define how to do this.

The **X.28** protocol defines the communication between the PAD and the character-oriented device. X.28 specifies commands that the terminal can give to the PAD and specifies the responses the PAD returns. For example, a user can enter a command to request a virtual call to a remote host (Figure 7.28a). The command then goes to the PAD, which must create an X.25 call request packet and send it over the network. When the call accepted packet returns (Figure 7.28b), the PAD returns

FIGURE 7.28    **Pad Responding to Virtual Call Requests**

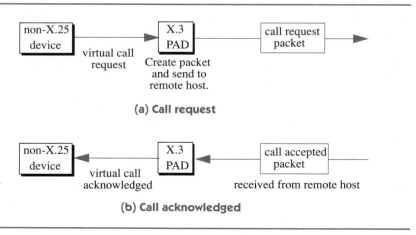

(a) **Call request**

(b) **Call acknowledged**

TABLE 7.10     **PAD Parameters**   (U. Black, *The X Series Recommendations*, McGraw-Hill, Inc., 1991. Reprinted with permission.)

| X.3 PARAMETER REFERENCE NUMBER | DESCRIPTION |
|---|---|
| **1. PAD recall** | Escape from data transfer mode to command mode in order to send PAD commands. |
| **2. Echo** | Controls the echo of characters sent by the terminal. |
| **3. Data forwarding** | Defines the characters to be interpreted by the PAD as a signal to forward data; indication to complete assembly and forward a complete packet. |
| **4. Idle timer delay** | Selects a time interval between successive characters of terminal activity as a signal to forward data. |
| **5. Ancillary device control** | Allows the PAD to control the flow of terminal data using X-ON/X-OFF characters. |
| **6. Control of PAD service signals** | Allows the terminal to receive PAD messages. |
| **7. Operation of the PAD on receipt of breaking signal from DTE** | Defines PAD action when a break signal is received from the terminal. |
| **8. Discard output** | Controls the discarding of data pending output to a terminal. |
| **9. Padding after carriage** | Control PAD insertion of padding characters after a carriage return is sent to the terminal. |
| **10. Line folding** | Specifies whether the PAD should fold the output line to the terminal; predetermined number of characters per line. |
| **11. Binary speed of DTE** | Indicates the speed of the terminal; cannot be changed by DTE. |
| **12. Flow control of the PAD** | Allows the terminal to flow control data being transmitted by the PAD. |
| **13. Line feed insertion** | Controls PAD insertion of line feed after a carriage return is sent to the terminal. |
| **14. Line feed padding** | Controls PAD insertion of padding characters after a line feed is sent to the terminal. |
| **15. Editing** | Controls whether editing by PAD is available during data transfer mode (parameters 16, 17, and 18). |
| **16. Character delete** | Selects character used to signal character delete. |
| **17. Line delete** | Selects character used to signal line delete |
| **18. Line display** | Selects character used to signal line display. |
| **19. Editing PAD service signals** | Controls the format of the editing PAD service signals. |
| **20. Echo mask** | Selects the characters that are not echoed to the terminal when echo (parameter 2) is enabled. |
| **21. Parity treatment** | Controls the checking and generation of parity on characters from and to the terminal. |
| **22. Page wait** | Specifies the number of lines to be displayed at one time. |

an acknowledgment to the user. Other example commands include those to clear or reset a virtual call or to send an interrupt packet. In these cases, the PAD responds by acknowledging receipt of the command. X.28 commands also allow the terminal to request the current PAD parameter values or to define new ones.

The **X.29** protocol defines how the PAD and a remote host communicate and specifies allowable commands and acknowledgments. Using X.29, the remote host can change PAD parameters. For example, PAD parameter 2 specifies whether user-entered characters are echoed back to the terminal. This is useful except when a user is entering a password as part of a login. Thus, when a remote host is ready to accept a password it can send a command to the PAD changing parameter 2 to suppress echoing. After the password has been entered the remote host resets the parameter to resume echoing.

The X.29 protocol is particularly useful when the user has no knowledge of the PAD or network. The user simply wants to use the terminal to connect to a remote device for some service. He or she does not want to worry about specific terminal characteristics (such as those described previously) or about setting PAD parameters. This way the remote host can instruct the PAD to set its parameters accordingly and allow the user to focus on the reason for the remote connection in the first place.

## 7.4   Internet Protocol

One of the most well known wide area networks actually consists of many networks and is collectively called the Internet. Its history dates back to the late 1960s, when the Advanced Research Projects Agency (ARPA) of the U.S. Department of Defense (DoD) began funding universities and private organizations for the purpose of developing communications systems. The research eventually led to the development of ARPANET, a small experimental network that demonstrated the feasibility of connecting different computers by a packet switching network. It has since grown and evolved into the Internet and connects thousands of universities, private institutions, and government agencies worldwide.

Many books use the term "internet" to refer to any collection of connected networks. The network that resulted from the ARPA project is commonly referred to as the Internet (with a capital I). The Internet currently consists of tens of thousands networks. Some estimates put the number of users at more than 1 million (Reference 10). It services people in almost every corner of the industrialized world.

### OVERVIEW OF TCP/IP

The Internet connects many networks each of which runs a protocol known as TCP/IP. **TCP (transmission control protocol)** and **IP (Internet protocol)** correspond roughly to layers 4 and 3 of the OSI model, respectively, although they are not part of the OSI model. They were developed along with the ARPA project and have become DoD standards. Some believe TCP/IP to be the most widely implemented protocol in the United States (Reference 10), one that runs on almost anything from PCs to supercomputers.

The TCP/IP pair of protocols is part of a protocol collection called the TCP/IP protocol suite (Figure 7.29). Three of the protocols are application protocols that provide specific services for Internet users. **SMTP (simple mail transfer protocol)** defines the protocol used for the delivery of mail messages over the Internet. The **TELNET** protocol allows users to log in to remote computers via the Internet. **FTP (file transfer protocol)** allows Internet users to transfer files from remote computers without having to log in to them. Section 8.1 discusses these protocols further. **DNS (domain name server)** provides a mapping of host names to addresses; it was discussed in Section 7.2.

TCP is a connection-oriented transport protocol designed to provide reliable communications over different network architectures. Its predecessor in the original ARPANET was **NCP (network control protocol)**, which was designed to run on top of a reliable network. ARPANET was sufficiently reliable, but as it evolved into an internetwork reliability was lost. Consequently, the transport protocol was forced to evolve as well. NCP, redesigned to run over unreliable networks, became TCP. **UDP (user datagram protocol)** provides a connectionless mode of communications over dissimilar networks. UDP and TCP provide the transport user with the two typical modes of communication. We will discuss both TCP and UDP in more detail in the next section.

### DoD Internet Protocol

The Internet protocol is a layer 3 protocol designed to provide a datagram service between stations. It is commonly, but not exclusively, used with TCP. Figure 7.30 shows how it works with TCP. Suppose two stations (*A* and *B*) need a connection-oriented

FIGURE 7.29    **Brief Overview of Internet Protocols**    (Marshall T. Rose, *The Simple Book: An Introduction to the Management of TCP/IP-based Internets*, ©1991, p. 23. Reprinted by permission of Prentice Hall, Englewood Cliffs, NJ.)

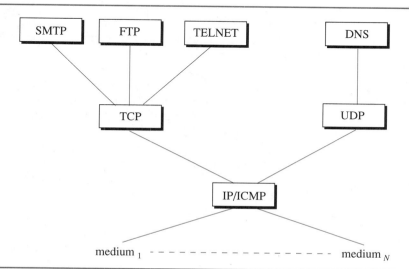

FIGURE 7.30    **IP Transmitting Packets Over Different Networks**

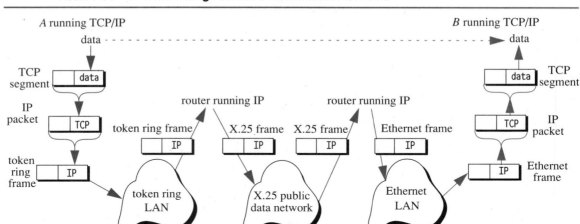

service. TCP provides the reliable connection independent of the network architectures in between the two, and IP does the work of dealing with different network architectures. Figure 7.30 shows three distinct network architectures between *A* and *B*. An X.25 network is in the middle, with a token ring and Ethernet LAN on either side. Each LAN runs LLC on top of its respective IEEE standard.

To begin, the TCP at station *A* creates a TCP segment[*] containing the user's data and "sends" the segment to station *B*. IP intercepts the segment and creates an IP packet (whose format we discuss shortly) containing the TCP segment. Next, data link protocols create a token ring frame and send it to a router via the token ring network. The router's data link layer extracts the IP packet from the token ring frame and gives it to the router's IP. IP examines the address in the packet and determines that it should go to another router over an X.25 public data network. The router's lower layers of X.25 embed the IP packet into an X.25 packet and send it over the public data network.

The second router does similar activities. Its lower-layer X.25 protocol accepts the packet and extracts the data (IP packet) from it. The IP layer determines it should be sent along an Ethernet LAN, and the router's data link layer for that LAN creates an Ethernet frame. Eventually the Ethernet frame reaches its destination, where the Ethernet data link protocols extract the data (IP packet) and give it to the IP. The IP interprets the packet and routes the TCP segment to TCP, which eventually gives the data to *B*. This simple description (which will be expanded as the chapter progresses) serves to show IP's role in routing packets over dissimilar networks.

---

[*] A TCP segment, similar to a packet, contains data and other overhead information. We discuss its format in Section 7.5.

**IP Packet**    An **IP packet** is similar in many ways to the packet and frame formats previously discussed. Still, there are some unique features that warrant discussion. Figure 7.31 shows the contents of an IP packet.

The following list explains the IP packet fields:

- **Version**. Specifies the current version of IP that created the packet. This allows different versions of IP to work together.

- **Header length**. Specifies the number of 32-bit words in the packet header (the fields preceding the data).

- **Service type**. Specifies transport layer requests regarding handling of the packet. This field allows four request options: **precedence**, **low delay**, **high throughput**, and **high reliability**. A 3-bit **precedence** field allows packets to be prioritized (0 for low and 7 for high priority). Protocols would allow high-priority (or precedence) packets to be transmitted before low-priority ones. This would be especially useful for exchanging control packets indicating status. It also could be used to execute distributed congestion control algorithms without being affected by the congestion it is trying to control (similar to a police vehicle making its way through a heavily congested traffic area to get to an accident so they can get traffic moving again.) Currently, most routers ignore precedence, but its implementation allows for changes in newer versions (Reference 11).

FIGURE **7.31**    **Internet Packet**    (Marshall T. Rose, *The Simple Book: An Introduction to the Management of TCP/IP-based Internets*, ©1991, p. 47. Reprinted by permission of Prentice Hall, Englewood Cliffs, NJ.)

| version | header length | service type | datagram length | | |
|---|---|---|---|---|---|
| identification | | | flags | fragment offset | |
| time to live | | protocol | header checksum | | |
| source IP address | | | | | |
| destination IP address | | | | | |
| options | | | | padding | |
| data | | | | | |

A transport protocol can request a **low-delay** transmission, useful when the transport user has logged into a remote computer and wants quick responses. IP protocols at various routers then can route the packets (containing user requests or remote system responses) over less-congested networks, thus reducing response time. On the other hand, a user may be using a file transfer protocol to get a large file. In this case choosing networks with a high bit rate may be more important than quick responses. Putting a high-throughput request in the packet causes the router's IP protocol to look for high-speed networks over which to route a packet. Finally, the high-reliability request specifies that the packet be delivered reliably. While IP is not designed to provide error-free service, it can look for networks that have a track record of providing more reliable service and make routing choices accordingly.

- **Datagram length**. Specifies the length of the entire IP packet. It is a 16-bit field, thus providing a maximum length of 65,535 octets.

- **Identification, flags, fragment offset**. These three fields are used in fragmentation (discussed shortly).

- **Time to live**. A station sending a packet into the Internet for the first time sets the time-to-live field specifying the maximum time the packet can remain in the Internet. When another router receives the packet it decrements the time-to-live field by the amount of time the packet spent in the router and sends the packet to the next router. If the time-to-live field reaches 0 or less the router discards the packet and sends an error message to the sending station. This step guarantees that routing or congestion problems do not cause packets to circulate endlessly within the Internet.

- **Protocol**. Specifies the higher-layer protocol using IP. It allows the destination IP to give the data to the appropriate entity at its end. For example, if the IP packet contains a TCP segment the protocol value is 6. Packets containing UDP or ICMP segments have protocol values of 17 or 1, respectively (Reference 12).

- **Header checksum**. Used for error detection of packet headers. Since the data corresponds to a TCP or other protocol segment it has its own error detection, which is done at a higher layer. Thus, IP needs to worry only about detecting errors in the header. An advantage of this is that error checking fewer bits allows each router to service the packet more quickly. To calculate the checksum, the header is interpreted as a sequence of 16-bit integers. The values are added using 1's complement arithmetic and the result is complemented and stored in the checksum field. On the receiving end, the checksum is recalculated from the arriving information. If it disagrees with the value stored in the checksum field it knows an error has affected the header. If a header is ever changed (in other words, due to fragmentation) the checksum is recalculated.

- **Source IP address and destination IP address**. They contain the addresses of the sending and receiving stations.

- **Options**. This field is not required in every packet but can be used to request special treatment for the packet. It consists of a series of entries each corresponding to a requested option. For example:

  **The record route option** traces the route a packet takes. The sending station reserves space for a list of IP addresses in the options field. Each router routing the packet inserts its own address in the list (space permitting), thus allowing the receiving station to determine which ones handled the packet.

  **The timestamp option** is similar to the record route option. In addition to storing its address, each router stores the time at which it routed the packet.

  **The source route option** allows the sender to specify the route to be taken by storing a sequence of IP addresses in the options field. Each router uses this information instead of its own routing tables. This is not the normal mode of routing as it requires knowledge of the physical topology. It can be useful if network administrators suspect there is a problem with a router and want to test a specific route.

  More extensive discussions of these options and their execution are found in Reference 11.

- **Padding**. Consists of 0, 1, 2, or 3 octects to make the IP header end on a 32-bit boundary.

- **Data**. Contains the data provided by the next-higher layer.

**Fragmentation**       One of the problems the Internet protocol faces is that different network architectures allow different maximum frame sizes (also called **maximum transfer units** or **MTUs**). If the IP packet length is smaller than each MTU encountered in a path there is no problem, but if an MTU is smaller the packet is divided into smaller units called **fragments**. The fragments travel to their eventual destination (possibly over different routes), where they must be reassembled. For fragmentation to work the destination IP must be able to distinguish fragments from unfragmented packets, and recognize which fragments correspond to the same packet, in which order they must be reassembled, and how many fragments are contained in each packet. The identification, flags, and fragment offset fields provide that information.

Suppose a router receives a packet and determines it must travel over a network with an MTU smaller than the packet length. It divides the packet into fragments each containing part of the packet's data. Furthermore, each fragment has a **fragment header** almost identical to the packet header to allow for subsequent routing. Many fields in the fragment header perform the same roles as their counterparts in the packet header. The following fields are relevant to the current discussion:

- The router puts the packet's identification value into each fragment's identification field.

- The flag field contains a **more fragments bit** (**mfb**). The router sets the mfb bit in each fragment except the last one. There is also a **do not fragment bit** that, if set, does not allow fragmentation. If a router receives such a packet, it discards the packet and sends an error message to the sending station. The sending station uses the message to determine threshold values where fragmentation occurs. That is if the current packet size is too large, the sender could repeat with smaller packet sizes to eventually determine where fragmentation occurs.

- Since a fragment contains part of a packet's data the router also determines the offset in the packet's data field from where the data was extracted and stores it in the **fragment offset field**. It measures offsets in units of 8-bytes each. Thus, offset 1 corresponds to byte number 8, offset 2 to byte 16, and so on.

Figure 7.32 shows a packet being divided into three fragments. It assumes the network has an MTU which allows no more than 1400 bytes of data. Consequently, the router divides an incoming packet with 4000 data bytes into three fragments. Each of the first two fragments has 1400 data bytes. The first one's fragment offset field is 0, indicating its data begins at offset 0 in the packet. The second one's fragment offset field is 175, indicating its data begins at byte 1400 (8*175) of the packet. The third has 1200 bytes of data and an offset of 350. The mfb bits in the first two fragments are 1, indicating that each is a fragment and more fragments exist. The last fragment's mfb is 0, indicating that it is the last fragment. The fact that it is a fragment at all is deduced from the value in the offset field.

When the destination IP sees two different fragments with the same identification, source, and destination address, it knows they came from the same packet. It

**FIGURE 7.32    Packet Fragmentation**

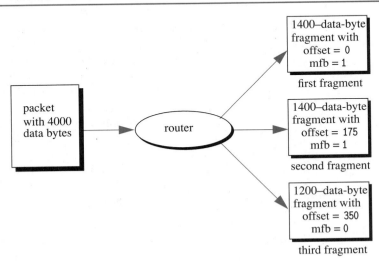

Fragments all have the same identification, source, and destination fields.

reassembles all such packets ordered by the values in their respective offset fields. It recognizes the last fragment as the one with the mfb equal to 0 and a non-zero offset. As part of the reassembly process it also sets a **reassembly timer** on receipt of the first fragment. If it does not receive all the fragments before the timer expires it assumes that one or more were lost. In that case, it discards the currently held fragments and sends an error message to the sending station. The result is that it gets all the fragments or none at all.

**IP Routing**     IP routing is based on routing tables stored at routers and the interpretation of IP addresses. Sections 6.5 and 7.2 have already dealt with these topics, and we will not reproduce those discussions here. Still, there are a couple of routing details that should be addressed while we are on the topic of the Internet. Recall from 7.2 that, to an Internet user, an **IP address** has the form

user@host.department.institution.domain

Domain name servers translate it to a 32-bit number that is typically expressed as a sequence of four 8-bit numbers separated by decimal points. For example, the IP address of Shayw@gbms01.uwgb.edu corresponds to the 32-bit number 10001111-11001000-10000000-00000011 or, using the equivalent dotted notation, as 143.200.128.3.

One issue we have not dealt with yet is the distinction between an IP address and a **physical address**. A unique 32-bit IP address is assigned to each host on the Internet. Its physical address is the one used by the underlying physical network. For example, stations connected to an Ethernet sense addresses stored in IEEE 802.3 frames to determine which ones are destined for it. However, these addresses are Ethernet addresses (48-bit numbers assigned to the interface board.) They have local significance but none on a global IP scale. How will such a station recognize a packet containing an IP address?

The answer is that it doesn't. Recall from Figure 7.30 that IP packets (IP address and all) are stored in frames as they travel the networks. Frames contain addresses depending on the data link control protocols. Within a network the frame's address specifies the frame's destination. If the frame goes to a router the IP there extracts the packet, examines the address, and determines where to send it next. It stores it into another frame containing the physical address of that destination. The next question must be: How does the router determine the physical address given the IP address? There are several ways, depending on specifics of the lower layers. We will outline a couple of common approaches here, but the interested reader should consult references 11 and 13 for more elaborate details.

When a router receives an IP packet there are two possibilities. Either the packet's destination is attached to a network to which the router is also attached, or it is not. The router recognizes the first case because the first number of each IP address specifies the network where the destination exists. If it recognizes the network as one to which it is attached it knows it can send the packet directly to its destination. This is called **direct routing**. It puts the destination's physical address in the frame and sends it. Another logical question is: How does the router determine the physical address given the IP address? One approach, **dynamic binding**, has the router transmit a broadcast frame containing an IP address to all stations on the network. The broadcast requests that the station with that IP address respond with its physical address. That station sends its physical address back to the router and the router stores it and the IP address locally. It then sends the frame (and any others with the same IP address) to the appropriate station.

Suppose the destination is not reachable directly through one of the router's networks. In that case the router uses hierarchical routing as discussed in Section 7.2 to determine another router and send the frame there. As before, the IP packet is encapsulated into a frame containing the router's physical address. The packet then travels from router to router until it reaches one connected to the destination's actual network.

To see how all of this works, consider the following example from Comer (Reference 11). Figure 7.33a shows several networks connected by several routers. Figure 7.33b shows part of a routing table at router *G*. Each network is identified by

**FIGURE 7.33**    **IP Routing**   (Douglas E. Comer, *Internetworking with TCP/IP*, Vol. I: Principles, Protocols, amd Architecture, 2e, ©1991, p.114. Reprinted by permission of Prentice Hall, Englewood Cliffs, NJ.)

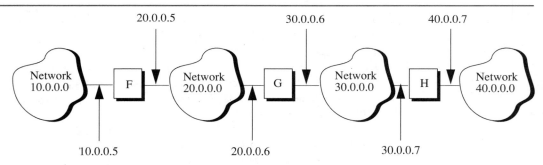

**(a) Example Internet with 4 networks and 3 routers**

| To reach hosts on network | Route to this address |
|---|---|
| 20.0.0.0 | deliver directly |
| 30.0.0.0 | deliver directly |
| 10.0.0.0 | 20.0.0.5 |
| 40.0.0.0 | 30.0.0.7 |

**(b) Routing table for router G**

the first of the four numbers in the IP address. Thus, every station on network 10.0.0.0 has an address of the form 10.x.y.z. This allows the routers to determine whether they can reach a destination directly.

Suppose router $G$ receives a packet with an IP address of 20.x.y.z. It knows it can deliver the packet to the destination directly and uses direct routing. It proceeds similarly for any packet containing an IP address of the form 30.x.y.z. On the other hand, suppose $G$ receives a packet containing address 10.x.y.z. Router $G$ knows it is not connected to that network and that it must route the packet to another router. According to the routing table in Figure 7.33b, it should create a frame containing IP address 20.0.0.5. This is the IP address of router $F$ via network 20.0.0.0.

We finish this section by describing a pseudo-coded IP routing algorithm (Figure 7.34), again from Comer (Reference 11). When a router receives a packet it determines the IP address of the destination network (lines 1 and 2). If the router is connected to the network, line 3 sends the frame directly to the station. If the sending station opted to specify the route (discussed previously), line 4 routes the packet according to the source route option field in the IP header. If the destination network's address appears in the router's routing table line 5 routes the packet

FIGURE 7.34    **IP Routing Algorithm**    (Douglas E. Comer, *Internetworking with TCP/IP*, Vol. I: Principles, Protocols, and Architecture, 2e, ©1991, p. 116. Reprinted by permission of Prentice Hall, Englewood Cliffs, NJ.)

Algorithm:

Route_IP_Datagram (datagram, routing_table)

1    Extract destination IP address, $I_D$, from datagram

2    Compute IP address of destination network, $I_N$

3    If $I_N$ matches any directly connected network address send datagram to
        destination over that network; (This involves resolving $I_D$ to a
        physical address, encapsulating the packet, and sending the frame.)

4    else if $I_D$ appears as a host-specific route*,

        route packet as specified in the table;

5    else if $I_N$ appears in routing table

        route datagram as specified in the table;

6    else if a default route has been specified

        route datagram to the default router;

    else declare a routing error;

    Given an IP datagram and a routing table, this algorithm selects the next machine to
    which the datagram should be sent. Routing tables always specify a next machine that
    lies on a directly connected network.

according to the routing table data. If neither of the previous cases occurs the router can send the packet to a default router (line 6), if one exists. This is useful for a small site with only one connection to the Internet or initially before a router has learned where others are. Rather than maintaining routing tables (all of which would point to the only Internet connection) it simply relies on the default. Finally, if all of these conditions fail the router drops the packet and sends an error message to the sender stating the packet could not be delivered.

## INTERNET CONTROL MESSAGE PROTOCOL

Because IP does not provide a guarantee of reliable service, the **Internet control message protocol (ICMP)** is a protocol used for reporting errors and for providing routers updates on conditions that can develop in the Internet. ICMP sends messages by encapsulating them in IP packets and setting the header's protocol field to 1.

The following list explains some typical control messages sent by ICMP:

- **Destination unreachable**. As we have stated previously, IP cannot guarantee delivery of a packet. The destination may not exist or it may be down; the sender may have made a source route request that cannot be carried out; a packet with its do not fragment bit set may be too large to be encapsulated into a frame. In such cases the router detecting the error sends an ICMP packet to the original sender. It contains the entire IP header of the undeliverable packet and the first 64 bits of its data, thus allowing the sender to recognize which packet was undeliverable.

- **Echo request**. ICMP uses this packet to determine whether a particular destination is reachable. For example, if *A* wants to know whether *B* is reachable it sends an echo request packet addressed to *B*. If *B* receives the packet it responds by sending an echo reply packet back to *A*. The echo reply packet will return any data placed in the echo request packet. This may be simpler than committing a protocol to sending a whole series of packets to a destination only to find out it is unreachable.

- **Echo reply**. Sent in response to an echo request.

- **Parameter problem**. Suppose an IP packet contains an error or an illegal value in one of its header fields. A router discovering the error sends a parameter problem packet back to the source. This packet contains the IP header in question and a pointer to the header field that is in error.

- **Redirect**. Suppose a host station sends a packet to a router and the router knows the packet could have been delivered faster via some other router. To facilitate future routing the router sends a redirect packet back to the host. It informs the host where the other router is and that it should send future packets with the same destination to it. This allows the host to update its routing tables dynamically and to take advantage of changing conditions in the network. The redirect packet is not used for router-to-router route updates because IP packets contain the source address but not the address of the most recent router that had it. When a router receives a packet from another router it does not know which one sent it.

- **Source quench**. If a router is receiving too many packets from a host it can send a message requesting a reduction in the rate at which packets are sent.

- **Time exceeded**. A time exceeded packet is sent when the time-to-live field in an IP packet reaches 0 or when the reassembly timer (set on receiving a packet's first fragment) expires. In either case, the packet or any unassembled fragments are dropped from the network. The guilty router then sends a time exceeded packet to the source indicating its packets were not delivered.

- **Timestamp request reply**. Timestamp packets allow a host to estimate the time required for a round trip between it and another host. A host creates and sends a timestamp packet containing the time of transmission (**original timestamp**). When the receiving host gets the packet it creates a **timestamp reply** packet. that contains the original timestamp, the time at which the receiving host got the packet (**receive timestamp**), and the time at which the receiving host sends the reply (**transmit timestamp**). When the original sender receives the reply it records the time it arrived. The difference between the arrival time and the original timestamp is the time required for the round trip. By calculating the difference between the receive timestamp and transmit timestamp the host also can determine how long the other host took to respond once it got the request. By subtracting this from the round-trip time the host can also estimate the transit time for both the request and the reply. Timestamp packets allow the host to estimate the network's efficiency in delivering packets.

## ISO INTERNET PROTOCOL

In order to be complete we must mention that ISO has its own version of an Internet protocol. Like the DoD IP, the **ISO internet protocol** is a connectionless protocol. In fact, the ISO IP is based on the DoD standard. It is designed to interface with the ISO transport layer using two primitives, **N-UNITDATA.request** and **N-UNITDATA.indication**. The first is a request made by the transport layer (network layer user) to transmit information. In response, the Internet protocol accepts the request, creates an IP packet, and proceeds similarly to previous discussions. Conversely, IP uses N_UNITDATA.indication to notify the transport layer that information has arrived.

At the level of discussion in this chapter the differences between the two Internet protocols are not significant. For example, the two IP packet formats differ, but the respective fields perform essentially the same functions. If you are interested in exploring the differences further, references 2,3, and 14 provide a broader coverage of the ISO IP.

## 7.5   Transport Protocols

So far we have primarily dealt with network operations. Frame formats, routing, congestion control, and addressing are all essential to allowing one station to talk to another. But how they talk with each other is equally important. A transport protocol is the lowest-layer protocol that defines what a station can say to another on behalf of the user. The lower three layers define how a network operates; the transport layer is the first to define the end-user protocol.

In some cases, the transport layer also provides the "connection" the user perceives. For example, users can logon to computers at remote sites, giving them the impression they are "connected." But the connection is not a physical one as it exists when connecting wires or making a telephone call. There is not necessarily a dedicated physical circuit devoted to transmitting information between the user and computer.

The transport layer can provide the perception of a connection by interfacing between the user and network protocols. It is similar to a secretary whose function is to place calls on behalf of an executive. The secretary gets the executive's request, makes the call, and reaches the desired person, thus making the connection. The executive then proceeds to have the conversation independent of any trouble the secretary may have had in finding the desired person who may have been in an important meeting, out to lunch, or on the racquetball court. When the executive has finished talking, the secretary may complete the connection by getting additional important information such as a client's address, phone number, or racquetball court location.

A transport protocol does more than make and break connections, however. The lowest three layers provide the means to connect separate devices, but the transport layer is the lowest layer that actually allows its users to communicate effectively and securely. Some transport layer functions are as follows:

- **Connection management**. This function defines the rules that allow two users to begin talking with one another as if they were connected directly. Defining and setting up the connection is also called **handshaking**.

- **Flow control**. It limits how much information one station can send to another without receiving some acknowledgment. If this sounds familiar, great! You are remembering some of the information from previous chapters. In Chapter 5 we discussed flow control and its relevance to the data link layer. To have flow control again in the transport layer seems strange at first, but remember that the transport layer must operate independently of the lower layers. Lower layers may allow more or less (or no) flow control. In order to preserve this independence a transport layer may use its own flow control. Thus, it may seem redundant, but independence often introduces redundancy.

- **Error detection**. This is another case that seems to duplicate lower-layer features. Some errors, however, escape lower-layer error detection. We know that data-link–level error detection techniques can detect point-to-point transmission errors. However, consider the router in Figure 7.35 (taken from Figure

FIGURE 7.35    **Error Undetected by Lower-Layer Detection Techniques**

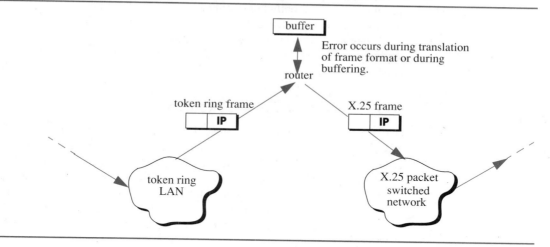

7.30). Suppose it receives a packet intact, but an error in the data occurs during reformatting of the packet. Any number of software or hardware errors can cause a problem. Since the checksum is calculated after the new packet is created it includes the erroneous data. Strictly speaking, it is not a transmission error because it occurred while the packet was in the possession of the router. But try telling that to the transport user, who saw her data changed while in transit. A transport layer error detection mechanism would detect this error.

- **Response to users' requests.** Examples include sending and receiving data, as well as specific requests. For example, a user may request high throughput, low delays, or reliable service. As discussed in the previous section, the IP can deal with these. The transport layer passes the request from the user to the IP.

- **Establishment of connectionless or connection-oriented communication.**

- **Reliable communications between end-users.** Since IP does not guarantee reliable service, transport protocols must provide acknowledgments and timers to make sure all of a user's data are sent and received. As with error detection, lower-layer protocols can determine when frames are lost in transit. But again, we want reliability to exist independent of lower layers. Besides, suppose an intermediate network node lost a frame after it received and acknowledged it but before it retransmitted the frame. As mentioned earlier, any number of on-site errors could cause this. Because there was no error in any point-to-point link it would be up to an end-to-end protocol to detect the error.

Two transport layer protocols that DoD designed specifically to run with its ARPANET IP are the **transmission control protocol (TCP)** and the **user datagram protocol (UDP)**. TCP is a connection-oriented protocol that forms the connection management facilities of the Internet. It is the most widely used transport layer protocol in the world. UDP is a connectionless transport layer protocol. It is used much less frequently but is still part of the TCP/IP suite. The rest of this section focuses on TCP and discusses UDP. To be complete, we must mention that the ISO also has defined its own layer-4 transport protocol. The Internet and TCP are such dominant forces in defining connections, however, that the DoD TCP is likely to be around for a long time.

### DoD TRANSMISSION CONTROL PROTOCOL

TCP provides a connection-oriented user-to-user service. It provides the hand-shaking by establishing, maintaining, and releasing connections. It handles requests to deliver information to a destination reliably, an important consideration since the lower layer (usually IP) does not guarantee delivery of packets. TCP receives data or requests from its user (Figure 7.36), stores it in a TCP segment format, and gives it to the IP. It plays no role in the subsequent routing and transfer of information. The receiver's TCP gets a segment, responds to the information in it, extracts the data, and gives it to the user.

**TCP Segment**    Figure 7.37 shows the contents of a **TCP segment**. The following list defines the fields:

- **Destination port**. Identifies the application to which the segment is sent. This is different from the IP address, which specifies an Internet address. Since many applications can run at the same Internet node, this field specifies which one.
- **Source port**. Specifies the application sending the segment.

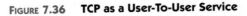

**FIGURE 7.36    TCP as a User-To-User Service**

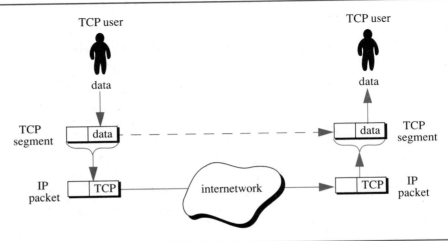

FIGURE 7.37 **TCP Segment** (Marshall T. Rose, *The Simple Book: An Introduction to the Management of TCP/IP-based Internets*, ©1991, p. 63. Reprinted by permission of Prentice Hall, Englewood Cliffs, NJ.)

| source port | | destination port | |
|---|---|---|---|
| sequence number | | | |
| acknowledgment number | | | |
| offset | reserved | flags | window |
| checksum | | urgent pointer | |
| options | | | padding |
| data | | | |

- **Sequence number**. If the segment contains data this field contains the sequence number of the segment's first data byte. In contrast to other protocols that number each packet or frame consecutively, TCP numbers the bytes. Thus, if each data segment contained 1000 data bytes the sequence numbers in consecutive segments would be $x, x + 1000, x + 2000$, and so on where $x$ is the sequence number of the first byte.[*] TCP also uses this field as part of the initial call connection strategy (discussed shortly).

- **Acknowledgment number**. Contains the byte sequence number the receiving TCP entity expects to receive. Effectively, it has acknowledged receiving all bytes prior to the one specified. This is similar to acknowledgments discussed in Sections 5.2 and 5.3 except that here the protocol is acknowledging bytes, not packets.

- **Offset**. Specifies the size of the TCP header and, consequently, where the data begins.

- **Flags**. This 6-bit flag field specifies when other fields contain meaningful data or specify certain control functions. For example two of the flags, ACK and URG (sounds like prehistoric sibling names), specify whether the acknowledgment and urgent point fields (discussed shortly) contain meaningful data. Four other flags are:

    **FIN (finish)**: Indicates the last TCP data segment.

---

[*]The initial sequence number is not necessarily 1 and is negotiated when the connection is established. We discuss this under connection management.

**PSH (push):** Ordinarily TCP decides when a segment contains enough data to warrant its transmission. In some cases an application can force TCP to send a segment earlier by issuing a push command. For example, an interactive application might issue a push after a user has entered a line from a keyboard. This provides a better and smoother response than allowing TCP to buffer several lines of input before sending any of them. When TCP receives a push command it sets the PSH field in the segment. When the PSH field is set in an incoming segment, the receiving TCP entity makes the segment's contents available to its application immediately. If the application is to display incoming data on a video screen, this mechanism provides a quick and smooth display.

**RST (reset):** Indication from the sending entity that the receiving entity should break the transport connection. Used when an abnormal condition occurs, it allows both entities to terminate the connection, stop the flow of data, and release buffer space associated with the connection.

**SYN (synchronize):** Used in the initial connection setup, it allows the two entities to synchronize (agree on) initial sequence numbers (discussed shortly).

- **Window.** This field tells the receiving TCP entity how many data bytes the sending TCP entity can accept in return. As we will discuss shortly, this corresponds roughly to the window size of a sliding window protocol (Sections 5.2 and 5.3) and allows the entities to alter how much they can receive dynamically.

- **Checksum.** Used for transport layer error detection.

- **Urgent Pointer.** If the URG bit is set, the segment contains **urgent data** meaning the receiving TCP entity must deliver it to the higher layers as quickly as possible. The urgent pointer points to the first byte following the urgent data and allows the receiving entity to distinguish the urgent data from nonurgent data.

- **Options/padding.** As of this writing the only option allows a TCP entity to specify the maximum segment size it will receive from the other entity. This value typically is specified during the initial connection setup. It is an important option because TCP may connect two computers with very different capabilities. Successful communication requires that each be aware of any limitations (such as buffer size) the other has. For example, a large IBM mainframe would not want to overwhelm a small PC with segments that are too large. The PC would establish the maximum segment it can receive when it establishes the connection. The padding is used to make sure the header ends on a 32-bit boundary.

- **Data.** User-supplied data.

**TCP Connection Management**    **Connection management** is the process of establishing, maintaining, and ending a connection. But what exactly is a connection? As indicated previously, a connection is more virtual than physical. (Isn't everything these days?). Basically, two TCP entities agree to exchange TCP segments and establish some parameters describing the segment exchange. Typical parameters describe the sequence numbers used for bytes and the number of bytes an entity can receive. The entities then send each other segments and do error checking, acknowledging, and flow control as if they were connected directly, leaving transmission details to the lower layers.

To begin, the two entities must agree to establish a connection. Initially, this seems straightforward: One entity makes a request to connect and the other says OK. This is a two-way handshake, discussed in Section 1.5. We also mentioned that it can cause problems if the first request is delayed and subsequently shows up at a much later time, thus causing an unintentional second connection. We responded by discussing a three-way handshake, in which one entity makes a connection request, the second acknowledges the request, and the first acknowledges the acknowledgment.

More is involved than simply sending connection requests and acknowledgments. We mentioned earlier that TCP treats data as a sequence of bytes to be divided and sent in segments. Rather than numbering each segment TCP stores the sequence number of the first data byte in the sequence field of a segment. The sequence field is a 32-bit field, thus allowing sequence numbers over 1 billion. To avoid the problems associated with a two-way handshake the three-way handshake establishes the initial sequence numbers each TCP entity uses. The following steps of the three-way handshake are illustrated in Figure 7.38:

1.  TCP entity $A$ transmits a TCP segment requesting a connection (time $t_1$). It sets the SYN field to indicate the segment represents a connection request and defines the sequence field to be $x$. It may determine $x$ using a timer or counter.

FIGURE 7.38    **Three-Way Handshake Protocol**

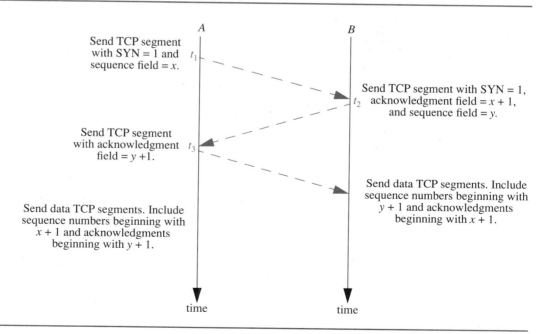

Send TCP segment with SYN = 1 and sequence field = $x$.     $t_1$

Send TCP segment with SYN = 1, acknowledgment field = $x + 1$, and sequence field = $y$.     $t_2$

Send TCP segment with acknowledgment field = $y + 1$.     $t_3$

Send data TCP segments. Include sequence numbers beginning with $y + 1$ and acknowledgments beginning with $x + 1$.

Send data TCP segments. Include sequence numbers beginning with $x + 1$ and acknowledgments beginning with $y + 1$.

time                    time

Each new request is accompanied by different and larger (modulo $2^{32}$) initial sequence numbers.

2.  TCP entity $B$ transmits a TCP segment acknowledging both the request and the sequence number (time $t_2$). It does this by setting the SYN field and defining the acknowledgment field $= x + 1$ and the sequence field $= y$. $B$ determines $y$ in much the same way $A$ determines $x$.

3.  TCP entity $A$ acknowledges the acknowledgment (time $t_3$). The next segment it sends contains sequence field $= x + 1$ and acknowledgment field $= y + 1$.

After the three segments have been sent and received, each entity knows what initial sequence number the other is using and, by way of the acknowledgment field, has told the other what it is expecting. Subsequent data segments contain increasing (modulo $2^{32}$) sequence numbers, where each increment is equal to the number of data bytes in the previous segment. We will elaborate shortly when we discuss flow control.

Terminating connections is similar to establishing them. TCP provides full-duplex communication, however, so one entity wanting to disconnect does not necessarily mean the other is ready. Basically, both parties must agree to disconnect before doing so. Consequently, another three-way handshake protocol to terminate connection is used (Figure 7.39):

1.  TCP entity $A$ gets a CLOSE request from its application (time $t_1$). It responds by sending a TCP segment with the FIN field set and sequence field $= x$. The FIN field indicates there is no more data and that the current segment represents a

**FIGURE 7.39    TCP Disconnect Protocol**

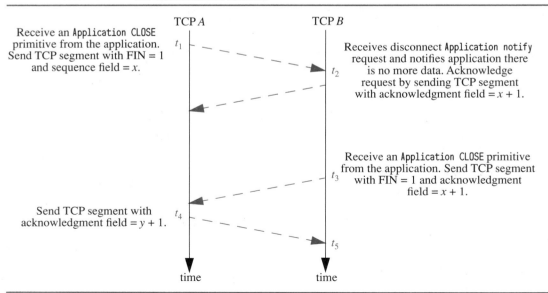

disconnect request. The parameter $x$ represents the current sequence count the TCP entity had been maintaining.

2.   TCP entity $B$ receives the segment (time $t_2$). It responds by notifying its application of the request to disconnect, effectively telling it no more data is on the way. It also sends a TCP segment back to $A$ acknowledging receipt of the request. Meanwhile $B$'s application could continue to send data or simply prepare to issue its own disconnect request.

3.   TCP entity $B$ gets a close request from its application (time $t_3$). It sends a TCP segment to $A$ with the FIN field set and acknowledgment field $= x + 1$.

4.   When TCP entity $A$ receives the acknowledgment (time $t_4$), it sends an acknowledgment and disconnects. When the acknowledgment arrives at $B$ (time $t_5$), it also disconnects.

**Flow Control**     Once the initial connection is made the two TCP entities can exchange segments using full-duplex communication buffering both the segments it sends and those it receives. It buffers segments it sends because there is no guarantee the segment will arrive. Therefore the TCP entity may have to retransmit it. It buffers the ones it receives because there is no guarantee segments arrive in order. Effectively the entities exchange segments using a variation of the sliding window protocols discussed in Chapter 5. We will not repeat a detailed discussion of flow control, but we do focus on a couple of differences between TCP flow control and flow control discussed in Chapter 5:

1.   Here, the sequence number refers to byte sequences instead of packet (or segment) sequences, and

2.   each entity can alter the size of its receiving window dynamically using the segment's window field.

Each entity implements flow control using a **credit mechanism**. A **credit**, stored in the segment's window field, specifies the maximum number of bytes the entity sending the segment can receive and buffer from the other entity. The TCP entity receiving the segment uses the credit to determine the maximum number of bytes it can send without having received an acknowledgment. Once it sends that many it must wait for some of them to be acknowledged or for the credit to increase. Figure 7.40 shows an example of this mechanism. We assume that the two stations have already negotiated the initial connection, initial sequence numbers, and credit using the three-way handshake. TCP entities $A$ and $B$ have initial sequence numbers 100 and 700, respectively. We also assume that each segment contains 100 bytes of data and that each entity has given an initial credit of 200 bytes. Entity $A$ starts by sending two segments, one with sequence number ($s$) 101 and the other with sequence number 201. The acknowledgments ($a$) indicate what $A$ is expecting from $B$ and the credit value ($c$) in the segments remains at 200.

After sending the second frame $A$ has used up its credit and must wait (time $t_1$). Later it receives a segment from $B$ containing a sequence number equal to 701 and an acknowledgment equal to 201. This means $B$ has received bytes sequenced up to 200

FIGURE 7.40     **Flow Control Using a Credit Mechanism**

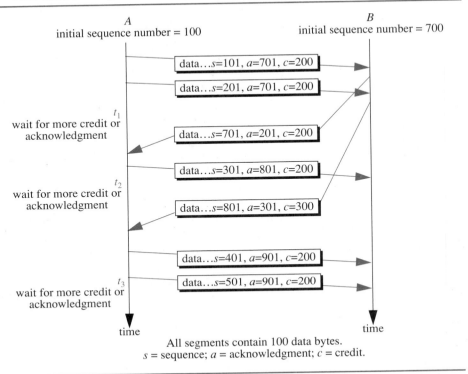

All segments contain 100 data bytes.
$s$ = sequence; $a$ = acknowledgment; $c$ = credit.

and is expecting byte number 201 next. The segment also reaffirms the credit of 200. At this point $A$ still has 100 bytes unacknowledged and a credit of 200. Consequently it sends another 100-byte segment and waits again (time $t_2$). After a while $A$ receives another segment from $B$ with acknowledgment equal to 301 and a credit equal to 300. At this point $A$ still has 100 bytes unacknowledged but has received an increase in credit to 300 bytes. Consequently, $A$ sends two segments for a total of 300 unacknowledged bytes before waiting at time $t_3$. To simplify, this example shows only $A$ being affected by credit limits, but be assured that credit limits apply to $B$ also.

The main advantage of the credit mechanism is that it allows the protocol to be more robust. Rather than living with a fixed window size the TCP entities can take advantage of changing conditions. If there is little activity at a particular site the TCP entity may acknowledge a segment with an increased credit to make better use of otherwise unused buffer space. On the other hand, if there is a lot of activity with other connections, it may send a segment reducing the credit to keep incoming information at a manageable level.

**TCP Primitives**     Up to now we have concentrated on the concepts behind TCP and have not addressed the interface between TCP and the application that uses it. Unlike previous topics we have discussed, there is no formal standard on how to use

TCP. (Of course, given the abundance of standards this is not necessarily a disadvantage.) For example, TCP documentation specifies several primitive operations to open/close connections, send/receive data, request/report status, and so on.

TCP performs many tasks and, to a certain degree, acts independently. Still, we should not lose sight of the fact that it is a middle-level protocol and must communicate with the next higher level protocol. In the OSI model this would be the session layer, but in practice could actually be a presentation or application layer. In any case, the TCP protocol allows for communication between TCP and that layer (which we call the TCP user). As with most protocols TCP defines requests its user may direct to TCP and responses that TCP can return. Table 7.11 shows primitives with a brief description of each. In the Type column, "request" means a user-to-TCP request, and "indication" or "confirm" means a TCP-to-user response.

**Sockets**    Because so many network applications run under the UNIX operating system, in particular **Berkeley UNIX**, a separate set of primitives was designed to be used by UNIX systems. Through these primitives UNIX applications communicate using a mechanism called a socket.

TABLE 7.11    **TCP Primitives**

| NAME | TYPE | DESCRIPTION |
| --- | --- | --- |
| ABORT | request | Close the connection because of error. |
| ACTIVE-OPEN | request | Initiate a connection. |
| ACTIVE-OPEN-W/DATA | request | Initiate a connection and include data with the request. |
| ALLOCATE | request | Increase buffer space for incoming data. |
| CLOSE | request | Close the connection normally. |
| CLOSING | indication | Tells TCP user that the remote TCP entity has issued a CLOSE. |
| DELIVER | indication | Tells TCP user that data has arrived. |
| ERROR | indication | Indicates an error has occurred. |
| FULL-PASSIVE-OPEN | request | Tells the TCP entity the user is able to accept connection requests from a specified remote site. |
| OPEN-FAILURE | confirm | Tells TCP user the previous ACTIVE-OPEN request failed. |
| OPEN-ID | confirm | Provides the name associated with the connection requested by the ACTIVE-OPEN request. Requires acceptance of the request by the remote site. |
| OPEN-SUCCESS | confirm | Tells TCP user the previous ACTIVE-OPEN request succeeded. |
| SEND | request | Request to send data over the connection. |
| STATUS | request | Requests connection status. |
| STATUS-RESPONSE | confirm | Responds to STATUS request with connection status. |
| TERMINATE | confirm | Tells the TCP user the connection has ended. |
| UNSPECIFIED-PASSIVE-OPEN | request | Tells the TCP entity the user is able to accept connection requests from any remote site. |

The **socket** is a UNIX construct and is the basis for UNIX network I/O. At a superficial level it is similar to UNIX pipes and files. A UNIX application creates a socket when it needs a connection to a network. It then establishes a connection to a remote station via the socket and communicates with the station by reading data from the socket and writing data to it. The comparison with pipes and files is superficial, as standard UNIX I/O works with byte streams whereas network communications require much more complex protocols. Having already discussed many of the protocols we won't elaborate again. Table 7.12 presents some of the socket commands and a brief description of each. If you are interested in a more complete description of the socket interface, references 11 and 15 present more commands and more detailed discussions of them.

**Limitations of TCP**     Although TCP is the most widely used transport protocol, it is not without its criticisms. Reference 2 lists the following limitations of DoD transport layer protocols:[*]

1.  An obvious weakness of TCP is its long headers. All data units have the same format, except for optional fields, with minimum header length 20 bytes. When TCP is used in conjunction with IP, at least 20 more bytes of header are added, giving total TCP/IP header overhead of at least 40 bytes. For short messages, as are often used for interactive applications, this can lead to very poor data transmission efficiency.

2.  The checksum for TCP is weak, failing to detect a substantial number of error patterns. How serious this is depends on the network layer and data link layer protocols underneath TCP. In many cases HDLC or an equivalent protocol, with strong error detecting capability, will be used at the data link layer. When this is true, the TCP checksum is largely superfluous. When transport layer checksums are really needed, though, it would be desirable to have a more powerful one.

3.  The urgent data feature in TCP is marginally adequate for delivering out of band or urgent data, since it does not cause normal flow control to be bypassed or otherwise greatly speed up delivery. Its primary function is to inform the user that some data are urgent and should be processed quickly.

4.  The stream orientation of TCP, treating data as a stream of bytes rather than as a sequence of message units, is unusual though it works reasonably well. It required the addition of the Push function to ensure timely delivery of short interactive messages; otherwise enough data to fill a normal size data unit would be accumulated before transmission.

5.  All in all, TCP has proved to be remarkably successful, especially when considering that it was the first general purpose transport layer protocol developed. With the addition of UDP for applications better adapted to datagram service, the DoD architecture satisfies most requirements for transport layer protocols reasonably well. At least two other types of transport layer protocols would be

---

[*] Reprinted by permission of Addison-Wesley Publishing Co.

TABLE 7.12   **UNIX Socket Commands**

| COMMAND | MEANING |
|---|---|
| socket | Creates a socket. The application specifies how to interpret network addresses, the protocol used (TCP is not the only protocol UNIX can interface with), and whether the communication is connection oriented or connectionless. If successful, it returns an integer (descriptor) of the socket. |
| close | Closes a socket. |
| bind | Associates a name to a socket. The name can be distributed to remote sites, thus allowing them to initiate connections with the local site via the socket. |
| connect | Requests a connection with a remote socket. The call must specify the local socket identifier and the remote socket address. This call is needed when a connection-oriented service is required. Connectionless services such as a datagram service do not require a connect. |
| listen | Often used by a server that responds to requests from many remote sites. Since it cannot have multiple connections simultaneously, it listens for incoming connection requests and puts them into a queue for subsequent processing. |
| accept | Used when a server is able to accept a connection request. |
| setsockopt | Gives the application some control over the socket. For example, the application can use this command to define timeout parameters or buffer limits. |
| getsockopt | Requests information regarding the specified socket. |
| write | Sends data via a connected socket. The call must specify the location and length of data and the socket identifier. It does not specify the destination because a previous connect command established the connection. |
| writev | Similar to write except it allows the application to send data that resides in noncontiguous locations. |
| send | Similar to write except it has an additional parameter, a set of bit flags that allow the application to control certain transmission functions. For example, the flags could indicate the presence of urgent data or request that routing tables not be used in order to let the user specify a route. |
| sendto | Similar to send except it is used with unconnected sockets. As such, it requires that the destination address and its length be specified as a parameter. |
| sendmsg | Similar to sendto except it allows the application to send data that resides in noncontiguous locations. It also consolidates several of sendto's parameters into a single structure to make it easier to use. |
| read, readv, recv, recvfrom, recvmsg | The read and receive (rec) commands are similar to their write and send counterparts. They accept data from remote sockets and store it. |
| select | Sometimes a server can interface with many sockets. In this case it needs a mechanism to determine which sockets are ready for I/O. The select call does this. |
| getpeername | Gets the address of the remote station to which the specified socket connects. |
| getsockname | Gets the local address for the corresponding socket. |

desirable, however; a speech protocol guaranteeing sequenced, timely delivery but without high reliability requirements and a real-time protocol guaranteeing high reliability and timeliness.

## USER DATAGRAM PROTOCOL

We have spent most of this section on the ARPANET TCP, but don't assume it is the only transport protocol in use. Although it is the most commonly used protocol, others warrant mention. One of these is the **user datagram protocol (UDP)**, a connectionless transport layer protocol. It is less complex than TCP, as indicated by the format of a **UDP segment** (Figure 7.41). It contains very little overhead which suggests limited abilities. The segment includes the usual source and destination addresses, the segment length, and a checksum for error detection. Because it is connectionless there is no handshake to establish a connection. When UDP has data to send it creates a UDP segment and gives it to the IP for delivery. At the receiving end, UDP gets the data from IP and does an error check. If there is no error UDP passes the data to its user; if there is an error UDP discards the data. There is no formal mechanism for acknowledging errors or a provision for flow control of segment sequencing. It is little more than an interface between a higher layer and IP.

## OSI TRANSPORT PROTOCOLS

The ISO has also defined several transport protocol standards for its OSI model. In fact, there are five classes, labeled **TP$i$** ($i$ = 0, 1, 2, 3, or 4), of transport services in the OSI model. Classes 0 through 3 are designed to work with networks that provide error-free service (unlike IP). They provide no error control and provide mainly connection and disconnection services. Their differences are relatively minor. For example, TP2 and TP3 can multiplex two or more transport connections over the same network connection. TP0 and TP1 do not. TP1 and TP3 allow the connected transport entities to be resynchronized in the event of network errors or congestion problems. Thus, they provide segment sequencing whereas TP0 and TP2 do not. TP3, but not TP1, provides flow control. Additional information on these protocols can be found in references 2,3,6, and 10.

FIGURE 7.41    **UDP Segment**

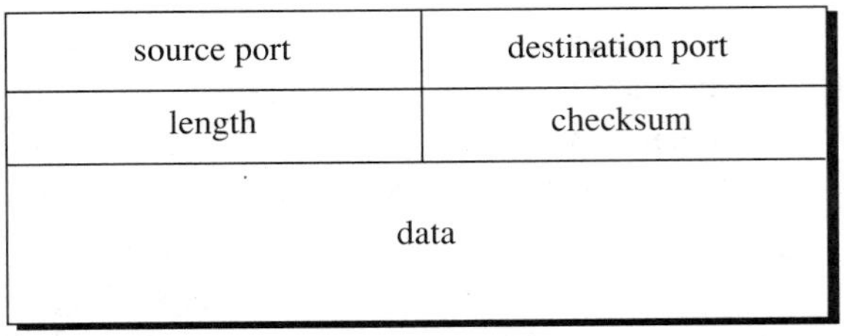

| source port | destination port |
|---|---|
| length | checksum |
| data | |

TP4 is designed to run on top of unreliable network services such as IP and is similar to TCP. Because of its similarity we do not go into detail but will outline some of the more important differences. One difference is in the terminology. For example, OSI uses the phrase **transport protocol data units** (**TPDUs**) to refer to the transport segments. Other areas of difference are:

- **Segment types**. TP4 allows ten different TPDU types (Table 7.13) for different functions. Each type is designated by a field in the segment header. This allows TP4 headers to be smaller as the header needs to contain only what is necessary for a particular function. On the other hand, the single-segment format makes TCP simpler.

- **Important data.** TCP uses urgent pointers to locate important data in the TCP segment. TP4's approach is to send important data in an ED TPDU ahead of any waiting DT TPDUs. An arriving ED TPDU alerts the receiving TP4 entity that the TPDU's contents should be processed quickly.

- **Graceful close.** As discussed earlier, the TCP disconnect protocol calls for both TCP entities to exchange disconnect requests and confirmations. This way if one entity receives a disconnect request but still has data to send, it may do so. TP4 does not provide the graceful close. If a station receives a disconnect request (DR TPDU) it sends a disconnect confirmation (DC TPDU) and informs the TP4 user. If TP4 still has data to send, it discards the data segments and the data is lost. In fairness to the OSI model, the data is not permanently lost as the session layer deals with the problem. However, some people have criticized the relegating of the solution to a higher layer.

- **Piggybacked acknowledgments**. TP4 does not provide for piggybacked acknowledgments, as does TCP, but instead uses AK TPDUs to acknowledge receipt of data (or an EA TPDU if acknowledging expedited data). However, TP4

**TABLE 7.13    TP4 TPDU Types**

| TPDU TYPE | FUNCTION |
|:---:|:---|
| **CR** | Connection request |
| **CC** | Connection confirmation |
| **DR** | Disconnect request |
| **DC** | Disconnect confirmation |
| **DT** | Data |
| **ED** | Expedited data |
| **AK** | Acknowledgment |
| **EA** | Expedited data acknowledgment |
| **ER** | Error |
| **RJ** | Rejection |

does allow the concatenation of a DT and AK TPDU into a single network protocol packet. The effect is the same as piggybacking and the distinction with TCP is primarily a matter of semantics.

- **Sequencing**. TP4 sequences by numbering the segments as opposed to the byte-oriented approach of TCP. DT TPDUs normally contain an 8-bit sequence field (although 32-bit fields are an option) that contains the TPDU number.

- **Flow control**. TP4 can use a credit mechanism much like TCP. However, it may also use no flow control and rely on flow control procedures at lower layers. Sending an ED TPDU affects flow control in two ways. First, the sending TP4 entity cannot have more than one ED TPDU outstanding. That is, it must receive an EA TPDU before it can send another ED TPDU. Second, a TP4 entity sends an ED TPDU ahead of any waiting DT TPDUs. The entity may send the waiting TPDUs afterward but cannot generate and send any new DT TPDUs until the expedited data is acknowledged. This is a bit unusual, but the idea is to expedite data transfer. Although TP4 can send an ED TPDU before other DT TPDUs it cannot guarantee it will arrive first. Consequently, TP4 really has no facility to speed up data delivery. Instead, it suspends sending new TPDUs in the hope that the absence of traffic will help the ED TPDU arrive faster.

## 7.6   Wide Area Networks in Operation

The actual number of wide area networks today is quite large. They are also quite diverse as they serve very different needs. This section lists many of the networks in operation and provide a few comments about each. We hope that this list will give you a sense of the many different types of networks that exist and an understanding of just how pervasive computer networks have become. Our main source for all of this information is Reference 10. If you are interested in more information on any of the networks listed here (or on many others not listed) that reference should be helpful.

**ACSnet** (Australian Computer Science network), the largest network in Australia, connects universities, government agencies, and private organizations. It relies in part on leased telephone lines and X.25 connections. Like Internet, it has no central administration (each site has the financial and technical responsibility of maintaining its host) and uses a domain naming system to access nodes. Internet users can access nodes on ACSnet via the domain name OZ.AU.

**AMPRNET** (Amateur Packet Radio Network) is a packet radio network. It uses the TCP/IP protocols and is registered with (although not connected to) the Internet as the domain ampr.org. AMPRNET users are primarily shortwave radio (ham) operators and must be licensed by the FCC. Using AMPRNET is a relatively low-cost venture as it requires primarily a terminal node controller (a device to modulate data into radio signals) and a shortwave radio to use with it.

**ARPANET** (Advanced Research Projects Agency Network) is perhaps the network that started it all. The Advanced Research Projects Agency was an agency of the U.S. Department of Defense and funded a research project in the 1960s to demonstrate the viability of packet switched computer networks. The research and protocols developed for the ARPANET have formed the basis for much of the OSI model and have evolved into protocols used in the Internet.

**BARRNet** (San Francisco Bay Area Regional Research Network) is a regional metropolitan network connecting (among others) several University of California campuses in the San Francisco area, Stanford University, and Lawrence Berkeley and Livermore laboratories. It is a high speed-network (using T1 transmissions) and uses the TCP/IP protocols. Its high speed was deemed necessary due to the supercomputer applications that would use its services. In addition, the relatively small area and the existence of T1 facilities in the area helped make its implementation possible.

**BCnet** (British Columbia Network) is a regional network connecting several Canadian Universities, the British Columbia Advanced Systems Institute, and Dominion Astrophysical Observatory. It uses telephone linkages and T1 optical fiber links. It also uses a variety of protocols such as TCP/IP, X.25, and DECNET.

**BITNET** (Because It's Time Network) started in 1981 when the City College of New York and Yale University connected two of their hosts using IBM network software. It is used largely by academic institutions and currently has over 2000 hosts in over 30 countries. It uses a protocol called Network Job Entry (NJE) that was developed by IBM and is incompatible with both TCP/IP and the OSI model. Its primary services are email and file transfer, although the file service generally applies to sending files rather than requesting them from remote sites. A university joins BITNET by leasing a telephone line (and paying for it) to another BITNET site. It also must agree to allow other universities to lease lines to it and to forward any information arriving via those lines.

**CDNnet** (Canada Network) is the first X.400 (email standard discussed in Chapter 8) network in the world and has its administrative headquarters at the University of British Columbia (UBC). CDNnet's primary function is electronic mail using the Ean implementation of X.400. This means it conforms to CCITT and ISO standards. The network resembles, in part, a star network with small organizations having a single link to the CDNnet headquarters at UBC. Larger organizations are permitted extra links to each other. Using gateways, CDNnet can connect to many other networks including the Internet.

**CERFnet** (California Education and Research Federation Network), founded in 1988, is a relative newcomer. Its members consist largely of California universities and research organizations. It is administered by officers of the California Education and Research Federation who are elected by member institutions. CERFnet supports both TCP/IP and DECNET protocols and has supercomputer access as one of its major goals. As such it supports link speeds up to the T1 range of 1.544 Mbps.

**CICNet** (Committee on Institutional Cooperation Network) is another relatively new network. Using T1 transmissions and the TCP/IP protocols, it connects educational institutions from seven midwestern states — Illinois, Indiana, Iowa, Michigan, Minnesota, Ohio, and Wisconsin. It is administered by a board of directors, one from each member institution.

**CompuServe** is not so much a computer network as it is an information service allowing subscribers to access a distributed database. It provides the service via a packet switching network, which allows a subscriber with a PC and modem to dial a local number and access a database providing a variety of services. Typical services allow subscribers to make airline reservations; get news, weather, or stock market information; participate in various forums; and do home shopping. Since it is an information service, subscribers are charged for their use based on time of day and modem speeds. It is similar to other information services such as Delphi, GEnie, and America on-line.

**CSNET** (Computer Science Network) connects academic, government, industrial, and nonprofit institutions primarily throughout the U.S. and Canada, although it does have overseas links. It was set up by the National Science Foundation and was designed to connect institutions involved in computer science or engineering related research. At the time this provided greater opportunities than did the DoD-owned ARPANET, which allowed only certain institutions to participate. CSNET is not actually a single network but, in fact, consists of several components (ARPANET, PHONENET, X25NET, and Cypress), each running its own lower-level protocols. CSNET is administered by the Coordination and Information Center at the BBN company in Cambridge, Massachusetts. The center provides the administrative, technical, and end-user support and makes all components act like a single network.

**Cypress** is a CSNET component and is similar to the ARPANET technology. It consists of UNIX-based packet switching nodes connected by leased lines.

**Datapac** is an example of a packet switched public data network. A public data network is one that provides network services for a fee and is used to gain access to many of the information services available. A Canadian network, Datapac was the first public X.25 network in the world.

**Dialcom** is an example of a public electronic mail service. It sells mailboxes and services allowing subscribers to communicate with each other. Dialcom is an X.400-based commercial mail service network and is used by groups such as the American Library Association, National Science Foundation, and Office of Naval Research.

**Dnet** (Deutschland Network) is the German component of EUnet, a UNIX-based European network. It uses the UUCP transport protocol on top of X.25 packet switched networks. It is a star network and is managed by a team of students and a faculty member who provide the technical support for the hub machine at Universität Dortmund.

**DREnet** (Defence Research Establishment Network) is a Canadian network linking sites doing research for the Canadian Department of National Defence (DND). As with other networks, the primary transport protocol is TCP/IP used on top of an X.25 packet switched network. The network was connected to the ARPANET in 1984 and is currently registered in the Internet under the domain name DND.CA.

**EASYnet** is a Digital Equipment Corporation product used largely by Digital employees. It provides file transfers, electronic mail, remote login, and intersystem resource sharing. It is administered by the Digital Telecommunications organization and is funded by the Digital Corporation. It uses 10 Mbps Ethernets and runs both the DECNET and TCP/IP protocols.

**EUnet** (European UNIX Network) began in the early 1980s by connecting sites in Denmark, the Netherlands, Sweden, and the United Kingdom. Today it spans Western Europe, with a backbone host in each member country, and provides connections to other countries and continents such as Japan, Korea, Australia, and North America. It is one of only three widely used networks in Western Europe. It is widely used by academic researchers in both universities and industry and is an important means of technology transfer. Like many European networks, it uses X.25 links but also uses TCP/IP in some locations. Representatives from each backbone host meet regularly to administer the network and plan for its growth and have implemented Internet DNS domains throughout EUnet.

**FidoNet** was developed in 1983 as an extension of the Fido Bulletin Board service. Most of the connections use a dialup protocol called Fido, which has features similar to those found in the XMODEM and ZMODEM protocols. FidoNet is accessible to anyone with a DOS machine. The network is worldwide and has a hierarchical organization, divided in zones dependent on geography. A unique feature is that administration is voluntary, being supported by various commercial organizations or computer clubs. FidoNet provides access to numerous mailer programs to provide message transfers. One example is a program named Arc, which uses Lempel-Ziv compression techniques to increase transfer rates. Most of the others are shareware, but a few are public domain.

**FNET** is the French component of EUnet. It is managed by the Institut de Recherche en Informatique et Automatique (INRIA), with the backbone machine located at inria.inria.fr. It supports the usual X.25 protocol, and has subnets that run the TCP/IP protocol.

**FUNET** (Finnish University Network) connects users in the Finnish universities and research establishments. It is a star network with the hub located at the Center for Scientific Computing in Helsinki. It uses the Ethernet technology heavily, connecting many sites with MAC-level bridges and network routers. The most commonly used higher-layer protocols are TCP/IP and DECNET, although it also supports NJE. Some of the FUNET sites are also experimenting with programs implementing OSI protocols.

**GEnie** (General Electric Network for Information Exchange), like Compuserve, is not really a network as much as an information service providing access to on-line databases. Users can get information on airline reservations, stock quotations, and hotel and automobile rates.

**HEPnet** (High Energy Physics Network), as the name suggests, connects laboratories where high-energy physics is researched. Originally it connected places such as Argonne National, Lawrence Berkeley, and the Fermi National Accelerator Laboratories and since has grown to connect sites in Europe and Japan. Much of the equipment is Digital, and the network depends heavily on the DECNET protocol.

**HP Internet**, a TCP/IP network operated by the Hewlett-Packard Corporation, is believed to be the largest TCP/IP network operated by a single organization. It is part of the Internet and connects sites throughout North America, Europe, Japan, and Australia. It was developed in the mid1980s because the then-current UUCP connections over dialup lines and X.25 links were too expensive and slow for corporate needs. Protocols below TCP/IP include Ethernet, X.25, T1 transmissions, and satellite links.

**Internet** is a collection of many networks all running the TCP/IP suite and connected by routers. The exact size of the Internet is difficult to know, but some estimates put it in excess of 500,000 hosts, 400 connected networks, and well over 1 million users. Participating networks run TCP/IP over X.25 networks, point-to-point, dialup, or T1 microwave links. Sites are accessed using the domain naming scheme discussed earlier in this chapter.

**JANET** (Joint Academic Network) originally connected universities and research institutions in the United Kingdom. Although primary sites are still research and educational institutions, it is connected to many other networks such as Internet, EUnet, and BITNET. Its services include file transfer, mail, remote login, and remote job entry. JANET uses a domain name system similar to that of the Internet but reverses the order of the components. Networks connected to JANET are typically Ethernets or X.25 networks using leased lines.

**JUNET** (Japan Unix Network), Japan's major network, allows its researchers to communicate with each other and with colleagues overseas. It connects all of Japan's major islands and has many sites near Tokyo and Osaka. It uses primarily UUCP over X.25, Ethernets, and dialup lines, although a few sites have implemented some OSI protocols. JUNET also uses the JIS (Japanese Industrial Standard) 16-bit codes for external communications. It defines codes for symbols used in several forms of Japanese writing, including Kanji, Hiragana, and Katakana, and also includes the ASCII code.

**MFEnet** (Magnetic Fusion Energy Network) was designed originally to connect physics departments doing nuclear fusion research. It uses several transport protocols to connect several underlying networks and provides access to supercomputers such as those at Lawrence Livermore National Laboratory and the Supercomputer Computations Research Institute at Florida State University. It has been expanded to provide service to all researchers funded by the Department of Energy.

**MIDnet** (Midwest Network) connects several midwestern universities from Illinois, Iowa, Nebraska, Kansas, Oklahoma, Arkansas, and Missouri in a ring using leased lines. Each of the links is a 56-Kbps leased line. The dominant protocol is TCP/IP, although some stations can support DECNET or SNA.

**MILNET** (Military Network) was developed using ARPANET research and is used primarily for military purposes. It connects military establishments throughout the U.S. with some in Japan, Korea, and the Philippines. MILNET and NFSNET are the backbone networks of the Internet. Although it uses TCP/IP, it uses static host tables rather than domain name servers for routing.

**MRNet** (Minnesota Regional Network) is an NFSNET regional network connecting several major Minnesota corporations and several of its colleges and universities. Included in these connections is a large proportion of the supercomputer industry in the U.S. It has an Ethernet backbone network connecting about a dozen sites and uses TCP/IP.

**NCSAnet** (National Center for Supercomputing Applications Network) is a regional TCP/IP network connecting NCSA supercomputers to the NFSNET backbone. Major sites are in Illinois, Indiana, and Wisconsin. It has two hubs, one at NCSA and the other at the University of Illinois–Chicago, with a T1 connection between the hubs. Each of these hubs, in turn, has links to other member sites.

**NORDUnet** (Nordic Network) is a cooperative effort by the Nordic countries to create an international network connecting Scandinavian universities with an international backbone Ethernet. It has a star organization with the Ethernet backbone located at Kungliga Tekniska Högskolan in Stockholm. The backbone runs all of X.25, TCP/IP, DECNET, and NJE. It also has or is planning connections to EUnet, HEPnet, NSFNET, and other networks.

**NSFNET** (National Science Foundation Network) is a large internet organized by the NSF designed to provide access to scientific resources and information. It consists of three levels of networks. First is a backbone network using T1 links to connect mid-level networks and NSF-funded supercomputer centers such as MIDnet, NCSA, and the John von Neumann Supercomputer Center. Second are the mid-level networks consisting of regional networks such as BARRNet and SURAnet, discipline-oriented networks such as USAN, and supercomputer consortium networks such as PSCnet and NCSA net. Third are the campus or commercial networks connected to the mid-level networks.

**OARnet** (Ohio Academic Resources Network) is a regional network connecting most of Ohio's academic institutions. It gives researchers access to libraries and supercomputers and facilitates cooperative research. Much of the funding is provided by the University of Ohio Board of Regents as part of the

Ohio Supercomputer Center budget. It supports the TCP/IP, DECNET, and NJE protocols and has access to the Internet via a T1 link to CICNet.

**PACNET** (Pacific Network) is an academic network connecting hosts throughout the Far East and southeast Asia. It uses the UUCP protocol and provides primarily mail and news services via dialup lines, the most common connections.

**PeaceNet** was founded on the premise of using computer conferencing to promote the peace movement. It is operated by the Institute for Global Communication, a division of the Tides Foundation, a public charity. Access to PeaceNet is primarily through dialup lines and allows access to a database containing information on various peace groups, speakers, and foundations. Conference topics include information on presidential candidates, nuclear weapons, and foreign affairs.

**PhoneNet** is a CSNET component and a store-and-forward electronic mail network. It is also a star network with the central hub at Bolt Baranek and Newman (BBN) in Cambridge, Massachusetts. Stations connect to the central location using low-speed telephone lines.

**PSCnet** (Pittsburgh Supercomputing Center Network) is the Pittsburgh Supercomputer Center's (PSC) network and connects to sites in Pennsylvania, Michigan, Oklahoma, and Maryland, providing access to supercomputer resources. Its establishment was a cooperative effort between Carnegie-Mellon University and the University of Pittsburgh.

**SPEARNET** (South Pacific Educational and Research Network) was developed by the universities in Australia and New Zealand for the purpose of academic research and teaching. It is the primary academic network in New Zealand. It is centrally administered and receives some government funding. It provides the usual services of remote login, mail, news, and file transfer, and work is under way that would eventually transform it into a backbone research network similar to NSFNET.

**SURAnet** (Southeastern Universities Research Association Network), developed in the late 1980s, connects sites throughout the southeastern states and the District of Columbia. It was supported by major research universities in that region for the primary purpose of promoting cooperative research. It provides access to supercomputers at some of the region's larger universities.

**Telenet** (not to be confused with the TELNET application layer protocol) is reported to be the world's largest public data network, spanning over 40 countries. It was developed in 1975 by General Telephone and Electric (GTE) and has been purchased by U.S. Sprint and renamed SprintNet. It provides access to many commercial information services and also offers telemail, an X.400-based mail service that is accessible using a portable terminal. It also offers a medical information service, Minet, that allows physicians to access a database covering medical practices.

**THEnet** (Texas Higher Education Network) is another regional network connecting academic, research, and private institutions throughout Texas. It is also one of the mid-level networks of NSFNET. DECNET is a common protocol, although many of the campuses use TCP/IP.

**TYMNET** is another very large public data network providing access to information services such Delphi, TRW Information Services, and Dow Jones News and Retrieval. It contains over 1400 packet switching nodes interconnected by leased lines, microwave, and satellite links. It supports numerous protocols such as X.25, BSC, X.75, and X.PC, a protocol similar to X.25 that allows PC access through dialup lines.

**UKnet** (United Kingdom UNIX Network) is the British branch of EUnet. It is run from the University of Kent at Canterbury in cooperation with the UK UNIX systems users group. It has a gateway machine providing access to JANET using UUCP connections.

**USAN** (University Satellite Network) connects several major U.S. universities and naval and oceanographic research institutes to the National Center for Atmospheric Research (NCAR) using satellite and VSAT technology. NCAR also has a link to BITNET and supports an Internet gateway capable of translating remote login, file transfers, and mail between DECNET and TCP/IP.

**USENET** (User's Network) is one of the largest networks connecting hosts on five continents. It is unique in several ways. First, it supports primarily one service. Its distributed conferencing service is a generalization of a mail or bulletin board service allowing people to "post" information or to initiate and participate in discussions. Second, it has no central funding or authority determining who can get access. All a site needs is its own resources and another computer with which to communicate.

**UUCP** (UNIX to UNIX Copy Program) refers to both a transport protocol and a network. It is worldwide and primarily connects machines ranging from PCs to supercomputers that run UNIX. It was the first UNIX network and was designed to use telephone lines. Like USENET, it has a very decentralized organization and provides a single primary service—mail.

**UUNET** began as an experiment proposed to the board of directors of the USENIX (the oldest and largest UNIX users group) association to enhance the service provided by UUCP and USENET. Its primary function is the transfer of mail and news between the UUCP and USENET networks. It also provides a gateway to the Internet and has direct connections to many networks worldwide allowing it to forward mail from its subscribers to almost any known network in the world.

**VNET** is IBM's internal network providing mail, file transfer, and remote login services to IBM employees. Anyone receiving mail on VNET must be a registered user. VNET is actually two networks consisting of the RSCS (remote spooling communications subsystem) network for mail and file transfer and the Passthru VM (virtual machine) network for remote login.

**X25Net** is a CSNET component and runs TCP/IP on top of X.25. It is part of the Internet and is also used for members outside the United States to connect to CSNET.

**XEROX Internet** consists of two highly interconnected networks, the Xerox Research Internet (RIN) and the Xerox Corporate Internet (CIN). RIN is designed for research needs and CIN is designed to be a stable backbone for the corporate needs. Both use the Xerox network services (XNS) protocol suite, an in-house protocol that is used little outside of the Xerox Corporation, to provide transparent connections and application sharing. RIN does use TCP/IP at some sites.

## 7.7   Summary

This chapter covered wide area networks and some of the common protocols that make them work. Specifically, we covered four aspects of wide area network operations: routing strategies, the X-series of protocols for public data networks, network layer protocols including the Internet Protocol, and transport layer protocols including TCP. We capped the section with a list and short description of several dozen actual networks in use today.

Routing strategies deal with how packets are transferred between two stations. We discussed four basic routing types:

1. Centralized: Routing information is maintained in a central location.
2. Distributed: Routing information is distributed among the nodes.
3. Static: Routing information does not change due to varying network conditions.
4. Adaptive: Changing network conditions alter routing information.

One way to manage routing information is to use routing tables that specify where to forward incoming packets. Maintaining them depends on the routing algorithms used. We discussed a few approaches such as

- Dijkstra's algorithm, a centralized algorithm designed to determine the cheapest path between two nodes.
- the Bellman-Ford algorithm, a distributed approach by which each node would communicate information on reachable nodes to each of its neighbors.
- hierarchical routing, in which nodes are divided into groups (domains), each of which has its own routing protocol.
- the Routing Information Protocol, used for interdomain communication where designated domain nodes exchange information with each other regarding reachable networks and the number of hops required to get there.

Finally, we discussed two problems that can occur during routing. Congestion develops when a node receives more packets than it can handle efficiently, thus causing an increase in the time required to forward them. Deadlock occurs when there is a circular list of nodes, each of which cannot forward any frames to the next one in the list.

Next, we discussed packet switched networks and two modes of operations. In a datagram service all packets are transmitted independently. In a virtual call service two stations must establish a connection during which a logical circuit (path) is defined. All subsequent packets transmitted follow that path. A popular standard for communicating with public data networks is the X.25 standard. It corresponds to the lower three protocol layers for communication between a DTE and network DCE. It defines packet format, connection establishment/termination, and the exchange of data packets.

For sites that do not have X.25 devices to communicate with a public data network, other protocols make communication possible. The X.3 packet assembler/disassembler (PAD) replaces the DCE as a network interface. The PAD then communicates with a non-X.25 device using the X.28 standard protocol and with a remote host using the X.29 standard protocol.

Another common layer 3 protocol is the DoD's Internet protocol (IP) used in the Internet. It allows the transfer of data over dissimilar networks and makes the differences transparent to higher-layer protocols. IP defines packet format, routing options, types of service, and ways to deal with fragmented packets too large to travel some networks. It uses hierarchical routing, thus requiring addresses to be specified using a "dotted" notation. The one thing that IP does not do is guarantee delivery of its packets. Consequently, another protocol, the Internet Control Message Protocol (ICMP), does error reporting and provides routers with updates on conditions that develop in the Internet. It defines different control/error messages and transmits them via the IP.

Transport protocols are the lowest-layer protocol that deal with end-user communication and work independently of network operations. A common protocol used in the Internet is the Transmission Control Protocol (TCP), a connection-oriented protocol. Some of the primary functions are connection management, flow control, and error detection. Effectively, TCP guarantees the reliable exchange of information. Some unique aspects of TCP are:

- Definition of a single-segment format for both data and control.
- Three-way handshake that requires not only an acknowledgment of a connection request but an acknowledgment of the acknowledgment.
- A credit mechanism for flow control similar to sliding window protocols.

There are no formal standards for interfacing with TCP at a higher layer, but there are two common approaches. One is to use TCP primitive operations that define the request/confirmation exchange between TCP and its users. The other is the socket interface used by many UNIX-based systems.

The ISO also has defined several transport protocols: TP0, TP1, TP2, TP3, and TP4. They differ in part in the type of networks over which they run. TP4 is most similar to TCP, but with several important differences: It defines multiple segment formats for greater flexibility, uses a different disconnect strategy, handles important data differently, and has a different flow control.

# Review Questions

1. What is a protocol converter?

2. At what OSI layers can protocol converters exist? List common ones and their names.

3. To what layer does TCP/IP correspond?

4. What is a routing table?

5. List the four major routing classifications and state what is characteristic of each.

6. Are the following TRUE or FALSE? Why?

   a. Distributed routing requires routing tables at each node.

   b. Adaptive routing allows a node to update its routing tables.

   c. Shortest path and cheapest path are generally the same.

   d. Hierarchical routing organizes all network nodes into a tree structure.

   e. Congestion means that all of a network's paths have become clogged with traffic.

   f. Congestion does not always lead to deadlock.

   g. The X.25 protocol defines packet switched network operations.

   h. Distinct virtual circuits may overlap.

   i. A datagram service will not deliver packets in the correct order.

   j. The triple-X protocols are typically used where there is not an X.25 device.

   k. The Internet protocol provides reliable delivery of packets.

   l. TCP provides reliable delivery of packets.

7. Distinguish between a forward search and a backward search algorithm.

8. What is hierarchical routing?

9. What is the purpose of using names and symbols in the Internet addressing rather than the assigned numerical numbers?

10. What is a domain name server?

11. List common Internet domains.

12. What do nodes that use the routing information protocol maintain in their routing tables?

13. Distinguish between network congestion and deadlock.

14. List some ways to deal with congestion.

15. What are the two types of deadlock?

16. Why does assigning packets to specific buffers, as shown in Figure 7.18, prevent store-and-forward deadlock?

17. What is a virtual circuit?

18. What is a packet switched network?

19. Why can't each node in a virtual circuit use the same number to identify the circuit?

20. What is a datagram service?

21. What does the X.25 standard define?

22. List the X.25 packet types related to call establishment.

23. How does a permanent virtual circuit differ from a virtual circuit?

24. What is a packet assembler/disassembler?

25. List the main functions of the triple-X protocols X.3, X.28, and X.29.

26. What is a virtual terminal?

27. Why is IP-packet fragmenting sometimes necessary?

28. List some major functions of IP.

29. What is the time-to-live field in an IP packet?

30. What is a maximum transfer unit? How does it affect the Internet protocol?

31. Distinguish between an Internet address and a physical address.

32. What is dynamic binding?

33. What is the Internet control message protocol used for?

34. List typical control messages defined by ICMP.

35. What is a timestamp request?

36. What is a handshake?

37. What is an urgent pointer?

38. Distinguish between a two-way and a three-way handshake.

39. What is a TCP credit?

40. List TCP primitives related to connection management.

41. What is a UNIX socket?

42. What is the User Datagram Protocol?

43. List and distinguish the five OSI transport protocol standards.

# Exercises

1. How many distinct routes are there from $X$ to $Y$ in the network of Figure 7.2?

2. Define the routing tables for all the nodes in the network in Figure 7.3.

3. Create a routing matrix for the following network. In cases where two routes have the cheapest cost, choose the one containing the fewest nodes. If both criteria are the same then choose one arbitrarily.

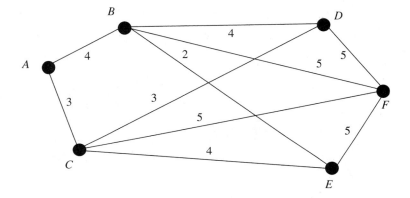

4. Apply Dijkstra's cheapest path algorithm to the following network. Create a table similar to Table 7.2 showing pertinent values at each step of the algorithm.

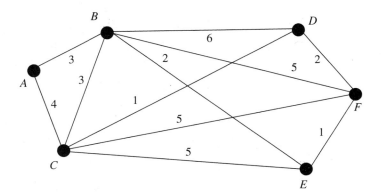

5. Design an algorithm that, when run after Dijkstra's algorithm, will list all nodes on the cheapest path to a given destination.

6. Using terminology from Dijkstra's algorithm, prove that whenever the Cost($V$) function is changed, it still represents the cheapest route from $A$ to $V$ via nodes in $S$.

7. The premise of the Bellman-Ford algorithm is that if Cost($A$, $Z$) is the cost of the cheapest route from node $A$ to $Z$ and $A$ has a direct connection to nodes $B$, $C$, $D$ then

$$\text{Cost}(A, Z) = \begin{cases} \text{cost of link from } A \text{ to } B + \text{cost of cheapest route from } B \text{ to } Z \\ \text{cost of link from } A \text{ to } C + \text{cost of cheapest route from } C \text{ to } Z \\ \vdots \\ \text{cost of link from } A \text{ to } D + \text{cost of cheapest route from } D \text{ to } Z \end{cases}$$

Why is this premise valid? That is, prove this assertion.

8. Create tables similar to Tables 7.4a through 7.4c by applying the Bellman-Ford algorithm to the following network.

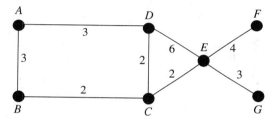

9. How is the routing information protocol similar to the Bellman-Ford algorithm?

10. Consider Figure 7.21. Suppose $A$ establishes a virtual circuit to $D$, and $B$ establishes a virtual circuit to $C$. If both virtual circuits go through $X$ and $Y$, what would $X$'s and $Y$'s routing tables look like?

11. Suppose a router at $A$ in the figure shown here receives an IP packet containing 4000 data bytes, fragments the packet, and routes the fragments to $B$ via network 1. $B$ in turn routes all the fragments except the second one to $C$ via network 3. However, it fragments the second one and sends the fragments to $C$ via network 2. Show the fragments that $C$ receives and specify relevant values in the fragment headers.

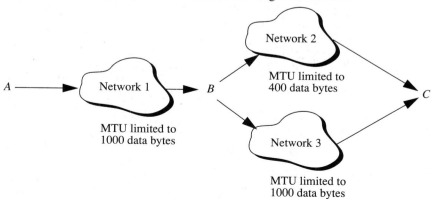

**12.** In IP fragmentation, why is the identification field in the fragment header necessary? Why can't the destination simply use the source address to determine related packets and reassemble them according to the offset field values?

**13.** What does the routing table from Figure 7.33b look like if Figure 7.33a is changed as follows?

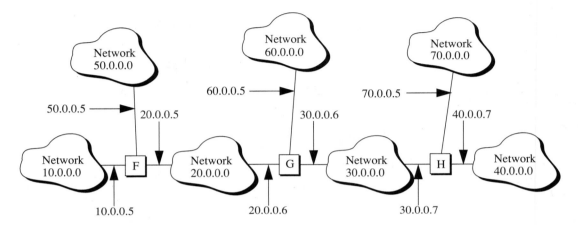

**14.** In the previous exercise, what do the routing tables for *F* and *H* look like?

**15.** Why don't TCP segments contain the number of data bytes each one has? How is the receiving TCP entity supposed to know how many data bytes to extract from it?

**16.** Suppose TCP entities *A* and *B* have initial sequence numbers 400 and 900, respectively; each segment contains 100 data bytes; and each has an initial credit of 200 bytes. Suppose *A* is capable (flow control permitting) of sending TCP segments at intervals of time *T* (starting at *T* = 0) and that *B* is capable of sending its segments at intervals of time 3*T* (starting at time 1.5*T*). Assuming the transmission time between *A* and *B* is negligible, sketch a diagram similar to Figure 7.40 showing the segment exchange up to time 12*T*.

**17.** Repeat Exercise 16 assuming *A*'s credit increases to 300 after it receives the second segment from *B*.

**18.** What actual networks are accessible at (or near) your school or place of business?

## REFERENCES

1. Aho, A., J. Hopcroft, and J. Ullman. *Data Structures and Algorithms*. Reading, MA: Addison-Wesley, 1983.

2. Spragins, J. D., J. L. Hammond, and K. Pawlikowski. *Telecommunications Protocols and Design*. Reading, MA: Addison-Wesley, 1991.

3. Stallings, W. *Data and Computer Communications,* 4th ed. New York: Macmillan, 1994.

4. Walrand, J. *Communications Networks: A First Course.* Boston: Richard D. Irwin, 1991.

5. Tsuchiya, P. F. and T. Eng. "Extending the IP Internet Through Address Reuse." *Computer Communication Review,* vol. 23, no. 1 (January 1993), 16–33.

6. Tanenbaum, A. S. *Computer Networks,* 2nd ed. Englewood Cliffs, NJ: Prentice-Hall, 1988.

7. Merlin, P. M. and P. J. Schweitzer. "Deadlock Avoidance in Store-and-Forward Networks I: Store-and-Forward Deadlock." *IEEE Transactions on Communications,* vol. COM-28 (March 1980), 345–54.

8. Black, U. *The X Series Recommendations.* New York: McGraw-Hill, 1991.

9. Russel, D. *The Principles of Computer Networking.* Cambridge University Press, 1989.

10. Quarterman, J. *The Matrix: Computer Networks and Conferencing Systems Worldwide.* Bedford, MA: Digital Press, 1990.

11. Comer, D. E. *Internetworking with TCP/IP. Volume I: Principles, Protocols, and Architecture,* 2nd ed. Englewood Cliffs, NJ: Prentice-Hall, 1991.

12. Rose, M. *The Simple Book: An Introduction to Management of TCP/IP.* Englewood Cliffs, NJ: Prentice-Hall, 1991.

13. Comer, D. E. *Internetworking with TCP/IP. Volume II: Design, Implementation, and Internals.* Englewood Cliffs, NJ: Prentice-Hall, 1991.

14. Black, U. *Data Networks: Concepts, Theory, and Practice.* Englewood Cliffs, NJ: Prentice-Hall, 1989.

15. Kochran, S. G. and P. H. Wood. *UNIX Networking.* Indianapolis: Hayden Books, 1989.

# CHAPTER 8

## ADDITIONAL NETWORK PROTOCOLS

### 8.1 TCP Applications

The purpose of this section is to discuss several applications designed to run on TCP/IP networks. Many of these applications involve interaction between programs running on different computers on the network, so we begin by introducing a common paradigm known as the **client-server model** used to support such interaction.

### CLIENT-SERVER MODEL[*]

A client-server model defines a basis for communication between two programs called, strangely enough, the client and server. A **server** is any application that provides a service to a network user. A **client** is any program that makes a request to a server. In general, a client and a server run on different computers. There are many examples of servers, including the following:

- **File server**. One of a network's most useful applications is the ability of users to share files. The actual files must be stored somewhere. Storing them locally near a user is one option, but not always a good one if many users need it. Instead, many networks designate one or more PCs as a file server whose sole purpose is storing, managing, and providing access to files. A network user who needs information from a file must go through the server to get it.

- **Print server**. In many ways, sharing a printer is like sharing a file. One or more printers are connected to the network and accessed when needed by network

---

[*] Portions of this section are reprinted from William A. Shay's *Introduction to Operating Systems* (Reference 1). Reprinted by permission of Harper Collins.

users. The server will handle and queue print requests and inform the user on completion of the print request.

- **Communications server**. A communications server manages communication lines to another device such as a network host computer. There are multiple connections between the device and the server. On request, the server establishes a connection between a user and the host, which allows the user and host to interact as though they were connected directly. The number of requests that can be handled at one time depends on the number of connections between server and host. Another common use for a communication server is to provide access to a modem pool (collection of modems). The intent, of course, is to provide modem capabilities to network users.

- **Fax server**. Fax machines digitize images and transmit them over telephone lines. Since the technology is well established, a growing trend is to digitize images and store them on a disk for later transmission. This system is useful where many people need fax capabilities. Rather than each user having a fax machine, a single fax machine can be connected to a network. A fax server then handles user requests and routes them to the fax for transmission.

Two common ways for a client and server to interact are message passing and the **remote procedure call** (**RPC**). An RPC resembles a conventional call in a language such as Pascal, but there are differences. For example:

- The client and server run on different computers.

- A client must pass all parameters by value rather than by reference. The reason is that passing a parameter by reference amounts to passing its address. If the server runs on a separate computer, however, it cannot access the client's memory.

- Servers often run with a higher or "privileged" priority, which allows them to access system resources that a client cannot. This is often required due to the nature of the service the server provides.

- Suspension and resumption mechanisms are necessary for timely execution of services. A service should not be provided before the client is ready, and the client often must be suspended until the service is completed.

RPCs are commonly implemented using send and receive communications primitives. The **send** primitive specifies a destination and a list of items to transmit. The client provides the list, but the destination information is usually determined by communication protocols. Ideally, a client should be able to specify which service is needed and depend on the protocol to make the connection. Hiding precise locations from the client makes these primitives especially useful in distributed systems.

The **receive** primitive specifies a source and a list of items to receive. The source is needed so that the server may eventually respond to the client. A server will not provide a service until after it executes a receive. When a client executes a send primitive, the list of items is sent, and it waits for the service to be done. When a receiver executes a receive, it receives the list of transmitted items. If they have not yet been sent, it waits. An example client and server outline follows.

| CLIENT | SERVER |
|---|---|
| : | : |
| : | : |
| send(server, list) | receive(client, list) |
| wait | do something |
| receive (server, list) | send(client, list) |
| : | : |
| : | : |

After the client executes the send primitive, it enters a wait state. It will remain there until the server provides the service and responds. After the server executes a receive, it performs its task, sends a message back to the client, and continues. When the client receives the message, it also continues. Problems can occur when processes run on different computers; for example:

- Messages may be lost or garbled due to transmission interference.
- The server or client could abort between its send and receive primitives.
- What if a server executes a receive, but there is no client asking for a service? More generally, how does a receiver know when to execute a receive?

Usually a timer mechanism prevents either process from waiting forever. In addition, conditional statements allow a server to execute a variety of receive primitives or to do other things if no calls are pending. Problems become even more complex when clients make many calls to different servers and servers receive many calls from different clients.

The other mode of interaction between a client and server, **message passing**, requires that they establish a session between them. Once it is established, they exchange information by passing messages back and forth according to a specified protocol. We will describe some of these protocols shortly.

Different types of server design can vary considerably. Simple servers handle requests as they arrive. That is, they provide their services sequentially. This is usually appropriate if the services can be done quickly and the number of requests is not excessive. Suppose, however, a file server receives two requests, one requiring the transfer of a very large file and the other requiring access to a single entry from a small file. If the short request arrives after the lengthy one, that user may wait an excessive amount of time given the nature of its request.

An alternative design is to divide the server into two parts: a master and slave server. The **master server** processes incoming requests from clients. When one arrives it activates a **slave server** to perform the service. Two features distinguish this approach from the sequential processing of requests. First, the master can continue accepting new requests, after activating the slave. Second, the master can activate multiple slaves, which can run concurrently, each providing a different service. Because of the concurrency, services are not necessarily handled in sequence. For example, the previously mentioned short and long file service requests correspond to two different processes running concurrently and sharing the computer's resources. Many operating system scheduling mechanisms allow its processes to take turns running. Consequently, the short process will not necessarily wait for the long one to finish.

Concurrent servers do provide the advantage of eliminating the strict sequentiality, but it is not without cost. Additional complexity is required to manage multiple requests concurrently. The underlying operating system must provide concurrent processing capabilities. Separate requests are not always independent. For example, what happens if two slave servers are attempting to update the same file? There are many interesting issues and problems in client-server computing. The interested reader can find more information in references 2 and 3.

## VIRTUAL TERMINAL

Networks provide communication between many types of equipment and software. One significant problem is that software is often written with specific equipment in mind. Full-screen text editors are examples. The editor displays text on a screen and allows the user to move the cursor and make changes. But the displayed number of rows and columns varies from one terminal type to another. Commands to move the cursor, delete, and insert text require control sequences that often vary by terminal type. Perhaps you have noticed that different terminals have different keyboards. Some sequences are not even available on some models.

Other examples include software that depends on screen formats for input. Often layouts provide a simple, uncluttered view of a user's options. Spacing, tabs, and highlighting help the user work with the software. But, again, such features are terminal dependent. In some cases the screen layout even is dependent on the font used and its size. It would be nice if programs could access a full range of screen-oriented functions, regardless of the terminal. But how can we achieve this?

Translation problems also apply to **smart terminals** that have local computing power. This is a typical approach in a client-server model in which computing power is provided in two locations, the user site and the remote site. A user runs a remote application (server program) that provides information to the user. The user then can make changes locally (using client software). For example, suppose that accounting software on a server can display a full screen of tax information from a remote database. An accountant can examine the information and determine its validity. Using the client, he or she can correct mistakes or make updates locally. The client's processor makes all the changes, and the server has no knowledge of them. When the changes are complete, the accountant sends the information to the server, which stores it in the remote database.

This approach has a major advantage: It does not require any communication during editing, thus reducing the network workload. Only the final version is transmitted. The problem is that client configurations vary considerably. How can we allow different ones to access common software?

One approach uses a **virtual terminal protocol**. A **virtual terminal** is a data structure maintained by either the application software or a local terminal. Its contents represent the state of the terminal. For example, they may include the current cursor position, reverse video indicator, cursor shape, number of rows and columns, and color. Both the user and the application can reference this structure. The application writes to the virtual terminal without worrying about terminal-specific matters. Virtual terminal software does the required translation, and the data is displayed. When a user enters data, the process works in reverse. Virtual terminal protocols define the format of the data structure, software converts user input to a standard form, and the application then reads the standard "screen."

Virtual terminals may contain more data than the screen can display. This is especially useful when scrolling. For example, suppose the virtual terminal can store 200 lines in a buffer but only 24 can appear on the screen at a time. Information in the virtual terminal will specify the first and last lines of displayed data (Figure 8.1). The displayed data is the **window** and it is marked by **window delimiters**. If the user enters a scroll command, the virtual terminal software simply changes the window delimiters. The result is that different text lines are displayed on the terminal.

## TELNET

One example of a network virtual terminal protocol is TELNET. It was designed for the ARPANET and is one of the protocols in the TCP/IP suite. Perhaps most people know TELNET as the application that allows **remote logins**.

To the user, a remote login appears to be no different than a login to a local computer (Figure 8.2a). However, Figure 8.2b reflects the situation more accurately. A user works at a PC (or is connected to another computer) that runs protocols to connect to a network. The protocols establish a connection over the network to a

FIGURE 8.1    **Windowing of Buffered Text**

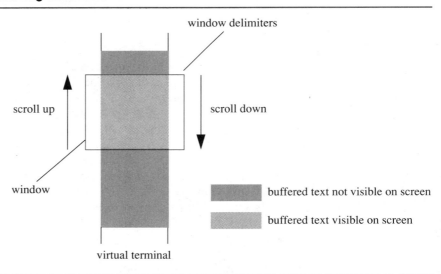

FIGURE 8.2     **Remote Connection**

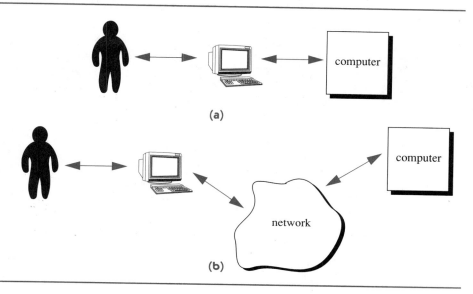

(a)

(b)

remote computer. The user and remote computer exchange commands and data using protocols such as those discussed in Chapter 7. The user is working at a higher layer, however, so this is all transparent and appears much like a local login. The only difference may be slight delays between responses, especially if the remote computer is far away or network traffic is heavy.

TELNET works in a **client-server** mode (Figure 8.3). That is, a PC (or other computer) runs TELNET (client) locally and transmits data between the user and network protocols. It also can format and send specific commands, some of which we will describe shortly. The remote computer also runs its version of TELNET (server). It performs similar functions, exchanging data between network protocols and the operating system and interpreting user-transmitted commands.

A user typically uses TELNET in one of two ways. First is to login to a local computer, wait for a system prompt ("$" in our example), and enter the command

$TELNET *internet-address*

The Internet address specifies the computer to which the user wants to connect. TELNET then calls on the transport protocol to negotiate and establish a connection with the remote site. Once connected, the user must login to the remote site by specifying the account number and password. The second way to use TELNET is to enter the command TELNET without an Internet address. The local system will respond with a TELNET prompt ("TELNET>"). At this point the user can enter TELNET commands or connect to the remote site by entering a "connect" or "open" command (depending on the local system) specifying the Internet address.

## FIGURE 8.3    Telnet Client-Server Relation

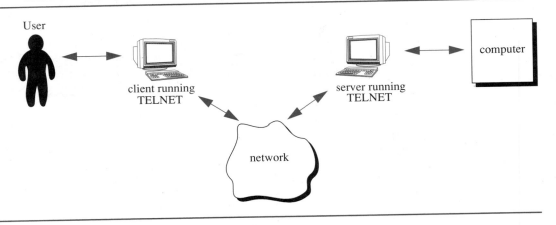

Once connected, TELNET works in the background completely transparent to the user. However, the user can "escape" from the remote login to give subsequent commands to TELNET. This is normally done by entering a control sequence such as "CTRL]". This returns the TELNET prompt back to the user but does not break the remote connection.

Table 8.1 shows some of the TELNET commands. Each command is coded and sent as an 8-bit number. To distinguish a command from data that may have the same 8-bit value, each command is preceded by the 8-bit IAC code (11111111). Consequently, receipt of this code tells TELNET to interpret the next byte as a command. In the event the IAC code appears in data, TELNET performs byte stuffing, inserting an extra IAC code in the stream, to distinguish data from command. In some cases TELNET may send a sequence of commands. In this case the IAC code is followed by the SB code (see Table 8.1), the list of coded commands, and finally the SE code. That is, SB and SE delimit the list of commands transmitted in one stream.

Let's give an example showing how a command may be sent. Suppose you have logged in to a remote host and are about to get a directory listing by entering the command "dir," but you inadvertently entered "dirr." Your usual response is to backspace or enter the delete key to eliminate the second 'r'. But what if the remote host does not recognize those keys? One option is to proceed as follows:[*]

```
$dirr <CTRL]>
TELNET>send EC
TELNET>resume
$hit return key
```

---

[*]This example was done using a VMS/Ultrix connection and may differ depending on the system on which you run.

TABLE 8.1    **TELNET Commands**

| COMMAND | ASCII VALUE | DESCRIPTION |
|---|---|---|
| Abort output (AO) | 245 | Terminates the output of a process initiated on the remote host while allowing the process to continue running. Can be used when the remote host does not recognize the "CTRL O" command. |
| Are you there (AYT) | 246 | Asks the remote host whether it is running. |
| Subnegotiation begin (SB) | 250 | The starting delimiter for a sequence of TELNET commands. |
| Break (BRK) | 243 | Terminates the process on the remote machine, a useful feature if the process is stuck in a loop or is generating more output than you care to have, such as the text for a political speech. |
| Do | 253 | Part of a negotiation that allows the client and server to agree on an option or set of parameters (discussed shortly). Can indicate a request for the other site to use a particular option. May also be a response to a "Will" command indicating that it will do the requested option. |
| Don't | 254 | A response to a "Will" command indicating that it will not do the requested option. |
| Subnegotiation end (SE) | 240 | The ending delimiter for a sequence of TELNET commands. |
| Erase character (EC) | 247 | Erases the most recent character entered on the remote host. Useful if the remote does not recognize your backspace or delete key. |
| Erase line (EL) | 248 | Erases the most recent line entered on the remote host. |
| Go ahead (GA) | 249 | Used when the remote host and user synchronize their exchanges, it tells the remote host it can send. |
| Interpret as command (IAC) | 255 | Instructs the receiving TELNET to interpret the next byte as a command. |
| Interrupt process (IP) | 244 | Terminates the process on the remote machine. |
| No operation (NOP) | 241 | Sends a no-operation command to the remote host. Technically a NOP does nothing, but it can be used to determine whether the connection exists. If the connection is broken and you send a NOP, you will get an error message. |
| Will | 251 | It can indicate a request that the other site use a particular option. It can also be a response to a "Do" command indicating that it will do the requested option. |
| Won't | 252 | A response to a "Do" command indicating that it will not do the requested option. |

TABLE 8.2   **TELNET Options**

| OPTION | MEANING |
|---|---|
| autoflush | When enabled and an interrupt character is sent, any data in the display buffers are flushed and the display terminated. Otherwise the display continues until the buffer is empty. |
| autosynch | When enabled the interrupt character is sent as urgent data. Otherwise it is sent in sequence with any other characters. |
| binary transmission | End-of-line characters are not mapped to the ASCII control characters <CR> and <LF>. This is necessary when transmitting binary data. |
| crlf | Causes the client to put the ASCII control characters <CR> and <LF> at the end of each line it sends. This is needed if the remote system expects these characters at the end of each line. |
| crmod | Causes the client to make sure that each line the user receives ends with the ASCII control characters <CR> and <LF>. This causes received lines to scroll upward on the screen. |
| local characters | Determines whether control sequences are interpreted by the client or the remote server. |
| terminal-type | Specifies information regarding the type of terminal and its characteristics. This is necessary for programs such as full-screen text editors that utilize cursor positions. |

The first line shows the system prompt ($) followed by the incorrectly entered command (dirr). If the user has discovered his typing error he can respond by entering the "control ]" sequence. This causes the user to escape to TELNET, where he can enter "send EC" (second line). This causes the EC command to be sent, effectively erasing the second 'r' in line 1. In line 3 the user enters a "resume" command to reestablish the TELNET session. Finally in line 4 the user presses the return key and gets the directory listing.

The number of TELNET options is extensive, and they vary depending on the software and hardware you run. Consequently, we do not attempt a complete description of them. Instead we list a few of the more common options in Table 8.2. The options have codes that are specified during the option negotiation phase. The best way to get detailed knowledge of how to use TELNET is through the documentation provided with your system.

## FILE TRANSFERS

One of the most common network applications is file transfer. It has many uses. People working on group projects or doing related research often must share files. The ability to access and transfer files is essential for information sharing. Instructors create files for students to use in programming assignments. Applications such as airline reservations and electronic banking also require the access and transfer of at least part of a file.

Logistics play an important role in file transfer. In some cases, different people may create files that are maintained on different computers. This is a **distributed file system**. In other cases, all files are in one place, and a **file server** manages them. In any case, when a user wants to transfer a file he or she makes a request to the appropriate application. It, in turn, observes the network's file transfer protocols. What must the protocol handle?

The first consideration is the file structure, which varies. For example, some files consist of a simple sequence of bytes. Others are flat files consisting of a linear sequence of records. Hashed files allow random access to a record through a key field value. Hierarchical files may organize all occurrences of a key field in a tree structure.[*] These differences pose a problem when transferring files.

One way to simplify transfers between incompatible systems is to define a **virtual file structure**, one supported by the network for the purpose of file transfer. Figure 8.4 shows the transfer process. User *A* wants to transfer a file to user *B*, but they work on computers that support different file systems. User *A*'s file must be translated into a network-defined structure. The file transfer protocol then handles the actual transfer, and the file finally is converted to a structure supported by user *B*'s computer.

Virtual files must preserve the essential ingredients of a file. For example, it must contain the file's name, attributes, and coded information on the actual structure to allow for proper translation. Of course, it must also contain the data.

Another issue in file transfer is accessibility. A file transfer system should not honor every request. It must consider protection. Is the file read-only? Can the user update the file or execute its contents? For that matter is the requester allowed access at all? Law enforcement and defense agencies would not want a system that

---

**FIGURE 8.4**    **File Transfer Between Computers Supporting Different File Structures**

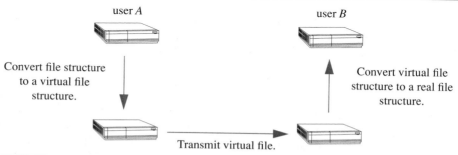

---

[*] Be sure to distinguish between a file's structure and its implementation. For example, a file may be hierarchical, but there are many implementations of a hierarchical structure.

allows access to all of their files. Multiple accesses to files also must be considered. Are they allowed? Passwords, locks, and keys are used for file protection and concurrency control.

**FTP—File Transfer Protocol**    One common file transfer protocol is called just that—**File Transfer Protocol** (**FTP**). It is another protocol in the TCP/IP suite. It is built on the same client-server paradigm as TELNET. A user, interacting with a local FTP program, connects to a remote site also running FTP. This is done in one of two ways. First is to simply enter the command

ftp *remote-host-address*

which will establish a connection to the specified remote computer, much as TELNET does. The second way is to enter

ftp

and wait for the prompt "ftp>". Next the user enters

ftp> open *remote-host-address*

to establish the connection. Sometimes "connect" is used instead of "open". Once connected, the user is asked to enter a user identification followed by a password. On entering the appropriate identification and password the user then can peruse subdirectories, get directory lists, and get copies of files.

Many sites make files available to the general Internet community. This means a user can access them without having an account on that machine. When a user connects to the site she usually enters "anonymous" for the account name and either "guest" or her Internet address as the password. The latter is to track use of accesses. This application is often called **anonymous FTP**.

On the surface, FTP looks just like TELNET: Both allow a user to establish a remote connection. The difference is that TELNET allows a legitimate login and FTP primarily provides access to certain files and directories.

Once the FTP connection is established the user sees the prompt "FTP>". At that point she has many choices. As before we do not try to cover all the commands; instead we summarize some of the most commonly used ones in Table 8.3. The user can get information on the commands by typing "help" or a question mark (?). Probably the most commonly used commands are "cd" to change the working directory in the remote host and "get", which copies a file from the remote to the local site.

Anonymous FTP allows files and technical reports to be made available to the general Internet community. Just what is available depends on what the remote site has put in the anonymous FTP account. There are hundreds of FTP sites, and their contents may change often, so we make no attempt to list them. We will, however, present an example showing how to use FTP to get access to a wide range of Internet information and how to use TELNET to determine FTP sites.

One series of documents available via FTP is the **request for comment** (**RFC**) series, research notes available in electronic or printed form. They cover a wide range of topics such as Internet protocols, network management and administration,

TABLE 8.3    **FTP Commands**

| COMMAND | MEANING |
| --- | --- |
| cd | Changes the working directory on the remote host. |
| close | Closes the FTP connection. |
| dir or ls | Provides a directory listing of the current working directory. |
| get | Copies the specified file from the remote host to the local system. The local file gets the same name as the one on the remote host. In the event there is incompatibility between naming conventions or the user simply wishes to give the transferred file a different name, he or she can specify a second parameter indicating a local file name. |
| glob | Acts as a toggle allowing or disallowing the use of wildcard characters. For example, if * is a wildcard character and its use is allowed then "mget *.TXT" would get all files with a "TXT" extension. |
| help | Displays a list of all client FTP commands. |
| mget | Copies multiple files from the remote host to the local system. |
| mput | Copies multiple files from the local system to the remote host, contingent on the remote host allowing the creation of new files. |
| put | Copies a specified file from the local system to the remote host if allowed by the remote host. |
| pwd | Displays the current working directory on the remote host. |
| quit | Quits FTP. |
| remotehelp | Displays a list of all server FTP commands. |
| struct | Specifies the file's structure. Some options are unstructured and random access. |
| type | Allows the user to specify the file type. Types ASCII and binary (sometimes called image) are most common. With ASCII files some control bytes may be changed to maintain readability on a different system. Binary files are transmitted with no changes in the contents. Other file types are EBCDIC and logical byte. EBCDIC is common on IBM mainframes and logical byte corresponds to systems with a byte size different than eight bits. |

email, network standards, and much more. Table 8.4 lists some of the repositories for RFC documents. The first column indicates the site to which you must connect via FTP; the second specifies the subdirectory containing RFC files.

RFCs are numbered and have the form RFC xxxx. The designation 'xxxx' is a 4-digit number. Table 8.5 lists a few RFCs that relate to topics covered in this book. As the numbers indicate, the list is very large. Reference 2 contains an extensive list of RFCs. An RFC list can be obtained as well from several FTP sites.

TABLE 8.4    **RFC Repositories**

| LOCATION | SUBDIRECTORY CONTAINING RFCS |
|---|---|
| ds.internic.net | rfc |
| nic.ddn.mil (DDN MILNET users) | rfc |
| ftp.nisc.sri.com | rfc |
| nis.nsf.net | internet/documents/rfc |
| nisc.jvnc.net | rfc |
| venera.isi.edu | in-notes |
| wuarchive.wustl.edu | doc/rfc |
| src.doc.ic.ac.uk | rfc |
| ftp.concert.net | rfc |

TABLE 8.5    **RFC Documents**

| RFC NUMBER | TOPIC |
|---|---|
| 764, 854 | TELNET protocol specification |
| 821, 822 | simple mail transfer protocol (SMTP) |
| 974 | mail routing and the domain system (DNS) |
| 768 | user datagram protocol (UDP) |
| 777, 792 | Internet control message protocol (ICMP) |
| 959 | file transfer protocol (FTP) |
| 1042 | transmitting IP datagrams over IEEE 802 Networks |
| 1098, 1157 | simple network management protocol (SNMP) |
| 877 | transmitting IP datagrams over public data networks |
| 1103 | transmitting IP datagrams over fiber distributed data interface (FDDI) |
| 874 | A critique of X.25 |
| 791, 963 | Internet protocol (IP) |
| 1058 | routing information protocol (RIP) |
| 793, 964 | transmission control protocol (TCP) |
| 1007, 1008 | ISO transport protocol |
| 987, 1026 | mapping between X.400 and RFC 822 |
| 1086 | ISO-TPO bridge between TCP and X.25 |

Most of the RFC repository sites maintain an RFC list that can be accessed using FTP or email. Figure 8.5 shows how this was done in one instance. Bold face characters represent those typed by the user and plain characters correspond to FTP responses. Line 1 shows the FTP command to connect to the remote site nis.nsf.net.

FIGURE 8.5    **Sample Use of FTP to Transfer a File**

```
1       $ ftp nis.nsf.net
2       220 nic.merit.edu FTP server (Version 4.1 Fri Aug 28 11:37:57 GDT 1987) ready.
3       Connected to NIS.NSF.NET.
4       Name (nis.nsf.net:shayw): anonymous
5       331 Guest login ok, send ident as password.
6       Password: shayw@uwgb.edu
7       230 Guest login ok, access restrictions apply.
8       ftp> cd /internet/documents/rfc
9       250 CWD command successful.
10      ftp> get INDEX.rfc
11      200 PORT command successful.
12      150 Opening ASCII mode data connection for INDEX.rfc (148427 bytes).
13      226 Transfer complete.
14      local: INDEX.rfc remote: INDEX.rfc
15      152496 bytes received in 00:00:59.12 seconds
16      ftp> quit
17      221 Goodbye.
```

Line 4 corresponds to the login request and the entry for the anonymous login. Line 6 requests the password, which in this case is the author's email address. As with most systems, the password was not echoed and is shown here only to illustrate the interaction. Line 8 changes the working directory to /internet/documents/rfc, the subdirectory containing RFC documents. Finally, line 10 requests that a copy of a file named "INDEX.rfc" be transferred to the local site. This file contains a list of all RFCs available in that repository as well as the topics covered. The copied file also will be named "INDEX.rfc". If you want a copy of a particular RFC the usual way is to enter

```
get rfcxxxx.txt
```

where "xxxx" represents the 4-digit RFC number. If you do this, be forewarned; some of them are very long files.

The remaining lines indicate the status of the file transfer as it occurs. Note that this is a very large file and will take some time (in this case, a little under one minute). As a courtesy to other Internet users you should transfer only files you need and transfer large files during off-hours (such as at night or on weekends) to minimize the effect of a lot of traffic.

When FTP is not a viable option RFCs can be mailed electronically on request. Each site has a contact email address to which requests can be made. Typically a request is an email message whose text body contains "get *filename*" where *filename* is the desired file. The site's service then mails the file to you. For example, instead of using FTP as in Figure 8.5, the file could be obtained by mailing such a message to rfc-mgr@merit.edu.

The hosts in Table 8.4 are not the only sites accessible via FTP, and RFCs are not the only files of interest. More than one thousand FTP sites are available. With this many sites, it can be difficult to know the useful ones and what they contain. Usually, people learn of sites through professional contacts, professional literature, or word of mouth. Another useful source of information is a service called **Archie**. Developed at McGill University, it was designed to scan existing FTP sites and maintain a database relating the sites and their contents.

Table 8.6 lists some of the Archie sites (from Reference 4). A user can access Archie by using TELNET to login to a remote site and entering "Archie" at the login prompt. Some of the useful Archie services are provided by the following commands:

- **help**. Lists Archie commands and describes what they do.
- **list**. Lists all FTP sites in the remote Archie database.
- **prog**. Performs a database search looking for all FTP sites containing information on a particular topic. For example, entering "prog X.400" causes the Archie service to list FTP sites and any of their files that contain information on the X.400 standard.

Another source of information is the **WAIS (Wide Area Information Servers)** system (Reference 5) developed by Dow Jones, Thinking Machines Corp., Apple Computer, and KPMG Peat Marwich. The WAIS architecture is based on a client-server model in which servers provide access to a variety of databases. Suppose a user wants to find information on a particular topic. He or she submits a request and client software translates it into a form prescribed by the WAIS protocol. WAIS routes it to various relevant databases, where servers search for any mention of the

TABLE 8.6    **Archie Sites**

| Host | Location |
| --- | --- |
| archie.ans.net | New York |
| archie.rutgers.edu | New Jersey |
| archie.sura.net | Maryland |
| archie.unl.edu | Nebraska |
| archie.mcgill.ca | Canada |
| archie.funet.fi | Finland |
| archie.au | Australia |
| archie.doc.ic.ac.uk | Great Britain |

requested topic. Each server responds to the user specifying documents related to the requested topic.

Gopher (Reference 6) is another information service. It was developed at the University of Minnesota. Like WAIS, it provides text searches, looking for documents related to a specific topic. It also provides a menu system allowing its users to browse, looking for topics of interest. Other information services include the World-Wide Web (WWW), developed at CERN in Switzerland; the Prospero File System, developed at the University of Washington; X.500 (which we describe in the next section); and INDIE (Distributed Indexing), developed at the University of Southern California. Reference 7 provides a nice survey of these (and other) systems, along with a general description and illustrations of some sample sessions. It's a nice place to start for someone trying to become acquainted with the Internet.

A potential disadvantage of the Internet is its ease of use. At first this may not seem to be a disadvantage, but each use implies more activity. In some cases, the activity is necessary; in others, it is not. Just as the post office delivers junk mail, the potential for electronic "junk" is very real. One must remember that the Internet was developed to let people communicate and get work done. The frivolous transferring of unnecessary files or mail affects those who need the services. Often the FTP sites request that, if possible, their services be accessed after normal working hours to help alleviate the load. In most cases, a site also limits the number of FTP users that can be logged on.

**TFTP—Trivial File Transfer Protocol**    Although FTP provides a wide range of options for the TCP/IP suite such as multiple file types, compression, and multiple TCP connections, many applications, such as LAN applications, do not need a full range of services. In these cases a simpler file transfer protocol, the **trivial file transfer protocol** (**TFTP**), will do the job. One difference between FTP and TFTP is that the latter does not use a reliable transport service. Instead, it runs on top of an unreliable one such as UDP. TFTP uses acknowledgments and timeouts to make sure all pieces of a file arrive.

Like other protocols, TFTP defines the communication rules between a client and a server. It defines five packet types to do this. They are:

- **Read request**. A request to read a file from a server.
- **Write request**. A request to write a file to the server.
- **Data**. A 512-byte (or less) block containing part of the file to be transferred. Blocks are numbered starting at 1.
- **Acknowledgment**. Acknowledges receipt of a data packet.
- **Error**. Communicates an error message.

When a client wishes to transfer a file it sends either a read request or write request packet, depending on which way the file transfer is to occur. The file then is transferred in 512-byte pieces using a stop and wait protocol. Only the last block may contain fewer than 512 bytes.

**SMTP—Simple Mail Transfer Protocol**      Certainly one of the most common uses of networks is electronic mail, the ability to send a message or file to a specific user at a local or remote site. Typically, you send a message by specifying the email address of the recipient. The message is buffered at the destination site and is accessible only by the intended user. The exact way to send mail varies slightly, but it usually takes one of the two following forms (boldface characters are typed by the user):

| MAILING A MESSAGE INTERACTIVELY | MAILING A MESSAGE ON A FILE |
| --- | --- |
| $**Mail** | $**Mail** |
| Mail> **Send** | Mail> **Send FileName** |
| To: **IN%"shayw@uwgb.edu"** | To: **IN%"shayw@uwgb.edu"** |
| Subject: **Test Mail** | Subject: **Test Mail** |
| Enter your message below. Enter <Ctrl Z> to exit or <Ctrl C> to quit | Mail> |
| **test test test test test** | |
| **<Ctrl Z>** | |
| Mail> | |

In both cases a user sends a message by invoking the mail utility at the system prompt ($), and the system responds with a mail prompt (Mail>). In the first case the user enters the command "Send". The system responds by requesting the email address of the recipient and a subject (short phrase giving some indication of the mail's contents). It then allows the user to type the message he wants to send, entering a control sequence when he is done. In the second case the user enters the mail command "Send FileName". Here the file contains the message to be sent. The first is useful for short, quick messages; the second for longer messages that must be carefully composed and edited (such as writing home and asking your parents for more money) using a text editor.

There are some similarities with file transfer protocols. For example, a client and server negotiate a file transfer. However, email typically sends the file to a specified user in whose account the message is buffered. Another difference is that the client and server work in the background. For example, if you get a file using FTP, you typically wait until the file arrives before doing another task. If you send (or receive) a file using email you can do other tasks while the client and server perform the mail delivery in the background. In the case of receiving mail you need not even be logged on. You will be notified of new mail the next time you login to the system.

The standard mail protocol in the TCP/IP suite is the **simple mail transfer protocol** (**SMTP**). It runs above TCP/IP and below any local mail service. Its primary responsibility to make sure mail is transferred between different hosts. By contrast, the local service is responsible for distributing mail to specific recipients.

Figure 8.6 shows the interaction between local mail, SMTP, and TCP. When a user sends mail, the local mail facility determines whether the address is local or requires a connection to a remote site. In the latter case, the local mail facility stores the mail (much as you would put a letter in a mailbox), where it waits for the client SMTP. When the client SMTP delivers the mail it first calls TCP to establish a con-

**FIGURE 8.6    SMTP Interacting with Local Mail and TCP**

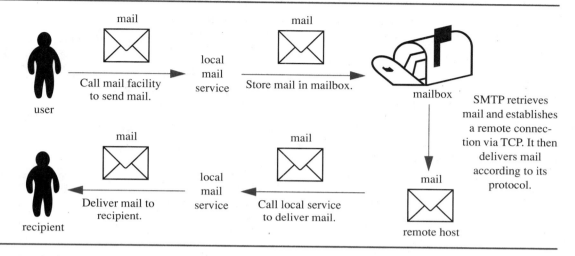

nection with the remote site. When the connection is made the client and server SMTPs exchange packets and eventually deliver the mail. At the remote end the local mail facility gets the mail and delivers it to the intended recipient.

Figure 8.7 shows the packet exchange between the client and server. The packets are also called SMTP **protocol data units** (**PDU**s) or simply commands. When the TCP connection is made the server sends a 220 PDU indicating it is ready to receive mail. The number 220 serves to identify the type of packet. Afterward, the client and server exchange the identities of their respective sites. Next, the client sends a "MAIL FROM" PDU indicating there is mail and identifying the sender. If the server is willing to accept mail from that sender it responds with a 250 "OK" PDU.

The server then sends one or more "RCPT TO" PDUs specifying the intended recipients to determine whether the recipients are there before sending the mail. For each recipient the server responds with a 250 "OK" PDU (recipient exists) or a 550 "recipient not here" PDU. After the recipients have all been identified the client sends a "DATA" PDU indicating it will begin mail transmission. The server's response is a 354 "start mail" PDU, which gives the OK to start sending and specifies a sequence the client should use to mark the mail's end. In this case the sequence is <CR> <LF> . <CR> <LF>.[*] The client sends the mail in fixed-size PDUs, placing this sequence at the mail's end. When the server gets the last PDU it acknowledges receipt of the mail with another 250 "OK" PDU. Finally, the client and server exchange PDUs indicating they are ceasing mail delivery and TCP releases the connection.

---

[*]This is the same as carriage return, line feed, period, carriage return, line feed. This sequence cannot appear in the body of the mail as SMTP disallows sending mail containing a single period on a separate line (Reference 2).

FIGURE 8.7     **Sending Email Using SMTP**

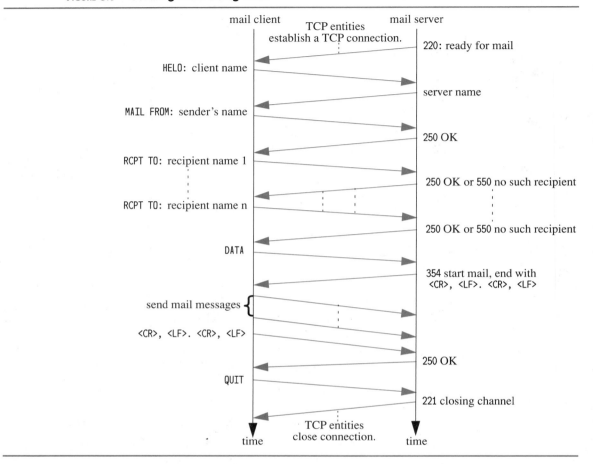

This description has outlined the basic functionality of SMTP and has not gone into the details of PDU format or issues such as forwarding mail or responding to nonexistent addressees. More information on SMTP can be found in references 2 and 8 and in RFC documents 821 and 822.

## SNMP—SIMPLE NETWORK MANAGEMENT PROTOCOL

The **simple network management protocol** (**SNMP**) is a management protocol designed to make sure network protocols and devices not only work but work well. It allows managers to locate problems and make adjustments by exchanging a sequence of commands between a client and a server. Unlike previous applications, it runs on top of UDP instead of TCP. Still, as it is an important part of Internet management it warrants a discussion.

FIGURE 8.8    **SNMP Architecture**

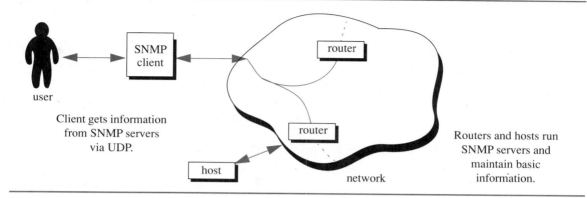

Figure 8.8 shows the SNMP architecture. A manager runs a management client program at a site that communicates with a management server program at another site. Typically the server programs are run on remote hosts and especially network routers. Both management programs use commands defined by the SNMP protocol. Primarily the commands define how to request information from a server and send information to a server or client.

SNMP has several goals (described in RFC 1157). The first is to simplify SNMP functions to reduce support costs and make SNMP easier to use. Second, it must be extensible to accommodate future updates in network operations and management. Third the protocol must be independent of design specifics of hosts or routers. The result is an application layer protocol that interfaces with transport services.

Because SNMP is a management application it must know what processes it is to manage and how to refer to them. The routers and hosts that SNMP manages are called **objects**. An object has a formal definition according to **ASN.1 (abstract syntax notation 1)**, a formal language designed expressly for the definition of PDU formats and object definition. A formal treatment of the objects and ASN.1 is far beyond the scope of this text, but if you are interested references 2, 9, and 10 provide such a treatment.

**Management Information Base**    Each object's server maintains a database of information that describes its characteristics and activities. Because there are different object types a standard defines precisely what should be maintained. This standard, the **management information base (MIB)** was defined by the group that proposed SNMP. There are eight categories of information specified by MIB. As before, a complete description of each one is very detailed, and references 2, 9, and 10 have more information. Here we will specify each of the categories and some examples of the information they contain:

- **System.** Describes the host or router operating system and contains information such as when the server was booted, description of the device it runs on, device location, and a contact person.

- **Interface.** Describes each network interface and contains items such as MTU (see Section 7.4) size, transmission rate, number of packets discarded for various reasons, number of octets transmitted and received, number of interfaces, and an interface description.

- **Address translation.** Contains a table used to change an IP address into a network-specific one.

- **IP.** Describes information specific to the Internet protocol. Examples of information maintained include default time-to-live value for IP packets, number of datagrams eliminated for various reasons, number of datagrams forwarded and delivered to the transport protocol and received from the data link protocol, number of fragments created, number of datagrams reassembled, and routing tables.

- **ICMP.** Describes information specific to the ICMP protocol. Primarily it contains many counters tracking the numbers of each type of control message (Section 7.4) sent by ICMP.

- **TCP.** Among the items it contains are timeout lengths, number of connections, number of segments sent and received, maximum number of simultaneous connections, IP address of each entity using TCP and the IP address of the remote connection, and number of failed connection attempts.

- **UDP.** Among the items it contains are the number of datagrams delivered, discarded, or received and the IP addresses of entities using UDP.

- **EGP (exterior gateway protocol).** This is a protocol to exchange routing information between two autonomous networks in an internet. As with other categories, it maintains counters tracking the number of EGP messages sent and received.

**SNMP Commands**     The management programs that use SNMP run asynchronously. That is, they send out requests but can do other things while waiting for responses. Generally the requests, or PDUs, request information from a server, send information to a remote management program, or respond to special conditions. SNMP defines five PDU formats:

1.  **GetRequest.** This command causes a GetRequest PDU[*] to be sent containing a command code, object name, and specification of an MIB variable. The receiving entity responds by sending a GetResponse PDU containing values of the variable requested or an error code in the event of an error.

2.  **GetNextRequest.** This command is similar to GetRequest except that the request is for values of variables that "follow" the ones specified in the PDU. The notion of "following" is based on a lexicographic order as determined by the MIB design. This is especially useful for traversing tables maintained by the management server.

---

[*]The specific PDU format and mechanism for identifying MIB variables is rather complex. References 2 and 10 contain fairly detailed discussions.

3.  **GetResponse**. A PDU sent in response to a previously received GetRequest PDU containing values requested or error codes.

4.  **SetRequest**. This command allows the manager to update values of MIB variables maintained by remote management programs and to remotely alter the characteristics of a particular object which, in turn, can affect network operations. The format does not violate any security measures that prevent unauthorized updates.

5.  **Trap**. This PDU is sent from a server to the manager when specific conditions or events have occurred. It allows the manager to stay abreast of changes in the operating environment. Some of the trap PDUs and their events are listed here:

    a.  **Coldstart trap**. The management program has been reinitialized with potential changes in the object's characteristics.

    b.  **Warmstart trap**. Reinitialization has occurred, but no characteristics have been altered.

    c.  **Linkdown trap**. A communications link has failed.

    d.  **Linkup trap**. A previously failed communication has been restored.

    e.  **EgpNeighborLoss trap**. The station has lost contact with an EGP peer neighbor.

    f.  **Authentication failure trap**. An SNMP PDU that failed an authentication check has been received.

A newer version of SNMP, **SNMP 2**, was designed to overcome some of the perceived weaknesses of SNMP. For example, one of the criticisms of SNMP is that, because of its simple command format, communication requires a large number of packets. SNMP 2 provides more messaging options, thus allowing the clients and hosts to communicate more efficiently. SNMP 2 also provides more security than the original SNMP through its implementation of message authentication and DES encryption. A third enhancement is increased flexibility to allow SNMP 2 to run on top of multiple protocols such as Appletalk, IPX, and OSI. These issues and others are discussed in more detail in references 11 and 12.

As with just about any protocol, SNMP and SNMP 2 are not the only management protocols. The ISO management protocol is the **common management information protocol (CMIP)**. When used over a TCP connection, CMIP is known as CMOT (**CMIP OVER TCP**). CMIP is more complex than SNMP and is reputed to be more suitable for larger networks. Further information may be found in references 13 and 10. Reference 11 is a textbook devoted completely to network management.

## 8.2    Electronic Mail: X.400 and X.500 Standards

Once again we visit the topic of electronic mail (email), not because we like being redundant, but because the SMTP of the previous section is not the only email protocol. An entire series of standards developed by CCITT describes the transfer and delivery of mail. Recall that electronic mail allows users to exchange messages. The sender enters a message and an identifier of the intended recipient. The message is then deposited in that person's "mailbox". The recipient can check the mailbox and display messages at any time.

Figure 8.9 shows how electronic mail works from the user's perspective. The electronic mail service is an application with which a user interacts. Sending mail means interacting with an electronic mail application that accepts mail and deposits it in local storage near the intended recipient. The recipient then can display the messages at her or his convenience.

Displaying messages is only a small part of the email service. For example, if a user is on vacation for several weeks, messages may accumulate. Rather than going through them sequentially, the user can request a list of them. The list reports attributes such as the size of each message and who sent it. It also displays a short comment describing the message. The comment could be "critical information about your future at this company" or "junk mail". The sender must include the comment because the electronic mail system has no idea what the message says. The list also may specify whether the message is new or has been answered or forwarded. So when you see 50 new "critical" messages from your boss, you might consider answering them before perusing your junk mail!

**FIGURE 8.9     Electronic Mail**

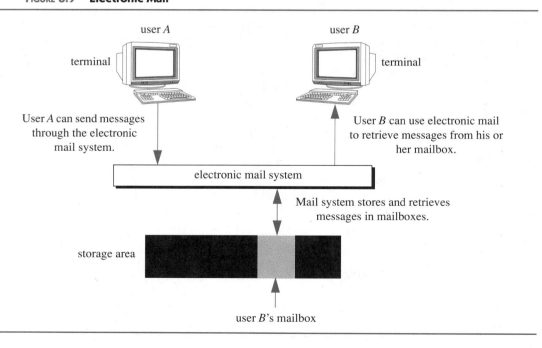

### X.400 Mail Standards

Due to the popularity of email, the CCITT issued its own standards for email in 1984. They are referred to collectively as the X.400 family of standards, and they operate at the OSI application layer. X.400 also forms the foundation of the ISO email system, MOTIS and is the ISO analog to TCP/IP's SMTP. It is based on a model for message handling systems illustrated by Figure 8.10. The model has four main parts: **user agent (UA)**, **message transfer agent (MTA)**, **message handling system (MHS)**, and **message transfer system (MTS)**.

Superficially, the user agent interacts with the user and essentially defines what the user can do. The MTAs defined a collection of nodes that execute a protocol to ensure proper routing of mail. They form the backbone of the mail system, and their

**FIGURE 8.10    Electronic Mail System Model**

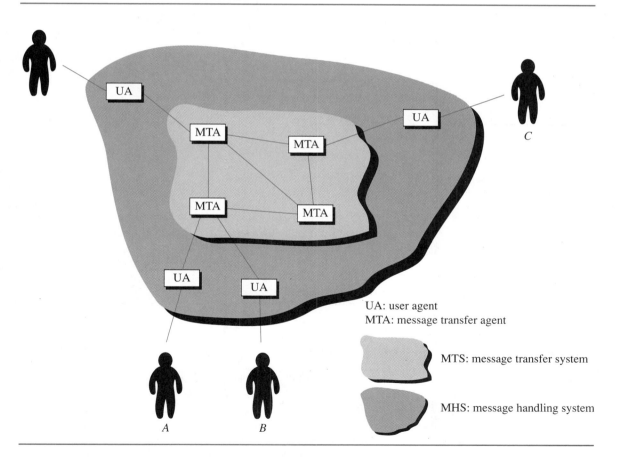

UA: user agent
MTA: message transfer agent

MTS: message transfer system

MHS: message handling system

physical connections vary. They play a role similar to that of routers in internetworks but operate at a higher OSI layer. Collectively the MTAs form the message transfer system. The MTAs and UAs form the message handling system, which ensures the eventual delivery of mail. Let's now examine each component in greater detail.

**User Agent**     The UA is the user interface. It has two main functions. First, it routes messages between the user and the local MTA, allowing the user to send and receive mail. Second, it manages the **message store** (**MS**) which, as you probably suspect, is used to store messages. The UA performs its function at the request of the user and, to the user at least, defines the system's capabilities. The following list includes some of the UA's functions.

- Send mail. The UA accepts a message and address from a user and gives it to the MTA for delivery. The UA will invoke an editor to allow the user to write a message or it will simply send the contents of a previously constructed file (which presumably contains the message). It also appends a header (Figure 8.11) to the user message containing the following information :

  a. sender

  b. recipients

  c. cc recipients (those who get copies)

  d. blind copy recipients (those who get copies secretly)

  e. subject (short note describing its contents)

  f. message ID

  g. reply-by date

  h. sensitivity (degree of confidentiality)

  i. priority

  This information is useful for the receiving UA to deliver the message to the appropriate users and for displaying a summary of all mail messages in a user's mailbox.

FIGURE 8.11   **Messages, Headers, and Envelopes**

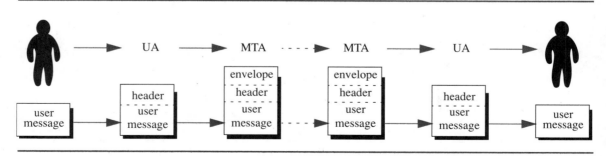

- Display a list of mail messages. This is similar to a directory list in a computer account that lists all files. In this case, the UA provides a list of all messages for the current user. Each entry in the list typically contains the following items:

    a. source of the message

    b. subject field

    c. message size

    d. various indicators indicating whether the message has been read, deleted, answered, or forwarded to another user

    e. message ID

    f. date received

- Display the contents of a message on the computer/workstation screen.

- Reply. The UA allows the user to respond to a currently displayed message by invoking an editor through which the user can construct a response. When the user is finished the UA automatically sends the response to the source of the previously displayed message.

- Forward the current message to one or more specified recipients.

- Extract the message and store it in a file. This is convenient if you want to save a message, print it, or make it available to others without explicitly forwarding it to them.

- Delete unwanted messages. Note that messages are not always physically deleted but are marked for deletion. Then another command such as a purge deletes all files marked for deletion. This allows accidentally deleted messages to be recovered.

- Undelete a message. Removes the deletion mark mentioned previously.

**Message Transfer Agent**     The MTA is software running on a dedicated workstation/computer and is part of the email system's backbone. Each MTA communicates with one or more UAs and other MTAs. Its basic function is to accept mail from a UA or another MTA, examine it, and route it. For example, when it receives mail from a UA it verifies the format of the mail. If it is not correct it informs the UA an error has occurred so the sender can be notified. If it is correct there are two possibilities. First, the recipient is reachable via another UA to which the MTA is connected. An example is user *A* sending mail to user *B* in Figure 8.10. In this case the MTA gives the mail to the appropriate UA for delivery. Second the UA that will deliver the mail is connected to another MTA. Here user *A* may have sent mail to user *C* in Figure 8.10. In this case the mail must be routed to another MTA. Collectively the MTAs execute a routing strategy that sends the mail through one or more MTAs until it reaches the desired one. Then the mail is sent to the appropriate UA for delivery.

Recall that the UA appends a header to a message sent from the user. If the MTA must route the mail to another MTA it also appends additional bytes to the message and header. These additional bytes are called the **envelope** (Figure 8.11).

This is similar to the terminology used by the postal system. Letters are inserted into envelopes that contain the necessary information for delivery or return. The envelope is used by the MTAs for routing, error checking, and verification. The following are some of the fields in the envelope:

- Destination address
- Sender address for possible acknowledgment or return
- Mail identification number
- Priority. As with regular mail, higher priorities may hasten delivery (at increased cost, of course) or may bring out the worst in the system, like putting "Fragile" on a package.
- Deferred date. A user may specify that delivery must occur after a given date.
- Delivery date. A user may specify that delivery must occur before a given date (Good luck!).
- Field specifying whether a message should be returned if it cannot be delivered
- Bytes for error detection
- Encryption information such as the location of a key
- Digital signatures. This field can provide authentication of the sender. For example, recall the encryption method from Section 4.6. This is useful if a sender later denies transmitting something, or at least "cannot recall" sending it. (It's amazing what people may forget in front of investigating committees, court-martials, tribunals, the press, or other unfriendly questioners.) Digital signatures also can be used to verify receipt of a message.

**Message Transfer System.**    The MTAs are physically connected in ways similar to the network topologies discussed earlier. They need not be part of the same computer system. Collectively they form the message transfer system (MTS). Mail travels through MTAs depending on its source and destination somewhat like files under FTP or mail under SMTP. X.400, however, operates on a **store-and-forward** concept. Each MTA runs the X.400 protocols transferring the message in its entirety from one MTA to the next. That is, each entire message is stored at each MTA between the originator and recipient.

This system differs from previous protocols in which individual packets or datagrams are stored at intermediate nodes but are assembled at the destination. This is not to say that X.400 messages are not divided into smaller packets at lower levels, but it does mean that each MTA node runs protocols up to the application layer and that messages are stored intact at each MTA (Figure 8.12). This approach may seem less efficient than simply reassembling them at the destination, but it is useful when the mail must go through networks running dissimilar network and transport layers. Protocols such as FTP and SMTP assume similar transport protocols (TCP).

**Message Handling System (MHS)**    The MHS, the most extensive part of the mail model, contains all the MTAs and UAs. It also includes specifications on,

FIGURE 8.12    **Store-and-Forward Routing**

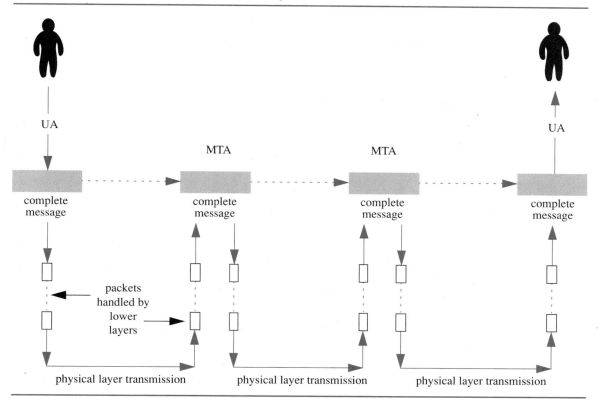

among other things, interaction between two UAs, two MTAs, and a UA and MTA. About the only thing not included is the interface between the UA and user.

The MHS can handle three types of protocol data units (PDUs): **messages**, **probes**, and **reports**. A message contains the user information, header, and envelope. A probe consists of an envelope only, a seemingly strange thing to have. Its purpose is to determine whether a specific destination is reachable without actually sending anything (perhaps similar to sending an empty envelope through the mail to see if a destination exists before shipping a warehouse full of furniture). The report (also called **reply**) is a response sent to the source of a previous message specifying whether it has been received.

CCITT has defined several standards for MHS operations. Some of those standards, which constitute the X.400 family, are summarized in Table 8.7.

MHS is defined in part by a series of protocols (called the P protocols) that define communication between various components. As we have discussed many times throughout this book, protocols are used to define the interaction between two

TABLE 8.7     Some of the X.400 Family of Protocols

| STANDARD | FUNCTION | MEANING |
| --- | --- | --- |
| X.400 | system service and overview | Describes MHS services, interactions among various components of the MHS, protocol layering, naming and address conventions. |
| X.402 | MHS architecture | Describes MHS architecture and rules for naming and addressing. |
| X.403 | testing | Describes testing requirements, timers, procedures, and protocol data units. |
| X.408 | code conversion | Specifies rules for converting between different codes and formats. |
| X.411 | MTS overview | Describes how MTS works. |
| X.413 | message store | Defines the message store (MS). |
| X.419 | MHS protocols | Describes MHS protocols P1, P3, and P7 defining communication among MTA components. |
| X.420 | interpersonal messaging | Describes both IPMs and P2 protocol. |

distinct entities. The MHS is no exception. Figure 8.13 shows some of the protocols and the agents that communicate using them.

The **P1 protocol** (**message transfer protocol**) defines communication between two MTAs. The first MTA creates the envelope according to P1 specifications and subsequent MTAs interpret the envelope's contents. P1 treats the message and header as data and makes no attempt to interpret anything in it. The **P2 protocol**, sometimes called the **interpersonal messaging (IPM) protocol**, deals with the header and body of a message and defines the exchange between two UAs. The sending UA creates the header, and the receiving UA interprets its contents.

When the UA and MTA reside in the same system they typically communicate using proprietary software. However, sometimes they may run remotely (in separate locations). For example, a UA may be in a PC with the MTA accessed via a dialup line or an X.25 connection. In such cases another CCITT protocol, the **P3 protocol** or **submission and delivery protocol**, defines the interaction between them. Finally, when a user wants to access mailed messages she does so through the UA. The UA, in turn, accesses the message store (MS), the place where messages are stored. The **P7 protocol** defines the interaction between the UA and MS.

These descriptions give you a basic outline of the structure of an X.400 mail system and introduce you to some of the terminology. The entire protocol contains vast amounts of information and could fill a textbook. It you are interested in more detailed discussions, Reference 14 has them.

FIGURE 8.13   **P Protocols**

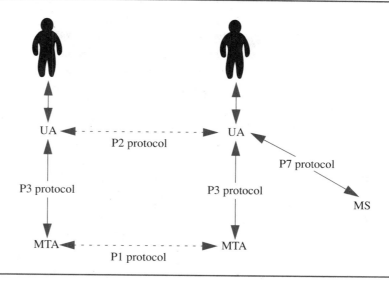

An X.400 system can provide the typical operations of sending and receiving mail as well as many more services such as those in the following list (actually specified by the X.401 protocol):

- **Alternate recipient allowed** lets the originating UA specify an alternate recipient in case the intended recipient cannot be found. In this case the mail goes to the alternate.

- **Authorizing users indication** allows the originator to specify who authorized the mail being sent.

- **Blind copy recipient indication** lets the originating UA cc (send copies of the mail to others). The difference between this and the normal cc function is that the blind recipients are not identified to those receiving the mail.

- **Cross referencing indication** specifies other mail related to the current message.

- **Deferred delivery service** lets the originator specify a time and date after which the mail should be delivered. The mail should not be delivered before that date.

- **Deferred delivery cancellation** lets the originating UA cancel a deferred delivery message.

- **Delivery notification** provides an acknowledgment to the originating UA when the mail has been delivered. Note that it does not mean the recipient has actually read the mail, just that the mail has been delivered.

- **Expiry date indication** allows the originator to specify to the recipient a time and date after which the message is invalid. MHS does not specify what happens when the time has passed.
- **Grade of delivery service** lets the sending UA specify whether the mail should be sent on an urgent, normal, or nonurgent basis. This is similar to the different classes of delivery defined by the postal system.
- **Hold for delivery service** lets a UA request that the MTS hold mail destined for it. This is useful when the UA is not available to receive mail. It is similar to an individual requesting that the post office hold all incoming mail while she is on vacation.
- **Latest delivery service** allows the originating UA to specify a time before which the mail must be delivered. This is useful when it absolutely, positively has to be there by a certain time.
- **Multidestination delivery service** allows mail to be sent to multiple recipients.
- **Nondelivery notification** allows the originating UA to be notified when mail was not delivered properly.
- **Probe service** lets a UA determine whether mail can be delivered to an address without actually sending any mail.
- **Proof of delivery service** allows the authentication of the recipients of a message and its contents using digital signature encryption techniques.
- **Proof of submission service** provides proof that a message has been submitted to the MTS for delivery.
- **Redirection of incoming messages service** allows a UA to redirect all incoming messages to another UA. This is similar to routing all your new work to a colleague while you are on vacation.
- **Reply request indication** requests that the recipient reply to the message.
- **Return of content service** provides for mail to be returned in the event it is not delivered.
- **Stored message deletion service** allows a UA to remove mail from its MS. It's like throwing away your unwanted mail.
- **Stored message listing service** provides a list of messages in the MS.
- **Stored message fetching service** lets the UA retrieve specific mail from the MS.

There are many more services available, but many are less common than those above. If you are interested, references 14 and 15 contain an extensive list of services.

## X.500 DIRECTORY SERVICE

One significant design aspect of any mail system is addressing, the method of identifying any one of the potential recipients. One approach to addressing is the domain system discussed in Section 7.2, familiar to anyone using email over the Internet. However, the growth of the Internet has created a serious address depletion problem (Reference 16), causing some to worry that soon there will be more users than allowable addresses. Since the CCITT recommendations are made with the intention of connecting the entire population of the industrialized world, CCITT standards take a different approach to addressing.

As we know, email systems allow users to send messages to others, but there is always one stipulation: the email address must be provided. Therefore, another important issue is the **mail directory** or **directory service** (Reference 17), which provides the address of an individual given that he/she is unambiguously identified. It is similar to the telephone system: You can call almost anywhere in the world, but you must know the number first. If you don't know the number resources such as telephone books or directory assistance can help, but even they are restrictive. Telephone books can be up to a year out of date. Using directory assistance requires that you first know the area code in which the desired person resides. Then you dial the directory assistance for that code and specify the name of the person you want to call. Typically you must also specify the person's address. Dialing directory assistance for the 312 area code (Chicago area) and asking for John Smith's number will not be very productive.

After developing the X.400 standards the CCITT wanted to define standards for a directory with functions similar to those of the telephone directory. The result is the **X.500 directory service** standard, which has several important features:

- **Distributed directory**. The actual directory would be distributed across many sites throughout the world. It appears as a single centralized directory to each user (Figure 8.14), but it is located and maintained at physically separate sites. This is unlike the telephone system in which a user has to call a different directory assistance depending on the area code.

FIGURE 8.14    **Distributed Directory**

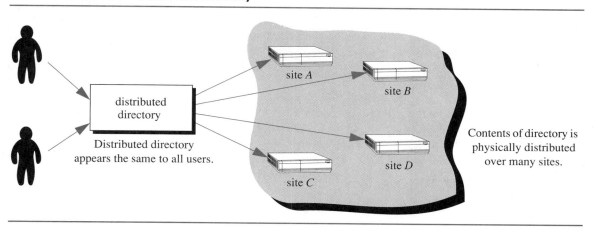

site *A*

site *B*

distributed
directory

Distributed directory
appears the same to all users.

site *C*

site *D*

Contents of directory is
physically distributed
over many sites.

- **Hierarchical structure**. This is similar to the telephone system in which the area code defines a geographic region. Even within the region telephones with the same three-digit prefix tend to be from the same area of town. It is unlike the Internet system, however. No, we haven't forgotten that we described the domain naming system of the Internet as a hierarchical organization, but it is more logical than physical. For example, two sites with the same ".edu" domain name can reside in the same city or at opposite ends of the United States. Don't conclude from this that there is no directory service for the Internet. The Network Information Center (NIC) maintains a WHOIS database with a query facility that allows users to search the database (Reference 4).

- **Consistency**. Some call it a homogeneous name space. Basically it means that all users see the same information presented the same way. On a global scale this is a daunting requirement. Telephone numbers in the United States all have the same format, but the format changes for international calls. Similarly, Internet addresses have the same format, but address formats of non-Internet sites differ.

- **Provide address lookup service**. Again, it is similar to the telephone service but more general. The user could get an address by specifying a variety of items that uniquely identify a person; For example, the person's name, where he works, the department he is in, or his telephone extension. Services also include abilities similar to those provided by the Yellow Pages. A user could get a range of addresses for businesses providing a particular type of service or addresses within a particular department in a large company.

The structure of the X.500 directory is primarily a distributed hierarchy. That is it has a logical hierarchical structure (tree), but parts of the tree are maintained at different sites. Collectively, all of the information in the directory is called the **directory information base** (**DIB**). The DIB consists of entries each of which contains information about a real-world entity such as a country, company, department, or person. The entries are organized in hierarchical fashion and form the **directory information tree** (**DIT**). The distributed aspect means that different branches of the tree are maintained by different organizations, but collectively the hierarchy is maintained. Each entry contains attributes describing the object it represents. Therefore, to specify an object represented in the DIB a user must uniquely identify attributes of the entries leading to it.

Figure 8.15 shows an example DIT. Here second-level nodes correspond to countries, third-level nodes to organizations within a country, fourth-level nodes to departments within an organization, and fifth-level nodes to a person within a department. The information shown means that Mary Smith works as a senior engineer in the engineering department at the ACME corporation in the United States. Thus, if someone wanted to send email to Mary Smith he would specify the following:

C = US,   O = ACME,   D = engineering,   N = Mary Smith

FIGURE 8.15    **Directory Information Tree**

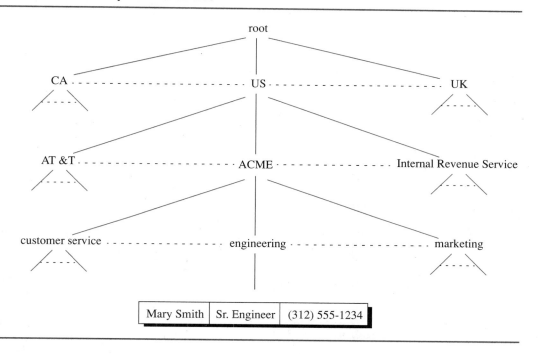

This format represents a key-word approach to referencing directory information, using C for country, O for organization, D for department, and N for name. The
key words and attributes define a path from the tree's root to the desired entry. If
there were several Mary Smiths working in the same department the format would
require additional attributes specifying the proper Mary Smith. They could include
Mary Smith's title, telephone number, or postal address. Somewhere there must be
an attribute distinguishing the two Mary Smiths. (Either that, or Mary Smith has a
clone.)

It is worth mentioning that X.500 uses object-oriented terminology to describe
its DIT. Each DIT node corresponds to an **object** and belongs to an **object class**. All
entries in an object class have the same attributes and the same parent in the DIT
(Figure 8.16). Furthermore, an object class inherits the attributes from the object
class of its parent and forms a subclass. Consequently, the attribute list that defines a
DIT entry also defines the path from the root to that entry. One main advantage of
using objects and object classes is the ability to create new classes by extending or
modifying other classes. This is one of the prime motivators of the object-oriented
paradigm in many fields of computer science.

Two more important components of the X.500 model are the **directory user
agent (DUA)** and **directory system agent (DSA)** (Figure 8.17). They play roles

FIGURE 8.16    **Object Class**

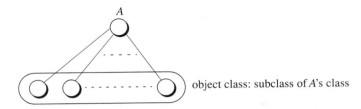

object class: subclass of $A$'s class

similar to the UA and MTA in the X.400 model. A network user typically makes a request through some application that interfaces with the DUA. The DUA, in turn, interacts with the distributed directory to provide whatever service the user requested. Typical services are finding the email address of a user, changing someone's address, or inserting/deleting addresses. Remember, however, that the directory is distributed over many sites (potentially hundreds) and that each site contains part of the directory managed by the DSA at that site. Thus the DUA, through network protocols, accesses the proper DSA in response to the user's request.

## SUMMARY

This section on X.400 and X.500 standards cannot begin to fully describe the complexity of managing and transmitting information on a global scale. In fact, you

FIGURE 8.17    **Directory Structure**

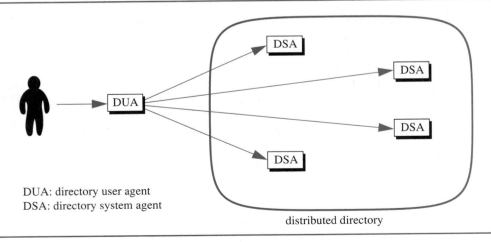

DUA: directory user agent
DSA: directory system agent

distributed directory

should not think of these standards as finished products. Much developmental work is still being done and X.400 is not without its detractors. Some cite its "lackluster performance as a platform for LAN applications" as a shortcoming (Reference 18). It also has stiff competition from other mail services such as SMTP and Novell's message handling service (MHS) (Reference 19). Even so, companies such as AT&T, IBM, Sun Microsystems, and Digital Equipment Corporation are manufacturing numerous X.400 products (Reference 20). Many believe they will form the foundation for future gateways that will be able to interpret a wide array of business documents and applications and pave the way for a truly global communications system.

## 8.3    Integrated Services Digital Network (ISDN)

Over 100 years ago people began stringing wires between houses and towns so they could communicate by telephone. Since then the telephone network has evolved into a global communications system using every communications medium we have described in this book. There is one more feature that distinguishes the telephone system from other networks we have discussed: It has a large analog component. We haven't forgotten that optical fibers and digital switching devices have introduced significant amounts of digital technology into the network. Telephones, however, are still analog devices transmitting analog signals to the local exchange office. This part of the telephone network is often called the **local loop** or the **last mile**. (The latter phrase refers to the largest impediment to an all-digital system.)

Initially, the analog system was a logical choice as the telephone was designed to transmit a person's voice. Since then the two fields of communications and computer science have been merging. Computers are critical to communications systems, and communications systems are commonly used to connect computers. Consequently, the CCITT is developing a standard for a global digital communications system called the **integrated services digital network** (**ISDN**). If fully implemented, it would allow the complete integration of both voice and nonvoice (e.g., data, fax, video) transmission within a single system. We will discuss the numerous advantages of such a system shortly.

Figure 8.18 shows the functionality of ISDN's **basic rate**. It provides three separate channels: two **B channels** transmitting at 64 Kbps and one **D channel** transmitting at 16 Kbps. It is often referred to as **2B+D**. The B channels transmit pure data such as PCM voice data or data generated by other devices such as a PC. The D channel is used for control and for some low-speed applications such as **telemetry** (remote reading of meters) or alarm systems. The three channels are time-division multiplexed onto a **bit pipe** providing the actual bit transmission.

CCITT also has developed a North American standard for a **primary rate** of **23 B+D** (23 B channels and one D channel), which fits nicely onto the T1 carrier system. It also has a European standard of 30B+D, which fits onto their 2.048 Mbps

FIGURE 8.18    **ISDN Basic Service**

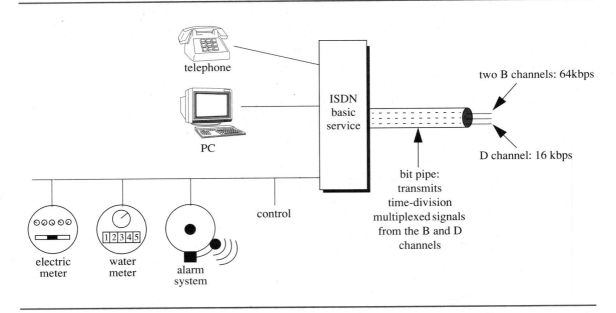

channel. The additional data channels provide the additional capacity for more data from different sources.

Oddly enough, the biggest impediments to eventually implementing a global digital communication are not the technical problems (but do not underestimate them). The main problems are logistical and economical. One significant problem is convincing telephone users that they will benefit from ISDN and that the conversion costs will be justified. Most people use their telephone systems for one thing: reaching out and talking with friends and neighbors. They don't care whether their voice is carried via analog or digital signals. On the other hand, the advantages of the ISDN basic service providing two data channels are easily articulated. For example, parents would no longer be stuck when their son or daughter monopolizes the line, because they would have a second line. (Of course, if they have two children they might still be out of luck.)

## ISDN SERVICES

This section lists some of the services that an all-digital system would provide. Some of them are already implemented in many parts of the world on a regional or company-wide basis. The eventual goal is to make them available to everyone. Furthermore, an all-digital system would facilitate the implementation of services.

Many of them, for example, would require an on-site video screen and some of the text-processing ability of a PC.

- One of the B channels could be used to send messages electronically. They could be routed depending on the recipient's telephone number and stored in a local repository near the recipient for eventual access.

- Telephone numbers of incoming calls could be displayed even before the telephone is answered. Remember, digital systems mean that both outgoing data and incoming signals are digitized. The source number could be encoded in the received signals. This feature would allow you to decide whether you want to answer the telephone and would deter obscene or crank phone calls. It also would facilitate the identification of incoming calls to a 911 emergency system, a particular advantage if the caller is incoherent or a very small child. The downside of this ability is that it defeats the purpose of unlisted numbers. Thus, provisions must be available to turn off the display of such numbers.

- Telephone numbers of incoming calls could also be used as a key to a database record. This has applications for professionals who deal with clients or patients (doctors, lawyers, brokers, insurance agents, and so on). Software could use the incoming source number to access the client's record and to display pertinent information on a screen. This feature would allow the professional to answer questions quickly and efficiently.

- Voice mail service similar to the service already provided by answering machines would allow callers to leave messages. The difference is that messages would be recorded and stored in a local repository.

- Fax transmission service would allow faxing of documents or video screens. In one possible application, photographs taken at automatic bank machines could be faxed to a bank for security.

- Every month utility companies send employees to neighborhood homes to read electric, gas, and water meters. ISDN telemetry service would allow the meters to be connected to the company and monthly readings accessed via a simple call. In addition, sensors could be placed in a home to detect fires or illegal entries. When they are activated telephone calls could be made automatically to the nearest fire or police station. At the station the number of the incoming call could be displayed or used to access a database providing the address from which the call is made.

- Videotex, interactive access to remote databases, would allow access to, for example, directory databases providing telephone listings such as those currently found in telephone books. Users could access library databases and query what they have in their collections and access encyclopedias or public records to get information on a particular topic.

- Users could transfer money between bank accounts, shop by entering product codes and credit card numbers, and pay off credit balances by transferring money from their bank accounts—all by telephone.

- Multiple B channels would allow some of these activities to be done simultaneously. If a family member is currently using the telephone to talk to a friend, another person could use the other channel to perform another activity.

The potential applications are staggering. Unfortunately, so are the potential abuses. Having so much information available by a simple phone call will require enormous security efforts. It also raises important social and ethical issues. How much information should be available? How do you prevent it from falling into the wrong hands? Could telemetry be extended to monitor (and control?) other events in the home? Capabilities already allow electric companies to remotely turn off power to air conditioners (with the customer's permission) during peak usage times. Could (should) this power be extended to control energy use during an energy crisis? (Who defines when a crisis exists?) These are topics of which any serious student of communications should be aware.

## ISDN ARCHITECTURE

An ISDN should work with a large variety of users and equipment, especially if it is to be integrated into an office environment. This includes both equipment designed with ISDN in mind and current equipment whose design predates ISDN and has little in common with it. To help in the design of connection strategies and the standardization of interfaces, CCITT has divided the equipment into **functional groups**. Devices within a group provide specific capabilities. CCITT has also defined **reference points** used to separate these groups, a useful aid to standardizing interfaces. Together they help categorize basic connection strategies and provide a basis on which to design more complex architectures. The following list describes the primary functional group designations:

- **NT1 (network termination 1)**. Nonintelligent devices concerned with physical and electrical characteristics of the signals. They primarily perform OSI layer 1 functions such as synchronizing and timing. NT1 devices typically form the boundary between a user's site and the **ISDN central office**. The central office, in turn, functions much as the telephone system's central office, providing access to other sites.

- **NT2 (network termination 2)**: Intelligent devices capable of performing functions specified in OSI layers 2 and 3. Among this group's functions are switching, concentration, and multiplexing. A common NT2 device is a digital PBX. It can be used to connect a user's equipment together or to an NT1 to provide access to the ISDN central office.

- **NT12**: Combination of NT1 and NT2 into a single device.

- **TE1 (terminal equipment 1)**: ISDN devices such as an ISDN terminal, digital telephone, or computer with an ISDN-compatible interface. Such devices typically connect directly to a network termination device.

- **TE2 (terminal equipment 2)**: Non-ISDN devices including printers, PCs, analog telephones, or anything that has a non-ISDN interface such as RS.232 or X.21.

- **TA (terminal adapter)**: Device designed to be used with TE2 equipment to convert their signals to an ISDN-compatible format. The purpose is to integrate non-ISDN devices into an ISDN network.

Figure 8.19 shows typical functional groups and how they can be connected. To standardize the interfaces CCITT has defined reference points between the groups. Although the connections shown are rather simple, they can be combined into much larger and more complex ones. However, the reference points will always divide the functional groups as shown. There are four reference points:

1.  **Reference point R** separates TE2 equipment from the TA (Figure 8.19a). Point R can correspond to several different interfaces according to the TE2's standard.

2.  **Reference point S** separates NT2 equipment from ISDN devices (Figure 8.19a,b). It supports a 2B+D channel and has a bit rate of 192 Kbps. * Effectively, it separates devices dedicated to user functions from devices devoted to communications functions.

3.  **Reference point T** is the access point to the customer's site (Figure 8.19a,c). Generally, it separates the customer's equipment from the network provider's equipment. Typically, if T is an interface between NT1 and either terminal equipment or adapter it corresponds to a 2B+D channel. If it lies between two NT devices it corresponds to a 23B+D channel.

4.  **Reference point U** defines the connection between NT1 and the ISDN central office (Figure 8.19d). Communication between different sites can go through one or more signal transfer points (a type of routing device) and are handled by a protocol known as signaling system # 7 (described shortly).

## PROTOCOLS

On the surface ISDN is similar to the current telephone system. To establish a connection to another site the user performs some control functions. In the conventional telephone system this means dialing a number; in ISDN it means sending control packets. The telephone uses **in-band signaling**; that is, the tones generated by pressing buttons are sent over the same channel that will later carry your voice. ISDN control information is sent over the D channel. Since this is a different channel from the ones used to carry your voice or data, it is called **out-of-band signaling**. A significant aspect of out-of-band signaling is that after a connection is made for a B channel the D channel can be used for another purpose. Activities such as telemetry or another call request can be made in parallel with the B channel's transmissions. Another significant aspect is that B channels transmit data (or digital voice) only. That is, ISDN does not specify the content of a B channel and treats all bits as pure data. If two users communicate over the B channel using a particular

---

*The bit rates from the two B channels and the D channel add up to 144 Kbps. Additional overhead bits push the bit rate up to 192 Kbps, as we will show soon.

FIGURE 8.19    ISDN Reference Points

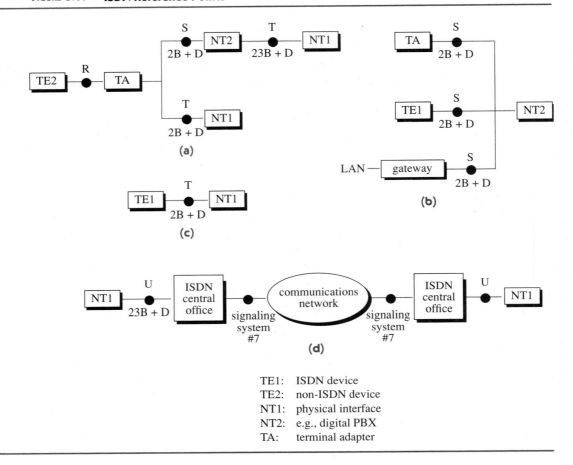

TE1:    ISDN device
TE2:    non-ISDN device
NT1:    physical interface
NT2:    e.g., digital PBX
TA:     terminal adapter

protocol such as packet switching, they must specify the packet formats and transmit them over the B channel. However, the actual packet format, including headers and control information, is transparent to ISDN.

Several types of connections can be made over a B channel. First is a **circuit switched connection** similar to that within the telephone system. All signaling and control information exchange occurs over the D channel. A second connection is a virtual circuit over a packet switched network. Again, all control information to establish the call and define the virtual circuit is done over the D channel. The third connection type is similar to a leased line service. The connection is ever present and does not require call establishment prior to sending data.

The D channel is another story. It carries control information such as call establishment or termination, the type of call, and the B channel assigned to that call.

Consequently, protocols must be defined to control transmission over the D channel. Before we discuss them, however, we will describe the physical transmission of the B and D channels.

A complete description of protocols that form the foundation of ISDN would easily fill at least one book (see references 21 and 22). Our approach, then, is to provide an introduction to some of the pertinent protocols. Relevant to ISDN, CCITT has developed two separate series of recommendations called the I-series and Q-series documents. The I-series, I.100–I.605, first issued in 1984 and updated in 1988 and 1992, consists of over 60 separate documents and describes topics such as ISDN network architecture, reference configurations, routing principles, and the user-network interface. We will describe a couple of these protocols shortly.

The Q-series, Q.700-Q.795, describes a layered protocol known as **signaling system #7 (SS7)**. First issued in 1980, SS7 defines a standard that provides functionality in an integrated digital network (IDN). Note the use of the term IDN as opposed to ISDN. An IDN represents an outgrowth of the old analog telephone system in which signal transmission and switching were handled separately. With the ability to put all the transmissions in a digital form, the two functions have been integrated. An ISDN will use an IDN but includes the ability to integrate digitized voice with many other types of digital data onto the digital links.

**Signaling System #7**     SS7 is a four-layer protocol (Figure 8.20). The bottom three layers make up the **message transfer part (MTP)** and perform functions similar to the X.25 protocol. Unlike X.25, however, SS7 is concerned with internal network functions such as routing and reliability. For example, it provides for the reliable transport of messages using a connectionless mode of transfer. The fourth layer, the **user part**, contains specifications for call control, message formats, various applications, and maintenance.

The lowest layer, the **signaling data link** (CCITT document Q.702) provides all the physical and electrical specifications and provides a 64-Kbps full-duplex transmission. The second layer, the **signaling link layer** (Q.703), provides reliable communications between two consecutive points in the network. As with other layer 2 protocols, it defines the frame format and provides error checking and flow control. It is similar to HDLC, and another discussion seems pointless here. If interested, you can find more details in references 21, 23, 24, and 25.

**FIGURE 8.20     Signaling System #7**

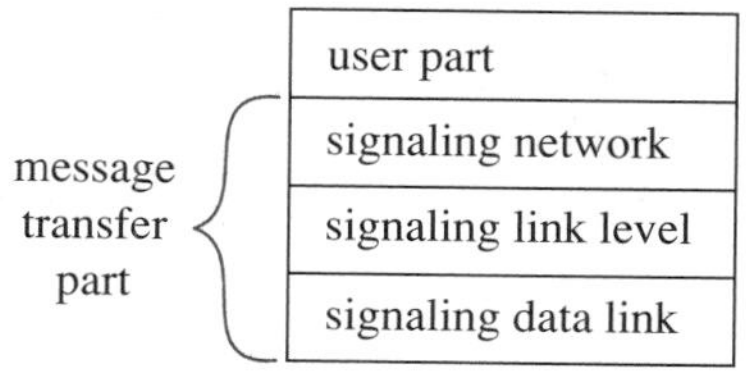

The third layer, the **signaling network layer** (Q.704), provides reliable message transfer between two signaling points (end points). It performs two major functions: routing and management. For example, it determines whether to transfer a message to another network node or to deliver it to the fourth layer (user part). In the former case, it must determine the next node. In the latter case, it must determine which user part gets the message. Management functions include the exchange of information among nodes regarding routes, error and congestion recovery, and rerouting.

The user part actually consists of a **telephone user part** (TUP) and an **ISDN user part** (ISUP). The TUP, described by documents Q.721–Q.725, describes the establishment of circuit-switched connections for telephone calls, including types of control messages and their format. Example messages include those that specify charges for a call, an indication that a call has been answered, or a message that a circuit has been released due to an error.

The ISUP, Q.761–Q.766, performs similar functions but is designed to be a service for ISDN users as opposed to telephone users. Some examples of ISUP messages are described in the following list:[*]

- **Initial address message (IAM).** A message sent in the forward direction to initiate seizure of an outgoing circuit and to transmit number and other information relating to the routing and handling of a call.

- **Subsequent address message (SAM).** A message that may be sent in the forward direction after an initial address message, to convey additional called party number information.

- **Information request message (INR).** A message sent by an exchange to request information in association with a call.

- **Information message (INF).** A message sent to convey information in association with a call requested in an INR message.

- **Address complete message (ACM).** A message sent in the backward direction indicating that all the address signals required for routing the call to the called party have been received.

- **Call progress message (CPG).** A message sent in the backward direction indicating that an event has occurred during call set-up which should be relayed to the calling party.

- **Answer message (ANM).** A message sent in the backward direction indicating that the call has been answered. This message is used in conjunction with charging information in order to: (1) start metering the charge to the calling customer, and (2) start measuring call duration for international accounting purposes.

- **Facility request message (FAR).** A message sent from an exchange to another exchange to request activation of a facility.

- **Facility accepted message (FAA).** A message sent in response to a facility request message indicating that the requested facility has been invoked.

---

[*] J. Griffith, *ISDN Explained*, ©1990, pp. 34–35. Reprinted by permission of John Wiley & Sons, New York.

- **Facility reject message (FRJ).** A message sent in response to a facility request message to indicate that the facility request has been rejected.
- **User-to-user information message (USR).** A message to be used for the transport of user-to-user independent of call-control messages.
- **Call modification request message (CMR).** A message sent in either direction indicating a calling or called party request to modify the characteristics of an established call (for example, change from data to voice).
- **Call modification completed message (CMC).** A message sent in response to a call modification request message indicating that the requested call modification (for example, from voice to data) has been completed.
- **Call modification reject message (CMRJ).** A message sent in response to a call modification request message indicating that the request has been rejected.
- **Release message (REL).** A message sent in either direction to indicate that the circuit is being released because of the reason (cause) supplied and is ready to be put into the IDLE state on receipt of the release complete message. In case the call was forwarded or is to be rerouted, the appropriate indicator is carried in the message together with the redirection address and the redirecting address.
- **Release complete message (RLC).** A message sent in either direction in response to the receipt of a release message, or if appropriate, to a reset circuit message, when the circuit concerned has been brought into the IDLE condition.

This list merely scratches the surface of SS7. If you would like to read more about SS7, consult any of references 22, 23, 24, and 25.

**ISDN Protocols**     There are over 60 documents in the CCITT I-series describing ISDN standards. Our approach is to introduce you to the user-network interface recommendations describing a three-layer protocol. The first layer (I.430) describes the physical bit stream for the ISDN basic service. There is a similar description (I.431) for the primary service. We will not discuss it here, but references 21 and 22 do.

The physical layer bit stream for the basic service corresponds to that at reference points S or T (Figure 8.19). Figure 8.21 shows how the basic service 2B+D channel is multiplexed over the bit pipe. Before we describe it we note several important facts:

1. The frame format for frames going from a TE to an NT differs from those going in the reverse direction. We will explain these differences shortly.

2. Communications between a TE and an NT are full duplex so that frames going in opposite directions do not collide.

3. The word "frame" carries a slightly different meaning than that used many times before. Its format is not defined by a layer 2 (or higher) protocol. Instead, it simply defines how bits from the two logical B and D channels are multiplexed into a single physical transmission stream.[*]

---

[*] An analogous format exists for a 23B+D channel. For further details see references 21, 22, and 23.

FIGURE 8.21    **ISDN Physical Frame Format**

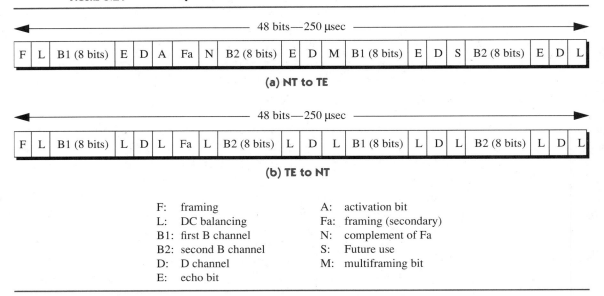

F:    framing
L:    DC balancing
B1:   first B channel
B2:   second B channel
D:    D channel
E:    echo bit

A:    activation bit
Fa:   framing (secondary)
N:    complement of Fa
S:    Future use
M:    multiframing bit

Each frame contains 48 bits and is sent every 250 μsec resulting in a bit rate of 192 Kbps. Each frame also contains two 8-bit fields from each of the B channels (labeled B1 and B2). A service using the B channel deposits 16 bits into the appropriate fields in each frame. The 16 bits sent every 250 μsec result in a data rate of 64 Kbps for each B channel. Four D bits are stored separately in each frame (labeled D), resulting in a data rate of 16 Kbps for the D channel. This means that when a TE has a packet of information to send over the D channel it does so four bits at a time.

The remaining bits are for some low-level control functions. As we describe them it is worth noting that ISDN uses a **pseudoternary coding** or **alternate mark inversion** technique in which a 1-bit is represented by zero volts and a 0-bit is represented by either a positive or a negative signal. Furthermore, each 0-bit has polarity opposite that of the most recent 0. This forces the signal representing a string of 0s to alternate between positive and negative.

The F-bit is a framing bit, a positive signal indicating the beginning of the frame. The L-bit is a DC balancing bit. After the F-bit it is a negative signal. Together they provide timing and synchronization of the incoming frame. The remaining L-bits are set to 0 if the number of preceding 0s is odd and set to 1 otherwise. This is a means of providing electrically balanced signals. For more information on the electrical significance of this you might consult references 21 and 22.

The E-bit is an echo bit, and there is one for each D-bit. In general, the NT uses it to echo back each D-bit it receives. In cases where several TEs are connected to an NT via a single physical bus (Figure 8.22), the E-bit also is used as a primitive form of contention for the D channel. When a TE has nothing to send on the D channel it

FIGURE 8.22    **Multiple TEs Connected to an NT via a Single Bus**

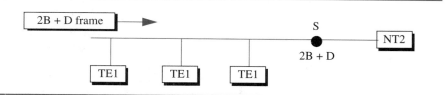

transmits a steady stream of 1s. Consequently, if none of the TEs are using the D channel the NT receives all 1s in the D-bit positions and echoes them back. Thus by checking the returning E-bits a TE can detect an idle D channel.

When a TE wants to send something on the D channel it monitors the returning E-bits. If it contains 0s the TE knows some other TE is using the D channel and waits. If the returning E-bits are all 1s either the D channel is idle or another TE is transmitting all 1s along it. However, a higher-layer protocol performs bit stuffing to limit the number of consecutive 1s that can be sent, so if a TE detects a number of 1s exceeding this value it concludes the D channel is idle and starts sending.

The problem is that another TE might start sending along the D channel, as well. However, the mechanism used and the fact that they compete for space in the same physical frame guarantees that one will be successful. To see how this works, suppose the leftmost TE of Figure 8.22 sent a D-bit equal to 1 (no signal). Suppose the physical frame reaches the next TE, which then deposits a 0 (high or low signal) into the D-bit position. The effect is that the 1 from the first TE is replaced with the 0 from the second TE. Both TEs (and any others that may also be sending) listen to the returning E-bits. If a TE detects an E-bit different from the D-bit it sent, it concludes that some other TE has grabbed the D channel and temporarily abandons its attempt at getting the D channel. If the TE sees its own D-bits echoed back as E-bits it continues sending along the D channel. Another contributing factor is that there is a 10-bit delay time between sending a D-bit and receiving the corresponding E-bit. Thus, because the D-bits are more than 10 bits apart in the physical frame the determination is made before the second D-bit is sent. If the first and subsequent D-bit from two TEs are the same, both continue sending until there is eventually a difference. At that point the unsuccessful TE stops transmitting.

Of the remaining physical frame bits, the A-bit is an activation bit and can be used to activate a TE. The Fa and M-bits are used for multiframing, which allows the addition of another channel (Q channel). The S and N-bits are reserved for future use.

The ISDN layer 2 protocol, defined by I.440 and I.441, is known as **link access protocol for channel D (LAP-D)**. If you have an absolutely fantastic memory you might recall its mention in Section 5.5. It is very similar to HDLC, and there is very little to say that has not already been said. References 21 and 22 contain detailed discussions of LAP-D.

The layer 3 protocol, defined by I.450 and I.451, includes the types and formats of ISDN messages sent over the D channel, protocols for establishing and clearing calls, management functions, and facility support. We will discuss ISDN messages and call control and refer you to references 21 and 23 for details on other functions.

Figure 8.23 shows the ISDN message format. The **protocol discriminator** allows the D channel to send messages from multiple protocols by identifying a protocol corresponding to a message. Currently the protocol discriminator can specify X.25 messages or the user-network call control messages we will describe shortly. However, the ability exists to include other layer 3 protocols in the future.

The **call reference field** specifies the call to which the message refers. This is necessary as the D channel is used to set up and clear calls from many other channels. Without it there is no way to specify to which call a control refers. The 4-bit field preceding the call reference specifies the number of octets in the call reference field. This is needed because the basic and primary services have different call reference lengths. The message type field is self-explanatory. The I.451 recommendation specifies about 30 different types of messages, some of which are listed in Table 8.8.

The remaining field's content and format depends on the message type and provides additional information. It contains information similar to that in other message types we have seen before such as source and destination address. It can also specify a B channel, redirection addresses, reasons for specific messages, and call status. Reference 21 contains an extensive list of the different parameters that can be stored here.

**Call Setup**     Setting up a call is not terribly different (at this level of discussion) than other initialization procedures we have discussed in this book. Figure 8.24 shows the exchange of messages during a typical setup. While going through this example keep in mind that each TE is operating on behalf of a user. If it helps to think of the user as someone making a telephone call over a circuit-switched network, go ahead.

When a user wants to place a call he makes a request to the TE. The telephone analogy would be pushing buttons to specify a number. The TE responds by sending a setup message to the NT. The setup message contains information such as the source and destination addresses, channel, whether the source address should be for-

FIGURE 8.23     **ISDN Layer 3 Message Format**

| protocol discriminator (8 bits) | |
|---|---|
| 0 0 0 0 | number of octets for call reference (4 bits) |
| call reference (variable length) | |
| message type (8 bits) | |
| additional information (variable length) | |

TABLE 8.8        **Some ISDN Layer 3 Messages**

| CALL | MEANING |
| --- | --- |
| **Call establishment** | |
| alert | Sent to calling TE that the called TE has alerted its user to an incoming call. |
| call proceeding | Sent by the network indicating the call request is in progress. |
| connect | Sent to calling TE indicating a call has been accepted. |
| connect ack. | Sent by calling TE indicating receipt of the connect message. |
| setup | Sent by the calling TE requesting call establishment. |
| setup ack. | Sent by the network to the calling TE indicating a previous setup message has been sent. It also requests that the calling TE send more information to process the call request. |
| **Call information** | |
| resume | Resume a suspended call. |
| resume ack. | Previously suspended call has been resumed. |
| resume reject | Previously suspended call could not be resumed. |
| suspend | Request suspension of call. |
| suspend ack. | Call has been suspended. |
| suspend reject | Call has not been suspended. |
| user information | Used to transfer information between two TEs. |
| **Call clearing** | |
| disconnect | Request to disconnect the call. It should be followed by a request to release the B channel. |
| release | Request to release a B channel. It is issued after a user "hangs up." |
| release complete | Indicates the B channel is released. |

warded, or who will be charged for the call. When the network gets the setup message it routes it according to the SS7 protocols, thus determining a route to the other end. It also sends a setup acknowledge message back to the TE. The latter informs the TE the call request has been forwarded and requests more information from the TE if the setup message contained insufficient information.

Once the network has the information it needs it sends a call proceeding message back to the TE. Meanwhile if all goes well the setup message travels through the network and reaches the destination TE. The destination TE then does two things. It sends an alert message back to the caller indicating it has received the setup message, and it notifies its user of the incoming call. In the case of a telephone call it does this by generating the familiar ringing sound. When the alert message returns to the calling TE the caller also hears the ringing sound.

FIGURE 8.24    ISDN Call Establishment

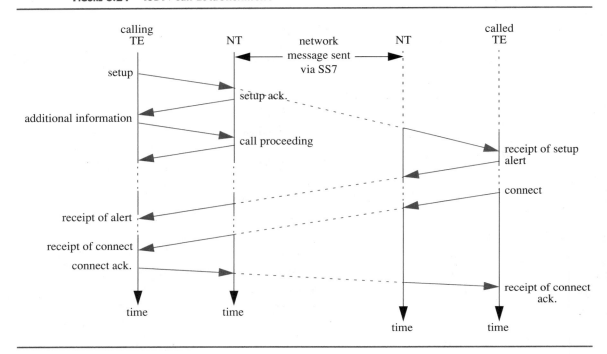

When the user being called answers, the called TE sends a connect message back to the caller. Once the calling TE receives it the ringing on its end stops and the TE responds with a connect acknowledgment. The exchange of the connect and connect acknowledgment messages identifies and confirms the B channel to be used and begins the time during which a charge will accrue. Each TE then routes the PCM-coded voice into the proper B channel as described in Figure 8.21 and the conversation begins.

A call ends when one TE sends a disconnect message to the network, typically after the user hangs up. The network routes the message over the network and sends a release message back to the TE. The TE then sends a release complete message back to the network, clearing the B channel at that end. When the disconnect message arrives at the other end the network and TE there also exchange release and release complete messages. This clears the B channel at that end also.

## BROADBAND ISDN (BISDN)

The digital nature of ISDN is attractive but some have criticized the establishment of a 64-Kbps data rate for B channels. Indeed, in an era of 10 Mbps (and higher) rates for LANs and rates approaching the gigabit range for optical fiber, there will be needs that ISDN cannot meet. Consequently, CCITT has been working on a new set of documents describing **broadband ISDN** (**BISDN**). The intent is to use current high bandwidth technologies to provide services requiring a high transfer rate.

Several services could be provided by a BISDN. Video conferencing and video telephones are two. Current ISDN standards could provide videophone service, but only for small screens. For larger screens with a high-quality video image, higher data rates are needed. Another example is pay television, similar to what already exists in many hotels. From your television you choose what you want to watch from a library of movies. At the end of the billing period you are charged depending on your choices.

One of the issues surrounding BISDN is the method of transfer. ISDN services use preallocated positions in the layer 1 frames for the channels (recall Figure 8.21). This approach, also called **synchronous transfer mode** (**STM**), is essentially time-division multiplexing. The disadvantage of it is that unassigned channels result in wasted bandwidth. Could other channels use the unassigned bandwidth to increase their own rates?

Another approach uses asynchronous transfer mode (ATM), a method similar to statistical TDM discussed in Section 3.3. ATM is a very fast packet switched protocol using small fixed-sized packets (called **cells**) optimized for multimedia use. It establishes logical connections similar to X.25, but the short fixed-sized packets allow them to be created and routed using underlying hardware. In addition, rather than preassigning slots for a channel's cells they are allocated to applications needing them. The advantage is that otherwise empty slots can be used. The disadvantage is the extra complexity and the fact that each slot requires a header. For example, the header would define a virtual circuit so that ATM packets could be routed quickly. ATM also defines multiplexing and switching functions and corresponds roughly to OSI layers 1 and 2. Other issues involve the definition of additional channels, the size of ATM slots, compression techniques, and the definition of bit rates. For more information on this topic see references 21, 22, and 26.

## SUMMARY

ISDN is in an early stage of development, and any realization of it on a massive scale will not be seen for a very long time if at all. Criticisms of ISDN include the complaint that the 64-Kbps rate is far too low to make it useful for the needs of high-quality video transmission (although BISDN addresses that issue). On the other hand, the 64-Kbps rate was originally established for PCM-coded voice. In the future, compression techniques probably will allow digitized voice to be transmitted using data rates as low as 16 Kbps (Reference 27). This development would underutilize the bandwidth significantly. Reference 28 presents a study of eight different applications and how they would be served in contrast to other methods of delivery.

Another problem is finding acceptance among the potential users. Many of them are used to doing things one way and find change difficult. The momentum caused by lack of change is a powerful force. In fact, the slow acceptance has elic-

ited the joke that ISDN really stands for I Still Don't Need it (Reference 29). Des
this, vendors and carriers believe ISDN will be a reality. Vendors are design
equipment to be used in ISDN environments (references 29 and 30) and carr
have been addressing the technical problems of implementing a national ISDN
vice. As with many other technologies, the reaction to ISDN will continue to
mixed, but ISDN almost certainly will be a significant player in an eventual glo
communications system.

## 8.4    Systems Network Architecture (SNA)

The OSI model is one that many references use for comparison, but do not be fool
into thinking it is the only one. For example, Chapter 7 discussed the TCP/IP suite
that evolved from the original ARPANET. There are many other proprietary protocols developed by different companies, however. Examples include **Digital Network Architecture** (**DNA**), also called **DECnet**, by the Digital Equipment
Corporation; **Manufacturing Automation Protocol** (**MAP**) by General Motors
Corporation; **Technical and Office Products** (**TOP**) system by Boeing Computer
Services; **Distributed Communications Architecture** (**DCA**) by Sperry Univac;
**Burroughs Network Architecture** (**BNA**) by Burroughs;[*] and **Distributed Systems** (**DS**) by Hewlett-Packard. For discussions of these protocols see references 31,
23, 26, and 15. The last protocol we will discuss is IBM's Systems Network Architecture (SNA). SNA is of interest because it predates OSI; it was first released in
1974. In addition, it is probably the most widely used proprietary network architecture. Originally it was designed to connect a single host with terminals, but was updated in 1976 to allow multiple hosts to communicate. In 1985 another update
included the support of LANs and arbitrary topologies.

Figure 8.25 shows the layered structure of SNA. It shows seven layers, but be
warned that some references present SNA as a six- or even a five-layer protocol. The
discrepancies occur because some people do not consider the lowest or highest
layers to be part of SNA. In some of the older versions the upper two layers were
considered one. At this level of discussion the number of layers is not important, as
we are not going to present a detailed discussion of the questionable layers anyway.
On the surface SNA resembles the OSI model. That is not surprising, because both
are designed to connect a variety of devices.

One difference between SNA and OSI is that each OSI layer has its own header
that it appends to data received from the next higher layer. This does not occur in
SNA. As with OSI, two SNA users communicate with the layers providing specified
tasks in the presentation and transmission of the data. Figure 8.26 illustrates the process. At the highest layer the user data is divided into one or more **request/response
units** (**RUs**). Each layer passes the RU down to a lower one, with some of them
adding extra headers. Transmission control adds an **RU header**; path control adds a

---

[*] Sperry Univac and Burroughs have merged and formed UNISYS.

FIGURE 8.25    SNA Seven-Layer Protocol

| transaction services |
| --- |
| presentation services |
| data flow control |
| transmission control |
| path control |
| data link control |
| physical link control |

**transmission header**, and data link control adds a **link header**. Some references show a function header added at the second-highest layer, but others consider it as part of the RU, as we have done here. Finally, the lowest layer transmits the RU with the appended headers as a bit stream.

In this last section we will summarize each of the layers and introduce some of the IBM terminology used in an SNA environment.

## LOWER LAYERS

**Physical Control**    The **physical control layer** provides the physical and electrical specifications. It allows a variety of communication modes including cable, optical fiber, and satellites. In some cases, it also allows multiple and distinct connections between two points, which lets the user specify a particular type of transmission, similar to the service type provided by the Internet protocol (Section 7.4). This layer also can be used to divide data from a long stream into separate units and transmit them separately. Typical transmissions use serial links, although parallel transmission can be used between a mainframe and a front-end processor (a special processor designed to handle requests on behalf of the mainframe).

**Data Link Control**    SNA's data link control uses **synchronous data link control (SDLC)**, the protocol on which HDLC is based. The two are very similar. As we discussed HDLC in Section 5.5, we will not repeat the discussion for SDLC. Reference 32 discusses SDLC in detail.

## PATH CONTROL

The **path control** like OSI's network layer, determines paths and makes routing decisions. One difference is that the paths are all virtual paths that are determined

FIGURE 8.26    **Packaging Data in SNA**

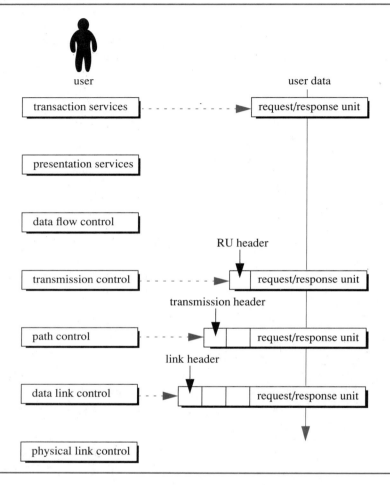

during the connection establishment phase by a higher layer. SNA does not provide a connectionless mode of transfer.

Describing path control requires the use of several SNA-related terms and an understanding of its components. In general we have used the word "node" to represent an entity in the network. An SNA node is a device capable of executing SNA protocols and storing data. It can be almost anything, including a terminal, device controller, workstation, mainframe, or front-end processor. SNA distinguishes between two types, a **peripheral node** which has limited processing capabilities and includes devices such as terminals, printers, and controllers, and a **subarea node**, which has more extensive capabilities and includes mainframes and communications processors.

Figure 8.27 shows how the two types of nodes typically are arranged and helps explain some other distinguishing features. SNA divides its network into domains or subareas, each containing one subarea node and many peripheral nodes. The subarea nodes from all of the subareas communicate and are capable of routing information to one another using the full range of SNA protocols. They form the network's backbone. Peripheral nodes in a subarea typically communicate directly only with the subarea node. If they want to communicate with a peripheral node in another subarea they must use intermediate subarea nodes. As a result, subarea nodes are sometimes called **boundary nodes**.

**Network Addressable Units**     Each node also contains several **network addressable units** (**NAUs**). As the name implies, an NAU is an entity having its own unique SNA address. Primarily an NAU is a software construct capable of executing SNA protocols on the node. In effect it defines the network access point for a user (Figure 8.28) or other application. In some cases an NAU is created when a user logs onto a system for the purpose of network access. In other cases an NAU is always present within the node for management, administration, or testing purposes. In all cases, they correspond to the entities among which SNA connections are established for the eventual exchange of RUs.

**FIGURE 8.27     SNA Node Arrangement**

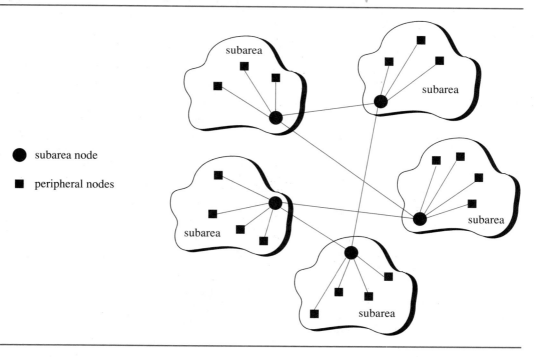

● subarea node

■ peripheral nodes

FIGURE 8.28    **Network Access via NAU**

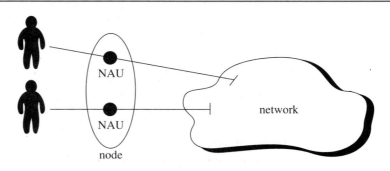

Each NAU's address contains two parts, the **subarea address** and the **element address**. Together they define the subarea and NAU within the subarea. The element address of an NAU is unique within its subarea. The subarea nodes route RUs along the backbone using only the subarea address.

Three types of NAUs are logical unit, physical unit, and system service control point. The **logical unit (LU)** defines the access point for an SNA user. It can also be called the user port. There is one LU for each session,[*] and it performs necessary functions for a user to communicate with another. The following list gives brief descriptions of the several types of LUs. If you are interested in a more detailed description of LUs, Reference 32 provides it.

- **LU 0** corresponds to sessions that use SNA transmission and data flow control layers. The higher layers are not part of the SNA architecture and are often specific to a particular device or user. Typically this would be used for devices that have their own proprietary high-layer protocols.

- **LU 1** corresponds to sessions involving certain types of terminals, printers, or storage devices. Typically, these devices send and receive data streams corresponding to the SNA character string codes, an EBCDIC-based code defining specific control and data characters.

- **LU 2** corresponds to sessions involving another type of device called a 3270 terminal. These terminals support the 3270 data stream, an old format used to define the data and how it is to be presented on the screen.

- **LU 3** is similar to LU 2 but corresponds to printers instead of terminals.

- **LU 4** corresponds to sessions between two terminals or between a terminal and a host.

---

[*] A session, created by higher layers, is analogous to the TCP connection discussed in Section 7.5. We will discuss the SNA session in more detail later, but for now just think of it as a connection through which two NAUs communicate.

- **LU 6** allows sessions between any two applications running on different mainframes.

- **LU 6.2** (also called **advanced program-to-program communication** or **APPC**) supports a session between any two applications running on one of many types of devices (hosts, PCs, minicomputers). It is predicted to be the only LU used, in the future and is designed for a truly distributed environment (some view LU 6.2 as a bona fide distributed operating system).

A **physical unit** (**PU**) is used for administration and testing functions. It generally manages a node's resources and performs control functions necessary to set up sessions and move information between the node and the network during the connection setup phase. It is responsible for activating or deactivating the node with regard to network access, and there is one PU for each node. As with LUs, there are several types of PUs. They are defined by the type of node in which they reside.

- **PU 1** is used in simple terminal nodes and supports non-SNA low-level protocols. They have limited capabilities and are essentially obsolete.

- **PU 2** is used in devices such as cluster controllers (devices that allow several terminals to connect to a common link), remote job entry stations, or printers connected to a host.

- **PU 2.1** may also be called a network node, peripheral node, or advanced cluster controller node. It is used in a variety of devices such as PCs or minicomputers such as Systems /36 and /38. PU 2.1 is significant because prior to its introduction hosts were needed to route traffic between two peer nodes that were not connected directly. The advent of PU 2.1 allowed a distributed environment using LU 6.2.

- **PU 4** is used in a communication controller or front-end processor.

- **PU 5** is used in host computers.

The last type of NAU, the **system service control point** (**SSCP**), is part of an IBM protocol called **virtual telecommunications access method** (**VTAM**). It has a much broader responsibility than either the LU or the PU. Whereas the LU and PU have responsibility for a particular node or device, the SSCP has responsibility for an entire domain or, in the absence of multiple domains, the entire SNA network. It does this in part by communicating with the various PUs within its domain. SSCP resides on a host, and its primary functions involve management of all communications within its subarea, network startup, session establishment, control of domain resources, maintenance, and error recovery.

With all the new and different terms being introduced, you may be having difficulty keeping them straight. Figure 8.29 attempts to help by showing some typical components, their connections in an SNA subarea, and where the various NAUs reside. It shows two terminal controllers, one with three active users at their respective terminals, and the other with none. Consequently the first controller has three LUs (one for each user) and the other has none. Each of the terminals contains a PU of type 1. The terminal controllers contain type 2 PUs, the communications controller

FIGURE 8.29     Relationship Among NAUs in an SNA Network

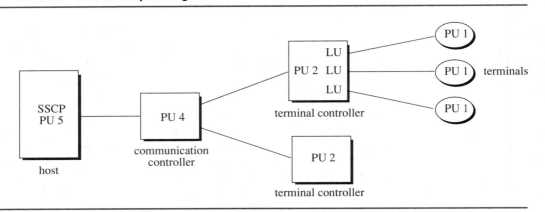

has a type 4 PU, and the host has a type 5 PU. The communication controllers and host here do not show an LU as the users' needs are met at the terminal controller. Certainly a variety of other configurations can exist, and references 31, 33, and 34 show some of them.

**Virtual Route Control**     One of the path control layer's main functions is the establishment of a path between two NAUs. It contains three components, the virtual route control, the explicit route control, and transmission group control.

Because all SNA communications are connection oriented, they require the establishment of a **virtual route** (similar to the virtual circuit of Section 7.3) before the exchange of user data. The **virtual route control** component does this by defining the logical connection between two NAUs. As with other networks we have discussed, no one component knows the route, and the route is transparent to the user. If the route crosses domain boundaries, routing tables at a subarea node transfer information to the next subarea node along the virtual route.

Each routing table entry contains a destination subarea address, a route number, and the location of the next node along the specified route to the specified address. The NAU's destination address and the route number to it are stored in a message's transmission header. On arrival, a subarea node looks for the subarea address and route number and compares them against its routing table's entries. From there it determines the next subarea node and stores the message in a queue to await transmission to it. In the event the message has arrived at the proper subarea, the node examines the element address and routes the message to the appropriate NAU.

Another virtual route control function is **pacing** (flow control). Pacing limits the number of **path information units** (**PIUs**) a node can send. As you probably guessed from the context, a PIU is the unit of information exchanged by the path control layers. Pacing uses a variation of a sliding window protocol, defining the maximum number of PIUs a node can send before it gets a response. The first PIU sent by a node contains a **virtual route pacing request** indicator, a request to the destination node to send a response called the **virtual route pacing response**.

There are now two possibilities. First is that the source node receives the response before it has sent all the PIUs in its window. In this case the source will begin sending PIUs from the next window after it sends all the PIUs in the current window. It assumes that since the destination responded so quickly it has the capacity to accept even more packets. (It's a lot like trying to please your boss by showing how much work you can get done. The more work you do, the more free time you are assumed to have. Therefore, you must not be busy enough.)

Suppose, on the other hand, the response does not arrive before the node sends the last PIU in the window. The node then puts a **virtual route pacing count indicator** in that last PIU. It is a signal to the destination that the source did not receive the response before sending the last PIU in the window. It is also a request that the destination send the response earlier if at all possible so the sending node can avoid waiting. In this case, the sending node increases its window by one (unless restricted by a maximum window size) and, when the response does arrive, resumes with the new and slightly larger window. The reason for the larger window is an attempt by the sender to increase its efficiency by waiting less. In the case where the response arrives promptly there is no point in increasing the window as the sender does not wait anyway.

The pacing technique also can respond to congestion. If a node along a route is congested it sets a **change window indicator** in the PIUs that it handles. When those PIUs reach their destination, the node sets a **change window reply indicator** in the **virtual route pacing response** it sends back to the source. When the source receives the response it decreases the window size by one (subject to a default minimum). This is a slow response to congestion, and there are more aspects to flow control at this level than presented here. As before, we refer the interested reader to references 32 and 26 for further details.

**Explicit Route Control**     The path control layer's **explicit route control** sublayer allows a user to specify a **class of service (COS)**. The COS allows a user to specify a high priority, a quick response, a secure line, a lower cost, or a higher throughput. This is similar to the Internet's type of service option in Section 7.4. Since SNA allows multiple connections between two subarea nodes (Figure 8.30), the COS partly determines which one to use. For example, a high throughput COS is better served by an optical fiber link, but a coaxial connection might be chosen for a low-cost COS. A quick response request would avoid a satellite link. The **explicit route** includes the virtual route further qualified by the actual transmission links between subarea nodes.

**Transmission Group Control**     The last component of path control is the transmission group control. A **transmission group** consists of one or more parallel transmission lines between two nodes that all can be assigned to the same explicit route. The purpose is to transmit different parts of user data in parallel to increase the overall transmission rate. Figure 8.31 shows an example. Two users at remote sites

FIGURE 8.30    **Explicit Routes Between Two Subarea Nodes**

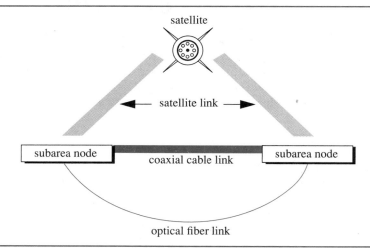

establish a connection and appear to communicate at a 50-Mbps rate. Unknown to each of them, the path control layers defined an explicit path with a three-line transmission group. One line has a 10-Mbps rate and the other two have 20-Mbps rates. Assuming everything works correctly and that information is transmitted over all three lines simultaneously, the perceived rate of transfer is 50 Mbps.

The transmission group control also can increase the data rate using **blocking** when there is only one transmission link available. It combines several

FIGURE 8.31    **Gaining Bandwidth via Multiple Links**

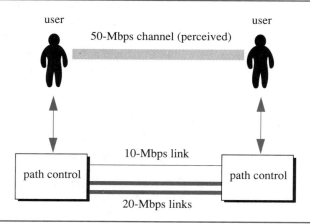

PIUs into a single but larger unit called the **basic transmission unit** (**BTU**). It then sends the BTU to the next lower layer for transmission as a single unit. The BTU is eventually sent where the receiving path control layer extracts the PIUs from it. Blocking several PIUs reduces the overhead bits required in sending otherwise separate units. It also eliminates the time between sending separate PIUs because they are sent together. You might review Section 5.2, which addressed the issue of effective data rates as a function of overhead, frame size, and overall bit rate.

### TRANSMISSION CONTROL

The **transmission control layer** is analogous to the OSI transport layer. It is an end-to-end protocol defining a logical connection (session) between two NAUs (Figure 8.32). Despite the similar terminology, the SNA **session** is more like the OSI transport connection than the OSI session. Once established, the session allows the two NAUs to communicate on a level transparent to the underlying network structure. The transmission control layer has two main components, the **session control** and the **connection point manager**.

**Session Control**     The **session control** has the responsibility for starting, maintaining, and ending sessions. Perhaps the logical place to start is to describe the five different session types. Meijer (Reference 32) defines the following five session types categorized by the types of NAUs at each end:[*]

- **LU-LU.** These are the sessions that are fulfilling the purpose of the network; through them the actual transfer of data between end-users can take place.

**FIGURE 8.32     Transmission Control Session Between Two NAUs**

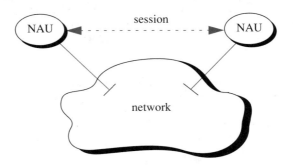

[*] A. Meijer, *Systems Network Architecture: A Tutorial,* ©1988, pp. 73, 75. Reprinted by permission of UCL Press, London.

- **PU-PU.** Between physical units no specific sessions are defined. There is, however, communication possible between PUs that are adjacent, in order to exchange Network Control information. Request Units that are supported are Network Control (NC) RUs, for the management of the explicit routes.

- **SSCP-SSCP.** These sessions are used for the communication between control domains in a multidomain network. They must be activated to make any cross-domain activities possible.

- **SSCP-PU.** These sessions must exist between the SSCP and all physical units in its control domain. They must be activated before any other activity, with the nodes controlled by the PUs if possible. The sessions are used to exchange network control information between the SSCP and the PU.

- **SSCP-LU.** These sessions are established between the SSCP and all logical units in its control domain. They must be activated before the LUs can get involved in any other activity.

Session establishment is not a simple task, and the approach varies depending on the NAU types and whether they reside in the same or different domains. We will describe one example of establishing a session between two LUs in different domains (Figure 8.33). References 26 and 32 provide details on other session types. During this discussion we assume that all necessary SSCP-LU, SSCP-PU, and SSCP-SSCP sessions already exist. As stated earlier, they are necessary before LUs can establish sessions with each other.

Similar to previous protocols there are different types of **BIUs (basic information units)** conveying different information. Session establishment defines the BIUs exchanged and the various responses to them. Suppose, in our example, LU *A* requests that a session be established with LU *B*. LU *A* might correspond to a user at a workstation trying to access a file server represented by LU *B*. When the user at *A* enters the command to request access the session control protocol goes into action.

Figure 8.34 outlines the series of BIUs the NAUs exchange. First, LU *A* indicates that it wants a session by sending an "**INITSELF**" request to the SSCP in its domain. LU *A* has no idea whether LU *B* is in its domain or not so the SSCP will make that determination. The request also identifies the LU making the request and

FIGURE 8.33    **Configuration for Example Session Establishment**

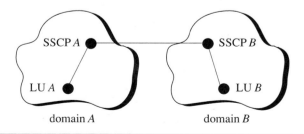

domain *A*    domain *B*

FIGURE 8.34    **Request/Response Exchange for LU-LU Session Establishment**

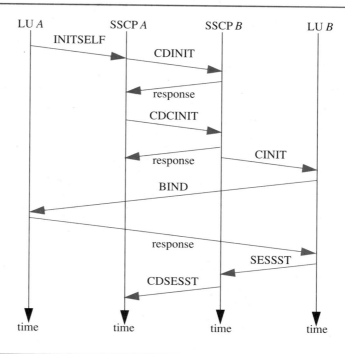

to whom the request is made. The SSCP in domain A gets the request and determines whether LU B is in its domain or another one. In this case, LU B is in another domain, adding complexity to the request. Now SSCP A must communicate with SSCP B and get it involved in the session establishment.

Consequently, SSCP A sends a "**CDINIT**" (**Cross Domain INITialize**) request to SSCP B. This is a preliminary indication to SSCP B that an LU from domain A wants a session with an LU in domain B. If SSCP B agrees to help in the session establishment (specified in the response) SSCP A follows with a "**CDCINIT**" (**Cross Domain Control INITialize**) request. This request contains all the details regarding the proposed session and provides information about the LU making the request. It may seem strange to do this with two separate requests, but it is common to make a request and get agreement before providing all the information. It's a bit like a student approaching an instructor and saying "May I ask a question?" before actually asking it.

When SSCP B gets the information in the "CDCINIT" request it responds to SSCP A and then sends a "**CINIT**" (**Control INITiate**) request to LU B. It tells LU B that LU A wants a session and requests that LU B send a "**BIND**" command all the way back to LU A. The BIND command actually initiates the session establishment and also contains some session parameters that B suggests (we will see some examples when we discuss the higher layers). When LU *A* gets the BIND, if it agrees with the controlling parameters it sends a response back to LU *B*. As far as LU *A* and LU *B* are concerned, the session is now established. The only task left is to inform the SSCPs that it is established. LU *B* sends SSCP *B* a "**SESSST**" (**SESS**ion **ST**arted) message and SSCP *B* sends a "**CDSESSST**" (**C**ross **D**omain **SESS**ion **ST**arted) message to SSCP *A*.

We know that much of this reads like an excursion through a large bowl of alphabet soup. SNA, along with much of the IBM industry, is loaded with acronyms. If necessary you should read it a second or even third time, take two aspirins, and call an IBM representative in the morning.

**Connection Point Manager**    The **connection point manager's (CPMGR)** main function is to provide support for data flow over a session. It has several specific responsibilities, among them:

- **Message sequencing**. As in previous protocols, messages are sequenced to make sure they arrive in order. It also uses message numbers to relate responses to previous requests.

- **Message buffering**. It maintains queues for incoming and outgoing messages.

- **Expedited messages**. Similar to the urgent indicator in TCP (Section 7.5), it allows certain "important" messages to be sent ahead of others following the normal sequence.

- **Pacing**. We haven't forgotten that we said that pacing is a function of the virtual route control sublayer. In that case, pacing refers to the traffic over a particular virtual route. However, a virtual route (or part of one) may support multiple sessions. In this case, pacing refers strictly to the flow rate between the two session partners. The pacing algorithm is basically the same as that used by virtual route control, except in this case the window size is fixed.

- **Encryption**. During session establishment the BIND message specifies whether none, some, or all messages will be encrypted. The CPMGR uses the DES algorithm to encrypt messages.

## DATA FLOW CONTROL

The fifth layer in SNA is the **data flow control** layer, whose functions are similar to the OSI session layer (Section 1.4). It is perhaps the lowest layer to provide services directly to the user. Despite the name, it has nothing to do with flow control as we have defined it. That is primarily a function of the lower layers. Responsibilities of this layer include:

- S**pecifying send/receive modes**. Specified in the BIND command, this function allows the LUs to exchange data using a half-duplex transfer mode, a useful feature if buffers must be shared by incoming and outgoing messages. There are two types of half-duplex modes: **half-duplex flip-flop** and **half-duplex contention**. Half-duplex flip-flop requires that the two LUs take turns sending with the

BIND command specifying who goes first. When the sending LU has finished sending it sets a bit (**change direction indicator**) in the last RU and enters a receive mode. When the receiving LU detects the indicator it enters the send mode. It is similar to passing a token back and forth. In this way they continue to take turns being in the sending and receiving modes.

With half-duplex contention mode either station can enter a send mode and transmit. However, if both do so at the same time a contention results. To address this, one of the LUs is designated a contention winner (by the BIND command) during session establishment. It is a bit like determining who is going to win before playing the game. When contention happens the winner rejects incoming messages and sends a reject response to the loser. The loser then must exit the send mode, dequeue the messages it sent, receive the incoming messages, and try sending later.

- **Chaining**. Chaining is a way of defining a sequence of RUs going in one direction (chain) that must be processed together. Chain indicators in the RU headers indicate the beginning and end of a chain. The idea is that a particular request might be made using several RUs. With chaining, the protocols could recover from an error by restarting the activity with the beginning of the chain. For example, suppose a small file was being transferred as a chain of RUs to a file server. If the drive failed and destroyed the information already written the protocols could recover, start from the beginning of the chain, and write all the information to a backup device.

  There are three types of chains: **no-response chain**, **exception-response chain**, and **definite-response chain**. The no-response chain means that no response is required for any RU in the chain. Exception-response requires a response only in the event of an error detected in one of the chain's RUs. The definite-response requires a response whether the chain was received intact or not.

- **Bracketing**. Chains can be generalized into **brackets** (Figure 8.35), providing another level of organizing RUs. A bracket typically corresponds to a **transaction**, a user-defined unit of work that might actually consist of several request/response exchanges. A typical example is a database query in which you enter a primary key, retrieve the information (and consequently lock the record), make updates, and store the result. An application layer could define these activities as a single transaction, thus causing all the associated RUs to be bracketed. The idea is to avoid a situation in which an error occurs after retrieving the record, thus severing the connection and leaving the record locked. With bracketing, the protocols would process all of the RUs or none at all. If an error occurred in the middle it would restart from the beginning of the bracket.

- **Defining request/response modes**. We stated earlier that there are two types of RUs, a request and a response. Generally a response will follow a request, but there are exceptions. Flags in an RU header can specify three types of responses: do not respond, respond only if an error occurs, respond always. Four request/response modes define the relationship between a request and a response.

FIGURE 8.35    **Relationship Between Chaining and Bracketing**

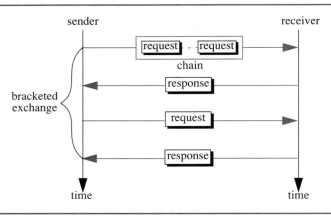

In **immediate request mode** if a sender sends a request (or a chain) requiring a definite response it may not send another until it receives the response. This rule does not apply to requests requiring exception responses or none at all. In other words, several of those requests can be pending. **Delayed request mode** allows the sender to have several requests requiring definite responses pending (there is an analogy here with the unrestricted and stop and wait flow control protocols if you think of responses as similar to acknowledgments). **Immediate response mode** requires the receiver to return responses in the same order the associated requests arrived. **Delayed response mode** allows them to be returned in any order. They largely define how much synchronization you want between the requests and responses.

The data flow control layer primarily provides a service for the layer above it, the presentation services. That is, the previous functions typically apply to RUs that data flow control receives from presentation services. However, in some cases the data flow control layers on each end can define and exchange their own RUs. For example, one end can stop the flow of incoming messages temporarily by sending a "QUIESCE AT END OF CHAIN" command. The other end will finish with its current chain but will send nothing more until it receives a "RELEASE QUIESCE" command.

An NAU also can prepare for session termination by sending a "SHUTDOWN" command to begin the session termination procedures at the transmission control layer. The other end will send any outstanding responses and then send a "SHUTDOWN COMPLETE" command, thus terminating the session. For information other examples of RUs that data flow control can exchange, we refer you to Reference 32.

## HIGHER LAYERS

Earlier we stated that references vary regarding the number of layers they attribute to SNA. In part this is due to developments within the SNA architecture itself. For example, in earlier versions of SNA there was one layer (**function management layer**) above the data flow control layer. With the development and release of LU 6.2, that layer was divided into the **presentation services** and **transaction services** layers (Figure 8.25).

We do not want to enter into discussions involving details that vary according to versions and the impact that LU 6.2 had on SNA. We do feel, however, that it is important to understand that such differences exist and to have a general idea of the impact of LU 6.2. Therefore, our approach here is to finish up this section, chapter, and book with brief summaries of these last two layers and refer you to more extensive readings.

At this level of discussion the presentation services layer is similar to the OSI presentation layer. It provides format translation to account for differences in the internal representation of data or in the control characters used to display data on a screen or print it. It also provides compression to increase transmission efficiency. A notable difference from OSI is encryption, a responsibility of the transmission control layer instead of the presentation services layer.

Transaction Services allows an operator to configure the network by adding or removing communication links. It also allows the gathering and display of network usage statistics, a useful feature in planning for future expansion or reconfiguration. This can include tracking various performance measures and providing accounting services to charge users for using the network. Applications also exist to provide testing and to help track down and isolate network errors. In some cases it can diagnose what went wrong and either provide a solution or bypass the problem until it can be fixed. The earlier versions of SNA had these services in the function management layer (also called NAU services layer). Reference 32 has an entire chapter devoted to these topics.

Finally, we mention LU 6.2 again because it has had a significant impact on the SNA architecture and its abilities. Prior to it, communicating entities were always involved in a master/slave relationship (a typical terminal-to-host connection). The slave entity had less processing power and had to make requests to the master regarding establishing and defining the protocols. With the advent of workstations and distributed computing environments, however, the need grew for more peer-to-peer sessions. This means that either end has significant computing power and can take the initiative in establishing sessions or making other requests. It also eliminates the need to exchange data in predefined formats and allows a two-way interactive ability between programs running on very different processors. We said it before but it bears repeating: LU 6.2 goes a long way toward making the underlying architecture completely transparent to the end user and providing distributed computing capabilities. The downside (and there is always a downside) is that it is expensive and may not be the best choice for environments that do not need a distributed environment. References 31, 32, 33, and 34 provide some different viewpoints on LU 6.2, how it works, and its role in future systems.

As with many protocols there is some disagreement as to whether SNA will eventually be superseded by other protocols such as OSI or even TCP/IP. Some feel that TCP/IP is better designed for decentralized computing environments (Reference 35).

IBM, of course, is not going to sit on its reputation and has developed its **Advanced Peer-to-Peer Networking** (**APPN**). Derived from SNA it allows a wide variety of computers to communicate across many different types of networks (including LANs and WANs). Some believe it will outperform current versions of TCP/IP and OSI protocols and will be in demand for a variety of applications from low-speed transport to multimedia applications (Reference 36). Yet others believe that TCP/IP still provides more flexibility and service to a greater variety of platforms (Reference 37). Regardless of the diverse views of many professionals, one thing is certain. There will continue to be many approaches to meeting network needs. Understanding them and their differences will challenge us well into the 21st century.

# Review Questions

1. Distinguish between a smart terminal and a virtual terminal.

2. Describe the client-server mode of computing.

3. What is TELNET?

4. Distinguish between a remote login and a conventional login.

5. What is a virtual file structure?

6. Are the following TRUE or FALSE? Why?

    a. TELNET allows you to login to any account on a remote machine as long as it is reachable via a network connection.

    b. TCP and IP are OSI model layer 3 and layer 4 protocols.

    c. Sending mail over Internet does not require a connection.

    d. Each message sent via the X.400 protocol is stored in its entirety at each intermediate X.400 node.

    e. Two user agents at the same site can communicate directly under the X.400 protocol.

    f. The all-digital capability of ISDN would provide immediate advantages to everyone who uses it.

    g. SNA pacing is the same as a sliding window protocol.

7. How does anonymous FTP differ from FTP?

8. What is an RFC?

9. Distinguish between TFTP and FTP.

10. What is SMTP?

11. Why are TCP and IP at different layers in the protocol hierarchy?

12. What is SNMP?

13. What is SNMP's management information base?

14. What is the exterior gateway protocol?

15. Distinguish among a coldstart trap, warmstart trap, and linkdown trap.

16. Why are there two standards for email, namely SMTP and X.400?

17. Distinguish between an X.400 user agent and a message transfer agent.

18. List four functions of X.400's user agent you think would be most useful to you.

19. What does the message transfer agent put in a message's envelope?

20. How does a store-and-forward protocol differ from previous protocols such as a packet switched protocol?

21. Distinguish among an MHS probe, message, and report.

22. Distinguish among MHS's P1, P2, and P3 protocols.

23. List four MHS services you think would be most useful to you.

24. Distinguish between the X.400 and X.500 protocol families.

25. What is a directory service?

26. Distinguish between X.500's directory information base and directory information tree.

27. Distinguish between a directory user agent and a directory system agent.

28. What is ISDN?

29. Distinguish between ISDN's basic and primary services.

30. List four ISDN services you think would be most useful to you.

31. List and summarize the four primary functional groups in ISDN.

32. List and summarize the four reference points in ISDN.

33. What is the difference between out-of-band and in-band signaling?

34. What is signaling system #7?

35. What is pseudoternary coding?

36. What is broadband ISDN?

37. What is SNA?

38. List each of SNA's seven layers and a brief description of its functions.

39. Distinguish between an SNA subarea node and peripheral node.

40. What is a network addressable unit?

41. Distinguish between an SNA logical unit and a physical unit.

42. How does the virtual route control change the size of an NAU's window?

43. Why is pacing done at both the path control layer and the transmission control layer?

44. What is the path control's transmission group?

45. Distinguish between explicit route control and virtual route control.

46. List and summarize the five types of SNA sessions.

47. What is a connection point manager?

48. List the major functions of SNA's data flow control layer.

49. Distinguish between the data flow control's chain and bracket.

# Exercises

1. Do a remote login to some account and experiment with some of the TELNET commands. For example, you can do the following:

   - Type a large file, escape to TELNET, and abort the output.
   - Determine the response to the AYT command.
   - Send EC commands to erase characters in an incorrectly typed command.
   - Run a long program, escape to TELNET, and interrupt the process.
   - Send an EL command to erase an incorrectly typed line.

   If you do not have access to an account on a remote machine you can login to your own account and access your account a second time via TELNET. It's a little like calling yourself on the telephone, but it works and allows you to become familiar with TELNET. (You will have to determine whether your site allows multiple logins to one account.)

2. Connect to a remote site via anonymous FTP; transfer a small file to your account; and write a short summary of the file's contents.

3. Connect to an Archie site and look for information on a topic of your choice. If it is more convenient, you may use Gopher, WAIS, or any of the other information sources.

4. Send someone you know an email message over Internet. If you don't know anyone at a remote site who has access to Internet, send an Internet mail message to someone locally, to the author of this text, indicating your opinion of the text, or to

yourself. (As in Exercise 1, this is a little like sending yourself a letter but, again, it helps you get familiar with Internet email.)

5. Suppose Mary Smith's (from Figure 8.15) husband is a marketing analyst in the same company. How would someone send him email using the X.500 directory service?

6. Suppose each of the TE1's in the following figure tries sending something to the NT2 at the same time.

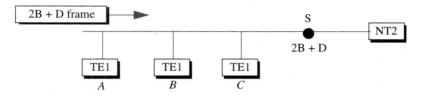

Suppose also that each is trying to send the following over the D channel.

- A sends 10011101.
- B sends 10001100.
- C sends 10011001.

Which TE1 wins the contention?

7. ISDN's B channel capacities were designed with the intention of transmitting voice. Section 2.4 showed that to capture most of a voice's characteristics 8-bit samples taken at a frequency of 8000 samples per second is sufficient and requires a bit rate of 64,000 bps. However, some encoding techniques actually allow voice data to be transmitted using 32,000 bps, and others will likely allow 16,000 bps to be sufficient. What effect will this have on the ISDN standard?

8. Draw a diagram similar to that of Figure 8.24 showing the ISDN disconnect procedure.

## REFERENCES

1. Shay, W. A. *Introduction to Operating Systems.* New York: Harper Collins, 1993.

2. Comer, D. E. *Internetworking with TCP/IP. Volume 1: Principles, Protocols, and Architecture,* 2nd ed. Englewood Cliffs, NJ: Prentice-Hall, 1991.

3. Comer, D. E. *Internetworking with TCP/IP. Volume III: Principles, Protocols, and Architecture.* Englewood Cliffs, NJ: Prentice-Hall, 1993.

4. Kehoe, B. P. *Zen and the Art of the Internet: A Beginner's Guide.* Englewood Cliffs, NJ: Prentice-Hall, 1993.

5. Kahle, B. and A. Medlar. "An Information System for Corporate Users: Wide Area Information Servers." *Connexions—The Interoperability Report,* vol. 5, no. 11 (November 1991) 2–9.

6.  McCahill, "The Internet Gopher Protocol: A Distributed Server Information System." *Connexions—The Interoperability Report*, vol. 6, no. 7 (July 1992) 10–14.

7.  Obraczka, K., P. Danzig, and S. Li. "Internet Resource Discovery Services." *Computer*, vol. 26, no. 9 (September 1993) 8–22.

8.  Russel, D. *The Principles of Computer Networking.* Cambridge, England: Cambridge University Press, 1989.

9.  Comer, D. E. *Internetworking with TCP/IP, Volume II: Design, Implementation, and Internals.* Englewood Cliffs, NJ: Prentice-Hall, 1991.

10. Rose, M. *The Simple Book: An Introduction to Management of TCP/IP.* Englewood Cliffs, NJ: Prentice-Hall, 1991.

11. Stallings, W. *SNMP, SNMPv2, and CMIP: The Practical Guide to Network-Management Standards.* Reading, MA: Addison-Wesley, 1994.

12. Jander, M. "SNMP 2: Coming Soon to a Network Near You." *Data Communications*, vol. 21, no. 16 (November 1992) 66–76.

13. Halsall, F. *Data Communications, Computer Networks and Open Systems*, 3rd ed. Reading, MA: Addison-Wesley, 1992.

14. Black, U. *The X Series Recommendations.* New York: McGraw-Hill, 1991.

15. Stallings, W. *Data and Computer Communications*, 4th ed. New York: Macmillan, 1994.

16. Tsuchiya, P. F. and T. Eng. "Extending the IP Internet Through Address Reuse." *Computer Communication Review*, vol. 23, no. 1 (January 1993) 16–33.

17. Weder, C., J. Reynolds, and S. Heker. "Technical Overview of Directory Services Using the X.500 Protocol." RFC Document 1309.

18. Saunders, S. and P. Heywood. "X.400's Last Windows of Opportunity." *Data Communications*, vol. 21, no. 8, (May 1992) 73–6.

19. Salamone, S. "Messaging Backbones: Making Sure the Mail (and More) Gets Through." *Data Communications*, vol. 22, no. 8 (May 1993) 54–62.

20. Scott, K. "X.400 Pushes the Envelope for Electronic Messaging." *Data Communications*, vol. 19, no. 7 (June 1990) 93–102.

21. Stallings, W. *ISDN: An Introduction.* New York: Macmillan, 1989.

22. Griffiths, J. M. *ISDN Explained.* New York: Wiley, 1990.

23. Black, U. *Data Networks Concept, Theory, and Practice.* Englewood Cliffs, NJ: Prentice-Hall, 1989.

24. Schlanger, G. G. "An Overview of Signaling System No. 7. " *IEEE Journal on Selected Areas in Communincation*, vol. SAC-4, no. 3 (May 1986) 360–5.

25. Appenzeller, H. R. "Signaling System No. 7, ISDN User Part." *IEEE Journal on Selected Areas in Communication*, vol. SAC-4, no. 3 (May 1986) 366–71.

26. Spragins, J. D., J. L. Hammond, and K. Pawlikowski. *Telecommunications Protocols and Design.* Reading, MA: Addison-Wesley, 1991.

27. Tanenbaum, A. S. *Computer Networks,* 2nd ed. Englewood Cliffs, NJ: Prentice-Hall, 1988.

28. Held, G. "Is ISDN an Obsolete Data Network?" *Data Communications*, vol. 18, no. 14 (November 1989) 103–10.

29. Johnson, J. T. "ISDN Goes Nationwide, But Will Users Want It?" *Data Communications*, vol. 21, no. 16 (November 1992) 93–8.

30. Hindin, E. M. "Hayes Unveils ISDN API, Which Could Become Standard." *Data Communications*, vol. 19, no. 2 (February 1990) 41–6.

31. Sherman, K. *Data Communications: A User's Guide*, 3rd ed. Englewood Cliffs, NJ: Prentice-Hall, 1990.

32. Meijer, A. "Systems Network Architecture: A Tutorial. " New York: Wiley, 1988.

33. Stallings, W. *Business Data Communications*. New York: Macmillan, 1990.

34. Fitzgerald J. *Business Data Communications Basic Concepts, Security and Design,* 3rd ed. New York: Wiley, 1990.

35. Friedman, N. "APPN Rises to the Enterprise Architecture Challenge." *Data Communications*, vol. 22, no. 3 (February 1993) 87–98.

36. Keough, L. "APPN: IBM's Bid for Multiprotocol Nets." *Data Communications*, vol. 21, no. 7 (May 1992) 55–8.

37. Snell, N. "Why TCP/IP Still Has the Edge. "*Datamation*, vol. 38, no. 20 (October 1 1992) 38–42.

# GLOSSARY

| | |
|---|---|
| abort | a sudden end to an activity, usually due to some type of error |
| abstract Syntax Notation 1 (ASN.1) | formal language designed expressly for the definition of protocol data unit formats and the representation of and operations on distributed information |
| access control (token ring) | octet in a token containing priority, reservation, token, and monitor bits |
| ack timer | timer used in flow control protocols to determine when to send a separate acknowledgment in the absence of outgoing frames |
| acknowledgment | indication that a station has received something from another |
| active monitor present frame | special frame used in the token ring protocol to indicate the presence of an active monitor station |
| adaptive routing | routing strategy that can respond to changes in a network |
| address field | field in a frame or packet identifying its sender or receiver |
| address learning | ability of a LAN bridge to update its routing tables dynamically |
| address lookup service | ability to get the email address of someone by specifying any of a variety of items that uniquely identify a person |
| address recognized bit | bit in a token ring frame indicating whether the destination address has been recognized |
| advanced peer-to-peer networking | an SNA derivative allowing a wide variety of computers to communicate across many types of networks |
| Advanced Research Projects Agency | agency of the U.S. Department of Defense |
| Advanced Research Projects Agency Network | network developed by the Advanced Research Projects Agency that evolved into protocols used in the Internet |

| | |
|---|---|
| all-routes broadcast frame | frame that a bridge will route onto all available LANs |
| Aloha | word used as a greeting or farewell |
| Aloha protocol | packet radio protocol in which a station sends a packet and, if it collides with another, will send another after a random amount of time |
| alternate mark inversion | digital encoding in which a 1-bit is represented by zero volts and a 0-bit is represented alternately by a positive and a negative signal |
| Amateur Packet Radio Network | packet radio network using TCP/IP and registered with the Internet |
| American National Standards Institute | private, nongovernmental standards agency whose members are manufacturers, users, and other interested companies |
| American Standard Code for Information Interchange (ASCII) | 7-bit code that assigns a unique combination to every keyboard character and to some special functions |
| amplitude | largest magnitude of an analog signal |
| amplitude modulation (amplitude shift keying) | method of representing bits using analog signals with different magnitudes |
| analog signal | continuously varying signal |
| analog-to-digital conversions | process of converting an analog signal to a digital one |
| anonymous FTP | application allowing remote users access to a set of files at a given site |
| application layer | seventh and highest layer of the OSI protocol, which works directly with a user or with application programs |
| Archie | information service designed to scan FTP sites and maintain a database relating the sites and their content |
| ARCNET | token passing protocol that uses a star topology |
| asynchronous balanced mode | mode for HDLC in which either station can send data, control information, or commands |
| asynchronous response mode | mode for HDLC in which a primary station can send data, control information, or commands, and a secondary station can send control information or data only |
| asynchronous transfer mode | very fast packet switched protocol using small fixed-sized packets optimized for multimedia use |
| asynchronous transmission | transmission mode in which bits are divided into small groups (bytes or octets) and sent independently |
| attenuate | degradation of a signal as it travels along a medium |

| | |
|---|---|
| Australian Computer Science network | largest network in Australia connecting universities, government agencies, and private organizations |
| authentication | verifying the sender of a message |
| autobaud modems | a modem capable of automatically choosing one of several modulation standards |
| automatic repeat request | error control whereby a station requests the sending station to resend a message if an error occurs |
| B channels | ISDN channel capable of transmitting at 64Kbps |
| backbone | that part of a network comprising the primary transmission paths |
| backward learning algorithm | routing algorithm in which a node learns from its neighbors the cheapest route to another node |
| balanced circuits | circuit using two lines carrying equal but opposite signals |
| bandpass filter | device used to extract individual modulated signals |
| bandwidth | difference between the highest and lowest frequencies that a medium can transmit |
| baseband mode | mode in which a cable's bandwidth is devoted to a single stream of data |
| baud rate | rate at which signal components can change |
| Baudot code | a 5-bit code originally designed for the French telegraph and still used today in telegraph and telex communications |
| Bay Area Regional Research Network (BARRNet) | a regional metropolitan network connecting (among others) several university campuses in the San Francisco area |
| beacon frame | token ring control frame used to inform stations a problem has occurred and the token-passing protocol has stopped |
| beam shaping | process of allowing a satellite signal to be concentrated in a small area |
| Because It's Time Network (BITNET) | a network used largely by academic institutions that runs an IBM-developed protocol |
| BEL | an ASCII control character causing a CRT or terminal to emit an audible sound |
| Bellman-Ford algorithm | a type of backward learning algorithm |
| binary coded decimal (BCD) | a code used in early IBM mainframes |
| binary exponential backoff algorithm | algorithm used to determine when a station should resend a frame after a collision |
| binary synchronous control (BSC) protocol | byte-oriented data link protocol made popular by IBM |

| | |
|---|---|
| bindery | Novell NetWare file containing file access rights for a user or group of users |
| bit-level ciphering | encryption by bit manipulation |
| bit oriented protocol | a protocol that treats frames as bit streams |
| bit pipe | the actual bit transmission in the ISDN protocol |
| bit stuffing | the insertion of an extra bit to avoid a long run of the same bit |
| bit-time | time required for one bit to be transmitted |
| block check character | character used by the BSC protocol for error checking |
| boundary nodes | nodes forming the backbone in the SNA protocol |
| bridge | an OSI layer 2 connection between two networks |
| bridge port | bridge to a LAN connection |
| bridge protocol data units | unit of information exchanged by bridges |
| bridge routing | the process a bridge uses to determine which frames to forward and where to forward them |
| British Columbia Network | a regional network connecting several Canadian universities, the British Columbia Advanced Systems Institute, and Dominion Astrophysical Observatory |
| broadband mode | mode in which a cable's bandwidth is divided into ranges, each carrying separately coded information |
| broadcast address | address indicating a frame should be sent to all stations on a network |
| brouter | device providing functions at both OSI layer 2 and layer 3 |
| buffering | temporary storage of information |
| bulletin boards | data banks allowing the exchange of software, files, or other information |
| burst error | error affecting a large number of bits |
| bus topology | way of connecting devices so they all communicate via a common cable |
| byte multiplexer | device that combines bytes from different sources onto a common data stream |
| byte-oriented protocol | protocol that treats frames as byte streams |
| byte stuffing | insertion of an extra byte to avoid misinterpreting a data byte as a control byte |
| Caesar cipher | simple encryption technique in which a character is replaced by another dependent only on the value of the original character |
| California Education and Research Federation Network | network consisting largely of California universities and research organizations |

| | |
|---|---|
| call confirmation | indication that a call has been accepted |
| call request | action taken by a device when it wants to establish a connection |
| Cambridge ring | ring network containing several rotating tokens |
| Canada Network | the first X.400 network in the world with its administrative headquarters at the University of British Columbia (UBC) |
| Carriage Return | ASCII control character causing a print mechanism or cursor to return to the left-most print position |
| carrier sense multiple access (CSMA) | protocol used to sense whether a medium is busy before attempting to transmit |
| carrier sense multiple access with collision detection (CSMA/CD) | same as carrier sense, multiple access but also has the ability to detect whether a transmission has collided with another |
| carrier signal | signal that is modulated by an input signal to create another signal |
| cells | geographic region having a reception and transmission station to communicate with cellular telephones |
| cellular telephone | portable telephone capable of connecting to the telephone system using radio communications |
| centralized routing | routing using information that is generated and maintained at a single central location |
| channel utilization | measurement specifying percentage of time a channel spends transferring information |
| channels | bandwidth range |
| Cheapernet | IEEE 802.3 network using 10 BASE 2 cable |
| checksum | field used for error detection formed by adding bit strings interpreted as integers |
| choke packets | control packet sent to a station causing it to reduce the number of packets it is transmitting |
| ciphertext | message that has been encrypted |
| circuit switching | a connection that is dedicated to the communication between two stations |
| cladding | part of an optical fiber that is optically less dense than the core, thus causing light to reflect back into the core |
| claim token frame | token ring control frame used to determine a monitor station |
| class of service | SNA path control option allowing a user to specify a high priority, quick response, secure line, lower cost, or higher throughput |
| clear to send | RS 232 signal from a DCE giving a DTE permission to send |
| client | device in a client-server model that sends requests to a server |
| client-server model | model of communication between two devices in which each has computing power |

| | |
|---|---|
| coaxial cable | conductive wire surrounded by an insulating layer, wire mesh, and a protective outer cover |
| code | association of bit patterns with specific information such as characters or actions |
| codec | device used to translate an analog signal to a digital equivalent |
| collision | the result when two or more stations both send a signal over a medium designed to transmit one signal at a time |
| collision detection | ability of a station to determine when a collision has occurred |
| combined station | station that can act as both a primary and a secondary station in the HDLC protocol |
| Comité Consultatif Internationale de Télégraphique et Téléphonique (CCITT) | standards organization whose members include various scientific and industrial organizations, telecommunication agencies, telephone authorities, and the ISO |
| common bus topology | way of connecting devices so they all communicate via a common cable |
| common management information protocol | ISO management protocol |
| communications subnet | collection of transmission media and switching elements required for routing and data transmission |
| compact disc | storage medium in which information is stored optically by making very small "pits" in a reflective material |
| compression | way to reduce the number of bits during transmission while retaining the meaning of the transmitted message |
| CompuServe | information service allowing subscribers to access a distributed database |
| computer hacker | person who likes to program just for sheer enjoyment of doing it |
| Computer Science Network | network connecting academic, government, industrial, and nonprofit institutions primarily throughout North America |
| concentrator | intelligent statistical multiplexer that can verify, acknowledge, and compress data |
| congestion | excessive amount of traffic over a network that causes a degradation of service and response times |
| connection | mechanism through which two stations exchange information |
| connection management | protocol used to establish, maintain, and release connections |
| connection request | request to establish a connection |
| connection strategy | strategy used to implement a connection |

| | |
|---|---|
| contention | term used when two or more stations want to transmit over a common medium at the same time |
| contention protocol | technique used to control access to a common medium from multiple entry points |
| control bits | the part of the data frame used for control functions such as routing and handling |
| control characters | binary codes that correspond to an action rather than data |
| control prefix character | special character inserted into a data stream by Kermit to avoid misinterpreting a data character as a control character |
| control-Q | control character used to tell a device to resume sending |
| control-S | control character used to tell a device to stop sending |
| credit | used in flow control, it specifies the number of bytes a TCP entity can receive from another |
| credit mechanism | method used to implement flow control in TCP |
| crosstalk | interference on a line caused by signals being transmitted along another one |
| cyclic redundancy check | error detection method based on interpreting bit strings as polynomials with binary coefficients |
| D channel | ISDN channel typically used for control and low-speed applications |
| data carrier detect | RS-232 signal indicating that a DCE is receiving a suitable carrier signal |
| data circuit-terminating equipment (DCE) | device used as an interface between a DTE and a network |
| data compression | way to reduce the number of bits during transmission while retaining the meaning of the transmitted message |
| data encryption standard | encryption technique developed by IBM and adopted as a standard by the U.S. government |
| data link escape | control character used as a toggle switch causing a device to interpret subsequently received characters differently |
| data link protocols | protocols operating at OSI layer 2 |
| data link layer | layer 2 of the OSI protocol |
| data rate | measurement specifying the number of data bits a medium can transmit per unit of time |
| data set ready | RS-232 signal indicating the DCE has connected to a communications medium |
| data terminal equipment (DTE) | device connected to a communications medium via a DCE |
| data terminal ready | RS-232 signal indicating a DTE is ready |
| datagram | independent transmission unit in a packet switching network |

| | |
|---|---|
| deadlock | situation in which stations are waiting for events to occur that cannot happen because of their own current states |
| deadly embrace | same as deadlock |
| decibel | measurement related to signal-to-noise ratio |
| decryption | process of restoring an encrypted message to its original form |
| defacto standards | standards that exist by virtue of their widespread use |
| demodulation | restoring a signal that has been modulated to its original form |
| designated bridge | during execution of the spanning tree algorithm for LAN interconnection, a bridge elected to forward frames from a LAN |
| destination address | address to which a frame or packet is to be delivered |
| Deutschland network | German component of EUnet and a UNIX-based European network |
| differential encoding | compression technique in which a frame is represented by the difference between it and a preceding frame |
| Differential Manchester encoding | Manchester encoding technique in which 0 and 1 are distinguished by whether the signal changes at the beginning of a bit interval |
| differential phase shift keying | distinguishing an analog signal by measuring its phase shift relative to that of a previous signal |
| Digital Equipment Corporation | major corporation perhaps best known for manufacture of its VAX line of computers |
| Digital Network Architecture | proprietary network protocol developed by the Digital Equipment Corporation |
| digital signal | square wave signal taking on only a high or low value |
| digital signature | method of authentication involving encrypting a message in a way only the sender would know |
| Dijkstra's algorithm | algorithm used to find the cheapest (shortest) path between two nodes in a graph |
| directory information base | distributed database containing information in an X.500 directory |
| directory service | service that provides the email address of an individual given that he/she is unambiguously identified |
| directory system agent | component of X.500 that manages part of the directory information base at a given site |
| directory user agent | component of X.500 providing the interface between an application and the distributed information base |
| disconnect | termination of a connection |

| | |
|---|---|
| disk duplexing | process of using two different controllers to make duplicate copies of data maintained by a file server |
| disk mirroring | process of using one controller to make duplicate copies of data maintained by a file server by writing it to two different disks |
| distortion | change in a signal due to electronic noise or interference |
| distributed directory | directory made up of components residing at different sites |
| distributed file system | collection of files in which files are maintained by different computers |
| distributed routing | routing strategy in which each node determines and maintains its routing information independently |
| do not fragment bit | control bit that disables fragmentation of a packet during its transmission |
| DoD Internet protocol | network layer protocol adopted by the Department of Defense and used in the Internet |
| domain name server | protocol that translates a symbolic Internet address to a 32-bit numeric address |
| domains | group of nodes in a network |
| double bit errors | transmission error affecting two bits |
| downstream neighbor | neighboring node within a ring in the direction the token travels |
| downward multiplexing | transport layer function that takes data from a single source and sends it to separate network nodes |
| DTE-DCE interface | protocol used to define communication between a DTE and a DCE |
| duplicate address test frame | token ring control frame used to look for stations with the same address |
| echo reply | ICMP packet sent in reply to an echo request |
| echo request | ICMP control packet used to determine whether a particular destination is reachable |
| effective data rate | measurement specifying the number of actual data bits that can be transmitted per unit of time |
| eighth-bit prefix character | character used in Kermit to precede some transmitted bytes from a binary file |
| electrical ground | voltage level with which all signal voltages are compared |
| Electronic Industries Association | standards agency consisting of members from electronics firms and manufacturers of telecommunications equipment and a member of ANSI |
| electronic mail (email) | service allowing the sending of files or messages to another site electronically |

| | |
|---|---|
| electronic numerical integrator and calculator | first completely electronic computer |
| electronic telephone directories | online database providing services similar to that of the conventional telephone directories |
| encryption | rendering of information into a different and unintelligible form |
| encryption key | data used to encrypt a message |
| End of Transmission | control character indicating the end of a transmission |
| End of Transmission Block | control character indicating the end of a block of data |
| envelope | additional control bytes added to a message by the message transfer agent in the X.400 email standard |
| erase character | TELNET command to erase the most recent character entered on a remote host |
| erase line | TELNET command to erase the most recent line entered on a remote host |
| error | unplanned event affecting accuracy of data or a protocol |
| error control | specification of how a station checks frames for errors and what it does if it finds them |
| error correction | process of correcting bits in a frame that were changed during transmission |
| error detection | process of determining whether bits in a frame have changed during transmission |
| error recovery | ability of a protocol to recover in the event of a failure in a network or lower-level protocol |
| escape | control character causing one or more subsequent characters to be associated with some action |
| Eskimo pies | warm-weather treat |
| Ether | imaginary substance that many once believed occupied all of outer space |
| Ethernet | local area network connected using a common bus and using a CSMA/CD contention protocol |
| EUnet | major network spanning western Europe and providing connections to Japan, Korea, Australia, and North America |
| even parity | method of error detection in which an extra bit is added whose value is 0 or 1 in order to make the total number of 1-bits in the transmission unit even |
| expedited messages | SNA mechanism that allows certain messages to be sent ahead of others |
| expiry date indication | MHS service allowing the sender of a message to specify a time and date after which the message is invalid |
| explicit route control | sublayer of SNA's Path Control layer that chooses actual transmission links between subarea nodes |

| | |
|---|---|
| extended binary coded decimal interchange code | 8-bit code for characters and control functions used heavily on IBM mainframes |
| exterior gateway protocol | SNMP protocol that exchanges routing information between two autonomous networks in an internet |
| extra low frequency | communication signals with a frequency less than 300 Hz |
| facsimile (fax) machine | device that scans and digitizes images for transmission over telephone lines |
| Federal Communications Commission | federal agency that regulates and licenses communications |
| fiber distributed data interface | ANSI standard for a ring network using optical fiber |
| file server | device responsible for the maintenance and security of a network's files |
| file transfer protocol | rules for the access and exchange of files between two sites |
| filter | device that allows signals of a certain frequency to pass |
| *fingerd* | UNIX utility that allows users to obtain information about others |
| finite state machine | formal model describing the set of all possible states and state transitions of a system |
| Finnish University Network | network connecting Finnish universities and research establishments |
| fire | activity corresponding to the movement of tokens in a Petri net |
| fixed routing | routing techniques based on information that does not change except by reprogramming |
| fixed routing bridges | bridges that do fixed routing |
| flags | bit indicators that indicate a function or status |
| flooding algorithm | routing algorithm that transmits a message to all possible locations |
| flow control | protocol that regulates the exchange of information between two devices |
| Form Feed | control character causing a print mechanism or cursor to advance to the beginning of the next form or screen |
| forwarding database | information used by a device to route frames from one network to another |
| Fourier Series | mathematical formula used to describe an arbitrary periodic signal |
| fragment | part of a packet formed by fragmentation |
| fragment header | control information in a fragment |

| | |
|---|---|
| fragment offset field | specifies the offset in a packet's data field from where the fragment's data was extracted |
| fragmentation | process of dividing a packet into pieces to maintain consistency with a network's protocol |
| frame | unit of information exchanged by low-level protocols |
| frame check sequence | field in a frame used for error checking |
| frame control | field in a token ring frame containing frame type and other control information |
| frame copied bit | bit indicating whether a token ring frame was copied by its intended destination |
| frame format | way in which bits are organized in a frame |
| frame reject | signal that an incoming frame was rejected by the receiving protocol |
| frame status | field in a token ring frame specifying whether a frame was copied or its destination address was recognized |
| frame timer | timer used in flow control protocols to determine when to resend a frame if it has not been acknowledged |
| frequency | rate at which a signal repeats |
| frequency dependent code | compression technique that assigns bits to a character depending on how frequently it appears in the text |
| frequency division multiplexing | process of accepting analog signals within distinct bandwidths and combining them into a more complex signal with a larger bandwidth |
| frequency modulation (frequency shift keying) | method of representing bits using analog signals with different frequencies |
| full duplex | transmission mode in which a device can send and receive simultaneously |
| fully connected topology | connection strategy in which every device in a network is connected directly to every other one |
| gateway | OSI layer 7 connection between two networks |
| generator polynomial | polynomial used as a divisor in the CRC method of error detection |
| GEnie | information service providing access to on-line databases |
| geosynchronous orbit | orbit at which a satellite moves at the same speed that the earth rotates, thus appearing stationary to a ground observer |
| getsockname | UNIX socket command requesting the local address for a socket |
| getsockopt | UNIX socket command requesting information for a socket |
| glob | FTP command allowing/disallowing the use of wildcard characters |
| go ahead | TELNET command telling a remote host it can send |

| | |
|---|---|
| go-back-n protocol | sliding window flow control protocol in which the receiver must receive frames in order |
| graded index multimode fiber | optical fiber whose cladding has a variable refractive index |
| graph | mathematical model consisting of nodes and edges connecting the nodes |
| gremlin | mythical creature responsible for all lost frames in a network |
| group address | address specifying several stations in a predefined group |
| guard band | unused frequency between two adjacent channels |
| guest station | secondary station in the HDLC protocol |
| hacker | person who likes to program just for sheer enjoyment of doing it |
| half duplex | transmission mode in which a device must alternate between sending and receiving |
| Hamming code | error correction method by doing several parity checks in prescribed positions |
| handshaking | process of defining and setting up a connection |
| Hayes compatible modem | intelligent modem capable of responding to a certain set of commands |
| Hertz (Hz) | signal measurement specifying the number of cycles per second |
| hierarchical routing | routing technique in which nodes are divided into groups called domains |
| high-definition television | television technology providing a much sharper image than conventional television |
| High Energy Physics Network | connects laboratories where high energy physics is researched |
| high-level data link control (HDLC) | data link protocol defined by ISO |
| hop count | a measurement in a routing technique that counts the number of stations along a route |
| horizontal tab | control character causing a print mechanism or cursor to move horizontally to the next tab setting |
| horn antenna | device used for microwave transmission |
| Huffman code | frequency-dependent compression technique |
| I-series | set of documents describing ISDN architecture, configurations, routing principles, and interfaces |
| IEEE 802 Networks | set of network standards for local and metropolitan area networks |
| in-band signaling | signaling technique in which the signals are sent in the same channel or bit stream as data |
| index of refraction | measurement specifying how much light will bend as it travels from one medium to another |

| | |
|---|---|
| information frames | HDLC frames carrying data |
| infrared light | electromagnetic waves with frequencies just below that of visible light |
| Institute of Electrical and Electronic Engineers (IEEE) | professional organization that publishes journals, runs conferences, and develops standards |
| integrated services digital network (ISDN) | standard for a proposed global digital communications system |
| intelligent modem | modem capable of responding to a certain set of commands |
| interface card (IC) | board placed into a PC for the purpose of interfacing with a network |
| International Consultative Committee for Telephony and Telegraphy (CCITT) | standards organization whose members include various scientific and industrial organizations, telecommunications agencies, telephone authorities, and the ISO |
| International Standards Organization (ISO) | world-wide organization consisting of standards bodies from many countries |
| Internet | collection of networks that run the TCP/IP protocol |
| Internet control message protocol (ICMP) | Internet protocol for error reporting and providing routers updates on conditions that can develop in the Internet |
| Internet packet exchange (IPX) | protocol used by Novell NetWare to establish and maintain connections between network devices |
| Internet protocol | network layer protocol originally developed by the Advanced Research Projects Agency |
| Internet worm | famous intrusion into the Internet that clogged systems and forced many to shut down |
| isochronous transmission | similar to asynchronous transmission, except the time between characters is equal to the amount of time needed to send an integral number of characters |
| Japan Unix Network | Japan's major network, which allows researchers to communicate with each other and with colleagues overseas |
| Kepler's laws of planetary motion | mathematical models used to describe planetary motion |
| Kermit | Muppet character and a file transfer protocol |
| key distribution | problem of sending encryption keys to those receiving encrypted messages |

| | |
|---|---|
| laser | very pure and narrow beam of light |
| Lempel-Ziv encoding | compression technique that replaces a repeated string with pointers to a location in which the string is stored |
| light emitting diode | device that produces less concentrated light than a laser and is often used as an alternative to a laser in fiber optic communication |
| line feed | control character that causes a print mechanism or cursor to advance to the next line |
| link access protocols (LAP) | data link layer protocol that handles logical links between stations |
| local area network (LAN) | network spanning a relatively small geographic area connecting a variety of devices |
| local exchange | local office containing switching logic to route telephone calls |
| local loop | wires connecting telephones to the local exchange office |
| lock-up | *see* deadlock |
| logical link control (LLC) | IEEE standard data link protocol used in local area networks that handles logical links between stations |
| login scripts | collection of commands (Novell NetWare) that are automatically executed each time a user logs in to the system |
| longitudinal redundancy check | error detection mechanism done by visualizing a two-dimensional array formed by storing each byte in a frame and then calculating a parity bit for all of the bits in each column |
| machine state | collection of values associated with a system at an instant in time |
| Magnetic Fusion Energy Network | network connecting supercomputer research centers and providing service to Department of Energy funded researchers |
| mail directory | service providing the address of an individual given that he/she is unambiguously identified |
| major synchronization points | error recovery mechanism that divides session layer transmissions into separate, and recoverable, dialog units |
| management information base | database used by SNMP that describes routers and hosts |
| Manchester code | digital encoding scheme in which the digital signal always changes state in the middle of an interval |
| Manufacturing Automation Protocol | proprietary network protocol for the General Motors Corp |
| maximum transfer unit | maximum frame size that can be transferred over a network |
| medium access control | lower sublayer of the data link protocol that controls access to the transmission medium. |

| | |
|---|---|
| medium attachment unit | PC-installable device containing the interfacing electronics and logic necessary to connect to an Ethernet |
| memory resident viruses | computer virus that waits in memory for an executable file to be placed there |
| Menehune | central facility used in the Hawaiian Islands' Aloha (packet radio) system |
| Merkle's puzzles | method of key distribution in which a receiver randomly chooses one of many transmitted messages to determine the encryption key |
| message age timer | timer maintained by a bridge specifying a maximum time during which it expects to hear from the root bridge elected by the spanning tree algorithm |
| message handling system | most extensive part of the X.400 mail system containing all of the message transfer agents and user agents |
| message sequencing | placing messages in a specified order |
| message store | place where an X.400 user agent stores its messages |
| message switching | alternative to packet switching or circuit switching in which a transmitted message is stored at each node, but different messages may travel different routes |
| message transfer agent | software running on a dedicated computer and part of the X.400 system's backbone whose major function is to accept mail from a user agent or another message transfer agent, examine it, and route it |
| message transfer part | bottom three layers of signaling system #7; performs function similar to X.25 |
| message transfer protocol | defines communication between two X.400 message transfer agents |
| message transfer system | that part of the X.400 mail system formed by the collection of message transfer agents |
| microwave transmissions | method of transmission using electromagnetic waves with a frequency below that of infrared light |
| Midwest network | network connecting several major midwestern universities. |
| Military Network | part of the Internet's backbone; connects military establishments throughout the U.S. and in some foreign countries |
| Minnesota Regional Network | regional network connecting some of Minnesota's major corporations and universities |
| minor synchronization points | mechanism used to subdivide a session layer's dialog units |
| modal dispersion | phenomenon resulting from light reflecting at different angles in an optical fiber causing some of the light to take a bit longer to get to the other end of the fiber |
| modem | device that converts analog signals to digital ones and vice versa |
| modem standards | standards defining how to convert between digital and analog signals |
| modulated signal | result of changing a carrier signal by another input signal |

| modulation | process of using one signal to change another one |
| monitor station | token ring station that has some maintenance and control responsibilities |
| mono-alphabetic cipher | primitive encryption technique in which a text character is replaced by another that is chosen dependent only on the character being replaced |
| more fragments bit | a bit indicator which is set in every fragment of an IP segment except the last one |
| Morse Code | transmission code developed for telegraph systems in which each character is represented by a series of "dots" and "dashes" |
| multidrop link | HDLC link in which a primary station can communicate with several secondary stations |
| multiplexer | device combining signals from several inputs and sending them out over a single channel |
| multipoint link | *see* multidrop link |
| narrowband radio | transmission using a single radio frequency in order to achieve a higher data rate |
| National Bureau of Standards | now called the National Institute of Standards and Technology, a standards making agency of the United States Department of Commerce |
| negative acknowledgment | flow control indication that a frame was not received correctly or was not received at all |
| neighbor identification procedure | token ring protocol allowing each station to learn the identity of its upstream neighbor |
| NetWare | commercial network operating system released by Novell |
| NetWare core protocol | procedures that a server uses to respond to a client's request |
| NetWare Directory Services | distributed database storing lists of NetWare user, resources, and access rights on all NetWare servers |
| NetWare loadable modules | collection of software modules that can be used to meet individual users' needs |
| NetWare shell | NetWare command interpreter that accepts commands entered from a workstation |
| network | collection of devices running software allowing them to communicate via some transmission medium |
| network addressable units | Systems Network Architecture (SNA) entity having its own address |
| Network control protocol | predecessor to TCP in the original ARPANET |
| network job entry | network protocol developed by IBM and used in BITNET |
| network layer | OSI layer 3 protocol responsible for routing packets through a network |
| network termination 1 | ISDN designation for nonintelligent devices concerned with physical and electrical characteristics of a transmission signal |

| | |
|---|---|
| network termination 2 | ISDN designation for intelligent devices capable of performing functions specified in OSI layers 2 and 3 |
| network topology | manner in which network devices are connected physically |
| network virtual terminal | application layer software that translates terminal-specific control sequences into standard forms |
| noise | unwanted signals that interfere with a transmitted signal |
| noiseless channel | channel impervious to noise |
| noisy lines | lines having more than a typical amount of noise |
| nonbroadcast frame | frame destined for a specific destination |
| non-data-*J*(also non-data-*K*) | digital signal that does not conform to any Manchester code for defining bits |
| Nondedicated file server | server that may also run applications |
| nondelivery notification | X.400 service indicating mail was not delivered properly |
| Non-persistent CSMA | protocol in which, after a collision has occurred, the station does not monitor the transmission medium, instead waiting for one time slot before checking for activity |
| non-return-to-zero | digital encoding scheme in which 0s and 1s are represented by specific voltage levels |
| Nordic Network | network connecting Scandinavian universities |
| normal response mode | HDLC mode in which the primary station controls the communication |
| Novell NetWare | commercial network operating system |
| null modem | device used to connect two DTEs directly |
| Nyquist theorem | theoretical result that relates the data rate to a signal's baud rate and the number of signal components |
| octet | group of eight bits |
| odd parity | method of error detection in which an extra bit is added whose value is 0 or 1 in order to make the total number of 1-bits in the transmission unit odd |
| Ohio Academic Resources Network | regional network connecting most of Ohio's academic institutions |
| Open Data-Link Interface | Novell NetWare package allowing multiple protocols to send their packets through a single board and network connection |
| open system | set of protocols that would allow any two different systems to communicate regardless of their underlying architecture |
| open systems interconnect (OSI) | protocol standard developed by the International Standards Organization to implement an open system |

| | |
|---|---|
| optical fiber | communications media consisting of a thin strand of glass through which light travels |
| orphan frame | token ring frame circulating endlessly because no station will remove it from the ring |
| out-of-band signaling | signaling technique in which the signals are sent in a separate channel or outside the data bit stream |
| outstanding frames | frames that have been sent but not yet acknowledged by a flow control protocol |
| P-persistent CSMA | protocol in which, after a collision has occurred, the station monitors the transmission medium and, when it is quiet, transmits with probability $p$ $(0 \leq p \leq 1)$ |
| Pacific Network | academic network connecting hosts throughout the Far East and southeast Asia |
| pacing | SNA virtual route control function controlling the number of transmission units a node can send |
| packet | transmission unit for a specified protocol |
| packet assembler/ disassembler (PAD) | protocol that accepts characters from character-oriented devices and assembles them into X.25 packets; it also accepts X.25 packets from a network, disassembles them, and transmits their data as a character stream to a character-oriented device |
| packet elimination | congestion control scheme that eliminates some packets if there is an excessive buildup of them at a node |
| packet header | control information in a packet |
| packet switched network | network over which messages are divided into pieces called packets and transmitted separately |
| parabolic dish reflector | microwave antenna whose dish is parabolic in shape |
| parallel transmission | transmission mode in which several bits are transmitted simultaneously |
| parity bit | extra bit in an error detection mechanism whose value is 0 or 1 in order to make the total number of 1-bits in the checked stream either even or odd |
| path | sequence of nodes in a network through which data must pass as it travels from sender to receiver |
| path control | layer 3 of the SNA protocol model responsible for determining paths and making routing decisions |
| Percent utilization | statistical measurement specifying the amount of time on an actual successful transmission as a percent of the total time spent on contending and sending |
| period | time required for a periodic signal to repeat a pattern once |
| periodic signal | signal that varies with time but repeats a certain pattern continually |
| peripheral node | SNA node that has limited processing capabilities |
| Petri nets | way to model a protocol using a graph to represent states and transitions |
| phase modulation | method of altering a signal by changing its phase shift |
| phase shift | horizontal shift in a periodic signal |

| | |
|---|---|
| phase shift keying | *see* phase modulation |
| physical layer | OSI layer 1 protocol responsible for defining the electrical and physical properties of the transmission medium |
| picture element | smallest visible component of an image on a television or video screen |
| piggyback acknowledgment | technique of sending an acknowledgment within a data frame |
| pixels | *see* picture element |
| plaintext | unencrypted message |
| point-to-point link | HDLC link in which a primary station communicates with one secondary station |
| poll bit | HDLC flag allowing a primary station to request a response from a secondary station |
| poly-alphabetic cipher | encryption technique in which each occurrence of a text character is replaced by a different character depending on the original character and its position in the message |
| polynomial | mathematical expression formed by adding terms each of which is a constant multiplied by an unknown term raised to a positive integral power |
| portable telephones | telephones that connect to the telephone system using radio communication |
| preamble | special bit pattern appearing at the beginning of some frame formats |
| predecessor | token bus term referring to the station from which a given station receives a token |
| prefix property | property stating that the bit code for a character never appears as the prefix of another code |
| presentation layer | OSI layer 6 protocol |
| presentation services | SNA layer 6 protocol |
| primary rate | CCITT standard for ISDN consisting of 23 B channels and one D channel |
| primary station | type of station designated by HDLC that manages data flow by issuing commands to other stations and acting on their responses |
| print server | network device that manages a printer and handles print requests |
| private branch exchanges (PBX) | private telephone system |
| probe service | X.400 service that lets a user agent determine whether mail can be delivered to an address |
| Project ELF | attempt by the Navy to install a large antenna in the upper peninsula of Michigan for the purpose of submarine communication using extra low frequency |
| proof of delivery service | X.400 service allowing the authentication of the recipients of a message |
| proof of submission service | X.400 service providing proof a message has been submitted to the message transfer system |

| | |
|---|---|
| protocol | set of rules by which two or more devices communicate |
| protocol converters | logic to convert one protocol to another |
| pseudoternary coding | *see* alternate mark inversion |
| public data networks | packet switched networks managed by a government or public utility |
| public key cryptosystem | encryption technique for which there is no attempt to protect the identity of the encryption key |
| pulse amplitude modulation | technique of sampling an analog signal at regular intervals and generating pulses with amplitude equal to that of the sampled signal |
| pulse code modulation | similar to pulse amplitude modulation, except the amplitude of the pulse must be one of a set of predefined values |
| pure Aloha | protocol developed at the University of Hawaii for a packet radio system |
| purge frame | token ring control frame that clears the ring of any extraneous signals |
| Q-series | series of CCITT documents describing a layered protocol called signaling system #7, a standard providing functionality in integrated digital networks |
| quadrature amplitude modulation | modulation technique in which bits are assigned to an analog signal dependent on a combination of its amplitude and phase shift |
| radio | device capable of sending or receiving electromagnetic signals in the 10 KHz – 100,000 MHz range |
| reassembly deadlock | deadlock caused by running out of buffer space while accepting packets from multiple sources |
| reassembly timer | timer used by the Internet protocol specifying the time in which it expects to receive all fragments from a packet |
| receive not ready | HDLC frame type used to stop the flow of incoming frames |
| receive ready | HDLC frame type used to indicate a station is ready to receive frames or to acknowledge frames already received |
| receiving window | flow control parameter specifying which frames can be received |
| receiving window size | flow control parameter specifying the maximum number of frames a receiving station can hold before passing them to the higher layer |
| record route option | Internet protocol parameter specifying that the route a packet takes be placed in the packet |
| reference points R, S, T, U | CCITT-defined reference points used to divide ISDN functional groups |
| refraction | phenomenon relating to the changing direction of light as it passes from one medium to another |

| | |
|---|---|
| regional center | telephone office covering (typically) a multistate region |
| relative encoding | *see* differential encoding |
| remote logins | process of logging in to a computer at a remote site |
| repeater | OSI layer 1 connection that receives signals and regenerates them before sending them on |
| reply | message sent in response to another |
| reply request indication | X.400 service requesting that a recipient reply to a transmitted message |
| request disconnect | protocol request from a station that a connection be terminated |
| request for comment (RFC) | series of documents containing research notes available via FTP |
| reservation system | token ring protocol mechanism allowing a station to try to reserve a token on its next pass |
| resolve contention frame | token bus control frame used in an arbitration protocol when two or more stations attempt to enter the logical ring simultaneously |
| return of content service | X.400 service providing for mail to be returned in the event it is not delivered |
| ring indicator | signal from a DCE to DTE indicating the DCE is receiving a ringing signal from the communications channel |
| ring initialization | token bus protocol that determines the logical order of the stations |
| ring topology | circular arrangement of devices each capable of communicating directly with its neighbor |
| root bridge | specially designated bridge determined by the spanning tree algorithm corresponding to the root of the spanning tree |
| root port | bridge port corresponding to the cheapest path to the root bridge |
| route | sequence of stations through which a frame must travel from its source to its destination |
| route designators | sequence of LAN and bridge IDs specifying a path |
| route discovery | process used by source routing bridges to determine the path to a particular station |
| route learning | process by which a bridge learns what to put in its routing table |
| Routed | routing program developed at the University of California at Berkeley to do routing on their local area network |
| router | OSI layer 3 connection between two networks |
| routing information protocol | routing strategy that uses a hop count to determine the path in a network |
| routing algorithm | method used to determine a route |
| routing directory | database used by a bridge or router to decide where to send frames it receives |

| | |
|---|---|
| routing table | *see* routing directory |
| RS-232 standard | rules defining communication between a DCE and DTE |
| RS-422 | electrical standard, using balanced circuits, for communication between a DCE and DTE |
| RS-423 | electrical standard, using unbalanced circuits, for communication between a DCE and DTE |
| RS-449 | operational standard, designed to replace RS-232, for communication between a DCE and DTE |
| run length encoding | compression technique that replaces a run of bits (or bytes) by the number of bits (or bytes) in the run |
| run length encoding prefix | special character used by Kermit to differentiate a data string from a run length encoded string |
| sampling frequency | rate at which analog signals are sampled |
| satellite | object orbiting the earth |
| satellite transmission | microwave transmission to/from an orbiting satellite |
| scripts | file containing a collection of commands to be executed |
| search drives | defines the directories that an operating system searches automatically when a user requests a file not in the current directory |
| secondary station | type of station designated by HDLC that responds to a primary station |
| security | pertaining to the protection or hiding of information from unauthorized people |
| selective reject | HDLC control frame requesting that a particular frame be resent |
| selective repeat protocol | sliding window flow control protocol in which the receiver defines a window specifying frames it can receive |
| self-synchronizing code | digital encoding scheme in which the signal always changes state in the middle of a bit interval |
| sending window | flow control parameter specifying which frames can be sent |
| sending window size | flow control parameter specifying the maximum number of frames a sending station can send before receiving acknowledgments |
| sequence number | number used for ordering frames or packets |
| serial transmission | mode of transmission in which all bits are sent in sequence |
| server | network device whose function is to respond to requests from the network users |
| service classes | mechanism used to prioritize data transmitted over a token bus network |
| service type | Internet packet field corresponding to transport layer requests regarding handling of the packet |
| session | logical connection between two end users |

| | |
|---|---|
| session control | component of SNA's Transmission Control layer |
| session layer | OSI layer 5 protocol |
| Shamir's method | method of key distribution such that a specified number of people must be present to determine it |
| shift down/up | Baudot code control character changing the interpretation of subsequently received characters |
| shift in/out | ASCII code control character changing the interpretation of subsequently received characters |
| shift register | part of a circuit used to implement cyclic redundancy checks |
| shortest path algorithm | logic used to determine the shortest path between two points |
| signal constellation | diagram using plotted points to define all legitimate signal changes recognized by a modem |
| signal ground | voltage level against which all other signals are measured |
| signal speed | speed at which a signal travels through a medium |
| signal-to-noise ratio | measurement used to quantify how much noise there is in the presence of a signal |
| signaling data link | lowest layer of signaling system #7 providing physical and electrical specifications |
| signaling link layer | second layer of signaling system #7 providing reliable communications between two adjacent points in the network |
| signaling network layer | third layer of signaling system #7 providing reliable message transfer between two signaling points |
| signaling system number 7 | four-layer protocol that defines a standard for functionality in an integrated digital network |
| simple mail transfer protocol | standard mail protocol in the TCP/IP suite |
| simple network management protocol | management protocol designed to make sure network protocols and devices work well |
| simplex communications | mode in which communication goes only one way |
| single-bit error | error affecting just one bit |
| single-mode fiber | optical fiber with a very small diameter designed to reduce to 1 the number of angles at which light reflects off the cladding |
| single-route broadcast frame | frame that is broadcast only through ports that are part of a spanning tree |
| sliding window protocol | flow control protocol where the sending and receiving stations restrict the frames they can send or receive |
| slot | time interval of length equal to the time required to transmit one frame |

| | |
|---|---|
| slotted Aloha protocol | Aloha protocol requiring a station to transmit at the beginning of a slot |
| slotted ring | similar to a token ring but with several rotating tokens |
| smart terminals | terminals with computing capability |
| socket | UNIX construct and a mechanism used to connect to a network |
| solicit successor frame | token bus control frame used to invite new stations to join the logical ring |
| source address | address of a station sending a message |
| source quench | ICMP control message requesting a reduction in the rate at which packets are sent |
| source routing bridge | bridge that routes a frame based on the contents of the frame's route designator |
| South Pacific Educational and Research Network | network developed by the universities in Australia and New Zealand for the purpose of academic research and teaching |
| Southeastern Universities Research Association Network | network providing service to major research universities in the District of Columbia and many southeastern states |
| spanning tree algorithm | distributed algorithm executed by bridges to determine a connection among all participating LANs that contains no redundant paths |
| spot beam | type of antenna allowing satellite signals to be broadcast to only a very small area |
| stacking station | token ring station that has raised the token's priority |
| standard | agreed-on way of doing something |
| standby monitor present (SMP) frame | token ring control frame used in the protocol's neighbor identification procedure |
| star topology | arrangement of devices in which all communication goes through a central computer or switch |
| starLAN | network that has a star topology but uses a bus protocol |
| start bit | single bit signal used in asynchronous transmission alerting the receiver that data is arriving |
| start of frame delimiter | special bit pattern indicating the start of a frame |
| Start of TeXt | control character indicating the beginning of a text transmission |
| state transition diagram | model of a system depicting all possible states and the events that cause the system to change states |
| state transition | changing of a system from one state to another due to the occurrence of some event |
| static routing | routing strategy that uses information that does not change with time |

| | |
|---|---|
| statistical multiplexer | time-division multiplexer that creates a variable sized frame |
| step index multimode fiber | optical fiber with a larger diameter allowing several angles at which light reflects off the cladding |
| stop and wait protocol | protocol in which a sender sends a frame and waits for the acknowledgment to return before sending the next frame |
| stop bit | single bit signal used in asynchronous transmission indicating the end of the transmission |
| store and forward | network protocol for which a message is stored in its entirety at each intermediate node along the path to the destination |
| store-and-forward deadlock | deadlock caused by a situation in which none in a circular list of nodes can send because the next one's buffers are full |
| subarea nodes | *see* boundary nodes |
| subareas | domains in an SNA network |
| submission and delivery protocol | protocol defining the interaction between X.400's user agent and message transfer agent |
| subnegotiation begin | starting delimiter for a sequence of TELNET commands |
| subnegotiation end | ending delimiter for a sequence of TELNET commands |
| successor | token bus term referring to the station to which a given station sends a token |
| supervisory frame | frame used by HDLC to indicate a station's status or to send negative acknowledgments |
| SYN character | character used in byte-oriented protocols indicating the start of a frame |
| synchronization points | *see* major synchronization points and minor synchronization points |
| synchronous data link control (SDLC) | bit-oriented data link protocol developed by IBM and similar to HDLC |
| synchronous transmission | transmission mode in which many bits are grouped into a specially formatted frame and sent as a single transmission unit |
| system login script | NetWare term applying to a file containing commands that are done for each user logging in to the system |
| Systems Network Architecture | IBM's seven-layer communications protocol |
| teleconferencing | communication system allowing people at different sites to not only hear but see each other as well |
| telegraph | primitive communication device consisting of a power source, switch, and sensor |
| telemetry | sensing of status or reading of data at remote sites |

| | |
|---|---|
| telenet | public data network purchased by U.S. Sprint and renamed SprintNet |
| telephone | device used for voice communication |
| TELNET | application layer virtual terminal protocol allowing remote logins |
| terminal adapter | device designed to be used with ISDN TE2 equipment converting their signals to an ISDN-compatible format |
| terminal equipment 1 (TE1) | ISDN primary functional group designation for ISDN devices |
| terminal equipment 2 (TE2) | ISDN primary functional group designation for non-ISDN devices |
| terminators (Schwarzeneggers) | electronic devices placed at the end of a medium preventing any electronic echoing of signals |
| Texas Higher Education Network | regional network connecting academic, research, and private institutions throughout Texas |
| three-way handshake | mechanism to establish a connection consisting of a connection request, acknowledgment to the request, and an acknowledgment to the acknowledgment |
| time-division multiplexing | process of accepting digital signals from several sources, storing them in a single frame, and sending the frame over a single channel |
| time exceeded | ICMP control message sent to a source station when a packet or unassembled fragments are dropped from the network due to a timer expiration |
| time to live | Internet protocol packet field specifying the maximum amount of time the packet can remain in the network |
| timestamp reply | ICMP control message sent in response to a timestamp request |
| timestamp request | ICMP control message sent to a remote host when a local host wants to estimate the round-trip time between it and the remote host |
| token | special frame circulating among all devices in a network used to determine when a station can send information over the network |
| token bus | bus topology network that controls access to the bus by using a token passing protocol |
| token holding timer | token bus timer specifying the maximum time a station may spend sending class 6 frames |
| token passing | process of circulating a token so that when a station captures the token, it may send data |
| token ring | ring topology network that controls access to the ring by using a token passing protocol |
| token rotation timer | token bus timer that determines the maximum time for a token to rotate around the logical ring |
| tone dialing | telephone dialing mechanism in which each digit sends a tone consisting of two frequencies |

| | |
|---|---|
| TP*i* | one of 5 classes of transport services in the OSI model |
| transaction | user-defined unit of work |
| transaction services | SNA layer 7 protocol |
| Transaction Tracking System | NetWare service allowing multiple updates to files to be regarded as a single transaction |
| transceiver | device that clamps onto an Ethernet cable for the purpose of interfacing between a PC and the cable |
| transceiver cable | cable connecting a transceiver to a PC |
| transmission control protocol | transport protocol used in the Internet |
| transmission group control | component of SNA's path control layer managing one or more parallel lines between two nodes |
| transmission rate | measurement specifying the number of bits per second that can be transmitted over a medium |
| transmit data | RS-232 circuit used to transmit data from the DTE to DCE |
| transparent bridge | bridge that creates and updates its own routing tables |
| transparent data | mode of transmission in which a receiving station does not react to the contents of incoming bytes |
| transport layer | OSI layer 4 protocol responsible for end-to-end communications |
| transport protocol data unit (TPDU) | transmission unit for the OSI transport protocol |
| transposition cipher | encryption technique that rearranges the plaintext characters |
| trunk | high-capacity lines capable of transmitting many telephone conversations simultaneously |
| trustee rights | rights granted by NetWare to a group of users allowing them to access specific directories and files |
| twisted pair | communication circuit consisting of two insulated wires twisted around each other |
| two-way handshake | mechanism to establish a connection consisting of a connection request and an acknowledgment to the request |
| TYMNET | public data network providing access to information services such as Delphi, TRW Information Services, and Dow Jones News |
| ultra high frequency | television transmission using electromagnetic waves between 300 MHz and 3 GHz |
| unbalanced circuit | circuit using one line for signal transmission and a common ground |
| undetected transmission errors | transmission errors that go unnoticed by the receiving station |

| | |
|---|---|
| University Satellite Network | network connecting several major U.S. universities, and naval and oceanographic research institutes to the National Center for Atmospheric Research using satellite and VSAT technology |
| unrestricted flow control | essentially a lack of flow control; the sending station sends frames making no effort to limit the number it sends |
| upstream neighbor | token passing term applying to the station from which a token is received |
| urgent data | data in a TCP segment that must be delivered to higher layers as quickly as possible |
| urgent pointer | TCP segment field pointing to urgent data |
| user agent | X.400 mail system component that interacts with the user and essentially defines what the user can do |
| user datagram protocol | connectionless transport layer protocol |
| user login script | NetWare term applying to a file containing commands that are done for a specific user logging into the system |
| verification | process of verifying the sender of a message |
| very high frequency (VHF) | television transmission using electromagnetic waves between 30 and 300 MHz |
| very small aperture terminal (VSAT) system | satellite communication system using small antenna dishes |
| videoconferencing | system allowing people in different locations to see and hear each other in a real-time setting |
| videotex | interactive access to remote databases |
| Vigenère cipher | substitution cipher in which the encryption key is a two-dimensional array of characters |
| virtual circuit (route) | logical connection that is established prior to any packet switched data transfer and for which all packets travel through the same network nodes |
| virtual route control | SNA path control layer function establishing a logical connection between two network addressable units |
| virtual terminal protocol | protocol defining communication between an application and terminal, independent of terminal characteristics |
| virus | unauthorized set of instructions that spreads from one computer to another, either through a network or through peripheral transfers |
| voice mail | system allowing telephone callers to leave messages in a local repository |
| waveguide | cylindrical tube that is part of a horn antenna |
| wide area information servers (WAIS) | client-server application in which servers provide access to a variety of databases |

| | |
|---|---|
| wide area network | network spanning a large geographic distance often connecting many smaller networks running a variety of different protocols |
| window | abstract concept defining a subset of frames for the purpose of flow control between two stations |
| wire center | central switch providing a physical connection between any two of a group of devices |
| wireless communications | communication independent of a physical connection |
| worm | program that intrudes into a system and has the potential to damage the system's security |
| X-OFF | flow control character causing incoming data to stop |
| X-ON | flow control character causing incoming data to resume |
| X.25 standard | standard for connecting stations to a packet switched network |
| X.400 standard | standard defining an electronic mail system |
| X.500 directory service | standard defining a distributed directory for an electronic mail system |

# Acronyms

**ABM,** asynchronous balanced mode

**ACK,** acknowledgment

**AM,** amplitude modulation

**ANSI,** American National Standards Institute

**APPC,** advanced program-to-program communication

**APPN,** advanced peer-to-peer networking

**ARM,** asynchronous response mode

**ARPA,** Advanced Research Projects Agency

**ARQ,** automatic repeat request

**ASCII,** American Standard Code for Information Interchange

**ASN.1,** abstract syntax notation 1

**ATM,** asynchronous transfer mode

**BCD,** binary coded decimal

**BCDIC,** binary coded decimal interchange code

**BISDN,** broadband integrated services digital network

**BITNET,** because it's time network

**BNA,** Burroughs network architecture

**BSC,** binary synchronous communication

**CBX,** computer branch exchange

**CCITT,** Comité Consultatif Internationale de Télégraphique et Téléphonique

**CDDI,** copper data distributed interface

**CMIP,** common management information protocol

**CMOT,** CMIP over TCP

**CPMGR,** connection point manager

**CRC,** cyclic redundancy check

**CSMA,** carrier sense, multiple access

**CSMA/CD,** carrier sense, multiple access with collision detection

**DARPA,** Defense Advanced Research Projects Agency

**DCE,** data circuit terminating equipment

**DES,** data encryption standard

**DIB,** directory information base

**DIT,** directory information tree

**DLE**, data link escape.

**DNS**, domain name server

**DoD**, Department of Defense

**DPSK**, differential phase shift keying

**DSA**, directory system agent

**DSR**, data set ready

**DTE**, data terminal equipment

**EBCDIC**, extended binary coded decimal interchange code

**EGP**, exterior gateway protocol

**EIA**, Electronic Industries Association

**ELF**, extra low frequency

**ENIAC**, electronic numerical integrator and calculator

**ESC**, escape

**FAX**, facsimile

**FCC**, Federal Communications Commission

**FDDI**, fiber distributed data interface

**FDM**, frequency division multiplexing

**FM**, frequency modulation

**FSK**, frequency shift keying

**FTP**, file transfer protocol

**HDLC**, high-level data link control

**HDTV**, high definition television

**IBM**, International Business Machines

**ICMP**, Internet control message protocol

**IDN**, integrated digital network

**IEEE**, Institute of Electrical and Electronic Engineers

**IP**, Internet protocol

**IPM**, interpersonal messaging

**IPX**, Internet packet exchange

**ISO**, International Standards Organization

**LAN**, local area network

**LAP**, link access protocol

**LED**, light emitting diode

**LLC**, logical link control

**MAC**, medium access control

**MAP**, manufacturing automation protocol

**MAU**, medium attachment unit

**MHS**, message handling system

**MIB**, management information base

**MILNET**, military network

**MTA**, message transfer agent

**MTS**, message transfer system

**MTU**, maximum transfer unit

**NAK**, negative acknowledgment

**NAU**, network addressable unit

**NBS**, National Bureau of Standards

**NCP**, network control protocol

**NIST**, National Institute of Standards and Technology

**NJE**, network job entry

**NLM**, NetWare loadable modules

**NRM**, normal response mode

**NRZ**, non-return to zero

**NSA**, National Security Agency

**ODI**, open data-link interface

**OSI**, open systems interconnect

**PABX**, private automatic branch exchange

**PAD,** packet assembler/disassembler

**PAM,** pulse amplitude modulation

**PBX,** private branch exchange

**PCM,** pulse code modulation

**PDU,** protocol data unit

**PM,** phase modulation

**PSK,** phase shift keying

**QAM,** quadrature amplitude modulation

**RFC,** request for comment

**RIP,** routing information protocol

**RPC,** remote procedure call

**RSA algorithm,** Rivest, Shamir, Adleman algorithm

**SDLC,** synchronous data link control

**SMTP,** simple mail transfer protocol

**SNA,** systems network architecture

**SNMP,** simple network management protocol

**SPX,** sequenced packet protocol

**SS7,** signaling system # 7

**SSCP,** system service control point

**STM,** synchronous transfer mode

**TCM,** trellis coded modulation

**TCP,** transmission control protocol

**TCP/IP,** transmission control protocol/Internet protocol

**TDM,** time division multiplexing

**TFTP,** trivial file transfer protocol

**TOP,** technical and office products

**TPDU,** transport protocol data unit

**TP$i$,** transport protocol $i$

**TRT,** token rotation timer

**TTS,** transaction tracking system

**UA,** user agent

**UDP,** user datagram protocol

**UHF,** ultra high frequency

**UUCP,** UNIX to UNIX copy program

**VHF,** very high frequency

**VSAT,** very small aperture terminal

**VTAM,** virtual telecommunications access method

**WAIS,** wide area information servers

**WAN,** wide area network

**WWW,** worldwide web

# INDEX

## Numerics

1 BASE 5, 328
10 BASE 2, 328
10 BASE 5, 328
10 BASE-T, 328
10 BROAD 36, 328
23 B+D, 517
25-pin connector, 142, 145
2B+D, 517, 525–27
37-pin connection, 147
4 of 5 code, 348–49
4B/5B encoder, 348
802.3 CSMA/CD (Ethernet), 167–73, 324–35
802.4 token bus, 352–62
802.5 token ring, 335–47
9-pin connector, 145

## A

ABM. *See* Asynchronous balanced mode.
ABORT, 461
Abort output, 489
Abstract syntax notation, 1, 501
Accept, 463
Access control, 339
ACK. *See* Acknowledgment
Acknowledgment, 89, 255–57, 260–62, 270–72, 279, 283, 289, 299. *See also* Sliding window protocols, High-level data link protocol, Transmission control protocol
Acknowledgment frames, 271
Acknowledgment number, 455
ACK timer, 264, 269, 277
ACSnet, 466
Active monitor present frame, 346
ACTIVE-OPEN, 461
ACTIVE-OPEN-W/DATA, 461
Activity, 41–42
Adaptive differential pulse code modulation, 162
Adaptive routing, 406, 408–09
Address. *See* Broadcast, Class B, Destination, Duplicate, Element, Group, IP, Physical, Source, Subarea
Address complete message, 524
Address depletion, 421
Address learning, 370–71
Address lookup service, 514
Address recognized bit, 339
Address reuse, 421
Advanced cluster controller node, 537
Advanced data communications control procedure (ADCCP), 301
Advanced Peer-to-Peer Networking, 548
Advanced program-to-program communication, 537
Advanced Research Projects Agency, 440

Advanced Research Projects Agency Network, 467
Algorithm. *See* Backward learning, Backward search, Bellman-Ford, Binary exponential back-off, Dijkstra's, Flooding, Forward learning, Forward search, RSA, Spanning tree
ALLOCATE, 461
All-routes broadcast frame, 379–80
Aloha Protocol, 163–67, 169, 178
Alternate mark inversion, 526
Alternate recipient allowed, 511
AM. *See* Amplitude modulation
Amateur Packet Radio Network, 466
American National Standards Institute, 15
American Standard Code for Information Interchange, 87–91
Amplitude, 100–01
Amplitude modulation, 111–12, 154
Amplitude shift keying, 111–12
AMPRNET, 466
Analog signals, 56, 99–101, 110, 153–55. *See also* Frequency division multiplexing, Fourier series.
Analog-to-digital conversions, 116–19
Anonymous FTP, 492
ANSI. *See* American National Standards Institute
Answer message, 524

Answer mode, 120
APPC. *See* Advanced program-to-program communication
Application layer 20, 44. *See also* Directory service, Electronic mail, File transfer protocol, TELNET, Virtual terminal
APPN. *See* Advanced Peer-to-peer networking.
Archie, 496
Arcnet, 381
Are you there, 489
ARM. *See* Asynchronous response mode
ARPA. *See* Advanced research projects agency
Arpanet, 404, 440, 467
ARQ. *See* Automatic repeat request
ASCII. *See* American standard code for information interchange
ASCII code, 138
ASK. *See* Amplitude shift keying
ASN.1. *See* Abstract syntax notation
Asynchronous balanced mode, 293
Asynchronous response mode, 293
Asynchronous transfer mode, 351, 531
Asynchronous transmission, 137
AT&T, 103
ATM. *See* Asynchronous transfer mode
ATTACH, 388
Attenuate, 59
Australian Computer Science network, 466
Authentication, 231–33
Authentication failure trap, 503
Authorizing users indication, 511
Autobaud modems, 123
Automatic repeat request, 250
AYT. *See* Are you there

**B**

Backbone 13, 325. *See also* Ethernet, Routers
Backward learning algorithm, 412, 423. *See also* Bellman-Ford algorithm

Balanced circuits, 147
Bandpass filters, 155
Bandwidth, 56, 108. *See also* Shannon's result
BARRNet, 467
Baseband mode, 60
Basic transmission unit, 541
Baud rate, 105. *See also* Nyquist result
Baudot code, 92
Bay Area Regional Research Network, 467
BCD. *See* Binary coded decimal
BCDIC. *See* Binary coded decimal interface code
B channels, 517–20, 525–26
BCnet, 467
Beacon frame, 346
Beam shaping, 73
Because It's Time Network, 467
Bel, 108. *See also* Bell
Bell, 89
Bellman-Ford algorithm, 412–17, 423
Berkeley Unix, 461
Bidirectional, 11
Binary coded decimal, 95
Binary Coded Decimal Interchange Code, 96
Binary exponential backoff algorithm, 173
BInary SYNchronous Communication, 301–06
    control characters, 303
    frame format, 302
BIND, 463, 543
BISDN. *See* Broadband ISDN
Bisync. *See* Binary synchronous communication
Bit. *See* Address recognized, DC balancing, Do-not-fragment, Echo, Frame copied, Framing, More-fragments, Parity, Priority, Reservation, Start, Stop, Token
Bit map, 86
Bit-oriented protocol, 293. *See also* High-level data link protocol
Bit pipe, 517

Bit stuffing, 295
BITNET, 467
Bit-time, 337
Blind copy recipient indication, 511
Block check character, 305
Blocking, 540
Boeing Computer Services, 532
Boundary nodes, 535
BPDU. *See also* Bridge protocol data unit
Bracket, 21, 545
Bracketing, 545
Break, 489
Bridge port, 374. *See also* Spanning tree algorithm
Bridge protocol data units, 375
Bridge, 14, 365–81, 402. *See also* Designated, Fixed routing, Root, Source routing, Transparent
British Columbia Network, 467
BRK. *See* Break
Broadband ISDN, 531
Broadband mode, 60
BROADCAST, 388
Broadcast address, 296
Broadcast television, 153
Brouter, 368
BS. *See* Backspace
BSC. *See* Binary synchronous communication
BTU. *See* Basic transmission unit
Buffer allocation, 424
Buffering, 32
Bulletin boards, 6
Burroughs Network Architecture, 532
Burst errors, 197–99, 206–08
Bus topology, 321. *See also* Ethernet, Token bus
Byte multiplexer, 157
Byte oriented I/O, 137
Byte stuffing, 304
Byte timing, 150

**C**

Caesar cipher, 215–17
California Education and Research Federation Network, 467

Call accepted packet, 433
Call confirmation, 434
Call connection, 433
Call modification completed message, 525
Call modification reject message, 525
Call modification request message, 525
Call reference field, 528
Call request packet, 433
Call waiting, 126
Cambridge ring 176, 351
Canada Network, 467
Cancel, 90
Car telephone, 82
Carriage Return, 90
Carrier Sense Multiple Access, 167–73
Carrier Sense Multiple Access with Collision Detection, 9, 170–73
Carrier signal, 154–55
CBX. *See* Computer branch exchange
CCITT, 15, 120, 149. *See also* X.21, X.21bis, X.25, X.26, X.27, X.28, X.29, X.3, X.400, X.500, I-series, Q-series, V.21, V.22, V.22bis, V.32, V.42bis, V.fast
CD. *See* Collision detection
CDNnet, 467
Cells, 531
Cellular radio, 82
Cellular telephones, 6, 48, 82
Centralized routing, 406, 409. *See also* Dijkstra's algorithm
CERFnet, 467
Chain, 545
Chaining, 545
Change direction indicator, 545
Change window indicator, 539
Change window reply indicator, 539
Channel utilization, 257–59. *See also* Percent utilization
Channels, 153. *See also* B channel, D channel
Cheapernet, 328
Cheapest route, 405. *See also* Routing algorithms

Checksum, 444, 456
Choke packets, 424
CICNet, 468
Cipher. *See* Caesar cipher, Mono-alphabetic cipher, Poly-alphabetic cipher, Transposition cipher, Vigenère cipher
Ciphertext, 215
Circuit switched connection, 522
Circuit switching, 28
Cladding, 62
Claim token (CT) frames, 345–46, 355
Class 1 regional centers, 79
Class B address, 419
Class of service, 539
Clear, 311
Clear confirmation packet, 435
Clear request packet, 435
Clear to send, 143, 148
Client, 382, 482, 484, 487, 499, 500
Client commands, 388
Client PCs, 382
Client workstations, 382
Client-server model, 482–85
CLOSE, 461, 463, 493
CMIP. *See* Common management information protocol
Coaxial cable, 59, 77, 78
Code. *See* Adaptive differential pulse code, ASCII code, Baudot code, BCD code, Differential code, Differential Manchester code, EBCDIC code, Frequency dependent code, 4-of-5 code, Hamming code, Huffman code, IAC code, Lempel-Ziv code, Manchester code, Morse code, Pulse code modulation, Self-synchronizing code
Codec, 110
Coder/decoder, 110
Coldstart trap, 503
Collision detection, 27, 170–73
Collisions, 27, 170, 327, 331
Combined station, 293
Comité Consultatif Internationale de Télégraphique et Téléphonique, 15

Committee on Institutional Cooperation Network, 468
Common bus topology. *See* Bus topology
Common management information protocol, 503
Communications server, 483
Communications subnet, 22
Compact disc, 118
CompuServe, 468
Computer Branch Exchange, 81
Computer hacker, 240
Computer Science Network, 468
Concentrator, 158
Conductive metal, 58
Configuration BPDU, 377
Congestion, 422–25
Connectionless service. *See* Datagrams, Routing, UDP
Connection management, 34, 452
Connection-oriented service. *See* Circuit switching, Connection management, TCP, Systems Network Architecture, Three-way handshake, Two-way handshake, Virtual circuit, X.25
Connection point manager, 541, 544
Connection request, 457
Connection strategy, 23
Console commands, 388
Contention, 27, 162–78. *See also* Aloha, Carrier Sense Multiple Access, Slotted Aloha, Token passing
Contention period, 332
Control characters, 89–92
Control INITiate, 543
Control prefix character, 309
Control station, 293
Control-Q, 90
Control-S, 90
COS. *See* Class of service
CPMGR. *See* Connection point manager
CR. *See* Carriage return
CRC. *See* Cyclic redundancy check
Credit, 459
Credit mechanism, 459–60

Cross Domain Control INITialize, 543
Cross Domain INITialize, 543
Cross Domain SESSion STarted, 544
Cross referencing indication, 511
Crosstalk, 58
Cryptography. *See* Caesar cipher, Data encryption standard, Digital signature, Key distribution, Mono-alphabetic cipher, Poly-alphabetic cipher, Public key cryptosystems, Transposition cipher, Vigenère cipher
CSMA. *See* Carrier sense multiple access
CSMA/CD. *See* Carrier sense multiple access with collision detection
CSNET, 468
CTS. *See* Clear to send
Cycle, 287
Cyclic redundancy check, 200–10
CRC-12, 207
CRC-16, 207
CRC-32, 207
Cypress, 468

**D**

DARPA. *See* Defense Advanced Research Projects Agency
Data carrier detect, 144
Data circuit-terminating equipment, 141, 431
Data compression, 44, 86, 178–87. *See also* Huffman code, Lempel-Ziv encoding, Run-length encoding, Relative encoding
Data encryption standard, 16, 222–26
Data flow control. *See* Flow control
Data link control protocols, 292. *See also* Binary synchronous communications, High-level data link control
Data link escape, 90, 303, 304
Data link layer 22, 27–30, 432. *See also* Binary synchronous communications, Bit stuffing,

Bridges, Byte stuffing, Error correction, Error detection, Flow control, Frame, High-level data link control, Logical link control, Medium access control
Data mode, 148
Data rate, 56, 77,105–09. *See also* Effective data rate
Data set ready,, 143
Data signal rate selector/indicator, 144
Data terminal equipment, 141
Data terminal ready, 143
Datagram, 26, 431
Datagram service, 430–31. *See also* X.25
Datapac, 468
DB-25 cable, 142
DC balancing bit, 526
DC1, 90
DC2, 90
DC3, 90
DC4, 90
DCA, 532
DCD. *See* Data carrier detect
DCE. *See* Data circuit-terminating equipment
D channel, 517
Deadlock, 425–26
Deadly embrace, 425–26
Decibel, 108
DECnet, 532
Decryption, 215. *See also* Encryption
Dedicated file server, 383
Defacto standards, 14
Defence Research Establishment Network, 469
Defense Advanced Research Projects Agency, 403
Deferred delivery cancellation, 511
Deferred delivery service, 511
Delay, 337
DELIVER, 461
Delivery notification, 511
Demodulation, 99, 109. *See also* Modulation
Department of Defense, 440
DES. *See* Data encryption standard

Designated bridge, 375–76
Destination address, 139, 262, 330
Destination port, 454
Destination unreachable, 450
Deutschland network, 468
Device controls, 90
Dialcom, 468
Dialog units, 40
DIB. *See* Directory information base
Differential encoding, 185
Differential Manchester Encoding, 98–99
Differential phase shift keying, 112
Digital Equipment Corporation, 532
Digital Network Architecture, 532
Digital signals, 55, 96–110. *See also* Modulation
Digital signature, 231–33
Digital telephone system, 48. *See also* Integrated Services Digital Network
Dijkstra's (shortest path) algorithm, 409–12, 423
Direct routing, 447
Directory information base, 514
Directory information tree, 514
Directory service, 513. *See also* X.500
Directory system agent, 515
Directory user agent, 515
DISABLE LOGIN, 388
DISC. *See* Disconnect
Disconnect, 298
Disconnect mode, 299
Disk duplexing, 386
Disk mirroring, 387
Distortion, 123
Distributed Communications Architecture, 532
Distributed directory, 513
Distributed file system, 491
Distributed indexing, 497
Distributed routing, 406, 407, 409. *See also* Bellman-Ford algorithm, routing information protocol
Distributed systems, 45, 532
DIT. *See* Directory information tree
DLE. *See* Data link escape

DNA. *See* Digital Network Architecture

Dnet, 468

DNS. *See* Domain name server

Do, 489

Do not fragment bit, 445

Document imaging, 392

DoD. *See* Department of Defense

Domain name server, 420, 441, 447

Domain system, 494

Domains, 417

Don't, 489

Double bit errors, 198

Downlinking, 72

Downstream neighbor, 346

Downward multiplexing, 32

DPSK. *See* Differential phase-shift keying

DREnet, 469

DS-1, 159

DSA. *See* Directory system agent

DSR. *See* Data set ready

DTE. *See* Data terminal ready

DTE-DCE interface, 141

DTR. *See* Data terminal ready

DUA. *See* Directory user agent

Duplicate address test frame, 345

Dynamic binding, 447

**E**

EASYnet, 469

EBCDIC. *See* Extended binary-coded decimal interchange code

Echo bit, 526

Echo reply, 450

Echo request, 450

Edwards Air Force Base, 76

Effective data rate, 259–60, 278–81

EGP. *See* Extended gateway protocol

EgpNeighborLoss trap, 503

EIA. *See* Electronic Industries Association

Eighth-bit prefix character, 309

Electrical ground, 143

Electronic Industries Association, 15, 142

Electronic locators, 50

Electronic mail, 4, 44, 48, 503. *See also* Directory service, Envelope, Message handling system, Message transfer agent, Message transfer system, P1, P2, P3, and P7 protocols, Simple mail transfer protocol, User agent, X.400, X.500

Electronic media access, 49

Electronic Numerical Integrator and Computer, 3

Electronic telephone directories, 47

Element address, 536

ELF. *See* Extra low frequency

email. *See* Electronic mail

ENABLE LOGIN, 388

Enabled, 288

Encoding. *See* Adaptive differential pulse code, ASCII code, Baudot code, BCD code, Differential code, Differential Manchester code, EBCDIC code, 4-of-5 code, Frequency dependent code, Hamming code, Huffman code, IAC code, Lempel-Ziv encoding, Manchester code, Morse code, Relative encoding, Run length encoding

Encryption, 44, 214–34, 544. *See also* Bit-level cipher, Caesar cipher, Data encryption standard, Digital signature, Merkle's puzzles, Poly-alphabetic cipher, Public key encryption, RSA algorithm, Shamir's method, Transposition cipher, Vigenère cipher

End of medium, 90

End of text, 90, 303

End of transmission, 90, 303

End of transmission block, 90, 304

Ending delimiter, 337

End-of-frame marker, 140

ENIAC. *See* Electronic numerical integrator and computer

Enquire, 90

Envelope, 507

Erase character, 489

Erase line, 489

ERROR, 461

Error control, 250. *See also* Acknowledgments, Automatic repeat request, Checksum, Cyclic reduncy check, Hamming code, Longitudinal redundancy check, Negative acknowledgment, Parity checking

Error correction, 196, 210–14

Error detection, 195–210

Error field, 255

Error recovery, 21

ESC. *See* Escape

Escape, 90

Eskimo pies, 208

ETB. *See* End of transmission block

ETB character, 304

Ether, 325

Ethernet, 10, 324–35. *See also* Binary exponential backoff, CSMA, Transceiver

cable specifications, 328–30

efficiency, 331–35

frame format, 330–31

Ethernet cable, 10, 328

Ethernet Frame Format, 330

ETX. *See* End of text

EUnet, 469

European Unix Network, 469

Even parity, 29, 196

Exception-response chain, 545

Exchange identification, 298

Expedited messages, 544

Expiry date indication, 512

Explicit route, 539

Explicit route control, 539

Extended Binary Coded Decimal Interchange Code, 16, 92

Exterior gateway protocol, 502

Extra low frequency, 66

**F**

Facility accepted message, 524

Facility reject message, 524

Facility request message, 524

Facsimile machine, 85

Factory automation, 177

FAX. *See* Facsimile machine

Fax server, 483

FCC. *See* Federal Communications Commission

FDDI. *See* Fiber distributed data interface

FDM. *See* Frequency division multiplexing

Federal Communications Commission, 3, 65, 73

Federal Express, 434

Fiber distributed data interface, 347–51, 494

Fiber optics. *See* Optical fiber

FidoNet, 469

File server, 8, 382, 482, 491

File transfer protocol, 441, 490–97

Filter, 104

Final bit, 297

Fingerd, 239

Finite state machine, 282–88

Finite state models, 250, 282–88

Finnish University Network, 469

Fire, 288

Firing sequence, 291

Fixed routing, 369

Fixed routing bridges, 368–70, 382

Flooding algorithm, 371

Flow control, 250–81. *See also* Acknowledgments, ACK timer, Credit mechanism, Frame timer, Go-back-n, Pacing, Selective repeat

FM. *See* Frequency modulation

FNET, 469

Focus, 67

Foreign-language logins, 392

Form feed, 90

Forward search algorithm, 409. *See also* Dijkstra's algorithm

Forwarding database, 368

Forwarding frames, 368

Fourier series, 102

FOZZIE BEAR, 220

Fragment header, 445

Fragment offset, 444

Fragment offset field, 446

Fragmentation, 445–47

Frame, 22, 29, 138, 163, 199, 257

Frame check sequence, 296, 331

Frame control, 339

Frame copied bit, 339

Frame format. *See* Binary Synchronous Communication, Ethernet, HDLC, Kermit, Token bus, Token ring

Frame number, 262

Frame reject, 299

Frame status, 339

Frame timer, 264, 269, 272, 277

Frame type, 139

Framing bit, 160, 526

Frequency, 57, 100. *See also* Analog signal

Frequency dependent code, 180. *See also* Hamming code

Frequency division multiplexing, 153

Frequency modulation, 111, 154

Frequency shift keying, 111

FSK. *See* Frequency shift keying

FTP. *See* File transfer protocol

Full duplex, 40, 141, 458

FULL-PASSIVE-OPEN, 461

Fully connected topology, 12, 321

Function management layer, 547

Functional groups, 520

FUNET, 469

**G**

Gateway, 403, 417

General Electric Network for Information Exchange, 470

General Motors Corporation, 532

Generator polynomial, 201, 203–208

GEnie, 470

Geosynchronous orbit, 71

Get, 311, 493

GetNextRequest, 502

Getpeername, 463

GetRequest, 502

GetResponse, 503

Getsockname, 463

Getsockopt, 463

Glob, 493

Go ahead, 489

Go-back-n protocol, 263–70

    algorithm code, 267–69

    features, 263–64

    window size, 264–66

Graceful close, 465

Grade of delivery service, 512

Graded index multimode fiber, 63

Graph, 287–88

Gremlin, 273

Group address, 296

Guard bands, 155

Guest station, 293

**H**

Hacker, 240

Hades, 275

Half duplex, 40, 140

Half-duplex contention, 544

Half-duplex flip-flop, 544

Hamming code, 210–13

Handshaking, 452. *See also* Two-way handshake, Three-way handshake

Hayes compatible modem, 124

Hayes Microcomputer Products, Inc., 123, 124

HDLC. *See* High-level data link control

HDTV. *See* High definition television

Help, 493

HEPnet, 470

Hertz (Hz), 57

Hewlett-Packard, 532

Hierarchical routing, 417–21

High Energy Physics Network, 470

High reliability, 443

High throughput, 443

High-definition television, 49

High-level data link control protocol, 293–301

    configurations, 294

    control fields, 296–97

    information frames, 297

    supervisory frames, 297

    unnumbered frames, 298–99

    frame format, 294, 296

Hold for delivery service, 512

Hop count, 421

Horizontal tab, 90

Horn antenna, 68

Host station, 293

HP Internet, 470
Huffman code, 180–83, 187

**I**

IAC. *See* Interpret-as command
IAC code, 488
IBM. *See* International Business Machines
ICMP. *See* Internet control message protocol
Identification, 444
Idle, 348
IDN. *See* Integrated digital network
IEEE. *See* Institute of Electrical and Electronic Engineers
IEEE Standard 802.3, 324–35. *See also* Ethernet
IEEE Standard 802.4, 352–62. *See also* Token bus
IEEE Standard 802.5, 335–47. *See also* Token ring
In-band signaling, 521
Incoming call, 148
Increased file management, 392
Increased memory protection, 392
Index of refraction, 61
INDIE, 497
Infected, 235
Information frame, 296, 297
Information message, 524
Information request message, 524
Information services, 6
Infrared light, 76
Inherited rights mask, 386
Initial address message, 524
Input place, 288
Installation utilities, 392
Institute for Global Communication, 472
Institute of Electrical and Electronic Engineers, 16
Integrated digital network, 523
Integrated Services Digital Network (ISDN), 49, 82, 517–32
    frame format, 525–27
    functional groups, 520–21
    layer three protocol, 527–30
    reference points, 521–22

services, 518–20
signaling system #7, 523–25
Intelligent file compression, 392
Intelligent modem, 124
Interface card (IC), 173, 327
Interfacing standards. *See* DTE-DCE interface, RS232, RS422, RS423, RS449, X.21, X.25
International Business Machines, 16
International Consultative Committee for Telephony and Telegraphy, 15
International Standards Organization, 16
Internet, 404, 419, 440, 470. *See also* Internet protocol transmission control protocol
Internet control message protocol, 450, 494
Internet management, 500. *See also* Simple network management protocol
Internet packet exchange, 384
Internet Protocol, 440–50
    fragmentation, 445–47
    packet format, 443–45
    routing, 447–50
Internetworking. *See* Arpanet, Bridges, Brouter, Datagram, Internet protocol, Routers, Routing algorithms, Spanning tree algorithm, Wide-area networks
Internet worm, 238
Interpersonal messaging, 510
Interpret-as command, 489
Interrupt mechanism, 237
Interrupt process, 489
Interrupt table, 237
Interrupt vector, 237
IP. *See* Internet protocol
IP address, 447
IPM. *See* Interpersonal messaging
IPX. *See* Internet packet exchange
ISDN. *See* Integrated Services Digital Network
ISDN basic rate, 517
ISDN central office, 520
ISDN user part, 524
I-series, 523

ISO. *See* International Standards Organization
ISO internet protocol, 451
ISO transport protocol, 464–66
Isochronous transmission, 140

**J**

JANET 470
Japan Unix Network, 470
Japanese Industrial Standard, 470
Joint Academic Network, 470
JUNET, 470

**K**

Kepler's laws of planetary motion, 71
KERMIT, 220, 250, 306
Kermit commands, 311
Kermit file transfer protocol, 306–12,
Kermit frame format, 308
Kermit frame types, 309
Key distribution, 226–27

**L**

LAN. *See* Local area networks
LAPB. *See* Link access protocol
LAPD. *See* Link access protocol
Laser, 62
Last mile, 81, 517
Latest delivery service, 512
Lawrence Berkeley Laboratory, 241
LED. *See* Light-emitting diode
Lempel-Ziv encoding, 186–87
Light-emitting diode, 62
Line feed, 89–90
Link access protocols (LAP), 301. *See also* Binary synchronous communications, High-level link control protocol
Link header, 533
Linkdown trap, 503
Linkup trap, 503
LISTDIR, 388
Listen, 463
LLC. *See* Logical link control

Local area network, 4, 8, 81, 207,
    321–400. *See also* Arcnet, Bridg-
    es, Bus topology, CSMA/CD,
    Ethernet, IEEE 802.3, IEEE
    802.4, IEEE 802.5, Medium-ac-
    cess control, Novell Netware,
    Ring topology, Starlan, Star to-
    pology, Token bus, Token ring
Local exchange, 79, 80
Local loop, 79, 517
Local loopback, 148
Lock up, 425
logical channel number, 432
Logical group number, 432
Logical link control (LLC), 301, 325,
    335. *See also* Binary synchro-
    nous communications, High-
    level data link control protocol
Logical order, 354
Logical unit, 536
Login scripts, 389
LOGIN/LOGOUT, 388
Longitudinal redundancy check, 305
Loop, 372
Lost token, 345
Low delay, 443

**M**

MAC. *See* Medium access control
Machine state, 282
Macros, 126
Magnetic Fusion Energy Network,
    470
Mail directory, 513. *See also* X.500
Major synchronization points, 40
Management Information Base, 501
Manchester code, 98–99
Manufacturing automation protocol,
    388, 532
MAP. *See* Manufacturing automation
    protocol
Master server, 484
MAU. *See* Medium attachment unit
Maximum transfer unit, 445
Medium access control, 325. *See
    also* CSMA/CD, Token bus, To-
    ken ring
Medium attachment unit, 328

Menehune, 163
Message age timer, 377
Message buffering, 544
Message handling system, 505, 508–
    512
Message passing, 483–84
Message sequencing, 544
Message store, 506, 510
Message switching, 25, 28
Message transfer agent, 505, 507–08
Message transfer part, 523
Message transfer protocol, 510
Message transfer system, 505, 508
MFEnet, 470
Mget, 493
MHS. *See* Message handling system
MIB. *See* Management information
    base
Microwave transmissions, 67–69,
    77–78
MIDnet, 471
Midwest Network, 471
Military Network, 471
MILNET, 241, 471
Mind Communications, 50
Minet, 472
Minimum frame sizes, 172
Minnesota Regional Network, 471
Minor synchronization points, 40
MISS PIGGY, 220
Modal dispersion, 63
Mode, 63. *See also* Answer, Asyn-
    chronous balanced, Asynchro-
    nous response, Asynchronous
    transfer, Baseband, Broadband,
    Delayed request, Delayed re-
    sponse, Disconnect, Immediate
    response, Normal response,
    Originate, Request initializa-
    tion, Synchronous transfer, Test
Modem, 99, 109, 119–26. *See also*
    Autoband, Hayes compatible,
    Intelligent, Null
Modem commands, 125
Modem standards, 119–26
Modulated signal, 154
Modulation, 99, 109. *See also* Adap-
    tive differential pulse code,
    Amplitude, Frequency, Phase,

Pulse amplitude, Pulse code,
    Quadrature amplitude, Trellis
    coded
Monitor station, 345
Mono-alphabetic cipher, 215–17
More fragments bit, 445
Morse code, 1, 92
MOTIS, 505
Mput, 493
MRNet, 471
MTA. *See* Message transfer agent
MTP. *See* Message transfer protocol
MTS. *See* Message transfer system
MTU. *See* Maximum transfer unit
Multidestination delivery service,
    512
Multidrop link, 293
Multiple bit error. *See* Burst error
Multiplexer, 152
Multiplexing, 32, 105. *See also* Byte,
    Downward, Frequency divi-
    sion, Statistical, Time division,
    Upward
Multipoint link, 293
Mux. *See* Multiplexer

**N**

NAK. *See* Negative acknowledg-
    ment
Narrowband radio, 76
National Bureau of Standards, 16
National Center for Atmospheric Re-
    search, 473
National Center for Supercomputing
    Applications Network, 471
National Institute of Standards and
    Technology, 16
National Science Foundation Net-
    work, 471
National Security Agency, 225
NAU. *See* Network addressable unit
NBS. *See* National Bureau of Stan-
    dards
NCP. *See* Network control protocol
NCSAnet, 471
Negative acknowledgment, 90, 263,
    272. *See also* Go-back-n proto-
    col, Sliding window protocol

Neighbor identification procedure, 346
NetWare, 381–92
NetWare core protocol, 384
NetWare directory services, 391
NetWare loadable modules, 384
NetWare shell, 384
Network, 8. *See also* IEEE 802, Integrated digital, Integrated services digital, Local area, Packet switched, Public data, Token bus, Token ring, Wide area
Network addressable units, 535–38
Network control protocol, 384, 441
Network job entry, 467
Network layer, 21, 30–36. *See also* Congestion, Internet protocol, Path control, Router, Routing, Signaling network, X.25
Network operating systems, 381
Network Switching Office, 83
Network termination 1, 520
Network termination 2, 520
Network topology, 8–14
Network virtual terminal, 438. *See also* TELNET
NETx.COM, 384
NIST. *See* National Institute of Standards and Technology
NJE. *See* Network job entry
NLM. *See* Netware loadable module
No operation, 489
Noise, 107
Noise power, 108
Noiseless channel, 106. *See also* Nyquist result
Noisy lines, 122. *see also* Shannon's result
Nonbroadcast frame, 379
Non-data-J, 338
Non-data-K, 338
Nondedicated file server, 383
Nondelivery notification, 512
Non-persistent CSMA, 168–69, 178
Nonreturn-to-zero invert, 348
Non-return-to-zero, 96
Nontransparent data, 302, 304
Nordic Network, 471
NORDUnet, 471

No-response chain, 545
Normal response mode, 293
Novell NetWare. *See* NetWare
NRM. *See* Normal response mode
NRZ. *See* Non-return-to-zero
NRZ coding, 138
NRZI. *See* Non-return-to-zero invert
NSA. *See* National Security Agency
NSFNET, 471
NT1, 520
NT2, 520
NT12, 520
NUL. *See* Null
Null, 90, 303
Null modem, 146–47
N-UNITDATA.indication, 451
N-UNITDATA.request, 451
Nyquist result, 105–07

**O**

OARnet, 471
Object class, 515
Object, 501, 515
Octet, 330
Odd parity, 29, 197
ODI. *See* Open data-link interface
Ohio Academic Resources Network, 471
Open data-link interface, 385
Open Systems Interconnect, 7,16, 17–47
    application layer, 20, 44–46
    data-link layer, 22, 27–30
    network layer, 21, 30–31
    physical layer, 22, 23–27
    presentation layer, 20, 42–44
    session layer, 21, 37–42
    transport layer, 21, 31–37
OPEN-FAILURE, 461
OPEN-ID, 461
OPEN-SUCCESS, 461
Optical fiber, 60–65, 77–78. *See also* Fiber distributed data interface, Graded index multimode, Laser, Light-emitting diode, Single mode, Step index multimode
Original timestamp, 451

Originate mode, 120
Orphan frame, 344
OSI. *See* Open systems interconnect
Out-of-band signaling, 521
Output place, 288
Outstanding frames, 260

**P**

P1 protocol, 510
P2 protocol, 510
P3 protocol, 510
P7 protocol, 510
PABX. *See* Private automatic branch exchange
Pacific Network, 472
Pacing, 538, 544
Packet assembler/disassembler, 436–40
Packet elimination, 423
Packet header (IP), 443
Packet switched network, 26, 427–31. *See also* X.25
Packet switching, 26, 28
PACNET, 472
PAD. *See* Packet assembler/disassembler
Pad field, 331
Padding, 445
PAD-host interface, 437
PAD-terminal interface, 436
PAM. *See* Pulse amplitude modulation
Parabolic dish reflector, 67
Parallel transmission, 136
Parameter problem, 450
Parity bits, 29, 197, 210
Parity checking, 196–200. *See also* Hamming code
Path, 287. *See also* Route
Path control, 533
Path information units, 538
Patron, 253, 261, 272, 277
PBX. *See* Private branch exchange
PCM. *See* Pulse code modulation
PC-to-modem connections, 145. *See also* RS232
PDU. *See* Protocol data unit
PeaceNet, 472

Peer-to-peer communications, 431

Percent utilization, 333–35

Period, 57, 100

Periodic signal, 57, 100

Peripheral node, 534

Permanent virtual circuit, 433

Petri nets, 288–92

Phase modulation, 112, 154

Phase shift 100, 101, 113, 120

Phase shift keying, 120

PhoneNet, 472

Physical address, 447

Physical control layer, 533

Physical Layer, 22, 23–27. *See also* Attenuation, Coaxial cable, Microwave transmission, Optical fiber, Repeater, Satellite transmission, Twisted pair

Physical unit, 537

Picture elements, 179

Piggybacked acknowledgments 269, 271, 297, 465

Pittsburgh Supercomputer Center's, 472

Pittsburgh Supercomputing Center Network, 472

PIU. *See* Path information unit

Pixels, 179

Plaintext, 215

PM. *See* Phase modulation

Point-to-point link, 293

Poll bit, 297

Poly-alphabetic cipher, 217–19

Polynomial, 201

Polynomial division, 201

Portable telephones, 48

P-persistent protocol, 168–69, 178

Preamble, 330

Precedence, 443

Predecessor, 353

Prefix property, 181

Presentation layer, 20, 42–44. *See also* Cryptography, Data compression

Presentation services, 547

Primary center, 80

Primary rate, 517

Primary station, 293, 299

Print server, 382, 482

PRINTER, 389

PRINTER ADD, 389

Priorities, 359

Priority bits, 339, 340

Private Automatic Branch Exchange, 81

Private Branch Exchanges, 5, 81

Probe service, 512

Probes, 509

Progress message, 524

Project ELF, 66

Proof of delivery service, 512

Proof of submission service, 512

Prospero File System, 497

Protective ground, 143

Protocol, 14. *See also* Aloha, Bit-oriented, BSC, Byte-oriented, CSMA, Data link, Data link control, Exterior gateway, FDDI, FTP, Go-back-n, HDCC, ICMP, IEEE 802.3, IEEE 802.4, IEEE 802.5, IP, ISDN, ISO internet, ISO transport, Link access, Message transfer, Netware core, OSI, P1, P2, P3, P7, RIP, RS232, RS422, RS423, RS449, Selective repeat, Sliding window, Slotted Aloha, SMTP, SNA, SNMP, Stop-and-wait, TCP, TELNET, TFTP, Three-way handshake, Transport, Two-way handshake, UDP, Unrestricted, Virtual terminal, X.3, X.25, X.28, X.29, X.400, X.500

Protocol converters, 402

Protocol data units, 499, 509

Protocol discriminator, 528

PSC, 472

PSCnet, 472

Pseudoternary coding, 526

PSH. *See* Push

PSK. *See* Phase shift keying

Public data networks, 427, 431–40, 494

Public key cryptosystems, 228–33

Pulse amplitude modulation, 116

Pulse code modulation, 117

Pulse dialing, 79

Pure Aloha, 163–67

Purge frame, 346

Push, 456

Put, 493

Puzzles, 226–27

**Q**

QAM. *See* Quadrature amplitude modulation

Q-series, 523. *See also* Signaling system #7

Quadrature amplitude modulation, 113–16

Quarantining, 42

QUEUE, 389

Queuing theory, 159

Quit, 493

**R**

Radio, 153

RD. *See* Receive data

Read, 463

Readv, 463

Reassembly deadlock, 426

Reassembly timer, 447, 451

Receive data, 143, 148, 150, 298

Receive not ready, 297

Receive ready, 297

Receive timestamp, 451

Receiving window, 271

Receiving window size, 272–74

Recv, 463

Recvfrom, 463

Recvmsg, 463

Redirect, 450

Redirection of incoming messages service, 512

Reference point R, 521

Reference point S, 521

Reference point T, 521

Reference point U, 521

Refraction, 61

Regional center, 80

REJ. *See* Reject

Reject, 297

Relative encoding, 185, 187

Release complete message, 525

Release message, 525

Remote logins, 486. *See also* TELNET
Remote loopback, 148
Remote procedure call, 483–85
Remote spooling communications
      subsystem, 473
Remotehelp, 493
Repeater, 59, 330, 364, 402
Reply, 509
Reply request indication, 512
Reports, 509
Request. *See* Automatic repeat, Con-
      nection, Echo, Timestamp, Vir-
      tual route pacing
Request disconnect, 298
Request for Comment, 492–95
Request initialization mode, 298
Request to send, 143, 148
Request/response modes, 545
Request/response units, 532
Reservation bits, 340
Reservation system (token ring),
      339–44
Reset, 298, 456
Resolve contention, 355
Resolve contention frame, 357
Resynchronize, 41
Return of content service, 512
RFC. *See* Request for comments
RIGHTS, 388
RIM. *See* Request initialization
      mode
Ring indicator, 144
Ring topology, 10, 321. *See also* To-
      ken ring network
RIP. *See* Routing information proto-
      col
RNR. *See* Receive not ready
Root bridge, 375, 376
Root port, 375, 376
Route designators, 378
Route determination, 30
Route discovery, 379
Route learning, 370
Routed, 421
Router, 368, 402, 417, 442, 448–50
Routing, 404–27, 447. *See also*
      Adaptive routing, Backward
      learning algorithm, Bell-Ford
      algorithm, Bridges, Broadcast,

Centralized routing, Conges-
      tion, Deadlock, Dijkstra's algo-
      rithm, Distributed routing,
      Explicit route control, Flood-
      ing, Forward search algorithm,
      Hierarchical routing, RIP, Rout-
      ers, Shortest path algorithm,
      Static routing, Transmission
      group control, Virtual route
      control
Routing directory, 368
Routing information protocol, 421–
      22, 494
Routing matrix, 406
Routing tables, 368, 370, 405, 429
RPC. *See* Remote procedure call
RR. *See* Receive ready
RS-232 standard, 142–47
RS-422, 147
RS-423, 147
RS-449, 147–49
RSA algorithm, 229–31
RTS. *See* Request to send
Run length encoding, 183–85, 187
Run-length encoding prefix, 310
RU. *See* Request/response unit

**S**

Sampling frequency, 117, 118
Samuel Morse, 92
Satellite transmission, 69–76
Scripts, 126
SDLC. *See* Synchronous data-link
      control
Search drives, 389
Secondary station, 293
Secondary station, 299
Sectional center, 80
Security, 196. *See also* Encryption,
      Viruses
Selective reject, 297
Selective repeat protocol, 270–81
Self-synchronizing code, 98
SEND, 311, 388, 461, 463
Send/receive modes, 544
Sender, 40
Sending window, 261, 264–66, 271–
      74, 281

Sendmsg, 463
Sendto, 463
Sequence number, 139, 455
Sequenced packed protocol, 385
Sequencing, 466
Serial transmission, 137
Server, 482, 485, 487, 499, 500
Service. *See* Address lookup, Class
      of, Datagram, Directory
Service classes, 359
Service type, 443
Session, 21, 541
Session control, 541
Session layer 21, 37–42. *See also*
      Activity, Dialog management,
      Quarantining, Synchronization
      points
SESSion STarted, 544
Set {send or receive} packet-length,
      312
Set {send or receive} timeout, 312
Set asynchronous balanced mode,
      298
Set asynchronous balanced mode ex-
      tended, 298
Set asynchronous response mode,
      298
Set asynchronous response mode ex-
      tended, 298
Set baud, 311
Set block-check, 311
Set delay, 311
Set duplex, 311
Set initialization mode, 298
Set normal response mode, 298
Set normal response mode extended,
      298
Set parity, 312
Set receive, 312
Set send, 312
Set successor, 355
Set successor frame, 356
Set timer, 312
Set window, 312
SETPASS, 388
SetRequest, 503
Setsockopt, 463
Shamir's method, 227
Shannon, 108

Shannon's result, 108–09
Shield, 150
Shift down, 93
Shift In, 90
Shift Out, 90, 91
Shift register (CRC), 208–10
Shift up, 94
Signal. *See* Analog, Carrier, Digital, Inband, Modulated, Out-of-band, Periodic
Signal constellation, 120–24
Signal element timing, 144, 150
Signal ground, 148
Signal quality, 148
Signal quality detector, 144
Signal rate selector, 148
Signal speed, 257, 279, 333
Signaling data link, 523
Signaling link layer, 523
Signaling network layer, 524
Signaling rate indicator, 148
Signaling system # 7, 523–25
Signal-to-noise ratio, 108
SIM. *See* Set initialization mode
Simple mail transfer protocol, 441, 494, 498–500
Simple network management protocol, 494, 500–03
Simplex communications, 140
Single bit errors, 197, 206, 210
Single mode fiber, 64
Single-route broadcast frame, 380
Slave server, 484
Sliding window protocol, 260–81. *See also* Selective repeat, Go-back-n
SLIST, 388
Slots, 165, 351
Slotted aloha protocol, 166–67
Slotted ring, 176, 351
Smart terminals, 485
Smartmodem 9600, 123
SMTP. *See* Simple mail transfer protocol
SNA. *See* Systems network architecture
SNMP. *See* Simple network management protocol
Socket, 462–63

Software distribution, 392
SOH. *See* Start of header
Solicit successor 1 frame, 356
Solicit successor 2 frame, 357
Source address, 139, 262, 331
Source port, 454
Source quench, 451
Source routing bridges, 377–81, 382
South Pacific Educational and Research Network, 472
Southeastern Universities Research Association Network, 472
Space (blank) character, 91
Spanning tree, 373
Spanning tree algorithm, 373–77
SPEARNET, 472
Spot beam, 73
Spread spectrum radio, 76
SprintNet, 472
Sputnik, 69
SPX. *See* Sequenced packet protocol
SREJ. *See* Selective reject
SS7. *See* Signaling system number 7
SSCP. *See* System service control point
Stacking station, 340
Standard format, 294
Standard protocol, 14
Standards organizations. *See* ANSI, CCITT, EIA, IBM, IEEE, ISO, NBS, NIST
Standby indicator, 148
Standby monitor present (SMP) frame, 346
Star topology, 10, 321
Star Trek, 49
StarLAN, 329
Start bit, 137
Start of frame delimiter, 330
Start of header, 91, 303
Start of text, 91, 303
Starting delimiter, 337
State transition, 282
State transition diagram, 282
Static routing, 406, 408, 409
Statistical multiplexer, 158
STATUS, 461
STATUS-RESPONSE, 461
Step index multimode fiber, 63

STM. *See* Synchronous transfer mode
Stop and go protocol, 163
Stop and wait protocol, 255–60, 281
Stop bit, 137
Store-and-forward, 508
Store-and-forward deadlock, 425
Stored message deletion service, 512
Stored message fetching service, 512
Stored message listing service, 512
STX. *See* Start of text
Subarea address, 536
Subareas, 535
Submission and delivery protocol, 510
Subnegotiation begin, 489
Subnegotiation end, 489
Subsequent Address Message, 524
Substitute character, 91
Success rate, 169
Successor, 353
Supervisory frame, 296–97
SURAnet, 472
Susceptibility to interference, 78
Switchboard, 2
SYN. *See* Synchronize
SYN characters, 138, 302
SYN field, 457
Synchronization points, 40
Synchronize, 456
Synchronous character, 91
Synchronous data link control (SDLC), 250, 301, 533
SYNchronous idle, 303
Synchronous transfer mode, 531
Synchronous transmission, 138
Synthetic division, 202–03
System service control point, 537
Systems Network Architecture, 16, 532
    data flow control, 544–46
    explicit route control, 539
    network addressable unit, 535–38
    path control, 533–41
    session control, 541–44
    transmission control, 541
    transmission group control, 539–41
    virtual route control, 538–39

**T**

T-1, 159
Target station, 293
TCM. *See* Trellis coded modulation
TCP. *See* Transmission control protocol
TCP disconnect protocol, 458–59
TCP primitives, 461
TCP segment, 454
TCP user, 461
TD. *See* Transmit data
TDM. *See* Time division multiplexing
TE1, 520
TE2, 520
Technical and Office Products, 532
Teleconferencing, 5
Telegraph, 1, 58
Telemail, 472
Telemetry, 517
Telenet, 472
Telephone, 77
Telephone system. *See* Cellular telephone, Circuit switching, ISDN, Local exchange, Local loop, PBX, Primary center, Regional center, Sectional center, T-1, Toll center
Telephone user part, 524
Television, 153
Television signals, 179
TELNET, 441, 486–90, 494
Telstar, 3
Terminal adapter, 521
Terminal equipment 1, 520
Terminal equipment 2, 520
Terminal in service, 148
Terminal ready, 148
Terminal timing, 148
TERMINATE, 461
Terminators, 326
TEST, 299
Test mode, 148
Texas Higher Education Network, 472
TFTP. *See* Trivial file transfer protocol
THEnet, 472

Three-dimensional imaging, 49
Three-way handshake, 36–37, 457–58
THT. *See* Token holding timer
Tides Foundation, 472
Time division multiplexing, 155, 159
Time exceeded, 451
Timeout period, 309
Timeout transitions, 290
Timestamp reply, 451
Timestamp request reply, 451
Time-to-live, 441, 451
Token, 12, 28, 173, 176, 228, 336
Token bit, 339
Token bus network, 176, 178, 352–62, 393
   adding stations, 356–57
   control frames, 355
   frame format, 354
   lost tokens, 357–58
   prioritizing frames, 359–62
   removing stations, 355–56
   ring initialization, 358–59
Token holding timer, 360
Token passing, 28, 173
Token ring network, 11, 178, 335–52, 393
   control frames, 345–46
   frame format, 337–39
   reserving and claiming tokens, 339–44
   ring maintenance, 344–47
Token rotation timer, 360
Toll center, 80
Tone dialing, 79
TOP. *See* Technical and office products
TP0, 464
TP1, 464
TP2, 464
TP3, 464
TP4, 465
TPDU. *See* Transport protocol data unit
TPDU types, 465
Transaction, 545
Transaction services, 547
Transaction tracking system, 386
Transceiver, 327

Transceiver cable, 327
Transitions 289
Transmission control layer, 541
Transmission control protocol, 404, 440, 454–64, 494
   connection management, 456–59
   flow control, 459–60
   primitives, 460–61
   segment format, 455
   sockets, 461–63
Transmission group, 539
Transmission group control, 539
Transmission header, 533
Transmission media. *See* Coaxial cable, Microwave, Optical fiber, Satellite, Twisted pair
Transmission modes, 136
Transmission rate, 257, 279, 333
Transmit data, 143, 150
Transmit timestamp, 451
Transparent Bridges, 370–71, 382
Transparent data, 304
Transport connection, 32
Transport layer, 21, 31. *See also* TCP, Three-way handshake, TP0, TP1, TP2, TP3, TP4
Transport protocol, 452–54
Transport protocol data units, 32, 465
Transposition cipher, 220–21
Trap, 503
Trellis coded modulation, 116
Trivial file transfer protocol, 497
TRT. *See* Token rotation timer
Trunk, 80
Trustee rights, 386
Trustees, 386
TTS. *See* Transaction tracking system
Twisted pair, 58, 77, 78
Two-way handshake, 34, 457
TYMNET, 473

**U**

UA. *See* User agent
Ubiquitous network cloud, 427
UDP. *See* User datagram protocol
UDP segment, 464

UHF. *See* Ultra-high frequency
UKnet, 473
Ultra-high frequency, 65
Unbalanced circuits, 147
Undetected error, 207
Undetected transmission errors, 206–08
Unidirectional, 11
United Kingdom Unix Network, 473
University of Cambridge, 176
University Satellite Network, 473
Unix to Unix copy program, 473
Unnumbered acknowledgment, 299
Unnumbered frames, 296, 297–299
Unnumbered information, 298
Unnumbered poll, 298
Unprintable characters, 89
Unrestricted flow control, 254–55, 258–60, 279, 281
UNSPECIFIED-PASSIVE-OPEN, 461
Uplinking, 72
Upstream neighbor, 346
Upward multiplexing, 32
Urgent data, 456, 463
Urgent pointer, 456
USENET, 473
User agent, 505, 506–07
User datagram protocol, 441, 453, 464, 494
User login script, 389
User part, 523
User's Network, 473
User-to-user information message, 525
User-to-user service, 454
UUCP. *See* Unix-to-Unix copy program
UUNET, 473

**V**

V.21 modem, 120
V.22 modem, 120
V.22bis standard, 121
V.32 standard, 121
V.42bis, 123
V.fast, 124

Verification, 231
Vertical tab, 91
Very high frequency, 65
Very small aperture terminal, 75
VHF. *See* Very High Frequency
Videoconferencing, 49
Videotex, 519
Vigenère cipher, 217–19
Virtual call, 433–35
Virtual call number, 431, 433
Virtual circuit, 26–27, 424, 427–29
Virtual file structure, 491
Virtual route, 538
Virtual route control, 538–39
Virtual route pacing count indicator, 539
Virtual route pacing request, 539
Virtual route pacing response, 539
Virtual telecommunications access method, 537
Virtual terminal protocol, 45, 485–86. *See also* TELNET
Virus, 234–38
VNET, 473
Voice & video communications, 5
Voice communications, 50
Voice mail, 519
VSAT. *See* Very small aperture terminal
VTAM. *See* Virtual telecommunication access method

**W**

WAIS. *See* Wide area information servers
WAN. *See* Wide area network
Warmstart trap, 503
Waveguide, 68
Who follows, 355
Who follows frame, 355
WHOAMI, 388
Wide area information servers, 496
Wide area networks (WANs), 4, 8, 321, 363, 401–81. *See also* Packet switched neworks, Public data networks, Routing, TCP/IP, X.25
Will, 489

Window. *See* Receiving window, Sending window, Sliding window protocol
Window-oriented stop and wait, 279–81
Wire center, 337
Wireless communications, 65. *See* also Microwave transmission, Satellite transmission
Wireless LAN, 75
Won't, 489
World-Wide Web, 497
Worm, 234, 238–40
Writev, 463
WWW. *See* World-Wide Web

**X**

X.3, 436–39
X.3 parameter, 439
X.21, 149–51
X.25 standard, 431–36. *See also* Virtual circuit
  packet format, 432
  virtual calls, 433–35
X.26, 149
X.27, 149
X.28, 436, 438–40
X.29, 437, 440
X.400, 503–12
  message handling system, 508–12
  message transfer agent, 507–08
  message transfer system, 508
  user agent, 506–07
X.500 directory service, 512–16
XEROX Internet, 474
X-OFF, 90, 252
X-ON, 90, 252